HMH Tennessee Science

This Write-In Book belongs to

adrianna Collins

Teacher/Room

Ms. Moliwa

Houghton Mifflin Harcourt™

Consulting Authors

Michael A. DiSpezio

Global Educator
North Falmouth, Massachusetts

Michael DiSpezio has authored many HMH instructional programs for science and mathematics. He has also authored numerous trade books and multimedia programs on various topics and hosted dozens of studio and location broadcasts for various organizations in the U.S. and worldwide. Most recently, he has been working with educators to provide strategies for implementing science and engineering practices, including engineering design challenges. To all his projects, he brings his extensive background in science, his expertise in classroom teaching at the elementary, middle, and high school levels, and his deep experience in producing interactive and engaging instructional materials.

Marjorie Frank

Science Writer and
Content-Area Reading Specialist
Brooklyn, New York

An educator and linguist by training, a writer and poet by nature, Marjorie Frank has authored and designed a generation of instructional materials in all subject areas, including past HMH Science programs. Her other credits include authoring science issues of an award-winning children's magazine, writing game-based digital assessments, developing blended learning materials for young children, and serving as instructional designer and co-author of pioneering school-to-work software. In addition, she has served on the adjunct faculty of Hunter, Manhattan, and Brooklyn Colleges, teaching courses in science methods, literacy, and writing.

Acknowledgments for Cover

Front cover: lava ©Bruce Omori/epa/Corbis

Tennessee Academic Standards courtesy of the Tennessee Department of Education.

Printed in the U.S.A.

ISBN 978-1-328-828620

7 8 9 10 0877 26 25 24 23 22 21 20

4500790426   B C D E F G

Michael R. Heithaus

Dean, College of Arts, Sciences & Education
Professor, Department of Biological Sciences
Florida International University
Miami, Florida

Mike Heithaus joined the FIU Biology Department in 2003, has served as Director of the Marine Sciences Program, and as Executive Director of the School of Environment, Arts, and Society, which brings together the natural and social sciences and humanities to develop solutions to today's environmental challenges. He now serves as Dean of the College of Arts, Sciences & Education. His research focuses on predator-prey interactions and the ecological importance of large marine species. He has helped to guide the development of Life Science content in this science program, with a focus on strategies for teaching challenging content as well as the science and engineering practices of analyzing data and using computational thinking.

Tennessee Reviewers

Emily C. Grayer
Richview Middle School
Clarksville, TN

Dale Land
Kenwood Middle School
Clarksville-Montgomery County
School System
Clarksville, TN

Patrece Morrow
Science, NBCT
Sherwood Middle School
Memphis, TN

Shari Myers
Academic Coach
Rossview Elementary School
Clarksville-Montgomery County
School System
Clarksville, TN

Sarah Becky Spain
Kenrose Elementary School
Brentwood, TN

Christy Walker, Ed.D., NBCT
Manley Elementary School
Morristown, TN

Content Reviewers

Paul D. Asimow, PhD
*Professor of Geology
and Geochemistry*
Division of Geological and Planetary Sciences
California Institute of Technology
Pasadena, CA

Laura K. Baumgartner, PhD
Postdoctoral Researcher
Molecular, Cellular, and Developmental
Biology
University of Colorado
Boulder, CO

Eileen Cashman, PhD
Professor
Department of Environmental Resources
Engineering
Humboldt State University
Arcata, CA

Hilary Clement Olson, PhD
Research Scientist Associate V
Institute for Geophysics, Jackson School of
Geosciences
The University of Texas at Austin
Austin, TX

Joe W. Crim, PhD
Professor Emeritus
Department of Cellular Biology
The University of Georgia
Athens, GA

Elizabeth A. De Stasio, PhD
*Raymond H. Herzog Professor
of Science*
Professor of Biology
Department of Biology
Lawrence University
Appleton, WI

Dan Franck, PhD
Botany Education Consultant
Chatham, NY

Julia R. Greer, PhD
*Assistant Professor of Materials Science and
Mechanics*
Division of Engineering and Applied Science
California Institute of Technology
Pasadena, CA

John E. Hoover, PhD
Professor
Department of Biology
Millersville University
Millersville, PA

William H. Ingham, PhD
Professor (Emeritus)
Department of Physics and Astronomy
James Madison University
Harrisonburg, VA

Charles W. Johnson, PhD
*Chairman, Division of Natural Sciences,
Mathematics, and Physical Education*
Associate Professor of Physics
South Georgia College
Douglas, GA

Tatiana A. Krivosheev, PhD
Associate Professor of Physics
Department of Natural Sciences
Clayton State University
Morrow, GA

Joseph A. McClure, PhD
Associate Professor Emeritus
Department of Physics
Georgetown University
Washington, DC

Mark Moldwin, PhD
Professor of Space Sciences
Atmospheric, Oceanic, and Space Sciences
University of Michigan
Ann Arbor, MI

Russell Patrick, PhD
Professor of Physics
Department of Biology, Chemistry, and Physics
Southern Polytechnic State University
Marietta, GA

Patricia M. Pauley, PhD
Meteorologist, Data Assimilation Group
Naval Research Laboratory
Monterey, CA

Stephen F. Pavkovic, PhD
Professor Emeritus
Department of Chemistry
Loyola University of Chicago
Chicago, IL

L. Jeanne Perry, PhD
Director (Retired)
Protein Expression Technology Center
Institute for Genomics and Proteomics
University of California, Los Angeles
Los Angeles, CA

Kenneth H. Rubin, PhD
Professor
Department of Geology and Geophysics
University of Hawaii
Honolulu, HI

Brandon E. Schwab, PhD
Associate Professor
Department of Geology
Humboldt State University
Arcata, CA

Marllin L. Simon, Ph.D.
Associate Professor
Department of Physics
Auburn University
Auburn, AL

Larry Stookey, PE
Upper Iowa University
Wausau, WI

Kim Withers, PhD
Associate Research Scientist
Center for Coastal Studies
Texas A&M University-Corpus Christi
Corpus Christi, TX

Matthew A. Wood, PhD
Professor
Department of Physics & Space Sciences
Florida Institute of Technology
Melbourne, FL

Adam D. Woods, PhD
Associate Professor
Department of Geological Sciences
California State University, Fullerton
Fullerton, CA

Natalie Zayas, MS, EdD
Lecturer
Division of Science and Environmental Policy
California State University, Monterey Bay
Seaside, CA

Contents in Brief

Tennessee Academic Standards for Science

Dear Students and Families,

    This book and this class are structured around the Tennessee Academic Standards for Science for Grade 8. As you read, experiment, and study, you will learn the concepts listed on these pages. You will also continue to build your science literacy, which will enrich your life both in and out of school.

Best wishes for a good school year,

The HMH Tennessee Science Team

PHYSICAL SCIENCES

8.PS2: Motion and Stability: Forces and Interactions

1) Design and conduct investigations depicting the relationship between magnetism and electricity in electromagnets, generators, and electrical motors, emphasizing the factors that increase or diminish the electric current and the magnetic field strength.

2) Conduct an investigation to provide evidence that fields exist between objects exerting forces on each other even though the objects are not in contact.

3) Create a demonstration of an object in motion and describe the position, force, and direction of the object.

4) Plan and conduct an investigation to provide evidence that the change in an object's motion depends on the sum of the forces on the object and the mass of the object.

5) Evaluate and interpret that for every force exerted on an object there is an equal force exerted in the opposite direction.

8.PS4: Waves and Their Applications in Technologies for Information Transfer

1) Develop and use models to represent the basic properties of waves including frequency, amplitude, wavelength, and speed.

2) Compare and contrast mechanical waves and electromagnetic waves based on refraction, reflection, transmission, absorption, and their behavior through a vacuum and/or various media.

3) Evaluate the role that waves play in different communication systems.

LIFE SCIENCES

8.LS4: Biological Change: Unity and Diversity

1) Analyze and interpret data for patterns in the fossil record that document the existence, diversity, extinction, and change in life forms throughout Earth's history.

2) Construct an explanation addressing similarities and differences of the anatomical structures and genetic information between extinct and extant organisms using evidence of common ancestry and patterns between taxa.

3) Analyze evidence from geology, paleontology, and comparative anatomy to support that specific phenotypes within a population can increase the probability of survival of that species and lead to adaptation.

4) Develop a scientific explanation of how natural selection plays a role in determining the survival of a species in a changing environment.

5) Obtain, evaluate, and communicate information about the technologies that have changed the way humans use artificial selection to influence the inheritance of desired traits in other organisms.

EARTH AND SPACE SCIENCES

8.ESS1: Earth's Place in the Universe

1) Research, analyze, and communicate that the universe began with a period of rapid expansion using evidence from the motion of galaxies and composition of stars.

2) Explain the role of gravity in the formation of our sun and planets. Extend this explanation to address gravity's effect on the motion of celestial objects in our solar system and Earth's ocean tides.

8.ESS2: Earth's Systems

1) Analyze and interpret data to support the assertion that rapid or gradual geographic changes lead to drastic population changes and extinction events.

2) Evaluate data collected from seismographs to create a model of Earth's structure.

3) Describe the relationship between the processes and forces that create igneous, sedimentary, and metamorphic rocks.

4) Gather and evaluate evidence that energy from the earth's interior drives convection cycles within the asthenosphere which creates changes within the lithosphere including plate movements, plate boundaries, and sea-floor spreading.

5) Construct a scientific explanation using data that explains the gradual process of plate tectonics accounting for A) the distribution of fossils on different continents, B) the occurrence of earthquakes, and C) continental and ocean floor features (including mountains, volcanoes, faults, and trenches).

8.ESS3: Earth and Human Activity

1) Interpret data to explain that earth's mineral, fossil fuel, and groundwater resources are unevenly distributed as a result of geologic processes.

2) Collect data, map, and describe patterns in the locations of volcanoes and earthquakes related to tectonic plate boundaries, interactions, and hotspots.

ENGINEERING, TECHNOLOGY, AND APPLICATIONS OF SCIENCE

8.ETS1: Engineering Design

1) Develop a model to generate data for ongoing testing and modification of an electromagnet, a generator, and a motor such that an optimal design can be achieved.

2) Research and communicate information to describe how data from technologies (telescopes, spectroscopes, satellites, and space probes) provide information about objects in the solar system and universe.

Contents

When can lying down help you go faster? When you are on a bicycle! Lowering your body reduces the energy you need to travel faster.

A horseshoe magnet is a type of permanent magnet. Its lifting strength is double that of most bar magnets.

© Houghton Mifflin Harcourt Publishing Company • Image Credits: ©Dorling Kindersley/Getty Images

Contents (continued)

Have you ever felt the vibrations when music is played loudly? Sound waves can make things, like this megaphone, vibrate.

Energy can travel through water as waves. The greater the amount of energy in a wave, the taller and more destructive the wave can be when it reaches shore.

Do you know a DJ? Disc jockeys, or DJs, rely on their knowledge of sound waves to "mix" music.

Contents (continued)

This astronaut's helmet has a special gold coating. The coating allows the astronaut to see while protecting him or her from harmful sun rays.

© Houghton Mifflin Harcourt Publishing Company • Image Credits: ©NASA

Amber fossils form when small creatures become trapped in tree sap that hardens.

There were all kinds of plants during the Paleozoic era. All except flowering plants that is, which hadn't developed yet.

© Houghton Mifflin Harcourt Publishing Company • Image Credits: (t) ©Howard Grey/Stone/Getty Images; (b) ©Publiphoto/Photo Researchers, Inc.

Contents (continued)

Stars and solar systems are born out of clouds of gas and dust, like the one seen here.

The huge White Cliffs of Dover were formed from the skeletons of organisms like the microscopic marine algae shown here.

Contents (continued)

Imagine how hot it must be for rock to melt and flow like water! That's lava for you.

Movement in Earth's crust releases tremendous amounts of energy, which can cause a lot of damage.

Motion and Forces

Big Idea

Unbalanced forces cause changes in the motion of objects, and these changes can be predicted and described.

The parachute helps slow the shuttle down.

8.PS2.3, 8.PS2.4, 8.PS2.5

What do you think?

How do you change the direction in which an object is moving? By applying force, of course. Can you tell what force helps the shuttle slow down? What allows the rocket in the photo to lift off?

Unit 1
Motion and Forces

What's in a Vane?

For hundreds of years, people have used the wind to do work, such as grind flour and pump water.

① Define The Problem

We need electricity to do work, such as power the lights and appliances that we use daily. As our need for electricity grows, many people are becoming more interested in new ways to generate electricity. Have you heard of using windmills to generate electricity?

A windmill vane, or sail, is a large structure that is attached to a rotating axle. The vane catches the wind and turns around. This turning motion can be used to generate electricity.

② Think About It

Designing a windmill vane

What characteristics of a windmill vane help it to catch the most wind? Create two different designs for windmill vanes that you can test to see which characteristics are the most beneficial.

Consider these factors as you design your vanes.

☐ the size of the vanes

☐ the shape of the vanes

☐ materials used to build the vanes

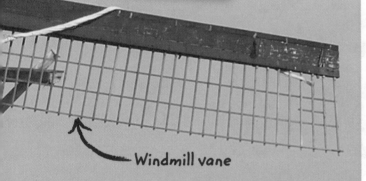
— Windmill vane

Take It Home

With the help of an adult, research windmills that are used to generate electricity for homes. Study the different designs and decide which would be best for your family. See *ScienceSaurus*® for more information about wind.

③ Plan and Test Your Design

A Your windmill designs should feature four windmill vanes attached to a straw or wooden spindle. The straw or spindle will be the axle. You should mount your axle so that it can spin freely. In the space below, sketch two designs that you would like to test.

B In the space below, identify what you will use as a wind source and the variables you must control.

_____
_____
_____
_____
_____
_____

C Conduct your test and briefly state your findings below.

_____
_____
_____
_____
_____

Motion and Speed

© Houghton Mifflin Harcourt Publishing Company • Image Credits: ©PCN Chrome/Alamy

ESSENTIAL QUESTION

How are distance, time, and speed related?

By the end of this lesson, you should be able to analyze how distance, time, and speed are related.

8.PS2.3, 8.PS2.4

The personal watercraft in this photo is going fast. How can we measure how fast it is going?

Lesson Labs

Quick Labs
• Investigate Changing Positions
• Create a Distance-Time Graph

S.T.E.M. Lab
• Investigate Average Speed

 Engage Your Brain

1 Predict Circle the correct words in the paragraph below to make true statements.

A dog usually moves faster than a bug. That means that if I watch them move for one minute, then the dog would have traveled a *greater*/*smaller* distance than the bug. However, a car usually goes *faster*/*slower* than a dog. If the car and the dog both traveled to the end of the road, then the *car*/*dog* would get there first.

2 Explain Draw or sketch something that you might see move. Write a caption that answers the following questions: How would you describe its motion? Is it moving at a constant speed, or does it speed up and slow down?

 Active Reading

3 Define Fill in the blank with the word that best completes the following sentences.

If an object changes its position, then it is

_____

The speed of a car describes

_____

_____

Vocabulary Terms

• position   • speed
• reference point   • vector
• motion   • velocity

4 Apply As you learn the definition of each vocabulary term in this lesson, make your own definition or sketch to help you remember the meaning of the term.

Location, location,

How can you describe the location of an object?

Have you ever gotten lost while looking for a specific place? If so, you probably know that the description of the location can be very important. Imagine that you are trying to describe your location to a friend. How would you explain where you are? You need two pieces of information: a position and a reference point.

With a Position

Position describes the location of an object. Often, you describe where something is by comparing its position with where you currently are. For example, you might say that a classmate sitting next to you is two desks to your right, or that a mailbox is two blocks south of where you live. Each time you identify the position of an object, you are comparing the location of the object with the location of another object or place.

With a Reference Point

When you describe a position by comparing it to the location of another object or place, you are using a reference point. A **reference point** is a location to which you compare other locations. In the example above of a mailbox that is two blocks south of where you live, the reference point is "where you live."

Imagine that you are at a zoo with some friends. If you are using the map to the right, you could describe your destination using different reference points. Using yourself as the reference point, you might say that the red panda house is one block east and three blocks north of your current location. Or you might say the red panda house is one block north and one block east of the fountain. In this example, the fountain is your reference point.

Active Reading **5 Apply** How would you describe where this question is located on the page? Give two different answers using two different reference points.

_____

_____

_____

_____

location

ZOO MAP

A B C D E F G H

1 Elephants

2 Cafe Gorillas

3 Zebras Rhino

Tigers

4 Reptiles

5 Monkey Island Red Panda

6 Birds

N

7 Petting Zoo Carousel Fountain

Guest Services

YOU ARE **HERE**

8 Gift Shop

Restrooms

Food

First Aid

9 Zoo Entrance Cafe

Information

Visualize It!

6 Apply One of your friends is at the southeast corner of Monkey Island. He would like to meet you. How would you describe your location to him?

I'd say I'm near the cafe and the fountain.

7 Apply You need to go visit the first aid station. How would you describe how to get there?

7

MOVE It!

What is motion?

An object moves, or is in motion, when it changes its position relative to a reference point. **Motion** is a change in position over time. If you were to watch the biker pictured to the right, you would see him move. If you were not able to watch him, you might still know something about his motion. If you saw that he was in one place at one time and a different place later, you would know that he had moved. A change in position is evidence that motion has happened.

If the biker returned to his starting point, you might not know that he had moved. The starting and ending positions cannot tell you everything about motion.

How is distance measured?

Suppose you walk from one building to another building that is several blocks away. If you could walk in a straight line, you might end up 500 meters from where you started. The actual distance you travel, however, would depend on the exact path you take. If you take a route that has many turns, the distance you travel might be 900 meters or more.

The way you measure distance depends on the information you want. Sometimes you want to know the straight-line distance between two positions, or the displacement. Sometimes, however, you might need to know the total length of a certain path between those positions.

When measuring any distances, scientists use a standard unit of measurement. The standard unit of length is the meter (m), which is about 3.3 feet. Longer distances can be measured in kilometers (km), and shorter distances in centimeters (cm). In the United States, distance is often measured in miles (mi), feet (ft), or inches (in).

The distance from point A to point B depends on the path you take.

Visualize It!

8 Illustrate Draw a sample path on the maze that is a different distance than the one in red but still goes from the start point, "A," to the finish point, "B."

This biker is in motion.

What is speed?

A change in an object's position tells you that motion took place, but it does not tell you how quickly the object changed position. The **speed** of an object is a measure of how far something moves in a given amount of time. In other words, speed measures how quickly or slowly the object changes position. In the same amount of time, a faster object would move farther than a slower moving object would.

What is average speed?

The speed of an object is rarely constant. For example, the biker in the photo above may travel quickly when he begins a race but may slow down as he gets tired at the end of the race. *Average speed* is a way to calculate the speed of an object that may not always be moving at a constant speed. Instead of describing the speed of an object at an exact moment in time, average speed describes the speed over a stretch of time.

Active Reading **9 Compare** What is the difference between speed and average speed?

_____

_____

_____

Think Outside the Book **Inquiry**

10 Analyze Research the top speeds of a cheetah, a race car, and a speed boat. How do they rank in order of speed? Make a poster showing which is fastest and which is slowest. How do the speeds of the fastest human runners compare to the speeds you found?

Speed It Up!

11 Identify As you read, underline sentences that relate distance and time.

How is average speed calculated?

Speed can be calculated by dividing the distance an object travels by the time it takes to cover the distance. Speed is shown in the formula as the letter s, distance as the letter d, and time as the letter t. The formula shows how distance, time, and speed are related. If two objects travel the same distance, the object that took a shorter amount of time will have the greater speed. An object with a greater speed will travel a longer distance in the same amount of time than an object with a lower speed will.

> The following equation can be used to find average speed:
>
> $$\text{average speed} = \frac{\text{distance}}{\text{time}}$$
>
> $$s = \frac{d}{t}$$

The standard unit for speed is meters per second (m/s). Speed can also be given in kilometers per hour (km/h). In the United States, speeds are often given in miles per hour (mi/h or mph). One mile per hour is equal to 0.45 m/s.

 Do the Math **Sample Problem**

A penguin swimming underwater goes 20 meters in 8 seconds. What is its average speed?

Identify

A. What do you know? $d = 20$ m, $t = 8$ s

B. What do you want to find out? average speed

Plan

C. Draw and label a sketch: |—— 20 m ——| 8 sec

D. Write the formula: $s = d/t$

E. Substitute into the formula: $s = \dfrac{20 \text{ m}}{8 \text{ s}}$

Solve

F. Calculate and simplify: $s = \dfrac{20 \text{ m}}{8 \text{ s}} = 2.5 \text{ m/s}$

G. Check that your units agree: Unit is m/s. Unit of speed is distance/time. Units agree.

Answer: 2.5 m/s

Do the Math You Try It

12 Calculate This runner completed a 100-meter race with a time of 13.75 seconds. What was her average speed?

Identify

A. What do you know?

B. What do you want to find out?

Plan

C. Draw and label a sketch:

D. Write the formula:

E. Substitute into the formula:

Solve

F. Calculate and simplify:

G. Check that your units agree:

Answer:

Fast Graphs

How is constant speed graphed?

A convenient way to show the motion of an object is by using a graph that plots the distance the object has traveled against time. This type of graph is called a distance-time graph. You can use it to see how both distance and speed change with time.

How far away the object is from a reference point is plotted on the y-axis. So the y-axis expresses distance in units such as meters, centimeters, or kilometers. Time is plotted on the x-axis, and can display units such as seconds, minutes, or hours. If an object moves at a constant speed, the graph is a straight line.

You can use a distance-time graph to determine the average speed of an object. The slope, or steepness, of the line is equal to the average speed of the object. You calculate the average speed for a time interval by dividing the change in distance by the change in time for that time interval.

Suppose that an ostrich is running at a constant speed. The distance-time graph of its motion is shown below. To calculate the speed of the ostrich, choose two data points from the graph below and calculate the slope of the line. The calculation of the slope is shown below. Since we know that the slope of a line on a distance-time graph is its average speed, then we know that the ostrich's speed is 14 m/s.

How can you calculate slope?

$$slope = \frac{change\ in\ y}{change\ in\ x}$$

$$= \frac{140\ m - 70\ m}{10\ s - 5\ s}$$

$$= \frac{70\ m}{5\ s}$$

$$= 14\ m/s$$

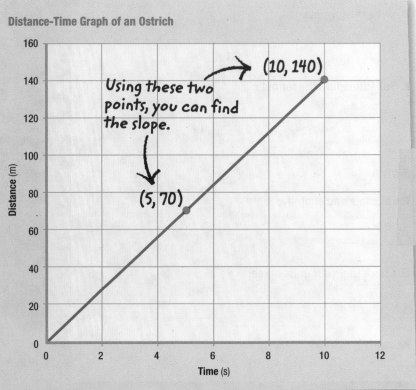

Distance-Time Graph of an Ostrich

Using these two points, you can find the slope.

(10, 140)

(5, 70)

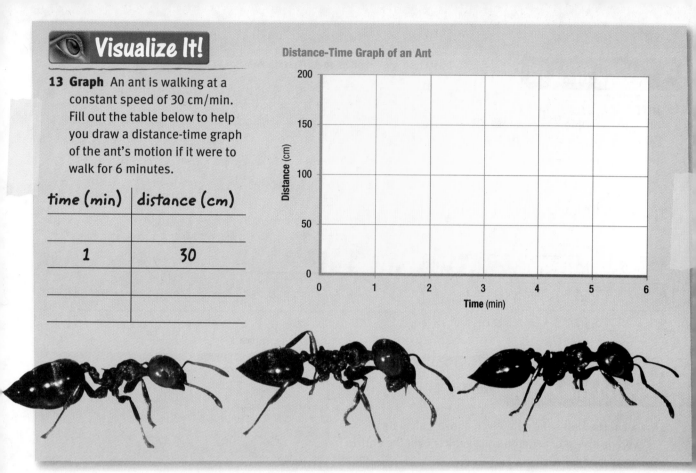

Visualize It!

13 Graph An ant is walking at a constant speed of 30 cm/min. Fill out the table below to help you draw a distance-time graph of the ant's motion if it were to walk for 6 minutes.

time (min)	distance (cm)
1	30

Distance-Time Graph of an Ant

How are changing speeds graphed?

Some distance-time graphs show the motion of an object with a changing speed. In these distance-time graphs, the change in the slope of a line indicates that the object has either sped up, slowed down, or stopped.

As an object moves, the distance it travels increases with time. The motion can be seen as a climbing line on the graph. The slope of the line indicates speed. Steeper lines show intervals where the speed is greater than intervals with less steep lines. If the line gets steeper, the object is speeding up. If the line gets less steep, the object is slowing. If the line becomes flat, or horizontal, the object is not moving. In this interval, the speed is zero meters per second.

For objects that change speed, you can calculate speed for a specific interval of time. You would choose two points close together on the graph. Or, you can calculate the average speed over a long interval of time. You would choose two points far apart on the graph to calculate an average over a long interval of time.

Active Reading **14 Analyze** If a line on a distance-time graph becomes steeper, what has happened to the speed of the object? What if it becomes a flat horizontal line?

_____

_____

_____

15 Graph Using the data table provided, complete the graph for the all-terrain vehicle. Part of the graph has been completed for you.

Time (s)	Distance (m)
1	10
3	10
4	30
5	50

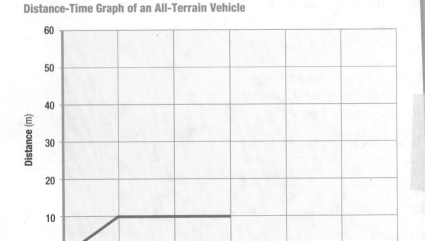

Distance-Time Graph of an All-Terrain Vehicle

 Do the Math **You Try It**

16 Calculate Using the data given above, calculate the average speed of the all-terrain vehicle over the entire five seconds.

Identify

A. What do you know?

B. What do you want to find out?

Plan

C. Draw and label a sketch:

D. Write the formula:

E. Substitute into the formula:

Solve

F. Calculate and simplify:

G. Check that your units agree:

Answer:

What would the distance-time graph of this ATV's motion look like?

Follow Directions

What is velocity?

Suppose that two birds start from the same place and fly at 10 km/h for 5 minutes. Why might they not end up at the same place? Because the birds were flying in different directions! There are times when the direction of motion must be included in a measurement. A **vector** is a quantity that has both size and direction.

In the example above, the birds' speeds were the same, but their velocities were different. **Velocity** [vuh•LAHS•ih•tee] is speed in a specific direction. If a police officer gives a speeding ticket for a car traveling 100 km/h, the ticket does not list a velocity. But it would list a velocity if it described the car traveling south at 100 km/h.

Because velocity includes direction, it is possible for two objects to have the same speed but different velocities. In the picture to the right, the chair lifts are going the same speed but in opposite directions: some people are going up the mountain while others are going down the mountain.

Average velocity is calculated in a different way than average speed. Average speed depends on the total distance traveled along a path. Average velocity depends on the straight-line distance from the starting point to the final point, or the displacement. A chair lift might carry you up the mountain at an average speed of 5 km/h, giving you an average velocity of 5 km/h north. After a round-trip ride, your average traveling speed would still be 5 km/h. Your average velocity, however, would be 0 km/h because you ended up exactly where you started.

These chair lifts have opposite velocities because they are going at the same speed but in opposite directions.

---

17 Compare Fill in the Venn diagram to compare and contrast speed and velocity.

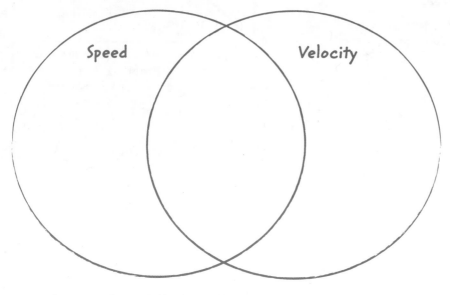

Speed

Velocity

Visual Summary

To complete this summary, check the box that indicates true or false. Then use the key below to check your answers. You can use this page to review the main concepts of the lesson.

Motion is a change in position over time.

YOU ARE HERE

	T	F	
18	☐	☐	A reference point is a location to which you compare other locations.
19	☐	☐	Distance traveled does not depend on the path you take.

Speed measures how far something moves in a given amount of time.

$$s = \frac{d}{t}$$

	T	F	
20	☐	☐	To calculate speed, you first need to find the mass of an object.
21	☐	☐	Average speed is a way to describe the speed of an object that may not always be moving at a constant speed.

Motion and Speed

A distance-time graph plots the distance traveled by an object and the time it takes to travel that distance.

	T	F	
22	☐	☐	In the graph at the right, the object is moving at a constant speed.

Answers: 18 T; 19 F; 20 F; 21 T; 22 T

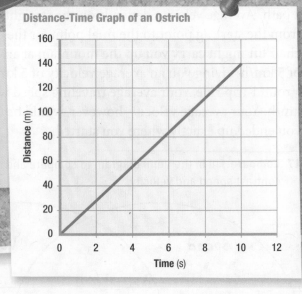

Distance-Time Graph of an Ostrich

23 Predict Amy and Ellie left school at the same time. Amy lives farther away than Ellie, but she and Ellie arrived at their homes at the same time. Compare the girls' speeds.

Lesson Review

Vocabulary

Draw a line to connect the following terms to their definitions.

1 velocity

2 reference point

3 speed

4 position

A describes the location of an object

B speed in a specific direction

C a location to which you compare other locations

D a measure of how far something moves in a given amount of time

Key Concepts

5 Describe What information do you need to describe an object's location?

_____

_____

_____

6 Predict How would decreasing the time it takes you to run a certain distance affect your speed?

_____

_____

_____

_____

7 Calculate Juan lives 100 m away from Bill. What is Juan's average speed if he reaches Bill's home in 50 s?

_____

_____

_____

_____

8 Describe What do you need to know to describe the velocity of an object?

_____

_____

_____

Use this graph to answer the following questions.

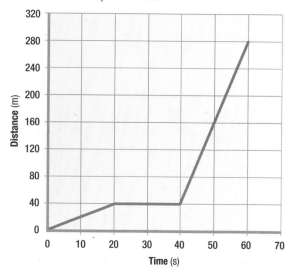

Distance-Time Graph of a Zebra

9 Analyze When is the zebra in motion? When is it not moving?

In motion: _____

Not moving: _____

10 Calculate What is the average speed of the zebra during the time between 0 s and 40 s?

_____

_____

_____

_____

Critical Thinking

11 Apply Look around you to find an object in motion. Describe the object's motion by discussing its position and direction of motion in relation to a reference point. Then explain how you could determine the object's speed.

_____

_____

_____

_____

My Notes

Interpreting Graphs

A visual display, such as a graph or table, is a useful way to show data that you have collected in an experiment. The ability to interpret graphs is a necessary skill in science, and it is also important in everyday life. You will come across various types of graphs in newspaper articles, medical reports, and, of course, textbooks. Understanding a report or article's message often depends heavily on your ability to read and interpret different types of graphs.

Tutorial

Ask yourself the following questions when studying a graph.

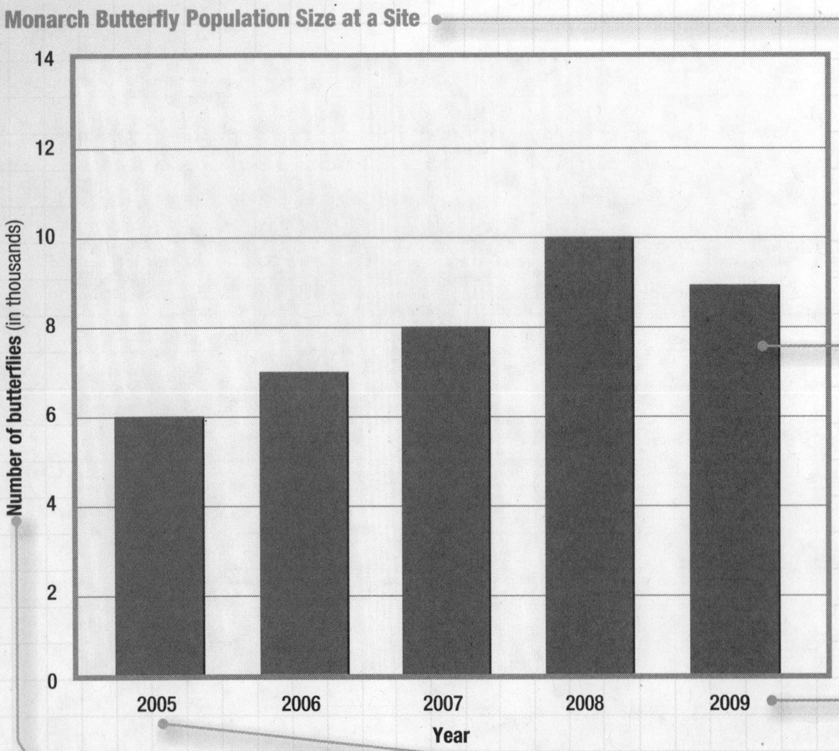

Monarch Butterfly Population Size at a Site

What is the title of the graph? Reading the title can tell you the subject or main idea of the graph. The subject here is monarch butterfly population.

What type of graph is it? Bar graphs, like the one here, are useful for comparing categories or total values. The lengths of the bars are proportional to the value they represent.

Do you notice any trends in the graph? After you understand what the graph is about, look for patterns. For example, here the monarch butterfly population increased each year from 2005 to 2008. But in 2009, the monarch butterfly population decreased.

What are the labels and headings in the graph? What is on each axis of the graph? Here, the vertical axis shows the population in thousands. Each bar represents a different year from 2005 to 2009. So from 2005 to 2009, the monarch butterfly population ranged from 6,000 to 10,000.

Can you describe the data in the graph? Data can be numbers or text. Analyze the information you read at specific data points. For example, the graph here tells us that there were 6,000 monarch butterflies in 2005.

You Try It!

A member of your research group has made the graph shown below about an object in motion. Study the graph, then answer the questions that follow.

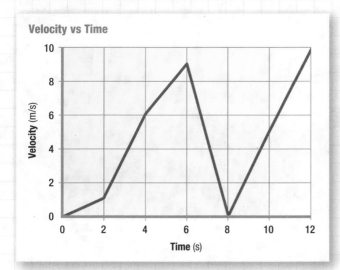

Velocity vs Time

1 Interpreting Graphs Study the graph shown above. Identify the title of this graph, the *x*-axis, the *y*-axis, and the type of graph.

A title of graph _____

B *x*-axis _____

C *y*-axis _____

D type of graph _____

2 Identify Study the graph shown above and record the velocity at the indicated times.

Time (s)	Velocity (m/s)
2	
4	
6	
8	
10	

3 Using Graphs Use the graph to answer the following questions.

A What is the approximate velocity of the object at 5 seconds?

_____

B During what time interval is the object slowing down? Explain how you can tell.

_____

_____

_____

_____

C At what time or times was the velocity of the object about 4 m/s?

_____

4 Communicating Results In a short paragraph, describe the motion of the object.

_____

_____

_____

_____

_____

_____

_____

_____

Take It Home

Find a newspaper or magazine article that has a graph. What type of graph is it? Study the graph and determine its main message. Bring the graph to class and be prepared to discuss your interpretation of the graph.

Acceleration

ESSENTIAL QUESTION

How does motion change?

By the end of this lesson, you should be able to analyze how acceleration is related to time and velocity.

8.PS2.3, 8.PS2.4

The riders on this roller coaster are constantly changing direction and speed.

Lesson Labs

Quick Labs
• Acceleration and Slope
• Mass and Acceleration

S.T.E.M. Lab
• Investigate Acceleration

Engage Your Brain

1 Predict Check T or F to show whether you think each statement is true or false.

T	F	
☐	☐	A car taking a turn at a constant speed is accelerating.
☐	☐	If an object has low acceleration, it isn't moving very fast.
☐	☐	An accelerating car is always gaining speed.

2 Identify The names of the two things that can change when something accelerates are scrambled together below. Unscramble them!

P E D S E

_____

C D E I I N O R T

_____

Active Reading

3 Synthesize You can often define an unknown word if you know the meaning of its word parts. Use the word parts and sentence below to make an educated guess about the meaning of the word *centripetal*.

Word part	Meaning
centri-	center
pet-	tend toward

Example Sentence:
Josephina felt the <u>centripetal</u> force as she spun around on the carnival ride.

centripetal:

_____

_____

_____

Vocabulary Terms

• acceleration
• centripetal acceleration

4 Distinguish As you read, draw pictures or make a chart to help remember the relationship between distance, velocity, and acceleration.

Getting up to

How do we measure changing velocity?

Imagine riding a bike as in the images below. You start off not moving at all, then move slowly, and then faster and faster each second. Your velocity is changing. You are accelerating.

Active Reading **5 Identify** Underline the two components of a vector.

Acceleration Measures a Change in Velocity

Just as velocity measures a rate of change in position, acceleration measures a rate of change in velocity. **Acceleration** (ack•SELL•uh•ray•shuhn) is the rate at which velocity changes. Velocity is a vector, having both a magnitude and direction, and if either of these change, then the velocity changes. So, an object accelerates if its speed, its direction of motion, or both change.

Keep in mind that acceleration depends not only on how much velocity changes, but also on how much time that change takes. A small change in velocity can still be a large acceleration if the change happens quickly, and a large change in velocity can be a small acceleration if it happens slowly. Increasing your speed by 5 m/s in 5 s is a smaller acceleration than to do the same in 1 s.

Each second, the cyclist's southward velocity increases by 1 m/s south.

| 1 m/s | 2 m/s | 3 m/s | 4 m/s | 5 m/s |

South

Speed

How is average acceleration calculated?

Acceleration is a change in velocity as compared with the time it takes to make the change. You can find the average acceleration experienced by an accelerating object using the following equation.

$$\text{average acceleration} = \frac{(final\ velocity - starting\ velocity)}{time}$$

Velocity is expressed in meters per second (m/s) and time is measured in seconds (s). So acceleration is measured in meters per second per second, or meters per second squared (m/s²).

As an example, consider an object that starts off moving at 8 m/s west, and then 16 s later is moving at 48 m/s west. The average acceleration of this object is found by the following equation.

$$a = \frac{(48\ m/s - 8\ m/s)}{16\ s}$$
$$a = 2.5\ m/s^2\ west$$

Active Reading

6 Identify Underline the units of acceleration.

This formula is often abbreviated as
$$a = \frac{(v_2 - v_1)}{t}$$

Visualize It!

7 Analyze What is the change in velocity of the cyclist below as he travels from point B to point C? What is his acceleration from point B to point C?

_____

_____

8 Calculate Find the average acceleration of the cyclist moving from point A to point B, and over the whole trip (from point A to point D).

Ⓐ 4 m/s
t = 0 s

Ⓓ 7 m/s
t = 3 s

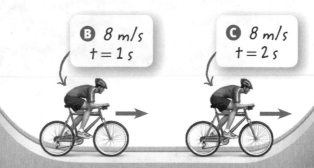

Ⓑ 8 m/s
t = 1 s

Ⓒ 8 m/s
t = 2 s

The cyclist is riding at 4 m/s. One second later, at the bottom of the hill, he is riding at 8 m/s. After going up a small incline, he has slowed to 7 m/s.

What a Drag!

How can accelerating objects change velocity?

Like velocity, acceleration is a vector, with a magnitude and a direction.

Accelerating Objects Change Speed

Although the word *acceleration* is commonly used to mean an increasing speed, in scientific use, the word applies to both increases and decreases in speed.

When you slide down a hill, you go from a small velocity to a large one. An increase in velocity like this is called *positive acceleration*. When a race car slows down, it goes from a high velocity to a low velocity. A decrease in velocity like this is called *negative acceleration*.

What is the acceleration when an object decreases speed? Because the initial velocity is larger than the final velocity, the term $(v_2 - v_1)$ will be negative. So the acceleration $a = \dfrac{(v_2 - v_1)}{t}$ will be a negative.

When acceleration and velocity (rate of motion) are in the same direction, the speed will increase. When acceleration and velocity are in opposing directions, the acceleration works against the initial motion in that direction, and the speed will decrease.

Active Reading

9 Identify Underline the term for an increase in velocity and the term for a decrease in velocity.

The parachute dragging on the air slows the car down, causing a negative acceleration.

Sliding down a hill causes a positive acceleration.

Accelerating Objects Change Direction

An object changing direction of motion experiences acceleration even when it does not speed up or slow down. Think about a car that makes a sharp left turn. The direction of velocity changes from "forward" to "left." This change in velocity is an acceleration, even if the speed does not change. As the car finishes the turn, the acceleration drops to zero.

What happens, however, when an object is *always* turning? An object traveling in a circular motion is always changing its direction, so it always experiences acceleration. Acceleration in circular motion is known as **centripetal acceleration**. (sehn•TRIP•ih•tahl ack•SELL•uh•ray•shuhn)

A skater rounding a curve experiences centripetal acceleration.

Inquiry

10 Conclude An acceleration in the direction of motion increases speed, and an acceleration opposite to the direction of motion decreases speed. What direction is the acceleration in centripetal acceleration, where speed does not change but direction does?

_____

_____

_____

Do the Math

11 Calculate The horse is galloping at 13 m/s. Five seconds later, after climbing the hill, the horse is moving at 5.5 m/s. Find the acceleration that describes this change in velocity.

$$a = \frac{(v_2 - v_1)}{t}$$

Running uphill is tough to do without slowing down!

5.5 m/s
5 seconds

13 m/s
0 seconds

Visual Summary

To complete this summary, complete the statements below by filling in the blanks. You can use this page to review the main concepts of the lesson.

Acceleration

Acceleration measures a change in velocity.

1 m/s   5 m/s

12 The formula for calculating average acceleration is

_____

Acceleration can be a change in speed or a change in direction of motion.

13 When acceleration and velocity are in the same direction, the speed will

_____

14 When acceleration and velocity are in opposing directions, the speed will

_____

15 Objects traveling in _____ motion experience centripetal acceleration.

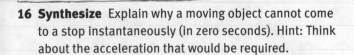

Answers: 12 $a = \dfrac{(v_2 - v_1)}{t}$; 13 increase; 14 decrease; 15 circular

16 **Synthesize** Explain why a moving object cannot come to a stop instantaneously (in zero seconds). Hint: Think about the acceleration that would be required.

Lesson Review

Vocabulary

Fill in the blank with the term that best completes the following sentences.

1 Acceleration is a change in _____

2 _____ occurs when an object travels in a curved path.

3 A decrease in the magnitude of velocity is called _____

4 An increase in the magnitude of velocity is called _____

Key Concepts

5 State The units for acceleration are
_____

6 Label In the equation $a = \dfrac{(v_2 - v_1)}{t}$, what do v_1 and v_2 represent?
_____
_____

7 Calculate What is the acceleration experienced by a car that takes 10 s to reach 27 m/s from rest?

8 Identify Acceleration can be a change in speed or _____

9 Identify A helicopter flying west begins experiencing an acceleration of 3 m/s² east. Will the magnitude of its velocity increase or decrease?
_____

Critical Thinking

10 Model Describe a situation when you might travel at a high velocity, but with low acceleration.
_____
_____
_____

Use this graph to answer the following questions. Assume Jenny's direction did not change.

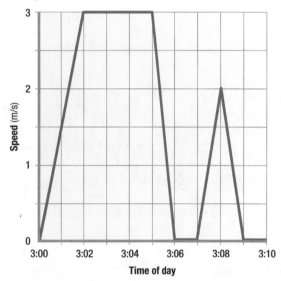

Jenny's Bike Ride

11 Analyze During what intervals was Jenny negatively accelerating?
_____
_____

12 Analyze During what intervals was Jenny positively accelerating?
_____
_____

13 Analyze During what intervals was Jenny not accelerating at all?
_____
_____

My Notes

Lesson 3

Forces

ESSENTIAL QUESTION

How do forces affect motion?

By the end of this lesson, you should be able to describe different types of forces and explain the effect force has on motion.

8.PS2.3, 8.PS2.4, 8.PS2.5

Even though this skydiver is not touching the ground, a force is still being exerted on him by Earth.

Lesson Labs

Quick Labs
• Net Force
• First Law of Skateboarding

S.T.E.M. Lab
• Newton's Laws of Motion

Engage Your Brain

1 Illustrate Draw a diagram showing how forces act on a ball tossed into the air.

2 Describe Write a caption for this photo.

Active Reading

3 Apply Many scientific words, such as *net*, also have everyday meanings. Use context clues to write your own definition for each meaning of the word *net*.

Example sentence
The fisherman scooped his catch out of the water with a <u>net</u>.

net:

Example sentence
Subtract the mass of the container from the total mass of the substance and the container to determine the <u>net</u> mass of the substance.

net:

Vocabulary Terms
• force
• net force
• inertia

4 Apply As you learn the definition of each vocabulary term in this lesson, create your own definition or sketch to help you remember the meaning of the term.

A Tour de Forces

What is a force, and how does it act on an object?

You have probably heard the word *force* used in conversation. People say, "Don't force the issue," or "Our team is a force to be reckoned with." Scientists also use the word *force*. What exactly is a force, as it is used in science?

A Force Is a Push or a Pull

 **Active Reading** **5 Identify** As you read, underline the unit that is used to express force.

In science, a **force** is simply a push or a pull. All forces have both a size and a direction. A force can cause an object to change its speed or direction. When you see a change in an object's motion, one or more forces caused the change. The unit used to express force is the newton (N). You will learn how to calculate force a little later in this lesson.

Forces exist only when there is an object for them to act on. However, forces do not always cause an object to move. When you sit in a chair, the chair does not move. Your downward force on the chair is balanced by the upward force from the floor.

Visualize It!

6 Identify Draw arrows to represent the pushing forces in the image at left and the pulling forces in the image at right.

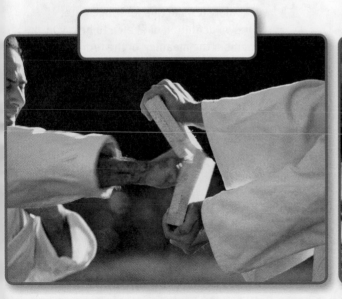

A Force Can Act Directly on an Object

It is not always easy to tell what is exerting a force or what is being acted on by a force. When one object touches or bumps into another object, we say that the objects are in contact with each other. A force exerted during contact between objects is a contact force. Friction is an example of a contact force between two surfaces. Suppose you slide a book across your desk. The amount of friction between the surface of the desk and the book cover determines how easily the book moves. Car tires rely on friction to keep a moving car from sliding off a road. Cars may slide on icy roads because ice lowers the force of friction on the tires.

A Force Can Act on an Object from a Distance

Forces can also act at a distance. One force that acts at a distance is called gravity. When you jump, gravity pulls you back to the ground even though you are not touching Earth. Magnetic force is another example of a force that can act at a distance. Magnetic force can be a push or a pull. A magnet can hold paper to a metal refrigerator door. The magnet touches the paper, not the metal, so the magnetic force is acting on the refrigerator door at a distance. Magnetic force also acts at a distance when the like poles of two magnets push each other apart. A magnetic levitation train floats because magnetic forces push the train away from its track.

Visualize It!

7 Identify The arrows in the picture below represent contact and distance forces. Label each arrow with a "C" if it is a contact force or "D" if it is a distance force.

In the Balance

What happens when multiple forces act on an object?

Usually, more than one force is acting on an object. The combination of all the forces acting on an object is called the **net force**. How do you determine net force? The answer depends on the directions of the forces involved.

When forces act in the same direction, you simply add them together to determine the net force. For example, when forces of 1 N and 2 N act in the same direction on an object, the net force is 1 N + 2 N = 3 N. When forces act in opposite directions, you subtract the smaller force from the larger force to determine the net force: 2 N – 1 N = 1 N.

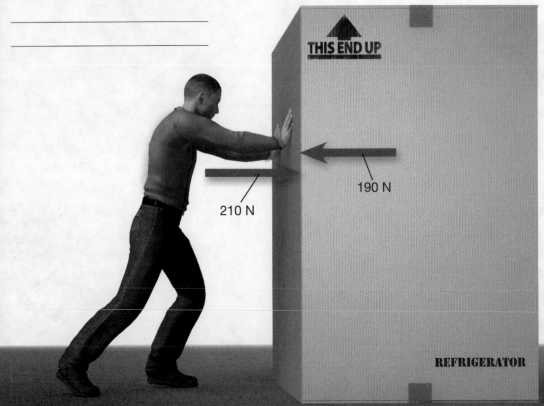

210 N

190 N

THIS END UP

REFRIGERATOR

The Forces Can Be Balanced

When the forces on an object produce a net force of 0 N, the forces are balanced. Balanced forces will not cause a change in the motion of a moving object or cause a nonmoving object to start moving. Many objects around you have only balanced forces acting on them. A light hanging from the ceiling does not move, because the force of gravity pulling downward on the light is balanced by the force of the chain pulling the light upward.

The Forces Can Be Unbalanced

When the net force on an object is not 0 N, the forces are unbalanced. Unbalanced forces produce a change in the object's motion. It could be a change in its speed or direction or both. This change in motion is called acceleration. The acceleration is always in the direction of the net force. For example, when a big dog and a small dog play with a tug toy, the bigger dog pulls with greater force, so the acceleration is in the direction of the bigger dog.

Visualize It!

10 Apply The arrows in the first image show that the forces on the rope are balanced. Draw arrows on the second image to show how the forces on the rope are unbalanced.

These two tug-of-war teams are pulling on the rope with equal force to produce a net force of 0 N. The rope does not move.

One of these teams is pulling on the rope with more force. The rope moves in the direction of the stronger team.

What is Newton's First Law of Motion?

Force and motion are related. In the 1680s, British scientist Sir Isaac Newton explained this relationship between force and motion with three laws of motion.

Newton's first law describes the motion of an object that has a net force of 0 N acting on it. The law states: *An object at rest stays at rest, and an object in motion stays in motion at the same speed and direction, unless it experiences an unbalanced force.* Let's look at the two parts of this law more closely.

An Object at Rest Stays at Rest

 **11 Identify** As you read, underline examples of objects affected by inertia.

Newton's first law is also called the law of inertia. **Inertia** (ih•NER•shuh) is the tendency of all objects to resist a change in motion. An object will not move until a force makes it move. So a chair will not slide across the floor unless a force pushes the chair, and a golf ball will not leave the tee until a force pushes it off.

Visualize It!

12 Explain In your own words, explain why the dishes remain in place when the magician pulls the cloth out from under them.

_____

_____

_____

An Object in Motion Stays in Motion

Now let's look at the second part of Newton's first law of motion. It states that an object in motion stays in motion at the same speed and direction, or velocity, unless it experiences an unbalanced force. Think about coming to a sudden stop while riding in a car. The car stops because the brakes apply friction to the wheel, making the forces acting on the car unbalanced. You keep moving forward until your seat belt applies an unbalanced force on you. This force stops your forward motion.

Both parts of the law are really stating the same thing. After all, an object at rest has a velocity—its velocity is zero!

Think Outside the Book Inquiry

13 Apply Create a model that demonstrates the concept of inertia. Share your results with the class.

When this car was in motion, the test dummy was moving forward at the same velocity as the car. When the car hit the barrier and stopped, the dummy kept moving until it, too, was acted on by a net backward force.

FO4305OZO2

000 1768

Visualize It!

14 Infer What forces acted on the test dummy to stop its forward motion?

_____

_____

_____

_____

_____

What is Newton's Second Law of Motion?

Active Reading

15 Identify As you read, underline Newton's second law of motion.

When an unbalanced force acts on an object, the object accelerates. Newton's second law describes this motion. The law states: *The acceleration of an object depends on the mass of the object and the amount of force applied.*

In other words, objects that have different masses will have different accelerations if the same amount of force is used. Also, a larger mass requires more force than a smaller mass to have the same acceleration. Imagine pushing a shopping cart. When the cart is empty, you need only a small force to accelerate it. But if the cart is full of groceries, the same amount of force causes a much smaller acceleration.

Force Equals Mass Times Acceleration

Newton's second law links force, mass, and acceleration. We can express this relationship using the equation $F = ma$, where F stands for applied force, m stands for mass, and a stands for acceleration. This equation tells us that a given force applied to a large mass will result in a small acceleration. When the same force is applied to a smaller mass, the acceleration will be greater.

Do the Math   Sample Problem

These players train by pushing a massive object. If the players push with a force of 150 N, and the object has a mass of 75 kg, what is the object's acceleration? One newton is equal to $1 \text{ kg}\cdot\text{m/s}^2$.

Use Newton's law:

$$F = ma$$
$$150 \text{ kg}\cdot\text{m/s}^2 = (75 \text{ kg})(a)$$
$$a = \frac{150}{75} \text{ m/s}^2$$
$$a = 2.0 \text{ m/s}^2$$

You Try It

16 Calculate For a more difficult training session, the mass to be pushed is increased to 160 kg. If the players still push with a force of 150 N, what is the acceleration of the object?

Use Newton's law:

$$F = ma$$
$$150 \text{ N} =$$

Newton's Second Law and You

Think about the last time you rode on a roller coaster or in a car on a hilly road. Did you feel like you were going to float out of your seat when you went over a big hill? Newton's second law can explain that feeling.

Going Up
When the roller coaster is going up a hill, you have two important forces acting on you—the force of gravity and the upward force exerted by the roller coaster seat.

Coming Down
Once the roller coaster starts down the other side, it accelerates downward, and your seat does not support your full weight.

flight path

Practicing for Space
Astronauts take special flights to train for space missions. The airplane's path looks like a roller coaster hill. As the plane accelerates downward, the astronauts lose contact with the plane and fall toward Earth. This condition is called free fall.

Extend

Inquiry

17 Infer Suppose you were standing on a scale in an elevator in free fall. What would the scale read?

18 Synthesize Explain why the feeling of weightlessness in free fall is not the same as truly being weightless.

19 Compare In what ways are roller coaster rides similar to and different from training simulations in a NASA plane?

What is Newton's Third Law of Motion?

Newton also devised a third law of motion. The law states: *Whenever one object exerts a force on a second object, the second object exerts an equal and opposite force on the first.*

So when you push against a wall, Newton's law tells you that the wall is actually pushing back against you.

Objects Exert Force on Each Other

Newton's third law also can be stated as: All forces act in pairs. Whenever one object exerts a force on a second object, the second object exerts an equal and opposite force on the first. There are action forces and reaction forces. Action and reaction forces are present even when there is no motion. For example, you exert a force on a chair when you sit on it. Your weight pushing down on the chair is the action force. The reaction force is the force exerted by the chair that pushes up on your body.

Forces in Pairs Have Equal Size but Opposite Directions

When an object pushes against another object, the second object pushes back equally hard, in the opposite direction. In the pool below, the swimmer's feet push against the wall as he moves forward. This push is the action force. The wall also exerts a force on the swimmer. This is the reaction force, and it moves the swimmer forward. The forces do not act on the same object. Read on to find out why the swimmer moves but the wall does not!

Visualize It!

20 Apply The arrow below represents the action force exerted by the swimmer. Draw an arrow that represents the reaction force.

When a swimmer pushes off against a wall, the wall pushes back against the swimmer.

Forces Acting in Pairs Can Have Unequal Effects

Even though action and reaction forces are equal in size, their effects are often different. Gravitation is a force pair between two objects. If you drop a ball, gravity in an action force pulls the ball toward Earth. But the reaction force pulls Earth toward the ball! It's easy to see the effect of the action force. Why don't you see the effect of the reaction force—Earth being pulled upward? Newton's second law answers this question. The force on the ball is the same size as the force on Earth. However, Earth has much more mass than the ball. So Earth's acceleration is much smaller than that of the ball!

21 Identify Label the action force and reaction force in the image below.

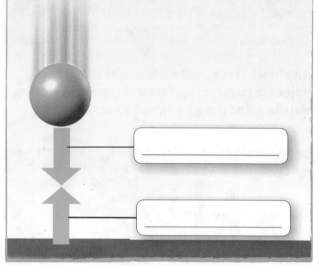

Forces Can Act in Multiple Pairs

An object can have multiple forces acting on it at once. When this happens, each force is part of a force pair. For example, when a baseball bat hits a baseball, the bat does not fly backward. A force is exerted on the ball by the bat. The bat does not fly backward, because the player's hands are exerting another force on the bat. What then keeps the player's hands from flying backward when the bat hits the ball? The bones and muscles in the player's arms exert a force on the hands. As you can see, a simple activity such as playing baseball involves the action of many forces at the same time.

22 Describe In your own words, explain Newton's third law of motion.

_____

_____

_____

Visual Summary

To complete this summary, fill in the blanks with the correct word or phrase. Then use the key below to check your answers. You can use this page to review the main concepts of the lesson.

Forces

An object at rest will remain at rest and an object in constant motion will remain in motion unless acted upon by an unbalanced force.

23 Newton's first law is also called the law of _____

When an unbalanced force acts on an object, the object moves with accelerated motion.

24 In the formula $F = ma$, m stands for _____

Whenever one object exerts a force on a second object, the second object exerts an equal and opposite force on the first.

25 Forces in the same pair have equal size but opposite _____

Answers: 23: inertia; 24: mass; 25: direction

26 Synthesize A car designer is designing a new model of a popular car. He wants to use the same engine as in the old model, but improve the new car's acceleration. Use Newton's second law to explain how to improve the car's acceleration without redesigning the engine.

Lesson Review

Vocabulary

Draw a line to connect the following terms to their definitions.

1 force

2 inertia

3 newton

A resistance of an object to a change in motion

B the unit that expresses force

C a push or a pull

Key Concepts

4 Describe What is the action force and the reaction force when you sit down on a chair?

_____

_____

_____

_____

_____

_____

_____

5 Summarize How do you determine net force?

_____

_____

_____

_____

_____

_____

6 Explain How do tests with crash dummies, seat belts, and air bags illustrate Newton's first law of motion?

_____

_____

_____

_____

_____

Critical Thinking

Use this photo to answer the following questions.

7 Identify This rock, known as Balanced Rock, sits on a thin spike of rock in a canyon in Idaho. Explain the forces that keep the rock balanced on its tiny pedestal.

_____

_____

_____

_____

8 Calculate Balanced Rock has a mass of about 36,000 kg. If the acceleration due to gravity is 9.8 m/s^2, what is the force that the rock is exerting on its pedestal?

_____

_____

_____

_____

_____

9 Infer What would happen to the moon if Earth stopped exerting the force of gravity on it?

_____

_____

_____

_____

_____

My Notes

Big Idea
Unbalanced forces cause changes in the motion of objects, and these changes can be predicted and described.

Lesson 1
ESSENTIAL QUESTION
How are distance, time, and speed related?

Analyze how distance, time, and speed are related.

Lesson 2
ESSENTIAL QUESTION
How does motion change?

Analyze how acceleration is related to time and velocity.

Lesson 3
ESSENTIAL QUESTION
How do forces affect motion?

Describe different types of forces and explain the effect force has on motion.

Connect ESSENTIAL QUESTIONS
Lessons 2 and 3

1 Synthesize How is force related to acceleration and gravity?

_____

_____

_____

_____

Think Outside the Book

2 Synthesize Choose one of these activities to help synthesize what you have learned in this unit.

☐ Using what you learned in lessons 1–3, create a brochure to explain why the following statement is false: An object's motion can change only if a force is applied to the object through direct contact.

☐ Using what you learned in lesson 3, make a poster presentation describing the forces acting on a falling skydiver with an open parachute.

Name _____

Vocabulary

Fill in each blank with the term that best completes the following sentences.

1 The _____ of an object describes the speed and the direction in which it is going.

2 The change in the velocity of an object is defined as its _____.

3 A location to which you compare other locations is a _____.

4 The _____ on an object is the combination of all the forces acting on the object.

5 Acceleration in circular motion is known as _____.

Key Concepts

Read each question below, and circle the best answer.

6 An airplane leaves New York to fly to Los Angeles. It travels 3,850 km in 5.5 hours. What is the average speed of the airplane?

A 700 km

C 700 km/hour

B 700 hours

D 700 hours/km

7 A vehicle's acceleration and velocity are in the same direction. What will happen to the speed of the vehicle?

A It will decrease.

B It will increase.

C It will remain the same.

D It will change direction.

8 This distance-time graph shows the speeds of four toy cars.

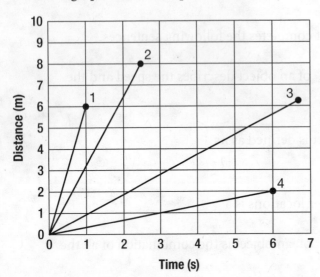

Which car is the fastest?

A Car 1   **C** Car 3

B Car 2   **D** Car 4

9 The diagram below shows the forces acting on a sneaker. As the force F is applied, the sneaker does not move.

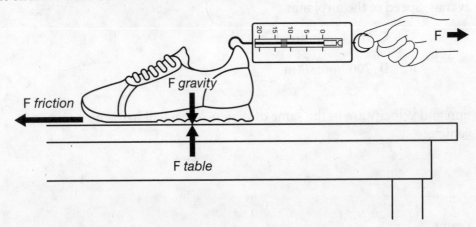

Which statement below correctly describes the forces?

A The net force is acting in an upward direction.

B The net force is acting to the left.

C The net force is moving to the right.

D The net force is zero and all the forces are balanced.

10 Elizabeth is wildlife biologist. She travels by boat to the Everglades to observe alligators. The following graphs show the motion of her boat at several times during the trip.

Graph A

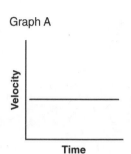

Graph B

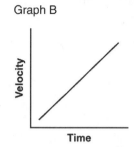

Graph C

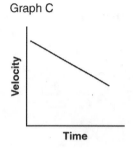

Graph D

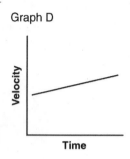

Which graph shows her boat traveling when it is not accelerating?

A Graph A

B Graph B

C Graph C

D Graph D

11 Julia is in a car with her father. The car is undergoing centripetal acceleration. What is happening to the car?

A The car is changing direction at a constant speed.

B The car is changing direction and speeding up.

C The car is stopping suddenly.

D The car is slowing down.

12 Consider two objects whose masses are 100 g and 200 g. The 100 g object strikes the 200 g object with a force of 500 N. According to Newton's third law of motion, what force does the larger object exert on the smaller object?

A 250 N.

B 500 N

C 1,000 N

D 1,500 N

Critical Thinking

Answer the following questions in the space provided.

13 Marek is trying to push a box of sports equipment across the floor. The arrow on the box is a vector representing the force that Marek exerts.

What are the forces acting upon the box?

_____

_____

_____

_____

14 What does the formula $F = ma$ mean, and which of Newton's three laws does it describe?

_____

_____

_____

Connect **ESSENTIAL QUESTIONS**
Lessons 1 and 2

Answer the following question in the space provided.

15 What is the difference between the speed of an object, the velocity of an object, and the acceleration of an object?

_____

_____

_____

_____

Electricity and Magnetism

Lightning is the discharge of static electricity that builds up in clouds during a storm.

Big Idea

An electric current can produce a magnetic field, and a magnetic field can produce an electric current.

8.PS2.1 ,8.PS2.2, 8.ETS1.1

What do you think?

Static electricity can make your hair stand on end. What other effects of static electricity can you think of?

This Van de Graaff generator makes a safe but hair-raising demonstration.

Unit 2
Electricity and Magnetism

Be Lightning Safe

Lightning can be an impressive display, but it is also very dangerous. Lightning strikes carry a great deal of energy that can split apart trees, damage property, and start fires. People can be injured or killed if they are struck by lightning.

1 Define the Problem

Research how people can protect themselves from lightning while participating in outdoor activities.

A What are some signs that lightning may occur?

_____

_____

_____

B Where and for how long should people take shelter from lightning?

_____

_____

_____

To be safe from lightning, people should wait out a storm by going inside a school building that is completely enclosed.

Game Canceled due to severe weather

② Ask Some Questions

A Where is your school's lightning-safety plan posted?

_____

_____

B Are students and teachers aware of your school's plan for lightning safety?

_____

_____

C What is your school's current policy for canceling outdoor events when there is a risk of lightning?

_____

_____

_____

D Is your school's current plan for lightning safety adequate?

_____

_____

_____

③ Make a Plan

A What are two ways in which your school's lightning-safety plan could be improved?

_____

_____

_____

_____

B Describe two steps that you could take to promote your improved lightning-safety plan at your school.

_____

_____

_____

_____

Take It Home

With an adult, make a lightning-safety plan for your family. And, discuss the weather conditions that would cause you to put your plan into action. See *ScienceSaurus*® for more information about weather.

Electric Charge and Static Electricity

ESSENTIAL QUESTION

What makes something electrically charged?

By the end of this lesson, you should be able to describe electric charges in objects and distinguish between electrical conductors and insulators.

8.PS2.2

This electrically charged metal dome is part of a device called a Van de Graaff generator. Touching the dome has made this student electrically charged.

Engage Your Brain

1 Predict Check T or F to show whether you think each statement is true or false.

T   F

☐   ☐   Electrons have a negative charge.

☐   ☐   Objects with like charges attract each other.

☐   ☐   Copper is an electrical conductor.

☐   ☐   Objects must be touching to exert an electric force on each other.

2 Describe Write your own caption describing what is happening to this student's hair.

_____

_____

_____

_____

 Active Reading

3 Synthesize Many scientific words, such as *charge*, also have everyday meanings. Use context clues to write your own definition for each meaning of the word *charge*.

Example sentence
The <u>charge</u> for entry to the zoo goes up every year.

charge:

_____

_____

Example sentence
When Andre touched the doorknob, the <u>charge</u> gave him a shock.

charge:

_____

_____

Vocabulary Terms
• electric charge
• static electricity
• electrical conductor
• electrical insulator
• semiconductor

4 Identify As you read, create a reference card for each vocabulary term. On one side of the card, write the term and its meaning. On the other side, draw an image that illustrates or makes a connection to the term. These cards can be used as bookmarks in the text so that you can refer to them while studying.

Opposites Attract

What is electric charge?

Have you ever touched a doorknob and felt a shock? Have you ever seen clothes cling to each other after they are taken from a dryer? Both of these events are due to a fundamental property of matter called *electric charge*. **Electric charge** is a property that leads to electromagnetic interactions between the particles that make up matter. An object can have a positive (+) charge, a negative (–) charge, or no charge. An object that has no charge is *neutral*.

The diagram below shows charges within an atom. All atoms have a dense center called a *nucleus*. The nucleus contains two types of particles: *protons* and *neutrons*. A proton has a charge of 1+. A neutron has no charge. *Electrons* are a third type of particle and are found outside the nucleus. An electron has a charge of 1–. When an atom has the same number of protons as electrons, the atom has no overall charge. This is because the charges of its protons and electrons add up to zero. However, atoms can lose or gain electrons. When this happens, the atom has an overall positive or negative charge and is called an *ion*. Positively charged ions have more protons than electrons. Negatively charged ions have fewer protons than electrons. The overall charge of an object is the sum of the charges of its atoms.

Pieces of paper cling to a ruler due to the electric charge of the ruler.

---

5 Apply An atom gains an additional electron. What is the overall charge of the ion that is formed? _____

Visualize It!

6 Label Complete the diagram by labeling the nucleus and an electron.

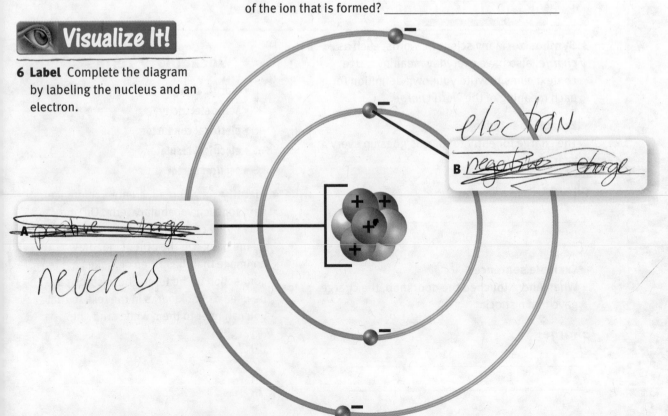

electron

B negative charge

A positive charge

nucleus

What affects the electric field between two objects?

Any two charged objects exert a force on each other called an *electric force*. The electric force acts through the electric field. Like gravity, the electric fields act between objects even when they do not touch. But gravity always pulls objects together. Unlike gravity, the electric field can either pull objects together or push them apart. How strongly the electric field pushes or pulls depends on the charge of each object and how close together the objects are.

Charge

If objects have like charges, they repel each other. The objects exert an electric field that pushes them apart. The balls in the diagram A at the right both have a positive charge. The arrows show the electric force acting on each ball.

Two objects with unlike charges attract each other. So an object with a positive charge and an object with a negative charge are attracted. Each object exerts a force on the other, pulling the objects together.

The amount of charge on each object also affects the strength of the electric field between them. The greater an object's charge is, the greater the electric force is. This is true whether the objects repel or attract each other.

Distance

The distance between two objects affects the strength of the electric field, too. The closer together the charged objects are, the greater the electric field is. As charged objects move farther apart, they attract or repel each other less strongly.

Active Reading **7 Identify** What factors affect how strong the electric field is between two charged objects?

distance and Charge

8 Analyze Label diagrams B and C with the missing charge signs. Then add a caption below each diagram to describe the forces between the objects.

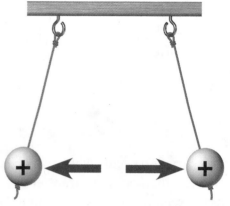

A *The balls have like positive charges. They push each other apart.*

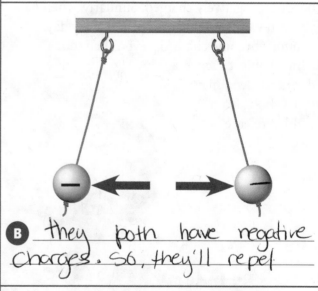

B *they both have negative charges. So, they'll repel*

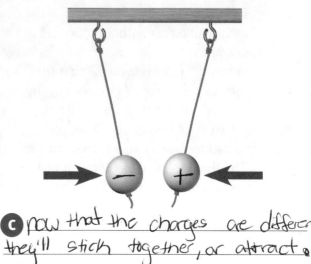

C *now that the charges are different they'll stick together, or attract.*

What a *Shock!*

Active Reading

9 Identify As you read, underline examples of objects becoming charged.

How can an object become charged?

Objects become charged when their atoms gain or lose electrons. Three ways that objects can gain or lose electrons are by friction, contact, or induction.

By Friction

Charging by friction occurs when two objects are rubbed together, causing a transfer of electrons between the objects. For example, rubbing a balloon on your hair moves electrons from your hair to the balloon. Your hair becomes positively charged, and the balloon becomes negatively charged. Similarly, when you rub your shoes on a carpet on a dry day, you may become charged. If you then touch a metal object such as a doorknob, you may feel a shock from the sudden release of electric charge.

By Contact

If a charged object and an uncharged object touch each other, the charged object can transfer some of its charge to the area it touches. The sphere at the right is part of a *Van de Graaff generator.* The generator places a charge on its dome. An uncharged object that touches the dome becomes charged by contact. This student's hair is standing on end because the charged hairs repel each other.

By Induction

Induction is a way of rearranging the charges within an object without touching it. For example, this ruler has a negative charge. When the ruler is brought near the metal knob, it repels electrons in the metal. Electrons move away from the ruler and down the metal rod. The knob now has a positive charge. The thin pieces of metal foil at the bottom of the metal rod now have a negative charge. Their like charges cause them to push each other apart.

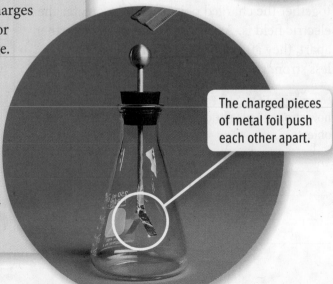

The charged pieces of metal foil push each other apart.

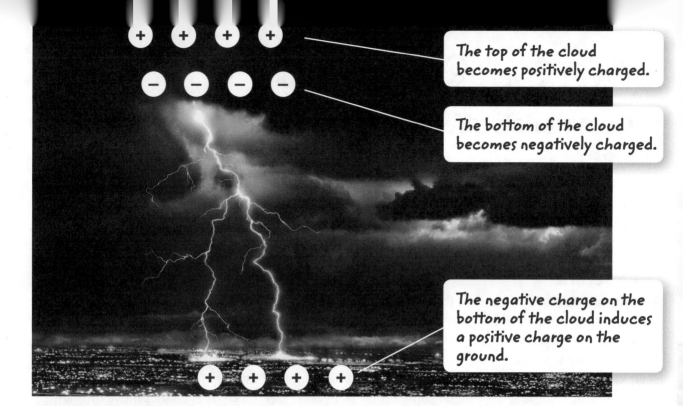

The top of the cloud becomes positively charged.

The bottom of the cloud becomes negatively charged.

The negative charge on the bottom of the cloud induces a positive charge on the ground.

What is static electricity?

After you take your clothes out of the dryer, they sometimes are stuck together. They stick together because of static electricity. **Static electricity** is the buildup of electric charge on an object. When something is static, it is not moving. Static electricity is the extra positive or negative charge that builds up on an object until it eventually moves elsewhere.

The Buildup of Charge on an Object

For an object to have static electricity, charge must build up on the object. For example, static electricity can build up inside storm clouds. The top of the cloud becomes positively charged. The bottom of the cloud becomes negatively charged. The negative charge in the bottom of the cloud can cause the ground to become positively charged by induction.

Charges that build up as static electricity eventually leave the object. This loss of charges is known as *electric discharge*. Electric discharge may happen slowly or quickly. Lightning is an example of rapid electric discharge. Lightning can occur between clouds. It can also occur between the negative part of the cloud and the positively charged ground. When lightning strikes, charged particles move toward places with opposite charge.

Active Reading **10 Analyze** During a lightning storm, what can cause the ground to become positively charged?

_____

_____

Think Outside the Book Inquiry

11 Apply Think of an everyday example of an object becoming charged. Draw and label a diagram that shows how charges moved. (Hint: You may need to use reference materials to learn more about the process you have chosen.)

Charging Ahead

What materials affect the flow of charge?

Have you ever noticed that electrical cords are often made from both metal and plastic? Different materials are used because electric charges move through some materials more easily than they move through others.

Conductors

An **electrical conductor** is a material through which charges can move freely. Many electrical conductors are metals. Copper is a metal that is used to make wires because it is an excellent electrical conductor. When an electrically charged plastic ruler touches a metal conductor, the charge it transfers to the metal can move freely through the metal.

Insulators

An **electrical insulator** is a material through which charges cannot move easily. The electrons are tightly held in the atoms of the insulator. Plastic, rubber, glass, and dry air are all good electrical insulators. Plastic is often used to coat wires because electric charges cannot move through the plastic easily. This stops the charges from leaving the wire and prevents you from being shocked when you touch the lamp cord.

Visualize It!

12 Identify What is the purpose of the material surrounding the metal inside the lamp cord?

a Conductor

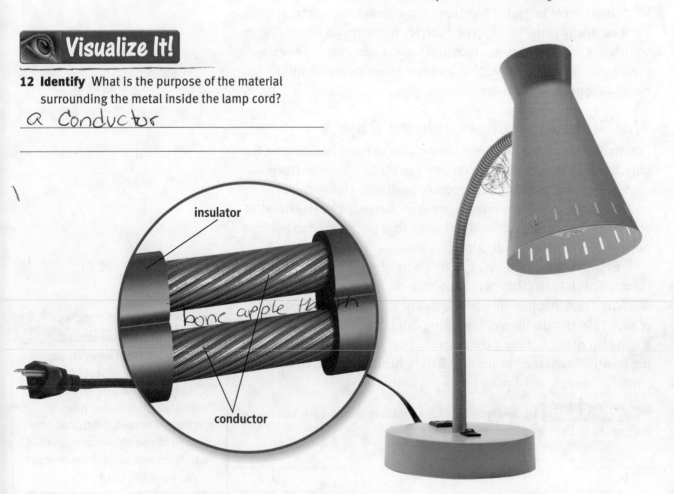

insulator

bone apple thorn

conductor

Semiconductors are used to make the computer chips found in electronic devices such as cell phones and calculators.

Semiconductors

Semiconductors are a special class of materials that conduct electric charge better than electrical insulators but not as well as electrical conductors. Their properties allow them to be used to control the flow of charge. Electrical devices use semiconductors to process electrical signals in many different ways. Silicon is the basis of many kinds of semiconductors. It is used to make computer chips found in electronic devices such as the ones shown above.

13 Summarize Fill in the table at the right to summarize what you have learned about conductors, insulators, and semiconductors.

	Example	Effect on the movement of charges
Conductor	copper wire	passes through
Insulator	threads	doesnt pass through
Semiconductor	photocell	

How is charge conserved?

All objects contain positive charges from the protons and negative charges from the electrons within their atoms. A neutral object becomes negatively charged when it gains one or more electrons and then has more negative charges than positive charges. Where do these electrons come from? They might come from a second object that loses the electrons and becomes positively charged. So electrons are not really lost. Charging objects involves moving electrons from one object to another. The total amount of charge always stays the same. This principle is called the conservation of charge.

Active Reading **14 Describe** What happens to the charge lost by an object?

_____

_____

Visual Summary

To complete this summary, fill in the blanks with the correct word. Then use the key below to check your answers. You can use this page to review the main concepts of the lesson.

Electric Charge and Static Electricity

Like charges repel each other, while unlike charges attract each other.

15 An object that has a positive charge equal to its negative charge is _____

Electrical conductors allow electric charges to move freely, while electrical insulators do not.

17 A _____ is a material whose conductivity is between that of an electrical conductor and an electrical insulator.

Objects can become charged by friction, contact, or induction.

16 _____ is the buildup of electric charges on an object.

Electric charge is always conserved.

18 The electrons lost by one object are _____ by another.

insulator

conductor

19 Predict Suppose an electrically charged ruler transfers some of its charge by contact to a tiny plastic sphere. Will the ruler and the sphere attract or repel afterwards? Why?

Lesson Review

Vocabulary

Draw a line to connect the following terms to their definitions.

1 electric charge

A a material that allows electrons to flow easily

2 electrical conductor

B a material that does not allow electrons to flow easily

3 electrical insulator

C property that leads to electromagnetic interactions

Key Concepts

4 Explain Describe electric discharge.

_____

_____

_____

_____

_____

_____

5 Compare What properties of semiconductors make them useful in electronic devices?

_____

_____

_____

_____

_____

6 Predict Two objects have unlike charges. How would the electric force between the two objects change as they are moved apart?

_____

_____

_____

_____

_____

_____

Critical Thinking

Use this diagram to answer the following questions.

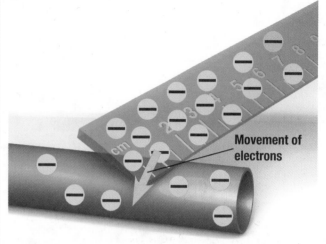

Movement of electrons

Not to scale

7 Analyze Describe how charge is transferred from the ruler to the metal rod.

_____

_____

_____

_____

_____

8 Describe Explain how this transfer observes the conservation of charge.

_____

_____

_____

_____

_____

_____

9 Evaluate A student places two charged objects near each other. The objects repel each other. The student concludes that the objects must both be negative. Do you agree? Explain.

_____

_____

_____

_____

My Notes

Electric Current

Electric current sent over wires from power plants supplies this city with energy for lights and other uses.

ESSENTIAL QUESTION

What flows through an electric wire?

By the end of this lesson, you should be able to describe how electric charges flow as electric current.

 8.PS2.2

✋ Lesson Labs

Quick Labs
- Investigate Electric Current
- Lemon Battery

S.T.E.M. Lab
- Voltage, Current, and Resistance

🧠 Engage Your Brain

1 Identify Unscramble the letters below to find terms related to electric current. Write your words on the blank lines.

SGARCHE _____

EGATOVL _____

EERPAM _____

EIRW _____

2 Describe Describe what makes this electric sign light up when it is in use.

_____

_____

_____

_____

✏️ Active Reading

3 Apply Many scientific words such as *resistance* also have everyday meanings. Use context clues to write your own definition for the word *resistance*.

Example sentence
John's request to go to the movies met with resistance from his friends.

resistance:

_____

_____

_____

Example sentence
The composition of a wire determines its electrical resistance.

resistance:

_____

_____

_____

Vocabulary Terms

- electric current
- resistance
- voltage

4 Identify As you read, place a question mark next to any words that you do not understand. When you finish reading the lesson, go back and review the text that you marked. If the information is still confusing, consult a classmate or a teacher.

Current Events

What is an electric current?

When you watch TV, use a computer, or even turn on a light bulb, you depend on moving charges to provide the electrical energy that powers them. *Electrical energy* is the energy of electric charges. In most devices that use electrical energy, the electric charges flow through wires. The rate of flow of electric charges is called **electric current**.

How is electric current measured?

To understand an electric current, think of people entering the seating area for a sporting event through turnstiles. A counter in each turnstile records the number of people who enter. The number of people who pass through a turnstile each minute describes the rate of flow of people into the stadium. Similarly, an electric current describes the rate of flow of charges, such as the slow flow of many electrons through a wire. Electric current is the amount of charge that passes a location in the wire every second. Electric current is expressed in units called *amperes* (AM•pirz), which is often shortened to "amps." The symbol for ampere is A. A wire with a current of 2 A has twice as much charge passing by each second as a wire with a current of 1 A.

© Houghton Mifflin Harcourt Publishing Company • Image Credits: ©Elsa/Staff/Getty Images Sport/Getty Images

Active Reading

5 Identify As you read, underline the units used to express electric current.

Visualize It!

6 Identify How can you express the rate of flow of people into a stadium? How can you express the rate of flow of charges through a wire?

like people, if the electricity is blocked by something the flow stops

What are two kinds of current?

Two kinds of electric current are *direct current* (DC) and *alternating current* (AC). Both kinds of current carry electrical energy. They differ in the way that the charges move.

Direct Current (DC)

In direct current, charges always flow in the same direction. The electric current generated by batteries is DC. Some everyday devices that use DC from batteries are flashlights, cars, and cameras.

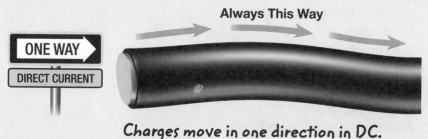

Always This Way

ONE WAY
DIRECT CURRENT

Charges move in one direction in DC.

Alternating Current (AC)

In alternating current, charges repeatedly shift from flowing in one direction to flowing in the reverse direction. The current *alternates* direction. The electric current from outlets in your home is AC. So, most household appliances run on alternating current. In the United States, the alternating current reverses direction and then returns back to the original direction 60 times each second.

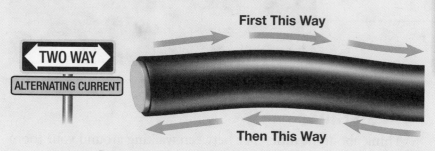

First This Way

TWO WAY
ALTERNATING CURRENT

Then This Way

Charges repeatedly change direction in AC.

 Active Reading

7 Explain What alternates in alternating current?

direction

_____

_____

You've Got *Potential*

What affects electric current?

Two factors that can affect the current in a wire are *voltage* and *resistance*.

Voltage

Compare the two drink containers below. If you pour lemonade from a full container, your glass fills quickly. If the container is nearly empty, the flow of lemonade is weaker. The lemonade in the full container exerts more pressure due to its weight, causing a higher rate of flow. This pressure can be compared to voltage. **Voltage** is the amount of work required to move each unit of charge between two points. Just as higher pressure produces a higher rate of flow of lemonade, higher voltage produces a higher rate of flow of electric charges in a given wire. Voltage is expressed in units of volts (V). Voltage is sometimes called *electric potential* because it is a measure of the electric potential energy per unit charge.

Visualize It!

8 Analyze How does the flow of the lemonade coming out of these containers relate to current and voltage?

the more voltage a current has the stronger the flow.

Resistance

Think about the difference between walking around your room and walking around in waist-deep water. The water resists your movement more than the air, so you have to work harder to walk through water. If you walked in waist-deep mud, you would have to work even harder. Similarly, some materials do not allow electric charges to move freely. The opposition to the flow of electric charge is called **resistance**. Resistance is expressed in ohms (Ω, the Greek letter *omega*). Higher resistance at the same voltage results in lower current.

© Houghton Mifflin Harcourt Publishing Company • Image Credits: (l) ©HMH; (r) ©MHM

What affects electrical resistance?

A material's composition affects its resistance. Some metals, such as silver and copper, have low resistance and are very good electrical conductors. Other metals, such as iron and nickel, have a higher resistance. Electrical insulators such as plastic have such a high resistance that electric charges cannot flow in them at all. Other factors that affect the resistance of a wire are thickness, length, and temperature.

- A thin wire has higher resistance than a thicker wire.
- A long wire has higher resistance than a shorter wire.
- A hot wire has higher resistance than a cooler wire.

Conductors with low resistance, such as copper, are used to make wires. But conductors with high resistance are also useful. For example, an alloy of nickel and chromium is used in heating coils. Its high resistance causes the wire to heat up when it carries electric current.

Like lemonade in a drinking straw, electric charges move more easily through a short, wide pathway than through a long, narrow one.

 **Visualize It!**

10 Predict For each pair of images, place a check mark in the box that shows the material that has higher electrical resistance.

Composition Wires made from different materials have different uses in electronic devices.	Pure copper  □	Nickel and chromium alloy  ☑
Thickness A three-way light bulb contains a thin filament and a thick filament. Charges move through one filament or the other or both to produce different brightness levels.	Thin filament 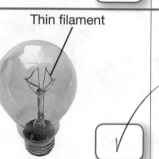 ☑	Thick filament 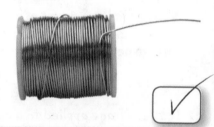 □
Temperature The electrical resistance of this heating element changes as its temperature increases.	 □	 ☑

Visual Summary

To complete this summary, fill in the blanks with the correct word or phrase. Then use the key below to check your answers. You can use this page to review the main concepts of the lesson.

Electric current is the rate of flow of electric charges.

First This Way

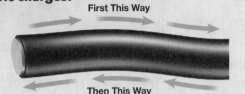

Then This Way

11 In _____ current, the flow of charge changes direction and then reverses back to the original direction.

The opposition to the flow of electric charges is called resistance.

13 Four factors that determine the resistance of a wire are

_____

_____

_____

_____

Voltage is the amount of work to move an electric charge between two points.

Electric Current

12 If the voltage applied to a given wire increases, its current will

_____

14 Apply What might happen if a wire in an electronic device is replaced with a thinner, longer wire? Explain.

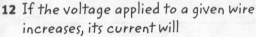

Lesson Review

Vocabulary

Draw a line to connect the following terms to their definitions.

1 electric current   **A** the opposition to the flow of electric charges

2 voltage   **B** the rate of flow of electric charges

3 resistance   **C** the amount of work required to move each unit of electric charge between two points

Key Concepts

4 Compare How does direct current differ from alternating current?

_____

_____

_____

_____

5 Summarize Describe how resistance affects electric current.

_____

_____

_____

_____

6 Apply What happens to the electric current in a wire as voltage is increased?

_____

_____

7 Apply List two everyday devices that use DC and two everyday devices that use AC.

_____

_____

_____

Critical Thinking

Use the diagram to answer the following questions.

Electrical Resistance of Various Materials

| Copper | Germanium | PVC Plastic |

Low resistance   High resistance

8 Analyze Which material is likely to slow the flow of electric charges the most? Explain.

_____

_____

9 Infer A certain voltage is applied to a copper wire and to a germanium wire of the same thickness and length. How will the current in the two wires compare?

_____

_____

_____

_____

10 Compare How do the currents produced by a 1.5 V flashlight battery and a 12 V car battery compare if the resistance is the same?

_____

_____

_____

11 Infer What does it mean to say that the electric current from a wall socket is "120 V AC?"

_____

_____

_____

My Notes

Electric Circuits

ESSENTIAL QUESTION

How do electric circuits work?

By the end of this lesson, you should be able to describe basic electric circuits and how to use electricity safely.

Microscopic electric circuits inside these computer chips carry electric charges that can power computers, video games, and home appliances.

Lesson Labs

Quick Labs
• Compare Parallel and Series Circuits
• Compare Materials for Use in Fuses

Exploration
• Model the Electric Circuits in a Room

Engage Your Brain

1 Predict Check T or F to show whether you think each statement is true or false.

T	F	
☐	☐	A circuit must form a closed loop to have an electric current.
☐	☐	Electricity is dangerous only when it is labeled as high voltage.
☐	☐	Every electric circuit must have an energy source.

2 Describe Write a caption explaining how these light bulbs are connected.

_____

_____

_____

_____

Active Reading

3 Apply Many scientific words, such as *current*, also have everyday meanings. Use context clues to write your own definition for each meaning of the word *current*.

Example sentence
The magazine covered <u>current</u> events.

current:

_____

_____

Example sentence
The circuit had an electric <u>current</u> in it.

current:

_____

_____

Vocabulary Terms

• electric circuit
• series circuit
• parallel circuit

4 Apply As you learn the definition of each vocabulary term in this lesson, create your own definition or sketch to help you remember the meaning of the term.

A Complete Circuit

What are the parts of an electric circuit?

Think about a running track. It forms a loop. The spot where you start running around the track is the same as the spot where you end. This kind of closed loop is called a circuit. Like a track, an electric circuit also forms a loop. An **electric circuit** is a complete, closed path through which electric charges can flow. All electric circuits contain three basic parts: an energy source, an electrical conductor, and a load.

Energy Source

The energy source converts some type of energy, such as chemical energy, into electrical energy. One common household energy source is a battery. A battery changes chemical energy stored inside the battery into electrical energy. A solar cell is an energy source that changes light energy into electrical energy.

Inside a power plant, a form of energy such as chemical or nuclear energy is changed into mechanical energy. Electric generators in the power plant change the mechanical energy into electrical energy. Power transmission lines deliver this energy to wall outlets in homes, schools, and other buildings.

Active Reading

5 Identify As you read this page and the next, underline examples of energy sources, electrical conductors, and electrical loads used in an electric circuit.

Solar cell

Battery

Power plant

Think Outside the Book Inquiry

6 Research Learn how your local power plant uses turbines and generators to produce electrical energy. Then write a short article about how the power plant generates the mechanical energy for the turbines.

Electrical Conductor

Materials in which electric charges can move easily are called *electrical conductors*. Most metals are good conductors of electric current. Electric wires are often made of copper. Copper is a metal that is a good conductor and is inexpensive compared to many other metals. Conducting wires connect all the parts of an electric circuit.

To protect people from harmful electrical shocks, copper wire is often covered with an insulator. An *electrical insulator* is a material, such as glass, plastic, or rubber, through which electric charges cannot move easily.

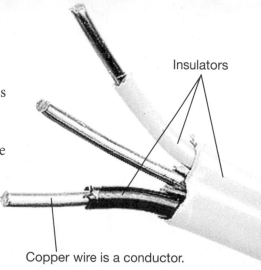

Insulators

Copper wire is a conductor.

Load

A complete circuit also includes a *load,* a device that uses electrical energy to operate. The conductor connects the energy source to the load. Examples of loads include light bulbs, radios, computers, and electric motors. The load converts electrical energy into other forms of energy. A light bulb, for example, converts electrical energy into light and energy as heat. A doorbell produces sound waves, energy that is transmitted through the air to your ear. A cell phone converts electrical energy into electromagnetic waves that carry information.

Visualize It!

7 Identify List the devices in the photograph that could be a load in an electric circuit.

_____

_____

_____

_____

_____

_____

_____

_____

Around and Around

How are electric circuits modeled?

Active Reading

8 Identify As you read, underline the descriptions of symbols used in circuit diagrams.

To make an electric circuit, you need only three basic parts: an energy source, an electrical conductor, and a load. Most electric circuits, however, have more than one load. A circuit in your home might connect a desk lamp, clock radio, computer, and TV set. The circuit may even include devices in more than one room. Circuits can be complex. A single computer chip can have many millions of parts. One tool that can be used to model electric circuits is a circuit diagram.

Circuit Diagram Symbols

Wire

Load

Energy Source

Open switch

Closed switch

With Circuit Diagrams

A circuit diagram helps engineers and electricians design and install electric circuits so that they function correctly and safely. Sometimes, special software is used to create complex circuit designs on computers. A diagram for an electric circuit shows all the parts in the complete circuit and the relationships among the different parts. The chart at the left shows how each part of a circuit can be represented in a circuit diagram. The energy source can be represented by two parallel lines of different length. A wire or other conductor is shown as a line. A load is represented by a zigzag line segment. A small circle shows where two wires are connected. A straight line between two circles shows an on-off switch. When the line of the switch symbol is slanted up, the switch is open. When the line for the switch symbol connects two dots, the switch is closed.

Symbols are put together to show the arrangement of parts in a circuit. A circuit diagram is like a road map for the moving charges.

How does current stop and start?

Electric charges move continuously in the closed loop of an electric circuit. What do you do if you want the charges to stop flowing? You open the switch! A switch is a device that turns electrical devices on and off. A switch is usually made of a piece of conducting material that can move. When the switch is open, the circuit is open. That means it does not form a closed loop, so charges cannot flow. When you turn a light switch on, the switch closes the circuit. Charges flow through the light bulb. If you turn a light switch off, the switch opens the circuit, and the charges stop flowing.

9 Explain Why does an open light switch turn off the light?

_____

_____

_____

_____

_____

Visualize It!

10 Identify Label the parts in this circuit diagram. Then draw a switch to match the circuit shown in the photograph.

B _____

A _____

A switch opens and closes a circuit to turn a light bulb off and on.

All Together?

How do series circuits and parallel circuits differ?

Most electric circuits have more than one load. Simple electric circuits that contain one energy source and more than one load are classified as either a series circuit or a parallel circuit.

In Series Circuits, Charges Follow a Single Path

The three light bulbs shown below are connected in a series circuit. In a **series circuit**, all parts are connected in a row that forms one path for the electric charges to follow. The current is the same for all of the loads in a series circuit. All three light bulbs glow with the same brightness. However, adding a fourth bulb would lower the current in the circuit and cause all the bulbs to become dimmer. If one bulb burns out, the circuit is open and electric charges cannot flow through the circuit. So all of the bulbs go out.

Active Reading

11 **Identify** As you read this page and the next, underline what happens if you add a bulb to a series circuit and to a parallel circuit.

Visualize It!

12 **Apply** In these two circuit illustrations, draw an X over the bulbs that would not glow if the bulb closest to the battery burned out.

Series circuit with battery and switch

The bulbs are connected to one another in a single loop.

In Parallel Circuits, Charges Follow Multiple Paths

Think about what would happen if all of the lights in your home were connected in series. If you needed to turn on a light in your room, all other lights in the house would have to be turned on, too! Instead of being wired in series, circuits in buildings are wired in parallel. In a **parallel circuit**, electric charges have more than one path that they can follow. Loads in a parallel circuit are connected side by side. In the parallel circuit shown below, any bulb can burn out without opening the circuit.

Unlike the loads in a series circuit, the loads in a parallel circuit can have different currents. However, each load in a parallel circuit experiences the same voltage. For example, if three bulbs were hooked up to a 12-volt battery, each would have the full voltage of the battery. Each light bulb would glow at the same brightness no matter how many more bulbs were added to the circuit.

13 Compare In the table below, list the features of series and parallel circuits.

Series circuits	Parallel circuits

Parallel circuit
with battery and switch

The bulbs are connected side by side.

Safety First!

How can I use electricity safely?

You use many electrical devices every day. It is important to remember that electrical energy can be hazardous if it is not used correctly. Electric circuits in buildings have built-in safeguards to keep people safe. You can stay safe if you are careful to avoid electrical dangers and pay attention to warning signs and labels.

By Avoiding Exposure to Current

Pure water is a poor conductor of electric current. But water usually has substances such as salt dissolved in it. These substances make water a better conductor. This is especially true of fluids inside your body. The water in your body is a good conductor of electric current. This is why you should avoid exposure to current. Even small currents can cause severe burns, shock, and even death. A current can prevent you from breathing and stop your heart.

Following basic safety precautions will protect you from exposure to electric current. Never use electrical devices around water. Do not use any appliance if its power cord is worn or damaged. Always pay attention to warning signs near places with high-voltage transmission lines. You do not actually have to touch some high-voltage wires to receive a deadly shock. Even coming near high-voltage wires can do serious harm to your body.

Active Reading

14 Identify As you read, underline the reason that electric currents can be harmful to people.

A damaged cord exposes the metal wires that conduct electric charges.

Stay away from places where there is high-voltage electrical equipment.

DANGER
High Voltage
Trespassers may
be electrocuted

By Using Electrical Safety Devices

Damage to wires can cause a "short circuit," in which charges do not pass through all the loads. When this happens, current increases and wires can get hot enough to start a fire.

Fuses, circuit breakers, and ground fault circuit interrupters (GFCIs) are safety devices that act like switches. When the current is too high in a fuse, a metal strip that is part of the circuit heats up and melts. Circuit breakers are switches that open when the current reaches a certain level. A GFCI is a type of circuit breaker. GFCIs are often built into outlets that are used near water, such as in a kitchen or bathroom.

Active Reading 15 **Identify** Name three safety devices that you might find in electric circuits at home.

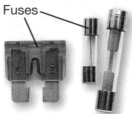

Fuses

When the current is too high in the fuse, the metal strip melts and opens the circuit.

Ground fault circuit interrupter (GFCI)

The lightning rod attached to the top of this building helps to protect it from a lightning strike.

By Taking Precautions during a Lightning Storm

When lightning strikes, electric charges can travel between a cloud and the ground. Lightning often strikes objects that are taller than their surroundings, such as skyscrapers, trees, barns, or even a person in an open field. During a thunderstorm, be sure to stay away from trees and other tall objects. The best place to seek shelter during a thunderstorm is indoors.

Many buildings have lightning rods. These are metal rods at the highest part of the building. The rod is connected to the ground by a thick conducting wire. The rod and wire protect the building by *grounding* it, or providing a path that allows charges to flow into the ground.

16 **Infer** What would happen if there were no electrical path from the top of the building to the ground?

Visual Summary

To complete this summary, fill in the blanks with the correct word or phrase. Then, use the key below to check your answers. You can use this page to review the main concepts of the lesson.

Electric Circuits

An electric circuit has three basic parts: an energy source, an electric conductor, and a load.

Circuits can be connected in series or in parallel.

19 When one of several bulbs in a series circuit burns out, the other bulbs _____

20 When one of several bulbs in a parallel circuit burns out, the other bulbs _____

17 Batteries are an example of an _____ in an electric circuit.

18 To open and close a circuit, a _____ can be used.

Taking precautions when using electricity and during a lightning storm can keep you safe from electrical dangers.

21 This outlet contains a GFCI, which acts as a _____ to protect people from short circuits.

22 **Synthesize** Compare the function of a switch in an electric circuit to the function of a water faucet. How are they alike and how are they different?

Lesson Review

Vocabulary

Draw a line to connect the following terms to their definitions.

1 series circuit

2 parallel circuit

A a circuit with two or more paths for charges

B a circuit with a single path for charges

Key Concepts

3 Explain Why is an energy source needed in order to have a working electric circuit?

_____

_____

_____

_____

4 Compare Describe the difference between a closed circuit and an open circuit.

_____

_____

_____

_____

5 Apply Why does removing one bulb from a string of lights in a series circuit cause all the lights to go out?

_____

_____

_____

_____

6 Describe How does a lightning rod protect a building from lightning damage?

_____

_____

_____

_____

Critical Thinking

Use this drawing to answer the following questions.

Energy source

7 Identify Circuits can be either series or parallel. What type of circuit is shown above?

_____

_____

8 Infer Imagine that a circuit breaker opened the circuit every time that you operated the light, coffee maker, and microwave at the same time. What could be causing this?

_____

_____

_____

_____

_____

9 Predict What electrical safety device could be used in this kitchen to decrease risk of electric shock? Explain.

_____

_____

_____

_____

_____

My Notes

Engineering Design Process

Skills
Identify a need
Conduct research
✓ Brainstorm solutions
✓ Select a solution
✓ Design a prototype
✓ Build a prototype
✓ Test and evaluate
✓ Redesign to improve
✓ Communicate results

Objectives

- Design an electric circuit to provide an answer to a problem.
- Test and modify a prototype circuit to achieve the desired result.

Building an Electric Circuit

Electric circuits are an essential part of many devices and technologies. Automobiles, televisions, digital watches, music players, cell phones, computers, and sports scoreboards all function, in part, because of carefully designed circuits.

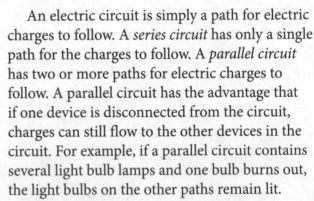

An electric circuit is simply a path for electric charges to follow. A *series circuit* has only a single path for the charges to follow. A *parallel circuit* has two or more paths for electric charges to follow. A parallel circuit has the advantage that if one device is disconnected from the circuit, charges can still flow to the other devices in the circuit. For example, if a parallel circuit contains several light bulb lamps and one bulb burns out, the light bulbs on the other paths remain lit.

In this activity, you will make an electric circuit of conducting wires, batteries, lamps, and switches. A switch can form a break in the circuit to stop the flow of electric charges and turn a device, such as a lamp, on and off.

1 Infer Do you think the lights in your home are wired in series circuits or parallel circuits? Explain.

_____

_____

_____

_____

_____

_____

This robotic device contains a number of electric circuits.

Modeling an Electric Circuit

Sketching a complex circuit could take a lot of time and expertise. Circuits are often drawn using simple symbols so that models or plans are easier to create and easier to read. You can use symbols like the ones shown below to show parts of a circuit such as wire, lamps, and switches.

2 Apply Compare the series circuit diagram shown on the left to the art of a series circuit on the right. Then, label the symbols in the circuit diagram with *wire, lamp,* or *energy source.*

closed switch

3 Apply Complete this parallel circuit diagram by drawing in the symbols for the missing switch and energy source.

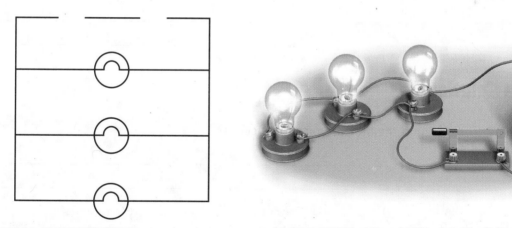

4 Explain What will happen if a light bulb is unscrewed from a lamp in the series circuit? What will happen if a light bulb is unscrewed from a lamp in the parallel circuit?

_____

_____

_____

 You Try It!

Now it's your turn to model and build a simple electric circuit.

You Try It!

Now it's your turn to model and build a simple electric circuit with three light bulb lamps and three switches.

1 Brainstorm Solutions

Brainstorm ideas for a simple circuit that lights up three light bulbs. The setup must include three switches so that one switch controls only one lamp, one switch controls two lamps, and one switch controls all three lamps.

A How will you decide whether to build a series circuit or a parallel circuit?

_____

_____

_____

B How can a switch turn on or off only one or two lamps in a three-lamp circuit?

_____

_____

_____

2 Select a Solution

Which of your ideas seems to offer the best promise for success?

_____

_____

3 Design a Prototype

In the space below, draw a circuit diagram for your three-lamp prototype. Be sure to include all the parts you will need, and show how they will be connected.

You Will Need

✓ batteries

✓ battery holders

✓ masking tape or duct tape

✓ small lamp bulbs, 1.5 V (3)

✓ small lamp bulb holders (3)

✓ switches (3)

✓ wires

(4) Build a Prototype

Now assemble your three-lamp circuit with the switches in place. Are there some parts of your design that cannot be assembled as you had predicted? What parts did you have to revise?

_____

_____

_____

_____

(5) Test and Evaluate

Open and close the switches and see what happens. Did one switch turn all the lamps on and off? Did the other two switches control only one or two lamps as predicted? If not, what parts of your setup could you revise?

_____

_____

(6) Redesign to Improve

Keep making revisions until your switches control only the specified number of lamps. What kinds of revisions did you have to make?

_____

_____

_____

(7) Communicate Results

In the space below, sketch a diagram of the successful circuit.

Magnets and Magnetism

ESSENTIAL QUESTION

What is magnetism?

By the end of this lesson, you should be able to describe magnets and magnetic fields and explain their properties.

8.PS2.1, 8.PS2.2

When cows are grazing, they may eat pieces of metal, such as nails. Farmers can feed the cows a smooth magnet to attract such objects. This prevents the objects from moving farther through the cow's system and causing damage.

Engage Your Brain

1 Predict Check Yes or No to show whether you think the object would be attracted to a magnet.

Yes	No	
☐	☐	A paper clip
☐	☐	A plastic water bottle
☐	☐	A piece of notepaper
☐	☐	Another magnet
☐	☐	Aluminum foil
☐	☐	A penny

2 Describe Write your own caption for this photo of a cow magnet.

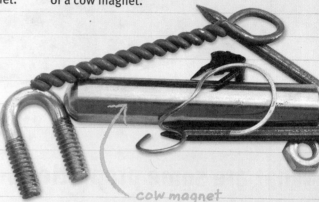

cow magnet

_____
_____
_____

Active Reading

3 Apply Many scientific words, such as *field*, also have everyday meanings. Use context clues to write your own definition for each meaning of the word *field*.

Example sentence
The farm animals in the <u>field</u> are eating grass and clover.

field:

_____
_____

Example sentence
The magnet attracted all the pins that were within its magnetic <u>field</u>.

field:

_____
_____

Vocabulary Terms
• magnet
• magnetic force
• magnetic pole
• magnetic field

4 Identify As you read, place a question mark next to any words you don't understand. When you finish reading the lesson, go back and review the text that you marked. If the information is still confusing, consult a classmate or a teacher.

What are some properties of magnets?

Have you wondered what a magnet is and why all materials are not magnets? The ancient Greeks discovered a mineral, called *magnetite* (MAG•nih•tyt), that would attract things made of iron. Today, we use the term **magnet** to describe any material that attracts iron or objects made of iron. Many magnets are made of iron, nickel, cobalt, or mixtures of these metals.

Magnetic Forces

When you bring two magnets together, they exert a push or pull called a **magnetic force** on each other. This force results from spinning electric charges in the magnets. The force can either push the magnets apart or pull them together. Magnetic force is one of only three forces in nature that can act at a distance— electromagnetic force and gravity are the other two.

Magnetic force explains why, when you hold a magnet close enough to a paper clip, the paper clip will start to move toward the magnet. You have probably noticed that either end of a magnet can pull on a paper clip. So why is it that when you place two magnets near each other, sometimes they pull together and sometimes they push each other apart?

 Active Reading 6 State Name two things magnetic force can do.

_____

_____

© Houghton Mifflin Harcourt Publishing Company • Image Credits: ©Dorling Kindersley/Getty Images

Inquiry

5 Infer What might be an advantage to making a magnet horseshoe-shaped?

_____

_____

_____

_____

_____

_____

Magnetic Poles

Two magnets can push each other apart because of their ends, or **magnetic poles**. Every magnet has a north pole and a south pole. If you place the north poles of two magnets together, they will repel, or push away. If you place the north pole and the south pole of two magnets near each other, they will attract, or come together. The saying "opposites attract" applies well to magnets.

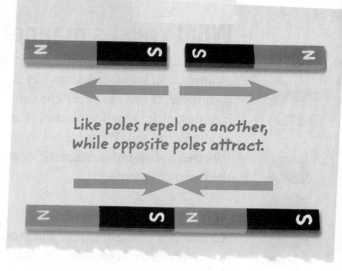

Like poles repel one another, while opposite poles attract.

Magnetic Fields

The area surrounding a magnet where magnetic forces can be detected is called the **magnetic field**. A magnetic object placed anywhere in the magnetic field will be affected by the magnet.

As you can see in the illustration below, the magnetic field is arranged in lines. Notice that the magnetic field lines enter the magnet at the south pole and exit at the north pole. The magnetic field is strongest near the poles where the field lines are closest together. The greater the distance from the poles, the weaker the magnetic field and the field lines are further apart.

Visualize It!

7 Diagram Draw an X on the illustration below to show one location in which a magnetic object would be attracted to the magnet. Draw an O to show one location in which a magnetic object would not be attracted to the magnet.

8 Relate Where are the magnetic field lines closest together, and what does that tell you about the strength of the magnetic field?

_____

_____

_____

_____

Lines with arrowheads are used to model a magnetic field.

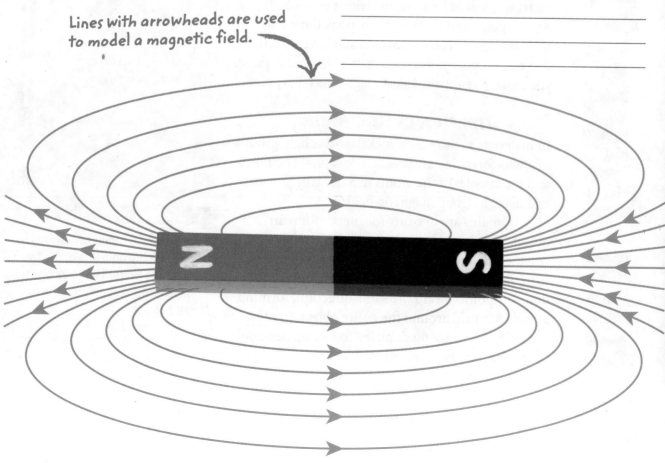

What causes magnetism?

Some materials are magnetic. Some are not. For example, you know that a magnet can pick up some metal objects such as paper clips and iron nails. But it cannot pick up paper, plastic, or even pennies or aluminum foil. What causes the difference? Whether a material is magnetic or not depends on the material's atoms.

The Type of Atom

All matter is made of atoms. Electrons are negatively charged particles of atoms. As an electron moves in an atom, it makes, or induces, a magnetic field. The electron will then have a north and a south magnetic pole. In most atoms, such as copper and aluminum, the magnetic fields of the individual electrons cancel each other out. These materials are not magnetic.

But the magnetic fields of the electrons in iron, nickel, and cobalt atoms do not completely cancel each other out. As a result, atoms of these materials have small magnetic fields. These materials are magnetic.

If you were to cut a magnet into two pieces, each piece would be a magnet with a north and a south pole. And if you were to break those two magnets into pieces, each would still have a north and a south pole. It does not matter how many pieces you make. Even the smallest magnet has two poles.

The Formation of Domains

In materials such as iron, nickel, and cobalt, groups of atoms form tiny areas called *domains*. The north and south poles of the atoms in a domain line up and make a strong magnetic field.

Domains are like tiny magnets within an object. The domains in an object determine whether the object is magnetic. When a magnetic material is placed in a magnetic field, most of the domains point toward the same direction, forming a magnetic field around the entire object. In other materials, there are no domains to line up because the atoms have no magnetic fields. These materials cannot become magnetized. Like the electric force, the strength of the magnetic force depends on the distance of the objects and the number of aligned magnetic domains.

Domains before magnetization

Domains after magnetization

Visualize It!

9 Compare Use your own words to compare the domains of the two nails. The bottom nail has been made into a magnet, but the top nail has not.

_____

_____

_____

_____

When Everything Lines Up

What are some types of magnets?

There are different types of magnets. Some materials are naturally magnetic, such as the mineral magnetite. Some materials can be turned into either permanent or temporary magnets.

Ferromagnets

A material that can be turned into a magnet is called *ferromagnetic* (fehr•oh•mag•NET•ik). Natural materials such as iron, nickel, cobalt, or mixtures of these materials have strong magnetic properties. They are considered ferromagnets.

A ferromagnetic material can be turned into a permanent magnet when placed in a strong magnetic field. Permanent magnets are difficult to make, but they keep their magnetic properties longer. Magnets can be made into various shapes such as bar magnets, disc magnets, and horseshoe magnets.

Electromagnets

Strong magnets are used to pick up metals in scrap yards, as shown in the photo below. To get a magnet powerful enough to do this, an *electromagnet* is used. An electromagnet is an iron core wrapped with electrical wire. When an electric current is in the wire, a magnetic field forms. When the current is turned off, the magnetic field stops. The strength of an electromagnet depends on the strength of the electric current.

This electromagnet uses electricity to produce a magnetic field.

Temporary Magnets

Some materials, such as soft iron, can be made into magnets temporarily when placed in a strong magnetic field. The material's domains line up, and the material is magnetized. You can make a temporary magnet by rubbing one pole of a strong magnet in one direction on a magnetic material, for example, a pair of scissors. The domains line up in the scissors, and it becomes a temporary magnet. Over time, the domains will lose their alignment. Banging or dropping a temporary magnet can also make it lose its magnetism.

Think Outside the Book Inquiry

10 Design Plan an investigation to find out how the strength of a temporary magnet is affected by the number of times you rub the object with a permanent magnet.

Polar Opposites

How is Earth like a giant magnet?

Earth acts like a giant magnet. Like a magnet, Earth has a magnetic field. Earth also has a north magnetic pole and a south magnetic pole. Earth's magnetic poles can attract another magnet, such as the needle of a compass.

It Has a Magnetic Field

 Active Reading **11 Identify** As you read, underline the text that explains why Earth has a magnetic field.

As early as the 1600s, scientists hypothesized that Earth has a magnetic field. This was before the properties of magnets were understood. Scientists now think that Earth's inner structure produces its magnetic field. Earth has an inner core and an outer core. The inner core is made of solid metals. The outer core is made of liquid iron and nickel, which are ferromagnetic. As Earth rotates, the liquid outer core moves. Charged particles, including electrons, move in the liquid and form a magnetic field. The constant rotation keeps Earth magnetized. Earth's magnetic field is strongest near its poles.

Inquiry

12 Infer Earth's magnetic poles do not stay in the same place. After reading about what causes Earth's magnetic field, write a possible explanation for why Earth's magnetic poles move.

_____

_____

_____

_____

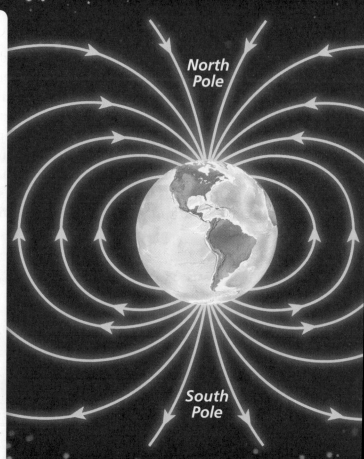

Like a magnet, Earth has magnetic poles and a magnetic field. Some animals may use Earth's magnetic field to navigate.

It Has Magnetic Poles

Earth's magnetic poles are not the same as Earth's geographic poles. The geographic poles mark the ends of Earth's axis. The geographic poles are near, but not exactly at, the magnetic poles. Navigators on airplanes and ships must take this small difference into account.

How can the north end of a compass point to the north magnetic pole? A compass needle is a magnet. If like poles repel, why do they not repel each other? The "north" pole of a magnet gets its name because it points toward Earth's geographic North Pole. A better term for the north pole of a magnet would be a "north-seeking" pole. Using these terms, the magnetic pole near Earth's North Pole is considered the south pole of a magnet. Likewise, the magnetic pole near Earth's South Pole is considered the north pole of a magnet.

Visualize It!

13 Illustrate Draw a bar magnet on the image of Earth to show Earth's magnetic poles.

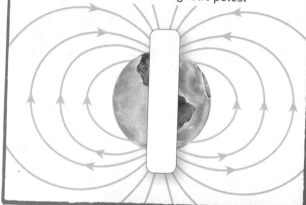

What is an aurora?

The beautiful displays of light that can be seen at northern or southern latitudes are related to Earth's magnetic field. The sun ejects charged particles. When they reach Earth, they are guided by its magnetic field. They enter Earth's upper atmosphere near the magnetic poles. There, the charged particles interact with atoms in the air, causing the atoms to emit visible light. This glow is called an *aurora*. In the Northern Hemisphere, an aurora is called an aurora borealis (bohr•ee•AL•is). In the Southern Hemisphere, it is called an aurora australis (aw•STRAY•lis).

This photo shows an aurora streaming across the night sky in Manitoba, Canada.

Visual Summary

To complete this summary, fill in each blank with the correct word or phrase. Then, use the key below to check your answers. You can use this page to review the main concepts of the lesson.

Magnets and Magnetism

A magnet is any material that attracts iron or any substance that contains iron.

14 Magnetic materials exert _____ and have magnetic _____ and _____

15 If the _____ of a material are lined up, the object will be magnetic.

There are different types of magnets.

16 A material such as iron is _____

17 A(n) _____ is a magnet produced by electricity.

18 An object can become a(n) _____ magnet by rubbing the object with the end of a magnet.

Earth acts like a magnet because it has properties similar to those of magnets.

19 Earth has a _____ and north and south _____

Answers: 14 forces, poles, fields; 15 domains; 16 ferromagnetic; 17 electromagnet; 18 temporary; 19 magnetic field, magnetic poles

20 **Synthesis** Explain how a compass can be used to find north.

Lesson Review

Vocabulary

Draw a line to connect the following terms to their definitions.

1 magnet

2 magnetic force

3 magnetic pole

4 magnetic field

A a magnet's push or pull

B the end of a magnet where the force is the strongest

C the lines of force surrounding a magnet

D a metal object that attracts iron or nickel

Key Concepts

5 List What are three properties of a magnet?

_____
_____
_____

6 Explain What causes some materials to have magnetic fields?

_____
_____
_____
_____

7 Identify List three types of magnets.

_____
_____
_____

8 Describe How is Earth like a magnet?

_____
_____
_____

9 Describe How do auroras form?

_____
_____
_____
_____

Critical Thinking

Use this drawing to answer the following question.

10 Illustrate The metal on the left has been magnetized, and the metal on the right has not. Draw the arrows in the domains of both.

11 Contrast What is the difference between the geographic North Pole and the magnetic north pole?

_____
_____
_____

12 Explain If opposite poles repel each other, why does the north end of a compass point to the North Pole?

_____
_____
_____
_____

13 Apply Food manufacturers want to prevent small bits of metal from entering their product. How might magnets be used?

_____
_____
_____

My Notes

Electromagnetism

When the strings on this guitar vibrate, small magnets in the pickups convert the vibrations into electrical signals.

pickups

ESSENTIAL QUESTION

What is electromagnetism?

By the end of this lesson, you should be able to describe the relationship between electricity and magnetism and how this relationship affects our world.

8.PS2.1, 8.PS2.2, 8.ETS1.1

Lesson Labs

Quick Labs
- Building an Electromagnet
- Making an Electric Generator

S.T.E.M. Lab
- Building a Speaker

Engage Your Brain

1 Predict Check T or F to show whether you think each statement is true or false.

T   F

☐   ☐   A moving magnetic field can produce electricity.

☐   ☐   Electricity can produce a magnetic field.

☐   ☐   Electricity and magnetism are the same thing.

2 Describe An electromagnet is a magnet produced from electric current. Describe what is happening in the photo.

_____

_____

_____

Active Reading

3 Apply Many scientific words, such as *induction*, also have everyday meanings. Use context clues to write your own definition for each meaning of *induction*.

Example sentence
There was a party after the baseball star's <u>induction</u> into the Hall of Fame.

induction:

_____

_____

Example sentence
<u>Induction</u> occurs when a wire moving near a magnet gains an electric current.

induction:

_____

_____

Vocabulary Terms

- electromagnetism
- solenoid
- electromagnet
- electric motor
- electromagnetic induction
- transformer
- electric generator

4 Apply As you learn the definition of each vocabulary term in this lesson, create your own definition or sketch to help you remember the meaning of the term.

MAGNETIC ATTRACTION

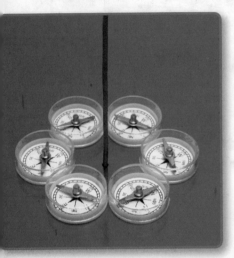

The compasses show that an electric current produces a circular magnetic field around the wire.

When the current is turned off, the needles align with Earth's magnetic field.

What is electromagnetism?

Electromagnetism is a relationship between electricity and magnetism. **Electromagnetism** results when electric currents and magnetic fields interact with each other.

The Interaction Between Magnets and Electricity

In 1820, physicist Hans Christian Oersted of Denmark made an interesting discovery by accident. He discovered that there is a connection between electricity and magnetism. No one at the time knew that electricity and magnetism were related. One day while preparing for a lecture, he brought a compass close to a wire carrying an electric current. Oersted was surprised to see the compass needle move. A compass needle is a magnet. It usually points north because of Earth's magnetic field. However, the compass moved because it was affected by a magnetic field other than Earth's.

Magnetism Produced by Electricity

Active Reading 5 **Identify** As you read, underline what caused Oersted's compass needle to move.

Oersted hypothesized that it was the electric current in the wire that had produced the magnetic field. He then did more experiments with electricity and magnetism. He found that when the wire is carrying a current, a magnetic field is produced around the wire. You can see this in the photograph on the top left. When the current is turned off, as shown in the bottom photograph, the magnetic field disappears. The compasses again point north.

Oersted found that the direction of the electric current also affects the magnetic field. Current in one direction caused a compass needle to move clockwise. Current in the other direction caused the compass needle to move counterclockwise. Oersted's hypothesis was confirmed.

© Houghton Mifflin Harcourt Publishing Company • Image Credits: (t) ©GIPhotoStock/Photo Researchers, Inc.; (b) ©GIPhotoStock/Photo Researchers, Inc.

How can you make a magnet using current?

An electric current in a single loop of wire produces a weak magnetic field. You can make a more powerful magnet by making a solenoid or an electromagnet.

With a Solenoid

A coil of wire that carries an electric current, and therefore produces a magnetic field, is called a **solenoid** (SOH•luh•noyd). The more loops, the stronger the magnetic field. A solenoid's magnetic field acts like a bar magnet. Increasing the number of loops or the current increases the strength of the magnetic field.

With an Electromagnet

Wrapping a solenoid around an iron core makes an **electromagnet**. An electromagnet combines the magnetic field of the solenoid with the magnetic field of the magnetized iron core. This combination creates a more powerful magnetic field than the solenoid alone. You can make it stronger by adding loops to the solenoid or increasing the current. Like with magnetic or electric fields, the strength of the magnetic field is greatly affected by distance.

> **Active Reading** **6 Solve** What benefit is gained by the addition of the iron core in an electromagnet?

_____

_____

_____

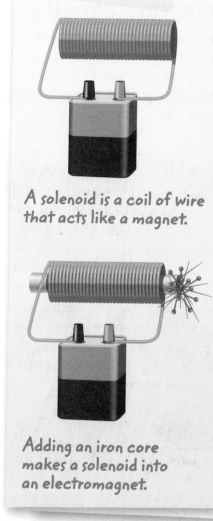

A solenoid is a coil of wire that acts like a magnet.

Adding an iron core makes a solenoid into an electromagnet.

Electromagnets lift this maglev train off the tracks and move it forward.

What are some uses for electromagnets?

Electromagnets are used in many devices that you may use every day. A solenoid around an iron piston makes a doorbell ring. Huge electromagnets are used in industry to move metal. Small electromagnets drive electric motors in objects from hair dryers to speakers. Physicists use electromagnets in "atom smashers" to study the tiny particles and high energies that make up an atom.

To Lift Metal Objects

Electromagnets are useful for lifting and moving large metal objects containing iron. When current runs through the solenoid coils, it creates a magnetic field that attracts the metal objects. Turning off the current turns off the magnetic field so that the metal can be easily dropped in a new place. Powerful electromagnets can raise a maglev train above its track. Just as poles of a bar magnet repel each other, electromagnets in the train and track repel each other when the electric current is turned on.

To Measure Current

A *galvanometer* (gal•vuh•NAHM•ih•ter) is a device that measures the strength and direction of an electric current in a wire. A galvanometer contains an electromagnet between the poles of a permanent magnet, such as a horseshoe magnet. When current is applied to the electromagnet, the two magnetic fields interact and cause the electromagnet to turn. The indicator, attached to the electromagnet, moves to one side of the zero on the scale, indicating the strength and direction of the current. The parts of a simple galvanometer are shown below.

Inquiry

7 Infer What is one advantage of using an electromagnet to move loads of metal?

_____

_____

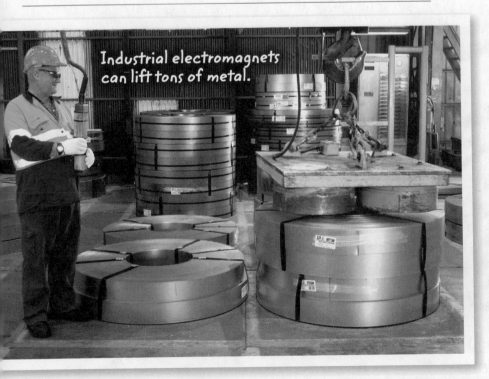
Industrial electromagnets can lift tons of metal.

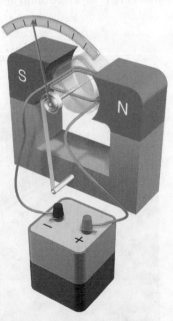
The indicator on a galvanometer shows current direction and strength.

© Houghton Mifflin Harcourt Publishing Company • Image Credits: ©Bloomberg/Getty Images

A Look Inside

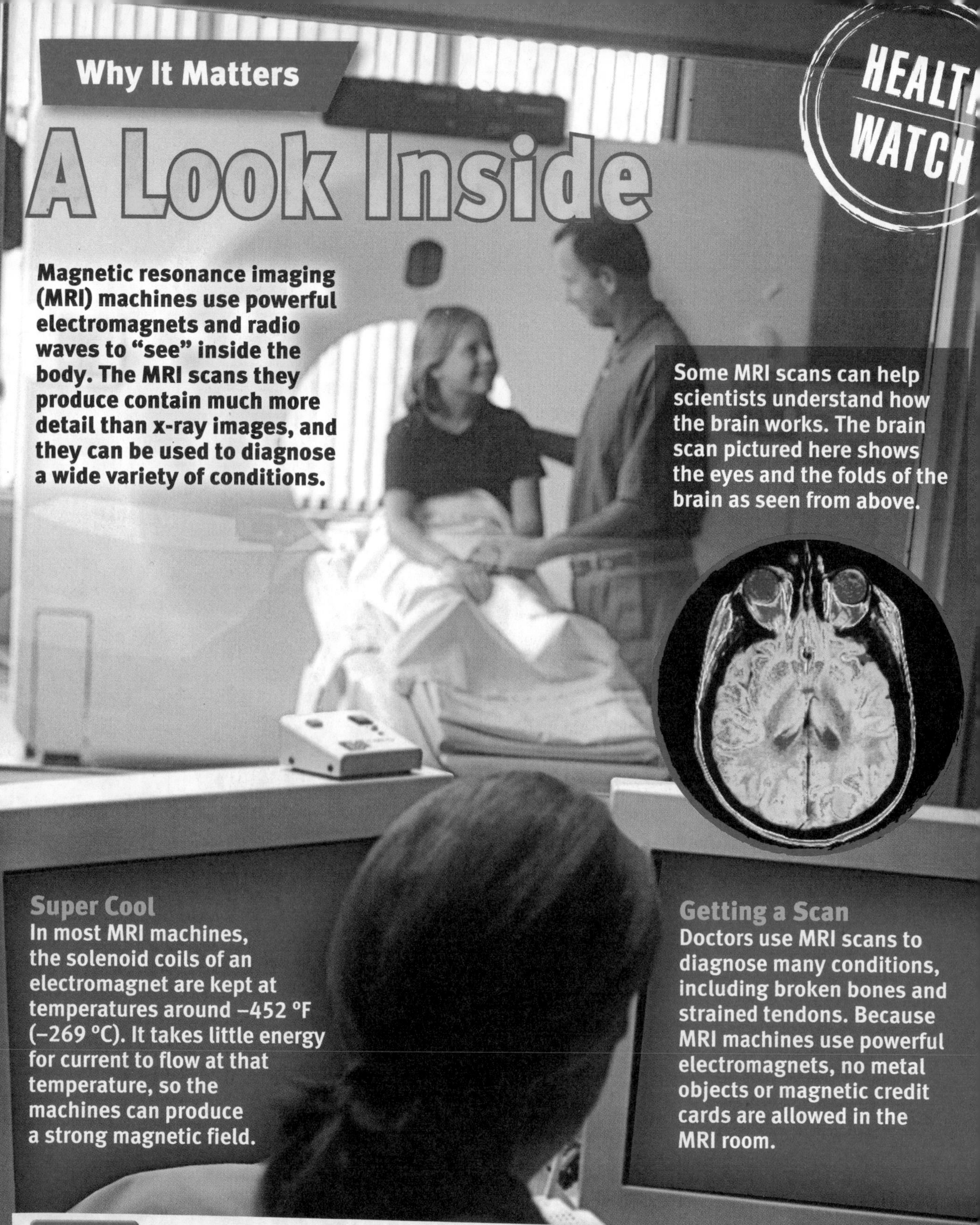

Magnetic resonance imaging (MRI) machines use powerful electromagnets and radio waves to "see" inside the body. The MRI scans they produce contain much more detail than x-ray images, and they can be used to diagnose a wide variety of conditions.

Some MRI scans can help scientists understand how the brain works. The brain scan pictured here shows the eyes and the folds of the brain as seen from above.

Super Cool

In most MRI machines, the solenoid coils of an electromagnet are kept at temperatures around −452 °F (−269 °C). It takes little energy for current to flow at that temperature, so the machines can produce a strong magnetic field.

Getting a Scan

Doctors use MRI scans to diagnose many conditions, including broken bones and strained tendons. Because MRI machines use powerful electromagnets, no metal objects or magnetic credit cards are allowed in the MRI room.

Extend

Inquiry

8 **Explain** Why are the electromagnets in MRIs kept at very low temperatures?

9 **Infer** Why are electromagnets, rather than permanent magnets, used in MRIs?

10 **Research** Investigate *magnetoencephalography* (mag•nee•toh•en•sef•uh•LAHG•ruh•fee), or MEG. Write about one way in which it is being used.

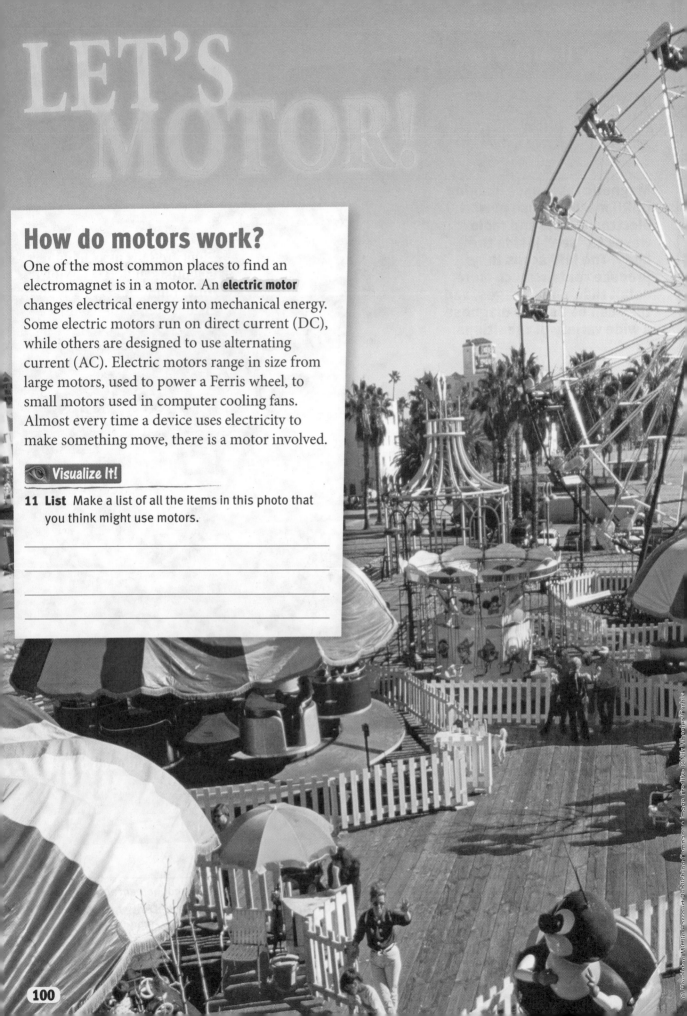

LET'S MOTOR!

How do motors work?

One of the most common places to find an electromagnet is in a motor. An **electric motor** changes electrical energy into mechanical energy. Some electric motors run on direct current (DC), while others are designed to use alternating current (AC). Electric motors range in size from large motors, used to power a Ferris wheel, to small motors used in computer cooling fans. Almost every time a device uses electricity to make something move, there is a motor involved.

Visualize It!

11 List Make a list of all the items in this photo that you think might use motors.

_____

_____

_____

_____

Motors Use Electromagnets

Electric motors are very similar to galvanometers. The main difference is that, in a motor, the electromagnet is made to rotate all the way around instead of back and forth in the magnetic field.

A simple motor has a coil or loop of wire called an armature (AR•muh•chur) mounted between the poles of a magnet. The armature becomes an electromagnet when current passes through it. The armature rotates because its poles are pushed and pulled by the opposite poles of the magnet. The armature turns until its north pole is opposite the magnet's south pole. Then, a device called a commutator reverses the direction of the current in the wire, causing the armature to complete its turn.

Visualize It!

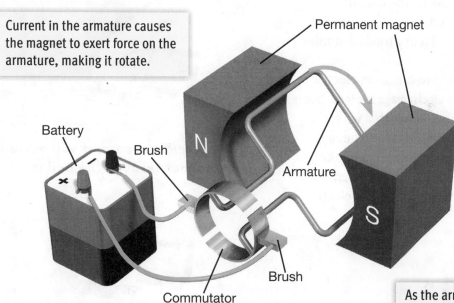

Current in the armature causes the magnet to exert force on the armature, making it rotate.

Permanent magnet

Battery

Brush

N

Armature

S

Brush

Commutator

As the armature rotates, the commutator causes the current to change direction. This reverses the direction of force and keeps the armature rotating.

12 Compare Analyze the illustration of the motor, and compare it to the galvanometer on the previous spread. Explain how they are alike.

_____

_____

_____

_____

_____

_____

What are some uses for induction?

Electric current can produce a magnetic field. In the early 1830s, scientists wondered if the opposite is true. Can a magnetic field create an electric current? English scientist Michael Faraday showed that it could. He connected a galvanometer to a wire coil. When he moved a magnet back and forth inside the coil, the galvanometer needle moved, indicating current. American physicist Joseph Henry made a similar discovery.

Using a magnetic field to create an electric current in a wire is called **electromagnetic induction**. When electric charges move through a wire, the wire carries a current. Magnetic force from a magnet moving inside a coil of wire can make the electric charges in the wire move. When the magnet stops moving inside the coil, the electric current stops.

An electric current is induced when you move a magnet through a coil of wire.

The current increases if you move the magnet through the coil faster.

The current also increases if you add more loops of wire.

The current can also be induced by reversing the motion—moving the coil over the magnet.

Visualize It!

13 State What are two ways to increase the current in the wire?

_____

_____

_____

14 Predict What would happen to the current if the magnet and coil were not moving?

_____

_____

To Change Voltage

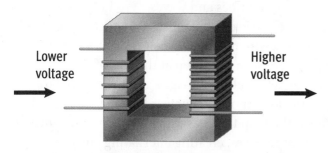

Active Reading

15 Identify As you read, underline the sentence that explains the purpose of transformers.

An important device that relies on electromagnetic induction is a transformer. **Transformers** use induction to increase or decrease the voltage of alternating current. For example, transformers on power lines increase voltage to send it miles away and then decrease it for a single home. Most transformers are iron "rings" with two coils of wire. The current in the wire on the primary side makes an electromagnet. Because the current alternates, the magnetic field changes. This induces a current in the wire on the secondary side.

Step-Up Transformer

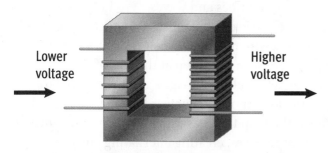

Lower voltage

Higher voltage

In a step-up transformer, there are more turns of wire on the secondary side.

Step-Down Transformer

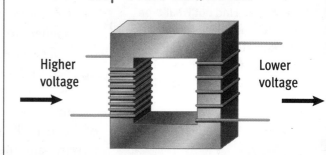

Higher voltage

Lower voltage

In a step-down transformer, there are more turns of wire on the primary side.

Do the Math

Sample Problem

Imagine the voltage on the primary side of a step-down transformer is 300 volts and the wire has 1,200 turns. The wire on the secondary side has 720 turns. What is the voltage on the secondary side?

The number of volts to wire turns on a transformer coil can be expressed as a ratio. This ratio is equal for both sides of the transformer. Cross-multiply to find the answer to the problem.

$$\frac{300 \text{ volts}}{1{,}200 \text{ turns}} = \frac{X \text{ volts}}{720 \text{ turns}}$$

$$300 \times 720 = 216{,}000$$

$$216{,}000 / 1{,}200 = 180$$

$$X = 180$$

Answer: 180 volts

You Try It

16 Calculate The voltage on the primary side of a step-down transformer is 500 volts, and the wire has 1,500 turns. The wire on the secondary side has 600 turns. What is the voltage on the secondary side?

To Generate Electricity

Did you know that most of the electricity you use every day comes from electromagnetic induction? **Electric generators** use induction to change mechanical energy into electrical energy. You can think of electric generators as being the "opposite" of electric motors.

In all different types of power plants, mechanical energy is used to rotate turbines. In some power plants turbines turn magnets inside coils of wire, generating electricity. Many power plants use rising steam to turn the turbines. The steam is produced from burning fossil fuels or using nuclear reactions to heat water. Other sources of mechanical energy to turn turbines are blowing wind, falling water, and ocean tides and waves.

Generators induce electric current when a magnet moves in a coil of wire or when a wire moves between the poles of a magnet. In a simple generator, a wire loop at the end of a rod moves through the magnetic field of a magnet. In the first half of the turn, one side of the loop moves downward. In the second half of the turn, the part of the loop that was moving down now moves upward, and the current reverses, creating alternating current.

Active Reading **18 Summarize** How does the function of a generator relate to the function of a motor?

_____

_____

Think Outside the Book

17 Research Find out what type of mechanical energy is used to generate electricity for your community. Share this information with somebody at home.

Generating Electricity

A generator induces electric current in wire that is moving in a magnetic field. A crank would be used to turn the wire in this generator.

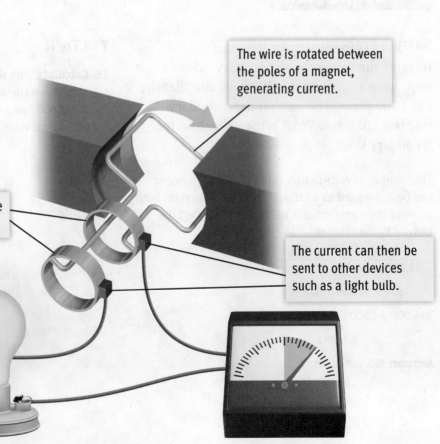

The wire is rotated between the poles of a magnet, generating current.

The current in the rotating wire is transferred to metal rings.

The current can then be sent to other devices such as a light bulb.

19 Diagram Fill in the chart below to help you organize the key concepts from this lesson.

Electromagnetism → Definition:
_____
_____

Uses:
  maglev train
  motor
_____
_____
_____
_____
_____
_____
_____

Electromagnetic induction → Definition:
_____
_____

Uses:
_____
_____
_____
_____
_____
_____

SMASHING ATOMS

How do electromagnets help us unlock the secrets of the universe?

Hundreds of feet beneath the countryside, on the border of France and Switzerland is a circular tunnel 17 miles in circumference. It contains one of the world's largest and most complex machines. The LHC (Large Hadron Collider) was built by over 10,000 scientists and engineers from over 100 different countries to recreate the conditions of the early universe and study its origin. It is designed to collide the protons of Hydrogen atoms at close to the speed of light so they release subatomic particles.

Accelerating Protons with Electromagnets

To prepare the hydrogen atoms for their journey, the electrons are split off, leaving the positively charged protons. Packets of protons are fed into two super-cooled vacuum tubes that run around the 17-mile circumference of the collider, and are accelerated in opposite directions.

The vacuum tubes are surrounded with more than 9,000 high-powered electromagnets that guide the the positively charged protons on their journey and accelerate them to an incredible speed of 99.999% the speed of light.

Inside the Hydrogen Atom

Hydrogen is the simplest and most abundant element in the universe. If we were to count all of the atoms in the universe we would find that 91% of them are hydrogen.

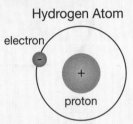

Hydrogen Atom

electron

proton

Hydrogen consists of two electrically-charged particles, one positively charged **proton**, and one negatively charged **electron**. Within this simple structure is a complex family of subatomic particles that are held together inside the proton.

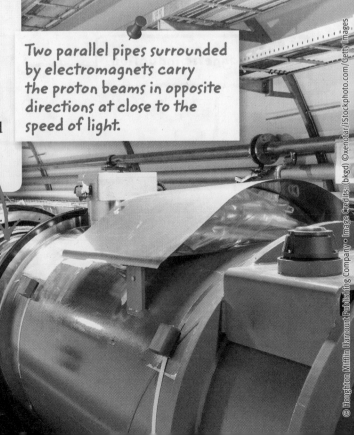

Two parallel pipes surrounded by electromagnets carry the proton beams in opposite directions at close to the speed of light.

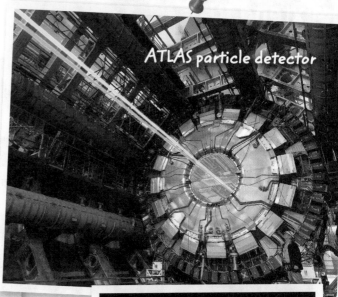
ATLAS particle detector

ATLAS Detector

The two beams of protons are guided by electromagnets into the massive ATLAS detector, where they collide and split apart. New particles are created out of the debris of the collision, some of which last for only a fraction of a second before annihilating themselves. Huge electromagnets in the ATLAS detector track and measure the paths of the new particles as they fly out of the colliding protons.

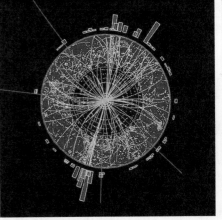

Particle tracks of a proton-proton collision inside the ATLAS Detector

Titan Supercomputer and Oak Ridge

It is only fitting that the story of the Large Hadron Collider ends up back in Tennessee. In many ways that was where it started. The first particle accelerators were built at the Oak Ridge National Laboratory, Tennessee, as part of the top secret Manhattan Project that helped end World War II.

Today, the massive amounts of data that are collected by the ATLAS detector are being sent back to the Oak Ridge National Laboratory team to be processed using its Titan supercomputer in Knoxville.

The ATLAS detector records 800 million collisions between protons every second, and some particles are only created once every two hours. It takes some serious computing power to find the needle in the haystack scientists are looking for.

Building an Electromagnet

Objectives

Answer the Focus Question by revising the electromagnet you built in the Quick Lab - Building an Electromagnet

Focus Question

How can the strength of an electromagnet be increased?

Challenge

See how many paper clips you can pick up with your modified electromagnet.

Skills

✓ modify design

✓ collect data

✓ analyze data

Part I Introduction

Engineers often modify and refine their designs to improve their effectiveness. Think about the changes that could be made to increase the strength of your electromagnet.

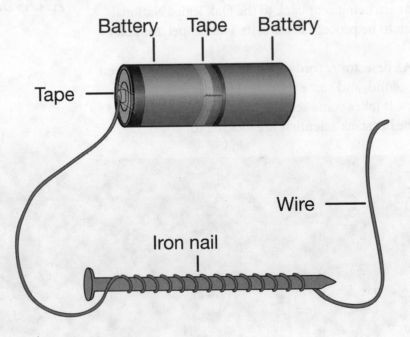

Brainstorm Questions

1 List the materials you will use in your modified electromagnet.

- tape
- batteries
- iorn nail
- wire

2 How could you increase the strength of the electromagnet by using the same type of materials? Describe what you would change about your design and explain why you think the change would affect the strength of the electromagnet.

maybe get a longer wire so you could create more loops around the yarn nail, to increase power. Make sure the wires don't touch.

Building an Electromagnet

Part II Modify/Redesign

Change the design of your electromagnet and collect data that supports
how your design met the challenge. Draw your data table below.

③ Draw your design and indicate the changes you made.

Part III Analysis

4 Refer to your data table. Which change(s) to your design had the greatest effect in increasing the strength of the electromagnet?

_____

_____

_____

_____

_____

_____

5 Refer to your data table. At what point did making further changes to your electromagnet stop making significant improvements to the strength of the electromagnet?

_____

_____

_____

_____

_____

_____

_____

_____

6 Describe the optimal design to meet the challenge of picking up the most paper clips.

_____

_____

_____

_____

_____

_____

_____

Making an Electric Generator

Objectives
Answer the Focus Question by modifying the electric generator you built in the Quick Lab - Making an Electric Generator.
Focus Question
How can a simple generator increase the amount of electricity produced?
Challenge
See how far you can move the needle of the galvanometer.

Skills
✓ *modify design*
✓ *collect data*
✓ *analyze data*

Part I Introduction

Engineers often modify and refine their designs to improve their effectiveness. Think about the changes that could be made to increase the strength of your electric generator.

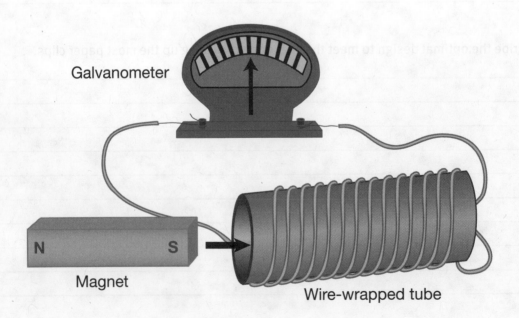

Galvanometer

N   S

Magnet

Wire-wrapped tube

Brainstorm Questions

1 List the materials you will use in your modified electric generator.

_____
_____
_____
_____
_____
_____
_____
_____

2 How could you increase the amount of electricity produced by your electric generator using the same type of materials? Indicate what you would change about your design and explain why you think the change would increase the amount of electricity of your generator.

_____
_____
_____
_____
_____
_____
_____
_____
_____
_____
_____
_____
_____
_____
_____
_____
_____
_____

Building an Electric Generator

Part II Modify/Redesign

Change the design of your electric generator and collect data that supports how your design met the challenge. Draw your data table below.

3 Draw your design and indicate the changes you have made.

Part III Analysis

4 Refer to your data table. Which modification had the greatest effect in increasing the strength of the electric current?

_____

_____

_____

_____

_____

_____

_____

5 Refer to your data table. At what point did making further changes to your design stop making significant improvements to the strength of the electric current?

_____

_____

_____

_____

_____

_____

_____

_____

6 Describe the optimal design to meet the challenge of maximizing the strength of the electric current.

_____

_____

_____

_____

_____

_____

_____

_____

Electric Motors

There is a large range and variety of electric motor design, as this versatile technology is used for so many purposes. They can be small enough to fit in a watch or large enough to power a locomotive.

A small hobby motor

A large industrial motor

A modern locomotive uses a diesel engine to power an electric generator, which then powers an electric motor on each axle. Transferring the power from a diesel engine to electrical motors makes the locomotive efficient as it eliminates the need for a mechanical transmission and a large gearbox. It is the ultimate hybrid vehicle.

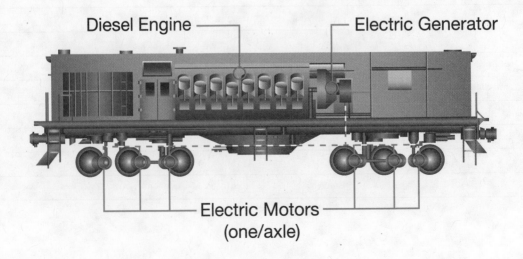

Diesel Engine — — Electric Generator

Electric Motors
(one/axle)

How It Works

Engineers consider several factors when designing an electric motor. The basic design includes magnets, a rotating shaft, and an electricity source. The more current that the motor can draw, the more power the electric motor can provide.

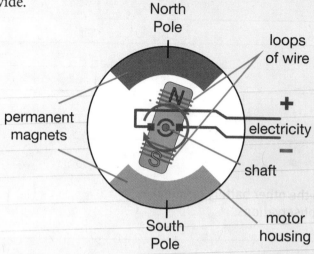

North Pole

loops of wire

permanent magnets

+ electricity −

shaft

South Pole

motor housing

Building an Electric Motor

In this lab, you will build an electric motor. An electric motor is a device that uses a magnetic field to cause rotational motion.

Proposed Procedure

You Will Need

✔ cardboard base

✔ tube

✔ insulated wire (approx 25 cm)

✔ electrical tape

✔ battery

✔ paper clip or thick, flexible wire (2)

✔ electrical tape or alligator clips

✔ permanent magnet

1. Using about 25 cm of wire, start tightly looping the wire around a tube or several fingers. Be sure to leave about 5 cm of un-looped wire on each end.

2. Take each paper clip (or piece of wire) and bend them so that they can form a loop on each end. These will hold the coil of wire you made in Step 1. Use tape to hold the paper clips down on the table or cardboard.

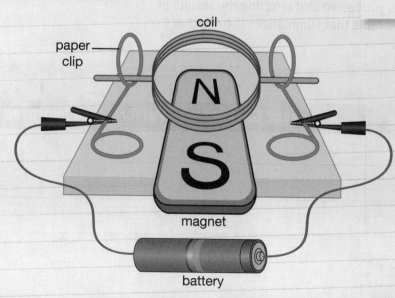

coil

paper clip

magnet

battery

Building an Electric Motor

3 Place the coil of wire on both paper clips. Attach one end of a wire to a paperclip and the other end of the wire to the negative end of the battery. Record your observations.

_____

_____

_____

_____

_____

4 Connect the other paper clip to the other battery terminal as you did in Step 3. Record your observations.

_____

_____

_____

_____

Once you have a functioning electric motor, consider how different factors affect the performance of the motor. Determine the factors that affect the performance of the motor by changing the design of the motor, keeping several variables constant and changing only one factor. Try different combinations of materials such as the number or orientation of magnets, number of turns, size of the loop, or number of batteries.

5 Identify which factors you tested and describe the results of each change. Create a table that summarizes the effect of the changes you tested.

Type of Change	Amount of Change	Performance Improved (y/n)

6 How did these changes affect the performance of the motor? Which combination of factors had the greatest effect?

_____

_____

_____

_____

Challenge

Based on your investigation so far, redesign your electric motor to improve its performance and make the loop of wire spin as fast as possible.

7 How did you you re-design your electric motor to spin faster? Briefly explain and make a sketch of your re-designed motor below.

8 What can make a stronger electric or magnetic field?

_____

_____

_____

_____

_____

Visual Summary

To complete this summary, check the box that indicates true or false. Then, use the key below to check your answers. You can use this page to review the main concepts of the lesson.

Electromagnetism results from the interaction of electric currents and magnetic fields.

	T	F	
20	☐	☐	Solenoids are magnetic.
21	☐	☐	The strength of an electromagnet decreases when you increase the current.
22	☐	☐	You can increase the number of coils to make an electromagnet stronger.
23	☐	☐	Electromagnets are used to lift heavy metal items.
24	☐	☐	Motors use electromagnets to produce movement.

Electromagnetism

Electromagnetic induction is electric current that results from magnetism.

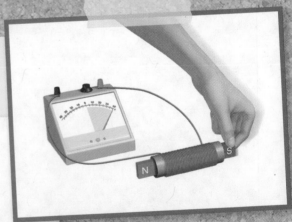

	T	F	
25	☐	☐	Generators use induction to produce electricity.
26	☐	☐	Transformers detect electric current.

Answers: 20 True; 21 False; 22 True; 23 True; 24 True; 25 True; 26 False

27 Synthesis Describe how you could use a motor in reverse to generate electricity.

Lesson Review

Vocabulary

Fill in the blank with the term that best completes the following sentences.

1 A(n) _____ is a coil of wire that produces a magnetic field when it carries an electric current.

2 A(n) _____ changes mechanical energy into electrical energy by means of electromagnetic induction.

3 A(n) _____ changes electrical energy into mechanical energy.

Key Concepts

4 Relate How do electricity and magnetism interact?

_____

_____

_____

5 Describe Describe how turning off the electric current in an industrial electromagnet affects its magnetic field.

_____

_____

6 Predict What effect would increasing the number of loops in a coil of wire have on an electromagnet?

_____

_____

7 Summarize How can a magnetic field be used to create an electric current?

_____

_____

_____

8 Identify List three everyday devices that could not have been developed without the discovery of electromagnetism.

_____

_____

Critical Thinking

9 Infer If Faraday had used a more powerful battery in his experiments with electromagnetic induction, what effect would this have had on his galvanometer's measurements of current when the battery was fully connected? Explain your reasoning.

_____

_____

_____

_____

Use the diagram to answer the following questions.

10 Illustrate Draw how the coils would look on a step-up transformer.

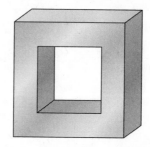

11 Identify On which side would the voltage be higher?

_____

_____

_____

_____

12 Describe How would the illustration look if it were showing a step-down transformer?

_____

_____

_____

_____

_____

My Notes

Unit 2

Lesson 1
ESSENTIAL QUESTION
What makes something electrically charged?

Describe electric charges in objects and distinguish between electrical conductors and insulators.

Lesson 2
ESSENTIAL QUESTION
What flows through an electric wire?

Describe how electric charges flow as electric current.

Lesson 3
ESSENTIAL QUESTION
How do electric circuits work?

Describe basic electric circuits and how to use electricity safely.

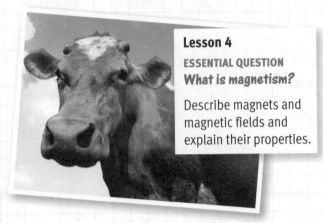

Lesson 4
ESSENTIAL QUESTION
What is magnetism?

Describe magnets and magnetic fields and explain their properties.

Lesson 5
ESSENTIAL QUESTION
What is electromagnetism?

Describe the relationship between electricity and magnetism and how this relationship affects our world.

Think Outside the Book

2 Synthesize Choose one of these activities to help synthesize what you have learned in this unit.

☐ Using what you learned in lessons 1 and 4, describe similarities between electricity and magnetism by making a poster presentation. Include captions and labels.

☐ Using what you learned in lessons 2, 3, and 5, explain how electric current, electric circuits, and electromagnetism have affected telecommunication by creating a timeline. Include specific examples from the lessons, your own experience, and history.

Connect ESSENTIAL QUESTIONS
Lessons 4 and 5

1 Synthesize Could a stationary magnet be used to generate an electric current? Explain.

_____

_____

_____

Name _____

Vocabulary

Fill in each blank with the term that best completes the following sentences.

1 A(n) _____ allows electrical charges to move freely.

2 The amount of work required to move a unit electric charge between two points is called _____.

3 A(n) _____ is an electric circuit in which all the parts are connected in a single loop.

4 Magnets exert forces on each other and are surrounded by a(n) _____.

5 A(n)_____ uses rotating magnets to produce electrical energy.

Key Concepts

Read each question below, and circle the best answer.

6 Objects can be charged in many ways. In the image below, a student is rubbing a balloon on his head.

What method is he using to charge the balloon?

A friction

C induction

B repulsion

D conduction

7 Which of the following is an electrical insulator?

A copper

C aluminum

B rubber

D iron

8 Which of the following wires has the lowest resistance?

A a short, thick copper wire at 25 °C

B a long, thick copper wire at 35 °C

C a long, thin copper wire at 35 °C

D a short, thin iron wire at 25 °C

9 There are many devices in the home that use electricity. Below is a diagram of four common electrical devices.

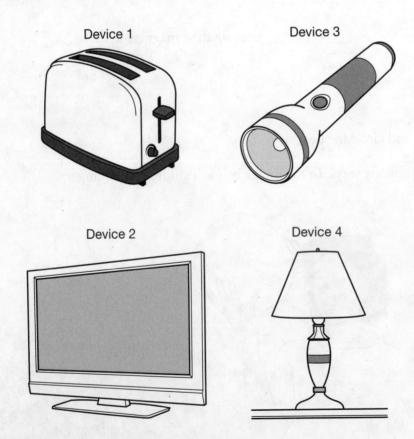

Device 1

Device 3

Device 2

Device 4

Which electrical device runs on direct current?

A Device 1

C Device 3

B Device 2

D Device 4

10 The diagram below shows two examples of electrical circuits.

Circuit 1

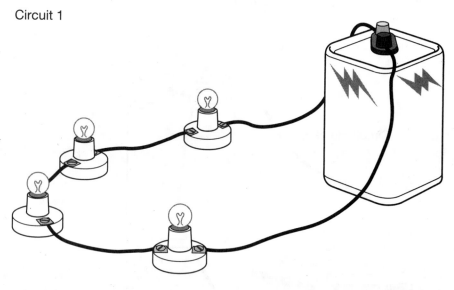

Circuit 2

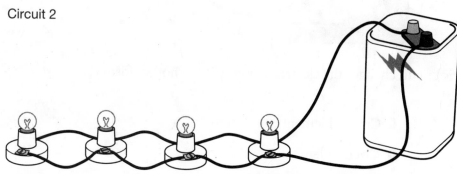

Which of the following statements about the circuits is correct?

A Circuit 1 is a parallel circuit, and Circuit 2 is a parallel circuit.

B Circuit 1 is a series circuit, and Circuit 2 is a parallel circuit.

C Circuit 1 is a parallel circuit, and Circuit 2 is a series circuit.

D Circuit 1 is a series circuit, and Circuit 2 is a series circuit.

11 It is important to practice electrical safety. Which of the following choices is unsafe?

A only using electrical cords that have proper insulation

B seeking shelter on a beach or under a tree during a lightning storm

C keeping electrical appliances away from sinks and bathtubs

D using ground fault circuit interrupters (GFCIs) in the home

12 Here is a diagram of a simple electric circuit. There are four elements to the circuit. They are labeled Circuit Element 1, Circuit Element 2, Circuit Element 3, and Circuit Element 4.

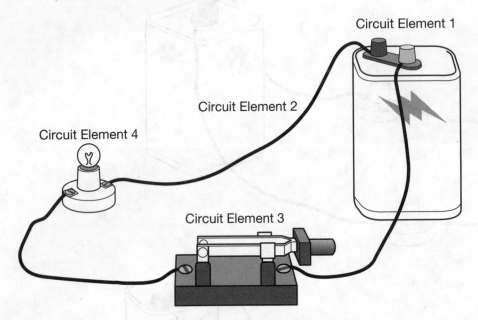

Circuit Element 1

Circuit Element 2

Circuit Element 4

Circuit Element 3

What part of an electric circuit changes the electrical energy into another form of energy?

A Circuit Element 1

C Circuit Element 3

B Circuit Element 2

D Circuit Element 4

13 Which of the following does not use an electromagnet?

A electric motor

C hand-held compass

B galvanometer

D doorbell

14 An object can become electrically charged if it gains or loses which particles?

A volts

C atoms

B neutrons

D electrons

15 Which device uses electricity to produce a rotational motion?

A computer

C magnet

B generator

D motor

16 What change would increase the strength of a generator?

A use thinner wire

C move the magnet faster

B add a larger battery

D move the magnet slower

17 Below is an image of a magnet showing the magnetic field.

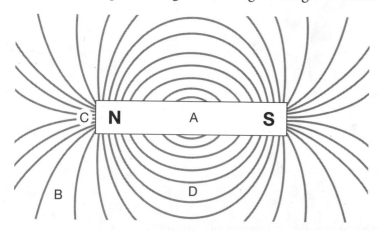

Where is the magnetic force the strongest?

A Position A

C Position C

B Position B

D Position D

Critical Thinking

Answer the following questions in the space provided.

18 Describe three properties of magnets.

_____

_____

_____

_____

_____

19 List two ways in which the strength of an electromagnet can be increased.

_____

_____

_____

_____

20 The image below shows Earth and its magnetic field.

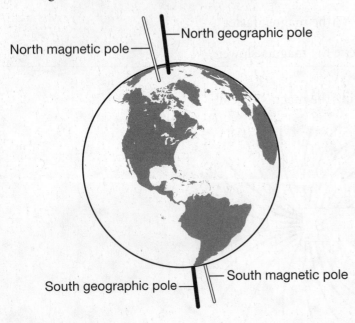

North magnetic pole —

— North geographic pole

South geographic pole —

— South magnetic pole

What is the difference between Earth's magnetic and geographic poles?
How do navigators take advantage of this?

_____

_____

_____

_____

_____

Connect ESSENTIAL QUESTIONS
Lessons 4 and 5

Answer the following question in the space provided.

21 There is a close relationship between magnetic forces and the generation of electricity. Explain how magnets can be used to generate electricity and how electric current can be used to create electromagnets. For each process, give an example of a device you would find around the home.

_____

_____

_____

_____

_____

Introduction to Waves

© Houghton Mifflin Harcourt Publishing Company • Image Credits: (bg) Gavin Hellier/Alamy Images; (inset) ©Greg Ewing/Getty Images

Big Idea

Waves transfer energy and interact in predictable ways.

8.PS4.1, 8.PS4.2, 8.PS4.3

The seven undulating waves of the Henderson Waves Bridge, a pedestrian walkway in Singapore, illustrate some of the properties of waves.

What do you think?

A surfer takes advantage of a wave's energy to catch an exciting ride. What other properties of waves might help a surfer catch a wave?

The higher the ocean wave, the farther the surfer can travel.

Unit 3
Introduction to Waves

Hit the Airwaves

When you hear the word *waves*, you probably think of waves in an ocean. But you encounter waves every day. For example, radio stations use airwaves to broadcast sounds to an audience.

1 Think about It

What do you know about the properties of waves? Sketch and label two full waves in the space below to show your current understanding of waves.

Each number on a radio dial represents a different wave frequency.

② Ask a Question

How does the Federal Communications Commission (FCC) assign the broadcast frequencies for radio and television stations? You might be surprised to discover that the FCC also assigns frequencies for devices that use radio waves. Such devices include garage-door openers and radio-controlled toys. With a partner, research this topic and share your findings with your class.

_____

_____

_____

③ Make a Plan

A Choose a call sign, broadcast frequency (has to be AM), and listening area for a campus radio station based on your research.

_____

_____

B List some other kinds of data you would need to research to start your own campus radio broadcasting station.

_____

_____

_____

C Could you increase the listening area of your radio station?

_____

_____

_____

The airwaves transmit the announcer's voice to listeners far and wide.

Take It Home

Talk with an adult about starting a radio station in your school. What types of programs would students want to hear? Could you actually create a school radio broadcasting station? Write a description of your radio station to turn in to your teacher. See *ScienceSaurus*® for more information about technology design.

Waves

ESSENTIAL QUESTION

What are waves?

By the end of this lesson, you should be able to distinguish between types of waves based on medium and direction of motion.

8.PS4.2

Ocean waves can cause great destruction. This woodblock print illustrates a great wave threatening boats off the coast of Japan.

Engage Your Brain

1 Predict Check T or F to show whether you think each statement is true or false.

T	F	
☐	☐	The air around you is full of waves.
☐	☐	Ocean waves carry water from hundreds of miles away.
☐	☐	Sound waves can travel across outer space.
☐	☐	Visible light is a wave.

2 Identify Make a list of items in the classroom that are making waves. Next to each item, write what kind of waves you think it is making.

_____

_____

_____

_____

_____

_____

_____

_____

_____

Active Reading

3 Distinguish Which of the following definitions of *medium* do you think is most likely to be used in the context of studying waves? Circle your answer.

A of intermediate size

B the matter in which a physical phenomenon takes place

C between two extremes

Vocabulary Terms

• wave
• medium
• longitudinal wave
• transverse wave
• mechanical wave
• electromagnetic wave

4 Apply As you learn the definition of each vocabulary term in this lesson, write your own definition or sketch to help you remember the meaning of the term.

What are waves?

The world is full of waves. Water waves are just one of many kinds of waves. Sound and light are also waves. A **wave** is a disturbance that transfers energy from one place to another.

Waves Are Disturbances

Many waves travel by disturbing a material. The material then returns to its original place. A **medium** is the material through which a wave travels.

You can make waves on a rope by shaking the end up and down. The rope is the medium, and the wave is the up-and-down disturbance. As the part of the rope nearest your hand moves, it causes the part next to it to move up and down too. The motion of this part of the rope causes the next part to move. In this way, the wave moves as a disturbance down the whole length of the rope.

Each piece of the rope moves up and down as a wave goes by. Then the piece of rope returns to where it was before. A wave transfers energy from one place to another. It does not transfer matter. The points where the wave is highest are called crests. The points where the wave is lowest are called troughs.

5 Identify Underline the names for the highest and lowest points of a wave.

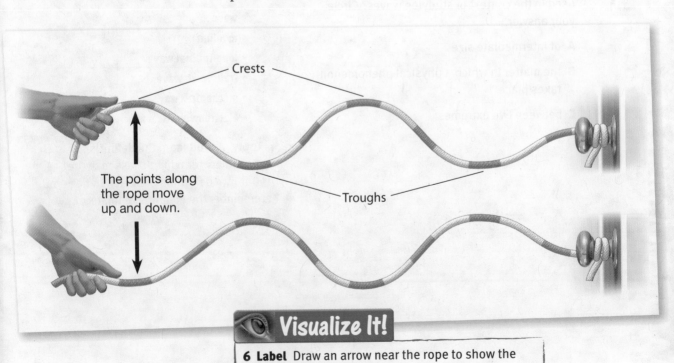

Crests

The points along the rope move up and down.

Troughs

Visualize It!

6 Label Draw an arrow near the rope to show the direction the wave travels.

Waves Are a Transfer of Energy

A wave is a disturbance that transfers energy. Some waves need a medium to transfer energy, such as waves in the ocean that move through water and waves that are carried on guitar or cello strings when they vibrate. Some waves can transfer energy without a medium. One example is visible light. Light waves from the sun transfer energy to Earth across empty space.

Visualize It!

Each snapshot below shows the passage of a wave. The leaf rises and falls as crests and troughs carry it.

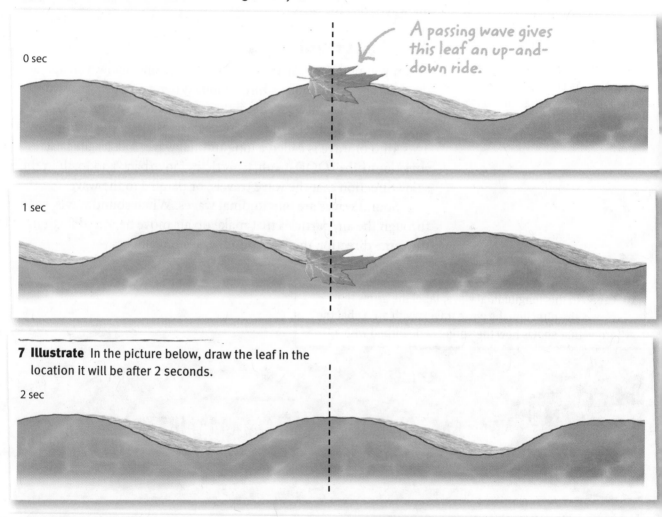

0 sec

A passing wave gives this leaf an up-and-down ride.

1 sec

7 Illustrate In the picture below, draw the leaf in the location it will be after 2 seconds.

2 sec

8 Model In the space below, draw the leaf and wave as they will appear after 3 seconds.

3 sec

How does a wave transfer energy?

A wave transfers energy in the direction it travels. However, the disturbance may not be in the same direction as the wave. Each wave can be classified by comparing the direction of the disturbance, such as the motion of the medium, with the direction the wave travels.

As a Longitudinal Wave

When you pull back on a spring toy like the one below, you spread the coils apart and make a *rarefaction*. When you push forward, you squeeze the coils closer together and make a *compression*. The coils move back and forth as the wave passes along the spring toy. This kind of wave is called a longitudinal wave. In a **longitudinal wave** (lahn•jih•TOOD•n•uhl), particles move back and forth in the same direction that the wave travels, or parallel to the wave.

Sound waves are longitudinal waves. When sound waves pass through the air, particles that make up air move back and forth in the same direction that the sound waves travel.

Visualize It!

10 Label In this longitudinal wave, label the arrow that shows the direction the wave travels with a *T*. Label the arrow that shows how the spring is disturbed with a *D*.

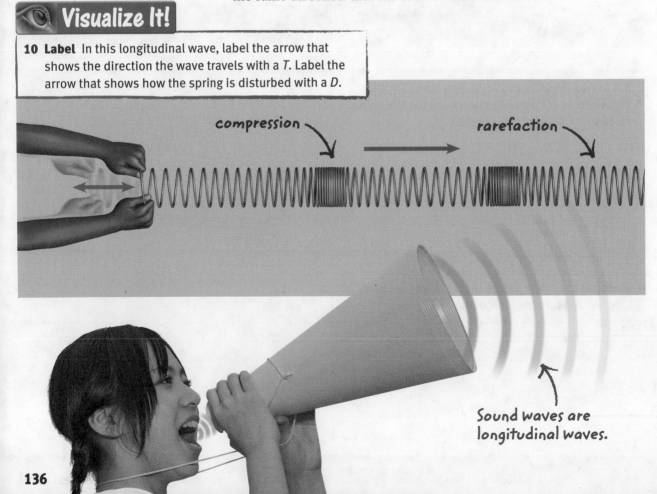

compression

rarefaction

Sound waves are longitudinal waves.

As a Transverse Wave

The same spring toy can be used to make other kinds of waves. If you move the end of the spring toy up and down, a wave also travels along the spring. In this wave, the spring's coils move up and down as the wave passes. This kind of wave is called a **transverse wave**. In a transverse wave, particles move perpendicularly to the direction the wave travels.

Transverse waves and longitudinal waves often travel at different speeds in a medium. In a spring toy, longitudinal waves are usually faster. An earthquake sends both longitudinal waves (called P waves) and transverse waves (called S waves) through Earth's crust. In this case, the longitudinal waves are also faster. During an earthquake, the faster P waves arrive first. A little while later, the S waves arrive. The S waves are slower but usually more destructive.

A transverse wave and a longitudinal wave can combine to form another kind of wave called a surface wave. Ripples on a pond are an example of a surface wave.

When these fans do "The Wave," they are modeling the way a disturbance travels through a medium.

12 Categorize Is the stadium wave shown above a transverse wave or a longitudinal wave?

© Houghton Mifflin Harcourt Publishing Company • Image Credits: (b) ©Derek Croucher/Alamy

Think Outside the Book · Inquiry

13 Identify What do the letters *S* in S waves and *P* in P waves stand for? Relate this to earthquakes and discuss it with a classmate.

Visualize It!

11 Label In this transverse wave, label the arrow that shows the direction the wave travels with a *T*. Label the arrow that shows how the spring is disturbed with a *D*.

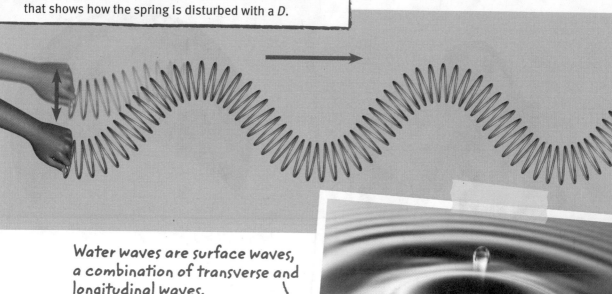

Water waves are surface waves, a combination of transverse and longitudinal waves.

Making Waves

What are some types of waves?

As you have learned, waves are disturbances that transfer energy. Waves can be classified by the direction of disturbance. But they can also be classified by what is disturbed.

Mechanical Waves

Most of the waves we have talked about so far are waves in a medium. For water waves, water is the medium. For earthquake waves, Earth is the medium. A wave that requires a medium through which to travel is called a **mechanical wave**.

Some mechanical waves can travel through more than one medium. For example, sound waves can move through air, through water, or even through a solid wall. The waves travel at different speeds in the different media. Sound waves travel much faster in a liquid or a solid than in air.

Mechanical waves can't travel without a medium. Suppose all the air is removed from beneath a glass dome, or bell jar, as in the photograph below. In a vacuum, there is no air to transmit sound waves. The vibrations made inside the bell jar can't be heard.

Electromagnetic Waves

Are there waves that can travel without a medium? Yes. Sunlight travels from the sun to Earth through empty space. Although light waves can travel through a medium, they can also travel without a medium. Light and similar waves are called electromagnetic (EM) waves. An **electromagnetic wave** is a disturbance in electric and magnetic fields. They are transverse waves. Examples of EM waves include

- visible light
- radio waves
- microwaves
- ultraviolet (UV) light
- x-rays

In empty space, all these waves travel at the same speed. This speed, referred to as the speed of light, is about 300 million meters per second!

The sound from the toy cannot be heard because there is no air to transmit the sound.

Visible light is a type of wave called an electromagnetic wave.

14 Classify Identify each example of waves in these three photographs as mechanical or electromagnetic.

Sunlight is a(n)
_____

Water waves are
_____

A towel waving displays a(n)
_____

Vocal sounds are
_____

Music is a(n)
_____

Firelight is a(n)
_____

Visual Summary

To complete this summary, fill in the lines below the statement to correct the statement so that it is true. You can use this page to review the main concepts of the lesson.

Waves are disturbances that transfer energy.

15 The water particles in the wave move to the right, along with the wave.

_____

_____

_____

Waves can be longitudinal or transverse.

16 The toy above and the toy below both show longitudinal waves.

_____

_____

_____

Waves

Waves can be mechanical or electromagnetic.

17 This picture shows only examples of mechanical waves.

_____

_____

_____

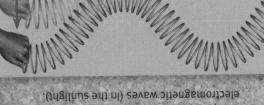

Answers: 15 The water particles in the wave move mostly up and down; 16 The toy above shows a longitudinal wave, but the toy below shows a transverse wave; 17 This picture shows mechanical waves and electromagnetic waves (in the sunlight).

18 **Support** Use an example to support the following statement: Waves transfer energy but not matter.

Lesson Review

Vocabulary

Circle the term that best completes the following sentences.

1 A wave is a disturbance that transfers *matter/energy*.

2 In a *longitudinal/transverse* wave, the disturbance moves parallel to the direction the wave travels.

3 *Mechanical/Electromagnetic* waves require a medium in which to travel.

Key Concepts

4–6 Identify Name the medium for each of the following types of waves.

Type of wave	Medium
ocean waves	**4**
earthquake waves	**5**
sound waves from a speaker	**6**

7 Describe Explain how transverse waves can be produced on a rope. Then describe how pieces of the rope move as waves pass.

_____

_____

_____

_____

8 Analyze Are the sun's rays mechanical waves or electromagnetic waves? How do you know?

_____

_____

Critical Thinking

9 Contrast Mechanical waves travel as disturbances in a physical medium. How do electromagnetic waves travel?

_____

_____

_____

Use this image to answer the following questions.

10 Infer Even though the phone is ringing, no sound comes out of the jar. What does this tell you about the space inside the jar?

_____

_____

_____

_____

11 Infer What does this same experiment tell you about light waves? Explain.

_____

_____

_____

_____

_____

My Notes

$2v + 11 = 41$

$4x - 13 = 47$

$55 = 2w + 17$

$5u - 14 = 76$

$68 = 3y + 17$

$2 = 3x - 9$

$109 = 5w + 14$

$56 = 3y + 14$

$$\begin{array}{r} {\scriptstyle 1}2 \\ \times\ 5 \\ \hline 6\,0 \end{array}$$

$$\frac{2}{7} \cdot \frac{3}{14} = \frac{6}{}$$

$$\frac{x+11}{7} \times \frac{2x+1}{-8}$$

$$\frac{5}{8} \cdot \frac{4}{1} = \frac{20}{8}$$

$$\begin{array}{c} 2.3 \\ \times 2.8 \end{array}$$

$$\frac{5}{8} \cdot \frac{6}{1} = \frac{30}{3}$$

600

$$\frac{12x}{7} \times \frac{3x}{-8}$$

$$\begin{array}{r} 259 \\ 372 \\ \hline 631 \end{array}$$

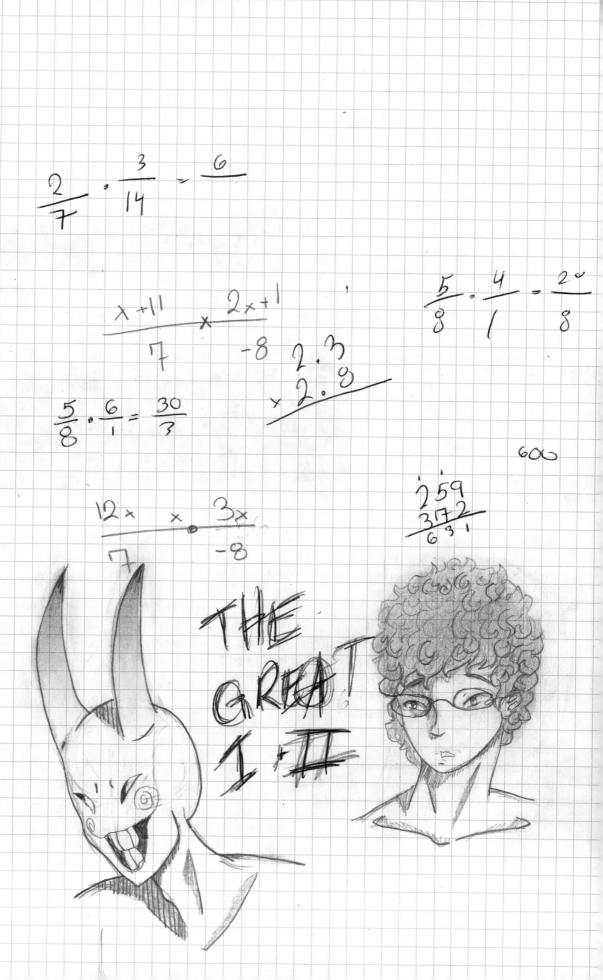

THE
GREAT
I · II

Mean, Median, Mode, and Range

You can analyze both the measures of central tendency and the variability of data using mean, median, mode, and range.

Tutorial

Imagine that a group of students records the light levels at various places within a classroom.

Classroom Light Levels	
Area	**Illuminance (lux)**
1	800
2	300
3	150
4	300
5	200

Mean

The mean is the sum of all of the values in a data set divided by the total number of values in the data set. The mean is also called the *average*.

$$\frac{800 + 300 + 150 + 300 + 200}{5}$$

mean = 350 lux

Median

The median is the value of the middle item when data are arranged in order by size. In a range that has an odd number of values, the median is the middle value. In a range that has an even number of values, the median is the average of the two middle values.

If necessary, reorder the values from least to greatest:

150, 200, **300**, 300, 800

median = 300 lux

Mode

The mode is the value or values that occur most frequently in a data set. If all values occur with the same frequency, the data set is said to have no mode. Values should be put in order to find the mode.

If necessary, reorder the values from least to greatest:

150, 200, 300, 300, 800

The value 300 occurs most frequently.

mode = 300 lux

Range

The range is the difference between the greatest value and the least value of a data set.

800 − 150

range = 650 lux

You Try It!

The data table below shows the data collected for rooms in three halls in the school.

Illuminance (lux)				
	Room 1	**Room 2**	**Room 3**	**Room 4**
Science Hall	150	250	500	400
Art Hall	300	275	550	350
Math Hall	200	225	600	600

Using Formulas Find the mean, median, mode, and range of the data for the school.

Analyzing Methods The school board is looking into complaints that some areas of the school are too poorly lit. They are considering replacing the lights. If you were in favor of replacing the lights, which representative value for the school's data would you use to support your position? If you were opposed to replacing the lights, which representative value for the school's data would you choose to support your position? Explain your answer.

___

Language Arts Connection

On flashcards, write sentences that use the keywords *mean, median, mode,* and *range*. Cover the keywords with small sticky notes. Review each sentence, and determine if it provides enough context clues to determine the covered word. If necessary, work with a partner to improve your sentences.

Properties of Waves

A heartbeat monitor c
a wave, the character
of which contain infor
about a patient's hear

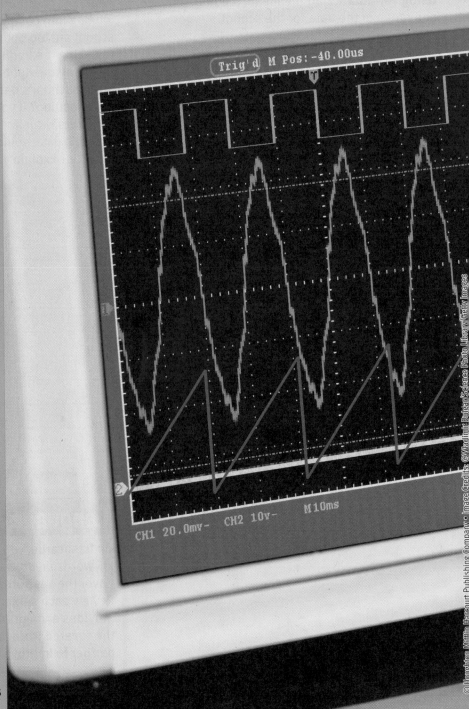

ESSENTIAL QUESTION

How can we describe a wave?

By the end of this lesson, you should be able to identify characteristics of a wave and describe wave behavior.

8.PS4.1. 8.PS4.2

Lesson Labs

Quick Labs
- Investigate Frequency
- Waves on a Spring

Exploration Lab
- Investigate Wavelength

Engage Your Brain

1 Describe Fill in the blank with the word that you think correctly completes the following sentences.

A guitar amplifier makes a guitar sound

_____

FM radio frequencies are measured in
mega-_____

The farther you are from a sound source,
the _____ the sound is.

Active Reading

3 Predict Many scientific words also have everyday meanings. For each of the following terms, write in your own words what it means in common use. Then try writing a definition of what it might mean when applied to waves.

length:

_____
_____
_____

_____

speed:

_____
_____
_____

_____

period (of time):

_____
_____
_____

2 Illustrate Draw a diagram of a wave in the space below. How would you describe your wave so that a friend on the phone could duplicate your drawing?

Vocabulary Terms

- wave
- amplitude
- wavelength
- wave period
- frequency
- hertz
- wave speed

4 Compare This list contains the vocabulary terms you'll learn in this lesson. As you read, circle the definition of each term.

Amp It UP!

How can we describe a wave?

Suppose you are talking to a friend who had been to the beach. You want to know what the waves were like. Were they big or small? How often did they come? How far apart were they? Were they moving fast? Each of these is a basic property that can be used to describe waves.

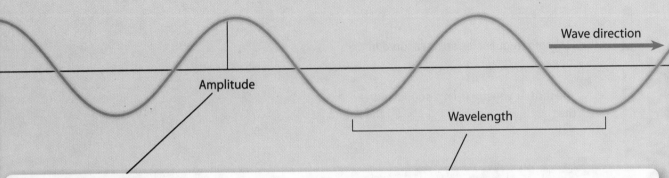

Wave direction

Amplitude

Wavelength

By Its Amplitude

A **wave** is a disturbance that transfers energy from one place to another. As a wave passes, particles in the medium move up and down or back and forth. A wave's **amplitude** is a measure of how far the particles in the medium move away from their normal rest position. The graph above shows a transverse wave. Notice that the amplitude of a wave is also half of the difference between the highest and lowest values.

By Its Wavelength

You can use amplitude to describe the height of an ocean wave, for example. But to describe how long the wave is, you need to know its wavelength. The **wavelength** is the distance from any point on a wave to an identical point on the next wave. For example, wavelength is the distance from one crest to the next, from one trough to the next, or between any other two corresponding points. Wavelength measures the length of one cycle, or repetition.

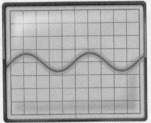 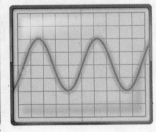 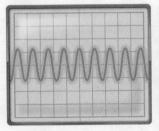 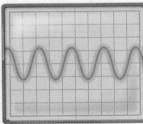

Visualize It!

5 Label Mark the amplitude in the two graphs above. Which wave has the greater amplitude?

6 Label Mark the wavelength in the two graphs above. Which wave has the greater wavelength?

By Its Frequency

Wavelength and amplitude tell you about the size of a wave. Another property tells you how much time a wave takes to repeat. The **wave period** (usually "period") is the time required for one cycle. You can measure the period by finding the time for one full cycle of a wave to pass a given point. For example, you could start timing when one crest passes you and stop when the next crest passes. The time between two crests is the period.

Another way to express the time of a wave's cycle is frequency. The **frequency** of a wave tells how many cycles occur in an amount of time, usually 1 s. Frequency is expressed in **hertz** (Hz). One hertz is equal to one cycle per second. If ten crests pass each second, the frequency is 10 Hz.

Frequency and period are closely related. Frequency is the inverse of period:

$$\text{frequency} = \frac{1}{\text{period}}$$

Suppose the time from one crest to another—the period—is 5 s. The frequency is then $\frac{1}{5}$ Hz, or 0.2 Hz. In other words, one-fifth (0.2) of a wave passes each second.

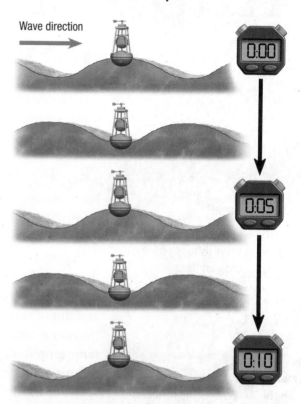

The buoy moves down and back up every five seconds as waves pass.

Wave direction

Frequency is equal to the number of cycles per unit of time:

$$\text{frequency} = \frac{\text{number of cycles}}{\text{time}}$$

Visualize It!

7 Illustrate On the grid below, draw a wave, and then draw another wave with twice the amplitude.

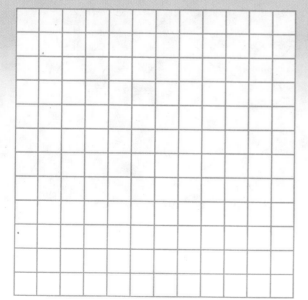

8 Illustrate On the grid below, draw a wave, and then draw another wave with half the wavelength.

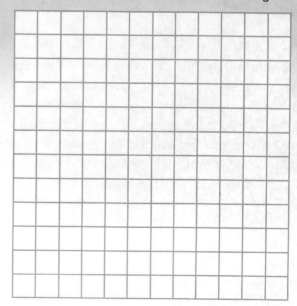

Amp It Down

What affects the energy of a wave?

All waves carry energy from one place to another, but some waves carry more energy than others. A leaf falling on water produces waves so small they are hard to see. An earthquake under the ocean can produce huge waves that cause great destruction.

The Amplitude or The Frequency

For a mechanical wave, amplitude is related to the amount of energy the wave carries. For two similar waves, the wave with greater amplitude carries more energy. For example, sound waves with greater amplitude transfer more energy to your eardrum, so they sound louder.

Greater frequency can also mean greater energy in a given amount of time. If waves hit a barrier three times in a minute, they transfer a certain amount of energy to the barrier. If waves of the same amplitude hit nine times in a minute, they transfer more energy in that minute.

For most electromagnetic (EM) waves, energy is most strongly related to frequency. Very high-frequency EM waves, such as x-rays and gamma rays, carry enough energy to damage human tissue. Lower-frequency EM waves, such as visible light waves, can be absorbed safely by your body.

Active Reading

9 Identify As you read, underline the kind of wave whose energy depends mostly on frequency.

Think Outside the Book

10 Apply An echo is the reflection of sound waves as they bounce back after hitting a barrier. How can the design of a building, such as a concert hall, reduce unwanted noises and echoes?

Energy Loss to a Medium

A medium transmits a wave. However, a medium may not transmit all of the wave's energy. As a wave moves through a medium, particles may move in different directions or come to rest in different places. The medium may warm up, shift, or change in other ways. Some of the wave's energy produces these changes. As the wave travels through more of the medium, more energy is lost to the medium.

Often, higher-frequency waves lose energy more readily than lower-frequency waves. For example, when you stand far from a concert, you might hear only the low-frequency (bass) sounds.

Some of the energy of these earthquake waves is lost to the medium when the ground shifts.

Energy Loss Due to Spreading

So far, we have mostly talked about waves moving in straight lines. But waves usually spread out in more than one dimension. The crests can be drawn as shapes, such as circles or spheres, called *wavefronts*. As each wavefront moves farther from the source, the energy is spread over a greater area. Less energy is available at any one point on the wavefront. If you measure a wave at a point farther from the source, you measure less energy. But the total energy of the wavefront stays the same.

Sound waves expand in three dimensions.

Inquiry

Ripples on a water surface expand in two dimensions.

11 Predict Which type of wave spreading do you think causes faster energy loss—two-dimensional or three-dimensional? Explain.

_____

_____

_____

As the student on the left knocks on the table, the students farther away feel the resulting waves less strongly.

Visualize It! Inquiry

12 Synthesize If these students repeated their experiment using a longer table, what differences would they observe? Explain your answer.

_____

_____

_____

A Happy Medium

What determines the speed of a wave?

Waves travel at different speeds in different media. For example, sound waves travel at about 340 m/s in air at room temperature, but they travel at nearly 1,500 m/s in water. In a solid, sound waves travel even faster.

The Medium in Which It Travels

The speed at which a wave travels—called **wave speed**—depends on the properties of the medium. Specifically, wave speed depends on the interactions of the atomic particles of the medium. In general, waves travel faster in solids than in liquids and faster in liquids than in gases. Interactions, or collisions, between particles happen faster in solids because the medium is more rigid.

How fast the wave travels between particles within the medium depends on many factors. For example, wave speed depends on the density of the medium. Waves usually travel slower in the denser of two solids or the denser of two liquids. The more densely packed the particles are, the more they resist motion, so they transfer waves more slowly.

In a gas, wave speed depends on temperature as well as density. Particles in hot air move faster than particles in cold air, so particles in hot air collide more often. This faster interaction allows waves to pass through hot air more quickly than through the denser cold air. The speed of sound in air at 20 °C is about 340 m/s. The speed of sound in air at 0 °C is slower, about 330 m/s.

Electromagnetic waves don't require a medium, so they can travel in a vacuum. All electromagnetic waves travel at the same speed in empty space. This speed, called the speed of light, is about 300,000,000 m/s. While passing through a medium such as air or glass, EM waves travel more slowly than they do in a vacuum.

Active Reading 13 **Identify** Does sound travel faster or slower when the air gets warmer?

14 Predict Air has been removed from the bell jar. Identify a type of wave that will travel through the bell jar and a wave that will not travel through the bell jar.

Wave that will pass through	Wave that won't pass through

Visualize It!

15 Diagram One diagram shows sound traveling through an air-filled tank. Draw a medium in the second tank in which sound will travel faster than in the air-filled tank.

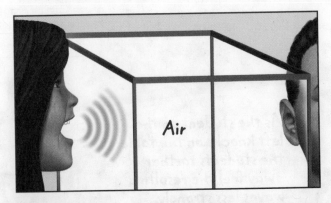

Air

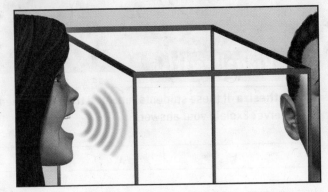

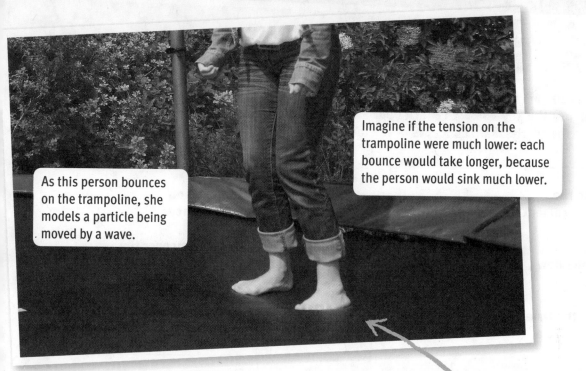

Imagine if the tension on the trampoline were much lower: each bounce would take longer, because the person would sink much lower.

As this person bounces on the trampoline, she models a particle being moved by a wave.

As a medium becomes more flexible, it carries waves more slowly.

Its Frequency and Wavelength

Wave speed can be calculated from frequency and wavelength. To understand how, it helps to remember that speed is defined as distance divided by time:

$$speed = \frac{distance}{time}$$

So if a runner runs 8 m in 2 s, then the runner's speed is 8 m ÷ 2 s = 4 m/s. For a wave, a crest moves a distance of one wavelength in one cycle. The time for the cycle to occur is one period. Using wavelength and period as the distance and time:

$$wave\ speed = \frac{wavelength}{wave\ period}$$

So if a crest moves one wavelength of 8 m in one period of 2 s, the wave speed is calculated just like the runner's speed: 8 m ÷ 2 s = 4 m/s.

Frequency is the inverse of the wave period. So the relationship can be rewritten like this:

$$wave\ speed = frequency \times wavelength$$
$$or$$
$$wavelength = \frac{wave\ speed}{frequency}$$

If you already know the wave speed, you can use this equation to solve for frequency or wavelength.

 Do the Math You Try It

16 Calculate Complete this table relating wave speed, frequency, and wavelength.

Wave speed (m/s)	Frequency (Hz)	Wavelength (m)
20		5
75	15	
	23	16
625		25
	38	20

© Houghton Mifflin Harcourt Publishing Company • Image Credits: ©Steppenwolf/Alamy Images

Visual Summary

To complete this summary, fill in the blanks with the correct word or phrase. Then use the key below to check your answers. You can use this page to review the main concepts of the lesson.

Amplitude tells the amount of displacement of a wave.

Wavelength tells how long a wave is.

Wave period is the time required for one cycle.

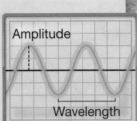

Amplitude

Wavelength

17 _____ $= \dfrac{1}{\text{wave period}}$

18 Hertz is used to express _____

19 One hertz is equal to _____

Wave energy depends on amplitude and frequency.

Most waves lose energy over time as they travel and spread.

21 Some of the wave's energy stays in the

_____

Wave Properties

Wave speed depends on the properties of the medium.

In a vacuum, electromagnetic waves all move at the speed of light.

20 wave speed = frequency × _____

Answers: 16 frequency; 17 frequency; 18 one cycle per second; 19 wavelength; 20 medium

22 **Synthesize** Describe how the properties of sound waves change as they spread out in a spherical pattern.

Lesson Review

Vocabulary

Fill in the blank with the correct letter.

1 frequency

_____

2 wavelength

_____

3 wave speed

_____

4 wave period

_____

5 amplitude

_____

A the distance over which a wave's shape repeats

B the maximum distance that particles in a wave's medium vibrate from their rest position

C the time required for one wavelength to pass a point

D the number of wavelengths that pass a point in a given amount of time

E the speed at which a wave travels through a medium

Key Concepts

6 Describe What measures the amount of displacement in a transverse wave?

_____

7 Relate How are frequency and wave period related?

_____
_____
_____
_____

8 Provide What does the energy of an electromagnetic wave depend on?

_____

9 Infer Sound travels slower in colder air than it does in warmer air. Why does the speed of sound depend on air temperature?

_____
_____
_____
_____

Critical Thinking

Use this diagram to answer the following questions. The frequency of the wave is 0.5 Hz.

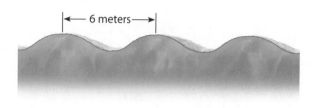

← 6 meters →

10 Analyze What is the wavelength of these waves?

_____

11 Calculate What is the speed of these waves?

_____

12 Solve If you were sitting in a boat as these waves passed by, how many seconds would pass between wave crests?

_____

13 Infer Why does the energy of a sound wave decrease over time?

_____
_____
_____

14 Infer A wave has a low speed but a high frequency. What can you infer about its wavelength?

_____
_____

15 Predict How do you know the speed of an electromagnetic wave in a vacuum?

_____
_____
_____

My Notes

hello
children.

HELLO
CHILDREN

Communication and Waves

ESSENTIAL QUESTION

How are waves used to communicate information?

By the end of this lesson, you should be able to evaluate the role that waves play in different communication systems.

8.PS.4.3

In the not so distant future, human beings will explore the red, dusty surface of Mars. Although millions of kilometers from home, carried by radio waves, their images will flash across television screens in every corner of Earth.

Engage Your Brain

1 Predict Check T or F to show whether you think each statement is true or false.

T F

Sound waves can be used to send signals through space. _____

Waves of the electromagnetic spectrum include radio waves. _____

All communication devices must be connected by wires. _____

Light waves travel faster than sound waves. _____

2 Explain Say you were at mission control on Earth. You use radio waves to say "Hello" to an astronaut on Mars when Mars is 84,000,000 km from Earth. The astronaut hears your "Hello" 280 seconds after you spoke the word. How do you explain this time lag?

_____

_____

_____

_____

_____

_____

Active Reading

3 Apply Scientific and technical terms often have a variety of meanings that can shed light on what they represent when spoken or written. In this lesson, you will come across the word *digital*. Use the word part, and the sentence below, to figure out the meaning of the word *digital*.

Word Part	Meaning
digit	finger; number

Example sentence

A digital signal is used to send certain messages.

Vocabulary Terms

- **communication**
- **analog signal**
- **digital signal**
- **wave**
- **frequency**

4 Apply As you learn the definition of each vocabulary term in this lesson, create your own definition or sketch to help you remember the meaning of the term.

A Word, A Wink.

What is communication?

In one way or another, people have always communicated with one another. They have shouted warnings. They have expressed affection with a smile. They have described their surroundings. They have taught one another how to survive and how to solve the riddles of the natural world. They have expressed and explained ideas. They have delivered news and information from one place to another. What does all this tell you about the meaning of communication? When it comes to human beings, **communication** is the transfer of information from one person, or group of people, to another person or group of people. By the way, communication is not only a characteristic of human beings. Animals also communicate. If you have a pet dog or cat, you can come up with all sorts of ways you and your pet communicate, and how your pet and other animals communicate. How are the ways you and an animal communicate similar and different?

Active Reading

5 Explain What is communication?

Visualize It!

6 Explain How is the driver of the ambulance communicating the urgency of her mission?

_____

_____

_____

_____

7 Identify What kinds of waves are indicating the urgency of the driver's mission?

_____

_____

_____

_____

_____

Emergency vehicles use sirens and lights to alert other drivers of their approach.

and a Wave

What are some different ways that people communicate?

The forms of communication people use vary. Some have depended on simple sounds. Grunts. Screams. Laughter. Giggles. Cries. Whistles. Some have depended on more complex mixtures of sounds, like spoken words. The words might be those of a rap or country singer. They might be those of an actress or actor. They might be those of a scientist or a politician. Others have depended on visual forms of communication. Gestures, like a raised fist, communicate anger or defiance. Open arms communicate welcome or acceptance. A waving hand might signal a greeting or a farewell. A wink might signal understanding or agreement. A drawing, painting, diagram, or graph communicates information, too. So does a mathematical or chemical equation. And, of course, the written word communicates a vast variety of information and expression.

The words of a country song communicate a story from the singer to his audience.

Smoke, Light

How do people communicate at a distance?

Long before the invention of telephones, radios, television, and cell phones, people invented ways to communicate over distances. Of course, the distances were not as far as Earth's moon, Mars, or the outer planets and beyond, distances over which signals can travel today. The distances were in kilometers. And light and sound were the tools of communication.

Communication Before Modern Times

More than two thousand years ago, the Greeks used smoke signals to transfer information from one place to another. About a thousand years later, Chinese warriors relayed smoke signals from one tower to the next along the Great Wall to alert soldiers to the approach of an enemy. Native Americans produced puffs of smoke on hilltops to signal danger or to gather people. The signals were sent in code that only the receiver could decode.

Talking Drums

People in Africa used the sounds of drumbeats to transfer information over long distances. The tones and patterns of the beats were a kind of code for the various languages of the people. The use of "talking drums" eventually traveled to the Caribbean islands along with African slaves. Slave owners and officials on the islands banned the use of 'talking drums" because the slaves used them to communicate with one another in a code that slave owners could not decipher.

This picture, painted by the Artist Frederic Remington, shows Native Americans sending messages encoded in puffs of smoke.

These drums were made out of hollowed logs. The bigger the log, the louder the sound would be made and the farther it could be heard.

and Sound!

Modern Communication at a Distance

Today, light and sound are still used to communicate information over distances that span our planet and its solar system. Just like using smoke signals and drumbeats, information sent by wired telephones, wireless cell phones, and computers also must be encoded when sent and decoded when received.

For example, an ordinary landline telephone setup has two essential parts: a handset and a phone base. The handset contains a microphone at its bottom and a speaker at its top. The microphone collects the sound waves produced by your voice and changes the energy carried by the sound waves into an electrical, coded, analog signal. The signal is then changed into a radio wave and transmitted to the phone base. The phone base converts the radio waves back into electrical signals that travel through wires to the switching stations.

An **analog signal** is a continuous wave that may vary in strength or frequency. Strength affects the loudness of a sound. Frequency affects its pitch, or whether the sound is high, like a screech, or low, like a growl.

Computers, video cameras, CD, and DVD players encode and decode messages using digital signals. A **digital signal** carries individual bits of information in separate units of time. The signal is represented by the numbers 0 and 1. A sound, or other **information**, is **encoded**, or changed into a code, as a series of 1s and 0s. The series of 0s and 1s can later be decoded to produce the original sounds or data. A cell phone also **transmits** information digitally. The phone converts the sound waves of your voice into a series of numbers. Eventually, the digital message reaches its destination and decoded into the sounds of a voice.

The series of numbers are transmitted by radio waves through the air to relay towers.

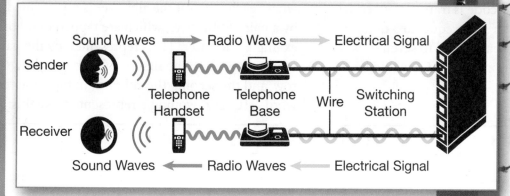

Sound Waves → Radio Waves → Electrical Signal

Sender

Telephone Handset Telephone Base Wire Switching Station

Receiver

Sound Waves ← Radio Waves ← Electrical Signal

Encode and Transmit a Message

Imagine that you want to communicate a message to a friend in an adjacent room, or across a field on a dark and windy night. The chances are that your voice would be very muffled, and the information that you tried to communicate would be lost, or garbled. This unwanted modification of the signal you are sending is called **noise**. You could try to amplify the signal by talking more loudly, but a more effective strategy is to make the signal very different from all the surrounding interference. This is what we do when we encode a signal for **transmission**.

In this Try it Out you are going to encode a simple message and transmit it to a partner using different kinds of waves.

Morse Code

A ●-	J ●---	S ●●●
B -●●●	K -●-	T -
C -●-●	L ●-●●	U ●●-
D -●●	M --	V ●●●-
E ●	N -●	W ●--
F ●●-●	O ---	X -●●-
G --●	P ●--●	Y -●--
H ●●●●	Q --●-	Z --●●
I ●●	R ●-●	

Morse code is a simple substitution code. It was developed in the 1830s for sending messages as pulses of electric current across wires using the newly invented telegraph. Each letter of the alphabet is represented by a series of dots and dashes. When Morse code is transmitted, each letter is separated by a space equal to 3 dots, and each word by a space equal to seven dots. In Morse code, the word "HELLO" would be represented like this:

H	E	L	L	O
●●●●	●	●-●●	●-●●	---

The Prisoner's Tap Code

	1	2	3	4	5
1	A	B	C/K	D	E
2	F	G	H	I	J
3	L	M	N	O	P
4	Q	R	S	T	U
5	V	W	X	Y	Z

The Prisoner's Tap Code was used by prisoners of war in World War II and Vietnam. It was developed as a way for them to communicate between cells by tapping messages on walls or pipes. The tap code is also a substitution code where each letter of the alphabet is represented by a pair of numbers, which are tapped out. For example, the letter "H" is represented by the pair of numbers (2,3); the first number being the row, and the second, the column. In tap code the word "HELLO" would be represented like this:

H	E	L	L	O
(2,3)	(1,5)	(3,1)	(3,1)	(3.4)

Procedure

1 Write a short message or a question on an index card in capital letters (about 20 words).

2 On a separate card, encode the question using either Morse Code or Prisoner's Tap code.

3 Give the encoded message to a partner to decode the message, and answer the question.

4 Trade roles with your partner using the other code.

You Will Need

✔ index cards
✔ pencils
✔ flashlight

If you want to make a secret message, you can **encrypt** it using an offset key. Choose a number between 1 and 10, and share the **key** with your partner. Substitute each letter in your message with the letter the same number of places away in the alphabet as your key. If the number you chose was 6, then the word "HELLO" becomes NKRRU ".

Encryption with offset key					
	H	**E**	**L**	**L**	**O**
Letter number	8	5	12	12	15
Offset key	+6	+6	+6	+6	+6
New letter number	14	11	18	18	21
Encrypted word	N	K	R	R	U

Analysis

5 Discuss with your partner how the message you encoded could be simply transmitted using a variety of mechanical waves, like sound, or electromagnetic waves like light. You could even transmit a message in Morse code using a closed hand for dots, and an open hand for dashes.

6 Transmit an encoded question to your partner using the type of wave you chose, and have them send an encoded answer back.

7 Give the encoded message to a partner to decode the message, and answer the question.

_____

_____

_____

_____

_____

_____

_____

_____

_____

_____

Riding the Wave

What are Waves?

If you have ever enjoyed a family vacation at a seashore, you may have ridden a wave to be knocked around by one. If so, you've learned first hand that waves carry energy. And that not only goes for ocean waves. Sound waves, light waves, radio waves, and microwaves all carry energy. People use that energy to communicate with one another.

But what, actually, is a wave? A wave is a disturbance that transfers energy through matter or space. Sound waves can only travel through matter, like air, water, or a metal. Light waves and radio waves do not need matter to travel, so they can travel through outer space. Sound waves transfer sounds from a source, such as the plucked strings of a guitar, to a receiver, such as your ear.

Radio waves are used to transfer a wide variety of information from a source to a receiver. Unlike sound and light waves, radio waves can transmit both sounds and images, making them useful for communication technologies such as radio, television, cell phones, and computers. Again, The properties of the waves determine the information they carry. By varying the properties of radio waves, a message is encoded. The code is decoded by receiver, such as a television set, and you observe sounds and pictures.

As a means of communication, radio waves have a number of advantages. Among these is the ability to travel at the speed of light (about 300,000 km/s) and the ability to pass through various materials, like the walls of your home. The speed of a sound wave, by contrast, varies with the medium through which it passes. For example, the speed of sound in air at 25°C is 346 m/s; in water at the same temperature, the speed is 1498 m/s.

Text messages use coded radio waves to send information from one person to another.

How do waves help cell phones communicate?

A cell phone lets you talk to a friend and listen to them at the same time. This is because it uses two different frequencies to send and receive messages. Frequency is the number of waves that pass a point in a given unit of time, usually a second. An outgoing message moves on a wave of one frequency while an incoming message moves on a wave of a different frequency.

Other kinds of devices that use radio waves, such as CB radios and walkie-talkies, allow only one person to talk at a time. These radios use the same frequency to send and receive messages. It's like using the same pipeline to move water in two different directions. You can't do both at the same time.

How do waves help satellites communicate?

At the beginning of a long trip in your family car, you tune into your favorite music radio station. But within a half-hour or so, the music begins to fade and static takes its place. What's going on, you wonder? It has to do with the radio waves bringing you music. They have a limited range, traveling in a straight line from a transmitting station to your car's radio. When your car slips over the horizon, perhaps less than 50 km from the transmitting station, the waves overshoot your car, and the music fades.

This could be a real problem for people who want to rapidly transmit information, like spoken words, TV pictures and sound, or data from a space station to places on Earth thousands of kilometers apart. The solution has been to place communication satellites in orbit 35,400 km above Earth's surface. The satellites are positioned so that together they can cover our entire planet.

Cell phone calls can be made half-way around the world and people can watch events on TV in far-off places.

Cell phone transmission

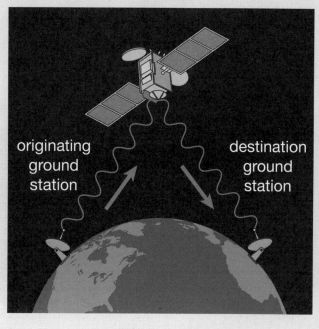

originating ground station

destination ground station

All of the technologies shown in the pictures use waves to transmit information. Some use radio waves. Some use sound waves. Some use both radio and sound waves.

8 Label Mark in the boxes with a **T** or **F** whether the technologies can receive and transmit sound waves, or can receive and transmit radio waves.

	Sound Waves	Radio Waves
Receive		
Transmit		

	Sound Waves	Radio Waves
Receive		
Transmit		

	Sound Waves	Radio Waves
Receive		
Transmit		

	Sound Waves	Radio Waves
Receive		
Transmit		

	Sound Waves	Radio Waves
Receive		
Transmit		

A Connected World

For some rural communities, there is little infrastructure to support technology, such as landline telephones and computers. Because of the far-reach of satellites and cell phone networks, farmers in these isolated places can take advantage of modern technology.

Farmers receive text alerts that provide tips and advice on pest and disease control, sustainable farming techniques, and weather forecasts to help them make informed decisions about planting, irrigating, and harvesting.

The alerts are in local languages and also recorded and accessed using an interactive voice response (IVR) because not all the farmers can read. Well-informed farmers become empowered and more prosperous, improving their lives, their communities, and the region.

In Pakistan, cell phone carriers are working with an aid agency and farmers to bring up-to-date information to their remote communities.

Extend

9 Describe Why can cell phones be used as an effective communication tool in these remote places?

_____

_____

_____

10 Research In some rural communities, there are more cell phones than people. Research other areas in the world where cell phone technology is helping remote communities to connect with the rest of the world.

_____

_____

_____

11 Propose Children in some isolated communities have to walk long distances to attend school. In these areas, schools may not have current educational materials. How would you use cell phone technology to provide these children with better access to education?

_____

_____

_____

Visual Summary

To complete this summary, circle the correct word or phrase. Then use the key below to check your answers. You can use this page to review the main concepts of this lesson.

Cell phone towers receive radio signals and transmit them back out.

Cell phones use radio waves to transmit, text, sounds, and pictures over distances.

9 Waves containing information are encoded/decoded so they can be transmitted to a receiver.

10 The transmitted signal is encoded/decoded by the receiver so it can be understood.

11 Radio waves travel at the speed of sound/speed of light.

12 Radio waves can travel through space, but not a medium/space and a medium.

Communication satellites use radio waves to relay messages from one point on Earth to another point on Earth.

13 One/more than one communication satellite is required to receive and relay radio waves to points at any location on Earth..

14 If a communication satellite is positioned 35,400 km above Earth's surface, a radio wave from the surface will take about 1/10 second/1 second/10 seconds to reach the satellite.

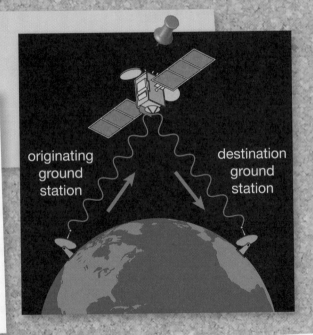

originating ground station

destination ground station

Answers: 9 encoded; 10 decoded; 11 light; 12 space and a medium; 13 more than one; 14 1/10 second

15 **Summarize** Explain how waves are used to communicate information.

Lesson Review

Vocabulary

In your own words, define the following terms.

1 analog sign

_____

_____

2 digital sign

_____

_____

3 frequency

_____

_____

Key Concepts

4 Describe What is the function of the phone base in a landline telephone system?

_____

_____

5 Explain Why are sound waves NOT used to communicate between objects in space?

_____

_____

_____

6 Explain Why do people riding in a car have to switch from one station to another to hear music as time passes?

_____

_____

_____

_____

7 Identify Which transmits information by light waves?

A	a grunt
B	a wink
C	a cry
D	a whisper

Critical Thinking

8 Apply Explain why certain locations in the United States are in "dead zones" where cell phones cannot send or receive messages.

_____

_____

_____

9 Apothesize As astronauts orbited the Moon, there was a period when they were unable to communicate with mission control on Earth using radio signals. Describe the conditions that might have led to the communications "blackout."

_____

_____

_____

_____

10 Explain You are sitting in the center field bleachers of a Major League baseball park. You see a batter strike a pitched ball. About 0.4 seconds later you hear the contact between the bat and the ball. In terms of the properties of light and sound waves, how do you explain the difference in the communications you received about the same event?

_____

_____

_____

11 Predict Assume you are responsible for determining the elevation of a communications satellite above Earth's surface. Predict and explain how elevation of the satellite would affect the area on Earth that transmitted radio waves can reach.

_____

_____

My Notes

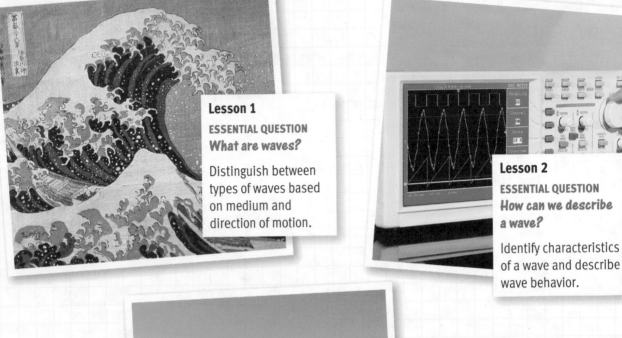

Lesson 1

ESSENTIAL QUESTION
What are waves?

Distinguish between types of waves based on medium and direction of motion.

Lesson 2

ESSENTIAL QUESTION
How can we describe a wave?

Identify characteristics of a wave and describe wave behavior.

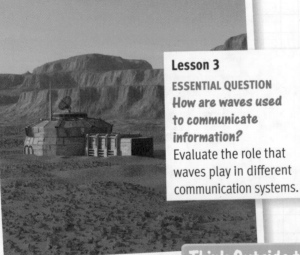

Lesson 3

ESSENTIAL QUESTION
How are waves used to communicate information?
Evaluate the role that waves play in different communication systems.

Connect   ESSENTIAL QUESTIONS
Lessons 1 and 2

1 Synthesize What are two properties of waves that affect the energy of waves?

_____

_____

Think Outside the Book

2 Synthesize Choose one of these activities to help synthesize what you have learned in this unit.

☐ Using what you learned in lessons 1 and 2, create a model that compares the parts of a mechanical wave to the parts of an electromagnetic wave.

☐ Using what you learned in lessons 1 and 2, design an experiment to compare mechanical wave speeds through different media. Include all of the steps in your process and provide illustrations where needed.

Name _____

Vocabulary

Fill in each blank with the term that best completes the following sentences.

1 Light travels as a(n) _____ wave.

2 The distance from the crest of one wave to the crest of the next wave is the _____

3 _____, the number of waves produced in a given amount of time, is expressed in hertz.

4 Sound is a(n) _____ wave because it cannot travel without a medium.

5 _____ is the transfer of information from one person, or group of people, to another person or group of people.

Key Concepts

Read each question below, and circle the best answer.

6 Sashita uses the volume control on her TV to make the sound louder or softer. Which property of waves is Sashita's volume control changing?

A amplitude

B wave period

C wavelength

D wave speed

7 Which statement best explains what an analog signal is?

A A signal that carries individual bits of information in separate units of time.

B A continuous wave that may vary in strength or frequency.

C A signal transmitted via light similar to a smoke signal.

D A wave that is used to transfer information using shape, colors, brightness, and dimness.

8 The diagram below shows the properties of a transverse wave.

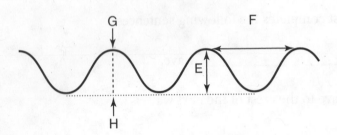

What property of the wave does F measure?

A period

C amplitude

B frequency

D wavelength

9 Which type of electromagnetic waves have the highest frequency?

A radio waves

C light waves

B gamma rays

D microwaves

10 Isabella researched how waves travel through the ground during an earthquake. She drew a diagram of one, called an S wave, moving through Earth's crust.

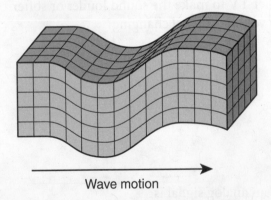

Wave motion

Based on her diagram, what kind of wave is an S wave?

A light

B sound

C longitudinal

D transverse

11 Visible, infrared, and ultraviolet light are electromagnetic waves that travel from the sun to Earth. There are other types of electromagnetic waves as well.

The Electromagnetic Spectrum
Typical frequency in hertz (1 hertz = 1 wavelength/second)

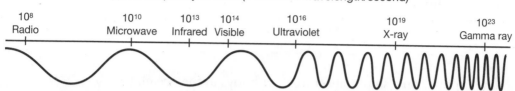

10^8	10^{10}	10^{13}	10^{14}	10^{16}	10^{19}	10^{23}
Radio	Microwave	Infrared	Visible	Ultraviolet	X-ray	Gamma ray

Which statement best explains what electromagnetic waves are?

A waves that vibrate through a medium

B disturbances in the atmosphere of space

C disturbances in electric and magnetic fields

D slow-moving waves

12 Which statement best describes how the frequency of waves act in a walkie-talkie and a cell phone?

A Walkie-talkies use the same frequency to send and receive messages while cell phones use two frequencies, one to send messages and one to receive messages.

B Walkie-talkies use two frequencies, one to send messages and one to receive messages, while cell phones use the same frequency to send messages and receive messages.

C Walkie-talkies and cell phones send and receive messages using the same single frequency.

D Walkie-talkies and cell phones send and receive messages using the same two frequencies, one to send and one to receive messages.

13 Which statement about the effects of medium on the speed of a mechanical wave is true?

A Medium has no effect on the speed of a mechanical wave.

B A mechanical wave generally travels faster in solids than liquids.

C A mechanical wave generally travels faster in gases than liquids.

D A mechanical wave always travels through liquids at the speed of light.

Unit 3 Review continued

Critical Thinking

Answer the following questions in the space provided.

14 Some waves carry more energy than others. Which wave has more energy, a loud sound or a quiet sound? Why?

_____

_____

15 Tafari worked one summer on a ship that set weather buoys in the ocean. He watched how the buoys moved in the water.

Which wave property describes why the buoys bobbed up and down?

Which wave property determines how fast the buoys bobbed in the water?

He observed that when the wind blew harder, the ocean waves were larger, and the buoys moved away from the ship. What effect, if any, did the waves have on how far the buoys moved? Explain your answer.

_____

_____

_____

_____

Connect ESSENTIAL QUESTIONS
Lessons 1 and 2

Answer the following question in the space provided.

16 Jung arrived at a concert in the park so late that the only seat she could get was almost a block from the stage. The music sounded much fainter to Jung than it did to people near the stage. She could hear the drums and bass guitar fairly well, but she had trouble hearing higher sounds from the singer. Explain the properties and behavior of waves that affected how Jung heard the music.

_____

_____

_____

_____

Sound

Big Idea

Sound waves transfer energy through vibrations.

8.PS4.1, 8.PS4.2, 8.PS4.3

The Singing Ringing Tree, located in rural England, enchants visitors with an eerie hum. The sound is created by the wind passing through the galvanized steel pipes.

What do you think?

Music is just one example of sound. Describe some sounds you heard today. Are these sounds produced by human activity or by nature?

The clarinetist uses "wind" to make music.

Sound It Out!

Have you ever felt a vibrating sensation during a really loud sound? That happens because sound waves transfer energy in the form of vibrations. You can learn how to make sounds louder and quieter by investigating sound sculptures.

① Do Additional Research

Investigate the Singing Ringing Tree by finding a book about it in the library or doing an Internet search. How does the sculpture produce sound?

_____

_____

_____

_____

_____

_____

The cheerleader uses a megaphone to make her voice louder.

② Think about It

What would make the sound louder?
What would make the sound quieter?
Write your ideas below.

Louder	Quieter

A mute is used to make the trumpet quieter.

③ Make A Plan

A You can make your own sound sculpture with everyday objects. Think about how you would create sound with some of the following items: spoons, drinking straws, plastic bottles, pencils, paper clips, sheets of paper, cellophane, rubber bands, or plastic cups. Will wind be the source of your sound? Write a prediction about how it will sound.

_____
_____
_____
_____
_____

B Sketch your sculpture in the space below.

ear trumpet

Take It Home

With an adult, research devices used by people who were hard of hearing in 1900, in 1960, and today. Over the years, how have these devices changed or stayed the same? See *ScienceSaurus*® for more information about sound.

Sound Waves and Hearing

ESSENTIAL QUESTION

What is sound?

By the end of this lesson, you should be able to describe what sound is, identify its properties, and explain how humans hear it.

8.PS4.1, 8.PS4.2

Musical instruments produce sound by making vibrations.

Lesson Labs

Quick Labs
• Investigate Sound Energy
• Different Instrument Sounds
• Investigate Loudness

Exploration Lab
• Sound Idea

 Engage Your Brain

1 Predict Check T or F to show whether you think each sentence below about sound is correct.

T	F	
☐	☐	Sound reaches our ears as waves.
☐	☐	Loud sounds are not harmful to humans.
☐	☐	All animals hear the same range of frequencies.
☐	☐	Sound can travel in outer space.
☐	☐	Sound can travel in water.

2 Describe Why is this woman wearing ear protection? Write your answer in the form of a caption for this photograph.

_____
_____
_____

 Active Reading

3 Apply Use context clues to write your own definition for the term *longitudinal wave*.

Example sentence:
The <u>longitudinal wave</u> traveled back and forth along the length of the coiled spring.

longitudinal wave:

_____
_____
_____
_____

Vocabulary Terms

• sound wave   • loudness
• longitudinal wave • decibel
• pitch   • Doppler effect

4 Identify As you read, create a reference card for each vocabulary term. On one side of the card, write the term and its meaning. On the other side, draw an image that illustrates or makes a connection to the term. Use your cards as bookmarks in the text so that you can refer to them while studying.

Listen Up!

What is sound?

When you beat a drum, the drum skin vibrates and causes the air to vibrate, as shown below. A *vibration* is the complete back-and-forth motion of an object. The vibrations in the air are interpreted as sounds by your brain. No matter how different they are, all sounds are created by vibrations.

What are sound waves?

5 Identify As you read, underline the properties of longitudinal waves.

A **sound wave** is a longitudinal wave that is caused by vibrations and travels through a medium. In a **longitudinal wave** the particles of a medium vibrate in the same direction that the wave travels. Longitudinal waves, also called *compression waves,* are made of compressions and rarefactions (rair•uh•FAK•shuhns). A *compression* is the part of a longitudinal wave where particles are close together. A *rarefaction* is the part where particles are spread apart. As the wave passes through a medium, its particles are compressed together and then spread apart.

6 Label Write labels for A and B on the sound wave in the diagram.

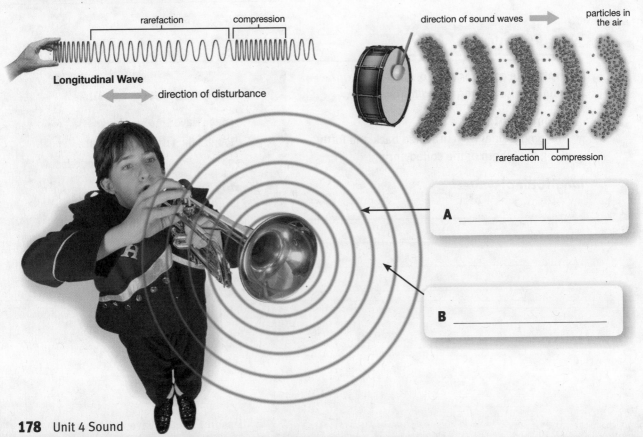

rarefaction   compression

Longitudinal Wave

← direction of disturbance →

direction of sound waves →   particles in the air

rarefaction   compression

A _____

B _____

How do sound waves travel?

Sound waves travel in all directions away from their source, as shown in the photo of the student playing the trumpet. But this is only possible if there is a medium through which the sound waves can travel.

Through a Medium

All matter—solids, liquids, and gases—is composed of particles. Sound waves travel by disturbing the particles in matter, or a medium. The particles of the medium do not travel with the sound waves themselves. The particles of a medium only vibrate back and forth along the path that the sound wave travels.

Most of the sounds that you hear travel through air at least part of the time. Sound waves can also travel through other materials, such as water, glass, and metal. You have probably heard people talking or dogs barking on the other side of a window or door. When you swim underwater, you may hear the sounds of your swim buddies as they splash and call to each other above the surface.

In a vacuum, there are no particles to vibrate. Therefore, no sound can be made in a vacuum. This fact helps to explain the effect shown in the photograph below. Sound must travel through air or some other medium to reach your ears and be detected.

Active Reading **7 Explain** Why can't sound travel through a vacuum?

_____

_____

_____

_____

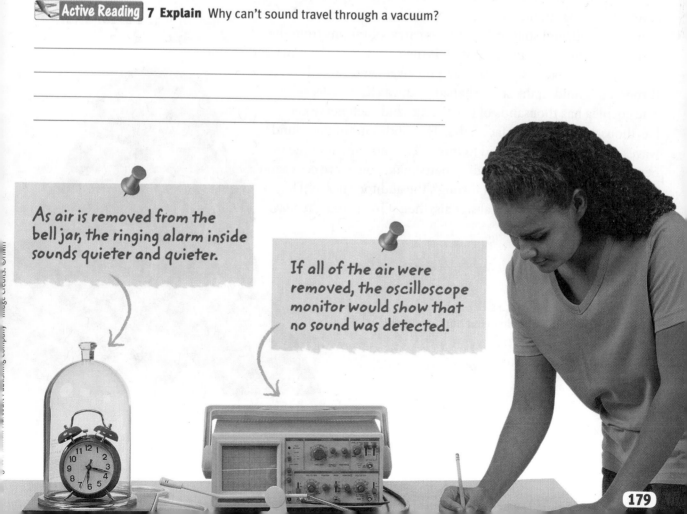

As air is removed from the bell jar, the ringing alarm inside sounds quieter and quieter.

If all of the air were removed, the oscilloscope monitor would show that no sound was detected.

Do You *Hear* That?

How do humans hear sound?

Humans detect sound with their ears. The ear acts like a funnel for sound waves. The ear directs sound vibrations from the environment into the inner ear, where the vibrations are converted to electrical signals. The electrical signals are sent to the brain, which interprets them as sound.

Humans Hear Sound Through Ears

Active Reading **8 Match** As you read, match each paragraph to the numbered part of the ear illustration on the facing page.

_____ Sound from the environment enters the outer ear, travels through the ear canal, and reaches the eardrum. The eardrum is a thin membrane that is stretched tightly over the entrance to the middle ear. The compressions and rarefactions in the sound waves make the eardrum vibrate.

_____ The eardrum transfers the vibrations to three tiny, connected bones in the middle ear. These bones are called the hammer, anvil, and stirrup. The bones carry vibrations from the eardrum to the oval window, which is the entrance to the inner ear.

_____ The vibrations pass through the oval window and travel through the fluid in the snail-shaped cochlea (KAHK•lee•uh). The cochlea has thousands of nerve cells, and each nerve cell has thousands of tiny surface hairs. The vibrations of the sound waves cause the cochlea fluid to move. The movement of the fluid bends the tiny hairs. The bending hairs make the nerve cells send electrical signals to the brain through the auditory nerve. The brain receives these electrical signals; then it interprets them as the sound that you hear.

The ear is the organ that detects sound.

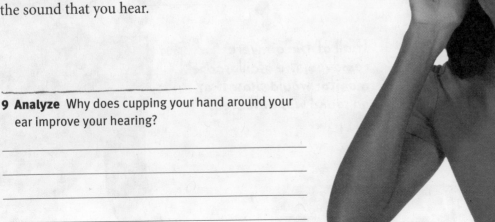

9 Analyze Why does cupping your hand around your ear improve your hearing?

_____

_____

_____

_____

The Human Ear

The human ear has many parts that all work together to capture and interpret sound waves.

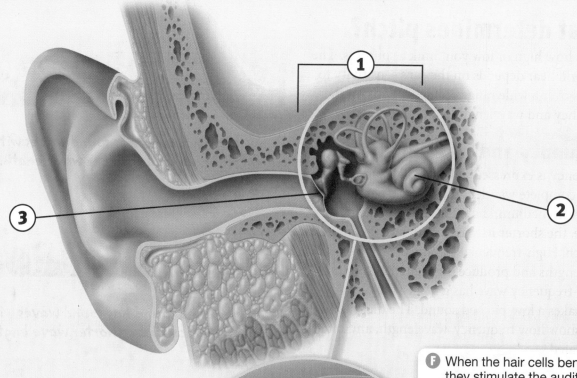

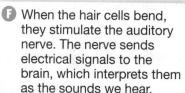

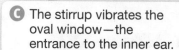

A Sound waves vibrate the eardrum—a tightly stretched membrane that forms the entrance to the middle ear.

B The eardrum vibrates, causing the hammer to vibrate. This in turn makes the anvil and the stirrup vibrate.

C The stirrup vibrates the oval window—the entrance to the inner ear.

D The vibrations of the oval window create waves in the liquid inside the cochlea.

E Movement of the liquid causes tiny hair cells inside the cochlea to bend.

F When the hair cells bend, they stimulate the auditory nerve. The nerve sends electrical signals to the brain, which interprets them as the sounds we hear.

 Inquiry

10 Predict If the nerve cells inside the cochlea were damaged, how might hearing be affected?

_____

_____

_____

Can You Hear Me NOW?

What determines pitch?

Pitch is how high or low you think a sound is. The pitch you hear depends on the ear's sensitivity to pitches over a wide range. Pitch depends on the frequency and wavelength of a sound wave.

Frequency and Wavelength

Frequency is expressed in hertz (Hz). One hertz is one complete wavelength, or cycle, per second. In a given medium, the higher the frequency of a wave, the shorter its wavelength and the higher its pitch. High-frequency waves have shorter wavelengths and produce high-pitched sounds. A low-frequency wave has a longer wavelength and makes a low-pitched sound. The diagrams at right show how frequency, wavelength, and pitch are related.

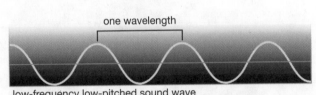

one wavelength

low-frequency low-pitched sound wave

A low-pitched sound has sound waves with a low frequency and a longer wavelength.

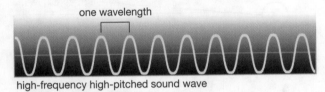

one wavelength

high-frequency high-pitched sound wave

A high-pitched sound has sound waves with a high frequency and a shorter wavelength.

Approximate Sound Frequencies Heard by Animals

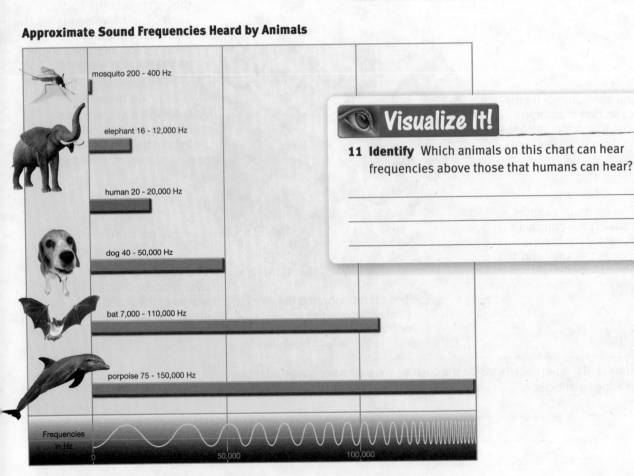

mosquito 200 - 400 Hz

elephant 16 - 12,000 Hz

human 20 - 20,000 Hz

dog 40 - 50,000 Hz

bat 7,000 - 110,000 Hz

porpoise 75 - 150,000 Hz

Frequencies in Hz

0   50,000   100,000

Visualize It!

11 Identify Which animals on this chart can hear frequencies above those that humans can hear?

_____

_____

_____

© Houghton Mifflin Harcourt Publishing Company • Image Credits: (t) ©Elvele Images Ltd/Alamy Images; (c) ©HMH; (bc) ©blickwinkel/Alamy Images; (b) ©Francois Gohier/Photo Researchers, Inc.; (r) ©Mark Bowler/Photo Researchers, Inc.

What makes a sound loud?

If you gently tap a drum, you will hear a soft rumbling. But if you strike the drum much harder, with more force, you will hear a much louder sound. By changing the force you use to strike the drum, you change the loudness of the sound it makes. **Loudness** is a measure of how well a sound can be heard.

Amplitude

The measure of how much energy a sound wave carries is the wave's intensity, or amplitude. The *amplitude* of a sound wave is the maximum distance that the particles of a wave's medium vibrate from their rest position. When you strike a drum harder, you increase the amplitude of the sound waves. The greater the amplitude, the louder the sound; the smaller the amplitude, the softer the sound.

One way to increase loudness is with an amplifier, as shown below. An amplifier receives sound signals in the form of electric current. The amplifier increases the sound wave's energy by increasing the wave's amplitude, which makes the sound louder.

Active Reading

12 Explain What is the relationship between amplitude and the loudness of a sound?

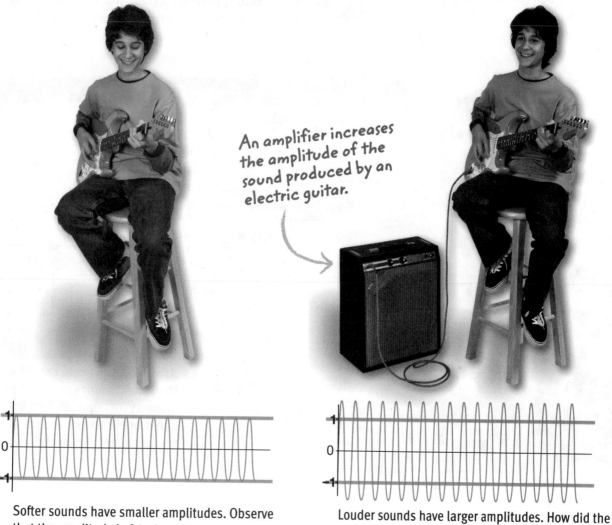

An amplifier increases the amplitude of the sound produced by an electric guitar.

Softer sounds have smaller amplitudes. Observe that the amplitude is 0 to 1, or 0 to −1.

Louder sounds have larger amplitudes. How did the amplitude change? Did the frequency change?

Turn That DOWN!

How is loudness measured?

Loudness is a characteristic of sound that can be calculated from the intensity of a sound wave. The most common unit used to express loudness is the **decibel** (DES•uh•bel). One decibel (dB) is one-tenth of a *bel*, the base unit, although the bel is rarely used. The bel is named after Alexander Graham Bell, who is credited with inventing the telephone.

The softest sounds most humans can hear are at a level of 0 dB. Sounds that are 120 dB or higher can be painful. The table below shows some common sounds and their decibel levels.

How loud is too loud?

Short exposures to sounds that are loud enough to be painful can cause hearing loss. Even loud sounds that are not painful can damage your hearing if you are exposed to them for long periods. Loud sounds can damage the hairs on the nerve cells in the cochlea. Once these hairs are damaged, they do not grow back.

There are simple ways to protect your hearing. Use earplugs to block loud sounds. Lower the volume when using earbuds, and move away from a speaker that is playing loud music. If you double the distance between yourself and a loud sound, you can reduce the sound's intensity by as much as one-fourth of what it was.

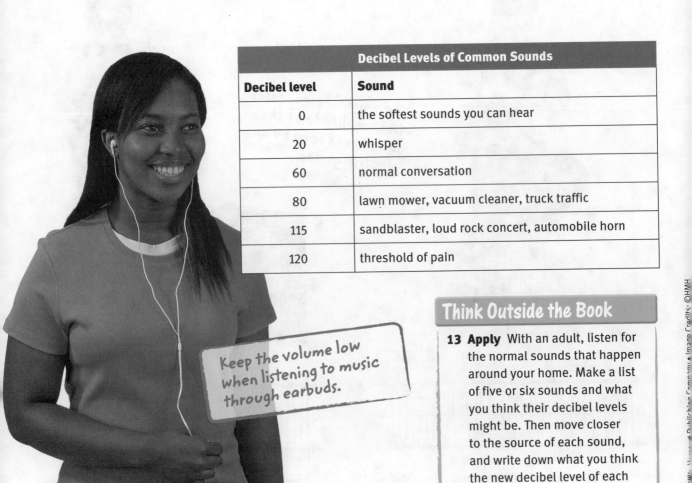

Decibel Levels of Common Sounds	
Decibel level	**Sound**
0	the softest sounds you can hear
20	whisper
60	normal conversation
80	lawn mower, vacuum cleaner, truck traffic
115	sandblaster, loud rock concert, automobile horn
120	threshold of pain

Keep the volume low when listening to music through earbuds.

Think Outside the Book

13 Apply With an adult, listen for the normal sounds that happen around your home. Make a list of five or six sounds and what you think their decibel levels might be. Then move closer to the source of each sound, and write down what you think the new decibel level of each sound is.

Image Credits: ©HMH

What is the Doppler effect?

Have you ever been stopped at a railroad crossing when a train with its whistle blowing went past? You probably noticed the sudden change in the pitch of the whistle as the train passed. This change in pitch is called the Doppler effect (DAHP•ler ih•FEKT). The **Doppler effect** is a change in the observed frequency of a wave when the sound source, the observer, or both are moving.

As shown in the diagram below, when you and the source of the sound are moving closer together, the sound waves are closer together. The sound has a higher frequency and a higher pitch. When you and the source are moving away from each other, the waves are farther apart. The sound has a lower frequency and a lower pitch.

Active Reading

14 Identify As you read, underline the main points that explain the Doppler effect.

Visualize It!

15 Label In the diagram below, consider the sound waves heard by the people as the train passes them. Label the sound wave that has a higher pitch and the sound wave that has a lower pitch.

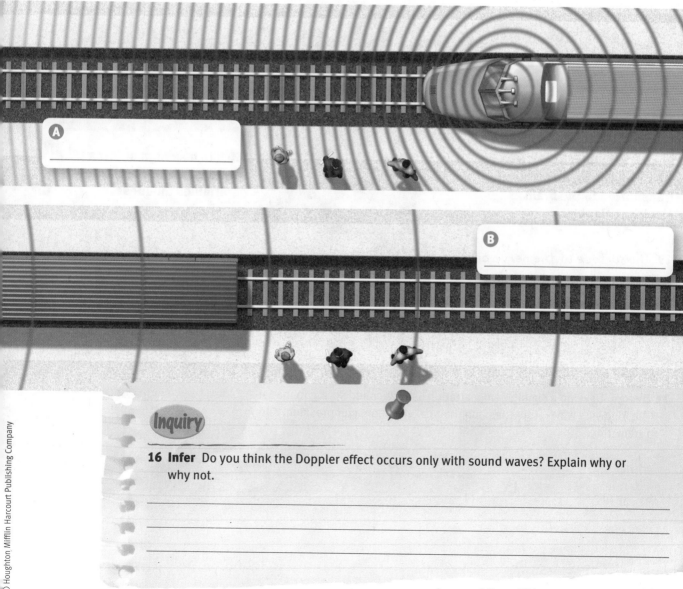

Ⓐ

Ⓑ

Inquiry

16 Infer Do you think the Doppler effect occurs only with sound waves? Explain why or why not.

_____

_____

_____

_____

Visual Summary

To complete this summary, fill in the blanks with the correct word or phrase. Then, use the key below to check your answers. You can use this page to review the main concepts of the lesson.

Sound waves are longitudinal waves that cause particles to vibrate.

17 Sound waves must travel through a _____

The Doppler effect is the change in pitch you hear when the source of a wave, the observer, or both are moving.

18 As a train approaches, the pitch of its whistle sounds _____

Sound Waves and Hearing

Human ears hear sound when vibrations of sound waves are transmitted to the brain as electrical signals.

19 The surface of the nerve cells in the cochlea contain thousands of _____

Pitch is how high or low a sound is, while amplitude determines loudness.

20 As the amplitude of a sound increases, the sound becomes _____

Answers: 17 medium; 18 higher; 19 tiny hair cells; 20 louder

21 Design Develop a simple demonstration using a coiled spring to model the following wave properties: longitudinal vibration, compression, and rarefaction.

© Houghton Mifflin Harcourt Publishing Company • Image Credits: ©HMH

Lesson Review

Vocabulary

Define Fill in the blank with the term that best completes the following sentences.

1 A _____ is an example of a longitudinal wave.

2 _____ is how high or low you think a sound is.

3 Loudness is expressed in _____

Key Concepts

4 Explain Describe the properties of a longitudinal wave.

_____

_____

_____

5 Sequence Describe how the human ear hears sound.

_____

_____

_____

_____

_____

6 Explain How are frequency, wavelength and pitch related?

_____

_____

_____

7 Summarize How does amplitude determine loudness?

_____

_____

_____

Critical Thinking

Use the illustration to answer the following questions.

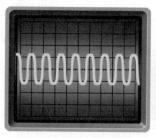 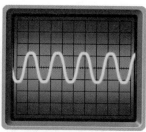

8 Analyze The screens show two sound waves that last the same amount of time. Which wave has a higher frequency? Explain your answer.

_____

_____

_____

9 Analyze Suppose these waves represent the sound of a siren on a passing ambulance. Which wave represents the sound of the siren *after* it has passed you? Explain your answer.

_____

_____

_____

_____

10 Analyze If a meteorite crashed onto the moon, would you be able hear it on Earth? Why or why not?

_____

_____

_____

11 Apply Is it safe to listen to music at a level of 115 decibels? Explain why or why not.

_____

_____

My Notes

Interactions of Sound Waves

ESSENTIAL QUESTION

How do sound waves travel and interact?

By the end of this lesson, you should be able to describe how sound waves interact, and how they can cause echoes and sonic booms.

→ 8.PS4.1, 8.PS4.2

Bats are one type of animal that uses sound waves to avoid obstacles and to find food.

✋ **Lesson Labs**

Quick Labs
- Resonance in a Bottle
- The Speed of Sound

S.T.E.M. Lab
- Echoes

 Engage Your Brain

1 Predict Check T or F to show whether you think each statement is true or false.

T   F

☐   ☐   Humans can hear sounds at any frequency.

☐   ☐   Sound waves can combine to become bigger or smaller.

☐   ☐   It is possible to break a crystal glass by singing a certain note.

☐   ☐   It is possible to travel faster than the speed of sound.

2 Draw A person standing on the edge of a canyon can make an echo by calling into the canyon. Draw how you think the sound waves travel to make the echo. Use arrows to represent the direction of the sound waves.

 Active Reading

3 Synthesize You can often determine the meaning of a term when you have heard some of the words in a different context. Draw a line from the terms on the left to their description on the right.

- constructive interference
  - causes sound waves to get smaller

- destructive interference
  - causes sound waves to get larger

Vocabulary Terms

- echo
- resonance
- interference

4 Apply As you learn the definition of each vocabulary term in this lesson, create your own definition or sketch to help you remember the meaning of the term.

Some Like It Hot

What affects the speed of sound?

Have you ever seen a flash of lightning, and then heard the sound of thunder a few seconds later? That happens because sound travels more slowly than light. Two main factors affect the speed of sound: the type of medium that the sound travels through, and the temperature of the medium. If we know these factors, we can predict the speed of sound.

Medium

The speed of sound depends on the type of matter, or medium, through which the sound wave travels. When you swim or bathe, you can hear sounds in more than one medium—air and water. The state of matter affects the speed of sound as well. In general, sound travels fastest through solids, slower through liquids, and slowest through gases. Sound travels fastest through solids because solids are denser than liquids or gases. That means that the particles are packed closer together in solids. A sound wave makes the particles of matter move as it travels along, so the wave is fastest when particles are close together.

Active Reading

5 Explain How does the state of matter affect the speed of sound?

_____

_____

_____

Visualize It!

6 Identify Through what medium shown below does sound travel fastest? _____

Slowest? _____

air (343 m/s)

water (1,482 m/s)

steel (5,200 m/s)

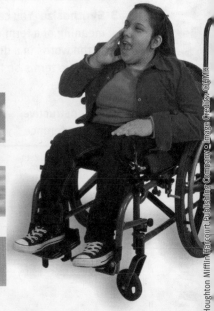

Temperature

The speed of sound also depends on the temperature of a medium. Sound in a medium travels faster at higher temperatures than at lower ones. Consider air, which is a mixture of gases. Particles in a gas are not held together as tightly as particles in a solid are. Instead, the gas particles bounce all around. The higher the temperature, the faster the gas particles move about. Particles of a material move more quickly and transfer energy faster at higher temperatures than at lower temperatures. Therefore, sound travels faster through hot air than through cold air.

 **Do the Math**

Sample Problem

Sound travels at 343 m/s through air at a temperature of 20 °C. How far will sound travel through 20 °C air in 5 s?

$$343 \text{ m}/1 \text{ s} = X \text{ m}/5 \text{ s}$$
$$343 \text{ m} \times 5 = X \text{ m}$$
$$X \text{ m} = 1{,}715 \text{ m}$$

You Try It

7 Calculate The speed of sound in steel at 20 °C is 5,200 m/s. How far can sound travel in 5 s through steel at 20 °C?

8 Apply Who will hear the sound of an approaching boat first: this diver or his friends above the water? Why?

_____

_____

_____

Speed of Sound in Different Media and Temperatures	
Medium	**Speed (m/s)**
Air (0 °C)	331
Air (20 °C)	343
Air (100 °C)	366
Water (20 °C)	1,482
Steel (20 °C)	5,200

Hello? Hello? Hello?

How do sound and matter interact?

Sound waves do not travel easily through all matter. When a sound wave runs into a barrier, some of the sound waves may bounce away from the front surface of the barrier, and some of the sound waves may be absorbed or transmitted through the barrier.

Matter Can Reflect Sound Waves

Sound waves, like all waves, can reflect off matter. Reflection is the bouncing back of a wave when the wave hits a barrier. The strength of a reflected sound wave depends on the reflecting surface. Sound waves reflect best off smooth, hard surfaces. A sound in a bare room can be loud because the sound waves are reflected off the walls, the floor, and the ceiling. If furniture, drapes, and carpet are added to the room, the same sound is much softer.

Matter Can Absorb Sound Waves

Some types of matter absorb sound waves much better than others. A rough wall will absorb sound better than a smooth wall will. And soft materials absorb sound better than hard materials do. If your school has a music room, it probably has sound-absorbing features, such as carpet and soft, rough acoustic tiles on walls and ceilings. These features help keep the music from being heard throughout the school.

Active Reading

9 Identify As you read, underline features that reflect or absorb sound.

Visualize It!

10 Identify Which features in this room reflect sound waves? Explain your reasoning.

_____
_____
_____
_____
_____
_____

The surfaces in room A interact differently with sound waves than do the surfaces in room B.

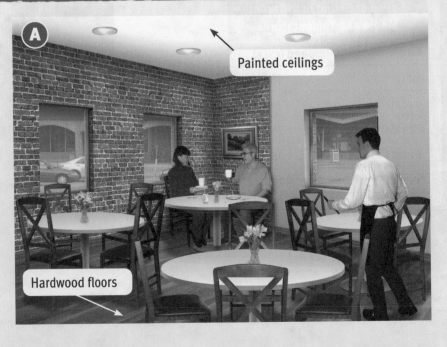

A

Painted ceilings

Hardwood floors

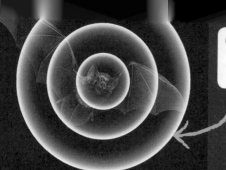

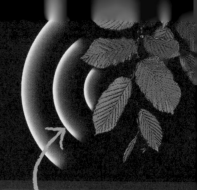

① The sound waves that bats emit while flying are at a higher frequency than humans can hear.

Bats use echoes to navigate.

② The sound waves meet an object and reflect back to the bat. The time it takes these echoes to reach the bat tells it how far the object is.

What is an echo?

Matter that absorbs sound waves will reduce echoes. An **echo** is a reflected sound wave. The strength of a reflecting sound wave depends on the reflecting surface. Echoes can be reduced by the presence of soft materials and rough or irregular surfaces. Rough surfaces reduce echoes by scattering sound waves.

Some animals—such as dolphins, bats, and beluga whales—use echoes to hunt food and to find objects in their paths. The use of reflected sound waves to find objects is called *echolocation*. The illustrations on this page show how echolocation works. Animals that use echolocation can tell how far away something is based on how long it takes sound waves to echo back to the animal.

One example of echolocation technology used by people is sonar (**so**und **n**avigation **a**nd **r**anging). *Sonar* is a type of electronic echolocation that uses echoes to locate objects underwater.

③ The bat can determine the direction an insect is flying in because the frequency of the echo changes as the insect moves.

Active Reading 11 **Describe** How do some animals use echoes?

_____
_____

B

Fabric curtains

Acoustic tiles

12 **Describe** Explain how the features in this room help reduce echoes.

_____
_____
_____
_____
_____
_____

Boom!

How do sound waves interact with each other?

Sound waves interact through interference. **Interference** happens when two or more waves overlap and combine to form one wave. In music, *beats* happen when two sound waves of nearly equal frequencies interfere. Since the wave frequencies are not quite equal, they form a repeating pattern of constructive and destructive interference that sounds alternately loud and soft.

Active Reading **13 Identify** As you read, underline the main characteristics of constructive interference and destructive interference.

Through Constructive Interference

When *constructive interference* occurs, waves overlap and combine to form a wave with a larger amplitude, or height. The greater amplitude causes the waves to produce a sound that is louder than before. Constructive interference can cause very loud sounds, such as sonic booms.

Through Destructive Interference

In *destructive interference*, waves combine to form a wave with a smaller amplitude. The sound will be softer because the amplitude is decreased. Some noise-canceling headphones use destructive interference. Electronics in the headphones create new sound waves that interfere with outside sounds, so the headphone wearer does not hear them.

When two speakers produce sound at the same frequency, the sound waves combine by both constructive and destructive interference.

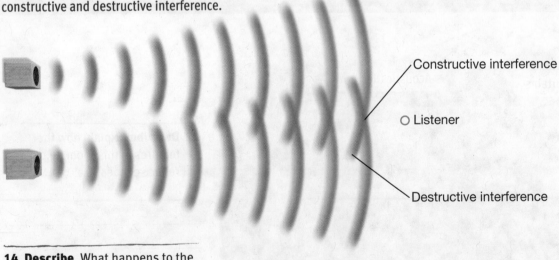

Constructive interference

○ Listener

Destructive interference

14 Describe What happens to the wave amplitude when there is constructive interference? What happens when destructive interference occurs?

_____

_____

_____

How does interference cause sonic booms?

Jet airplanes moving faster than the speed of sound can produce a very loud sound called a *sonic boom*. The sonic boom from a low-flying airplane can rattle and even break windows! When a jet reaches very high speeds, it actually catches up to its own sound waves. The waves pile up as a result of constructive interference. They form a high-pressure area, called the *sound barrier*, in front of the plane. If the jet is going fast enough, it breaks through the barrier. The jet moves at *supersonic* speeds—speeds faster than the speed of sound—and gets ahead of both the pressure barrier and the sound waves. The sound waves behind the jet form a single shock wave as a result of constructive interference. When the shock wave reaches people's ears, they hear it as a loud boom!

Traveling at very high speeds, a jet can break through a barrier of its own sound waves.

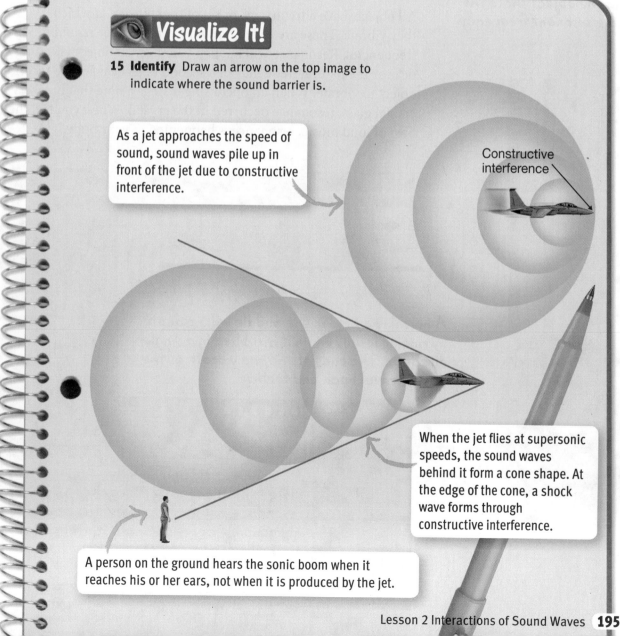

Visualize It!

15 Identify Draw an arrow on the top image to indicate where the sound barrier is.

As a jet approaches the speed of sound, sound waves pile up in front of the jet due to constructive interference.

Constructive interference

When the jet flies at supersonic speeds, the sound waves behind it form a cone shape. At the edge of the cone, a shock wave forms through constructive interference.

A person on the ground hears the sonic boom when it reaches his or her ears, not when it is produced by the jet.

Good Vibrations

Active Reading

16 Identify As you read, underline the main characteristics of resonance.

A vibrating tuning fork can cause another object to start vibrating if the fork and the object share the same resonant frequency.

What is resonance?

Have you ever held a seashell to your ear and listened to the "ocean"? What you actually are hearing is resonance. **Resonance** happens when a sound wave matches the natural frequency of an object and causes the object to vibrate. The air in the seashell vibrates at certain frequencies because of the shape of the shell. If a sound wave in the room forces air in the seashell to vibrate at its natural frequency, resonance occurs. This resonance results in a big vibration that sounds like the ocean when you hear it.

Where can resonance occur?

All objects have a frequency, or set of frequencies, at which they vibrate. These are called *natural frequencies,* or *resonant* frequencies. Resonance will happen wherever an object vibrating at or near the natural frequency of a second object causes the second object to vibrate. When an opera singer sings a note that breaks a crystal glass, resonance occurred in the crystal. When you feel the bass of loud music, resonance is happening in your body.

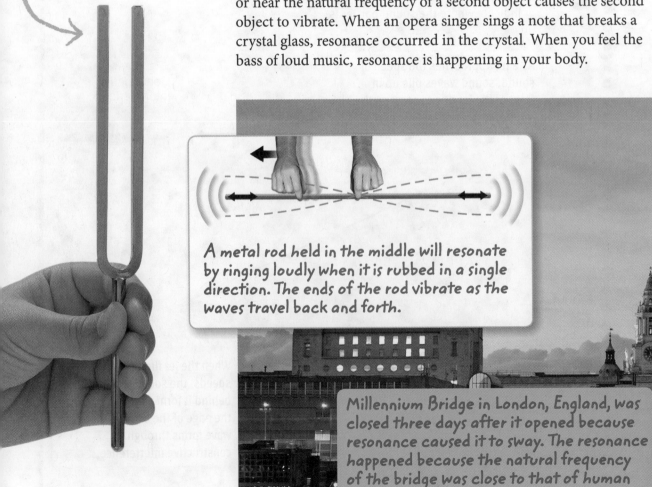

A metal rod held in the middle will resonate by ringing loudly when it is rubbed in a single direction. The ends of the rod vibrate as the waves travel back and forth.

Millennium Bridge in London, England, was closed three days after it opened because resonance caused it to sway. The resonance happened because the natural frequency of the bridge was close to that of human footsteps walking across it.

In Musical Instruments

Active Reading **17 Identify** As you read, underline how resonance occurs in wind instruments.

Resonance is important for making music. In wind instruments, blowing air into the mouthpiece causes vibrations. The vibrations make a sound that gets louder when it forms a standing wave inside the instrument. A *standing wave* is a pattern of vibration that looks like a wave that is standing still. Resonance occurs when standing waves are formed. Waves and reflected waves of the same frequency go back and forth in standing waves inside the instrument.

String instruments also resonate when played. An acoustic guitar has a hollow body. When the strings make a standing wave, the sound waves enter the body of the guitar. Standing waves also form inside the body, and the sound becomes louder.

In Bridges

Resonance can even occur in buildings, towers, and bridges. Because resonance could cause a structure to collapse, engineers plan their designs carefully. For example, some bridges are built in sections with overlapping plates. When the plates move together, they create friction. This friction can change the frequency from one plate to another and keep the resonant wave from becoming destructive. Even simple human activity can create resonance on bridges. For example, rhythmic marching can create resonance and cause a bridge to sway or even collapse. That's why troops always stop marching before crossing a bridge.

This musician creates music by making standing waves on the strings of her cello.

Think Outside the Book Inquiry

18 Apply To better understand how marching can resonate with bridges, form a line with your classmates and march in time around your classroom. As you march, try to be aware of the vibrations and resonance of the classroom floor. Then repeat, but "break step"—march out of time. Do the floor and other objects respond the way they did in the first trial?

Visual Summary

To complete this summary, fill in the word to finish each sentence. Then, use the key below to check your answers. You can use this page to review the main concepts of the lesson.

The speed of sound depends on the medium it travels through and on the temperature of the medium.

Sound waves interact with each other through interference.

19 Sound waves travel _____ in solids than in liquids.

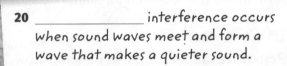

20 _____ interference occurs when sound waves meet and form a wave that makes a quieter sound.

Some surfaces reflect sound waves, while other surfaces absorb sound waves.

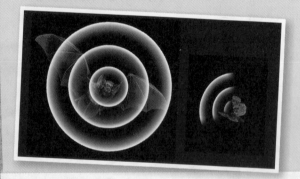

Resonance occurs when the frequency of a sound wave matches the natural frequency of an object and makes the object vibrate.

21 Sound waves reflect better off _____ surfaces.

22 Resonance happens when two objects vibrate at _____ frequency.

Answers: 19 faster; 20 Destructive; 21 hard; 22 the same

23 Summarize What are the results of the two ways that sound waves can interact with each other?

Lesson Review

Vocabulary

Fill in the blank with the term that best completes the following sentence.

1 _____ is the combination of two or more waves, which results in a single wave.

2 _____ happens when a sound wave causes an object to vibrate.

3 A(n) _____ is a reflected sound wave.

Key Concepts

4 Identify How does the state of matter affect the speed of a sound wave traveling through it?

_____

_____

_____

5 Describe How could you reduce the echoes in a music studio?

_____

_____

_____

6 Explain Describe how a jet can create a sonic boom.

_____

_____

_____

7 Summarize In your own words, explain how resonance occurs when you play a horn.

_____

_____

_____

Critical Thinking

Use this table to answer the following questions.

Speed of Sound in Some Materials	
Material	**Speed of sound (m/s)**
air	330
water	1,480
brain	1,540
blood	1,570

8 Analyze Ultrasound uses high-frequency sound waves to get images of the insides of our bodies. Sound waves would travel the fastest through which of the materials listed in the chart?

_____

9 Infer What two types of matter are closest in density? How do you know?

_____

_____

_____

_____

10 Relate Ultrasound waves do not transmit easily through bone. What do you think happens to ultrasound waves when they reach a bone in the body? Give reasons for your answer.

_____

_____

_____

_____

_____

My Notes

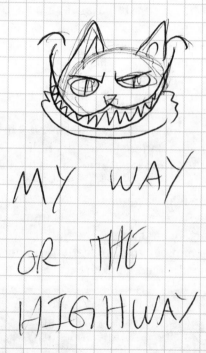

MY WAY

OR THE

HIGHWAY

James West

RESEARCH SCIENTIST

James West's parents wanted him to be a medical doctor, but he wanted to study physics. His father was sure he'd never find a job that way. But Dr. West wanted to study what he loved. He did study physics, and he did find a job. He worked for Bell Laboratories and developed a microphone called the electret microphone. Today, Dr. West's microphone is in almost all telephones, cell phones, and other equipment that records sound.

Dr. West's interest in the microphone started with a question about hearing. A group of scientists wanted to know how close together two sounds could be before the ear would not be able to tell them apart. At the time, there was no earphone sensitive enough for their tests. Dr. West and fellow scientist Dr. Gerhard Sessler found that they could make a more sensitive microphone by using materials called *electrets*. Electrets are the electrical counterparts of permanent magnets. Electrets can store electric charge. This eliminates the need for a battery. The new microphones were cheaper, more reliable, smaller, and lighter than any microphone before them.

Dr. West enjoys the thrill of discovery. He should know. To date, he holds more than 250 U.S. and foreign patents. In 1999 he was inducted into the National Inventors Hall of Fame. Dr. West retired from Bell Laboratories in 2001 and is now on the faculty at Johns Hopkins University. He has won many awards for his work, including both the Silver and Gold Medals from the Acoustical Society of America, The National Medal of Technology and Innovation, and the Benjamin Franklin Medal in Electrical Engineering.

Dr. West's research into sound waves and hearing has helped make microphones smaller.

JOB BOARD

Dispensing Optician

What You'll Do: Help select and then fit eyeglasses and contact lenses.

Where You Might Work: Medical offices, or optical, department, or club stores

Education: Most training is on the job or through apprenticeships that last two years or longer. Some employers prefer graduates of postsecondary training programs in opticianry.

Other Job Requirements: A good eye for fashion, face shape, and color is a plus, as opticians help people find glasses they like.

Lighting Designer

What You'll Do: Work in theater, television, or film to make what happens on stage or on set visible to audiences. Lighting designers also use lighting and shadow to create the right tone or mood.

Where You Might Work: Theaters, television and film studios and sets, concerts and other special events

Education: A diploma or certificate in lighting design or technical stage management from a college or performing arts institute

Other Job Requirements: Experience lighting stage productions, the ability to work in a team

PEOPLE IN SCIENCE NEWS

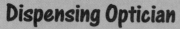

ELY Stone

A New Light on Microscopy

Doctors and medical researchers use fluorescent microscopes to see colored or fluorescent dyes in medical research. These microscopes use expensive and dangerous mercury light bulbs to illuminate the dyes. But Ely Stone, a retired computer programmer and inventor in Florida, found a less expensive source of light.

When the mercury bulb on his microscope died, Ely replaced it with many differently colored light-emitting diodes (LEDs). Each inexpensive LED emits light of a different wavelength. The LEDs cost only a couple of dollars each and are much safer than mercury bulbs. Yet they still provide the light needed to view the fluorescent dyes. Now, researchers can use the LED microscopes to really light up their dyes!

Lesson 3

Sound Technology

ESSENTIAL QUESTION

How does sound technology work?

By the end of this lesson, you should be able to describe how sound technology is used to extend human senses.

8.PS4.3

Many radio programs are recorded so that you can listen to them whenever you want.

Engage Your Brain

1 Predict Check T or F to show whether you think each statement is true or false.

T	F	
☐	☐	Some animals use sound to find food.
☐	☐	Reflected sound waves can be used to make images.
☐	☐	Sound waves are sent from one telephone to another telephone.
☐	☐	Computers can save and store sound waves.

2 Describe List three devices that produce sound waves that you use in your everyday life. Describe how your life would be different without these devices.

_____

_____

_____

_____

_____

_____

_____

Active Reading

3 Synthesize You can often define an unknown word if you know the meaning of its word parts. Use the word part and sentence below to make an educated guess about the meaning of the word *ultrasound*.

Word Part	Meaning
ultra-	beyond

Example sentence
Humans cannot hear <u>ultrasound</u> waves.

ultrasound:

_____

_____

Vocabulary Terms
- echolocation
- sonar
- ultrasound

4 Apply As you learn the definition of each vocabulary term in this lesson, create your own definition or sketch to help you remember the meaning of the term.

How are echoes used?

You would have difficulty using your sense of hearing to find objects around you. But some animals find food and other objects using *echolocation*. **Echolocation** is the use of echoes, or reflected sound waves to find objects. Animals that use echolocation produce **ultrasound**, which are sound waves that have frequencies greater than 20,000 Hz. The frequencies of these ultrasonic sound waves are too high for humans to hear. But, animals that use echolocation can tell how far away an object is by the time it takes for their ultrasonic waves to bounce off an object and return to them, or *echo*. For example, the dolphin shown below can tell how far away the fish is by sensing the echoes that bounce off of the fish. It takes more time for ultrasonic sound waves to reach and return from objects that are farther away.

 **Active Reading** 5 **Explain** What are ultrasonic waves?

_____

_____

 **Visualize It!**

6 **Illustrate** Draw the sound waves that are reflected from the fish.

7 **Analyze** Will the echo from the fish or from the boat reach the dolphin first?

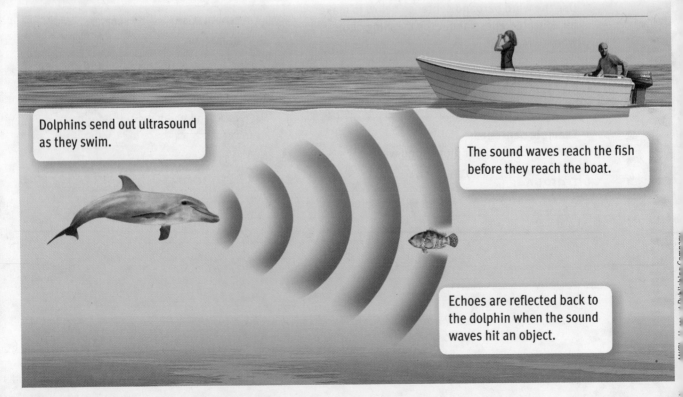

Dolphins send out ultrasound as they swim.

The sound waves reach the fish before they reach the boat.

Echoes are reflected back to the dolphin when the sound waves hit an object.

To Locate Objects

You may not be able to send out or hear ultrasonic waves, but people can use echolocation through various technologies. **Sonar** is a system that uses sound waves to determine the location of objects or to communicate. Visually impaired people can use sonar technology to navigate. Sonar is also used to find shipwrecks, to avoid icebergs, to find fish, and to map the ocean floor as shown in this diagram. An instrument on the boat sends out ultrasonic waves. Then it detects any echoes, or reflected sound waves. The short wavelengths of ultrasonic waves provide more information about objects than the longer wavelengths of sound do.

Emitted Sound Waves

Reflected sound waves are used to map the ocean floor. The red areas are closer to the ship. The blue areas are farther away.

A *more time / less time*

8 Label Circle the correct phrase in each box on the map to show where the reflected sound waves will take more time to return to the ship and where they will take less time to return to the ship.

Reflected Sound Waves

B *more time / less time*

To Make Ultrasound Images

Echoes are used in medicine, too. Ultrasound procedures use ultrasonic sound waves to produce images of the inside of a person's body. Ultrasound that has a frequency of 1 million to 10 million hertz can pass safely into a patient's body. These sound waves reflect when they meet the patient's internal organs. The echoes are detected and used to make images of organs, such as the heart and bladder. Ultrasonic waves do not damage human cells like x-rays can. Ultrasound procedures do not harm fetuses. So ultrasound is often used to check how a fetus is growing inside the mother's body. Health professionals can use ultrasound images to determine the age and sex of a fetus and to diagnose certain disorders.

This ultrasound image shows a 20-week-old fetus.

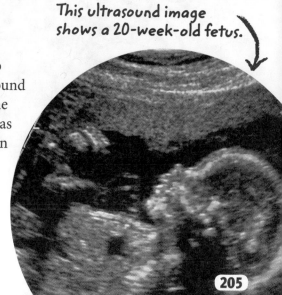

How do telephones transmit sound?

Sound waves lose energy over time. The sound waves of your voice will not reach a friend who is far away. But, you can use a telephone to talk to your friend. Phones change sound waves into other types of signals that can be sent over long distances. Phones also change the signals they receive back into sound waves that you can hear.

All telephones change sound waves into electrical signals. However, electrical signals cannot travel through air. A cell phone is a type of mobile telephone used by millions of people today. Cell phones convert the sound waves from your voice into an electrical signal. The signal travels as radio waves which are then picked up by a cell tower. These radio waves travel at the speed of light. The cell tower then sends the radio waves to your friend's phone, which converts the waves back into sound waves.

Active Reading

9 Identify As you read, underline the types of signals sound waves are changed into by telephones.

Think Outside the Book (Inquiry)

10 Apply Create a short cartoon with captions that shows the changes the sound waves go through during a telephone call.

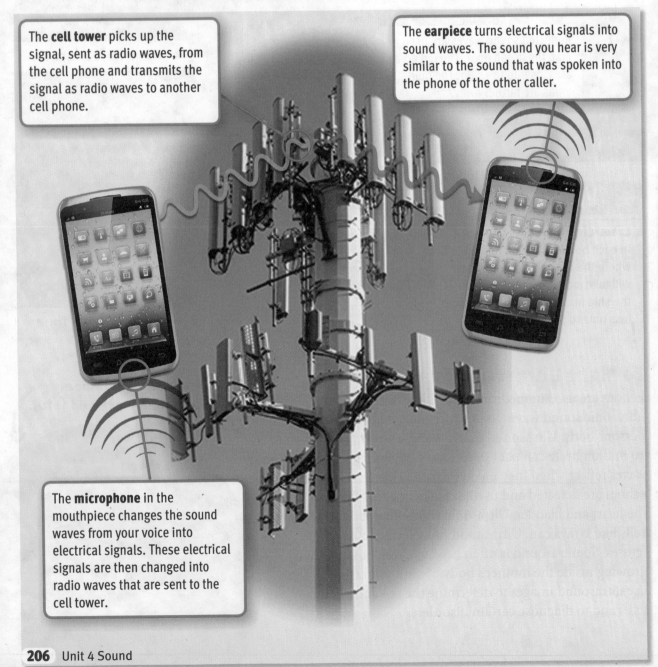

The **cell tower** picks up the signal, sent as radio waves, from the cell phone and transmits the signal as radio waves to another cell phone.

The **earpiece** turns electrical signals into sound waves. The sound you hear is very similar to the sound that was spoken into the phone of the other caller.

The **microphone** in the mouthpiece changes the sound waves from your voice into electrical signals. These electrical signals are then changed into radio waves that are sent to the cell tower.

Hello, Operator

For most of human history, people had no way of sending their voices farther than they could shout. The invention of the telephone in 1876 made long-distance communication possible. How has telephone technology changed since then?

Manual Switching

People used to have to call telephone operators whenever they wanted to make a call. The operator plugged wires into a switchboard to connect one phone to another. The switchboard allowed many phone calls to be connected at one time.

Dialing Around

The invention of the rotary dial phone made it possible for people to call a number directly. Human operators were replaced by automated switching centers.

Cell Phones

Cell phones use radio waves to send signals. The signals are sent to cell phone towers, which transfer the signals to underground phone cables. Cell phone towers are part of cellular networks which cover large geographic areas. This means that you can travel very long distances and not lose the signal. Cell phones can also send images and text.

Extend

Inquiry

11 Infer What was a main advantage of a dial phone over an operator-controlled switchboard?

12 Research Make a timeline that shows the following major inventions related to telephones: the telephone, the telephone switching center, the rotary phone, the push-button phone, and the mobile phone. Include pictures and an interesting detail about each invention in your timeline.

13 Compose Write a short paragraph describing how you use telephones in your everyday life. Include one way you would improve your phone.

Groovy

How is sound recorded and played back?

Once sound waves lose their energy, they are gone forever. People make recordings to preserve sound information, such as interviews and music. Thomas Edison invented the phonograph, which could record and play back sound. Later, information in sound was recorded in the grooves of records or on the surface of compact discs. Today, most sound recordings are stored in computer files.

On Compact Discs

A compact disc, or CD, is made of hard plastic. The information in sound waves is stored by pressing microscopic pits into the plastic. The pits and lands, which are the spaces between the pits, form a spiral pattern on the CD. This pattern stores digital signals as 1s and 0s that are used to recreate sound waves.

A CD player uses light to read the information stored on the CD. The plastic layer of a CD is coated with a thin layer of shiny aluminum. The light from a laser reflects off the shiny surface as the CD rotates. The pattern on the CD surface produces a pattern of light and dark reflected light. The detector changes this pattern into an electrical signal. The CD player then changes the electrical signal back into sound waves.

Active Reading

14 Identify As you read, underline why people record sound.

Music can be stored in the grooves of records.

Visualize It!

This image shows the pattern on the surface of a CD. Different patterns produce different sounds. CD players use reflected light to read the pattern on CDs.

15 Analyze Suppose the pattern near the arrow represents part of a word of an audio book. How do you think the pattern will appear on the CD the next time that word is repeated? Explain.

_____

_____

_____

_____

_____

Compact disc

An image made by a scanning electron microscope (SEM) shows the pattern in the back side of a CD.

CD pit

In Computers

Sound can also be stored as digital files in a computer. Digital sound files, such as MP3 files, can store a large amount of sound information. To record sound as a computer file, the original sound is first changed into an electrical signal. Then it is stored as a digital file on the computer hard drive. The digital file is a series of 1s and 0s, similar to the pattern stored on a CD.

Software reads the digital files and produces an electrical signal that is sent to the speakers. The speakers change the signal back into sound waves. Personal MP3 players store and play back sound files in a similar way as larger computers do. But they make it very easy to carry a lot of recordings with you. You would need several CDs to store the hundreds of songs that can be stored in a tiny MP3 player.

Sound is stored in digital files in computers.

---

16 Summarize Complete the following process chart to show how sound waves can be digitally recorded and played back.

| Original sound waves are played. | → | | → | | → | Sound waves come out of speaker. |

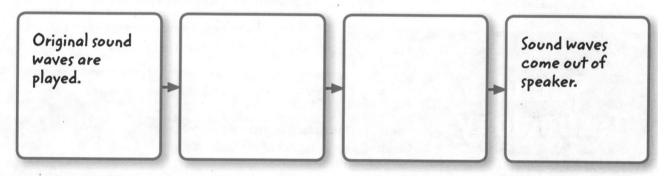

❶ The laser shines on a CD that is spinning. Light is reflected back to the detector.

CD

❷ The reflected light is darker where there are pits. The detector picks up a pattern of light and dark spots.

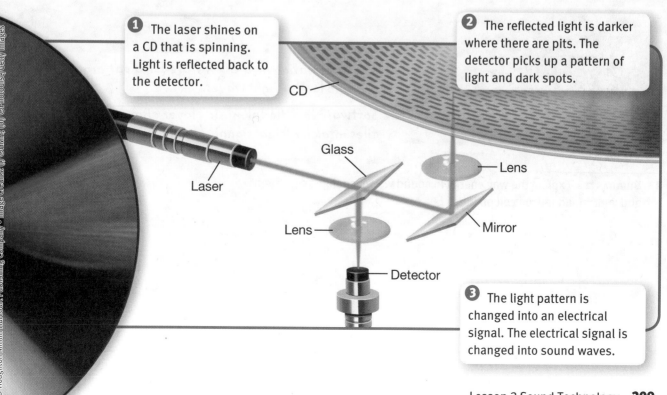

Glass

Lens

Laser

Lens

Mirror

Detector

❸ The light pattern is changed into an electrical signal. The electrical signal is changed into sound waves.

Visual Summary

To complete this summary, circle the correct word or phrase. Then, use the key below to check your answers. You can use this page to review the main concepts of the lesson.

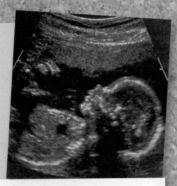

Echolocation is the use of ultrasound to locate objects.

Telephones change sound waves into electrical signals and electrical signals back into sound waves.

17 A fetus can be viewed using an infrasound / ultrasound procedure.

18 Sonar / Laser light is used to locate objects underwater.

19 A cell phone sends sound / radio waves between the phone and the tower.

20 A telephone's earpiece / microphone changes sound waves into electrical signals.

Sound Technology

Sound information is stored digitally on compact discs and in computer files.

21 The information on a CD is stored in a pattern of pits and lands / light waves.

22 Software in a digital music player changes music files into electrical signals / radio waves.

Answers: 17 ultrasound; 18 Sonar; 19 radio; 20 microphone; 21 pits and lands; 22 electrical signals

23 Summarize Explain the way energy in sound waves changes when you and your friend talk on cell phones.

Lesson Review

Vocabulary

In your own words, define the following terms.

1 echolocation

_____

_____

2 ultrasound

_____

_____

3 sonar

_____

_____

Key Concepts

4 Identify Which device can store sound information?

A CD player

B telephone wires

C microphone

D computer

5 Describe How does a cell phone change the incoming signals from a caller into sound that you can hear?

_____

_____

6 Infer Why do people use echolocation technology to locate objects?

_____

_____

_____

7 Explain Why are sound recordings needed to preserve sound information?

_____

_____

_____

Critical Thinking

8 Explain Describe what happens inside a CD player when you listen to an audio CD.

_____

_____

_____

_____

_____

9 Apply Explain how a doctor can use ultrasound to look at a patient's kidneys.

_____

_____

_____

_____

Use this drawing to answer the following questions.

10 Describe How is sound technology being used by the people in the boat?

_____

_____

11 Analyze Why are the sound waves in the drawing shown to be reflecting from the larger fish but not from the smaller fish under the boat?

_____

_____

My Notes

Unit 4 Sound waves transfer energy through vibrations.

Lesson 1
ESSENTIAL QUESTION
What is sound?

Describe what sound is, identify its properties, and explain how humans hear it.

Lesson 2
ESSENTIAL QUESTION
How do sound waves travel and interact?

Describe how sound waves interact, and how they can cause echoes and sonic booms.

Lesson 3
ESSENTIAL QUESTION
How does sound technology work?

Describe how sound technology is used to extend human senses.

Connect ESSENTIAL QUESTIONS
Lessons 1 and 2

1 Synthesize If you bounce a basketball in an empty gym, you will hear it echo. Describe the path that the sound wave travels from the basketball to your eardrum.

_____
_____
_____
_____

Think Outside the Book

2 Synthesize Choose one of these activities to help synthesize what you have learned in this unit.

☐ Using what you learned in lessons 2 and 3, create a brochure to sell a sound absorbing material, explaining why recording studios need this material for the walls and ceiling. Use illustrations with captions and labels.

☐ Using what you learned in lessons 1 and 3, make a poster to explain why communicating in space is a challenge, and show how space scientists have met this challenge.

Unit 4 Review

Vocabulary

Check the box to show whether each statement is true or false.

T	F	
☐	☐	**1** A Sound wave is a <u>longitudinal wave</u> that is caused by vibrations in a medium.
☐	☐	**2** <u>Decibels</u> are units that measure the pitch of a sound.
☐	☐	**3** An <u>echo</u> is a sound wave that is absorbed by a soft material.
☐	☐	**4** <u>Interference</u> occurs when two or more waves overlap and combine to form one wave.
☐	☐	**5** <u>Ultrasound</u> technology is used to create medical images and it is based on sound waves with frequencies so high that human ears cannot hear them.

Key Concepts

Read each question below, and circle the best answer.

6 Which statement best describes how humans hear sound?

A Sound waves enter the ear canal and increase in amplitude, which causes you to hear the sound.

B Sound waves cause parts of the ear to vibrate until the waves are converted to electrical signals, which are sent to the brain.

C Sound waves travel into people's ears, and the eardrum sends the sound waves to the brain.

D Sound waves become sounds when they strike the eardrum inside the ear.

7 When Consuelo struck a tuning fork and held it close to a string on a guitar, the string began to vibrate on its own and make a sound. Which statement best explains why the string vibrated without anyone touching it?

A The string vibrated because of destructive inference between its sound waves and those of the tuning fork.

B The tuning fork produced ultrasonic frequencies beyond human hearing.

C The tuning fork and the guitar string both created mechanical waves.

D The string vibrated because of resonance, which happened because the tuning fork and guitar string have the same natural frequency.

8 The diagram below shows a sound wave traveling through a medium.

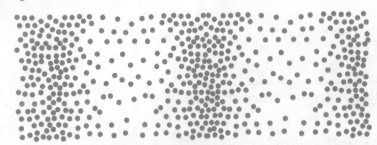

Which statement best describes how the sound wave is moving through a medium?

A The sound wave is creating tensions and accumulations in the medium.

B The sound wave is creating an echo inside the medium.

C The sound wave is creating compressions and rarefactions in the medium.

D The sound wave is creating a mechanical wave in the medium.

9 Which material best absorbs sound waves in a room?

A heavy curtains

B hardwood floors

C brick walls

D cement floors

10 Yorgos drew a diagram of a wave and labeled its parts, as shown below.

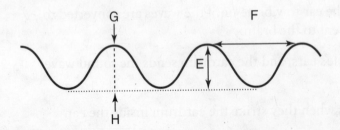

Wavelength is typically measured between the crests to two successive waves. Which labels represent a crest and a wavelength?

A G points to a crest; F is a wavelength

B G points to a crest; E is a wavelength

C H points to a crest; E is a wavelength

D H points to a crest; F is a wavelength

11 Which of the following is not a way in which echolocation is used?

   A flying bats avoiding trees and houses at night

   B sending messages over telephone lines

   C dolphins finding fish in deep water

   D mapping the ocean floor

12 Josh observed a bolt of lightning during a thunderstorm. It took more than 15 seconds for Josh to hear the sound of thunder. Why did Josh see the lightning strike before he heard the thunder?

   A Thunder always takes 15 seconds to travel through the air after lightning strikes.

   B Light waves from the lightning and sound waves from the thunder moved through different media.

   C Light waves are electromagnetic waves that travel much faster than mechanical waves, such as the sound waves he heard as thunder.

   D The conditions in the air at the time allowed light waves to move faster than the sound waves he heard as thunder.

13 The diagram below shows the distribution of particles in two different kinds of media.

Liquid   **Gas**

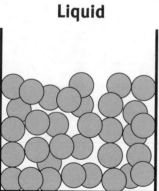 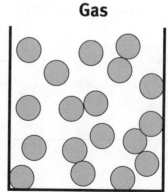

Which statement best compares how sound waves travel through the media shown above?

   A Sound waves travel at the same speed through both of the media shown.

   B Sound waves move faster through the closely packed medium on the left than the loosely packed medium on the right.

   C Sound waves move faster through the loosely packed medium on the right than the closely packed medium on the left.

   D Sound waves cannot travel through either medium that is shown above.

Critical Thinking

Answer the following questions in the space provided.

14 Describe where the cochlea is located, what parts it contains, and explain the role these parts play in human hearing.

_____

_____

_____

15 Suppose you are at a train station. What changes would you hear in the sound of the whistle as a train comes toward you and then moves away? What causes the changes, and what is this effect called?

_____

_____

_____

_____

Connect **ESSENTIAL QUESTIONS**
Lessons 1 and 2

16 A fighter jet breaks the sound barrier. What is the sound barrier, and how can a jet break through it? Where does the sound around the jet come from? What causes the sonic boom, and how can you hear it?

_____

_____

_____

_____

_____

_____

Light

Big Idea

Visible light is the small part of the electromagnetic spectrum that is essential for human vision.

8.PS.4.1, 8.PS4.2, 8.PS4.3

What do you think?

Waves can travel great distances. This large radio telescope gathers radio waves from space. Other telescopes use mirrors to gather light waves. What have people learned about space from light waves?

Unit 5
Light

Looking Into Space

The first telescopes were refracting telescopes, which used a pair of lenses to gather light. Today, astronomers also use reflecting telescopes, which gather light with large mirrors, to observe distant objects.

Galileo observing space

1609
Galileo Galilei used a refracting telescope to observe phases of Venus, the moons of Jupiter, the surface of the moon, sunspots, and a supernova.

List other tools that use lenses and think of a use for each one.

_____

_____

_____

_____

Telescope similar to Isaac Newton's

Skylab image of the sun

1973

Telescopes that operate from space, like the sun-observing telescope that was aboard Skylab, can see all kinds of things we can't see from Earth.

1668

Isaac Newton built a reflecting telescope that used a curved mirror to gather light. Newton's mirror did not split light into colors as did the lenses in early refracting telescopes.

Hubble Space Telescope

1990

The orbiting Hubble Space Telescope can capture detailed images of objects very far from Earth. The Hubble Space Telescope has taken images of the most distant galaxies astronomers have ever seen.

Take It Home · Eyes to the Sky

Use a pair of binoculars or a telescope to look at the night sky. Compare what you can see with magnification to what you can see when looking at the same part of the sky without magnification. Draw or write your observations in the chart. See *ScienceSaurus*® for more information about astronomy.

Unmagnified Night Sky	Magnified Night Sky

Lesson 1

The Electromagnetic Spectrum

ESSENTIAL QUESTION

What is the relationship between various EM waves?

By the end of this lesson, you should be able to distinguish between the parts of the electromagnetic spectrum.

8.PS.4.1, 8.PS4.2

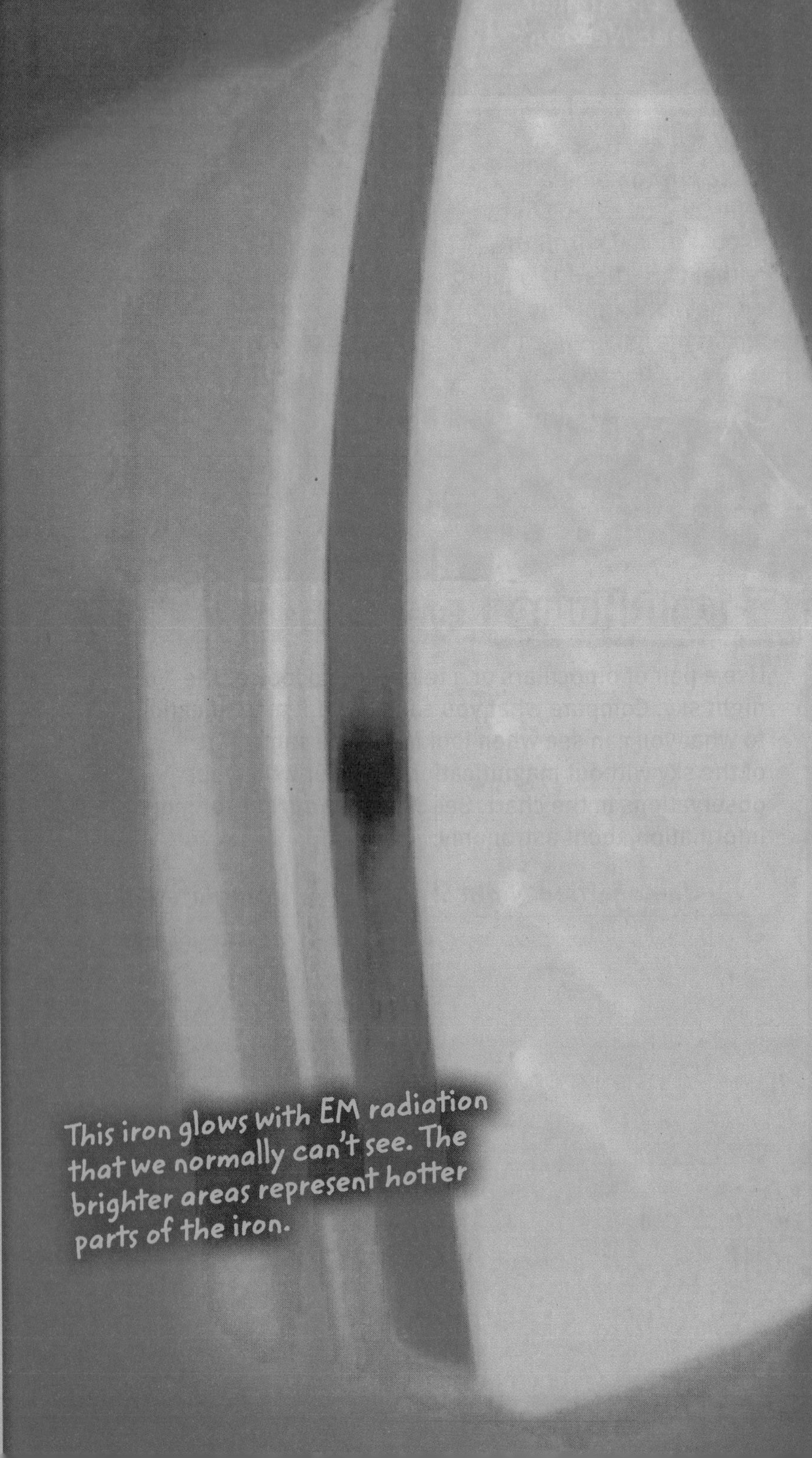

This iron glows with EM radiation that we normally can't see. The brighter areas represent hotter parts of the iron.

Engage Your Brain

1 Select Circle the word or phrase that best completes each of the following sentences:

Radio stations transmit (*radio waves*/*gamma rays*).

The dentist uses (*infrared light*/*x-rays*) to examine your teeth.

Intense (*visible light*/*ultraviolet light*) from the sun can damage your skin.

2 Predict Imagine that humans had not realized there are other parts of the electromagnetic spectrum besides visible light. How would your day today be different without technology based on other parts of the EM spectrum?

_____

_____

_____

_____

_____

_____

 ## Active Reading

3 Synthesize You can often define an unknown word if you know the meaning of its word parts. Use this table of word parts to make an educated guess about the meanings given.

Word part	Meaning
ultra-	beyond
infra-	below
electro-	related to electricty
-magnetic	related to magnetism

What word means "beyond violet"?

_____

What word means "below red"?

_____

What word means "related to electricity and magnetism"?

_____

Vocabulary Terms
- radiation
- electromagnetic spectrum
- infrared
- ultraviolet

4 Apply As you learn the definition of each vocabulary term in this lesson, think of an example of a real-world use. Practice writing the term and its definition, and then writing or drawing a sketch of the example next to the definition.

Electromagnetic Light Show

What is the nature of light?

Light is a type of energy that travels as waves, but light waves are not disturbances in a medium. Light waves are disturbances in electric and magnetic fields. If you have felt the static cling of fabric and the pull of a magnet, then you have experienced electric and magnetic fields. Because these fields can exist in empty space, light does not need a medium in which to travel.

When an electrically charged particle vibrates, it disturbs the electric and magnetic fields around it. These disturbances, called electromagnetic (EM) waves, carry energy away from the charged particle. The disturbances are perpendicular to each other and to the direction the wave travels. **Radiation** (ray•dee•AY•shuhn) is the transfer of energy as EM waves.

In a vacuum, all EM waves move at the same speed: 300,000,000 m/s, called the speed of light. That's fast enough to circle Earth more than seven times in one second!

Although light and other EM waves do not need a medium, they can travel through many materials. EM waves travel more slowly in a medium such as air or glass than in a vacuum.

Active Reading

5 Identify Underline what produces EM waves.

6 Synthesize Why do we see lightning before we hear the accompanying thunder?

_____

_____

_____

_____

Visualize It!

7 Label Mark and label the wavelength and amplitude of the disturbances in the fields.

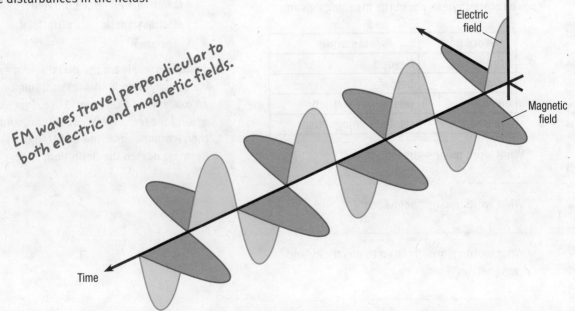

EM waves travel perpendicular to both electric and magnetic fields.

Electric field

Magnetic field

Time

The color with the shortest wavelengths is violet. Violet light has the highest frequencies.

What determines the color of light?

Light comes in many colors, from red to violet. But what is different about each color of light? Like all waves, light has wavelengths. Different wavelengths of light are interpreted by our eyes as different colors. The shortest wavelengths are seen as violet. The longest wavelengths are seen as red. Even the longest wavelengths we can see are still very small—less than one ten-thousandth of a centimeter.

White light is what we perceive when we see all the wavelengths of light at once, in equal proportions. A prism can split white light into its component colors, separating the colors by wavelength. The various wavelengths of light can also be combined to produce white light.

Our eyes only register three color ranges of light, called the primary colors—red, green, and blue. All other colors we see are a mixture of these three colors. A television or computer screen works by sending signals to make small dots, called pixels, give off red, green, and blue light.

The color with the longest wavelengths is red. Red light has the lowest frequencies.

Visualize It!

8 Arrange List the colors of the spectrum in order of increasing wavelength.

_____

_____

_____

_____

_____

_____

Red, green, and blue light combine to appear white.

9 Select What combination of primary colors do we perceive as yellow?

_____

_____

Invisible Colors

What are the parts of the EM spectrum?

EM waves are measured by frequency or by wavelength. The light waves we see are EM waves. However, visible light represents only a very small part of the range of frequencies (or wavelengths) that an EM wave can have. This range is called the **electromagnetic (EM) spectrum**. These other EM waves are the same type of wave as the light we're used to. They're just different frequencies.

Two parts of the spectrum are close to visible light. **Infrared**, or IR, light has slightly longer wavelengths than red light. **Ultraviolet**, or UV, light has slightly shorter wavelengths than violet light.

The Electromagnetic Spectrum

Microwaves
Despite their name, microwaves are not the shortest EM waves. Besides heating food, microwaves are used by cellular phones.

Infrared Light
Infrared means "below red." The amount of infrared light an object gives off depends on its temperature. Below, colors indicate different amounts of infrared light.

Radio Waves
Radio waves have the longest wavelengths. They are used to broadcast signals for radios, televisions, alarm systems, and other devices.

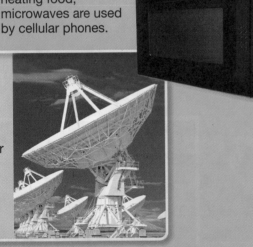

Frequency in hertz (1 hertz = 1 cycle/second)

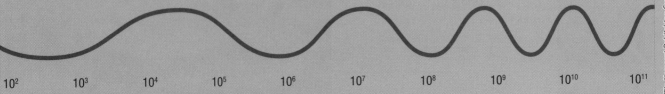

10^2	10^3	10^4	10^5	10^6	10^7	10^8	10^9	10^{10}	10^{11}

Radio Waves

Microwaves

The inner part of these flowers reflects UV light differently than the outer part. A bee's eyes are sensitive to UV light, and the bee can see the difference. However, human eyes cannot detect UV light. Our eyes can detect yellow light, and the center and edges of the flower reflect yellow light equally, so we see an all-yellow flower.

Human eyes see the flowers as entirely yellow.

A bee's eyes see a pattern in UV light.

Think Outside the Book

10 Incorporate The flower shows designs that are visible to bees, which can see light in the ultraviolet range. Research and explain how this adaptation leads to a symbiotic relationship between the flowers and bees.

Visible Light
Visible light is all the colors of the EM spectrum we can see. It is the narrowest part of the EM spectrum.

Ultraviolet Light
Ultraviolet means "beyond violet." Some animals can see ultraviolet light.

X-Rays
X-rays can pass through most living tissue, but are absorbed by bones.

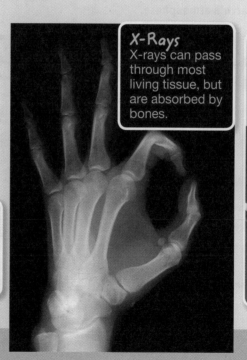

Gamma Rays
Gamma rays can be used to treat illnesses and in making medical images.

| 10^{12} | 10^{13} | 10^{14} | 10^{15} | 10^{16} | 10^{17} | 10^{18} | 10^{19} | 10^{20} |

Infrared Light   **Ultraviolet Light**   **Gamma Rays**

Visible Light   **X-Rays**

Star Light,

How much of the sun's energy reaches us?

The sun gives off huge amounts of energy in the form of EM radiation. More of this energy is in the narrow visible light range than any other part of the spectrum, but the sun gives off some radiation in every part of the spectrum.

 **Active Reading** 11 **Identify** What prevents most of the sun's gamma rays from reaching us?

_____

Visualize It!

The illustration shows how far down each part of the EM spectrum penetrates Earth's atmosphere.

The Earth Shields Us from Some EM Radiation

Between the sun and us lies Earth's atmosphere. In order for us to see anything, some of the sun's light must make it through the atmosphere. However, not all wavelengths of light penetrate the atmosphere equally. The atmosphere blocks most of the higher-frequency radiation like x-rays and gamma rays from reaching us at the ground level, while allowing most of the visible light to reach us. There is a "window" of radio frequencies that are barely blocked at all, and this is why the most powerful ground-based telescopes are radio telescopes.

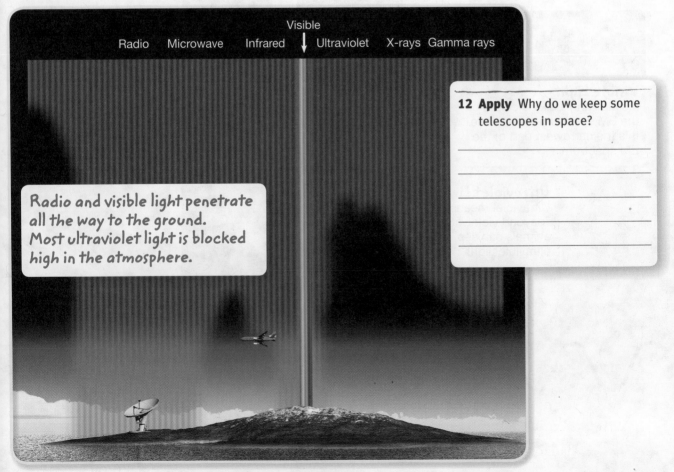

Radio | Microwave | Infrared | Visible ↓ | Ultraviolet | X-rays | Gamma rays

Radio and visible light penetrate all the way to the ground. Most ultraviolet light is blocked high in the atmosphere.

12 Apply Why do we keep some telescopes in space?

_____

_____

_____

_____

Star Bright

Inquiry

13 Hypothesize Why might it be less dangerous to wear no sunglasses than to wear sunglasses that do not block UV light?

_____

_____

_____

_____

Astronauts need extra protection from EM radiation in space.

We Shield Ourselves from Some Radiation

The atmosphere blocks much of the sun's radiation, but not all. Some EM radiation can be dangerous to humans, so we take extra steps to protect ourselves. Receiving too much ultraviolet (UV) radiation can cause sunburn, skin cancer, or damage to the eyes, so we use sunscreen and wear UV-blocking sunglasses to protect ourselves from the UV light that passes through the atmosphere. Hats, long-sleeved shirts, and long pants can protect us, too.

We need this protection even on overcast days because UV light can travel through clouds. Even scientists in Antarctica, one of the coldest places on Earth, need to wear sunglasses, because fresh snow reflects about 80% of UV light back up to where it might strike their eyes.

Outer space is often thought of as being cold, but despite this, one of the biggest dangers to astronauts is from overheating! Outside of Earth's protective atmosphere, the level of dangerous EM radiation is much higher. And, in the vacuum of space, it's much harder to dispose of any energy, because there's no surrounding matter (like air) to absorb the extra energy. This is one reason why astronauts' helmets have a thin layer of pure gold. This highly reflective gold layer reflects unwanted EM radiation away.

Frequency Asked Questions

How much energy does EM radiation have?

What makes some EM waves safe, and some dangerous? The answer is that different frequencies of EM waves carry different amounts of energy.

Higher Frequency Means More Energy

The energy of an EM wave depends on its frequency. High-frequency, short-wavelength EM waves have more energy than low-frequency, long-wavelength waves.

More Energy Means More Dangerous

A high-frequency EM wave carries a lot of energy, so it has the possibility of damaging living tissue. But a low-frequency wave carries much less energy, and is safer. This is why radio waves (which have the lowest frequencies) are used so often, such as in walkie-talkies and baby monitors. In contrast, UV light causes sunburn unless you have protection, and when working with even higher-energy waves like x-rays, special precautions must be taken, such as wearing a lead apron to block most of the rays.

> **Active Reading** **14 Conclude** What kind of EM waves are most dangerous to humans?

Radio waves pass through humans safely.

UV waves can cause damage to living tissue.

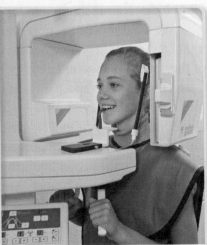

X-rays require extra safety.

Fire in the Sky

The sun constantly streams out charged particles. Earth has a strong magnetic field. When particles from the sun strike Earth, the magnetic field funnels them together, accelerating them. When these particles collide with the atmosphere, they give off electromagnetic radiation in the form of light, and near the poles where they usually come together, a beautiful display called an *aurora* (uh•RAWR•uh) sometimes lights up the sky.

Winds of Change
The stream of electrically charged particles from the sun is called the *solar wind*.

What a Gas!
An aurora produced by nitrogen atoms may have a blue or red color, while one produced by oxygen atoms is green or brownish-red.

Pole Position
At the North Pole, this phenomenon is called the *aurora borealis* (uh•RAWR•uh bawr•ee•AL•is), or northern lights. At the south pole, is it called the *aurora australis* (uh•RAWR•uh aw•STRAY•lis), or southern lights.

Extend

16 Relate Which color of aurora gives off higher-energy light, green or red?

17 Explain Why don't we see auroras on the moon?

18 Hypothesize Based on what you have learned about auroras, do you think auroras occur on other planets? Why or why not?

Visual Summary

To complete this summary, fill in the blanks with the correct word or phrase. Then use the key below to check your answers. You can use this page to review the main concepts of the lesson.

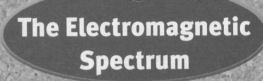

The Electromagnetic Spectrum

Different wavelengths of light appear as different colors.

19 The color of the longest visible wavelength is _____

20 The color of the shortest visible wavelength is _____

Higher-frequency waves carry more energy. This makes them more dangerous.

21 The energy of an electromagnetic (EM) wave is proportional to its _____

EM waves exist along a spectrum.

22 The waves with the longest wavelengths are _____ waves.

23 The waves with the shortest wavelengths are _____

10^0

10^{19}

Radio Waves

Gamma Rays

Answers: 19 red; 20 violet; 21 frequency; 22 radio; 23 gamma rays

24 Synthesize Suppose you are designing a device to transmit information without wires. What part of the EM spectrum will your device use, and why?

Lesson Review

Vocabulary

Fill in the blanks with the terms that best complete the following sentences.

1 The transfer of energy as electromagnetic waves is called _____

2 The full range of wavelengths of EM waves is called the _____ _____

3 _____ radiation lies at frequencies just below the frequencies of visible light.

Key Concepts

4 Describe What is an electromagnetic wave?

_____

_____

_____

5 Organize What are the highest-frequency and lowest-frequency parts of the EM spectrum?

_____

_____

_____

6 Compare How fast do different parts of the EM spectrum travel in a vacuum?

_____

_____

_____

Suppose you like to listen to two different radio stations. The opera station broadcasts at 90.5 MHz and the rock and roll station broadcasts at 107.1 MHz.

7 Apply Which station's signal has waves with longer wavelengths?

_____

_____

8 Apply Which station's signal has waves with higher energy?

_____

_____

Use the graph to answer the following questions.

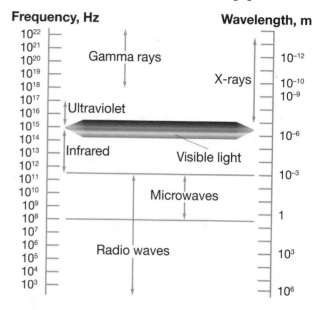

9 Classify How would you classify an EM wave with a frequency of 10^7 Hz?

_____

10 Classify How would you classify an EM wave with a wavelength of 10^{-12} m?

_____

_____

11 Apply What is white light?

_____

_____

Critical Thinking

12 Recommend If you wanted to detect x-rays coming from the sun, where would you place the detector? Why?

_____

_____

_____

_____

_____

_____

My Notes

Interactions of Light

ESSENTIAL QUESTION

How does light interact with matter?

By the end of this lesson, you should be able to explain how light and matter can interact.

8.PS4.2

These windows allow different colors of light to pass through. The colorful pattern is then reflected off the floor inside.

 Lesson Labs

Quick Labs
- Why is the Sky Blue?
- Refraction with Water

Exploration Lab
- Comparing Colors of Objects in Different Colors of Light

Engage Your Brain

1 Predict Check T or F to show whether you think each statement is true or false.

T	F	
☐	☐	Light cannot pass through solid matter.
☐	☐	A white surface absorbs every color of light.
☐	☐	Light always moves at the same speed.

2 Identify Unscramble the letters below to find words about interactions between light and matter. Write your words on the blank lines.

OCRLO _____

RIORMR _____

NABORIW _____

TTRACSE _____

CENFOLRETI _____

 ## Active Reading

3 Synthesize You can often define an unknown word if you know the meaning of its word parts. Use the word parts and sentence below to make an educated guess about the meanings of the words *transmit*, *transparent*, and *translucent*.

Word part	Meaning
trans-	through
-mit	send
-par	show
-luc	light

Vocabulary Terms

- transparent
- translucent
- opaque
- absorption
- reflection
- refraction
- scattering

4 Apply As you learn the definition of each vocabulary term in this lesson, create your own definition or sketch to help you remember the meaning of the term.

transmit: _____

_____

transparent: _____

_____

translucent: _____

_____

Shedding Light

How can matter interact with light?

Interactions between light and matter produce many common but spectacular effects, such as color, reflections, and rainbows. Three forms of interaction play an especially important role in how people see light.

Matter Can Transmit Light

Recall that light and other electromagnetic waves can travel through empty space. When light encounters a material, it can be passed through the material, or transmitted. The medium can transmit all, some, or none of the light.

Matter that transmits light is **transparent** (tranz•PAHR•uhnt). Air, water, and some types of glass are transparent materials. Objects can be seen clearly through transparent materials.

Translucent (tranz•LOO•suhnt) materials transmit light but do not let the light travel straight through. The light is scattered into many different directions. As a result, you can see light through translucent materials, but objects seen through a translucent material look distorted or fuzzy. Frosted glass, some lamp shades, and tissue paper are examples of translucent materials.

Active Reading

5 Identify As you read, underline three words that describe how well matter transmits light.

Objects can be seen clearly through transparent glass.

Objects look distorted when seen through translucent glass.

Think Outside the Book

6 Discuss Write a short story in which it is important that a piece of glass is translucent or transparent.

on the Matter

Matter Can Absorb Light

Opaque (oh•PAYK) materials do not let any light pass through them. Instead, they reflect light, absorb light, or both. Many materials, such as wood, brick, or metal, are opaque. When light enters a material but does not leave it, the light is absorbed. **Absorption** is the transfer of light energy to matter.

The shirt at right absorbs the light that falls on it, and so the shirt is opaque. However, absorption is not the only way an object can be opaque.

The shirt is opaque, because light does not pass through it. We can't see the table underneath.

👁 Visualize It!

7 Explain Is the table in the photo at right transparent, translucent, or opaque? Explain how you know.

_____

_____

_____

Matter Can Reflect Light

You see an object only when light from the object enters your eye. However, most objects do not give off, or emit, light. Instead, light bounces off the object's surface. The bouncing of light off a surface is called **reflection**.

Most objects have a surface that is at least slightly rough. When light strikes a rough surface, such as wood or cloth, the light reflects in many different directions. Some of the reflected light reaches your eyes, and you see the object.

Light bounces at an angle equal to the angle at which it hit the surface. When light strikes a smooth or shiny surface such as a mirror, it reflects in a uniform way. As a result, a mirror produces an image. Light from a lamp might be reflected by your skin, then be reflected by a mirror, and then enter your eye. You look at the mirror and see yourself.

👁 Visualize It!

8 Identify What is the difference between the way light interacts with the shirt above and the way light interacts with the mirror at right?

_____

_____

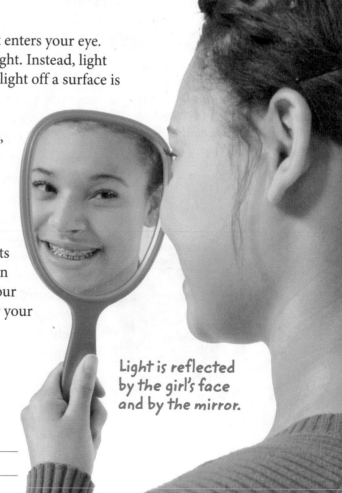

Light is reflected by the girl's face and by the mirror.

Color Me Impressed!

What determines the color of objects we see?

Visible light includes a range of colors. Light that includes all colors is called white light. When white light strikes an object, the object can transmit some or all of the colors of light, reflect some or all of the colors, and absorb some or all of the colors.

The frog's body is green because it reflects green light while absorbing other colors of light.

The Light Reflected or Absorbed

The perceived color of an object is determined by the colors of light reflected by the object. For example, a frog's skin absorbs most colors of light, but reflects most of the green light. When you look in the direction of the frog, the green light enters your eyes, so the frog appears green.

An object that reflects every color appears white. An object that absorbs every color appears black.

> **Think Outside the Book**
>
> 9 **Diagram** Use colored pencils, crayons, or markers to draw light shining on an object. Draw arrows showing the colors of incoming light and arrows showing which colors are reflected.

The Light Transmitted

The color of a transparent or translucent object works differently than it does for opaque objects. Some materials may absorb some colors but let other colors pass through. Green plastic, for example, does not appear green because it reflects green light, but rather, because it transmits green light while absorbing other colors of light. When you look toward a bottle made of green plastic, the transmitted green light reaches your eyes. Therefore, the bottle looks green.

Some matter can absorb visible light but let other kinds of electromagnetic waves pass through. For example, radio waves can easily pass through walls that are opaque to visible light. X-rays pass through skin and muscle, but are stopped by denser bone.

The bottle is green because it allows green light to pass through while absorbing other colors of light.

The Available Light

Sometimes the perceived color of an object depends on the light available in the area. You may have been in a room with a red light bulb. The glass around the bulb filters out all colors except red, plus some orange and yellow. An object that reflects red light would still appear red under such a light bulb. But an object that absorbed all red, orange, and yellow light would appear gray or black. We can't see colors of light that aren't there to be reflected to our eyes!

Filtered Light

Below, the light from the bulb is being filtered before shining on a frog.

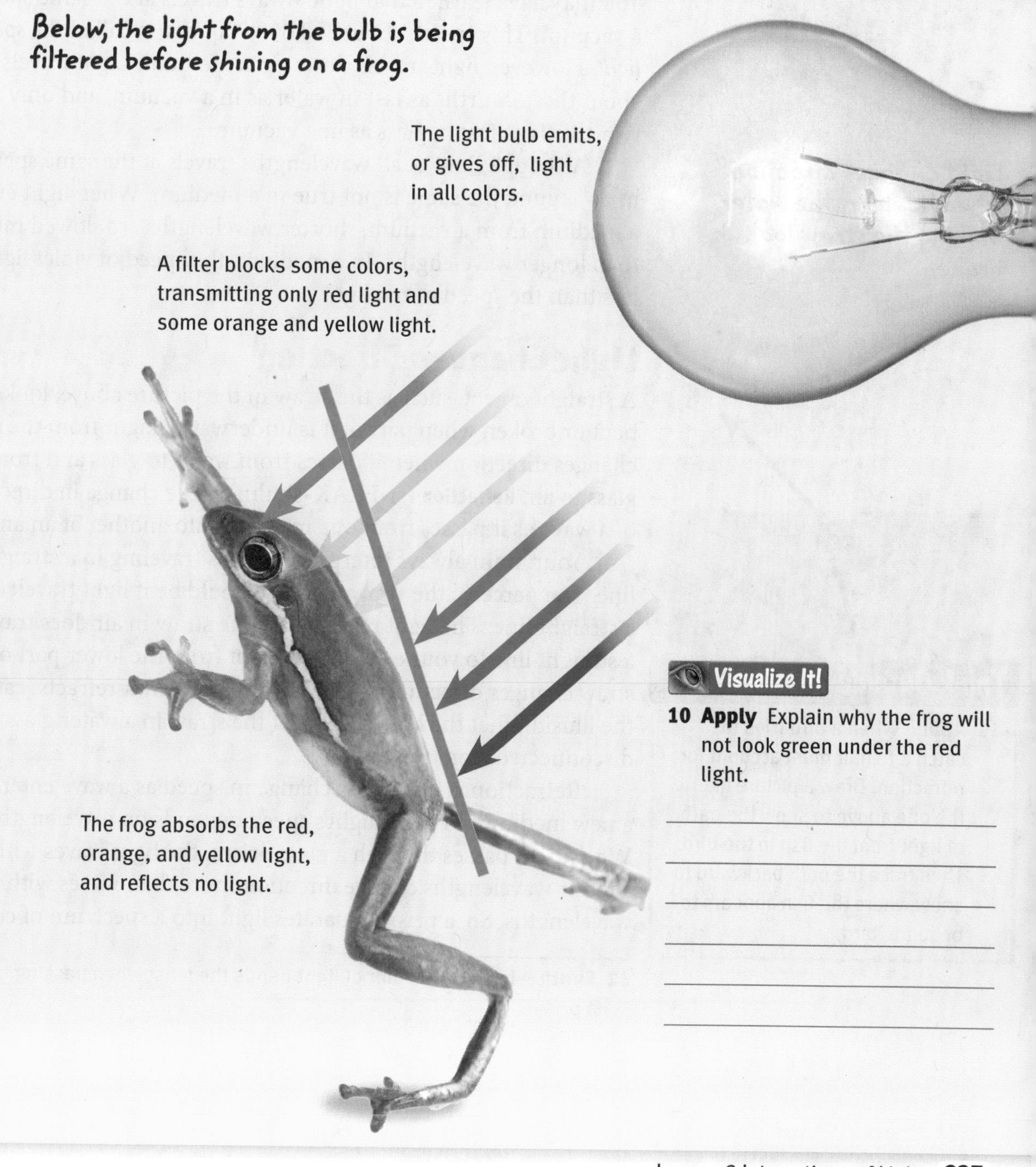

The light bulb emits, or gives off, light in all colors.

A filter blocks some colors, transmitting only red light and some orange and yellow light.

The frog absorbs the red, orange, and yellow light, and reflects no light.

Visualize It!

10 Apply Explain why the frog will not look green under the red light.

_____

_____

_____

_____

_____

Matter Scatter

What happens when light waves interact with matter?

You have already learned that light can pass through a transparent medium. But when light waves pass through a medium, the medium can change properties of the light.

Light Slows When It Passes Through Matter

You may have learned that light always travels at the same speed in a vacuum. This speed, about 300,000,000 m/s, is called the *speed of light*. However, light travels slower in a medium. Light travels only about three-fourths as fast in water as in a vacuum, and only about two-thirds as fast in glass as in a vacuum.

Although light of all wavelengths travels at the same speed in a vacuum, the same is not true in a medium. When light enters a medium from a vacuum, shorter wavelengths are slowed more than longer wavelengths. In a medium, the speed of violet light is less than the speed of red light.

Light changes direction when it leaves the water, making the straw look broken.

Light Changes Direction

A straight object, such as the straw in the picture above, looks bent or broken when part of it is underwater. Light from the straw changes direction when it passes from water to glass and from glass to air. **Refraction** (ri•FRAK•shuhn) is the change in direction of a wave as it passes from one medium into another at an angle.

Your brain always interprets light as traveling in a straight line. You perceive the straw where it would be if light traveled in a straight line. The light reflected by the straw in air does travel in a straight line to your eye. But the light from the lower part of the straw changes direction when it passes into air. It refracts, causing the illusion that the bottom part of the straw in a water glass is disconnected from the top part.

Refraction is due to the change in speed as a wave enters a new medium. In glass, light's speed depends on wavelength. When light passes through a glass prism, the light waves with shorter wavelengths change direction more than waves with longer wavelengths. So, a prism separates light into a spectrum of colors.

Think Outside the Book

11 **Apply** When a bird tries to catch a fish, it must account for refraction. Draw a picture like the one above to show the path of light from the fish to the bird. Then trace the path backward to show where the fish appears to be to the bird.

12 **Synthesize** Which color of light bends the least when passing through a prism?

_____

© Houghton Mifflin Harcourt Publishing Company • Image Credits:; ©Keith Leighton/Alamy

Light Scatters

You don't see a beam of light shining through clear air. But if the beam of light shines through fog, some of the light is sent in many different directions. Some enters your eye, and you see the beam. **Scattering** occurs when light is sent in many directions as it passes through a medium. Dust and other small particles can scatter light.

The color of the sky is due to scattered light. Particles of air scatter short wavelengths—blue and violet light—more than long wavelengths. As sunlight passes through air, blue light is scattered first. The blue light appears to come from all directions, and so the sky appears blue. When the sun is near the horizon in the sky, sunlight passes through more of the atmosphere. As the light passes through more and more air, almost all light of short wavelengths is scattered. Only the longest wavelengths are left. The sun and the sky appear yellow, orange, or red.

 **Active Reading**

13 Identify What color of light is scattered most easily by the atmosphere?

We can see the light beam coming out of the lighthouse because the fog scatters the light.

In the diagram below, the red lines represent paths of light from the sun. The black brackets show the amount of atmosphere the light must pass through to reach our eyes.

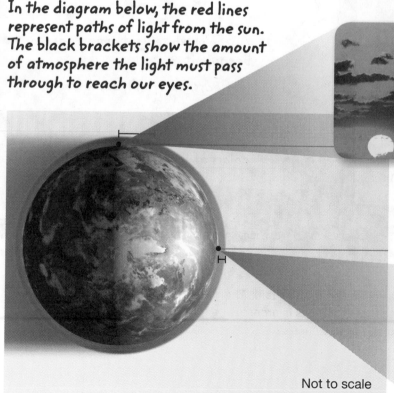

Not to scale

In the evening, sunlight travels through a lot of air. The blue light scatters, leaving only redder light.

The daytime sky appears blue because air scatters blue light more than it does other colors.

Visual Summary

To complete this summary, circle the correct word to complete each statement. Then, use the key below to check your answers. You can use this page to review the main concepts of the lesson.

Interactions of Light and Matter

Matter can transmit, reflect, or absorb light.

14 Matter that transmits no light is (transparent/translucent/opaque).

The color of an object depends on what colors of light it reflects or transmits.

15 A frog in white light appears green because it

(reflects/absorbs/transmits) green light and

(reflects/absorbs/transmits) other colors of light.

A transparent medium can bend, scatter, or change the speed of light.

16 The bending of light is called (reflection/refraction/scattering).

Answers: 14 opaque; 15 reflects, absorbs; 16 refraction

17 Synthesize Suppose you are looking at a yellow fish in a fish tank. The tank is next to a window. Describe the path that light takes in order for you to see the fish, starting at the sun and ending at your eyes.

Lesson Review

Vocabulary

Fill in the blank with the term that best completes the following sentences.

1 An object appears fuzzy when seen through a(n) _____ material.

2 A(n) _____ material lets light pass through freely.

3 The bouncing of light off a surface is called _____

4 The bending of light when it changes media is called _____

5 _____ occurs when light changes direction after colliding with particles of matter.

Key Concepts

6 Identify For each picture below, identify the material enclosing the sandwich as transparent, translucent, or opaque.

a. _____

b. _____

c. _____

d. _____

7 Identify Which material in the pictures above reflects the most light?

_____

8 Identify Which material in the pictures above absorbs the most light?

_____

Critical Thinking

9 Infer Is a mirror's surface transparent, translucent, or opaque? How do you know?

_____

_____

_____

_____

_____

10 Apply Why does a black asphalt road become hotter than a white cement sidewalk in the same amount of sunlight?

_____

_____

_____

_____

_____

11 Explain Why is the sky blue?

_____

_____

_____

_____

_____

_____

_____

12 Explain Red, green, and blue light rays each enter a drop of water from the same direction. Which light ray's path through the drop will bend the most, and which will bend the least? Why?

_____

_____

_____

_____

_____

My Notes

Engineering Design Process

Skills
Identify a need
Conduct research
✓ Brainstorm solutions
✓ Select a solution
Design a prototype
✓ Build a prototype
✓ Test and evaluate
✓ Redesign to improve
✓ Communicate results

Objectives

- Identify different uses of mirrors and lenses.
- Use mirrors and lenses to design and build a periscope.
- Test and evaluate the periscope you built.

Building a Periscope

A *periscope* is a device that uses mirrors and lenses to help people see around obstacles. You might be surprised to learn how many other important technologies benefit from mirrors and lenses.

Early Uses of Mirrors and Lenses

For many centuries, people have used mirrors and lenses to bend light. In ancient times, people used shiny metal to see their reflections and pieces of curved glass to start fires. In the 17th century, scientists began using lenses and mirrors to make telescopes, microscopes, and other devices that helped them make new discoveries.

In 1610, Italian astronomer Galileo used a two-lens telescope to discover Jupiter's moons.

1. **Identify** List devices that use mirrors, lenses, or a combination of both. Then describe the purpose of each device, and identify whether it uses mirrors, lenses, or both.

Device	Purpose	Mirrors, Lenses, or Both
telescope	magnifies far away objects	both

Lasers

Mirrors bend light by reflecting it in a different direction. Lenses bend light by slowing it as it passes through the lens material. Many modern technologies also take advantage of mirrors and lenses. Devices such as DVD players and barcode scanners operate by using laser light. A *laser* is a device that produces a coherent beam of light of a specific wavelength, or color. Laser light is created in a chamber that has mirrors on each end. A single color of light is produced by reflecting light back and forth between the two mirrors. The distance between the mirrors determines the wavelength of light that is amplified. When the light is of the proper wavelength, it can exit the transparent center of one of the mirrors. Lenses are often found in devices that use laser light. Lenses can focus the laser light in devices such as DVD players.

2 Identify Conduct research about the uses of laser light. What are some objects that use lasers?

_____

_____

_____

This device uses mirrors and lasers to measure the wind speed during an aircraft test. Wind speed is measured as the laser interacts with dust in the wind.

Periscopes

A periscope is another type of device that uses mirrors and lenses. The mirrors in a periscope bend light in order to allow a person to see around obstacles or above water. Most people think of periscopes in submarines, but periscopes are also used to see over walls or around corners, to see out of parade floats, and to see inside pipes or machinery.

Submarine periscopes use lenses and mirrored prisms to allow people to see above the water without surfacing.

 You Try It!

Now it's your turn to use mirrors and lenses to design and build a periscope.

 # You Try It!

Mirrors are used to bend light, and lenses are used to focus light. Now it's your turn to use mirrors and lenses to design and build a periscope that can see at least six inches above eye level.

You Will Need

✓ cardboard boxes or poster board

✓ cardboard or plastic tubes

✓ lenses

✓ mirrors

✓ scissors

✓ tape

① Brainstorm Solutions

A You will build a periscope to see things at least six inches above eye level. Brainstorm some ideas about how your periscope will work. Check a box in each row below to get started.

Length of periscope: ☐ 6 inches ☐ 12 inches ☐ other _____

Shape of periscope: ☐ tube ☐ box ☐ other _____

User will look with: ☐ one eye ☐ both eyes

Your periscope: ☐ will ☐ will not magnify objects

B Once you have decided what your periscope needs to do, look at the materials available to you, and brainstorm how you can build your periscope. Write down the materials you will use and how you will use them.

_____

_____

_____

② Select a Solution

Choose one of the ideas that you brainstormed. In the space below, draw a sketch of how your prototype periscope will be constructed. Include arrows to show the path of light through your periscope.

(3) Build a Prototype

Use your materials to assemble the periscope according to your design. Write down the steps you took to assemble the parts.

_____

_____

_____

_____

(4) Test, Evaluate, and Redesign to Improve

Test your periscope, and fill in the first row of the table below. Make any improvements, and test your periscope again, filling in an additional row of the table for each revised prototype.

Prototype	What I saw through the periscope	Improvements to be made
1		
2		
3		

(5) Communicate Results

Write a paragraph summarizing what you wanted the periscope to do, how you designed and built it, whether the finished periscope worked as planned, and how you made improvements.

_____

_____

_____

_____

_____

_____

Light Technology

ESSENTIAL QUESTION

How can light be used?

By the end of this lesson, you should be able to apply knowledge of light to describe light-related technologies.

8.PS4.3

The searchlights on these buildings can be seen from miles away.

Lesson Labs

Quick Labs
• Total Internal Reflection
• Light Technology in Color Monitors

Exploration Lab
• Investigating Artificial Light

Engage Your Brain

1 Predict Check T or F to show whether you think each statement is true or false.

T	F	
☐	☐	Light can be used to perform surgery.
☐	☐	Light cannot be used to transmit sound or data.
☐	☐	Lasers emit light of all frequencies.
☐	☐	Light technology has stayed the same for decades.
☐	☐	Telescopes can use either lenses or mirrors to manipulate light.

2 Describe Do you think this fiber optic lamp is an example of light technology? Explain.

_____

_____

_____

_____

Active Reading

3 Apply Many scientific words, such as *fiber*, also have everyday meanings. Use context clues to write your own definition for each meaning of the word *fiber*.

Example sentence
Clothes can be made of wool <u>fibers</u>.

fiber:

_____

_____

Example sentence
Optical <u>fibers</u> use light to transmit information.

fiber:

_____

_____

Vocabulary Terms
• incandescent light
• fluorescent light
• LED
• laser
• optical fiber

4 Identify As you read, place a question mark next to any words you don't understand. When you finish reading the lesson, go back and review the text that you marked. If the information is still confusing, consult a classmate or a teacher.

I Can See the LIGHT

What are some ways to produce light?

Throughout history, people have developed different ways of producing light to help see things, store and transfer information, and interact with matter. These are considered light technologies. For example, candles were an early invention that helped people see and work even after the sun went down. We now have a wider variety of technologies that produce and use light.

Think Outside the Book (Inquiry)

5 **Research** Investigate light pollution. Write a public service announcement about light pollution, or communicate a new way to produce light while preventing light pollution.

Incandescent Lights

Visible light produced from a very hot material is **incandescent light** (in•kuhn•DES•uhnt LYT). In a typical incandescent bulb, electric current is passed through a thin wire, called a *filament*, inside the bulb. The filament gets hot enough to *emit*, or give off, visible light. Incandescent bulbs are inefficient in producing light compared with other types of bulbs. Only about 8% of the energy given off by an incandescent light bulb is in the form of light. The rest is in the form of heat.

Fluorescent Lights

Electric current can energize some gases and produce ultraviolet light, which is invisible to humans. **Fluorescent light** (flu•RES•uhnt LYT) is produced when a fluorescent coating inside a bulb converts the ultraviolet light into visible light. About 80% of the energy given off by fluorescent bulbs is in the form of visible light. Fluorescent bulbs last about 10 times longer than incandescent bulbs. Because of their energy efficiency, many light bulbs sold in stores for household use are CFL, or Compact Fluorescent Light Bulbs. The screens of many devices produce light using similar technologies.

6 **Compare** Fill in the Venn diagram to compare and contrast incandescent and fluorescent light bulbs.

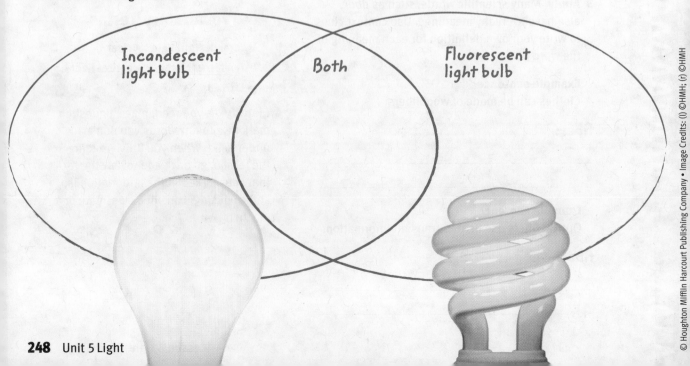

Incandescent light bulb   Both   Fluorescent light bulb

Light-Emitting Diodes

The tiny indicator light on many electronic devices is a *light-emitting diode*, or *LED*. **LEDs** contain solid materials that emit light when energized by an electric current. Unlike other light sources, an LED emits only one color of light. Almost 100% of the energy given off by LEDs is in the form of visible light. This means that LEDs are very efficient and last a long time. Most traffic lights in the United States now use LEDs.

A string of LEDs can provide light for many years.

Lasers

A **laser** is a device that produces intense light of a very small range of wavelengths. Lasers produce light in such a way that causes the light to be more concentrated, or intense, than other types of light. Unlike non-laser light, laser light is *coherent*. When light is coherent, light waves stay together as they travel away from their source. The crests and troughs of coherent light waves are aligned. So the individual waves behave as one wave. The diagram below shows how lasers produce coherent light.

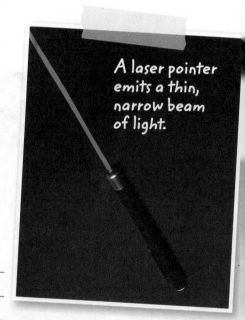

A laser pointer emits a thin, narrow beam of light.

7 Infer What might be an advantage of focusing light into a narrow beam?

_____

_____

How a Helium-Neon Laser Works

A The inside of the laser is filled with helium and neon gases. An electric current in the laser "excites" the atoms of the gases.

B Excited neon atoms release photons of red light. When these photons strike other excited neon atoms, more photons are released that travel together.

C Plane mirrors on both ends of the laser reflect the photons back and forth along the tube.

D Because the photons travel back and forth many times, many more photons are released, and the laser light gets brighter.

E A partial coating on one mirror allows the laser light to escape and form a coherent beam.

Light SPEED

What are some ways light can transfer information?

Some light technologies use light to encode, send, or read signals. For example, a laser inside a CD or DVD player reads the information stored on the disc. Other examples are the bar code scanners in retail stores that record the price of your purchase and TV remote controls that are used to transfer information. Remote controls typically use infrared light.

Infrared Technologies

Infrared radiation is invisible electromagnetic radiation with a wavelength longer than what our eyes can detect. However, several technologies make use of infrared radiation. Some night vision goggles can emit infrared radiation, allowing people to see objects without the help of visible light. Weather satellites can track storms forming at night by taking infrared pictures. Space-based telescopes can determine the temperatures of stars and dust clouds by measuring the infrared radiation coming from them.

Active Reading **8 Identify** As you read, underline three uses of optical fibers.

Fiber Optic Technologies

A thin, transparent glass thread that transmits light over long distances is an **optical fiber**. A bundle of optical fibers is shown on the left. Transmitting information through telephone cables is the most common use of optical fibers. They are also used to network computers and to allow doctors to see inside patients' bodies without performing major surgery.

Optical fibers are like pipes that carry light. Light stays inside an optical fiber because of *total internal reflection*. Total internal reflection is the complete reflection of light back and forth along the inside surface of the material through which it travels. Light is emitted out the end of the fiber.

An optical fiber is flexible and can transmit light with little loss.

Visualize It!

9 Diagram Draw a circle on the fiber optic diagram to show where light is emitted.

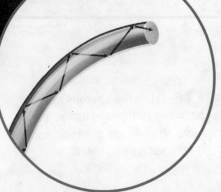

Light traveling through an optical fiber reflects off the sides thousands of times each meter.

© Houghton Mifflin Harcourt Publishing Company • Image Credits: ©Kulka/zefa/Corbis

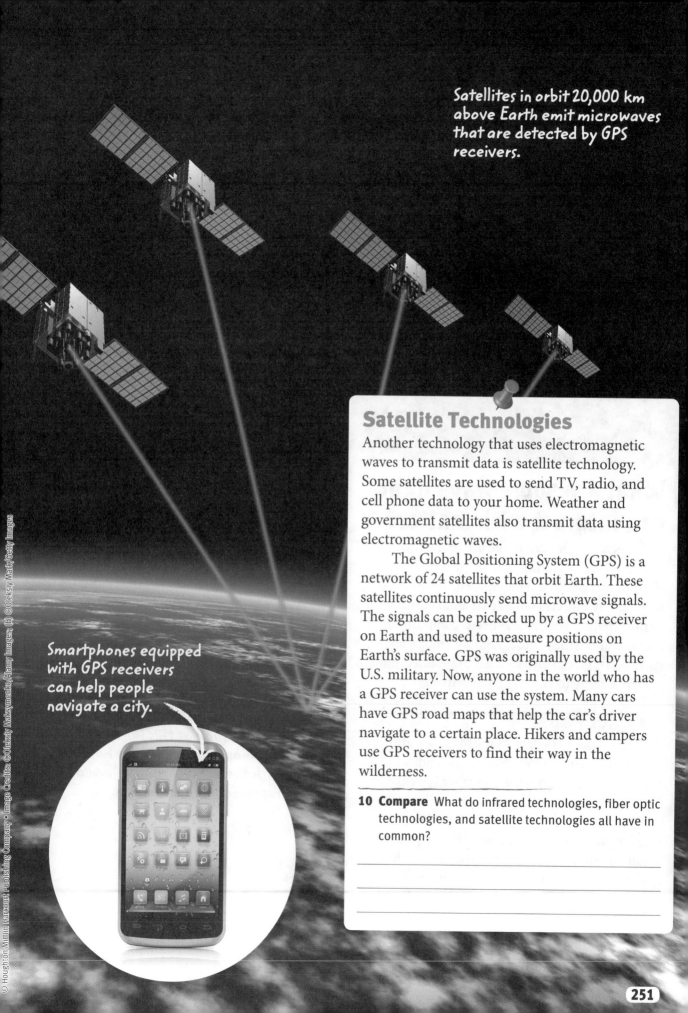

Satellites in orbit 20,000 km above Earth emit microwaves that are detected by GPS receivers.

Smartphones equipped with GPS receivers can help people navigate a city.

Satellite Technologies

Another technology that uses electromagnetic waves to transmit data is satellite technology. Some satellites are used to send TV, radio, and cell phone data to your home. Weather and government satellites also transmit data using electromagnetic waves.

The Global Positioning System (GPS) is a network of 24 satellites that orbit Earth. These satellites continuously send microwave signals. The signals can be picked up by a GPS receiver on Earth and used to measure positions on Earth's surface. GPS was originally used by the U.S. military. Now, anyone in the world who has a GPS receiver can use the system. Many cars have GPS road maps that help the car's driver navigate to a certain place. Hikers and campers use GPS receivers to find their way in the wilderness.

10 Compare What do infrared technologies, fiber optic technologies, and satellite technologies all have in common?

_____

_____

_____

Light WORK

A truck with a radar dish can follow storm clouds and gather information about them.

What are some ways light can interact with matter?

Light technologies can make use of the ways light interacts with matter to get information about materials. The light emitted, absorbed, or reflected by objects contains an amazing amount of information about the objects' composition, motion, and temperature. Light technologies, such as lasers, can also be used to produce and control energy to actually change matter.

Doppler Radar

Doppler radar uses light in the form of radio waves to measure weather patterns. Radio waves are sent out toward a weather system. They bounce off of the clouds and back to the transmitter, which captures them for analysis. The frequency of the radio waves changes a small amount, depending on how the weather system is moving. The reflected radio waves are received, and the image is used to make a picture of the entire moving weather system. The speed and intensity of the moving system can be determined.

Doppler radar uses light to measure the intensity, location, and movement of a storm system, such as this hurricane. On the radar map, blue is used to show the areas with the lightest rain. Yellow and green represent moderate rain.

Active Reading

11 Identify What form of light does Doppler radar use?

© Houghton Mifflin Harcourt Publishing Company • Image Credits: (t) ©Ryan McGinnis/Alamy Images; (b) ©NOAA

Laser Technologies

The light from lasers can be accurately pointed. The intense energy of the light beam can be used to melt and cut different materials. For example, lasers can be used in manufacturing to cut, weld, and engrave certain metals. Doctors sometimes use lasers for surgery because a laser can be used to make very precise incisions. Lasers are used to shape the cornea of the eye to correct eyesight.

Lasers are found in many everyday devices, too. They are used in the CD drive of computers and in many printers. Laser pointers can be used from a distance, and laser levelers can help you hang pictures in a straight line. Lasers are also used to make holograms, the three-dimensional images seen on credit cards.

Active Reading

12 Identify As you read, underline five specific uses of laser technology.

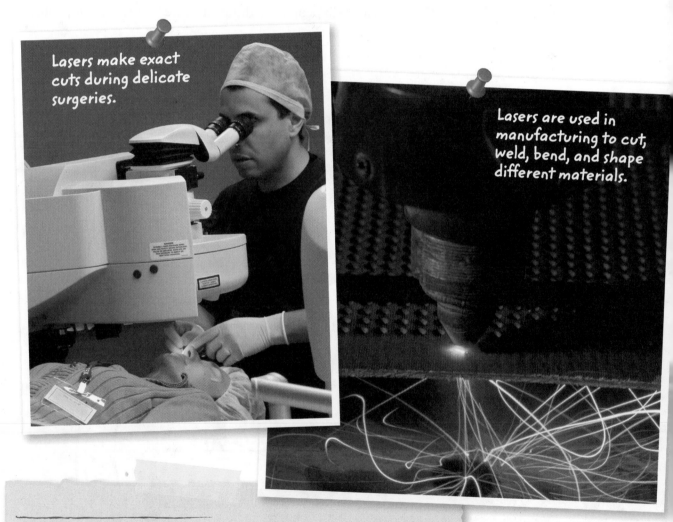

Lasers make exact cuts during delicate surgeries.

Lasers are used in manufacturing to cut, weld, bend, and shape different materials.

13 Infer The photographs on this page show medical and industrial applications of laser technology. Describe a household use of lasers.

_____

_____

_____

_____

Seeing is BELIEVING

What are some ways light can change what people see?

Optical instruments are devices that use mirrors and lenses to control the path of light and change what people can see. These light technologies help people see objects that cannot be observed with the eye alone. Microscopes allow people to see the very small; binoculars and telescopes can allow people to see the very far. Cameras can help people see things that are fast, slow, dangerous, or hard to reach.

Microscopes

Microscopes are used to see magnified images of tiny, nearby objects. Simple light microscopes have two convex lenses. An objective lens is close to the object being studied. An eyepiece lens is the lens you look through. Light from a lamp or mirror at the bottom shines through the object being studied. The user looks through the eyepiece and focuses on the object.

Visualize It!

15 Identify Label the lenses in the illustration.

A

B

Green chloroplasts inside plant cells.

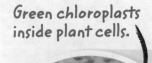

Microscopes allow us to see the very small objects in our world.

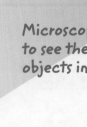

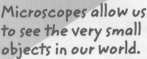

Telescopes

Telescopes are used to see images of large, distant objects. Astronomers use telescopes to study known objects, like the moon, and to search for undiscovered objects. Telescopes that use visible light are classified as either refracting or reflecting. Refracting telescopes use lenses to collect light. Reflecting telescopes use mirrors to collect light. Large telescopes are often housed in observatories, high on mountaintops. The less atmosphere the light travels through, the clearer the image appears.

Telescopes allow people to observe objects that are billions of light-years away.

Cameras

Cameras are used to record images. A digital camera controls the light that enters the camera and uses sensors to detect the light. The sensors send an electrical signal to a computer in the camera. This signal contains data about the image that can be stored and transferred. Some cameras also record video using computers. Cameras are useful for scientists who need to see and record things that are fast, slow, dangerous, or hard to reach.

The lens of a digital camera focuses light on the sensors. Moving the lens focuses light from objects at different distances.

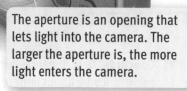

The aperture is an opening that lets light into the camera. The larger the aperture is, the more light enters the camera.

Video cameras can record motion data, which can be analyzed later in a laboratory.

Think Outside the Book

16 Summarize Choose one of the technologies on these two pages and research its history. Write a report of your findings.

Visual Summary

To complete this summary, fill in each blank with the correct word or phrase. Then use the key below to check your answers. You can use this page to review the main concepts of the lesson.

Light Technology

Light is produced in many different ways.

17 A(n)_____bulb produces light more efficiently than a(n)_____ bulb does.

Light can be used to transfer information.

18 _____ can transmit telephone calls, network computers, and allow doctors to see inside the body.

Interactions between light and matter help humans perform tasks.

19 Lasers are useful in manufacturing because the light beam is narrow and carries a great amount of _____

Light can be manipulated to change what people can see.

20 A _____ telescope uses lenses to manipulate light and allow people to see far away objects.

Answers: 17 fluorescent, incandescent; 18 Optical fibers; 19 energy; 20 refracting

21 **Conclude** Describe three areas of human knowledge that would not be as advanced without light technology.

Lesson Review

Vocabulary

Fill in the blank with the term that best completes the following sentences.

1 The coating in a(n) _____ light bulb emits light when it interacts with ultraviolet light.

2 The material inside a(n) _____ light bulb emits light when it is very hot.

3 A(n) _____ contains solid materials that emit light when energized by an electric current.

4 Intense light of a narrow range of wavelengths is called _____ light.

Key Concepts

5 List Give three examples of infrared technologies.

_____

_____

_____

6 Identify What light technology is used by GPS systems?

_____

7 Explain How can a camera help someone see something he or she wouldn't normally be able to see?

_____

_____

_____

_____

8 Distinguish In what way is laser light different from the light produced by other sources?

_____

_____

_____

_____

Critical Thinking

Use this drawing to answer the following questions.

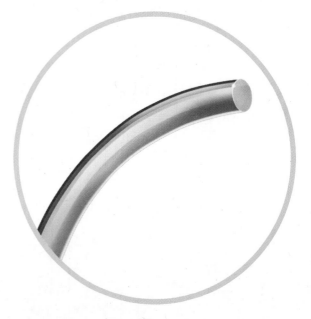

9 Illustrate Draw light rays on the fiber to show how light travels through, and is emitted from, an optical fiber.

10 Evaluate What are some advantages of optical fibers?

_____

_____

_____

_____

11 Recommend Some streetlights use incandescent bulbs, and others use LEDs. Which would you recommend and why?

_____

_____

_____

_____

_____

My Notes

Unit 5

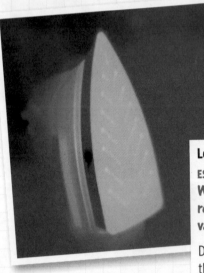

Lesson 1

ESSENTIAL QUESTION
What is the relationship between various EM waves?

Distinguish between the parts of the electromagnetic spectrum.

Lesson 3

ESSENTIAL QUESTION
How can light be used?

Apply knowledge of light to describe light-related technologies.

Lesson 2

ESSENTIAL QUESTION
How does light interact with matter?

Explain how light and matter can interact.

Think Outside the Book

2 Synthesize Choose one of these activities to help synthesize what you have learned in this unit.

☐ Using what you learned in lessons 3 and make a poster presentation describing the ways in which people use the way light interacts with matter.

☐ Using what you learned in lessons 1, 2, and 5, and research, create a timeline showing how understanding the electromagnetic spectrum and the ways in which to apply it has affected communications technology.

Connect ESSENTIAL QUESTIONS
Lessons 1, 2, and 3

1 Synthesize What type of light forms a rainbow? Would you expect that a rainbow could form with ultraviolet light? Explain.

_____

_____

_____

_____

Name _____

Vocabulary

Check the box to show whether each statement is true or false.

T	F	
☐	☐	**1** Radiation is the transfer of energy as electromagnetic (EM) waves.
☐	☐	**2** Laser light is more intense than other types of light because it comes from a very small range of wavelengths in the visible spectrum.
☐	☐	**3** Electromagnetic waves travel through a medium by radiation.
☐	☐	**4** Scattering occurs when certain wavelengths of light are reflected by particles, causing the light to spread out in all directions
☐	☐	**5** A material that allows light to pass through it completely is transparent.

Key Concepts

Read each question below, and circle the best answer.

6 What is proportional to the energy of an electromagnetic (EM) wave?

   A its gamma rays

   B its total amount of charged particles

   C its frequency

   D its longest visible wavelength

7 What form of light does Doppler radar use?

   A optical fiber

   B laser light

   C radio waves

   D microscopes

8 The table below lists electromagnetic waves.

	A	B	C	D
Low frequency	Radio waves	Gamma rays	Laser light	Visible light
	Microwaves	x-rays	Visible light	x-rays
	Infrared waves	Ultraviolet light	Ultraviolet light	Ultraviolet light
	Visible light	Visible light	x-rays	Radio waves
High frequency	Ultraviolet light	Infrared light	Gamma rays	Microwaves

Which column correctly lists waves from lowest to highest frequencies?

A Column A

B Column B

C Column C

D Column D

9 Which statement best tells the ways in which light interacts with matter?

A Light can come from the sun, fire, or a light bulb.

B Light waves can be reflected, refracted, or absorbed by matter.

C Laser light goes through matter, and all other light gets stopped by matter.

D Only visible light can interact with matter.

10 Waves of red light and yellow light go through air and strike a piece of glass. The diagram shows how the two kinds of light interact with the glass.

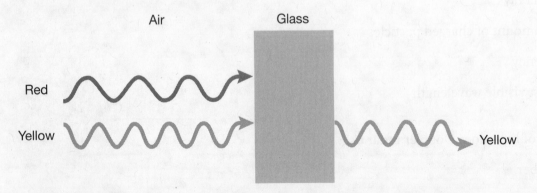

Which statement describes how the glass interacts with red and yellow light?

A The glass absorbs red light and transmits yellow light.

B The glass transmits red light and absorbs yellow light.

C The glass reflects both red and yellow light.

D The glass transmits both red and yellow light.

11 Use the graph to answer the following question.

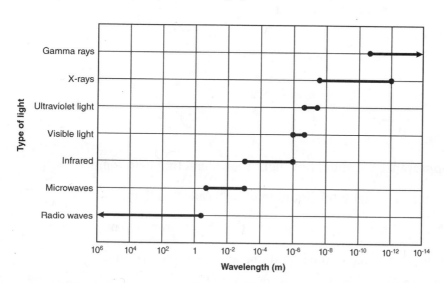

How would you classify an electromagnetic (EM) wave that has a longer wavelength than infrared light?

A as an x-ray

B as a gamma ray

C as a radio wave

D as ultraviolet light

12 The electromagnetic spectrum includes all electromagnetic waves, from radio waves with long wavelengths and low frequencies to gamma rays with short wavelengths and high frequencies. Which statement best describes how fast these waves travel in a vacuum?

A Gamma rays travel much faster than others because they have the highest frequencies.

B High frequency waves travel somewhat faster than low frequency waves.

C Infrared waves travel faster than ultraviolet waves.

D All electromagnetic waves travel at the same speed.

13 When Juan shined a light through the liquid in glass A and then glass B, he saw that the liquids in the two glasses looked different.

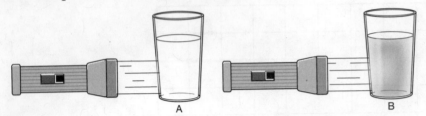

What did the liquids' appearance tell about how light was interacting with them?

A The liquid in glass A absorbed light; the liquid in glass B reflected light.

B The liquid in glass A was transparent; the liquid in glass B was translucent.

C The liquid in glass A was translucent; the liquid in glass B was transparent.

D The liquids looked different because the liquid in glass A scattered more light than the liquid in glass B.

Critical Thinking

Answer the following questions in the space provided.

14 Explain why a black asphalt road becomes hotter than a white cement sidewalk in the same amount of sunlight.

_____

_____

15 How fast do different parts of the electromagnetic (EM) spectrum travel in a vacuum?

_____

_____

Connect **ESSENTIAL QUESTIONS**
Lessons 1, 2, and 3

Answer the following question in the space provided.

16 Give two examples of natural light and two examples of artificial light. How is natural light transmitted? How is artificial light produced?

_____

_____

_____

Life over Time

Big Idea

The types and characteristics of organisms change over time.

8.LS4.1, 8.LS4.2, 8.LS4.3, 8.LS4.4, 8.LS4.5, 8.ESS2.1

Fossils provide valuable information about life over time. Some species, such as the ginkgo tree, have lived on Earth for millions of years.

Modern ginkgo leaf

What do you think?

Over Earth's history, life forms change as the environment changes. What kinds of organisms lived in your area during prehistoric times?

Unit 6
Life over Time

Prehistoric Life

Scientists have learned a lot about prehistoric times from fossils. We know that life on Earth was very different in the geologic past, and that it changes over time. A changing environment causes changes in the types of organisms that are able to survive.

Jurassic Period
206 mya–140 mya

The central United States was covered by a huge ocean during the age of the dinosaurs! Many fossils from that time period are from aquatic organisms.

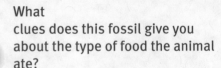

Mosasaurs found in the Midwest are fossils of extinct marine reptiles.

What clues does this fossil give you about the type of food the animal ate?

Wood fossilizes when minerals replace all the organic material.

Mammals such as this saber-toothed cat once roamed Indiana grasslands.

Great white egrets live in Indiana's wetlands.

Tertiary Period
65 mya–2 mya

Land began to emerge from the water. Early mammals and some plants left many kinds of fossils behind, telling us a lot about this period.

Early Holocene
12,000–10,000 years ago

As humans occupied the land, many large animals, including mammoths, mastodons, saber-toothed cats, and giant sloths, disappeared.

Present Day

Humans have a large impact on the organisms living in the Midwest. Some species, such as the piping plover, are threatened with extinction due to human activities. Protecting these species helps to ensure that Midwestern habitats will remain diverse.

Take It Home — Your Neighborhood over Time

Your neighborhood has also changed over time. Do some research to find out when your town was founded. Create a timeline similar to the one above that shows the details of what changes your neighborhood and town might have experienced in the time since it was founded. See *ScienceSaurus*® for more information about change and diversity of life.

Introduction to Living Things

ESSENTIAL QUESTION

What are living things?

By the end of this lesson, you should be able to describe the necessities of life and the characteristics that all living things share.

Living things need energy to survive. This bluebird gets energy by eating insects like this dragonfly.

Engage Your Brain

1 Compare Both of these pictures show living things. How are these living things different?

_____

_____

_____

_____

_____

2 List Many of the things that people need to stay alive are not found in space. List the things that the International Space Station must have to keep astronauts alive.

_____

_____

_____

_____

_____

_____

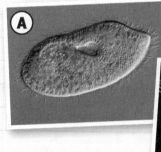

A

B

Active Reading

3 Synthesize Many English words have their roots in other languages. Use the Greek words below to make an educated guess about the meaning of the word _homeostasis_.

Greek word	Meaning
hómoios	similar
stásis	standing still

Example sentence
On a hot day, your body sweats to maintain <u>homeostasis</u>.

homeostasis:

_____

_____

_____

Vocabulary Terms
- cell
- stimulus
- homeostasis
- DNA
- sexual reproduction
- asexual reproduction

4 Identify This list contains the vocabulary terms you'll learn in this lesson. As you read, underline the definition of each term.

Share and Share Alike

What characteristics do living things share?

An amazing variety of living things exists on Earth. These living things may seem very different, but they are all alike in several ways. What does a dog have in common with a bacterium? What does a fish have in common with a mushroom? There are five characteristics that all living things share.

Living Things Are Made of Cells

All living things are made of one or more cells. A **cell** is a membrane-covered structure that contains all of the materials necessary for life. Cells are the smallest unit of life, which means they are the smallest structures that can perform life functions. Most cells are so small they cannot be seen without a microscope. The membrane that surrounds a cell separates the cell's contents from its environment. Unicellular organisms are made up of only one cell. Multicellular organisms are made up of more than one cell. Some of these organisms have trillions of cells! Cells in a multicellular organism usually perform specialized functions.

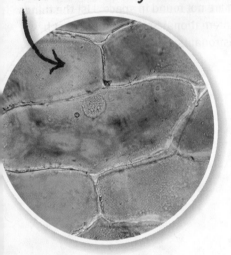

This is a microscopic view of cells in an onion root. An onion has many cells, so it is a multicellular organism.

Visualize It!

5 Categorize Identify each organism in the picture as unicellular or multicellular.

I'm an amoeba. I am:
☐ unicellular ☐ multicellular

I'm a cattail. I am:
☐ unicellular ☐ multicellular

I'm a turtle. I am:
☐ unicellular ☐ multicellular

Living Things Respond to Their Environment

All living things have the ability to sense change in their environment and to respond to that change. A change that affects the activity of an organism is called a **stimulus** (plural: stimuli). A stimulus can be gravity, light, sound, a chemical, hunger, or anything else that causes an organism to respond in some way. For example, when your pupils are exposed to light—a stimulus—they become smaller—a response.

Even though an organism's outside environment may change, conditions inside its body must stay relatively constant. Many chemical reactions keep an organism alive. These reactions can only happen when conditions are exactly right. An organism must maintain stable internal conditions to survive. The maintenance of a stable internal environment is called **homeostasis**. Your body maintains homeostasis by sweating when it gets hot and shivering when it gets cold. Each of these actions keeps the body at a stable internal temperature.

Visualize It!

6 Analyze Why are these sunflowers all facing in the same direction?

_____

_____

_____

_____

Dogs respond to stimuli in their environment.

7 Infer Fill in the response that a dog might have to each stimulus listed in the table.

Stimulus	Response
Hunger	
Hot Day	
Owner with Leash	
Squirrel in Yard	
Friendly Dog	
Stranger	

Living Things Reproduce

How does the world become filled with plants, animals, and other living things? Organisms make other organisms through the process of reproduction. When organisms reproduce, they pass copies of all or part of their DNA to their offspring. **DNA**, or deoxyribonucleic acid, is the genetic material that controls the structure and function of cells. DNA is found in the cells of all living things. Offspring share characteristics with their parents because they receive DNA from their parents.

Living things reproduce in one of two ways. Two parents produce offspring that share the characteristics of both parents through the process of **sexual reproduction**. Each offspring receives part of its DNA from each parent. Most animals and plants reproduce using sexual reproduction.

A single parent produces offspring that are identical to the parent through the process of **asexual reproduction**. Each offspring receives an exact copy of the parent's DNA. Most unicellular organisms and some plants and animals reproduce using asexual reproduction. Two methods of asexual reproduction are binary fission and budding. A unicellular organism splits into two parts during binary fission. During budding, a new organism grows on the parent organism until it is ready to separate.

A father pig is needed to produce piglets.

Visualize It!

9 Identify Use the check boxes to identify which offspring are identical to the parent or parents and which offspring are not identical.

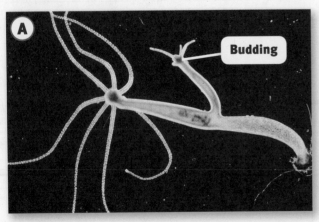

A

Budding

A hydra produces offspring using asexual reproduction.

☐ identical   ☐ not identical

B

A mother pig feeds her piglets. Pigs reproduce using sexual reproduction.

☐ identical   ☐ not identical

Living Things Use Energy

Living things need energy to carry out the activities of life. Energy allows organisms to make or break down food, move materials into and out of cells, and build cells. Energy also allows organisms to move and interact with each other.

Where do living things get the energy they need for the activities of life? Plants convert energy from the sun into food. They store this food in their cells until they need to use it. Organisms that cannot make their own food must eat other organisms to gain energy. Some organisms eat plants. Others eat animals. Organisms such as fungi break down decaying material to gain energy.

10 Describe List three activities that you have done today that require energy.

_____

_____

_____

Living Things Grow and Mature

All living things grow during some period of their lives. When a unicellular organism grows, it gets larger and then divides, forming two cells. When a multicellular organism grows, the number of cells in its body increases, and the organism gets bigger.

Many living things don't just get larger as they grow. They also develop and change. Humans pass through different stages as they mature from childhood to adulthood. During these stages, the human body changes. Frogs and butterflies have body shapes that look completely different during different stages of development.

Visualize It!

11 Describe How does a frog grow and develop? Write a caption for each picture to describe each stage in a frog's life.

Younger Tadpoles (A)

_____

_____

Older Tadpole (B)

_____

_____

Adult Frog (C)

_____

_____

Stayin' Alive

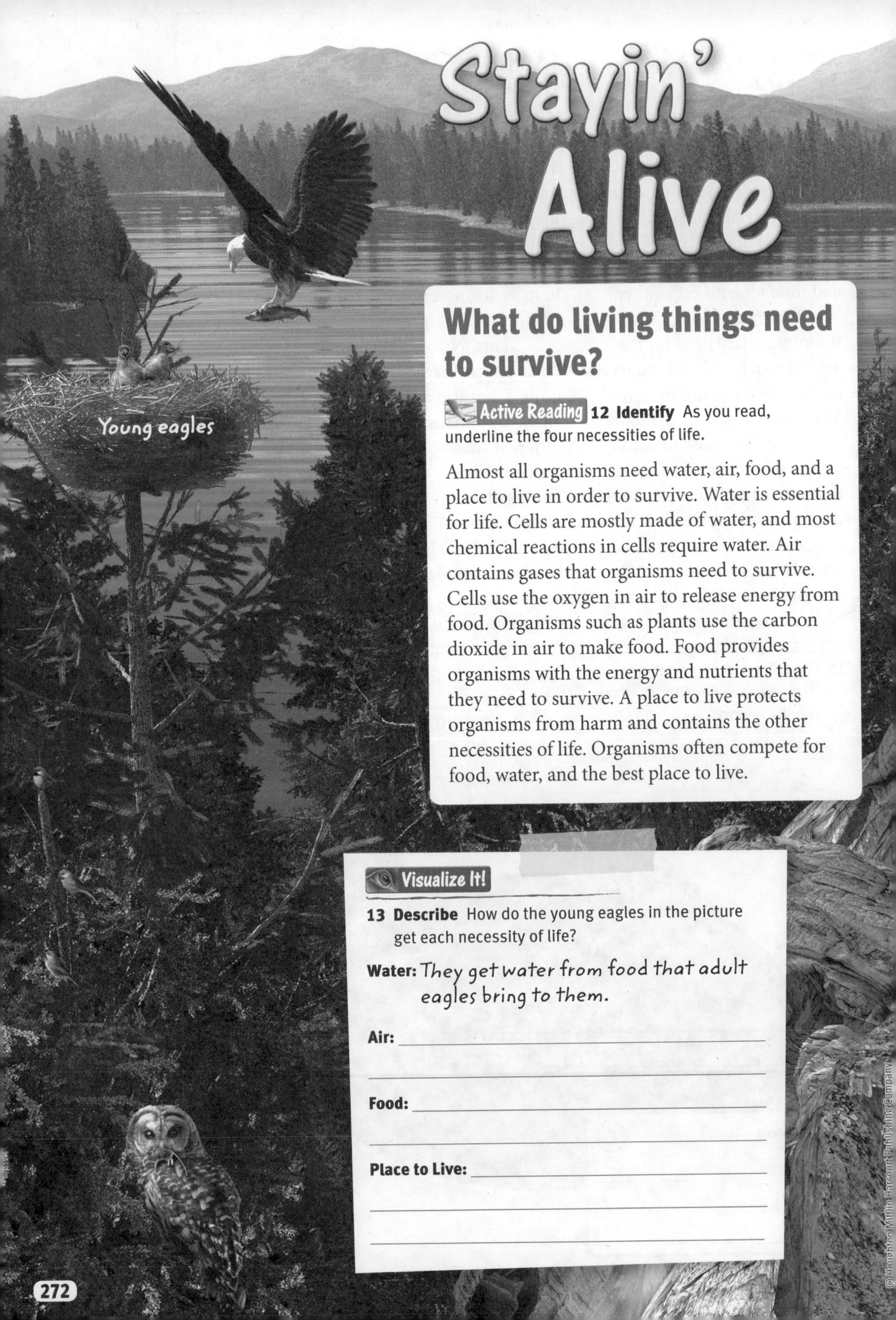

Young eagles

What do living things need to survive?

Active Reading 12 **Identify** As you read, underline the four necessities of life.

Almost all organisms need water, air, food, and a place to live in order to survive. Water is essential for life. Cells are mostly made of water, and most chemical reactions in cells require water. Air contains gases that organisms need to survive. Cells use the oxygen in air to release energy from food. Organisms such as plants use the carbon dioxide in air to make food. Food provides organisms with the energy and nutrients that they need to survive. A place to live protects organisms from harm and contains the other necessities of life. Organisms often compete for food, water, and the best place to live.

Visualize It!

13 Describe How do the young eagles in the picture get each necessity of life?

Water: They get water from food that adult eagles bring to them.

Air: _____

_____

Food: _____

_____

Place to Live: _____

_____

How do living things get food?

Food gives living things the energy and nutrients that they need to perform life processes. Nutrients include carbohydrates, lipids, and proteins. Fruits, vegetables, and grains provide carbohydrates. Nuts and fats provide lipids. Meats, nuts, and vegetables provide proteins.

Not all organisms get food in the same way. Producers make their own food. Consumers eat other organisms to get food. Decomposers break down dead organisms or wastes to get their food. Plants and algae are examples of producers. They use energy from the sun to make food. Animals such as deer are consumers that eat plants. Mice and squirrels are consumers that eat seeds from plants. Owls and eagles are consumers that eat other animals. Worms, bacteria, and fungi are examples of decomposers. They return nutrients to the soil, which other organisms can use.

Visualize It!

14 Describe Look for these four organisms in the picture. How does each organism get its food?

Organism	Classification	Way of Getting Food
Barred Owl	Consumer	Eats mice and other small animals
Earthworm		
Red Squirrel		
Fern		

Visual Summary

To complete this summary, circle the correct word. Then use the key below to check your answers. You can use this page to review the main concepts of the lesson.

Introduction to Living Things

All living things are made of cells that contain DNA. Living things use energy, grow and develop, and reproduce. They also respond to changes in their environment.

15 Sunlight is an example of (a) homeostasis / stimulus.

16 Binary fission is an example of asexual / sexual reproduction.

Almost all living things need water, air, food, and a place to live.

17 Plants are producers / consumers.

18 Decomposers return organisms / nutrients to the environment.

Answers: 15 stimulus; 16 asexual; 17 producers; 18 nutrients

19 **Hypothesize** How do some producers and consumers each rely on light from the sun?

Lesson Review

Vocabulary

In your own words, define the following terms.

1 homeostasis

_____

_____

2 asexual reproduction

_____

_____

3 cell

_____

_____

Key Concepts

4 Explain What is the relationship between a stimulus and a response?

_____

_____

_____

_____

5 Describe What happens to DNA during sexual reproduction?

_____

_____

_____

_____

6 Contrast What are the differences between producers, consumers, and decomposers?

_____

_____

_____

_____

Critical Thinking

Use the pictures to answer the questions below.

7 Describe What is happening to the birds in the picture above?

_____

_____

_____

_____

8 Explain How do nutrients and energy allow the changes shown in the picture to happen?

_____

_____

_____

_____

_____

9 Compare How is a fish similar to an oak tree?

_____

_____

_____

10 Making Inferences Could life as we know it exist on Earth if air contained only oxygen? Explain.

_____

_____

_____

_____

My Notes

The Process of Natural Selection

ESSENTIAL QUESTION

What is the process of natural selection?

By the end of this lesson, you should be able to describe the role of genetic and environmental factors in the process of natural selection.

8.LS4.3, 8.LS4.4

Because this grass snake's skin color looks like the plant stalk, it is able to hide from predators! This form of camouflage is the result of natural selection.

Lesson Labs

Quick Labs
- Model Natural Selection
- Analyzing Survival Adaptations
- The Opposable Thumb

Exploration Lab
- Environmental Change and Evolution

Engage Your Brain

1 Predict Check T or F to show whether you think each statement is true or false.

T   F

☐ ☐ Fur color can help prevent an animal from being eaten.

☐ ☐ The amount of available food can affect an organism's survival.

☐ ☐ Your parents' characteristics are not passed on to you.

☐ ☐ A species can go extinct if its habitat is destroyed.

2 Infer How do you think this bird and this flower are related? Explain your answer.

_____

_____

_____

_____

Active Reading

3 Synthesize You can often define an unknown word by clues provided in the sentence. Use the sentence below to make an educated guess about the meaning of the word *artificial*.

Example sentence:
Many people prefer real sugar to <u>artificial</u> sweeteners made by humans.

artificial:

_____

_____

_____

Vocabulary Terms

- evolution
- artificial selection
- natural selection
- variation
- mutation
- adaptation
- extinction

4 Apply As you learn the definition of each vocabulary term in this lesson, create your own definition or sketch to help you remember the meaning of the term.

Darwin's Voyage

What did Darwin observe?

Charles Darwin was born in England in 1809. When he was 22 years old, Darwin graduated from college with a degree in theology. But he was also interested in plants and animals. Darwin became the naturalist—a scientist who studies nature—on the British ship HMS *Beagle*.

During his voyage, Darwin observed and collected many living and fossil specimens. He made some of his most important observations on the Galápagos Islands of South America. He kept a log that was later published as *The Voyage of the Beagle*. With the observations he made on this almost five-year journey, Darwin formed his idea about how biological evolution could happen.

In biology, **evolution** refers to the process by which populations change over time. A population is all of the individuals of a species that live in an area at the same time. A species is a group of closely related organisms that can mate to produce fertile offspring. Darwin developed a hypothesis, which eventually became a theory, of how evolution takes place.

Darwin left England on December 27, 1831. He returned 5 years later.

ENGLAND

EUROPE

NORTH AMERICA

ATLANTIC OCEAN

AFRICA

The plants and animals on the Galápagos Islands differed from island to island. This is where Darwin studied birds called finches.

Galápagos Islands

Equator

SOUTH AMERICA

Cape of Good Hope

Think Outside the Book Inquiry

5 Explore Trace Darwin's route on the map, and choose one of the following stops on his journey: Galápagos Islands, Andes Mountains, Australia. Do research to find out what plants and animals live there. Then write an entry in Darwin's log to describe what he might have seen.

Differences among Species

Darwin collected birds from the Galápagos Islands and nearby islands. He observed that these birds differed slightly from those on the nearby mainland of South America. And the birds on each island were different from the birds on the other islands. Careful analysis back in England revealed that they were all finches! Eventually, Darwin suggested that these birds may have evolved from one species of finch.

Darwin observed differences in beak size among finches from different islands. Many years later, scientists confirmed that these differences related to the birds' diets. Birds with shorter, heavier beaks could eat harder foods than those with thinner beaks.

This cactus finch has a narrow beak that it can use in many ways, including to pull grubs and insects from holes in the cactus.

This vegetarian finch has a curved beak, ideal for taking large berries from a branch.

Visualize It!

6 Infer How do you think the pointed beak of this woodpecker finch helps it to get food?

_____

_____

_____

Woodpecker finch

ASIA

INDIAN OCEAN

Darwin saw many plants and animals that were found only on certain continents such as Australia.

AUSTRALIA

Equator

NEW ZEALAND

km 0   1,000 2,000
mi 0   1,000   2,000

Darwin's Homework

What other ideas influenced Darwin?

The ideas of many scientists and observations of the natural world influenced Darwin's thinking. Darwin drew on ideas about Earth's history, the growth of populations, and observations of how traits are passed on in selective breeding. All of these pieces helped him develop his ideas about how populations could change over time.

This chicken has been bred to have large tail feathers and a big red comb.

Organisms Pass Traits On to Offspring

Farmers and breeders have been producing many kinds of domestic animals and plants for thousands of years. These plants and animals have traits that the farmers and breeders desire. A *trait* is a form of an inherited characteristic. For example, the length of tail feathers is an inherited characteristic, and short or long tail feathers are the corresponding traits. The practice by which humans select plants or animals for breeding based on desired traits is **artificial selection**. Artificial selection shows that traits can change. Traits can also spread through populations.

This chicken has been bred to have large head feathers.

7 List Darwin studied artificial selection in the pigeons that he bred. List three other domestic animals that have many different breeds.

_____

_____

_____

_____

_____

This chicken has been bred to have feathers on its feet.

© Houghton Mifflin Harcourt Publishing Company • Image Credits: (t) ©Dorling Kindersley/Getty Images; (c) ©Joel Sartore/National Geographic/Getty Images; (b) ©Purestock/Getty Images

8 Identify As you read, underline the names of other important thinkers who influenced Darwin's ideas.

Organisms Acquire Traits

Scientist Jean-Baptiste Lamarck thought that organisms could acquire and pass on traits they needed to survive. For example, a man could develop stronger muscles over time. If the muscles were an advantage in his environment, Lamarck thought the man would pass on this trait to his offspring. Now we know that acquired traits are not passed on to offspring because these traits do not become part of an organism's DNA. But the fact that species change, and the idea that an organism's traits help it survive, shaped Darwin's ideas.

9 Apply Explain why the size of your muscles is partly an acquired trait and partly dependent on DNA.

_____

_____

_____

_____

These rock layers formed over millions of years.

Earth Changes over Time

The presence of different rock layers, such as those in the photo, show that Earth has changed over time. Geologist Charles Lyell hypothesized that small changes in Earth's surface have occurred over hundreds of millions of years. Darwin reasoned that if Earth were very old, then there would be enough time for very small changes in life forms to add up.

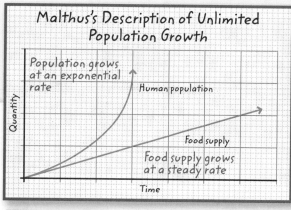

A Struggle for Survival Exists

After his journey, Darwin read an essay about population growth by economist Thomas Malthus. The essay helped Darwin understand how the environment could influence which organisms survive and which organisms die. All populations are affected by factors that limit population growth, such as disease, predation, and competition for food. Darwin reasoned that the survivors probably have traits that help them survive and that some of these traits could be passed on from parent to offspring.

Visualize It!

10 Summarize What can you conclude from the two red growth lines on this graph?

_____

_____

_____

Natural Selection

What are the four parts of natural selection?

Darwin proposed that most evolution happens through the natural selection of advantageous traits. **Natural selection** is the process by which organisms that inherit advantageous traits tend to reproduce more successfully than other organisms do.

Overproduction

When a plant or animal reproduces, it usually makes more offspring than the environment can support. For example, a female jaguar may have up to four pups at a time. Only some of them will survive to adulthood, and a smaller number of them will successfully reproduce.

---

11 Infer A fish may have hundreds of offspring at a time, and only a small number will survive. Which characteristics of fish might allow them to survive?

_____

_____

_____

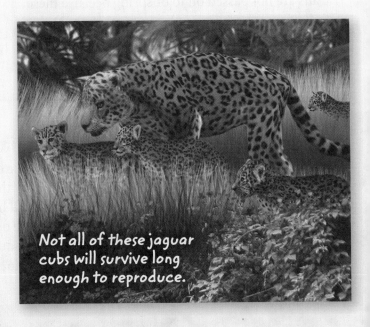

Not all of these jaguar cubs will survive long enough to reproduce.

Variation exists in the jaw sizes of these two jaguars. This variation will be passed on to the next generation.

Genetic Variation

Within a species there are naturally occurring differences, or **variations**, in traits. For example, in the two jaguar skulls to the left, one jaw is larger than the other. This difference results from a difference in the genetic material of the jaguars. Genetic variations can be passed on from parent to offspring. An important source of variation is a **mutation**, or change in genetic material.

As each new generation is produced, genetic variation may be introduced into a population. The more genetic variation in a population, the more likely it is that some individuals might have traits that will be advantageous if the environment changes. Also, genetic variation can lead to diversity of organisms as a population adapts to changing environments.

Selection

Individuals try to get the resources they need to survive. These resources include food, water, space and, in most cases, mates for reproduction. About 11,000 years ago, jaguars faced a shortage of food because the climate changed and many prey species died out. A genetic variation in jaw size then became important for survival. Jaguars with larger jaws could eat hard-shelled reptiles when other prey were hard to find.

Darwin reasoned that individuals with a particular trait, such as a large jaw, are more likely to survive long enough to reproduce. As a result, the trait is "selected" for, becoming more common in the next generation of offspring.

A larger jaw makes it easier for this jaguar to eat hard-shelled turtles.

12 Summarize How did large jaws and teeth become typical traits of jaguars?

_____

_____

_____

Adaptation

An inherited trait that helps an organism survive and reproduce in its environment is an **adaptation**. Adaptation is the selection of naturally occurring trait variations in populations. Jaguars with larger jaws were able to survive and reproduce when food was hard to find. As natural selection continues, adaptations grow more common in the population with each new generation. Over time, the population becomes better adapted to the environment.

Large jaw size is one adaptation of jaguars.

13 Explain In the table below, explain how each part of natural selection works.

Principle of natural selection	How it works
overproduction	
genetic variation	
selection	
adaptation	

Well-adapted

How do species change over time?

In order for a population to change, some individuals have to be different from other members of the population. Mutations are one of the main sources of genetic variation. Offspring sometimes inherit a gene that has a slight mutation, or change, from the gene the parent has. Mutations can be harmful, helpful, or have no effect. Beneficial mutations help individuals survive and reproduce.

Over Generations, Adaptations Become More Common

Active Reading **14 Identify** Underline examples of adaptations.

Adaptations are inherited traits that help organisms survive and reproduce. Some adaptations, such as a duck's webbed feet, are internal or external structures. Other adaptations are inherited behaviors that help an organism find food, protect itself, or reproduce. At first, an adaptation is rare in a population. Imagine a bird population in which some birds have short beaks. If more birds with shorter beaks survive and reproduce than birds with longer beaks, more birds in the next generation will probably have short beaks. The number of individuals with the adaptation would continue to increase.

Visualize It!

15 Write a caption to describe how this butterfly's long mouth part helps it to survive.

_____

_____

_____

Genetic Differences Add Up

Parents and offspring often have small differences in genetic material. Over many generations, the small differences can add up. These differences accumulate so that organisms alive now are often very different from their ancestors. As a result, there is great diversity among organisms. For example, the antibiotic penicillin was able to kill many types of bacteria in the 1950s. Today, some of those species of bacteria are now completely resistant to penicillin. The genetic makeup of these bacterial populations has changed. New fossil discoveries and new information about genes add to scientists' understanding of natural selection and evolution.

The male frigate bird uses his red throat pouch to attract a female, which could lead to reproduction.

What happens to species as the environment changes?

Certain environments favor certain traits. Consider a snake population with either brown- or green-colored snakes. In a forest that has many dead leaves on the ground, brown snakes will blend in better than green snakes will. But in an area with more grass, the green snakes may be better at hiding from predators. Changes in environmental conditions can affect the survival of organisms with a particular trait. Environmental changes can also lead to diversity of organisms by increasing the number of species.

Dinosaurs went extinct 65 million years ago.

Adaptations Can Allow a Species to Survive

All organisms have traits that allow them to survive in specific environments. For example, plants have xylem tissue that carries water up from the roots to the rest of the plant.

If the environment changes, a species is more likely to survive if it has genetic variation. For example, imagine a species of grass in which some plants need less water than others. If the environment became drier, many grass plants would die, but the plants that needed less water might survive. These plants might eventually become a new species if they cannot reproduce with the plants that needed more water.

Some Species May Become Extinct

If no individuals have traits that help them to survive and reproduce in the changed environment, a species will become extinct. **Extinction** occurs when all members of a species have died. Greater competition, new predators, and the loss of habitat are examples of environmental changes that can lead to extinction. Some extinctions are caused by natural disasters. Because a natural disaster can destroy resources quickly, organisms may die no matter what adaptations they have. The fossil record shows that many species have become extinct in the history of life on Earth.

Visualize It!

Environmental change has affected the environmental conditions near the North Pole.

16 Summarize How has ice cover near the North Pole changed in the last few decades?

_____

_____

17 Infer How do you think this environmental change will affect species that live in the surrounding area?

_____

_____

_____

Bering Sea

km 0   300   600
mi 0   300   600

ASIA

Minimum ice cover
☐ 1979–2000 median
☐ 2005
☐ 2007

+ North Pole

Barents Sea

EUROPE

NORTH AMERICA

Baffin Bay

Norwegian Sea

Source: National Aeronautics and Space Administration, 2007

Machimosaurus rex

Scientists who study the evolution of organisms look at phenotypes to better understand how an organism survived in its environment over time. A phenotype includes all of the traits of an animal or plant, such as physical characteristics and behaviors. For example, an elephant's phenotypes would include the length of its trunk, the shape of its tusks, the size of its body, and the use of its long trunk to spray water on itself.

Skills

✓ Analyze evidence

✓ Develop a scientific conclusion using evidence

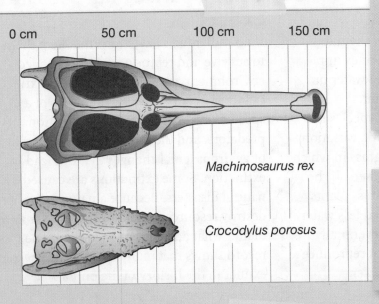

0 cm   50 cm   100 cm   150 cm

Machimosaurus rex

Crocodylus porosus

The fossils of *Machimosaurus rex* were dated to be from 125-135 Mya. It is believed that there was a massive eruption of lava around 200 mya, causing many marine species to become extinct.

Scientists can look at the skulls of modern crocodiles (*Crocodylus porosus*) and compare them to the fossils of ancient crocodiles like *Machimosaurus rex*.

Crocodylus porosus

Then and Now

In 2016, the fossil of a crocodile was discovered in a desert in Tunisia. Over 30 feet long, the ancient animal was massive. Its head alone was about five feet in length! Recently named *Machimosaurus rex*, it lived millions of years ago near the sea.

It was a saltwater animal that survived by eating other sea creatures. In addition to its big body, it had short, rounded teeth with strong jaws that could take a big bite! It mostly ate a variety of animals, including ancient sea turtles. This crocodile of long ago was likely an "ambush predator." That means it hid and waited for the right moment to strike to catch a meal.

How does the *Machimosaurus rex* compare to saltwater crocodiles living now? Today's crocodiles that live by the sea are big. They're the biggest members of the crocodilian family and males can be up to 17 feet long. To feed, they tend to wait patiently in the water just out of sight. When potential prey arrives to get a drink, the crocodile leaps out and attacks!

The chart show how the shapes and sizes of *Machimosaurus rex* and the modern saltwater crocodile compare to each other and to an adult male.

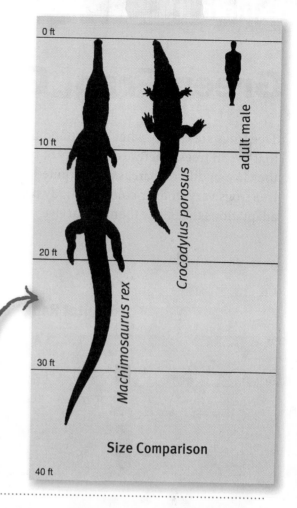

Size Comparison

Analysis

1. Take a closer look at the different images and descriptions. Which traits does the saltwater crocodile of today have in common with its ancient ancestor? What is similar about their phenotypes?

_____

_____

_____

_____

2. What is different about the two organisms? Using the different types of evidence, explain how the phenotypes of the crocodile helped the species survive changes in the environment and resulted in adaptation.

_____

_____

_____

_____

_____

_____

Green Frog, Gray Frog

Tree frogs are exactly what they sound like. They are frogs that live in trees. There are a variety of types of tree frogs and they live in different areas of the United States. Populations of tree frogs vary in their color and body parts. All tree frogs have adaptations that allow them to survive in their environments.

Skills

✓ Analyze evidence

✓ Develop a scientific explanation using evidence

Habitat Range of Green and Gray Tree Frogs

Green Tree Frog   Gray and Green Tree Frog   Gray Tree Frog

① Study these maps that show the distribution of the habitats for two types of tree frogs. Where do green tree frogs live? Where do gray tree frogs live?

_____

_____

_____

_____

_____

_____

_____

_____

Green and gray tree frogs have some characteristics in common. For example, they both need water and plants to survive. Some regions where they live overlap and both are hunted by snakes and birds. However, they differ in a number of important ways, including their habitat and appearance.

Green Tree Frogs

Green tree frogs tend to live in wetland areas. They make a home among the vegetation found in marshes or near lakes and streams. They can be found clinging to tall grasses or leaves.

2 Describe the green tree frog's appearance.

_____

_____

_____

_____

_____

3 Describe the environment of the green tree frog seen here.

_____

_____

_____

_____

4 How does the green tree frog's appearance compare to its environment?

_____

_____

_____

_____

_____

_____

Gray Tree Frogs

On the other hand, gray tree frogs tend to live in wooded areas, thick with bark-covered trees. These areas have smaller or temporary bodies of water, unlike the wetlands where green tree frogs are found.

Gray Tree Frog

5 Describe the gray tree frog's appearance.

_____

_____

_____

_____

6 Describe the environment of the gray tree frog seen here.

_____

_____

_____

_____

7 How does the gray tree frog's appearance compare to its environment?

_____

_____

_____

_____

_____

_____

_____

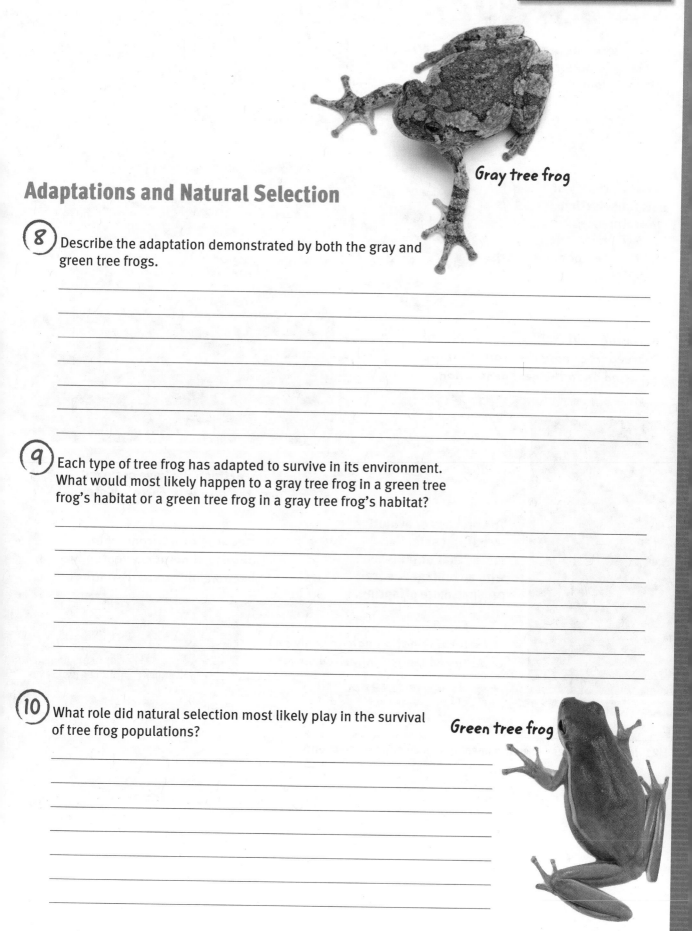

Gray tree frog

Adaptations and Natural Selection

(8) Describe the adaptation demonstrated by both the gray and green tree frogs.

_____

_____

_____

_____

_____

_____

_____

(9) Each type of tree frog has adapted to survive in its environment. What would most likely happen to a gray tree frog in a green tree frog's habitat or a green tree frog in a gray tree frog's habitat?

_____

_____

_____

_____

_____

_____

_____

(10) What role did natural selection most likely play in the survival of tree frog populations?

Green tree frog

_____

_____

_____

_____

_____

_____

Visual Summary

To complete this summary, circle the correct word. Then use the key below to check your answers. You can use this page to review the main concepts of the lesson.

Evolution is Change over Time

Darwin's theory of natural selection was influenced by his own observations and the work of other scientists.

18 Through natural / artificial selection, breeders choose the traits that are passed on to the next generation.

The process of evolution by natural selection states that organisms with advantageous traits produce more offspring.

19 Natural selection can act only on acquired traits / inherited variation.

Many extinctions have occurred over the course of Earth's history.

20 Because of environmental change, dinosaurs eventually became mutated / extinct.

Answers: 18 artificial; 19 inherited variation; 20 extinct

21 **Infer** How does the environment influence natural selection?

Lesson Review

Vocabulary

Use a term from the lesson to complete the sentences below.

1 The four parts of natural selection are overproduction, _____, selection, and adaptation.

2 _____ is the process by which populations change over time.

3 The hollow bones of birds, which keep birds lightweight for flying, is an example of a(n) _____

Key Concepts

4 Summarize Describe Darwin's observations on the Galápagos islands during his voyage on the HMS *Beagle*.

_____

_____

_____

_____

5 Explain How does environmental change affect the survival of a species?

_____

_____

_____

_____

6 Compare Why are only inherited traits, not acquired ones, involved in the process of natural selection?

_____

_____

_____

7 Describe What is the relationship between mutation, natural selection, and adaptation?

_____

_____

_____

_____

Critical Thinking

Use the diagram to answer the following question.

8 Apply How is each of these lizards adapted to its environment?

_____

_____

_____

_____

_____

_____

_____

9 Infer What might happen to a population of rabbits in a forest if a new predator moved to the forest?

_____

_____

_____

_____

_____

_____

My Notes

Lesson 3

Evidence of Common Ancestry

ESSENTIAL QUESTION

What evidence supports the concept of common ancestry?

By the end of this lesson, you should be able to describe the evidence that supports the concept that species have common ancestors.

8.LS4.1, 8.LS4.2, 8.LS.4.3

Fossils show us what a dinosaur looks like. This dinosaur lived millions of years ago!

Lesson Labs

Quick Labs
• Comparing Anatomy
• Genetic Evidence for Evolution

Field Lab
• Mystery Footprints

Engage Your Brain

1 Predict Check T or F to show whether you think each statement is true or false.

T	F	
☐	☐	Fossils provide evidence of organisms that lived in the past.
☐	☐	The wing of a bat has similar bones to those in a human arm.
☐	☐	DNA can tell us how closely related two organisms are.
☐	☐	Whales are descended from land-dwelling mammals.

2 Infer This is a Petoskey stone, which is made up of tiny coral fossils. What can you infer if you find a coral fossil on land?

Petoskey stone

_____
_____
_____
_____

Active Reading

3 Synthesize You can often define an unknown word if you understand the parts of the word. Use the words below to make an educated guess about the meaning of the word *fossil record*.

Word	Meaning
fossil	the remains or trace of once-living organisms
record	an account that preserves information about facts or events

fossil record:

_____
_____
_____

Vocabulary Terms

• fossil   • fossil record

4 Apply As you learn the definition of each vocabulary term in this lesson, create your own definition or sketch to help you remember the meaning of the term.

Fossil Hunt

How do fossils form?

Evidence that organisms have changed over time can be found in amber, ice, or sedimentary rock. Sedimentary rock is formed when particles of sand or soil are deposited in horizontal layers. Often this occurs as mud or silt hardens. After one rock layer forms, newer rock layers form on top of it. So, older layers are found below or underneath younger rock layers. The most basic principle of dating such rocks and the remains of organisms inside is "the deeper it is, the older it is."

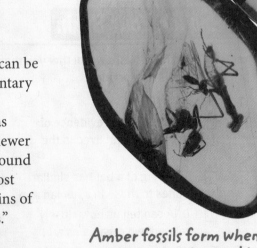

Amber fossils form when small creatures are trapped in tree sap and the sap hardens.

5 Examine What features of the organism are preserved in amber?

_____

_____

_____

This flying dinosaur is an example of a cast fossil.

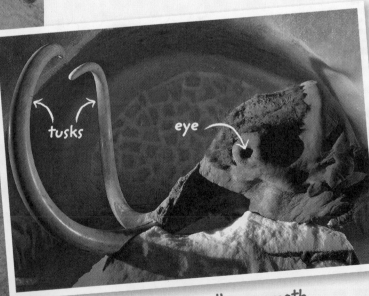

tusks

eye

Because this woolly mammoth was frozen in ice, its skin and hair were preserved.

Many Fossils Form in Sedimentary Rock

Rock layers preserve evidence of organisms that were once alive. The remains or imprints of once-living organisms are called **fossils**. Fossils commonly form when a dead organism is covered by a layer of sediment or mud. Over time, more sediment settles on top of the organism. Minerals in the sediment may seep into the organism and replace the body's material with minerals that harden over time. This process produces a cast fossil. Many familiar fossils are casts of hard parts, such as shells and bones. If the organism rots away completely after being covered, it may leave an imprint of itself in the rock. Despite all of the fossils that have been found, it is rare for an organism to become a fossil. Most often, the dead organism is recycled back into the biological world by scavengers, decomposers, or the process of weathering.

 **Active Reading**

6 Identify As you read, underline the steps that describe how a cast fossil forms.

How do fossils show change over time?

All of the fossils that have been discovered make up the **fossil record**. The fossil record provides evidence about the order in which species have existed through time, and how they have changed over time. By examining the fossil record, scientists can learn about the history of life on Earth.

Despite all the fossils that have been found, there are gaps in the fossil record. These gaps represent chunks of geologic time for which a fossil has not been discovered. Also, the transition between two groups of organisms may not be well understood. Fossils that help fill in these gaps are *transitional fossils*. The illustration on the right is based on a transitional fossil.

Fossils found in newer layers of Earth's crust tend to have physical or molecular similarities to present-day organisms. These similarities indicate that the fossilized organisms were close relatives of the present-day organisms. Fossils from older layers are less similar to present-day organisms than fossils from newer layers are. Most older fossils are of earlier life-forms such as dinosaurs, which don't exist anymore.

Visualize It!

A transitional form between fish and four-legged land vertebrates may be this creature called *Tiktaalik roseae*.

7 Identify Describe the environment in which this organism lives.

_____

_____

8 Infer How is this organism like both a fish and a four-legged vertebrate, such as an amphibian?

_____

_____

Image Credits: ©Zina Deretsky, National Science Foundation

More clues . . . .

What other evidence supports evolution?

Many fields of study provide evidence that modern species and extinct species share an ancestor. A *common ancestor* is the most recent species from which two different species have evolved. Structural data, DNA, developmental patterns, and fossils all support the theory that populations change over time. Sometimes these populations become new species. Biologists observe that all living organisms have some traits in common and inherit traits in similar ways. Evidence of when and where those ancestors lived and what they looked like is found in the fossil record.

Active Reading

9 List What is a common ancestor?

Common Structures

Scientists have found that related organisms share structural traits. Structures reduced in size or function may have been complete and functional in the organism's ancestor. For example, snakes have traces of leglike structures that are not used for movement. These unused structures are evidence that snakes share a common ancestor with animals like lizards and dogs.

Scientists also consider similar structures with different functions. The arm of a human, the front leg of a cat, and the wing of a bat do not look alike and are not used in the same way. But as you can see, they are similar in structure. The bones of a human arm are similar in structure to the bones in the front limbs of a cat and a bat. These similarities suggest that cats, bats, and humans had a common ancestor. Over millions of years, changes occurred. Now, these bones perform different functions in each type of animal.

front limb of a bat

front limb of a cat

Visualize It!

10 Relate Do you see any similarities between the bones of the bat and cat limbs and the bones of the human arm? If so, use the colors of the bat and cat bones to color similar bones in the human arm. If you don't have colored pencils, label the bones with the correct color names.

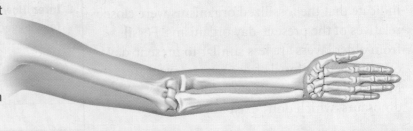

Similar DNA

The genetic information stored in an organism's DNA determines the organism's traits. Because an organism's DNA stays almost exactly the same throughout its entire lifetime, scientists can compare the DNA from many organisms. The greater the number of similarities between the molecules of any two species, the more recently the two species most likely shared a common ancestor.

Recall that DNA determines which amino acids make up a protein. Scientists have compared the amino acids that make up cytochrome c proteins in many species. Cytochrome c is involved in cellular respiration. Organisms that have fewer amino acid differences are more likely to be closely related.

Frogs also have cytochrome c proteins, but they're a little different from yours.

Cytochrome C Comparison	
Organism	Number of amino acid differences from human cytochrome c
Chimpanzee	0
Rhesus monkey	1
Whale	10
Turtle	15
Bullfrog	18
Lamprey	20

Source: M.Dayhoff, *Atlas of Protein Sequence and Structure*

👁 **Visualize It!**

11 Infer The number of amino acids in human cytochrome c differs between humans and the species at left. Which two species do you infer are the least closely related to humans?

_____

_____

_____

_____

Developmental Similarities

The study of development is called *embryology*. Embryos undergo many physical and functional changes as they grow and develop. If organisms develop in similar ways, they also likely share a common ancestor.

Scientists have compared the development of different species to look for similar patterns and structures. Scientists think that such similarities come from an ancestor that the species have in common. For example, at some time during development, all animals with backbones have a tail. This observation suggests that they shared a common ancestor.

These embryos are at a similar stage of development.

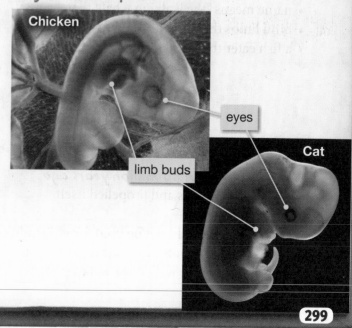

Chicken

eyes

Cat

limb buds

How do we know organisms are related?

Scientists examine organisms carefully for clues about their ancestors. In a well-studied example, scientists looked at the characteristics of whales that made them different from other ocean animals. Unlike fish and sharks, whales breathe air, give birth to live young, and produce milk. Fossil and DNA evidence support the hypothesis that modern whales evolved from hoofed mammals that lived on land.

Fossil Evidence

Scientists have examined fossils of extinct species that have features in between whales and land mammals. None of these species are directly related to modern whales, but are called *transitional forms*. Their skeletons suggest how a gradual transition from land mammal to aquatic whale could have happened.

Ⓐ Pakicetus   52 million years ago
- whale-shaped skull and teeth adapted for hunting fish
- ran on four legs
- ear bones in between those of land and aquatic mammals

Ⓑ Ambulocetus natans   50 million years ago
- name means "the walking whale that swims"
- hind limbs that were adapted for swimming
- a fish eater that lived on water and on land

Ⓒ Dorudon   About 40 million years ago
- lived in warm seas and propelled itself with a long tail
- tiny hind legs could not be used for swimming
- pelvis and hind limbs not connected to spine, could not support weight for walking

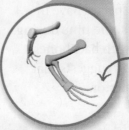

Unused Structures
Most modern whales have pelvic bones and some have leg bones. These bones do not help the animal move.

Molecular Evidence

The DNA of whales is very similar to the DNA of hoofed mammals. Below are some DNA fragments of a gene that makes a type of milk protein.

Hippopotamus   **TCC TGGCA GTCCA GTGGT**
Humpback whale   **CCC TGGCA GTGCA GTGCT**

12 Identify Circle the pairs of nitrogen bases (G, T, C, or A) that differ between the hippopotamus and humpback whale DNA.

13 Infer How do you think these bones are involved in a whale's movement?

_____

_____

_____

D Modern Whale   *Present day*

- no hind limbs, front limbs are flippers
- some whales have tiny hip bones left over from their hoofed-mammal ancestors
- breathe air with lungs like other mammals do

14 Analyze Examine the four skeletons. Indicate which species appears to be best adapted for swimming underwater for a long time. Which characteristics allow the animal to behave this way?

_____

_____

_____

_____

_____

_____

_____

Visual Summary

To complete this summary, circle the correct word. Then use the key below to check your answers. You can use this page to review the main concepts of the lesson.

Evidence of Common Ancestry

Fossil evidence shows that life on Earth has changed over time.

15 The remains of once-living organisms are called fossils / ancestors.

Scientists use evidence from many fields of research to study the common ancestors of living organisms.

Evolutionary theory is also supported by structural, genetic, and developmental evidence.

16 Similarities / Differences in internal structures support evidence of common ancestry.

17 The tiny leg bones / large dorsal fins of modern whales are an example of unused structures.

Answers: 15 fossils; 16 similarities; 17 tiny leg bones

18 Summarize How does the fossil record provide evidence of the diversity of life?

Lesson Review

Vocabulary

1 Which word means "the remains or imprints of once-living organisms found in layers of rock?"

_____

2 Which word means "the history of life in the geologic past as indicated by the imprints or remains of living things?"

_____

Key Concepts

3 Identify What are two types of evidence that suggest that species have changed over time?

_____

_____

_____

4 Explain How do fossils provide evidence that species have changed over time?

_____

_____

_____

5 Apply What is the significance of the similar number and arrangement of bones in a human arm and a bat wing?

_____

_____

_____

_____

_____

Critical Thinking

6 Imagine If you were a scientist examining the DNA sequence of two unknown organisms that you hypothesize share a common ancestor, what evidence would you expect to find?

_____

_____

_____

Use this table to answer the following questions.

Cytochrome C Comparison	
Organism	Number of amino acid differences from human cytochrome c
Chimpanzee	0
Turtle	15
Tuna	21

Source: M. Dayhoff, *Atlas of Protein Sequence and Structure*

7 Identify What does the data suggest about how related turtles are to humans compared to tuna and chimpanzees?

_____

_____

_____

8 Infer If there are no differences between the amino acid sequences in the cytochrome c protein of humans and chimpanzees, why aren't we the same species?

_____

_____

_____

_____

9 Apply Explain why the pattern of differences that exists from earlier to later fossils in the fossil record supports the idea that species change over time?

_____

_____

_____

_____

My Notes

Scientific Debate

Not all scientific knowledge is gained through experimentation. It is also the result of a great deal of debate and confirmation.

Tutorial

As you prepare for a debate, look for information from the following sources.

Controlled Experiments Consider the following points when planning or examining the results of a controlled experiment.

- Only one factor should be tested at a time. A factor is anything in the experiment that can influence the outcome.

- Samples are divided into experimental group(s) and a control group. All of the factors of the experimental group(s) and the control group are the same except for one variable.

- A variable is a factor that can be changed. If there are multiple variables, only one variable should be changed at a time.

Independent Studies The results of a different group may provide stronger support for your argument than your own results. And using someone else's results helps to avoid the claim that your results are biased. Bias is the tendency to think about something from only one point of view. The claim of bias can be used to argue against your point.

Comparison with Similar Objects or Events If you cannot gather data from an experiment to help support your position, finding a similar object or event might help. The better your example is understood, the stronger your argument will be.

Read the passage below and answer the questions.

Many people want to protect endangered species but do not agree on the best methods to use. Incubating, or heating eggs to ensure hatching, is commonly used with bird eggs. It was logical to apply the same technique to turtle eggs. The Barbour's map turtle is found in Florida, Georgia, and Alabama. To help more turtles hatch, people would gather eggs and incubate them. However, debate really began when mostly female turtles hatched. Were efforts to help the turtles really harming them? Scientists learned that incubating eggs at 25°C (77°F) produces males and at 30°C (86°F) produces females. As a result, conservation programs have stopped artificially heating the eggs.

1 What is the variable described in the article about Barbour's map turtles?

_____

2 Write a list of factors that were likely kept the same between the sample groups described in the article.

_____

_____

_____

3 What argument could people have used who first suggested incubating the turtle eggs?

_____

_____

_____

© Houghton Mifflin Harcourt Publishing Company • Image Credits: (bl) ©Suzanne L. Collins/Science Source

You Try It!

Fossils from the Burgess Shale Formation in Canada include many strange creatures that lived over 500 million years ago. The fossils are special because the soft parts of the creatures were preserved. Examine the fossil of the creature *Marrella* and the reconstruction of what it might have looked like.

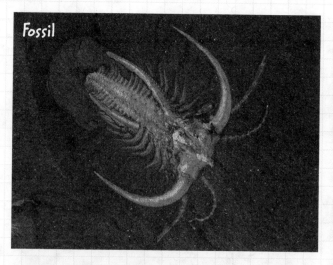
Fossil

Reconstruction

1 Recognizing Relationships Find four features on the reconstruction that you can also identify in the fossil. Write a brief description of each feature.

_____

_____

_____

_____

_____

_____

2 Applying Concepts *Marrella* is extinct. How do you think *Marrella* behaved when it was alive? What did it eat? How did it move? On what do you base your argument?

_____

_____

_____

_____

_____

_____

_____

3 Communicating Ideas Share your description with a classmate. Discuss and debate your positions. Complete the table to show the points on which you agree and disagree.

Agree	Disagree

Take It Home

Research more about the creatures of the Burgess Shale Formation. Find at least one other fossil creature and its reconstruction. What do you think the creature was like?

The History of Life on Earth

ESSENTIAL QUESTION

How has life on Earth changed over time?

By the end of this lesson, you should be able to describe the evolution of life on Earth over time, using the geologic time scale.

8.LS4.1, 8.ESS2.1

Trilobites like this one lived on Earth about 400 million years ago. This fossil preserved great detail of the trilobite's body parts.

Engage Your Brain

1 Predict Check T or F to show whether you think each statement is true or false.

T F

☐ ☐ A mass extinction occurs when a large number of species go extinct during a relatively short amount of time.

☐ ☐ The largest division of the geologic time scale is the era.

☐ ☐ We currently live in the Cenozoic era.

☐ ☐ Fossils show that the first living things were very tiny.

☐ ☐ Variations in species can occur over long periods of time and in spurts during short periods of time.

2 Draw Imagine you find a fossil of a fish. Which parts of the fish could you see in the fossil? Draw what you think you would see below.

Active Reading

3 Apply Use context clues to write your own definition for the words *fossil record* and *extinction*.

Example sentence
Scientists develop hypotheses about Earth's history based on observable changes in the <u>fossil record</u>.

fossil record:

_____

_____

Example sentence
Endangered species are protected by law in an effort to preserve them from <u>extinction</u>.

extinction:

_____

_____

Vocabulary Terms
- fossil
- fossil record
- extinction
- geologic time scale

4 Identify As you read, place a question mark next to any words that you don't understand. When you finish reading the lesson, go back and review the text that you marked. If the information is still confusing, consult a classmate or a teacher.

Uncovering Clues

How do we learn about ancient life?

Paleontologists look for clues to understand what happened in the past. These scientists use fossils to reconstruct the history of life. A **fossil** is a trace or imprint of a living thing that is preserved by geological processes. Fossils of single-celled organisms date as far back as 3.8 billion years.

What can we learn from fossils?

All of the fossils that have been discovered worldwide make up the **fossil record**. By examining the fossil record, scientists can identify when different species lived and died. There are two ways to describe the ages of fossils. *Relative dating* determines whether a fossil formed before or after another fossil. When an organism is trapped in mud or sediment, the resulting fossil becomes part of that sedimentary layer of rock. In rock layers that are not disturbed, newer fossils are found in layers of rock that are above older fossils. *Absolute dating* estimates the age of a fossil in years. Estimations are based on information from radioactive elements in certain rocks near the fossil.

Visualize It!

The abbreviation Ma stands for mega annum. A mega annum is equal to 1 million years. Ma is often used to indicate "million years ago."

5 Infer What does relative dating tell you about fossil A?

_____

_____

_____

6 Solve What does absolute dating tell you about fossil A?

_____

_____

_____

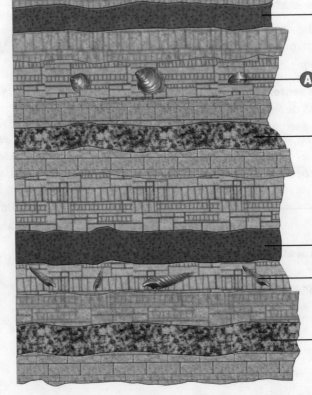

75 Ma

A

130 Ma

170 Ma

B

195 Ma

385 Ma

Eusthenopteron   **Tiktaalik**   **Ichthyostega**

365 Ma

Fossils (names of the species shown above) indicate changes in limb structure as adaptations allowed movement on land.

How Life Forms Have Changed over Time

The fossil record gives evidence of many of the different organisms that have lived during Earth's long history. Each fossil gives information about a single organism. But the overall fossil record helps us understand larger patterns of change.

Over many generations, populations change. These changes can be preserved in fossils. For example, fossils show the gradual change in limb structure, over many millions of years, of animals such as the ones shown in the drawing above.

Some species are present in the fossil record for a relatively short period of time. Other species have survived for long time spans without much change. The hard-plated horseshoe crab, for example, has changed little over the last 350 million years.

When Extinctions Occurred

An **extinction** happens when every individual of a species dies. A mass extinction occurs when a large number of species go extinct during a relatively short amount of time. Gradual environmental and geographic changes can cause mass extinctions. Catastrophic events, such as the impact of an asteroid, can also cause mass extinctions.

Extinctions and mass extinctions are documented in the fossil record. Fossils that were common in certain rock layers may decrease in frequency and eventually disappear altogether. Based on evidence in the fossil record, scientists form hypotheses about how and when species went extinct.

Visualize It!

7 Describe What changes do you see in the limb structure of the three animals above?

_____

_____

_____

_____

_____

_____

_____

_____

Active Reading

8 Describe How can the extinction of an organism be inferred from evidence in the fossil record?

_____

_____

_____

_____

Way Back When

9 Identify Underline one reason why it is hard for scientists to study the early history of Earth.

What is the geologic time scale?

After a fossil is dated, a paleontologist can place the fossil in chronological order with other fossils. This ordering allows scientists to hypothesize about relationships between species and how organisms changed over time. To keep track of Earth's long history, scientists have developed the geologic time scale. The **geologic time scale** is the standard method used to divide Earth's long 4.6-billion-year natural history into manageable parts.

Paleontologists adjust and add details to the geologic time scale when new evidence is found. The early history of Earth has been poorly understood, because fossils from this time span are rare. As new evidence about early life on Earth accumulates, scientists may need to organize Earth's early history into smaller segments of time.

Visualize It!

10 Identify When did the Paleozoic era begin and end?

_____

_____

_____

Precambrian time (4600 Ma to 542 Ma)

EONS	Hadean eon	Archean eon	
4600 Ma	3850 Ma		2500 Ma

Ma = million years ago

ERAS	Paleozoic era					
PERIODS	Cambrian	Ordovician	Silurian	Devonian	Carboniferous	Permian
	542 Ma	488 Ma	444 Ma	416 Ma	359 Ma	299 Ma	251 Ma

At the beginning of the Paleozoic era, life flourished in the oceans.

A Tool to Organize Earth's History

Boundaries between geologic time intervals correspond to significant changes in Earth's history. Some major boundaries are defined by mass extinctions or significant changes in the number of species. Other boundaries are defined by major changes in Earth's surface or climate.

The largest divisions of the geologic time scale are eons. Eons are divided into eras. Eras are characterized by the type of organism that dominated Earth at the time. Each era began with a change in the type of organism that was most dominant. Eras are further divided into periods, and periods are divided into epochs.

The four major divisions that make up the history of life on Earth are Precambrian time, the Paleozoic era, the Mesozoic era, and the Cenozoic era. Precambrian time is made up of the first three eons of Earth's history.

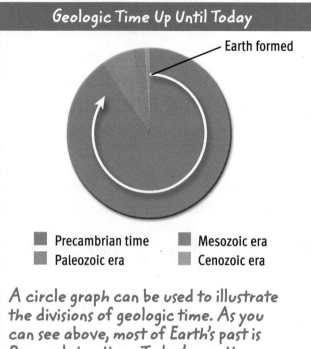

Geologic Time Up Until Today

Earth formed

■ Precambrian time   ■ Mesozoic era
■ Paleozoic era   ■ Cenozoic era

A circle graph can be used to illustrate the divisions of geologic time. As you can see above, most of Earth's past is Precambrian time. Today's era, the Cenozoic era, makes up just a very small percentage of Earth's history.

👁 Visualize It!

11 List Which three periods make up the Mesozoic era?

_____

_____

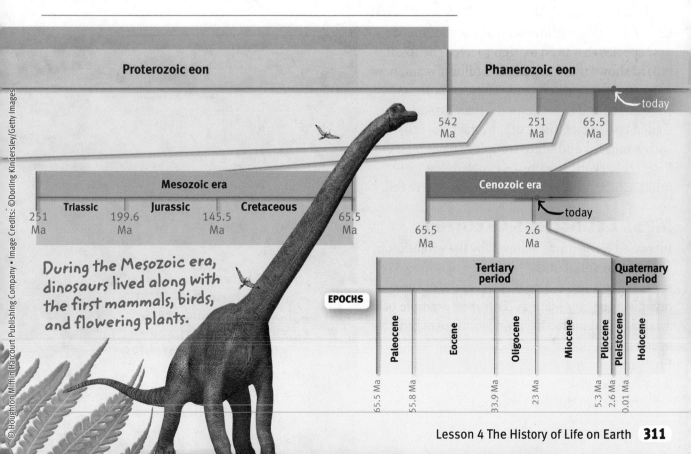

Proterozoic eon | Phanerozoic eon

today

542 Ma | 251 Ma | 65.5 Ma

Mesozoic era

| Triassic | Jurassic | Cretaceous |

251 Ma | 199.6 Ma | 145.5 Ma | 65.5 Ma

During the Mesozoic era, dinosaurs lived along with the first mammals, birds, and flowering plants.

Cenozoic era

today

65.5 Ma | 2.6 Ma

Tertiary period | Quaternary period

EPOCHS

Paleocene | Eocene | Oligocene | Miocene | Pliocene | Pleistocene | Holocene

65.5 Ma | 55.8 Ma | 33.9 Ma | 23 Ma | 5.3 Ma | 2.6 Ma | 0.01 Ma

Ancient Wisdom

What defined Precambrian time?

Precambrian time started 4.6 billion years ago, when Earth formed, and ended about 542 million years ago. Life began during this time. *Prokaryotes*—single-celled organisms without a nucleus—were the dominant life form. They lived in the ocean. The earliest prokaryotes lived without oxygen.

Life Began to Evolve and Oxygen Increased

Fossil evidence suggests that prokaryotes called *cyanobacteria* appeared over 3 billion years ago. Cyanobacteria use sunlight to make their own food. This process releases oxygen. Before cyanobacteria appeared, Earth's atmosphere did not contain oxygen. Over time, oxygen built up in the ocean and air. Eventually, the oxygen also formed *ozone,* a gas layer in the upper atmosphere. Ozone absorbs harmful radiation from the sun. Before ozone formed, life existed only in the oceans and underground.

Multicellular Organisms Evolved

Increased oxygen allowed for the evolution of new species that used oxygen to live. The fossil record shows that after about 1 billion years, new types of organisms evolved. These organisms were larger and more complex than prokaryotes. Called *eukaryotes,* these organisms have cells with a nucleus and other complex structures. Later, eukaryotic organisms evolved that were multicellular, or made up of more than one cell.

Mass Extinctions Occurred

Increased oxygen was followed by the evolution of some organisms, but the extinction of others. For some organisms, oxygen is toxic. Many of these organisms became extinct. This is an example of a gradual change affecting populations of organisms over a longer period of time. Less is known about Precambrian life than life in more recent time intervals, because microscopic organisms did not preserve well in the fossil record.

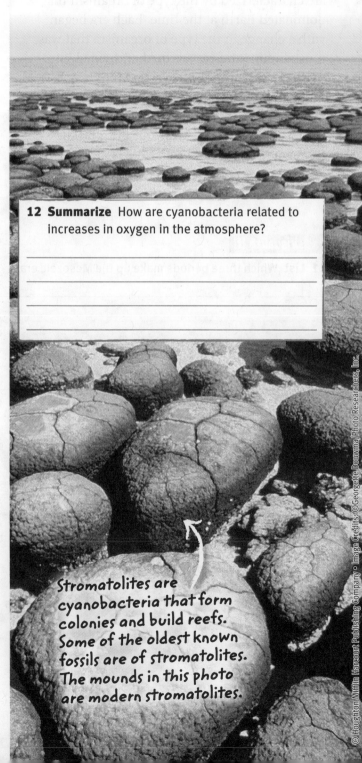

12 Summarize How are cyanobacteria related to increases in oxygen in the atmosphere?

_____

_____

_____

Stromatolites are cyanobacteria that form colonies and build reefs. Some of the oldest known fossils are of stromatolites. The mounds in this photo are modern stromatolites.

What defined the Paleozoic era?

The word *Paleozoic* comes from Greek words that mean "ancient life." When scientists first named this era, they thought it was the time span in which life began.

The Paleozoic era began about 542 million years ago and ended about 251 million years ago. Rocks from this era are rich in fossils of animals such as sponges, corals, snails, and trilobites. Fish, the earliest animals with backbones, appeared during this era, as did sharks.

Think Outside the Book Inquiry

13 Compose Select one of the organisms that lived during the Paleozoic era and find out more about it. Make a poster with information about the organism.

Life Moved onto Land

Plants, fungi, and air-breathing animals colonized land during the Paleozoic era. Land dwellers had adaptations that allowed them to survive in a drier environment. All major plant groups except flowering plants appeared. Crawling insects were among the first animals to live on land, followed by large salamander-like animals. By the end of the era, forests of giant ferns covered much of Earth, and reptiles and winged insects appeared.

A Mass Extinction Occurred

The Permian mass extinction took place at the end of the Paleozoic era about 299 million years ago. It is the largest known mass extinction. During this time the Earth experienced sudden changes in temperature and prolonged extreme conditions. By 251 million years ago, as many as 96% of marine species had become extinct. The mass extinction wiped out entire groups of marine organisms such as trilobites. Oceans were completely changed. Many other species of animals and plants also became extinct. However, this caused geographic changes that opened up new habitats to those organisms that survived.

Visualize It!

14 Describe Based on this drawing, describe the landscape that existed during the Carboniferous period of the Paleozoic era.

_____

_____

_____

_____

_____

_____

Giant winged insects such as this one were common during the Carboniferous period.

This drawing is an artist's impression of life during the Carboniferous period.

Time Marches On

15 Identify As you read, underline the names of animals that lived in the Mesozoic era.

What defined the Mesozoic era?

The Mesozoic era lasted about 185.5 million years. *Mesozoic* comes from Greek words that mean "middle life." Scientists think the reptiles that survived the Paleozoic era evolved into many different species during the Mesozoic era. Because of the abundance of reptiles, the Mesozoic era is commonly called the *Age of Reptiles*.

Dinosaurs and Other Reptiles Dominated Earth

Dinosaurs are the most well-known reptiles that evolved during the Mesozoic era. They dominated Earth for about 150 million years. A great variety of dinosaurs lived on Earth, and giant marine lizards swam in the ocean. The first birds and mammals also appeared. The most important plants during the early part of the Mesozoic era were conifers, or cone-bearing plants, which formed large forests. Flowering plants appeared later in the Mesozoic era.

A Mass Extinction Occurred

Why did dinosaurs and many other species become extinct at the end of the Mesozoic era? Different hypotheses are debated. Evidence shows that an asteroid hit Earth around this time. A main hypothesis is that this asteroid caused extreme rapidly occurring changes like giant dust clouds and worldwide fires. With sunlight blocked by dust, many plants would have died. Without plants, plant-eating dinosaurs also would have died, along with the meat-eating dinosaurs that ate the other dinosaurs. In total, about two-thirds of all land species went extinct.

16 Explain Analyze the following data. Then use the data as evidence to explain how a rapid geographic change can lead to drastic changes in populations.

- Dinosaur fossils have been found on all continents.

- No dinosaur fossils have been found in rock that formed after the Mesozoic era.

- Iridium is an element that is rare in rocks on Earth, but is more common in meteorites and asteroids.

- A layer of sediment that contains relatively high concentrations of iridium has been found in many parts of the world. This layer is about 65 million years old.

- Structures near Mexico indicate that an asteroid crashed into Earth about 65 million years ago.

_____

_____

_____

_____

_____

_____

_____

_____

What defines the Cenozoic era?

The Cenozoic era began about 65 million years ago and continues today. *Cenozoic* comes from Greek words that mean "recent life." More is known about the Cenozoic era than about previous eras, because the fossils are closer to Earth's surface and easier to find.

Primates evolved during the Cenozoic era.

Birds, Mammals, and Flowering Plants Dominate Earth

Mammals have dominated the Cenozoic the way reptiles dominated the Mesozoic. Early Cenozoic mammals were small, but larger mammals appeared later. Humans appeared during this era. Birds and flowering plants have also flourished.

The climate has changed many times during the Cenozoic. During ice ages, ice sheets covered vast areas of land, and geographic changes occurred. Many populations migrated toward the equator because of these changes. Other populations gradually adapted to the geographic changes and the cold or they went extinct.

Primates Evolved

Primates are a group of mammals that includes humans, apes, and monkeys. Primates' eyes are located at the front of the skull. Most primates have five flexible digits, one of which is an opposable thumb.

The ancestors of primates were probably nocturnal, mouse-like mammals that lived in trees. The first primates did not exist until after dinosaurs died out. Millions of years later, primates that had larger brains appeared.

17 **Hypothesize** How might the mass extinction that occurred at the end of the Mesozoic era relate to the dominance of mammals in the Cenozoic era?

_____

_____

_____

The Cenozoic era has been dominated by mammals. Woolly mammoths were well-adapted to surviving in a cold climate.

How the Mysticeti Lost Their Teeth

Fossils provide evidence about what life was like on Earth in the past. The study of fossils is called *paleontology*. Evidence from paleontology helps scientists understand how plants and animals lived on the planet. Fossils can also show how populations changed over time to evolve into new species.

Modern whales are classified into two distinct suborders of the class Mammalia: baleen whales (Mysticeti) and toothed whales (Odontocetes). Baleen whales are characterized by the fact that they have large hairy plates attached to the roof of their mouths rather than teeth. The baleen plates enable these whales to filter out and feed on small crustaceans in the oceans.

Modern Whales

Odontocetes

Mysticeti

Features	Modern Odontoceti Toothed Whales	Modern Mysticeti Baleen Whales
Upper Jaw Attachment	Teeth	Baleen Teeth
Number of Blowholes	One Blowhole	Two Blowholes
Skull Shape	Asymmetrical	Symmetrical
Relative Mouth Size	Small	Large
Relative Body Size	Smaller	Larger

Fossil Evidence

With fossil evidence, scientists can determine how baleen whales have evolved over time from their toothed ancestors. Modern baleen whales and toothed whales differ from each other in a number of ways besides having baleen or teeth.

(1) What evidence would we look for to determine if the fossil of an ancient whale species could be an ancestor of modern baleen whales?

_____

_____

_____

_____

Many fossils and living organisms show evidence of an intermediate state between one set of characteristics and another. These are called **transitional forms.** Transitional forms give us abundant evidence that organisms change over time.

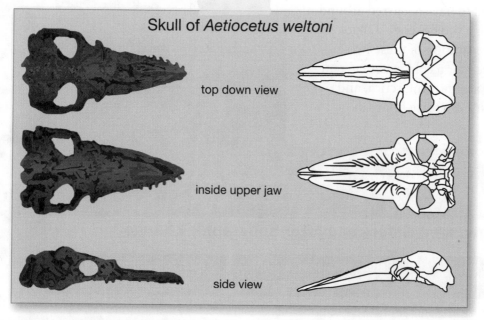

Skull of *Aetiocetus weltoni*

top down view

inside upper jaw

side view

(2) Look at the drawing of a fossil of an ancient whale *Aetiocetus weltoni,* that lived about 25 mya.

The eye sockets are on the side of the head. Where do you think the blowhole is?

We can see that this fossil has teeth, but it also has ridges on the roof of its mouth suggesting that something was attached there. What might that be?

Is there any other evidence from examining the skull of this fossil that indicates that it might be a transitional form?

_____

_____

_____

Geographic Change over Time

Modern baleen whales and toothed whales have very different diets and feeding strategies. When species change over time, they are adapting to a changing environment. This may be due to an environmental pressure, or environmental opportunity, that may give individual organisms the opportunity to exploit a new source of food or adopt a new strategy for survival.

In the case of whales, the separation of South America from Antarctica as a result of the break-up of Gondwana was just that opportunity. This geographic change is believed to have occurred around 30 – 35 mya during the Eocene – Oligocene transition. The separation of these two continents allowed for a cold water current to begin to form around Antarctica, and eventually a drastic decrease in ocean temperature.

Baleen whale feeding

Environment Before and After Geographic Change

Characteristics	Before Separation of South America and Antarctica	After Separation of South America and Antarctica
Ocean Temperature	Relatively warm, temperate	Cooler
Ocean Currents	Shallow, warm-water current; no upwelling	Formation of deep, cold-water current; upwelling of cold-water
Food Resources Available	Fish and squid	Plankton near surface; deep-water fish
Specialized Adaptations Related to Feeding	Teeth, elongated body	*Mystecetis*: baleen-plates for filter-feeding plankton *Odontocetes*: ability to echolocate to find individual prey

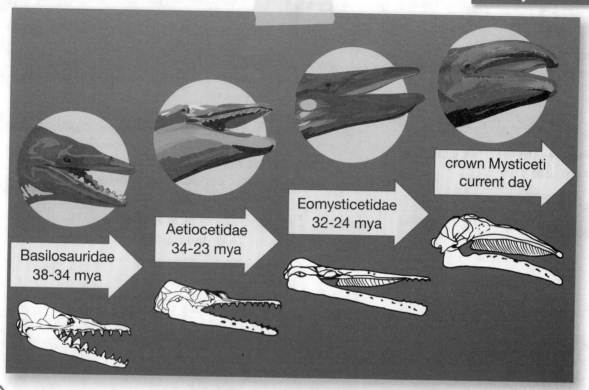

Basilosauridae
38-34 mya

Aetiocetidae
34-23 mya

Eomysticetidae
32-24 mya

crown Mysticeti
current day

3 What do you observe about the changes in the shape of the skull and mouth of these baleen whale populations over time?

_____

_____

_____

4 Which evidence supports the conclusion that a gradual geographic change, which caused changes in the environment, led to changes in the whale population?

_____

_____

_____

5 How does this fossil evidence support the conclusion that changes in the environment led to changes in the whale population?

_____

_____

_____

_____

6 What would have happened to the whale species if, after the environment changed, the population could not adapt? What evidence would you see in the fossil record?

_____

_____

Visual Summary

To complete this summary, circle the correct word. Then, use the key below to check your answers. You can use this page to review the main concepts of the lesson.

The fossil record provides evidence of ancient life.

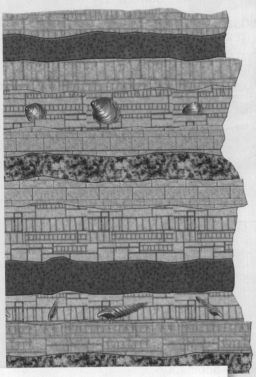

18 Absolute/Relative dating estimates the age of a fossil in years.

The geologic time scale divides Earth's history into eons, eras, periods, and epochs.

19 Epochs/Eras are characterized by the type of organism that dominated Earth at the time.

The **History** of **Life** on **Earth**

Four major divisions of Earth's past are Precambrian time, the Paleozoic era, the Mesozoic era, and the Cenozoic era.

20 Primates evolved during the Mesozoic era/Cenozoic era.

Answers: 18 Absolute; 19 Eras; 20 Cenozoic era

21 Synthesize Starting with Precambrian time, briefly describe how life on Earth has changed over Earth's long history.

Lesson Review

Vocabulary

Draw a line to connect the following terms to their definitions.

1 fossil

2 geologic time scale

3 fossil record

4 extinction

A all of the fossils that have been discovered worldwide

B death of every member of a species

C trace or remains of an organism that lived long ago

D division of Earth's history into manageable parts

Key Concepts

5 List What four major divisions make up the history of life on Earth in the geologic time scale?

_____

_____

_____

6 Explain What is one distinguishing feature of each of the four major divisions listed in your previous answer?

_____

_____

_____

_____

_____

_____

_____

_____

Critical Thinking

7 Contrast How do the atmospheric conditions near the beginning of Precambrian time contrast with the atmospheric conditions that are present now? Which organism is largely responsible for this change?

_____

_____

Use this drawing to answer the following question.

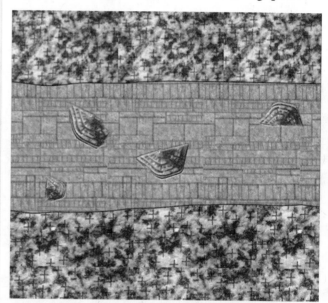

8 Explain The fossils shown are of a marine organism. In which of the three rock layers would you expect to find fossils of an organism that went extinct before the marine organism evolved? Explain your answer.

_____

_____

9 Describe While dating fossils, scientists observed evidence that some species changed gradually, but in others, they observed evidence of changes occurring rapidly. Describe one event that caused gradual changes and one that caused rapid changes to species.

_____

_____

_____

My Notes

Dr. Erica Bree Rosenblum

EVOLUTIONARY BIOLOGIST

Think about watching a little frog hop around. Now, imagine a world of children who have neither seen nor heard of a frog, except in very old videos. It is true that the world's amphibian population is declining. But thanks to scientists such as Dr. Erica Bree Rosenblum, frogs will likely be part of the world for kids in future generations.

Dr. Rosenblum does research in the areas of biological diversity and adaptive evolution at the University of California, Berkeley. Her research includes studying both the emergence of new species and the extinction of existing species. In the case of frogs, her work will hopefully prevent their extinction.

A fungus known as Bd (*Batrachochytrium dendrobatidis*) is killing many amphibians, including frogs. Since the 1980s, amphibians have declined about 70%, and this fungus is partially responsible for the decline. Dr. Rosenblum and her colleagues are studying frogs' responses to the Bd fungus under certain conditions. With continued effort, these researchers may be able to help amphibians survive this widespread fungal infection.

Frogs range in size from about one inch long to one foot long.

© Houghton Mifflin Harcourt Publishing Company • Image Credits: (bg) ©Pierre Steenberg/Alamy; (b) ©Tom Brakefield/Photodisc/Getty Images

Social Studies Connection

Find ten different countries that report amphibian declines due to the Bd fungus. On a world map, shade in the countries you find. Share your map with classmates to get an idea of the widespread nature of the amphibian decline.

JOB BOARD

Vet Technician

What You'll Do: Assist veterinarians in taking care of the health of animals.

Where You Might Work: In a veterinary clinic, animal humane society, pet hospital, or zoo.

Education: A veterinarian technician license is preferred.

Other Job Requirements: You should have compassion for animals and an ability to perform a variety of tasks, including surgical assistance, laundry and exam-room cleaning, animal feeding, and dog walking.

Student Research Assistant

What You'll Do: Assist in molecular/genome research under the supervision of university faculty by recording and inputting data into the computer.

Where You Might Work: In a lab within a university building on your college campus.

Education: You must be a student within a science-based degree program at the university.

Other Job Requirements: You should be willing to work odd hours with short notice, have attention to detail, excellent data-entry skills, and an ability to follow directions carefully.

Wildlife Photographer

What You'll Do: Take photos of wildlife in their natural habitat.

Where You Might Work: For a publishing company, advertising agency, magazine, or as a freelance photographer. If you work as a freelancer, you would have to secure contracts with companies in order to be paid for your work.

Education: No degree is required; however, having an associate's or bachelor's degree in photojournalism would make it easier to get a job as a wildlife photographer. With or without a degree, you will need a portfolio of your work to take to interviews.

Classification of Living Things

ESSENTIAL QUESTION

How are organisms classified?

By the end of this lesson, you should be able to describe how people sort living things into groups based on shared characteristics.

8.LS4.2

Scientists use physical and chemical characteristics to classify organisms. Is that a spider? Look again. It's an ant mimicking a jumping spider!

Lesson Labs

Quick Labs
- Using a Dichotomous Key
- Investigate Classifying Leaves

Exploration Lab
- Developing Scientific Names

Engage Your Brain

1 Predict Check T or F to show whether you think each statement is true or false.

T F
- ☐ ☐ The classification system used today has changed very little since it was introduced.
- ☐ ☐ To be classified as an animal, an organism must have a backbone.
- ☐ ☐ Organisms can be classified according to whether they have nuclei in their cells.
- ☐ ☐ Scientists can study genetic material to classify organisms.
- ☐ ☐ Organisms that have many physical similarities are always related.

2 Analyze The flowering plant shown above is called an Indian pipe. It could be mistaken for a fungus. Write down how the plant is similar to and different from other plants you know.

_____

_____

_____

_____

Active Reading

3 Word Parts Many English words have their roots in other languages. Use the Latin suffix below to make an educated guess about the meaning of the word *Plantae*.

Latin suffix	Meaning
-ae	a group of

Example sentence
Maples are part of the kingdom <u>Plantae</u>.

Plantae:

_____

_____

Vocabulary Terms
- species
- genus
- domain
- Bacteria
- Archaea
- Eukarya
- Protista
- Fungi
- Plantae
- Animalia

4 Apply As you learn the definition of each vocabulary term in this lesson, write your own definition or make a sketch to help you remember the meaning of each term.

Sorting Things Out!

Why do we classify living things?

There are millions of living things on Earth. How do scientists keep all of these living things organized? Scientists *classify* living things based on characteristics that living things share. Classification helps scientists answer questions such as:

- How many kinds of living things are there?
- What characteristics define each kind of living thing?
- What are the relationships among living things?

Sharks have fins and gills.

Dolphins also have fins, but not gills.

Visualize It!

5 Analyze The photos show two organisms. In the table, place a check mark in the box for each characteristic that the organisms have.

Yellow pansy butterfly

American goldfinch

	Wings	Antennae	Beak	Feathers
Yellow pansy butterfly				
American goldfinch				

6 Summarize What characteristics do yellow pansy butterflies have in common with American goldfinches? How do they differ?

_____

_____

_____

How do scientists know living things are related?

If two organisms look similar, are they related? To classify organisms, scientists compare physical characteristics. For example, they may look at size or bone structure. Scientists also compare the chemical characteristics of living things.

Physical Characteristics

How are chickens similar to dinosaurs? If you compare dinosaur fossils and chicken skeletons, you will see that chickens and dinosaurs share many physical characteristics. Scientists look at physical characteristics, such as skeletal structure. They also study how organisms develop from an egg to an adult. For example, animals with similar skeletons and development may be related.

Chemical Characteristics

Scientists can identify the relationships among organisms by studying genetic material such as DNA and RNA. They study mutations and genetic similarities to find relationships among organisms. Organisms that have very similar gene sequences or have the same mutations are likely related. Other chemicals, such as proteins and hormones, can also be studied to learn how organisms are related.

The two pandas below share habitats and diets. They look alike, but they have different DNA.

Red panda

The red panda is a closer relative to a raccoon than it is to a giant panda.

Raccoon

Giant panda

Spectacled bear

The giant panda is a closer relative to a spectacled bear than it is to a red panda.

7 List How does DNA lead scientists to better classify organisms?

_____

_____

_____

_____

_____

_____

What's in a Name?

How are living things named?

Early scientists used names as long as 12 words to identify living things, and they also used common names. So, classification was confusing. In the 1700s, a scientist named Carolus Linnaeus (KAR•uh•luhs lih•NEE•uhs) simplified the naming of living things. He gave each kind of living thing a two-part *scientific name*.

Scientific Names

Each species has its own scientific name. A **species** (SPEE•sheez) is a group of organisms that are very closely related. They can mate and produce fertile offspring. Consider the scientific name for a mountain lion: *Puma concolor*. The first part, *Puma*, is the genus name. A **genus** (JEE•nuhs; plural, *genera*) includes similar species. The second part, *concolor*, is the specific, or species, name. No other species is named *Puma concolor*.

A scientific name always includes the genus name followed by the specific name. The first letter of the genus name is capitalized, and the first letter of the specific name is lowercase. The entire scientific name is written either in italics or underlined.

HELLO
my name is
Carolus Linnaeus

The A.K.A. Files

Some living things have many common names. Scientific names prevent confusion when people discuss organisms.

Scientific name:
Puma concolor

Common names:
Mountain lion
Puma
Cougar
Panther

Scientific name:
Acer rubrum

Common names:
Red maple
Swamp maple
Soft maple

8 Apply In the scientific names above, circle the genus name and underline the specific name.

9 Identify As you read, underline the levels of classification.

What are the levels of classification?

Linnaeus's ideas became the basis for modern taxonomy (tak•SAHN•uh•mee). *Taxonomy* is the science of describing, classifying, and naming living things. At first, many scientists sorted organisms into two groups: plants and animals. But numerous organisms did not fit into either group.

Today, scientists use an eight-level system to classify living things. Each level gets more specific. Therefore, it contains fewer kinds of living things than the level above it. Living things in the lower levels are more closely related to each other than they are to organisms in the higher levels. From most general to more specific, the levels of classification are domain, kingdom, phylum (plural, *phyla*), class, order, family, genus, and species.

Classifying Organisms

Domain **Domain Eukarya** includes all protists, fungi, plants, and animals.

Kingdom **Kingdom Animalia** includes all animals.

Phylum Animals in **Phylum Chordata** have a hollow nerve cord in their backs. Some have a backbone.

Class Animals in **Class Mammalia**, or mammals, have a backbone and nurse their young.

Order Animals in **Order Carnivora** are mammals that have special teeth for tearing meat.

Family Animals in **Family Felidae** are cats. They are carnivores that have retractable claws.

Genus Animals in **Genus** *Felis* are cats that cannot roar. They can only purr.

From domain to species, each level of classification contains a smaller group of organisms.

Species The species *Felis domesticus*, or the house cat, has unique traits that other members of genus *Felis* do not have.

Visualize It!

10 Apply What is true about the number of organisms as they are classified closer to the species level?

_____

_____

_____

_____

_____

Triple Play

What are the three domains?

© Eye of Science/Photo Researchers, Inc.; (tr) ©Tom Murphy/National Geographic/Getty Images;

Once, kingdoms were the highest level of classification. Scientists used a six-kingdom system. But scientists noticed that organisms in two of the kingdoms differed greatly from organisms in the other four kingdoms. So scientists added a new classification level: domains. A **domain** represents the largest differences among organisms. The three domains are Bacteria (bak•TIR•ee•uh), Archaea (ar•KEE•uh), and Eukarya (yoo•KAIR•ee•uh).

Bacteria

All bacteria belong to Domain Bacteria. Domain **Bacteria** is made up of prokaryotes that usually have a cell wall and reproduce by cell division. *Prokaryotes* are single-cell organisms that lack a nucleus in their cells. Bacteria live in almost any environment—soil, water, and even inside the human body!

Archaea

Domain **Archaea** is also made up of prokaryotes. They differ from bacteria in their genetics and in the makeup of their cell walls. Archaea live in harsh environments, such as hot springs and thermal vents, where other organisms could not survive. Some archaea are found in the open ocean and soil.

Bacteria from the genus Streptomyces are commonly found in soil.

Archaea from the genus Sulfolobus are found in hot springs.

© Houghton Mifflin Harcourt Publishing Company • Image Credits: (l) ©Chris Leschinsky/Digital Vision/Getty Images; (bl) ©Eye of Science/Photo Researchers, Inc.; (r) ©Tom Murphy/National Geographic/Getty Images; (tr) ©Eye of Science/Photo Researchers, Inc.

Eukarya

What do algae, mushrooms, trees, and humans have in common? All of these organisms are *eukaryotes*. Eukaryotes are made up of cells that have a nucleus and membrane-bound organelles. The cells of eukaryotes are more complex than the cells of prokaryotes. For this reason, the cells of eukaryotes are usually larger than the cells of prokaryotes. Some eukaryotes, such as many protists and some fungi, are single-celled. Many eukaryotes are multicellular organisms. Some protists and many fungi, plants, and animals are multicellular eukaryotes. Domain **Eukarya** is made up of all eukaryotes.

It may look like a pinecone, but the pangolin is actually an animal from Africa. It is in Domain Eukarya.

Visualize It!

12 Identify Fill in the blanks with the missing labels.

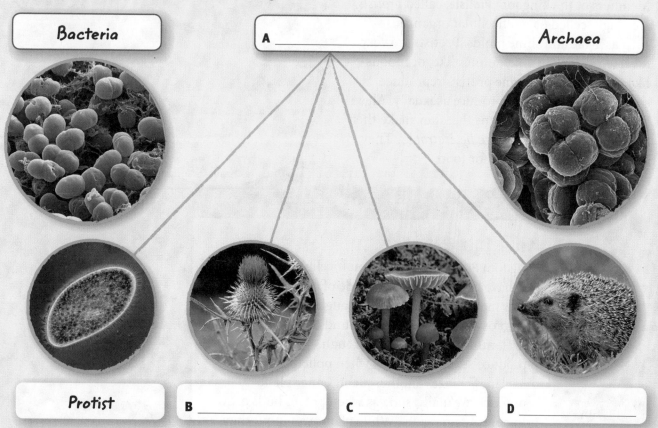

Bacteria

A _____

Archaea

Protist

B _____

C _____

D _____

13 Compare What are the differences between Bacteria and Eukarya?

_____

_____

_____

My Kingdom for a

What are the four kingdoms in Eukarya?

Scientists have classified four types of Eukarya. They ask questions to decide in which kingdom to classify an organism.

- Is the organism single-celled or multicellular?
- Does it make its food or get it from the environment?
- How does it reproduce?

Kingdom Protista

Members of the kingdom **Protista**, called *protists*, are single-celled or multicellular organisms such as algae and slime molds. Protists are very diverse, with plant-like, animal-like, or fungus-like characteristics. Some protists reproduce sexually, while others reproduce asexually. Algae are *autotrophs*, which means that they make their own food. Some protists are *heterotrophs*. They consume other organisms for food.

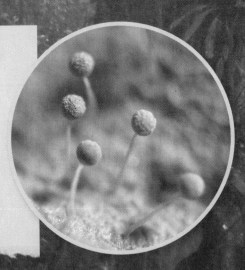

Kingdom Plantae

Kingdom **Plantae** consists of multicellular organisms that have cell walls, mostly made of cellulose. Most plants make their own food through the process of photosynthesis. Plants are found on land and in water that light can pass through. Some plants reproduce sexually, such as when pollen from one plant fertilizes another plant. Other plants reproduce asexually, such as when potato buds grow into new potato plants. While plants can grow, they cannot move by themselves.

14 Compare How are protists different from plants?

_____

_____

_____

Eukaryote!

Kingdom Fungi

The members of the kingdom **Fungi** get energy by absorbing materials. They have cells with cell walls but no chloroplasts. Fungi are single-celled or multicellular and include yeasts, molds, and mushrooms. Fungi use digestive juices to break down materials around them for food. Fungi reproduce sexually, asexually, or in both ways, depending on their type.

Active Reading 15 **Identify** As you read, underline the characteristics of the kingdom Animalia.

Kingdom Animalia

Kingdom **Animalia** contains multicellular organisms that lack cell walls. They do not have chloroplasts like plants and algae, so they must get nutrients by consuming other organisms. Therefore, they are heterotrophic. Animals have specialized sense organs, and most animals are able to move around. Birds, fish, reptiles, amphibians, insects, and mammals are just a few examples of animals. Most animals reproduce sexually, but a few types of animals reproduce asexually, such as by budding.

16 Classify Place a check mark in the box for the characteristic that each kingdom displays.

Kingdom	Cells		Nutrients		Reproduction	
	Unicellular	Multicellular	Autotrophic	Heterotrophic	Sexual	Asexual
Protista						
Plantae						
Fungi						
Animalia						

How do classification systems change over time?

Millions of organisms have been identified, but millions have yet to be named. Many new organisms fit into the existing system. However, scientists often find organisms that don't fit. Not only do scientists identify new species, but sometimes these species do not fit into existing genera or phyla. In fact, many scientists argue that protists are so different from one another that they should be classified into several kingdoms instead of one. Classification continues to change as scientists learn more about living things.

Active Reading

17 Predict How might the classification of protists change in the future?

_____

_____

_____

_____

How do branching diagrams show classification relationships?

How do you organize your closet? What about your books? People organize things in many different ways. Linnaeus' two-name system worked for scientists long ago, but the system does not represent what we know about living things today. Scientists use different tools to organize information about classification.

Scientists often use a type of branching diagram called a *cladogram* (KLAD•uh•gram). A cladogram shows relationships among species. Organisms are grouped according to common characteristics. Usually these characteristics are listed along a line. Branches of organisms extend from this line. Organisms on branches above each characteristic have the characteristic. Organisms on branches below lack the characteristic.

Visualize It!

18 Apply How can you use the branching diagram to tell which plants produce seeds?

_____

_____

_____

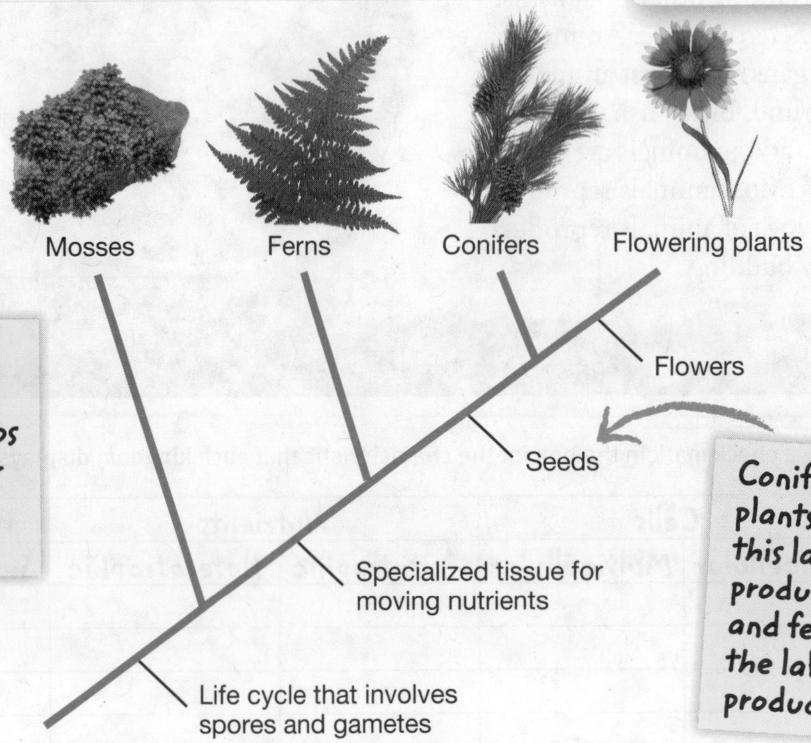

_____

Mosses   Ferns   Conifers   Flowering plants

Flowers

Seeds

This branching diagram shows the relationships among the four main groups of plants.

Specialized tissue for moving nutrients

Conifers and flowering plants are listed above this label, so they both produce seeds. Mosses and ferns, listed below the label, do not produce seeds.

Life cycle that involves spores and gametes

A Class by Themselves

As scientists find more living things to study, they find that they may not have made enough classifications, or that their classifications may not describe organisms well enough. Some living things have traits that fall under more than one classification. These organisms are very difficult to classify.

Sea spider

Sea Spider

The sea spider is a difficult-to-classify animal. It is an arthropod because it has body segments and an exoskeleton. The problem is in the sea spider's mouth. They eat by sticking a straw-like structure into sponges and sea slugs and sucking out the juice. No other arthropod eats like this. Scientists must decide if they need to make a new classification or change an existing one to account for this strange mouth.

Euglena

Euglena

An even stranger group of creatures is Euglena. Euglena make their own food as plants do. But, like animals, they have no cell walls. They have a flagellum, a tail-like structure that bacteria have. Despite having all of these characteristics, Euglena have been classified as protists.

Extend

Inquiry

19 Explain In which domain would the sea spider be classified? Explain your answer.

20 Research Investigate how scientists use DNA to help classify organisms such as the sea spider.

21 Debate Find more information on Euglena and sea spiders. Hold a class debate on how scientists should classify the organisms.

Keys to Success

How can organisms be identified?

Imagine walking through the woods. You see an animal sitting on a rock. It has fur, whiskers, and a large, flat tail. How can you find out what kind of animal it is? You can use a dichotomous key.

Dichotomous Keys

A *dichotomous key* (dy•KAHT•uh•muhs KEE) uses a series of paired statements to identify organisms. Each pair of statements is numbered. When identifying an organism, read each pair of statements. Then choose the statement that best describes the organism. Either the chosen statement identifies the organism, or you will be directed to another pair of statements. By working through the key, you can eventually identify the organism.

22 Apply Use the dichotomous key below to identify the animals shown in the photographs.

Dichotomous Key to Six Mammals in the Eastern United States

1	**A** The mammal has no hair on its tail.	**Go to step 2**
	B The mammal has hair on its tail.	**Go to step 3**
2	**A** The mammal has a very short naked tail.	**Eastern mole**
	B The mammal has a long naked tail.	**Go to step 4**
3	**A** The mammal has a black mask.	**Raccoon**
	B The mammal does not have a black mask.	**Go to step 5**
4	**A** The mammal has a flat, paddle-shaped tail.	**Beaver**
	B The mammal has a round, skinny tail.	**Possum**
5	**A** The mammal has a long furry tail that is black on the tip.	**Long-tailed weasel**
	B The mammal has a long tail that has little fur.	**White-footed mouse**

A _____

B _____

23 Apply Some dichotomous keys are set up as diagrams instead of tables. Work through the key below to identify the unknown plant.

Think Outside the Book Inquiry

24 Summarize With a partner, choose six plants or animals in a local ecosystem. Then design a dichotomous key that can be used to identify the organisms. When you have finished, trade keys with your classmates and work through their keys with your partner.

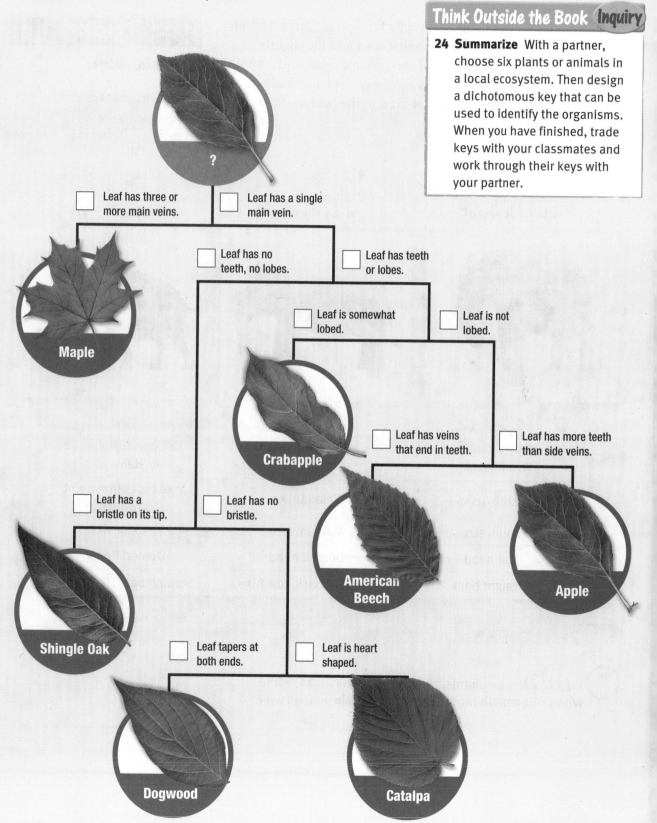

Leaf has three or more main veins.

Leaf has a single main vein.

Leaf has no teeth, no lobes.

Leaf has teeth or lobes.

Leaf is somewhat lobed.

Leaf is not lobed.

Leaf has veins that end in teeth.

Leaf has more teeth than side veins.

Leaf has a bristle on its tip.

Leaf has no bristle.

Leaf tapers at both ends.

Leaf is heart shaped.

Maple

Crabapple

American Beech

Apple

Shingle Oak

Dogwood

Catalpa

Deep-freeze DNA

When we think of elephants we usually think of the large African Elephant with its big ears and wrinkled skin, and the slightly smaller Asian Elephant with small ears, domed head, and smooth skin. About 4,000 years ago theses ago these elephants had a close cousin, the Woolly Mammoth, that lived in the cold north.

Skills
✓ Analyze evidence
✓ Construct an explanation using evidence

African Elephant

Asian Elephant

Woolly Mammoth

African Elephant	Asian Elephant	Woolly Mammoth
Wrinkled skin	Smooth Skin	Hairy
Large tusks	Small tusks	Large tusks that point upwards
Large size	Medium size	Medium size
Flat head	Domed head	Domed Head
Straight back	Straight back, low hips	Sloping back, low hips

1) Which of the elephants, the African or the Asian, is the Woolly Mammoth most similar to? Explain your answer.

_____

_____

_____

_____

_____

Woolly Mammoths

Woolly Mammoth populations decreased very rapidly about 10,000 years ago. The last surviving mammoths probably died out about 1650 B.C.E on the isolated Wrangle Island in Siberia.

We know that Woolly Mammoths and humans had a lot of contact and that humans hunted the mammoths. Of the 250 drawings of animals in the Rouffignac cave, 62% of them were of mammoths, so we know that they were important animals for humans.

The Rouffignac Cave in France is known as The Cave of the Hundred Mammoths for its many drawings of Mammoths by Paleolithic hunters.

Frozen

Fossils are preserved impressions of long dead organisms in rock. On rare occasions, remains of extinct animals can be preserved in other ways.

In 2012, the remains of a 10,000-year-old female mammoth were discovered trapped in ice in northern Siberia. It was intact and had remarkably well-preserved hair, skin and even blood.

Remains preserved in ice.

(2) How do you think our Paleolithic ancestors used the Woolly Mammoth?

_____

_____

_____

_____

(3) What could you learn by examining the remains of an extinct organism that was preserved in ice that you could not learn by other fossil evidence?

_____

_____

_____

_____

_____

Trapped DNA

Trapped inside the cells of every animal is a wealth of information. DNA, or deoxyribonucleic acid, is a long-chained molecule that is found in the nucleus of every cell. It contains the genetic information of the organism. Think of it as a blueprint, or a set of instructions thousands of lines long, on how to build an organism.

Unfortunately, DNA breaks apart very rapidly when an organism dies, so sometimes all we are left with are fragments. Scientists from Japan are trying to reconstruct the sequence of mammoth DNA from the fragments they have found.

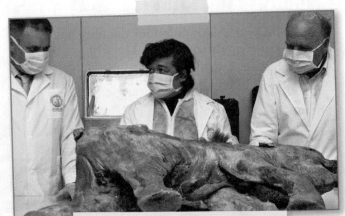

Scientists are able to extract DNA from blood and tissue and write out its sequence.

Sequence of a Fragment of Woolly Mammoth DNA

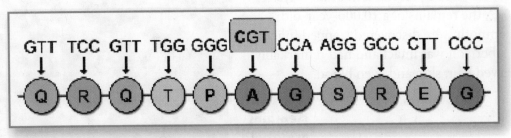

4 What do you think scientists could discover by examining the fragments of mammoth DNA and comparing them to the DNA of similar organisms?

_____
_____
_____
_____
_____
_____
_____
_____
_____
_____
_____
_____

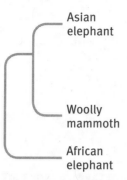

Asian
elephant

Woolly
mammoth

African
elephant

This cross between a donkey
and a zebra is a cross-species
hybridization.

Manipulating Nature

It has been disputed for some time which animals were the closest relatives to woolly mammoths. Recent DNA evidence has shown that woolly mammoths share more DNA with Asian elephants than Asian elephants do with African elephants.

Recent advances in biotechnology have allowed scientists to manipulate the DNA of living organisms, creating hybrids of different species that would not normally reproduce. This cross-species hybridization does happen occasionally in nature with some interesting results.

Since the DNA from mammoths is fragmentary, scientists are looking to splice those fragments into the DNA of Asian elephants to create an offspring that is more like a mammoth than its Asian elephant mother.

Some people believe this is a good idea. They think it will help us learn how to protect endangered animals living today. Other people worry about the possible effects on the environment. Where would woolly mammoths live? What kind of food would they need to survive? These are just some of the questions people have.

(5) What do you think? Would it be a good idea to bring back the woolly mammoth from extinction? Why or why not?

_____

_____

_____

_____

_____

_____

_____

Visual Summary

To complete this summary, check the box that indicates true or false. Then, use the key below to check your answers. You can use this page to review the main concepts of the lesson.

Classification of Living Things

Scientists use physical and chemical characteristics to classify organisms.

	T	F	
25	☐	☐	Scientists compare skeletal structure to classify organisms.
26	☐	☐	Scientists study DNA to classify organisms.

All species are given a two-part scientific name and classified into eight levels.

	T	F	
27	☐	☐	A scientific name consists of domain and kingdom.
28	☐	☐	There are more organisms in a genus than there are in a phylum.

Branching diagrams and dichotomous keys are used to help classify and identify organisms.

	T	F	
29	☐	☐	Branching diagrams are used to identify unknown organisms.

The highest level of classification is the domain.

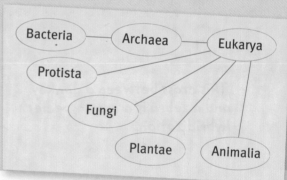

	T	F	
30	☐	☐	Domains are divided into kingdoms.

31 Summarize How has the classification of living things changed over time?

Lesson Review

Vocabulary

Fill in the blanks with the term that best completes the following sentences.

1 A _____ contains paired statements that can be used to identify organisms.

2 The kingdoms of eukaryotes are _____, Fungi, Plantae, and Animalia.

3 Domains _____ and _____ are made up of prokaryotes.

Key Concepts

4 List Name the eight levels of classification from most general to most specific.

_____
_____
_____

5 Explain Describe how scientists choose the kingdom in which a eukaryote belongs.

_____
_____
_____
_____

6 Identify What two types of evidence are used to classify organisms?

_____
_____

7 Compare Dichotomous keys and branching diagrams organize different types of information about classification. How are these tools used differently?

_____
_____
_____
_____
_____

Critical Thinking

Use the figure to answer the following questions.

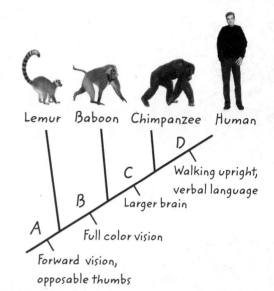

Lemur   Baboon   Chimpanzee   Human

D — Walking upright; verbal language

C — Larger brain

B

A — Forward vision, opposable thumbs

Full color vision

8 Identify Which traits do baboons have?

_____
_____

9 Analyze Which animal shares the most traits with humans?

_____

10 Synthesize Do both lemurs and humans have the trait listed at point D? Explain.

_____
_____
_____
_____

11 Classify A scientist finds an organism that cannot move. It has many cells, produces spores, and gets food from its environment. In which kingdom does it belong? Explain.

_____
_____
_____
_____
_____

My Notes

Biotechnology

ESSENTIAL QUESTION

How does biotechnology impact our world?

By the end of this lesson, you should be able to explain how biotechnology impacts human life and the world around us.

8.LS4.5

These glowing bands contain fragments of DNA that have been treated with a special chemical. This chemical glows under ultraviolet light, allowing scientists to see the DNA.

✋ **Lesson Labs**

Quick Labs
• Modeling DNA
• Building a DNA Sequence
• Mutations Cause Diversity
• How Can a Simple Code Be Used to Make a Product
• Observing Selective Breeding

Exploration Labs
• Extracting DNA

🧠 Engage Your Brain

1 Predict Fill in the blanks with the word or phrase you think correctly completes the following sentences.

A medical researcher might study DNA in order to learn _____

_____

_____

A crime scene investigator might study DNA in order to learn _____

_____

_____

2 Apply *GMO* stands for "genetically modified organism." Write a caption to accompany the following photo.

_____

_____

_____

📖 Active Reading

3 Apply Use context clues to write your own definition for the words *inserted* and *technique.*

Example sentence
Using special technologies, a gene from one organism can be inserted into the DNA of another.

inserted:

_____

_____

Example sentence
Cloning is a technique in which the genetic information of an organism is copied.

technique:

_____

_____

Vocabulary Terms

• **biotechnology**
• **artificial selection**
• **genetic engineering**
• **clone**

4 Apply As you learn the definition of each vocabulary term in this lesson, create your own definition or sketch to help you remember the meaning of the term.

Bio**TECHNOLOGY**

Protective clothing keeps this geneticist safe as he works with infectious particles.

This scientist works inside of a greenhouse. He breeds potato plants.

What is biotechnology?

A forensic scientist makes copies of DNA from a crime scene. A botanist breeds flowers for their bright red blooms. A geneticist works to place a human gene into the DNA of bacteria. What do these processes have in common? They are all examples of biotechnology. **Biotechnology** is the use and application of living things and biological processes. In the past 40 years, new technologies have allowed scientists to directly change DNA. But biotechnology is not a new scientific field. For thousands of years, humans have been breeding plants and animals and using bacteria and yeast to ferment foods. These, too, are examples of biotechnology.

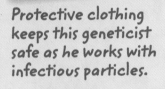 **Active Reading** **6 Identify** Name three examples of biotechnology.

_____

_____

_____

Different dog breeds are produced by artificial selection.

What are some applications of biotechnology?

Biotechnology processes fall into some broad categories. Artificial selection, genetic engineering, and cloning are some of the most common techniques.

Artificial Selection

For thousands of years, humans have been carefully selecting and breeding certain plants and animals that have desirable traits. Over many generations, horses have gotten faster, pigs have gotten leaner, and corn has become sweeter. **Artificial selection** is the process of selecting and breeding organisms that have certain desired traits. Artificial selection is also known as *selective breeding*.

Artificial selection can be successful as long as the desirable traits are controlled by genes. Animal and plant breeders select for alleles, which are different versions of a gene. The alleles being selected must already be present in the population. People do not change DNA during artificial selection. Instead, they cause certain alleles to become more common in a population. The different dog breeds are a good example of artificial selection. All dogs share a common ancestor, the wolf. However, thousands of years of selection by humans have produced dogs with a variety of characteristics.

Visualize It!

These vegetables have been developed through artificial selection. Their common ancestor is the mustard plant.

kale

broccoli

cabbage

cauliflower

Brussels sprouts

7 Infer Why might farmers use artificial selection to develop different types of vegetables?

_____

_____

_____

_____

Scientists have disabled a gene in the mouse on the right. As a result, this mouse cannot control how much food it eats.

Genetic Engineering

Within the past 40 years, it has become possible to directly change the DNA of an organism. **Genetic engineering** is the process in which a piece of DNA is modified for use in research, medicine, agriculture, or industry. The DNA that is engineered often codes for a certain trait of interest. Scientists can isolate a segment of DNA, change it in some way, and return it to the organism. Or, scientists can take a segment of DNA from one species and transfer it to the DNA of an organism from another species.

Active Reading **8 Describe** For what purposes can genetic engineering be used?

_____

_____

_____

These genetically modified plant cells produce tiny, biodegradable plastic pellets. The pellets are then collected to make plastic products.

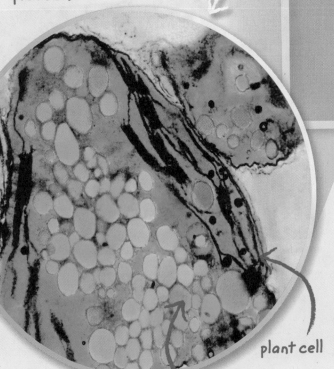

plant cell

plastic pellets

9 Infer Traditional plastics are made from petroleum, a nonrenewable resource. What benefit could plastic made by plants have over traditional plastic?

_____

_____

_____

_____

_____

_____

Cloning

A **clone** is an organism, cell, or piece of genetic material that is genetically identical to the one from which it was derived. Cloning has been used to make copies of small traces of DNA found at crime scenes or on ancient artifacts. Also, cloning can be used to copy segments of DNA for genetic engineering.

In 1996, scientists cloned the DNA from one sheep's body cell to produce another sheep named Dolly. The ability to clone a sheep, which is a mammal, raised many concerns about the future uses of cloning, because humans are also mammals. It is important that people understand the science of genetics. Only then can we make informed decisions about how and when the technology should be used.

Dolly was cloned from a body cell of an adult sheep.

10 Apply Review each of the examples of biotechnology below. Then classify each as artificial selection, genetic engineering, or cloning.

	Scientists have introduced a gene to the DNA of these fish that causes the fish to glow.	☐ artificial selection ☐ genetic engineering ☐ cloning
	A scientist is gathering DNA from clothing found at a crime scene. Then many copies of the DNA sample will be made. This will allow the scientist to better study the DNA. Then the scientist might be able to confirm the identity of the person at the crime scene.	☐ artificial selection ☐ genetic engineering ☐ cloning
	Wild carrots have thin, white roots. Over time, carrot farmers have selected carrots that have thick, bright orange roots.	☐ artificial selection ☐ genetic engineering ☐ cloning
	Diabetes can be treated in some people with injections that contain the hormone insulin. The gene responsible for producing insulin in humans has been inserted into the DNA of bacteria. These bacteria then produce the human insulin that is used in the injection.	☐ artificial selection ☐ genetic engineering ☐ cloning

Feel the IMPACT!

How does biotechnology impact our world?

Scientists are aware that there are many ethical, legal, and social issues that arise from the ability to use and change living things. Biotechnology can impact both our society and our environment. We must decide how and when it is acceptable to use biotechnology. The examples that follow show some concerns that might be raised during a classroom debate about biotechnology.

---

11 Evaluate Read the first two examples of biotechnology and what students had to say about their effects on individuals, society, and the environment. Then complete Example 3 by filling in questions or possible effects of the technology.

Example 1

A Glowing Mosquito?

This is the larva of a genetically engineered mosquito. Its DNA includes a gene from a glowing jellyfish that causes the engineered mosquito to glow. Scientists hope to use this same technology to modify the mosquito's genome in other ways. For example, it is thought that the DNA of the mosquito could be changed so that the mosquito could not spread malaria.

Effects on Individuals and Society

"If the mosquito could be engineered so that it does not spread malaria, many lives could be saved."

Effects on Environment

"Mosquitoes are a food source for birds and fish. Are there health risks to animals that eat genetically modified mosquitoes?"

Think Outside the Book — Inquiry

12 Debate As a class, choose a current event that involves biotechnology. Then hold a debate to present the benefits and risks of this technology.

© Houghton Mifflin Harcourt Publishing Company • Image Credits: ©Sinclair Stammers/Photo Researchers, Inc.

Example 2

Cloning the Gaur

The gaur is an endangered species. In 2001, a gaur was successfully cloned. The clone, named Noah, died of a bacterial infection 2 days after birth.

Effects on Individuals and Society

"How will we decide when it is appropriate to clone other types of organisms?"

Effects on Environment

"Cloning could help increase small populations of endangered species like the gaur and save them from extinction."

Example 3

Tough Plants!

Much of the corn and soybeans grown in the United States is genetically engineered. The plants have bacterial genes that make them more resistant to plant-eating insects.

Effects on Individuals and Society

Effects on Environment

Cracking the Code

With biotechnology, scientists manipulate the biological processes of organisms for a specific purpose. One purpose might be artificial selection. Through artificial selection, crops can be grown to be resistant to pests, cows can be made to produce more milk, and hens can be made to lay more eggs. It can also produce new kinds of medicine, allow people with allergies to own cats and dogs, and lead to bugs that can fight off diseases.

Different techniques make artificial selection possible. Take a look at the different types of technology on the following pages. You will research each one, and then explain what it is and how researchers use the technique to carry out the process of artificial selection.

Skills

✓ Obtain scientific information

✓ Evaluate scientific information

✓ Communicate scientific information

Part of a complex DNA code

Technique 1 DNA Sequencing

Being able to sequence and understand DNA is an important part of artificial selection.

Research Questions

1. How does this type of technology work?

2. How do scientists use the information it provides?

A DNA Sequencer

1. Write a short response on the lines below. Include supporting facts and details from your research.

_____

_____

_____

_____

_____

_____

Technique 2 Gene Editing

"Test tube babies"–genetically altered Salmon eggs being prepared for release into containers to hatch.

In order to create a larger salmon, scientists use the genes from three different species: the Chinock salmon, the ocean pout, and the Atlantic salmon.

A larger genetically modified salmon is made with a process called CRISPR.

CRISPR stands for *Clustered Regularly Interspaced Short Palindromic Repeats*.

More important than its name is the fact that it is a form of genome, or gene editing.

Research Questions

1. What is gene editing?
2. How do scientists use it?
3. Do you think this is a good idea? Why or why not?

2. *Write a short response on the lines below. Include supporting facts and details from your research.*

_____

_____

_____

_____

_____

_____

_____

_____

_____

_____

Technique 3 Gene Gun

A gene gun might look like something out of a science fiction movie, but scientists who work in the field of artificial selection, use it to insert the DNA of one living organism into another.

Research Questions

1. How does this type of technology work?

2. How does it help in the process of artificial selection?

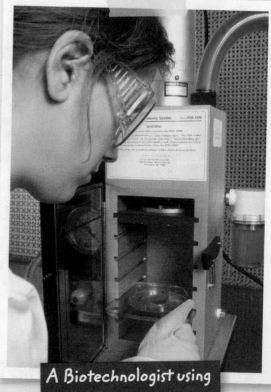

A Biotechnologist using a gene gun.

3. *Write a short response on the lines below. Include supporting facts and details from your research.*

_____

_____

_____

_____

_____

_____

_____

_____

_____

_____

Technique 4 Cloning

Cloning is used in artificial selection. Like twins, clones are exact genetic copies of each other.

In 1996, Dolly was the first mammal to be successfully cloned through reproductive cloning.

Dolly had three mothers: one provided the egg, one provided the DNA, and one carried the fertilized egg to term. Which one was Dolly's genetic mother?

Some people think it could lead to scientific breakthroughs. Others worry that cloning might be too dangerous to practice.

Research Questions

1. What is cloning?
2. Do you think cloning is a good idea? Why or why not?

Dolly, the sheep, was the first cloned mammal.

4. Write your responses on the lines below. Include supporting information from your research and a reason for your point of view on the issue.

_____
_____
_____
_____
_____
_____
_____

Visual Summary

To complete this summary, circle the correct word or phrase. Then use the key below to check your answers. You can use this page to review the main concepts of the lesson.

Biotechnology

Biotechnology is the use of living things and biological processes.

13 Modern biotechnology techniques can change an organism's DNA / environment.

Aritifical selection, genetic engineering, and cloning are three types of biotechnology.

14 The DNA of the mouse on the right has been modified through a technique called cloning / genetic engineering.

Biotechnology impacts individuals, society, and the environment.

15 Creating a clone / gene of an endangered species could impact the environment.

Answers: 13 DNA; 14 genetic engineering; 15 clone

16 **Compare** Both artificial selection and genetic engineering produce organisms that have traits that are different from the original organism. Explain how these two techniques differ.

Lesson Review

Vocabulary

In your own words, define the following terms.

1 biotechnology

_____

_____

_____

2 artificial selection

_____

_____

_____

3 clone

_____

_____

_____

Key Concepts

4 Identify Wheat has been bred by farmers for thousands of years to improve its ability to be ground into flour. This is an example of what kind of biotechnology?

A artificial selection

B genetic engineering

C cloning

D PCR

5 Identify Which of the following statements correctly describes why society must carefully consider the use of biotechnology?

A Biotechnology is a relatively new scientific field.

B Biotechnology can impact individuals and the environment.

C The methods of genetic engineering are not well understood.

D Artificial selection is an example of biotechnology.

Critical Thinking

Use this graph to answer the following questions.

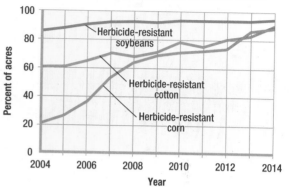

Genetically Modified Crops Grown in the United States

Source: *USDA, 2009*

6 Analyze In 2004, what percentage of soybean crops in the United States were genetically engineered to be herbicide resistant?

_____

7 Analyze From 2004 to 2008, which genetically engineered crop had the greatest increase in acreage?

_____

_____

8 Synthesize Some salmon have been genetically engineered to grow more quickly. The salmon are raised in pens set in rivers or in the sea. Describe how these salmon might impact society and the environment.

_____

_____

_____

_____

_____

_____

_____

My Notes

Unit 6

Lesson 1
ESSENTIAL QUESTION
What are living things?

Describe the necessities of life and the characteristics that all living things share.

Lesson 4
ESSENTIAL QUESTION
How has life on Earth changed over time?

Describe the evolution of life on Earth over time, using the geologic time scale.

Lesson 2
ESSENTIAL QUESTION
What is the process of natural selection?

Describe the role of genetic and environmental factors in the process of natural selection.

Lesson 5
ESSENTIAL QUESTION
How are organisms classified?

Describe how living things can be grouped by shared characteristics.

Lesson 3
ESSENTIAL QUESTION
What evidence supports the concept of common ancestry?

Describe the evidence that supports the theory of evolution by natural selection.

Lesson 6
ESSENTIAL QUESTION
How does biotechnology impact our world?

Explain how biotechnology impacts human life and the world around us.

Think Outside the Book

2 Synthesize Choose one of these activities to help synthesize what you have learned in this unit.

☐ Using what you learned in lessons 2, 3, and 4, explain why a scientist studying evolution might be interested in how the environment has changed over time.

☐ Using what you learned in lessons 1 and 2, write a short paragraph that compares sexual and asexual reproduction and explain why sexual reproduction is important to evolution.

Connect ESSENTIAL QUESTIONS
Lessons 2 and 3

1 Identify Describe two types of evidence that support the theory of evolution.

_____

_____

_____

_____

Name _____

Vocabulary

Fill in each blank with the term that best completes the following sentences.

1 A _____ is a membrane-covered structure that contains all of the materials necessary for life.

2 In _____ reproduction, a single parent produces offspring that are genetically identical to the parent.

3 _____ is the difference in inherited traits an organism has from others of the same species.

4 The process of selecting and breeding organisms that have certain desired traits is called _____.

5 In the most recent classification system, Bacteria, Archaea, and Eukarya are the three major _____ of life.

Key Concepts

Read each question below, and circle the best answer.

6 The teacher makes an argument to the class for why fire could be considered a living thing and then asks what is wrong with that argument. Tiana raises her hand and replies with one characteristic of life that fire does not have. Which of these could have been Tiana's response?

A Fire does not grow and develop.

B Fire cannot reproduce.

C Fire does not have genetic material.

D Fire does not use energy.

7 A mushroom grows on a dead, rotting oak tree lying in the forest. Which of the following best describes the tree and the mushroom?

A The oak tree was a producer, and the mushroom is a producer.

B The oak tree was a consumer, and the mushroom is a consumer.

C The oak tree was a decomposer, and the mushroom is a producer.

D The oak tree was a producer, and the mushroom is a decomposer.

8 Darwin's theory of natural selection consists of four important parts. Which of these correctly lists the four essential parts of natural selection?

A living space, adaptation, selection, and hunting

B overproduction, genetic variation, selection, and adaptation

C selection, extinction, underproduction, and competition

D asexual reproduction, genetic variation, selection, and adaptation

9 Charles Darwin studied the finches of the Galápagos Islands and found that their beaks vary in shape and size.

   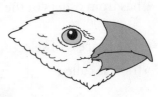

Darwin found that the finches that ate mostly insects had long, narrow beaks. Finches that ate mostly seeds had shorter, broad beaks to crush seeds. Which statement below best describes how natural selection resulted in the four types of finches shown above?

A The residents of the Galápagos Islands selectively bred together finches having the traits that they wanted them to have.

B The narrow-beaked finches came first and evolved into the broad-beaked finches through a series of natural mutations.

C The broad-beaked finches wore down their beaks digging for insects and passed these narrower beaks on to their offspring.

D Over time, the finches that were born with beaks better suited to the available food supply in their habitats survived and reproduced.

10 Which of these describes a likely reason why a species would become extinct after a major environmental change?

A There are not enough members of the species born with a trait necessary to survive in the new environment.

B The environmental changes mean fewer predators are around.

C The change in the environment opens new resources with less competition.

D There are more homes for the species in the changed environment.

11 Which of the following provides structural evidence for the concept a common ancestor?

A A fossil from the Mesozoic era shows an extinct animal similar to a modern animal.

B A comparison of similar bones in the legs of a human, a dog, and a bat.

C A genetic analysis of two animals shows similar sequences of DNA.

D The embryos of two animals look similar at similar stages.

12 The pictures below show four types of sea organisms.

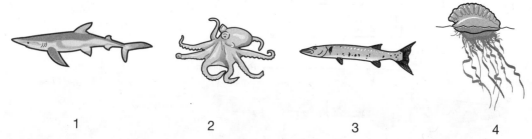

1   2   3   4

Which of these would you most expect to be true if these organisms were classified by their physical characteristics only?

A Organisms 1 and 3 would be in the same species.

B Organisms 2 and 4 would be in the same genus.

C Organisms 1 and 3 would be more closely related than organisms 2 and 4.

D Organisms 2 and 4 would be more closely related than organisms 1 and 3.

13 Scientists introducing a gene to the DNA of these fish that causes the fish to glow is an example of which application of biotechnology?

A artificial selection

B genetic engineering

C cloning

D artificial intelligence

Critical Thinking

Answer the following questions in the space provided.

14 The dichotomous key below helps identify the order of some sharks.

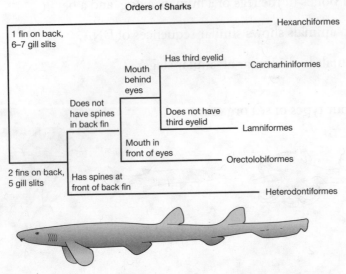

Orders of Sharks

Hexanchiformes

1 fin on back, 6–7 gill slits

Has third eyelid — Carcharhiniformes

Mouth behind eyes

Does not have spines in back fin

Does not have third eyelid — Lamniformes

Mouth in front of eyes — Orectolobiformes

2 fins on back, 5 gill slits

Has spines at front of back fin — Heterodontiformes

Use the diagram to determine the order to which this shark belongs. Then name its domain and kingdom.

Order: _____

Domain: _____   Kingdom: _____

15 Describe how the changes that happened during the first division of the geologic time scale affected the evolution of organisms on Earth.

_____

_____

_____

_____

Connect **ESSENTIAL QUESTIONS**
Lessons 2, 3, 4, and 5

Answer the following question in the space provided.

16 Explain why mass extinctions occur and why it makes sense to measure geologic time between mass extinctions.

_____

_____

_____

Space

Big Idea

The universe rapidly expanded and is held together by gravity. Technology provides information about the universe's origin and structure.

8.ETS1.2, 8.PS4.1, 8.ESS1.1, 8.ESS1.2,

Viewing the night sky from an observatory

What do you think?

A telescope can be used to observe the night sky. What observations can you make about the universe from your own backyard?

Using high-powered binoculars

Exploring Space

The human eye is far better at identifying characteristics of galaxies than any computer. So Galaxy Zoo has called for everyday citizens to help in a massive identification project. Well over a hundred thousand people have helped identify newly discovered galaxies. Now you can, too.

① Think About It

The scientists using the Sloan Digital Sky Survey telescope can gather far more information than they can review quickly. Humans are better at galaxy identification than computers. Why might this be a difficult task for computers?

_____

_____

_____

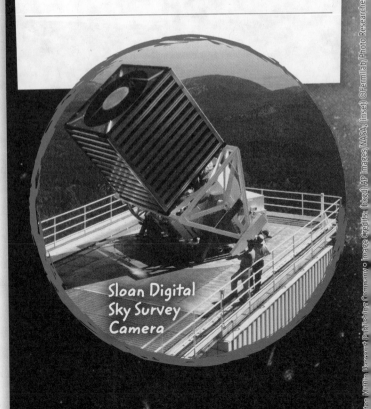

Sloan Digital
Sky Survey
Camera

A galaxy seen edge-on

Spiral galaxy

② Ask A Question

How can people who aren't scientists help aid in galaxy identification?

With a partner, review the instructions on Galaxy Zoo's website and practice identifying galaxies. You will need to pay attention to the Galaxy Zoo classification system. Record your observations about the process.

_____

_____

_____

_____

_____

Things to Consider

Many different people review and classify each image of a galaxy at Galaxy Zoo. This way, scientists are able to control the mistakes that individuals may make.

✔ How can having many different people look at each galaxy help prevent errors?

③ Apply Your Knowledge

A List the characteristics you will be looking for when you examine a galaxy photo.

_____

_____

_____

_____

_____

_____

_____

B Review and classify galaxies on Galaxy Zoo's website.

C Create a classroom guide to the galaxies that you have identified.

Take It Home

What has the Citizen Science project known as Galaxy Zoo accomplished so far? Find out how many people have participated and compare that to the number of scientists working on the project. See _ScienceSaurus®_ for more information about galaxies.

Technology for Space Exploration

ESSENTIAL QUESTION

How do we explore space?

By the end of this lesson, you should be able to analyze the ways people explore space, and assess the role of technology in these efforts.

8.ETS1.2

Space probes, like the artist's rendition shown here, visit distant planets in our solar system and transmit data back to Earth.

Lesson Labs

Quick Labs
• Analyzing Satellite Images
• Design a Spacecraft

S.T.E.M. Lab
• Build a Rocket

Engage Your Brain

1 Predict Check T or F to show whether you think each statement is true or false.

T	F	
☐	☐	Astronauts can travel to distant planets in the solar system.
☐	☐	The space shuttle orbits the moon.
☐	☐	Artificial satellites in space can help you find locations on Earth.
☐	☐	Rovers explore the surfaces of planets and moons.

2 Describe Write your own caption to this photo.

_____

_____

_____

Active Reading

3 Apply Use context clues to write your own definition for the words *analyze* and *transmit*.

Example sentence
Some spacecraft carry technology that can <u>analyze</u> soil and rock samples from objects in space.

analyze:

_____

_____

Example sentence
Satellites <u>transmit</u> data back to Earth.

transmit:

_____

_____

Vocabulary Terms
• space shuttle   • lander
• probe   • rover
• orbiter   • artificial satellite

4 Identify As you read, place a question mark next to any words that you don't understand. When you finish reading the lesson, go back and review the text that you marked. If the information is still confusing, consult a classmate or a teacher.

Beyond the Clouds

How do people travel to space?

On April 12, 1961, Yuri Gagarin became the first human to orbit Earth. Since then, people have continued to travel into space. Large rockets were the first method used to transport humans into space. The space shuttle was developed later and allowed people more time to live and work in space.

With Rockets

To travel away from Earth, large rockets must overcome the pull of Earth's gravity. A *rocket* is a machine that uses gas, often from burning fuel, to escape Earth's gravitational pull. Rockets launch both crewed and uncrewed vehicles into space. During early space missions, the capsules that contained the crews detached from the rockets. The rockets themselves burned up. The capsules "splashed down" in the ocean and were recovered but not reused.

With Space Shuttles

A **space shuttle** is a reusable spacecraft that launches with the aid of rocket boosters and liquid fuel. The shuttle glides to a landing on Earth like an airplane. It carries astronauts and supplies back and forth into orbit around Earth. *Columbia*, the first space shuttle in a fleet of six, was launched in 1981. Since then, more than 100 shuttle missions have been completed. Two white, solid rocket boosters (SRBs) help the shuttle reach orbit. These booster rockets detach and are reused.

Active Reading 5 **Explain** What is the purpose of SRBs?

_____

_____

How do people live in space?

People live and work in space on space stations. A *space station* is a long-term crewed spacecraft on which scientific research can be carried out. Currently, the *International Space Station* (ISS) is the only space station in Earth's orbit. Six-member crews live aboard the ISS for an average of six months. Because crews live in a constant state of weightlessness, the ISS is the perfect place to study the effects of weightlessness on the human body. Many other scientific experiments are conducted as well. Observations of Earth and Earth systems are also made from the ISS.

Booster rockets launch the space shuttle. Following launch, they detach and fall into the ocean. They are retrieved for use again.

What are some challenges people face in space?

Active Reading **6 Identify** As you read, underline challenges humans face when traveling in space.

Astronauts have traveled to the moon, but no human has yet traveled to more distant objects in the solar system. There are many technological challenges to overcome, such as having the fuel necessary for a long return voyage. Other challenges include having sufficient supplies of air, food, and water available for a long journey. Also, the spacecraft must be insulated from the intense cold of space as well as harmful radiation from the sun.

Spacesuits protect astronauts when they work outside a spacecraft. But astronauts still face challenges inside a spacecraft. In space, everything seems weightless. Simple tasks like eating and drinking become difficult. Astronauts must strap themselves to their beds to avoid floating around. The human body experiences problems in a weightless environment. Bones and muscles weaken. So, astronauts must exercise daily to strengthen their bodies.

Visualize It!

Spacesuits protect astronauts from extreme temperatures and from micrometeoroid strikes in space. They provide oxygen to astronauts and remove excess carbon dioxide.

7 Identify What are some technologies humans use to survive outside in space?

A life support pack supplies oxygen and removes carbon dioxide.

Pressurized suits protect the astronaut from the vacuum of space.

The astronaut is tethered to the shuttle at the waist.

The helmet contains communication gear and a protective visor.

© Houghton Mifflin Harcourt Publishing Company • Image Credits: (bg) ©Gene Blevins/LA Daily News/Corbis; (b) ©Stocktrek/Getty Images

The Hubble Space Telescope took this amazing image of Supernova SN1987A in the Large Magellanic Cloud and transmitted the image back to Earth.

Looking Up

What uncrewed technologies do people use to explore space?

Most objects in space are too far away for astronauts to visit. Scientists and engineers have developed uncrewed technologies to gather information about these objects. These technologies include space telescopes, probes, orbiters, landers, and rovers.

Telescopes in Space

Earth's atmosphere distorts light that passes through it. This makes it difficult to obtain clear images of objects in deep space. So some telescopes are placed in Earth's orbit to obtain clearer images. Computers in the telescopes gather data and transmit it back to Earth. For example, the *Hubble Space Telescope* is a reflecting telescope that was placed in orbit in 1990. It detects visible light, and ultraviolet and infrared radiation as well. It has greatly expanded our knowledge of the universe.

Other space telescopes collect data using different types of electromagnetic radiation. The *Chandra X-Ray Observatory* and *Compton Gamma-Ray Observatory* were placed in space because Earth's atmosphere blocks most X-rays and gamma rays.

Active Reading **8 Relate** What is one advantage of placing a telescope in space?

_____

_____

_____

Space Probes

A space **probe** is an uncrewed vehicle that carries scientific instruments to distant objects in space. Probes carry a variety of data-collecting instruments, and on-board computers handle data, which are sent back to Earth.

Probes have been especially useful for studying the atmospheres of the gas giant planets. An atmospheric entry probe is dropped from a spacecraft into a planet's atmosphere. These probes relay atmospheric data back to the spacecraft for a short period of time before they are crushed in the planet's atmosphere. Remember, the gas giant planets do not have solid surfaces on which to land, and the pressure within their atmospheres is much greater than the atmospheric pressure on Earth.

Some probes can collect and return materials to Earth. In 2004, NASA's *Stardust* probe collected dust samples as it flew by a comet. The particles were returned to Earth for analysis two years later. It was the first time samples from beyond the moon were brought back to Earth!

The **Mars Curiosity** rover is searching for evidence of past life. This photo shows the rover's tracks across a sand dune.

This artist's rendition shows the encounter of the space probe **Stardust** with Comet Wild 2 in 2004.

Orbiters

An **orbiter** is an uncrewed spacecraft that is designed to enter into orbit around another object in space. As an orbiter approaches its target, rocket engines are fired to slow down the spacecraft so it can go into orbit. Controllers on Earth can place a spacecraft into orbit around a distant planet or its moons.

Orbiters can study a planet for long periods of time. On-board cameras and other technology are used to monitor atmospheric or surface changes. Instruments are also used to make measurements of temperature and to determine the altitudes of surface features. Orbiters can photograph an entire planet's surface. The data allow scientists to create detailed maps of solar system bodies.

Active Reading **10 Describe** What information can scientists obtain from orbiters?

_____

_____

_____

Visualize It!

9 Compare How are probes and landers alike? How are they different?

_____

_____

_____

_____

Landers and Rovers

Orbiters allow astronomers to create detailed maps of planets. They do not touch down on a planet or moon, however. That task is accomplished by landers that are controlled by scientists from Earth. A **lander** is a craft designed to land on the surface of a body in space. Landers have been placed successfully on the moon, Venus, Mars, and on Saturn's moon Titan. Some, such as the *Mars Pathfinder*, transmitted data for years. The images taken by a lander are more detailed than those taken by an orbiter.

In addition, a lander may carry a rover. A **rover** is a small vehicle that comes out of the lander and explores the surface of a planet or moon beyond the landing site. Both landers and rovers may have mechanical arms for gathering rock, dust, and soil samples.

In 2004, the rovers *Spirit* and *Opportunity* landed on Mars. They found evidence that water and wind once shaped Mars' surface. In 2012, *Curiosity* landed on Mars. After analyzing rock on the surface, *Curiosity* found that Mars likely had suitable conditions for life to have begun in the past.

Looking Down

How are satellites used to observe Earth?

A satellite is any object in space that orbits another object. An **artificial satellite** is any human-made object placed in orbit around a body in space. Some examples of artificial satellites include remote-sensing satellites, navigation satellites, weather satellites, and communications satellites. Artificial satellites orbit Earth and send data about our planet back to ground stations.

To Study Earth's Features

Scientists use remote-sensing satellites to study Earth. Remote sensing is a way to collect information about something without physically being there. Remote-sensing satellites map and monitor Earth's resources. For example, these satellites identify sources of pollution and monitor crops to track the spread of disease. They also monitor global temperatures, ocean and land heights, and the amount of freshwater ice and sea ice.

Astronauts in the *International Space Station* have photographed volcanoes during different stages of eruption. These photos from space are valuable because scientists can see and study views that are not possible from Earth.

11 Identify As you read, underline examples of four different kinds of satellites.

Inquiry

12 Identify List two different features on Earth's surface not given as an example here that might be studied from space.

_____

_____

Using satellites, scientists can study images of Earth's features taken from space, such as the eruption of the Gaua volcano in the South Pacific.

To Monitor Changes in Earth Systems

Remote-sensing data provide valuable information on how Earth systems change over time. For example, for more than 30 years, satellites have been observing Arctic sea ice. Images from the European Space Agency's ENVISAT satellite show that a large decline in Arctic sea ice has occurred over the past several years. By analyzing these images, scientists can better determine why the changes are happening.

Images taken by remote-sensing Landsat satellites show changes in the Mississippi River delta over time. When comparing an image taken in 1973 with an image taken in 2003, scientists can see how the delta has changed shape. They can also keep track of changes in the amount of land that is underwater.

The blue shows the shape of the delta in 1973. The green shows the land surface.

This image shows the shape of the delta in 2003. The black represents the water in the Gulf of Mexico.

Visualize It!

13 Analyze Identify changes in the land surface along the Mississippi River delta using the photos.

_____
_____
_____
_____

To Collect Weather Data

It is difficult to imagine life without reliable weather forecasts. Every day, millions of people make decisions based on information provided by weather satellites. Weather satellites give scientists a big-picture view of Earth's atmosphere. These satellites constantly monitor the atmosphere for events that lead to severe weather conditions. For example, weather satellites are able to provide images of hurricanes. These images help scientists predict the path of the hurricane. People living in the projected pathway can be warned to move to a safer place until the hurricane passes.

Weather satellites also monitor changes in cloud formation and in energy coming from Earth. Information from weather satellites helps airplanes avoid dangerous weather and provides farmers with information that can help them to grow their crops.

Weather satellites monitor the path of Hurricane Igor churning over the Atlantic Ocean in 2010.

For Search and Rescue Operations

The U.S. National Oceanic and Atmospheric Administration (NOAA) has many different satellites. NOAA's environmental satellites carry an instrument package called *SARSAT*. The SARSAT instruments detect distress signals from emergency beacons (BEE•kuhnz). Many ships, airplanes, and individuals on land have emergency beacons. The beacons can be used anywhere in the world, at any time of day. Once the distress signals are received, the satellites relay the signals to a network of ground stations, as shown in the illustration. In the end, the signals go to the U.S. Mission Control Center in Maryland. The Mission Control Center processes the emergency and puts the search and rescue operation into action.

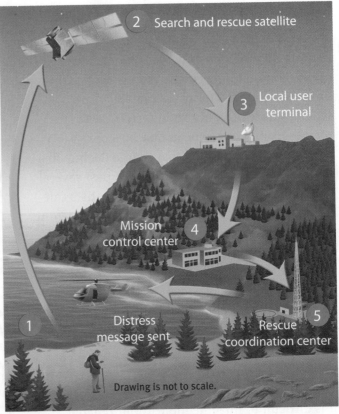

2 Search and rescue satellite

3 Local user terminal

Mission control center 4

1

Distress message sent

5 Rescue coordination center

Drawing is not to scale.

Steps involved in a search and rescue operation

The white areas indicate the most light.

To Provide Composite Images

Data from satellites can be combined to form one image that shows more complete information. The combined image is called a *composite* image. Composite satellite images can give very detailed information about an area's surface features and other features. For example, satellite images can be combined to produce a dramatic image that shows where most of the sources of artificial light are located, as shown here. In this false-color image, data were combined to produce the different colors. A composite image that shows artificial light sources would include images of Earth with no cloud cover.

Think Outside the Book

14 Research Investigate a satellite map that shows surface features for your town or city. What kinds of data does this map contain?

© Houghton Mifflin Harcourt Publishing Company • Image Credits: ©P. Cinzano, Fabio Falchi & Chris D. Elvidge/Blackwell Science/Photo Researchers, Inc.

Exploring the Ocean

NEW FRONTIER

They may not seem related, but deep-sea exploration and space exploration have something in common. Both use advanced technologies to observe locations that are difficult or dangerous for humans to explore.

Ocean Submersibles
Both marine scientists and space scientists investigate areas most humans will never visit. Ocean submersibles can be crewed or uncrewed.

Black Smokers
Hydrothermal vents are on the ocean floor where the pressure is too great for humans to withstand.

Tube Worms
In the 1970s, scientists aboard a submersible discovered giant tube worms living near an ocean vent. NASA scientists examine the extreme conditions of Mars and other planets for any signs of life.

Extend

Inquiry

15 Identify List two similarities between deep-sea exploration and space exploration.

16 Research and Record List some features of an ocean submersible, for example, *Alvin*. How is the submersible's structure similar to that of spacecraft?

17 Recommend Support more funding for deep-sea exploration by doing one of the following:
• write a letter
• design an ad for a science magazine
• write a script for a radio commercial

For Communication

Communications satellites relay data, including Internet service and some television and radio broadcasts. They are also used to relay long-distance telephone calls. One communications satellite can relay thousands of telephone calls or several television programs at once. Communications satellites are in use continuously.

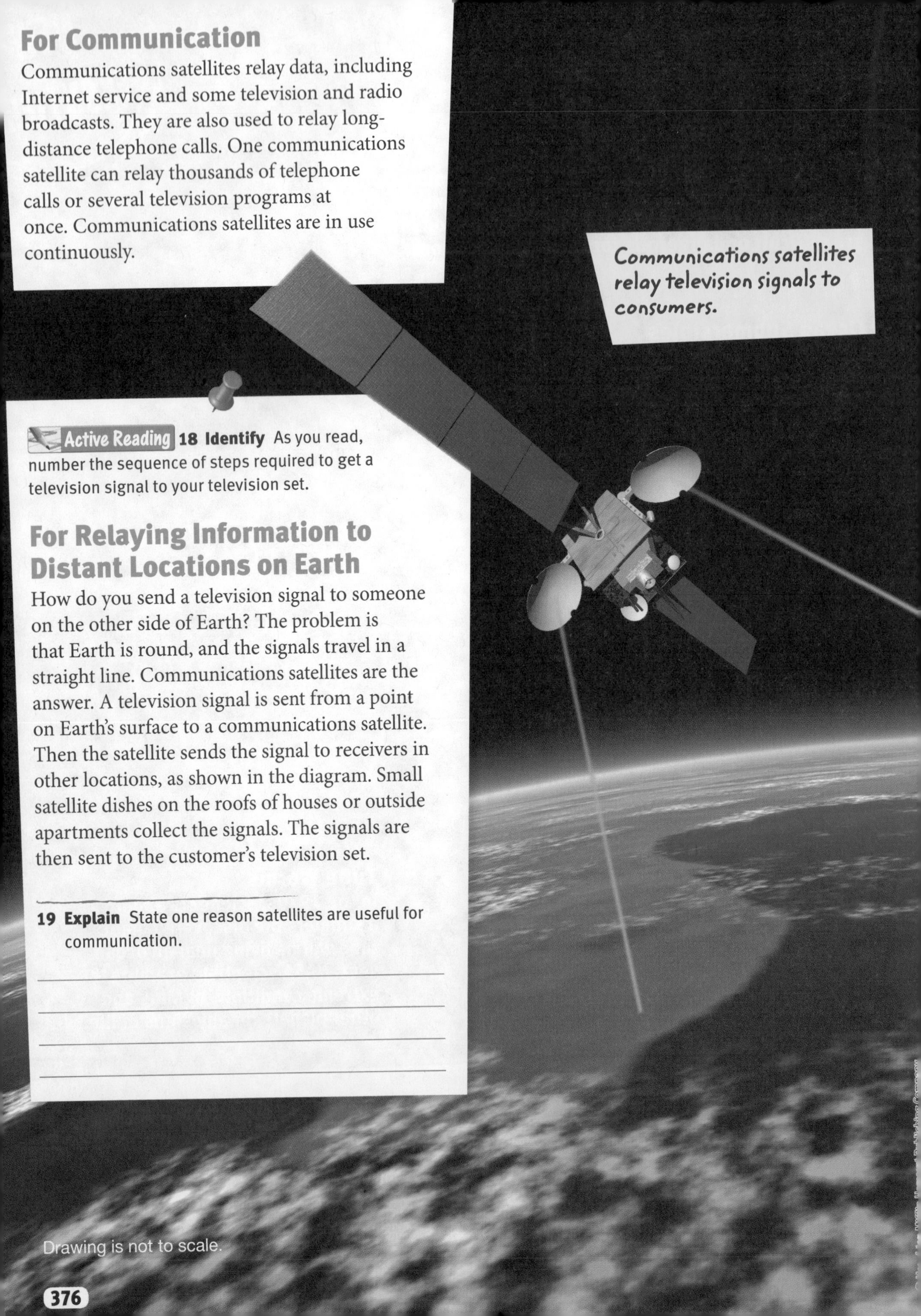

Communications satellites relay television signals to consumers.

Active Reading **18 Identify** As you read, number the sequence of steps required to get a television signal to your television set.

For Relaying Information to Distant Locations on Earth

How do you send a television signal to someone on the other side of Earth? The problem is that Earth is round, and the signals travel in a straight line. Communications satellites are the answer. A television signal is sent from a point on Earth's surface to a communications satellite. Then the satellite sends the signal to receivers in other locations, as shown in the diagram. Small satellite dishes on the roofs of houses or outside apartments collect the signals. The signals are then sent to the customer's television set.

19 Explain State one reason satellites are useful for communication.

_____

_____

_____

_____

Drawing is not to scale.

20 Apply Write a caption for the image shown here.

_____
_____
_____
_____

For Navigating and Locating

Did you know that satellite technology can actually help keep you from getting lost? The Global Positioning System (GPS) is a network of 24 satellites that orbit Earth. GPS satellites continuously send microwave signals. A GPS receiver receives signals from at least four satellites at one time. Once a GPS receiver on Earth picks up the signals, the technology in the receiver can determine the location of the receiver on Earth's surface. Airplane and boat pilots use GPS for navigation. Many cars now have GPS units that show information on a screen on the dashboard.

GPS satellites send signals that help a receiver calculate its location.

Modern GPS units are small enough to hold in your hand, so you can take them with you and know your location anywhere you go!

Eye in the Sky

How can an airplane packed full of the most modern communications technology disappear without a trace? In March 2014 that is exactly what happened with Malaysia Airlines Flight MH370 bound for Beijing, China, from Malaysia.

While we may never know exactly what happened, it did make us more aware of the limitations of ground-based plane tracking technology, and has led to calls for big changes in the industry on how planes are tracked.

Most airplanes are tracked using ground-based radar (RAdio Detection And Ranging), which bounces radio waves off objects to determine where they are and how fast they are moving. However, because of the curvature of the Earth these land-based technologies have limited range; a limitation not shared by satellites high above the Earth's surface.

Skills

✔ **Research information about technologies**

✔ **Communicate by describing how data from technologies provides information about the solar system and universe**

What You'll Do

- Quickly read through the different technologies discussed on the next few pages.

- Working with your teacher, make a plan to research the technologies to help you answer the questions.

(1) In the diagram below, mark the area where using radar from ground stations A and B would not be effective. Draw arrows to show how airplane C could broadcast its position to ground stations A and B using the satellite D.

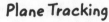

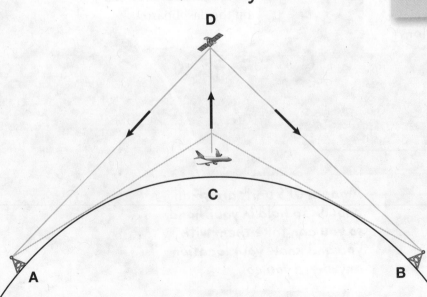

Looking into Space

Even the best ground-based telescopes in the world have a great limitation when they look deep into space because of our turbulent atmosphere. Light from distant stars scatters in the atmosphere, creating a fuzzy blob rather than a clear point of light. Astronomers have sought to overcome this by placing their telescopes high in the mountains where the atmosphere is thin.

Some observatories have sought to deal with the problem of atmospheric disturbance directly with a technique called **adaptive optics**. At the Keck Observatory in Hawai'i, astronomers fire laser beams into the upper atmosphere to gauge the amount of disturbance in the column of air. The data from the laser beams is fed into a computer, which then distorts the telescope's mirror to compensate for atmospheric disturbance, providing a much clearer image.

The Very Large Telescope (VLT) site at Cerro Paranal, Chile

The laser beams at the Keck Observatory in Hawai'i

(2) What are the advantages and disadvantages of placing an observatory on a high mountaintop?

_____

_____

_____

_____

_____

(3) What other atmospheric effect is adaptive optics not able to compensate for?

_____

_____

_____

_____

Hubble Space Telescope

Perhaps the best way to deal with the disturbances in the atmosphere is to get far above it altogether. In 1990, NASA launched the Hubble Space telescope high above the atmosphere into low Earth orbit. It has provided astronomers with some truly astonishing images, and a wealth of data about distant galaxies.

One of the most remarkable images was taken of a small patch of sky near the constellation Ursa Major. Over a period of ten days the Hubble telescope took 342 images to create this view seen in the background of theses two pages. The process was repeated looking in the southern skies. The images showed over 3,000 galaxies!

The Hubble Space telescope is approxinmately 540km above the surface of the earth.

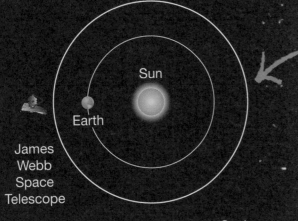

Sun

Earth

James
Webb
Space
Telescope

Not to Scale

James Webb Space Telescope

In 2018, NASA plans to launch the James Webb Telescope into space. Its destination is a point almost 1,000,000 miles from Earth. That is almost four times the distance of the moon. Unlike the Hubble Space Telescope, the James Webb telescope will orbit the Sun, not the Earth, travelling with the Earth as it makes its year-long journey around the solar system.

---

4 With the Hubble Space Telescope being in low Earth orbit there are times that it can't be used, and places that it cannot look. Explain.

_____

_____

_____

_____

5 What is the advantage of the James Webb telescope being in a solar orbit?

_____

_____

_____

_____

_____

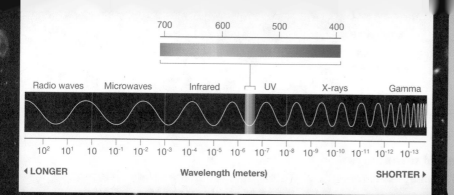

Radio waves	Microwaves	Infrared	UV	X-rays	Gamma

| 10² | 10¹ | 10 | 10⁻¹ | 10⁻² | 10⁻³ | 10⁻⁴ | 10⁻⁵ | 10⁻⁶ | 10⁻⁷ | 10⁻⁸ | 10⁻⁹ | 10⁻¹⁰ | 10⁻¹¹ | 10⁻¹² | 10⁻¹³ |

◄ LONGER   Wavelength (meters)   SHORTER ►

Light You Don't See

Visible light is only a small portion of the electromagnetic spectrum. We know from sensors and special telescopes that the objects in the universe emit electromagnetic radiation from other frequencies in the spectrum.

The Crab

In the constellation of Taurus there is a small fuzzy patch known as The Crab Nebula. Its location was recorded by the Chinese in 1054 as it marked the appearance of a "guest star" that shone as brightly as Venus for almost a month.

What the Chinese astronomers had witnessed was a supernova, a star that exploded and collapsed 7,000 light years away. As the star faded, so did its memory until it was rediscovered as a nebula in 1774 and named "The Crab".

So massive was the explosion that it emitted electromagnetic radiation across the spectrum that we can detect today with different instruments.

CRAB NEBULA

| RADIO | INFRARED | VISIBLE LIGHT | ULTRAVIOLET | X-RAYS | GAMMA RAYS |

6 What can the data from different wavelengths show you about the Crab Nebula that you would not be able to show from visible light alone?

_____

_____

_____

_____

_____

Visual Summary

To complete this summary, fill in the blanks with the correct word or phrase. Then, use the key below to check your answers. You can use this page to review the main concepts of the lesson.

Technology for Space Exploration

Humans use crewed technology to travel to and from space.

21 To escape from Earth's gravity, the space shuttle uses liquid fuel and _____

Telescopes in space study different types of electromagnetic radiation.

23 To obtain clearer images, space telescopes orbit above _____

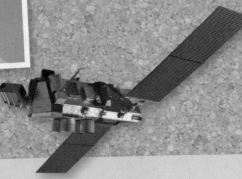

Artificial satellites provide a wealth of information about Earth.

22 Satellites provide images for military purposes, remote sensing, communications, navigation, and _____

Uncrewed spacecraft can explore distant planets.

24 Examples of uncrewed spacecraft include probes, orbiters, landers, and _____

Answers: 21 solid rocket boosters; 22 weather; 23 Earth's atmosphere; 24 rovers

25 Provide Give examples of the kind of information scientists can obtain from each type of uncrewed spacecraft.

Lesson Review

Vocabulary

Circle the term that best completes the following sentences.

1 A *rocket / space shuttle* is a reusable crewed spacecraft.

2 A(n) *lander / orbiter* is a kind of artificial satellite.

3 A(n) *orbiter / rover* often has mechanical arms to gather rock samples.

4 A(n) *orbiter / probe* is more suited to the long-term study of a planet or moon.

5 A *rocket / space shuttle* had detachable capsules that contained the crew.

Key Concepts

6 List Give an example of how satellites are used for communication.

_____

_____

7 Explain Why is most space exploration accomplished with spacecraft that do not have crews on board?

_____

_____

_____

8 Apply How could you benefit from using a GPS unit in your daily life?

_____

_____

_____

9 Explain What is one advantage of using an orbiter to study objects in space?

_____

_____

_____

_____

Critical Thinking

Use the diagram to answer the following questions.

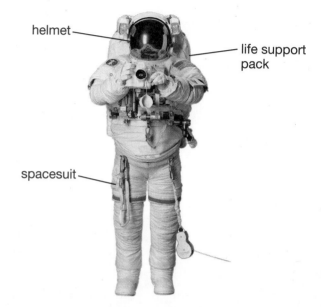

helmet

life support pack

spacesuit

10 Identify Which spacesuit feature provides oxygen to an astronaut?

_____

11 Infer How is the spacesuit designed to protect the astronaut outside of a spacecraft?

_____

_____

_____

12 Infer Why do you think it's important to map a planet's surface before planning a lander mission?

_____

_____

_____

13 Conclude Could a lander be used to study the surface of Saturn? Explain.

_____

_____

_____

My Notes

Testing and Modifying Theories

When scientists develop a theory, they use experiments to investigate the theory. The results of experiments can support or disprove theories. If the results of several experiments do not support a theory, it may be modified.

Tutorial

Read below about the Tomatosphere Project to find out more about how theories are tested and modified. This project exposes tomato seeds to simulated Martian conditions to observe later seed germination.

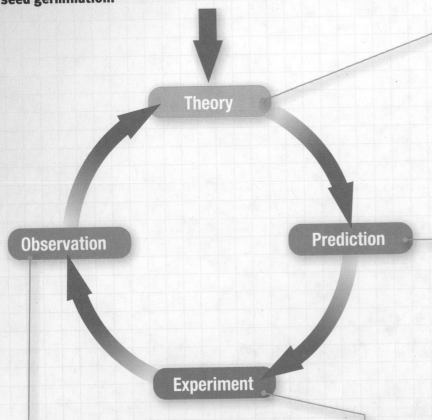

A theory is created/modified.
Sometimes, two well-supported theories explain a single phenomenon. A theory might be modified based on new data. Scientists can figure out how to supply long-term space missions with food, water, oxygen, and other life-support needs.

A prediction is made.
Predictions are based on prior knowledge. Scientists might predict that if tomato seeds are exposed to Martian conditions, they will still be able to germinate and grow into healthy, fruit-bearing plants.

Observations are made.
Scientists evaluate their observations to see whether or not the results support their hypothesis. If any data disprove the original prediction, scientists may have to modify their theory. The results of the blind studies are gathered and analyzed to see whether exposure to harsh conditions affected the germination of the seeds.

Experiments are done.
Setting up the proper scientific procedure to test the prediction is important. In the Tomatosphere Project, a set of exposed seeds, along with a control group of regular seeds, are planted in thousands of classrooms. At least 20 of each type were planted, to ensure a large enough sample size. The type of seeds were not revealed, as part of a blind study.

© Houghton Mifflin Harcourt Publishing Company

You Try It!

Two scientists describe theories that try to explain the motion of galaxies. Use the information provided to answer the questions that follow.

Background

Any objects that have mass, such as Earth and you, exert a gravitational force that pulls them toward each other. An unexpected motion of an object in space, such as a galaxy, could be the result of an unseen object pulling on it. Scientists use electromagnetic radiation, such as visible, infrared, and ultraviolet light, to detect and study visible matter. However, dark matter is a hypothetical material that does not give off electromagnetic radiation that we can detect.

Scientist A

There is more dark matter than visible matter in galaxies. There is just too little visible matter to exert the force that would explain how the galaxies move. The additional force exerted by dark matter would explain the motion we see without having to change our understanding of gravitational force.

Scientist B

We must change our understanding of gravitational force. The farther away from the center of a galaxy you go, the stronger (not weaker) the gravitational force becomes. With this change, the amount of visible matter is enough to explain how the galaxies move. Dark matter is not needed.

1 Predicting Outcomes How would proof that dark matter exists affect each scientist's theory?

_____

_____

_____

_____

2 Predicting Outcomes If experiments fail to detect dark matter, does Scientist A's theory need to be modified? Explain why.

_____

_____

_____

_____

3 Making Inferences What evidence would require both scientists to modify their theories?

_____

_____

_____

_____

Take It Home

Using the Internet, research a scientific theory that has been reproduced in two different experiments. Write a short report that explains how the observations helped develop the theory. How else could this theory could be investigated?

Observing the Universe

ESSENTIAL QUESTION

What can we learn from space images?

By the end of this lesson, you should be able to describe ways of collecting information from space and analyze how different wavelengths of the electromagnetic spectrum provide different information.

8.ETS1.2, 8.PS4.1

This blue object is the sun. The image was not produced using visible light.

✋ **Lesson Labs**

Quick Labs
• Using Invisible Light
• A Model of the Universe
• Splitting White Light

S.T.E.M. Lab
• Making a Telescope

Engage Your Brain

1 Predict Check T or F to show whether you think each statement is true or false.

T F

☐ ☐ Visible light is a type of electromagnetic radiation.

☐ ☐ Artificial satellites can produce images of Earth only.

☐ ☐ Earth's atmosphere blocks all ultraviolet radiation from space.

☐ ☐ Optical telescopes are used to study objects in the universe.

2 Identify Look at the picture below. Write a caption that explains what the picture shows.

_____
_____
_____
_____
_____

Active Reading

3 Synthesize You can often define an unknown word if you know the meaning of its word parts. Use the word parts and sentence below to make an educated guess about the meaning of the word *microwave*.

Word part	Meaning
micro-	small
-wave	an up-and-down or back-and-forth movement

Example sentence

microwave:
_____
_____

Vocabulary Terms

• wavelength
• electromagnetic spectrum
• spectrum

4 Apply As you learn the definition of each vocabulary term in this lesson, create your own definition or sketch to help you remember the meaning of the term.

What is electromagnetic radiation?

Energy traveling as electromagnetic waves is called *electromagnetic radiation*. Waves can be described by either their wavelength or frequency. **Wavelength** is the distance between two adjacent crests or troughs of a wave. *Frequency* measures the number of waves passing a point per second. Higher-frequency waves have a shorter wavelength. Energy carried by electromagnetic radiation depends on both the wavelength and the amount of radiation at that wavelength. A higher-frequency wave carries higher energy than a lower-frequency wave.

How is electromagnetic radiation classified?

Active Reading **5 Identify** As you read, underline the name of each part of the electromagnetic spectrum.

There are many different wavelengths and frequencies of electromagnetic radiation. All these wavelengths and frequencies make up what is called the **electromagnetic spectrum**. A **spectrum** (plural, *spectra*) is a continuous range of a single feature, in this case wavelength. The form of electromagnetic radiation with the longest wavelength and the lowest frequency is radio waves. Radios and televisions receive radio waves. These devices then produce sound waves. Sound waves are not electromagnetic radiation. Microwaves have shorter wavelengths and higher frequencies than radio waves. The next shortest wavelength radiation is called *infrared*. Infrared is sometimes called "heat radiation." Visible light has a shorter wavelength than infrared. You see an object when visible light from the object reaches your eyes. Images produced in visible light are the only images we can see without computer enhancement. Even shorter in wavelength is ultraviolet radiation. The shortest wavelengths belong to x-rays and gamma rays.

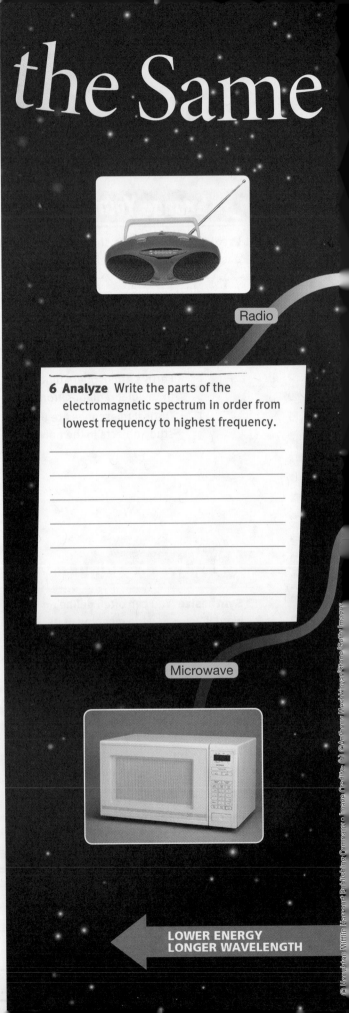

On the Same

Radio

6 Analyze Write the parts of the electromagnetic spectrum in order from lowest frequency to highest frequency.

_____

_____

_____

_____

_____

_____

_____

Microwave

**LOWER ENERGY
LONGER WAVELENGTH**

Wavelength?

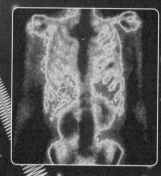

Gamma rays

Infrared

7 Complete Electromagnetic
_____ that
has a shorter wavelength has a
_____ frequency.

Ultraviolet

X-rays

Visible light

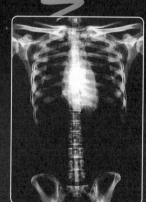

**HIGHER ENERGY
SHORTER WAVELENGTH**

A Rainbow of Colors

What is a spectroscope?

The visible light that you see from distant stars is made up of many colors of light, even though it appears white. Scientists use spectroscopes to collect light from stars and separate the colors in the light. Some spectroscopes contain prisms. Light first passes through a slit so that only a very narrow beam of light reaches the prism. The prism separates the colors of light to make a spectrum of visible light. The light then travels to a detector that is attached to a computer.

In a simple spectroscope, light passes through a slit to a prism. Before the light travels to the detector, a prism separates the colors.

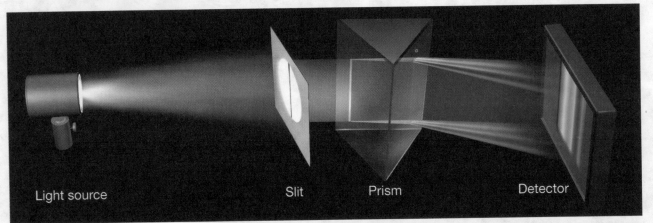

Light source   Slit   Prism   Detector

How is spectral analysis used in astronomy?

Astronomers analyze spectra from all parts of the electromagnetic spectrum. Because different wavelengths have different energies per wave, different types of radiation interact with matter in different ways. These interactions provide scientists with information about the components of the universe. For example, scientists can analyze spectra to learn about the motion and distance of objects. They can also learn about the properties of objects, such as composition and temperature.

8 Summarize Complete the concept map by filling in the circles below to show how spectral analysis is used to gain information about the universe.

Spectral analysis can reveal

9 Identify As you read, underline the characteristics of the different types of visible spectra.

What are types of visible spectra?

Spectra are produced when matter emits or absorbs light. As with all spectra, the visible spectrum is ordered by wavelength or frequency. Violet light has the shortest wavelength and the highest frequency. Red light has the longest wavelength and lowest frequency. The types of visible spectra that scientists study to learn about matter are continuous spectra, emission spectra, and absorption spectra.

A Continuous Spectrum

A continuous spectrum is produced when a light source emits all of the colors of visible light. It is made up of all of the wavelengths of visible light with no gaps or breaks between the wavelengths. So, it appears as an unbroken band of colors. The colors are always in the same order in a continuous spectrum, the order of the colors of the rainbow—red, orange, yellow, green, blue, and violet.

A continuous spectrum shows all of the colors of light without any gaps.

An Emission Spectrum

A real neon sign always glows red. Neon gas emits only certain wavelengths of light. You could look at the emission spectrum of neon to see these colors. An emission spectrum is a series of unevenly spaced lines of different colors and brightnesses. Each color corresponds to a certain wavelength of light that is emitted. The emission spectrum of neon has many bands at wavelengths that correspond to red light. Each element has a unique emission spectrum. Therefore, bright lines will appear at different wavelengths in the spectrum of helium than of hydrogen.

An emission spectrum of hydrogen shows the colors of light that heated hydrogen gas emits.

An Absorption Spectrum

Gaseous elements also absorb certain wavelengths of light when light from a glowing object passes through the gas. An absorption spectrum looks similar to a continuous spectrum, except it has dark lines at certain wavelengths. The dark lines represent the wavelengths that a gas absorbs. Scientists have standard absorption and emission spectra of elements. They can determine the composition of stars by comparing the patterns of spectra taken from stars to the standard spectra.

An absorption spectrum of hydrogen shows dark lines where hydrogen gas absorbs light that passes through it.

10 Explain How are an absorption spectrum and an emission spectrum used to determine the elements that make up a star?

_____

_____

_____

Changing Waves

What is the Doppler effect?

The pitch of a siren that you hear as an ambulance passes by changes from higher to lower because of the Doppler effect. The Doppler effect is an observed change in frequency or wavelength when the source is moving with respect to the observer.

As the source of the sound moves forward, the sound waves in front of the source become closer together. So, the wavelength decreases and the frequency increases. As a result, the sound is higher. The source of the sound is also moving away from the sound waves behind it. These waves are farther apart than they would be if the source of the sound were not moving. An observer behind an ambulance hears a lower sound because the waves have a longer wavelength and lower frequency.

Visualize It!

11 Analyze Look at the sound waves emitted by the ambulance siren. How does the sound of the siren change as the vehicle approaches and then moves away from the observer in front of the ambulance?

_____

_____

_____

_____

What information about stars can be gained using the Doppler effect?

The Doppler effect also applies to electromagnetic radiation. When a star is moving toward Earth, the wavelengths emitted by the star are compressed and appear blue to an observer on Earth. A blueshift occurs. When a star is moving away from Earth, the wavelengths are stretched out. A redshift occurs.

Astronomers use redshifts and blueshifts in the hydrogen spectra of stars to determine the direction the star is moving relative to Earth. Even though the emitted light shifts to higher or lower wavelengths, the pattern of the emitted light does not change. By comparing the wavelengths of the spectrum of a star to a standard spectrum, scientists can determine whether a redshift or blueshift occurred. They also analyze how far the wavelengths shifted in order to determine how fast the star is moving. The faster the star is moving, the greater the change in wavelength.

The faster a distant galaxy is moving away from Earth, the farther it is from Earth. The speed at which a galaxy is moving away from Earth is used to estimate its distance. The distance equals the speed divided by a constant called the *Hubble constant*.

Visualize It! Inquiry

Hydrogen absorbs and emits the same wavelengths. Absorption spectra can be compared to a standard emission spectrum to see if and how the wavelengths that are absorbed have shifted.

Emission spectrum of hydrogen

This hydrogen emission spectrum was taken from a hydrogen source in a lab.

Redshift

The lines of this absorption spectrum have shifted slightly toward the red end of the spectrum.

Blueshift

The lines of this absorption spectrum have shifted slightly toward the blue end of the spectrum.

12 Analyze The hydrogen spectrum of the Andromeda galaxy is similar to the bottom spectrum. How is this galaxy moving relative to Earth?

_____

_____

_____

To See or Not to See

What are telescopes?

One reason that human knowledge of the universe increases is that scientists develop new technology to observe space. One important tool for observing space is the telescope. A telescope is an instrument that is used to collect and concentrate electromagnetic radiation. Optical telescopes were the first instruments used to extend human observations of space. These telescopes gather visible light. Today, there are also non-optical telescopes. These types of telescopes are used to collect electromagnetic radiation outside of the visible region, such as radio waves or x-rays.

What are two types of optical telescopes?

Optical telescopes use mirrors or lenses to collect visible light. They can make distant objects appear closer and larger than they appear to the unaided eye. You could use an optical telescope to observe the larger moons of Jupiter or the rings of Saturn, just as Galileo did 400 years ago. There are also much larger, more powerful optical telescopes that can be used to collect light from distant galaxies. The two types of optical telescopes are reflecting telescopes and refracting telescopes.

Reflecting Telescopes

A reflecting telescope uses a curved mirror to collect light. The light that enters one end of the telescope strikes the curved mirror at the opposite end. The light is concentrated when it reflects from this mirror. The light then travels to a flat mirror that is at an angle. The light reflects from the flat mirror into the eyepiece, where it makes an image at the focal point. Reflecting telescopes are helpful when observing very dim objects. Larger mirrors can be used to collect more light. The Hubble Space Telescope is a type of reflecting telescope.

A reflecting telescope uses mirrors to produce an image from light that is collected.

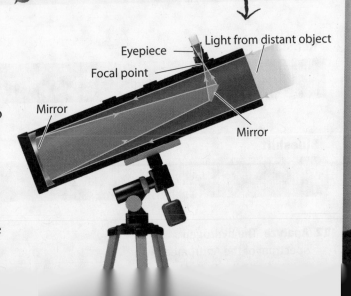

Light from distant object

Eyepiece

Focal point

Mirror

Mirror

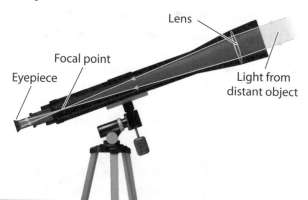

A refracting telescope uses lenses to produce a magnified image for the viewer.

Lens

Focal point

Eyepiece

Light from distant object

Refracting Telescopes

A refracting telescope uses a lens to collect light. The lens also magnifies the image seen by the observer. It bends, or refracts, light that enters the telescope. The light is focused to make an image near the back of the telescope. Another lens in the eyepiece makes the image appear larger for the observer. Larger lenses produce more detailed images than smaller lenses do because they can collect more light. These telescopes help observers view details of the moon and planets in the solar system.

14 Contrast How do reflecting telescopes and refracting telescopes differ?

_____

_____

_____

_____

Where are telescopes located?

Although visible light does pass through the atmosphere, some ultraviolet light is absorbed. The atmosphere also affects light that passes through it, which is why stars twinkle. Telescopes may also collect the light pollution from nearby urban areas. Therefore, powerful telescopes are located far away from urban centers. Telescopes are also often located on the tops of mountains, where the atmosphere is thinner. Some telescopes, including the Hubble Space Telescope, orbit Earth.

The GranTeCan is a reflecting telescope. It is far away from city lights and at an altitude of 2,267 m.

15 Explain What is the advantage of placing telescopes on high mountains or in space?

_____

_____

_____

How are other parts of the electromagnetic spectrum observed?

All of the parts of the electromagnetic spectrum can be analyzed to learn about the universe. Non-optical telescopes are used to collect wavelengths that are outside of the visible region. Different types of radiation can provide different information about the same structure in the universe. Non-optical telescopes include radio, microwave, x-ray, ultraviolet, and other types of telescopes.

Remember, you cannot see electromagnetic radiation collected by non-optical telescopes. Most telescopes have digital sensors, or detectors. Different detectors are used for various parts of the electromagnetic spectrum. Computers assign colors, called *false color*, to images to represent information in the image.

With Radio Telescopes

Radio telescopes detect radio waves from objects in space. Most of these telescopes have smooth, curved surfaces that look like a satellite dish. The curved surface collects and focuses radio waves to a receiver similar to the way that a curved mirror in a reflecting telescope does. Radio telescopes are usually very large so that they can collect weak radio waves from space.

Radio telescopes are used to gain information about many components in the universe. Data from radio telescopes can be analyzed to learn about the properties of dust clouds where stars, planets, and new solar systems form. The data provide details about the temperature and density of the dust clouds and the size of the structures in the clouds. Radio telescopes are also used to study the activity on the sun, including solar flares.

Think Outside the Book

17 Apply Research a particular telescope that collects wavelengths in the non-optical part of the electromagnetic spectrum. Find out where the telescope is located and what information can be gained by analyzing the data it collects. Identify one recent discovery made using the telescope. Make a poster presentation to share your findings.

Visualize It!

16 Compare How is the surface of a radio telescope similar to a mirror in a reflecting telescope?

_____

_____

The huge, curved surface of this telescope collects radio waves.

With Microwave Telescopes

Microwave telescopes detect microwave radiation. Earth's atmosphere is transparent to microwaves in the higher wavelengths, so some microwave telescopes are located on Earth. However, microwave telescopes have been launched into space to collect both short and long microwave radiation.

Microwave telescopes have collected data about the properties of the very early universe. These telescopes help scientists gain information about the age of the universe as well as how matter and energy were spread out. Images of the surface of Venus have been made using microwaves. Unlike visible wavelengths, microwaves are able to pass through Venus's thick atmosphere.

With X-ray Telescopes

X-ray telescopes detect very short wavelengths that are usually produced in hot areas in the universe. They must be launched into space, because x-rays are blocked by Earth's atmosphere. Data from x-ray telescopes can be analyzed to determine the elements found in exploding stars and to study black holes. No matter or energy escapes black holes. However, scientists can gain information about a black hole by studying the x-rays that are emitted by the matter around it.

With Other Non-Optical Telescopes

Other kinds of non-optical telescopes can detect infrared, ultraviolet, and gamma radiation. The atmosphere prevents these wavelengths from reaching Earth's surface. So, these telescopes must be flown high in the atmosphere or launched into space.

Infrared telescopes can be used to determine the composition of the atmospheres of planets and moons. They can also collect data about the temperature and density of disks of dust around stars. These data give scientists information about the type of star at the center of the dust as well as whether planets are forming.

Ultraviolet telescopes are used to learn about solar cycles, young stars, and star formation rates in galaxies. Infrared, visible, and ultraviolet images of galaxies are compared to learn about the shape of galaxies and how galaxies change.

Gamma-ray telescopes are used to learn about components of the universe with very high energy. They have observed very intense bursts of energy called *gamma-ray bursts*, which may be the explosions of the most massive stars in the universe.

© Houghton Mifflin Harcourt Publishing Company • Image Credits: (b) ©NASA Johnson Space Center; (t) ©MSFC/NASA

Active Reading

18 Describe What information about Venus have scientists gained using microwaves?

_____

_____

_____

The Chandra X-ray Observatory orbits Earth. False-color images are produced using the x-ray data it collects.

A jet aircraft is used to fly an infrared telescope high into the atmosphere.

Seeing Is Believing

What can you learn from space images?

Visible light allows you to see the surfaces of planets and how other objects in space might look. Different types of radiation can be used to produce images to reveal features not visible to the eye. For example, infrared radiation can reveal the temperature of objects. Dust blocks visible light, but some wavelengths of infrared pass through dust. So scientists can see objects normally hidden by dust clouds in space. High-energy objects may be very bright in x-ray or gamma-ray radiation but difficult to see at longer wavelengths. The three images of the Andromeda galaxy on the right were produced using wavelengths other than visible light, so the colors are all false colors.

 **Visualize It!**

19 Analyze Compare one image of the Andromeda galaxy on the opposite page with the image in visible light on this page.

_____

_____

_____

_____

_____

_____

_____

↑ This image of the Andromeda galaxy was produced using visible light.

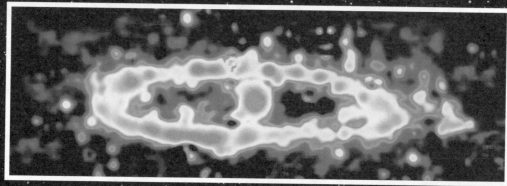

This image of the Andromeda galaxy was produced using radio waves. The reddish-orange color in the center and in the ring represents a source of radio waves. New stars are forming in the ring area.

In this infrared image of the Andromeda galaxy, you can see more detail in the structure of the galaxy. The dark areas within the bright rings are dust. The dust is so thick in some areas that radiation behind the dust is not getting through.

This image of the Andromeda galaxy was produced with a combination of ultraviolet and infrared radiation. The blue areas represent large, young, hot stars. The green areas represent older stars. The bright yellow spot at the very center of the galaxy represents an extremely dense area of old stars.

Visual Summary

To complete this summary, fill in the blanks with the correct word or phrase. Then, use the key below to check your answers. You can use this page to review the main concepts of the lesson.

The electromagnetic spectrum is all the wavelengths and frequencies of electromagnetic radiation.

20 Two parts of the electromagnetic spectrum between visible light and gamma rays are

_____

_____

Spectral analysis can tell scientists the properties of stars and their motion and distance relative to Earth.

21 A redshift or blueshift in the spectra from a star occurs because of the

_____

Telescopes can be used to observe every portion of the electromagnetic spectrum.

22 Radiation from structures that have a very high temperature is collected by

_____

Different types of radiation reveal various properties that are not observable with visible light.

23 This false-color image of the Andromeda galaxy was made using infrared and ultraviolet

_____

Answers: 20 ultraviolet, x-rays; 21 Doppler effect; 22 x-ray telescopes; 23 radiation

24 **Describe** For each part of the electromagnetic spectrum, identify one component of the universe that scientists learn about using that type of radiation.

Lesson Review

Vocabulary

Fill in the blank with the term that best completes the following sentences.

1 The distance between two adjacent crests of a wave is called its _____.

2 The _____ is all the wavelengths of electromagnetic radiation.

3 A _____ is a continuous range of a single feature, such as a wavelength.

Key Concepts

4 Explain State why telescopes that detect non-optical radiation are useful for studying objects in space. Give an example.

_____

_____

_____

_____

_____

5 Identify What are three properties of components of the universe that can be determined using electromagnetic radiation?

_____

_____

_____

6 Explain Describe how wavelength, frequency, and energy are related.

_____

_____

_____

_____

7 Contrast How does an emission spectrum differ from an absorption spectrum?

_____

_____

_____

Critical Thinking

Use this diagram to answer the following questions.

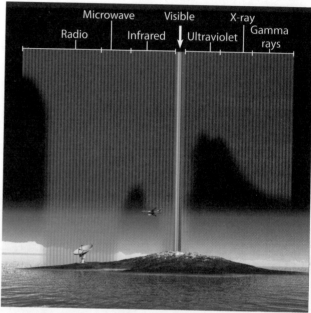

8 Analyze Some infrared radiation reaches Earth, and some does not. Which part does reach Earth—longer wavelength infrared or shorter wavelength infrared?

_____

_____

9 Analyze List two other types of electromagnetic radiation that can reach telescopes on Earth's surface.

_____

_____

10 Analyze Describe the Doppler effect and how it relates to the distance of a galaxy from Earth.

_____

_____

_____

_____

My Notes

Hakeem Oluseyi

ASTROPHYSICIST

Dr. Oluseyi's work has helped advance our understanding of the universe.

Dr. Hakeem Oluseyi always thought scientists were "supercool." Still, he didn't start right out of high school trying to become a scientist. He spent some time in the Navy before going to college. In college he studied physics and eventually earned a Ph.D. in astrophysics.

Dr. Oluseyi has worked on the manufacture of computer chips, developing ways to both make them smaller and make them operate more quickly. He has also assisted in the development of very sensitive detectors that go on spacecraft. These detectors measure different types of electromagnetic radiation that come from bodies in outer space. Dr. Oluseyi came up with ways to make these detectors more sensitive and stable. This made them better able to work in outer space.

Currently, Dr. Oluseyi is helping to develop the Large Synoptic Survey Telescope (LSST). This telescope will observe the entire sky every night for 10 years. (Other all-sky surveys typically take several years to complete!) Dr. Oluseyi plans to use the data to map out the galactic structure and to search for planets around pulsating stars. Pulsating stars are stars that show changes in brightness due to internal processes happening within the star.

Through work like Dr. Oluseyi's we are gaining a better understanding of the planets and stars. But Dr. Oluseyi would tell you, there is still plenty more he'd like to know.

Crab Nebula

Potentially hazardous near-Earth asteroids could be identified using the Large Synoptic Survey Telescope.

Social Studies Connection

The Crab Nebula is what remains of an exploding star. Research when the earliest observations of the Crab Nebula were made. Create a timeline of this discovery.

JOB BOARD

Public Education Space Specialist

What You'll Do: You will design, develop, and teach programs on different space topics for an organization. You will also give presentations and tours of space-related workplaces for teachers, students, and the media.

Where You Might Work: Observatories, museums, government buildings, NASA, and the National Science Foundation are places you might work.

Education: Specialists must have a bachelor's degree in astronomy, physical science, science education, or a related field. Experience in public speaking, teaching, and developing educational programs is a plus.

Other Job Requirements: You should be able to present information in a clear and interesting way to people of all ages.

Information Technology (IT) Technician

What You'll Do: Monitor computer systems and help other people use them.

Where You Might Work: Large organizations with mainframe computer systems, like multinational companies, government agencies, hospitals, or colleges.

Education: IT technicians usually have a college certificate in information systems, data processing, electronics technology, mainframe operations, or microcomputer systems.

Other Job Requirements: You need to be able to work on a team and have excellent problem-solving skills.

PEOPLE IN SCIENCE NEWS

Caroline Moore

Seeking Supernovae

Caroline Moore was only 14 years old when she discovered Supernova 2008ha, a new type of supernova, from her backyard observatory. Because the one she discovered is different from other supernovae, her discovery has encouraged scientists to reconsider how stars die. Moore continues to search for supernovae, and is now helping to teach and inspire other young people to take an interest in astronomy.

The Origin of the Universe

ESSENTIAL QUESTION

How did the universe begin?

By the end of this lesson, you should be able to summarize the evidence that has led scientists to accept the Big Bang theory to explain the origin of the universe.

8.ESS1.1

The dark clouds in this image are part of the Eagle Nebula. Stars and the nebulae in which they form are part of the universe.

Engage Your Brain

1 Predict Check T or F to show whether you think each statement is true or false.

T F

☐ ☐ A galaxy is the largest structure in the universe.

☐ ☐ Albert Einstein developed the law of universal gravitation.

☐ ☐ The universe is between 13 and 15 billion years old.

☐ ☐ The universe is expanding in all directions.

2 Describe In your own words, define the word *universe*.

_____

_____

_____

_____

_____

_____

_____

_____

Active Reading

3 Synthesize You can often define an unknown compound word if you know the meaning of the words it contains. Use the words and sentence below to make an educated guess about the meaning of the word *redshift*.

Word part	Meaning
red	the color of the visible spectrum with the longest wavelengths
shift	to move from one position to another

Example sentence
The wavelengths of a star that is moving away from Earth appear longer because of a <u>redshift</u>.

redshift:

_____

Vocabulary Terms

• universe
• redshift
• Big Bang theory
• cosmic microwave background (CMB)

4 Apply As you learn the definition of each vocabulary term in this lesson, create your own definition or sketch to help you remember the meaning of the term.

The Stars at Night...

This string of galaxies may be made up of thousands of galaxies. Each galaxy contains millions to billions of stars.

What is the universe?

The **universe** is space and all of the matter and energy in it. That means you are as much a part of the universe as the sun and Earth are. Scientists can detect energy in the form of electromagnetic radiation from visible matter, such as stars. Scientists study this electromagnetic radiation to learn about the structures in the universe as well as to gather evidence of how the universe formed.

What large-scale structures make up the universe?

The universe is made up of several types of large-scale structures, each one larger than the last. A solar system is the smallest of the large-scale structures and consists of at least one star and the objects that orbit it. The next-largest structure is a star cluster, which is a group of stars bound together by gravitational attraction. Star clusters may contain a few hundred to many thousands of stars. A galaxy is larger than a star cluster. Galaxies contain millions to billions of stars. Still larger is a galaxy cluster, which is made up of dozens of galaxies. A supercluster is the largest structure. It is made up of hundreds of galaxies.

Active Reading

5 Identify As you read, underline each large-scale structure in the universe.

6 Identify The images below show a portion of the structures of the universe. Label each image with the correct term on the right.

solar system   galaxy

star cluster   galaxy cluster

A _____

B _____

C _____

D _____

Who's Who in the Universe?

Who are some scientists who contributed to our understanding of the universe?

People once thought that Earth was the center of the universe. The work of many scientists who followed changed our understanding of the universe. Scientists including Sir Isaac Newton, Albert Einstein, Georges Lemaître, Edwin Hubble, and George Gamow built upon the knowledge of earlier scientists. Our knowledge of the universe continues to grow as scientists today continue to build upon their work.

 Active Reading

7 Identify As you read the next two pages, underline the contributions of each scientist.

Sir Isaac Newton

Sir Isaac Newton (1643–1727) was an English scientist. He developed the law of universal gravitation. This law states that every object in the universe attracts other objects. It also states that the force of the attraction depends on the masses of the objects and the distance between them. Newton's law explains why objects fall toward the center of Earth. It also explains why planets orbit stars and stars are held together in galaxies.

Not all of Newton's ideas have stood the test of time. He thought that the universe did not change. He also believed that every star was fixed in one place in space and that stars were spread out evenly throughout the universe.

Newton's law of universal gravitation helps to explain the motions of objects in space.

Albert Einstein

Albert Einstein (1879–1955) developed the theory of special relativity. This theory states that space and time are relative. *Relative* means that they depend on the motion of the observer and the object being observed. He also developed a new theory of gravity called *general relativity*. This theory explains how gravity causes space and time to curve. Although this seems like a strange idea, it is supported by many observations of the universe.

Newton's thinking still influenced Albert Einstein. Einstein's studies indicated that the universe was expanding. However, he adjusted his equations to fit Newton's idea that the universe stays the same over time.

Einstein won the Nobel Prize in Physics in 1921 for his contributions to science.

© Houghton Mifflin Harcourt Publishing Company • Image Credits: (l) ©Universal Images Group/Getty Images; (r) ©Topical Press Agency/Hulton Archive/Getty Images

Lemaître's work convinced most astronomers that the universe was not unchanging, as Newton had thought.

Georges Lemaître

Belgian scientist Georges Lemaître (1894–1966) used Einstein's equations to show that the universe is expanding. Lemaître explained the relationship between the distances of galaxies and the speeds at which those galaxies are moving away from Earth. He proposed a hypothesis that was later developed into the currently accepted theory of the origin of the universe. He thought that if the universe was expanding, all matter must have been packed into a very small space—a "primeval atom"—at some time in the past.

8 Explain How did Lemaître's reasoning lead him to develop the concept of the "primeval atom"?

_____

_____

Edwin Hubble

American astronomer Edwin Hubble (1889–1953) was the first scientist to present observational evidence that supported the idea that the universe is expanding. Hubble observed a redshift in the light that was coming from distant galaxies. A **redshift** is an apparent shift toward longer (red) wavelengths of light in an object's spectrum. This shift is caused when the object moves away from an observer. His observations showed that most galaxies were moving away from Earth. Hubble also determined that the redshifts of galaxies depended on their distances from Earth. He discovered that the fainter and farther away a galaxy appeared, the greater its redshift. Therefore, the greater a galaxy's distance from Earth, the faster it is moving away from Earth.

Hubble's observations showed that the universe is expanding.

9 Explain How does the redshift of galaxies provide evidence that the universe is expanding?

_____

_____

George Gamow

George Gamow (1904–1968) outlined a theory that explained how elements formed in the universe. He knew that most of the visible matter in the universe is hydrogen and helium. Gamow and his student proposed that the isotopes of light elements, including hydrogen and helium, formed between 3 and 20 minutes after the universe began. In that brief period, no elements heavier than beryllium were formed. Heavier elements formed later in stars.

Gamow helped develop a mathematical explanation for the formation of light elements in the universe.

Getting Started with a Bang!

According to the Big Bang theory, the universe began with a rapid expansion.

What evidence supports the Big Bang theory?

The **Big Bang theory** states that the universe began with a tremendous expansion 13–15 billion years ago. It is the currently accepted scientific theory of the origin of the universe. According to the Big Bang theory, all of the contents of the universe existed in a tiny volume that suddenly began expanding in all directions. Scientific evidence that supports the Big Bang theory comes from several sources. Evidence includes the abundance of light elements in the universe, the redshift of galaxies, and the Cosmic Microwave Background (CMB).

Light Element Abundance

The Big Bang theory predicts certain percentages of light elements in the universe. These predictions are supported by data. The abundance of light elements in the early universe can be compared with the abundance of light elements in stars today. To do this, scientists study stars that are very far from Earth and in the early stages of development. Scientists analyze the spectral lines of these stars to determine the amounts of elements being produced within their cores. The percentages of light elements in these stars are very close to the theoretical values predicted by the Big Bang theory.

Active Reading

10 Identify As you read this page, underline the statements that describe the Big Bang theory.

Think Outside the Book

11 Research Work with a partner to find out more about how scientific data provide evidence about the origin of the universe. Write an essay that relates how scientific research has led to the Big Bang theory being the currently accepted theory.

The Redshift of Galaxies

The expansion of the universe also supports the Big Bang theory. Edwin Hubble found redshifts, such as the example shown at the upper right, in the spectra of the galaxies he observed. The redshifts show that galaxies are moving away from Earth in all directions. Also, galaxies are moving at speeds proportional to their distance from Earth. The farther away a galaxy is, the faster it is moving. Hubble concluded that the distances between galaxies and galaxy clusters have been increasing over time. Because galaxies are moving apart, they must have been closer together in the past. This is consistent with the idea that the universe has been expanding since the Big Bang.

Cosmic Microwave Background

The early universe was made of very hot particles. These particles absorbed and emitted visible and ultraviolet radiation. The universe cooled rapidly as it expanded. The radiation also spread out and cooled. Its wavelengths stretched into the microwave range. The universe today should be filled with traces of this early radiation, called the **Cosmic Microwave Background (CMB)**.

The CMB can be detected by infrared and radio telescopes. In 1965, radio engineers Arno Penzias and Robert Wilson were using an antenna that transmitted telephone calls to orbiting satellites. They noticed a faint background signal from every direction in the sky. They discovered that they were picking up the CMB. The temperature of the radiation is a very cold 2.73 K. This temperature is similar to what scientists predicted the temperature would be after the universe cooled for billions of years.

The most distant galaxies in the universe are shown in the background of this photo.

Visualize It!

12 Predict Which galaxies in this photo will have the largest redshift?

_____

_____

_____

_____

Visualize It!

13 Explain What information does the WMAP temperature map give scientists about the structure of the universe?

_____

_____

_____

_____

_____

_____

_____

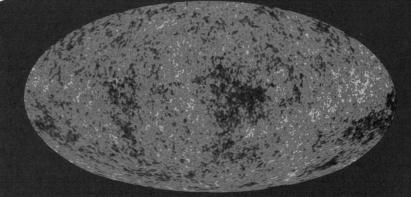

This sky map was made by NASA's WMAP (Wilkinson Microwave Anisotropy Probe) mission. It shows the temperatures of the CMB increasing from dark blue to red. Small temperature differences indicate the first major structures in the universe, such as galaxies and superclusters.

In the Beginning...

Active Reading

14 Identify As you read, underline the conditions that existed at the very beginning of the universe.

What were the conditions of the early universe?

Immediately after the Big Bang, the universe was no bigger than an atom. It was extremely dense and hot. It had an estimated temperature of about 1×10^{32} K. Matter and energy began to spread out rapidly in all directions. The temperature and density of the universe decreased quickly. This brief period of very rapid expansion immediately after the Big Bang is called *inflation*. Inflation lasted only a few fractions of a second. After inflation, the universe began to expand at a slower rate.

Scientists use particle accelerators to model the conditions in the early universe. Data from experiments have provided evidence of the particles that first existed in the universe. Scientists are also trying to find out how those particles combined to form atoms.

Scientists use particle accelerators to model conditions that existed during the Big Bang. The image to left shows a high-energy particle collision, similar to collisions scientists think happened during the Big Bang.

Inquiry

15 Compare How does a model of the Big Bang differ from the actual event?

_____

_____

_____

_____

_____

This is an artist's concept of how the universe may have looked when the first stars were forming some 200 million years after the Big Bang.

How can scientists estimate the age of the universe?

You can use the speed of a car to determine the time it takes the car to reach its current position from its starting point. Similarly, scientists can estimate the age of the universe by using the present rate of expansion of the universe. To determine this rate, scientists measure how fast distant galaxies are moving away from Earth. Current data show that the rate of expansion is increasing, or accelerating. Scientists use the present rate of expansion to estimate past rates of expansion. Then, they use these rates to determine the distances between galaxies in the early stages of the universe. Current estimates place the age of the universe at between 13 and 15 billion years old. The most widely accepted estimate is 13.75 billion years.

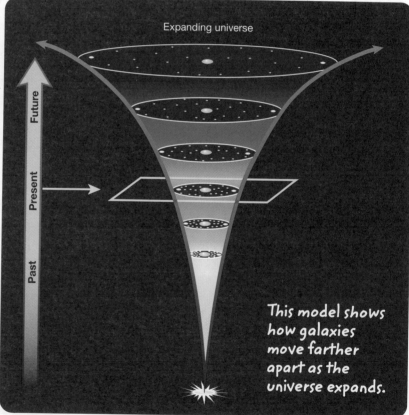

Expanding universe

Future

Present

Past

This model shows how galaxies move farther apart as the universe expands.

16 Explain How do scientists use the rates of expansion of the universe to estimate the age of the universe?

_____

_____

_____

_____

Researching the Big Bang

The **Big Bang** theory is a model describing the origin of the universe. Based on observations from space and light technologies, and mathematical models, scientists have hypothesized about the conditions of the early universe. While the model itself has evolved and been refined over the last 100 years, the fundamental explanation that the universe began as a single, small, dense, hot, singularity, is still being confirmed by new evidence.

Skills

- ✓ Research scientific information
- ✓ Communicate scientific information

What You'll Do

- Work with a partner to find out more about the Big Bang theory and the scientific evidence that supports it.
- Use the information below to help you plan out your research.
- Present what you have learned about the Big Bang.

Presentation Ideas

- ✓ Write an essay
- ✓ Perform a song
- ✓ Make a poster
- ✓ Make a skit
- ✓ Come up with your own idea!

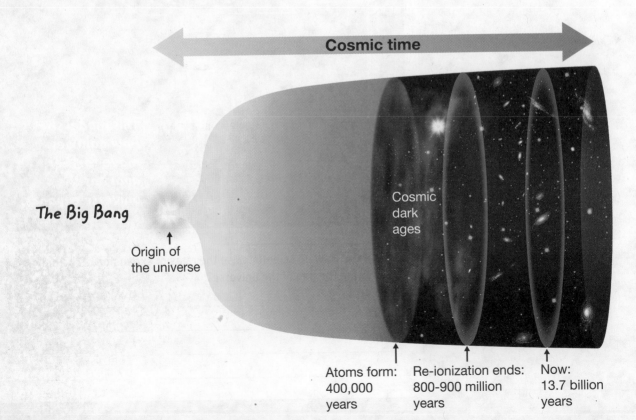

Cosmic time

The Big Bang

Origin of the universe

Cosmic dark ages

Atoms form: 400,000 years

Re-ionization ends: 800-900 million years

Now: 13.7 billion years

Brainstorm

① With your partner, discuss some ideas you would like to explore. Ideas might include:

- Which scientists are responsible for developing the theory?

- What is the evidence supporting the theory and how does it confirm the theory?

- How was this evidence found?

- What implications does this theory have on our understanding of the origin and future of the universe?

- Why is the theory called "Big Bang"? Does that name really apply?

This Hubble Telescope Ultra-Deep Field (HUDF) image shows galaxies that are 13 billion years old.

_____

_____

_____

_____

_____

_____

Organize Research Plan

② Discuss ideas you have with your partner. Determine how you are going to do your research and what sources you will use. Make a graphic organizer to show what you will be doing and who is responsible for each item.

Make sure your plan includes information about:

✓ how the universe formed

✓ the evidence scientists used to confirm their theory

_____

_____

_____

_____

_____

_____

_____

_____

Outline

3 Now that you have done your research, write an outline to organize your thoughts. The organizer shown here is for writing an essay, but you can modify it. Answer the questions below to fill out the organizer.

✓ **Main Ideas**: What information will you present first? What other main ideas will you present?

✓ **Support**: What details support the main idea(s)?

✓ **Key Points**: What are the major points that you want to communicate in your presentation?

Main Ideas	Support #1	Major #1
		Major #2
		Major #3
	Support #2	Major #1
		Major #2
		Major #3
	Support #3	Major #1
		Major #2
		Major #3

Rough Draft

④ Now for the fun part! Use your outline to write or sketch out a rough draft of your final presentation. You might be writing an essay, a script, or you might be sketching out what you'll show. You and your partner will both be presenting, so you'll need to decide which parts you are each going to work on.

Note: You'll want more paper for this part.

Prepare Final Presentation

⑤ Now is when you are making sure your final presentation includes all the information you need to share about the Big Bang, and that you are ready to either hand in something written or present your information to the class.

Make sure your presentation includes information about:

✔ how the universe formed

✔ the evidence scientists used to confirm the Big Bang theory

Visual Summary

To complete this summary, circle the correct word. Then, use the key below to check your answers. You can use this page to review the main concepts of the lesson.

Large-scale structures make up the universe.

17 A supercluster / solar system is made up of many galaxies.

Evidence indicates that the universe is expanding in all directions.

18 Albert Einstein / Edwin Hubble was the first scientist to discover observational evidence that supported the concept of an expanding universe.

The Big Bang theory is the most widely accepted scientific theory about the origin of the universe.

19 The Big Bang theory is supported by the abundance of heavy / light elements in the universe.

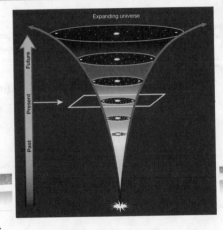

Answers: 17. supercluster, 18. Edwin Hubble, 19. light

20 Summarize Relate the contributions of scientists to our understanding of the universe. Include the names of at least two scientists and how their research had an impact on scientific thought about the universe.

Lesson Review

Vocabulary

Fill in the blank with the term that best completes the following sentence.

1 According to the _____, the universe began as a tiny volume that suddenly and rapidly began expanding.

2 The _____ _____ is the remnant of the early radiation that filled the universe.

3 The _____ is space and all energy and matter in it.

4 A _____ is an apparent shift toward longer wavelengths of light caused when an object moves away from an observer.

Key Concepts

5 Describe Which statement best describes how scientific thought about the universe has changed over time? Circle your answer.

A. Scientists now know that Earth, not the sun, is the center of the universe.

B. Scientists now know that the universe changes over time rather than remaining unchanging.

C. Scientists now know that a solar system, not a star, is the largest structure in the universe.

D. Scientists now know that the universe was made of only matter, not matter and energy.

6 Identify Who discovered that hydrogen and helium formed during the early stages of the Big Bang?

_____

7 Describe What was Georges Lemaître's major contribution to the current understanding of the universe?

_____

_____

_____

Critical Thinking

Use the map to answer the following question.

8 Apply What does this map of the CMB show about radiation from the Big Bang?

_____

_____

_____

_____

9 Summarize What evidence other than the CMB provides support for the Big Bang theory?

_____

_____

_____

_____

_____

_____

10 Explain How does Newton's law of universal gravitation help scientists describe the universe?

_____

_____

_____

_____

_____

_____

_____

My Notes

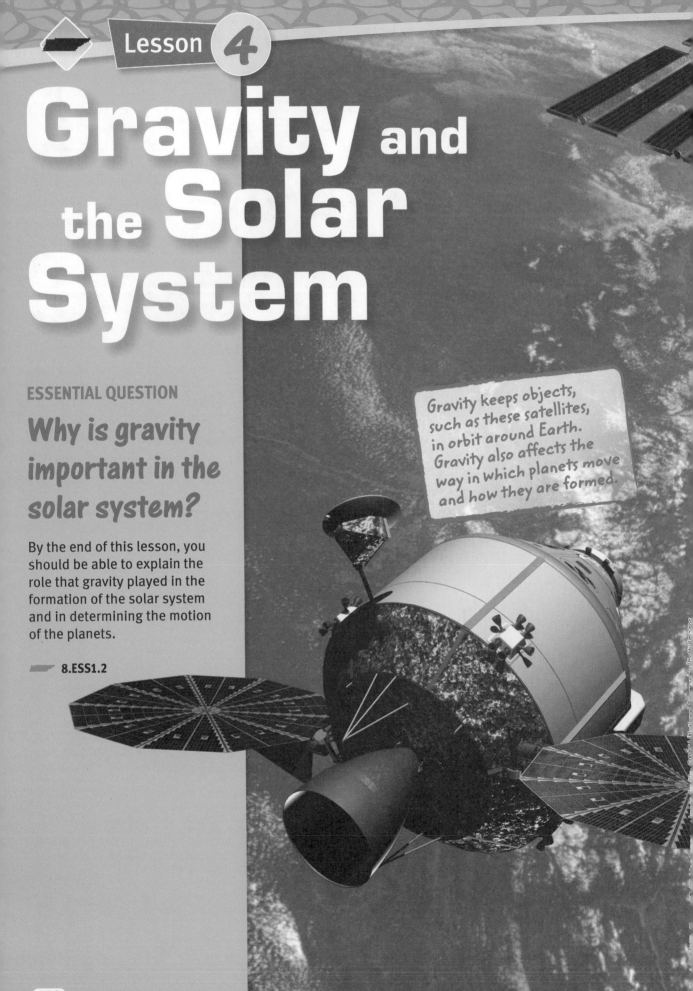

Gravity and the Solar System

ESSENTIAL QUESTION

Why is gravity important in the solar system?

By the end of this lesson, you should be able to explain the role that gravity played in the formation of the solar system and in determining the motion of the planets.

8.ESS1.2

Gravity keeps objects, such as these satellites, in orbit around Earth. Gravity also affects the way in which planets move and how they are formed.

 **Lesson Labs**

Quick Labs
• Gravity's Effect
• Gravity and the Orbit of a Planet

Exploration Lab
• Weights on Different Celestial Bodies

Engage Your Brain

1 Predict Check T or F to show whether you think each statement is true or false.

T   F

☐   ☐   Gravity keeps the planets in orbit around the sun.

☐   ☐   The planets follow circular paths around the sun.

☐   ☐   Sir Isaac Newton was the first scientist to describe how the force of gravity behaved.

☐   ☐   The sun formed in the center of the solar system.

☐   ☐   The terrestrial planets and the gas giant planets formed from the same material.

2 Draw In the space below, draw what you think the solar system looked like before the planets formed.

Active Reading

3 Synthesize You can often define an unknown word if you know the meaning of its word parts. Use the word parts and sentence below to make an educated guess about the meaning of the word *protostellar*.

Word part	Meaning
proto-	first
-stellar	of or having to do with a star or stars

Example sentence
The <u>protostellar</u> disk formed after the collapse of the solar nebula.

protostellar:

_____

_____

Vocabulary Terms

• gravity
• orbit
• aphelion
• perihelion
• centripetal force
• solar nebula
• planetesimal

4 Apply This list contains the key terms you'll learn in this section. As you read, circle the definition of each term.

Gravity

What is gravity?

Active Reading 5 **Identify** Underline the definition of and the effects of gravity.

Gravity is a force of attraction between objects that is due to their masses and the distances between them. Every object in the universe pulls on every other object. Objects with greater masses have a greater force of attraction than objects with lesser masses have. Objects that are close together have a greater force of attraction than objects that are far apart have.

Gravity is the weakest force in nature. A toy magnet can overcome the gravitational force acting on a paperclip by the entire mass of Earth. Yet, gravity is one of the most important forces in the universe. It accounts for the formation of planets, stars, and galaxies. It also keeps smaller bodies in orbit around larger bodies. An **orbit** is the path that a body follows as it travels around another body in space. For example, the moon orbits Earth, and Earth orbits the sun.

When astronauts are in orbit, Earth's gravity still pulls them downward toward the planet. However, they appear to be weightless and floating. They "float" because everything around them is falling at the same speed.

What are Kepler's laws?

The 16th-century Polish astronomer Nicolaus Copernicus (nik•uh•LAY•uhs koh•PER•nuh•kuhs) (1473–1543) changed our view of the solar system. He discovered that the motions of the planets could be best explained if the planets orbited the sun. But, like astronomers who came before him, Copernicus thought the planets followed circular paths around the sun.

Danish astronomer Tycho Brahe (TY•koh BRAH) (1546–1601) built what was at the time the world's largest observatory. Tycho used special instruments to measure the motions of the planets. His measurements were made over a period of 20 years and were very accurate. Using Tycho's data, Johannes Kepler (yoh•HAH•nuhs KEP•luhr) (1571–1630) made discoveries about the motions of the planets. We call these *Kepler's laws of planetary motion.*

Kepler found that objects that orbit the sun follow elliptical orbits. When an object follows an elliptical orbit around the sun, there is one point, called **aphelion** (uh•FEE•lee•uhn), where the object is farthest from the sun. There is also a point, called **perihelion** (perh•uh•HEE•lee•uhn), where the object is closest to the sun. Today, we know that the orbits of the planets are only slightly elliptical. However, the orbits of objects such as Pluto and comets are highly elliptical.

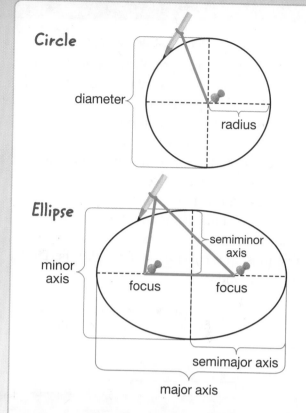

Circle

diameter

radius

Ellipse

semiminor axis

minor axis

focus   focus

semimajor axis

major axis

Visualize It!

6 Compare How is a circle different from an ellipse?

_____

_____

_____

_____

Kepler's First Law

Kepler's careful plotting of the orbit of Mars kept showing Mars' orbit to be a deformed circle. It took Kepler eight years to realize that this shape was an ellipse. This clue led Kepler to propose elliptical orbits for the planets. Kepler placed the sun at one of the foci of the ellipse. This is Kepler's first law.

Active Reading **7 Contrast** What is the difference between Copernicus' and Kepler's description of planetary orbits?

_____

_____

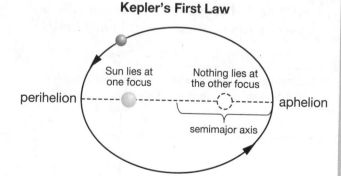

Kepler's First Law

Sun lies at one focus

Nothing lies at the other focus

perihelion

aphelion

semimajor axis

Each planet orbits the sun in an ellipse with the sun at one focus. (For clarity, the ellipse is exaggerated here.)

Kepler's Second Law

Using the shape of an ellipse, Kepler searched for other regularities in Tycho's data. He found that an amazing thing happens when a line is drawn from a planet to the sun's focus on the ellipse. At aphelion, its speed is slower. So, it sweeps out a narrow sector on the ellipse. At perihelion, the planet is moving faster. It sweeps out a thick sector on the ellipse. In the illustration, the areas of both the thin blue sector and the thick blue sector are exactly the same. Kepler found that this relationship is true for all of the planets. This is Kepler's second law.

Active Reading **8 Analyze** At which point does a planet move most slowly in its orbit, at aphelion or perihelion?

As a planet moves around its orbit, it sweeps out equal areas in equal times.

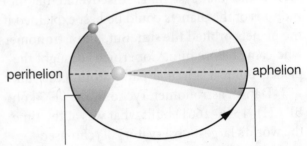

Kepler's Second Law

perihelion --------- aphelion

Near perihelion, a planet sweeps out an area that is short but wide.

Near aphelion, in an equal amount of time, a planet sweeps out an area that is long but narrow.

Kepler's Third Law

When Kepler looked at how long it took for the planets to orbit the sun and at the sizes of their orbits, he found another relationship. Kepler calculated the orbital period and the distance from the sun for the planets using Tycho's data. He discovered that the square of the orbital period was proportional to the cube of the planet's average distance from the sun. This law is true for each planet. This principle is Kepler's third law. When the units are years for the period and AU for the distance, the law can be written:

$$(\text{orbital period in years})^2 = (\text{average distance from the sun in astronomical units [AU]})^3$$

The square of the orbital period is proportional to the cube of the planet's average distance from the sun.

Kepler's Third Law

$$p^2 \text{ yrs} = a^3 \text{ AU}$$

perihelion ----a---- aphelion

9 Summarize In the table below, summarize each of Kepler's three laws in your own words.

First law	Second law	Third law

What is the law of universal gravitation?

Using Kepler's laws, Sir Isaac Newton (EYE•zuhk NOOT'n) became the first scientist to mathematically describe how the force of gravity behaved. How could Newton do this in the 1600s before the force could be measured in a laboratory? He reasoned that gravity was the same force that accounted for both the fall of an apple from a tree and the movement of the moon around Earth.

In 1687, Newton formulated the *law of universal gravitation*. The law of universal gravitation states that all objects in the universe attract each other through gravitational force. The strength of this force depends on the product of the masses of the objects. Therefore, the gravity between objects increases as the masses of the objects increase. Gravitational force is also inversely proportional to the square of the distance between the objects. Stated another way this means that as the distance between two objects increases, the force of gravity decreases.

Sir Isaac Newton
(1642–1727)

Do the Math

Newton's law of universal gravitation says that the force of gravity:
- increases as the masses of the objects increase and
- decreases as the distance between the objects increases

In these examples, M = mass, d = distance, and F = the force of gravity exerted by two bodies.

Sample Problems

A. In the example below, when two balls have masses of M and the distance between them is d, then the force of gravity is F. If the mass of each ball is increased to 2M (to the right) and the distance stays the same, then the force of gravity increases to 4F.

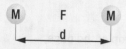

B. In this example, we start out again with a distance of d and masses of M, and the force of gravity is F. If the distance is decreased to ½ d, then the force of gravity increases to 4F.

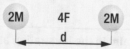

You Try It

Recall that M = mass, d = distance, and F = the force of gravity exerted by two bodies.

10 Calculate Compare the example below to the sample problems. What would the force of gravity be in the example below? Explain your answer.

> 2M ——— 2d ——— 2M

_____

_____

_____

_____

_____

How does gravity affect planetary motion?

The illustrations on this page will help you understand planetary motion. In the illustration at the right, a girl is swinging a ball around her head. The ball is attached to a string. The girl is exerting a force on the string that causes the ball to move in a circular path. The inward force that causes an object to move in a circular path is called **centripetal** (sehn•TRIP•ih•tuhl) **force**.

In the illustration at center, we see that if the string breaks, the ball will move off in a straight line. This fact indicates that when the string is intact, a force is pulling the ball inward. This force keeps the ball from flying off and moving in a straight line. This force is centripetal force.

In the illustration below, you see that the planets orbit the sun. A force must be preventing the planets from moving out of their orbits and into a straight line. The sun's gravity is the force that keeps the planets moving in orbit around the sun.

As the girl swings the ball, she is exerting a force on the string that causes the ball to move in a circular path.

Centripetal force pulls the ball inward, which causes the ball to move in a curved path.

direction centripetal force pulls the ball

direction ball would move if string broke —

— Center of rotation

String

path ball takes when — moving around the center of rotation

Just as the string is pulling the ball inward, gravity is keeping the planets in orbit around the sun.

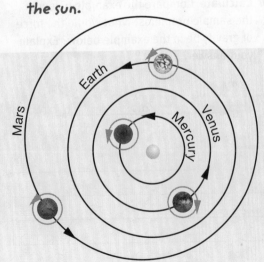

Mars

Earth

Venus

Mercury

11 Explain In the illustration at the top of the page, what does the hand represent, the ball represent, and the string represent? (Hint: Think of the sun, a planet, and the force of gravity.)

_____

_____

_____

How did the solar system form?

The formation of the solar system is thought to have begun 4.6 billion years ago when a cloud of dust and gas collapsed. This cloud, from which the solar system formed, is called the **solar nebula** (SOH•ler NEB•yuh•luh). In a nebula, the inward pull of gravity is balanced by the outward push of gas pressure in the cloud. Scientists think that an outside force, perhaps the explosion of a nearby star, caused the solar nebula to compress and then to contract under its own gravity. It was in a single region of the nebula, which was perhaps several light-years across, that the solar system formed. The sun probably formed from a region that had a mass that was slightly greater than today's mass of the sun and planets.

Active Reading **12 Define** What is the solar nebula?

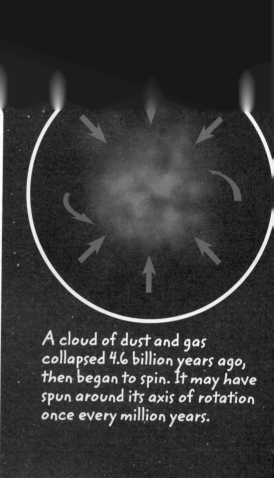

A cloud of dust and gas collapsed 4.6 billion years ago, then began to spin. It may have spun around its axis of rotation once every million years.

A Protostellar Disk Formed from the Collapsed Solar Nebula

As a region of the solar nebula collapsed, gravity pulled most of the mass toward the center of the nebula. As the nebula contracted, it began to rotate. As the rotation grew faster, the nebula flattened out into a disk. This disk, which is called a *protostellar disk* (PROH•toh•stehl•er DISK), is where the central star, our sun, formed.

As a region of the solar nebula collapsed, it formed a slowly rotating protostellar disk.

The Sun Formed at the Center of the Protostellar Disk

As the protostellar disk continued to contract, most of the matter ended up in the center of the disk. Friction from matter that fell into the disk heated up its center to millions of degrees, eventually reaching its current temperature of 15,000,000 °C. This intense heat in a densely packed space caused the fusion of hydrogen atoms into helium atoms. The process of fusion released large amounts of energy. This release of energy caused outward pressure that again balanced the inward pull of gravity. As the gas and dust stopped collapsing, a star was born. In the case of the solar system, this star was the sun.

 Active Reading **13 Identify** How did the sun form?

_____
_____
_____
_____
_____

This is an artist's conception of what the protoplanetary disk in which the planets formed might have looked like.

Visualize It!

14 Describe Use the terms *planetesimal* and *protoplanetary disk* to describe the illustration above.

_____
_____
_____
_____
_____
_____

Planetesimals Formed in the Protoplanetary Disk

As the sun was forming, dust grains collided and stuck together. The resulting *dust granules* grew in size and increased in number. Over time, dust granules increased in size until they became roughly meter-sized bodies. Trillions of these bodies occurred in the protostellar disk. Collisions between these bodies formed larger bodies that were kilometers across. These larger bodies, from which planets formed, are called **planetesimals** (plan·ih·TES·ih·muhls). The protostellar disk had become the *protoplanetary disk*. The protoplanetary disk was the disk in which the planets formed.

Dust grains collided and stuck together.

Over time, dust granules grew to become meter-sized bodies.

Planetesimals formed from the collisions of meter-sized bodies.

Visualize It! (Inquiry)

15 Explain How can objects as small as dust grains become the building blocks of planets?

_____

_____

_____

_____

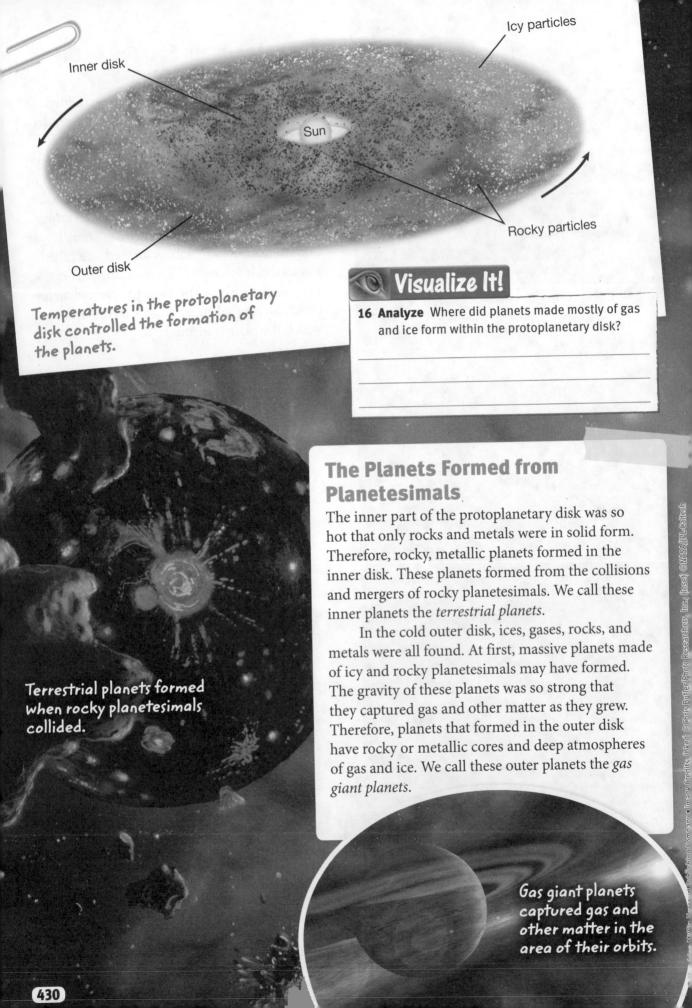

Inner disk

Icy particles

Sun

Rocky particles

Outer disk

Temperatures in the protoplanetary disk controlled the formation of the planets.

Visualize It!

16 Analyze Where did planets made mostly of gas and ice form within the protoplanetary disk?

_____

_____

_____

Terrestrial planets formed when rocky planetesimals collided.

The Planets Formed from Planetesimals

The inner part of the protoplanetary disk was so hot that only rocks and metals were in solid form. Therefore, rocky, metallic planets formed in the inner disk. These planets formed from the collisions and mergers of rocky planetesimals. We call these inner planets the *terrestrial planets*.

In the cold outer disk, ices, gases, rocks, and metals were all found. At first, massive planets made of icy and rocky planetesimals may have formed. The gravity of these planets was so strong that they captured gas and other matter as they grew. Therefore, planets that formed in the outer disk have rocky or metallic cores and deep atmospheres of gas and ice. We call these outer planets the *gas giant planets*.

Gas giant planets captured gas and other matter in the area of their orbits.

17 Describe In the spaces on the left, describe steps in the
formation of the solar system. In the spaces on the right, draw
the last two steps in the formation of the solar system.

Steps in the Formation of the Solar System

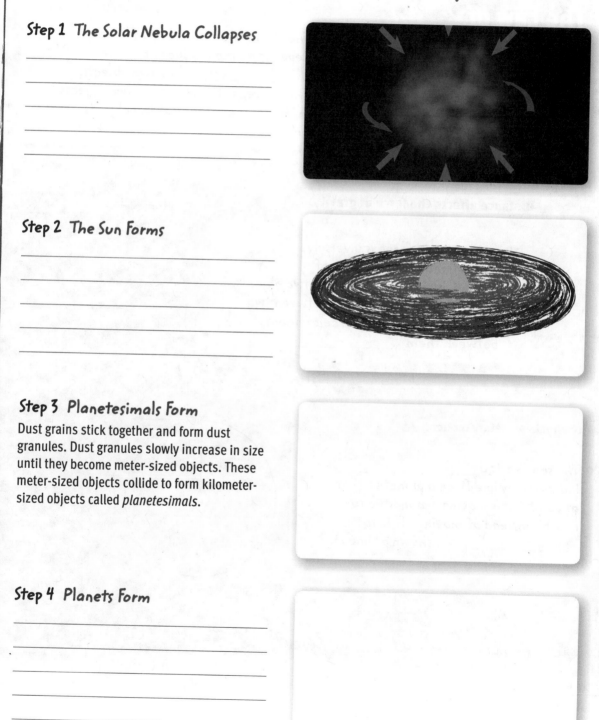

Step 1 The Solar Nebula Collapses

_____
_____
_____
_____
_____

Step 2 The Sun Forms

_____
_____
_____
_____
_____

Step 3 Planetesimals Form

Dust grains stick together and form dust
granules. Dust granules slowly increase in size
until they become meter-sized objects. These
meter-sized objects collide to form kilometer-
sized objects called *planetesimals*.

Step 4 Planets Form

_____
_____
_____
_____
_____

Visual Summary

To complete this summary, fill in the blank with the correct word or phrase. Then use the key below to check your answers. You can use this page to review the main concepts of the lesson.

The Law of Universal Gravitation

Mass affects the force of gravity.

18 The strength of the force of gravity depends on the product of the _____ of two objects. Therefore, as the masses of two objects increase, the force that the objects exert on one another _____.

Distance affects the force of gravity.

19 Gravitational force is inversely proportional to the square of the _____ between two objects. Therefore, as the distance between two objects increases, the force of gravity between them _____.

Gravity affects planetary motion.

20 The sun exerts a _____, indicated by line B, on a planet so that at point C it is moving around the sun in orbit instead of moving off in a _____ as shown at line A.

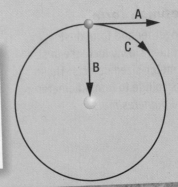

21 **Explain** In your own words, explain Newton's law of universal gravitation.

© Houghton Mifflin Harcourt Publishing Company

Lesson Review

Vocabulary

Fill in the blank with the term that best completes the following sentences.

1 Small bodies from which the planets formed are called _____

2 The path that a body follows as it travels around another body in space is its _____

3 The _____ is the cloud of gas and dust from which our solar system formed.

Key Concepts

4 Define In your own words, define the word *gravity*.

_____

_____

_____

5 Describe How did the sun form?

_____

_____

_____

_____

_____

_____

_____

_____

_____

6 Describe How did planetesimals form?

_____

_____

_____

_____

_____

_____

_____

Critical Thinking

Use the illustration below to answer the following question.

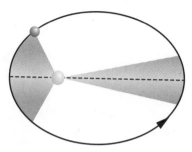

7 Identify What law is illustrated in this diagram?

_____

8 Analyze How does gravity keep the planets in orbit around the sun?

_____

_____

_____

_____

_____

_____

9 Explain How do temperature differences in the protoplanetary disk explain the arrangement of the planets in the solar system?

_____

_____

_____

_____

_____

_____

_____

My Notes

Earth's Tides

ESSENTIAL QUESTION

What causes tides?

By the end of this lesson, you should be able to explain what tides are and what causes them in Earth's oceans and to describe variations in the tides.

8.ESS1.2

You may wonder why this boat is sitting in such shallow water. This photo was taken at low tide, when the ocean water is below average sea level.

Engage Your Brain

1 Describe Fill in the blank with the word that you think correctly completes the following sentences.

The motion of the _____ around Earth is related to tides.

The daily rotation of _____ is also related to tides.

During a _____ tide, the water level is higher than the average sea level.

During a _____ tide, the water level is lower than the average sea level.

2 Label Draw an arrow to show where you think high tide might be.

Low tide ▶

Active Reading

3 Synthesize The word *spring* has different meanings. Use the meanings of the word *spring* and the sentence below to make an educated guess about the meaning of the term *spring tides*.

Meanings of *spring*
the season between winter and summer
a source of water from the ground
jump, or rise up
a coiled piece of metal

Example Sentence
During spring tides, the sun, the moon, and Earth are in a straight line, resulting in very high tides.

spring tides:

_____

_____

Vocabulary Terms
- tide
- tidal range
- spring tide
- neap tide

4 Apply As you learn the definition of each vocabulary term in this lesson, create your own definition or sketch to help you remember the meaning of the term.

A Rising Tide of Interest

What causes tides?

The photographs below show the ocean at the same location at two different times. **Tides** are daily changes in the level of ocean water. Tides are caused by the difference in the gravitational force of the sun and the moon across Earth. This difference in gravitational force is called the *tidal force*. The tidal force exerted by the moon is stronger than the tidal force exerted by the sun because the moon is much closer to Earth than the sun is. So, the moon is mainly responsible for tides on Earth.

How often tides occur and how tidal levels vary depend on the position of the moon as it revolves around Earth. The gravity of the moon pulls on every particle of Earth. These statements support a misconception that the water is pulled; the moon's gravitational pull on Earth decreases with the moon's distance from Earth. The part of Earth facing the moon is pulled toward the moon with the greatest force and causes a bulge in the crust. The solid Earth is pulled more strongly toward the moon than the ocean water on Earth's far side is.

Active Reading

5 Identify Underline the sentences that identify which object is mainly responsible for tides on Earth.

At low tide, the water level is low, and the boats are far below the dock.

At high tide, the water level has risen, and the boats are close to the dock.

What are high tides and low tides?

High tide is a water level that is higher than the average sea level. Low tides form in the areas between the high tides. *Low tide* is a water level that is lower than the average sea level. At low tide, the water levels are lower because the water is in high-tide areas.

As the moon moves around Earth and Earth rotates, the tidal bulges move around Earth. The tidal bulges follow the motion of the moon. As a result, many places on Earth have two high tides and two low tides each day.

6 Identify Label the areas where high tides form and the area where the other low tide forms.

Note: Drawing is not to scale.

Moon

A _____

B _____

Earth

Low tide

C _____

This grizzly bear in Alaska is taking advantage of low tide by digging for clams.

7 Predict What happens to the bear when high tide comes in?

_____

_____

Tide Me Over

What are two kinds of tidal ranges?

Active Reading

8 Identify As you read, underline the two kinds of tidal range.

Tides are due to the *tidal force,* the difference between the force of gravity on one side of Earth and the other side of Earth. Because the moon is so much closer to Earth than the sun is, the moon's tidal force is greater than the sun's tidal force. The moon's effect on tides is twice as strong as the sun's effect. The combined gravitational effects of the sun and the moon on Earth result in different tidal ranges. A **tidal range** is the difference between the levels of ocean water at high tide and low tide. Tidal range depends on the positions of the sun and the moon relative to Earth.

Spring Tides: The Largest Tidal Range

Tides that have the largest daily tidal range are **spring tides**. Spring tides happen when the sun, the moon, and Earth form a straight line. So, spring tides happen when the moon is between the sun and Earth and when the moon is on the opposite side of Earth, as shown in the illustrations below. In other words, spring tides happen during the new moon and full moon phases, or every 14 days. During these times, the gravitational effects of the sun and moon add together, causing one pair of very large tidal bulges. Spring tides have nothing to do with the season.

Note: Drawings are not to scale.

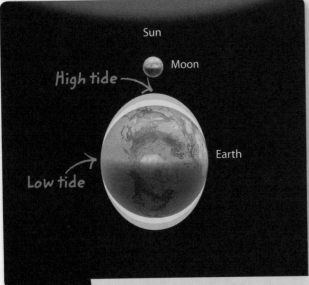

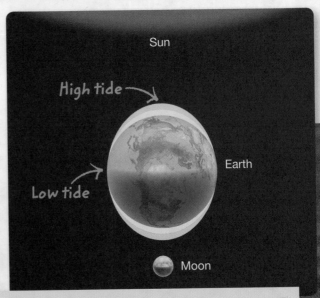

During spring tides, the tidal force of the sun on Earth adds to the tidal force of the moon. The tidal range increases.

Inquiry

9 Inquire Explain why spring tides happen twice a month.

_____

_____

_____

Neap Tides: The Smallest Tidal Range

Tides that have the smallest daily tidal range are **neap tides**. Neap tides happen when the sun, Earth, and the moon form a 90° angle, as shown in the illustrations below. During a neap tide, the gravitational effects of the sun and the moon on Earth do not add together as they do during spring tides. Neap tides occur halfway between spring tides, during the first quarter and third quarter phases of the moon. At these times, the sun and the moon cause two pairs of smaller tidal bulges.

Note: Drawings are not to scale.

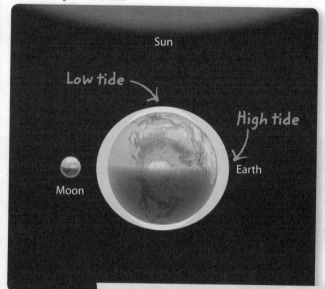

During neap tides, the gravitational effects of the sun and the moon on Earth do not add together. The tidal range decreases.

10 Compare Fill in the Venn diagram to compare and contrast spring tides and neap tides.

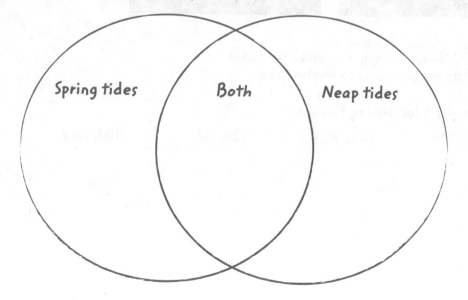

Spring tides   Both   Neap tides

What causes tidal cycles?

The rotation of Earth and the moon's revolution around Earth determine when tides occur. Imagine that Earth rotated at the same speed that the moon revolves around Earth. If this were true, the same side of Earth would always face the moon. And high tide would always be at the same places on Earth. But the moon revolves around Earth much more slowly than Earth rotates. A place on Earth that is facing the moon takes 24 h and 50 min to rotate to face the moon again. So, the cycle of high tides and low tides at that place happens 50 min later each day.

In many places there are two high tides and two low tides each day. Because the tide cycle occurs in 24 h and 50 min intervals, it takes about 6 h and 12.5 min (one-fourth the time of the total cycle) for water in an area to go from high tide to low tide. It takes about 12 h and 25 min (one-half the time of the total cycle) to go from one high tide to the next high tide.

Note: Drawings are not to scale.

Tuesday 11:00 a.m.

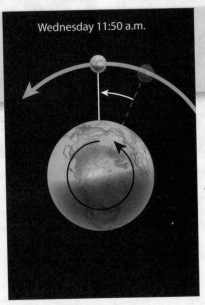

Wednesday 11:50 a.m.

The moon moves only a fraction of its orbit in the time that Earth rotates once.

Think Outside the Book Inquiry

11 Inquire Draw a diagram of Earth to show what Earth's tides would be like if the moon revolved around Earth at the same speed that Earth rotates.

12 Predict In the table, predict the approximate times of high tide and low tide for Clearwater, Florida.

Tide Data for Clearwater, Florida

Date (2009)	High tide	Low tide	High tide	Low tide
August 19	12:14 a.m.		12:39 p.m.	
August 20	1:04 a.m.	7:17 a.m.		
August 21				

Extreme Living Conditions

Some organisms living along ocean coastlines must be able to tolerate extreme living conditions. At high tide, much of the coast is under water. At low tide, much of the coast is dry. Some organisms must also survive the constant crashing of waves against the shore.

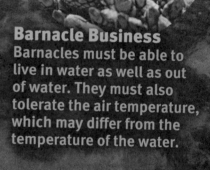

Barnacle Business

Barnacles must be able to live in water as well as out of water. They must also tolerate the air temperature, which may differ from the temperature of the water.

Ghostly Crabs

Ghost crabs live near the high tide line on sandy shores. They scurry along the sand to avoid being underwater when the tide comes in. Ghost crabs can also find cover between rocks.

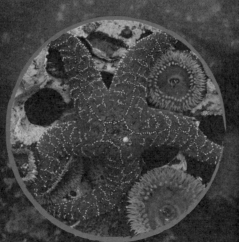

Stunning Starfish

Starfish live in tidal pools, which are areas along the shore where water remains at low tide. Starfish must be able to survive changes in water temperature and salinity.

Extend

Inquiry

13 Identify Describe how living conditions change for two tidal organisms.

14 Research and Record List the names of two organisms that live in the high tide zone or the low tide zone along a coastline of your choice.

15 Describe Imagine a day in the life of an organism you researched in question 14 by doing one of the following:
- make a poster
- write a play
- record an audio story
- make a cartoon

A Closer Look at Tides

The pictures below show the same location at two different times of day. Do you notice what's different between the two pictures? The abbey at Mont Saint Michelle in France has extreme high and low tides twice a day. Did you know that Earth's tides are not all the same? What determines the height of a tide or how many times a day a tide occurs?

Skills
✓ Explain a scientific phenomenon

Low Tide

HighTide

The combined effects of topography and gravity cause variations in tides worldwide. Some places have two tides a day, other places have one tide, and some have no ocean tidal changes at all.

Tides that occur once a day are called **diurnal** and the heights of high and low tide are about the same. **Semidiurnal** tides occur twice a day with the high and low tide height about the same. Mixed semidiurnal refers to two tides a day but the high and low tides are not the same height.

Types of Tides

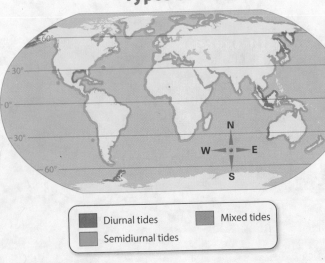

■ Diurnal tides	■ Mixed tides
■ Semidiurnal tides	

What does gravity have to do with it?

To understand these variations, let's look at the cause of tides more closely. Gravity's effect on Earth is greatest where the mass is large, especially on Earth's crust, mantle and core. In comparison, the oceans are only a very small amount of mass, and gravity's effect is weaker.

The Moon's Pull on Earth

When the mass of Earth is pulled by the moon, a **tidal bulge** is formed in Earth's crust. It's only about 30 cm, but it's enough to cause the crust to change shape and water to move. This means that in places with tides, the tide doesn't occur because the moon's gravity is pulling on the water, but because it's pulling on Earth!

Visualize It!

1 Analyze Identify two areas that have no tides. What do many of the locations with no tides have in common?

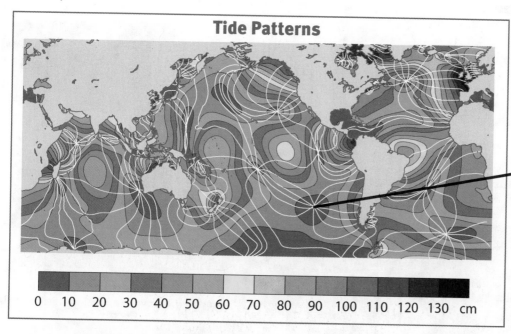

Tide Patterns

0 10 20 30 40 50 60 70 80 90 100 110 120 130 cm

Where the height is 0 cm, there is no tide!

When the moon's gravity pulls on Earth, it causes Earth's crust to flex and deform. The ocean water responds to the tidal bulge in the crust by "sloshing around". Different locations on Earth experience this movement of water and may have one tide, two tides or no tides per day.

Fun Fact

The moon has a tidal bulge caused by Earth's gravitational pull, even though there is no liquid water on the moon.

2 Synthesize What is the relationship between tidal bulges in the crust and tides?

_____

_____

_____

_____

_____

_____

3 Explain What is the role of gravity for tides that occur once per day?

_____

_____

_____

_____

_____

_____

Visual Summary

To complete this summary, fill in the blanks with the correct word. Then use the key below to check your answers. You can use this page to review the main concepts of the lesson.

Tides on Earth

In many places, two high tides and two low tides occur every day.

16 The type of tide shown here is

____

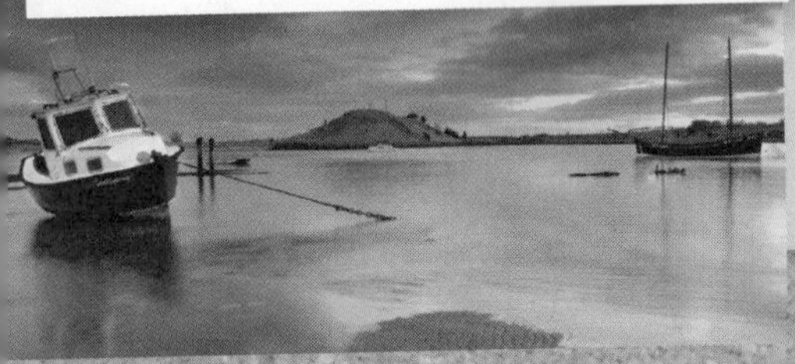

The gravitational effects of the moon and the sun cause tides.

17 Tides on Earth are caused mainly by the

____

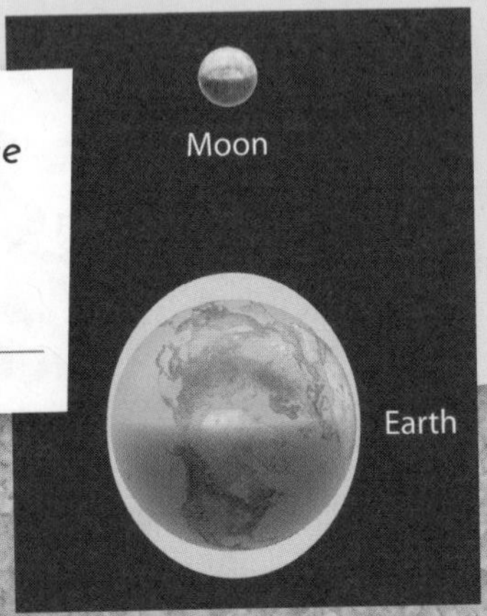

Note: Drawings are not to scale.

There are two kinds of tidal ranges: spring tides and neap tides.

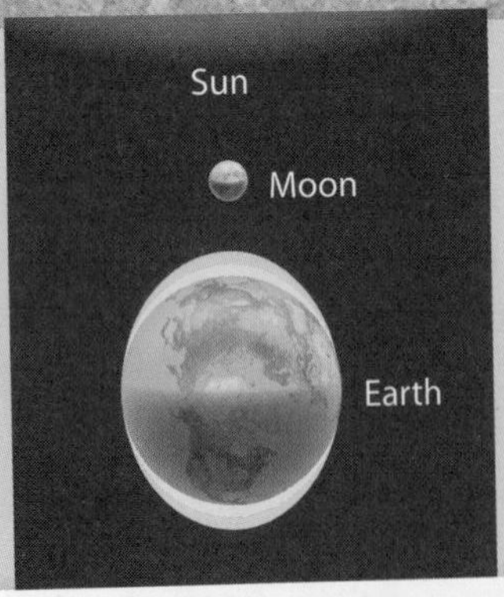

18 During a spring tide, the sun, moon, and Earth are in a/an

____

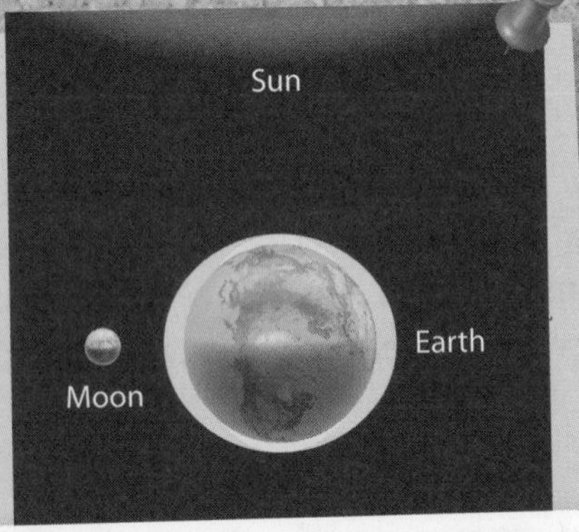

19 During a neap tide, the sun, moon, and Earth form a/an

____

Answers: 16 low tide; 17 moon; 18 straight line; 19 90° angle

20 Describe State how the moon causes tides.

Lesson Review

Vocabulary

Answer the following questions in your own words.

1 Use *tide* and *tidal range* in the same sentence.

_____

_____

_____

2 Write an original definition for *neap tide* and for *spring tide*.

_____

_____

_____

_____

Key Concepts

3 Describe Explain what tides are. Include *high tide* and *low tide* in your answer.

_____

_____

_____

_____

_____

4 Explain State what causes tides on Earth.

_____

_____

_____

5 Identify Write the alignment of the moon, the sun, and Earth that causes a spring tide.

_____

_____

_____

6 Describe Explain why tides happen 50 min later each day.

_____

_____

_____

Critical Thinking

Use this diagram to answer the next question.

Note: Drawing is not to scale.

Last quarter moon

7 Analyze What type of tidal range will Earth have when the moon is in this position?

_____

8 Apply How many days pass between the minimum and the maximum of the tidal range in any given area? Explain your answer.

_____

_____

_____

_____

_____

_____

9 Apply How would the tides on Earth be different if the moon revolved around Earth in 15 days instead of 30 days?

_____

_____

_____

_____

_____

_____

My Notes

Unit 7

Big Idea   The universe rapidly expanded and is held together by gravity. Technology provides information about the universe's origin and structure.

Lesson 1
ESSENTIAL QUESTION
How do we explore space?

Describe the ways that people use technology to explore space.

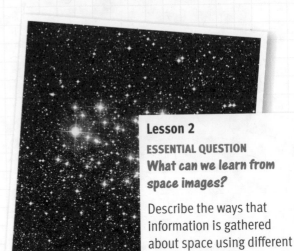

Lesson 2
ESSENTIAL QUESTION
What can we learn from space images?

Describe the ways that information is gathered about space using different wavelengths of light.

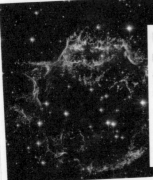

Lesson 3
ESSENTIAL QUESTION
How did the universe begin?

Describe the evidence that supports the Big Bang theory.

Lesson 5
ESSENTIAL QUESTION
What causes tides?

Describe what tides are and what causes the variety of tides.

Lesson 4
ESSENTIAL QUESTION
Why is gravity important in the solar system?

Describe the role that gravity plays in the formation and motion of the planets.

Connect ESSENTIAL QUESTIONS
Lessons 2 and 3

1 Synthesize Describe how data about the origin of the universe is gathered and why this data supports the Big Bang theory. Include an explanation of the importance of Doppler shift in interpreting this data.

_____

_____

_____

_____

Think Outside the Book

2 Synthesize Choose one of these activities to help synthesize what you have learned in this unit.

☐ Using what you learned in lessons 4 and 5, write a short essay describing the role of gravity in the formation of Earth and its role with ocean tides.

☐ Using what you learned in lessons 4 and 5, create a poster presentation that describes the role of the sun, moon and Earth in the formation of different ocean tides around Earth.

Name _____

Vocabulary

Fill in the blanks with the term that best completes the following sentences.

1 An _____ is any human-made object placed in orbit around a body in space, either with or without a crew.

2 A _____ is the periodic rise and fall of the water level in the oceans and other large bodies of water.

3 A(n) _____ is a large group of stars, gas, and dust bound together by gravity.

4 The solar system formed from a _____, which is a rotating cloud of gas and dust that formed into the sun and planets.

5 An increase in the wavelength of light as a galaxy moves away from Earth is called a(n) _____.

Key Concepts

Read each question below, and circle the best answer.

6 What does Kepler's first law of planetary motion state?

A the orbit of a planet around the sun is an ellipse with the sun at one focus

B the orbit of a planet is dependent on heat

C the difference between centripetal force and elliptical force

D the orbital period is infinite

7 Satellites in orbit around Earth are used for various purposes. For which one of the following purposes are satellites **not** used?

A transmitting signals over large distances to remote locations

B monitoring changes in Earth's environment over time

C changing Earth's orbit

D collecting different types of weather data

8 Why do astronauts who live on the space station have to exercise every day?

A There is not much else to do, and exercising passes the time.

B It prevents their bones and muscles from weakening.

C Astronauts need to stay in good shape.

D It helps them to sleep better at night.

9 Look at the table of tide information.

Date	High tide time	High tide height (m)	Low tide time	Low tide time height (m)
June 3	6:04 a.m.	6.11	12:01 a.m.	1.76
June 4	6:58 a.m.	5.92	12:54 a.m.	1.87
June 5	7:51 a.m.	5.80	1:47 a.m.	1.90
June 6	8:42 a.m.	5.75	2:38 a.m.	1.87
June 7	9:30 a.m.	5.79	3:27 a.m.	1.75
June 8	10:16 a.m.	5.90	4:13 a.m.	1.56
June 9	11:01 a.m.	6.08	4:59 a.m.	1.32
June 10	11:46 a.m.	6.28	5:44 a.m.	1.05
June 11	12:32 p.m.	6:47	6:30 a.m.	0.78

What was the tidal range on June 9?

A 1.32 m

B 4.76 m

C 6.08 m

D 7.40 m

10 How are telescopes used in space science?

A Telescopes help in looking at cells.

B Telescopes are used to communicate over long distances.

C Telescopes are used to transmit visible light over long distances.

D Telescopes help to gather data about space for use by astronomers.

11 Where do stars form?

A in nebulae

B on asteroids

C in a planet's core

D in sun spots on the surface of the sun

12 The dot in the diagram is a source of light waves. It is moving from right to left across the diagram.

How does the diagram relate to the expanding universe? (Hint: Step 1. Compare the characteristics of the waves in front of the source with those behind the source. Step 2. Think about evidence scientists used to conclude that the universe is expanding. Step 3. Relate the diagram to the evidence.)

A It shows that light produced during the Big Bang is still in motion.

B It shows that objects move faster depending on the type of light they produce.

C It shows that a source produces light of different wavelengths in different positions.

D It shows that wavelengths are increased behind an object that is moving away from an observer.

13 Which statement best supports the Big Bang theory?

A Microwave radiation is observed to be even throughout the sky.

B The largest stars are also the hottest stars.

C Some galaxies are moving toward us and have blue shifted light.

D Gamma radiation is observed from the most distant galaxies

14 Which describes an effect of centripetal force?

A objects break apart in space

B objects burn at very high temperatures

C objects move in a circular path

D objects move in an elliptical path

15 Which is a similarity between a neap tide and a spring tide?

A Neap tides occur once a year in fall and spring tides once a year in spring.

B Each occurs twice a year and relates to the phases of the moon.

C A neap tide occurs at night, and a spring tide occurs during the day.

D Each tide occurs twice a month, and is determined by the pull of gravity of the moon.

Critical Thinking

Answer the following questions in the space provided.

16 Outline a brief history of space exploration, and discuss some problems humans encounter when they explore space.

_____

_____

_____

_____

17 Janais lives near the ocean. How do Earth, the sun, and the moon interact to affect Janais's life?

_____

_____

_____

_____

_____

Connect **ESSENTIAL QUESTIONS**
Lessons 1, 2, 3, 4, and 5

Answer the following question in the space provided.

18 Scientists' understanding of the universe changed over time as new evidence was discovered. How did each of the following scientists affect the understanding of the universe?

- Isaac Newton

- Albert Einstein

- George Lemaître

- Edwin Hubble

_____

_____

_____

_____

_____

Minerals and Rocks

The rock in this abandoned Australian copper mine has been colored by different compounds of copper.

Big Idea

Minerals and rocks are basic building blocks of Earth and can change over time from one type of mineral or rock to another.

8.ESS2.3

What do you think?

Minerals and rocks have a variety of uses in products that people use every day. What minerals or rocks are mined in your community?

Copper was one of the first metals used by humans, because it can be found in a nearly pure form, like this native copper.

Unit 8
Minerals and Rocks

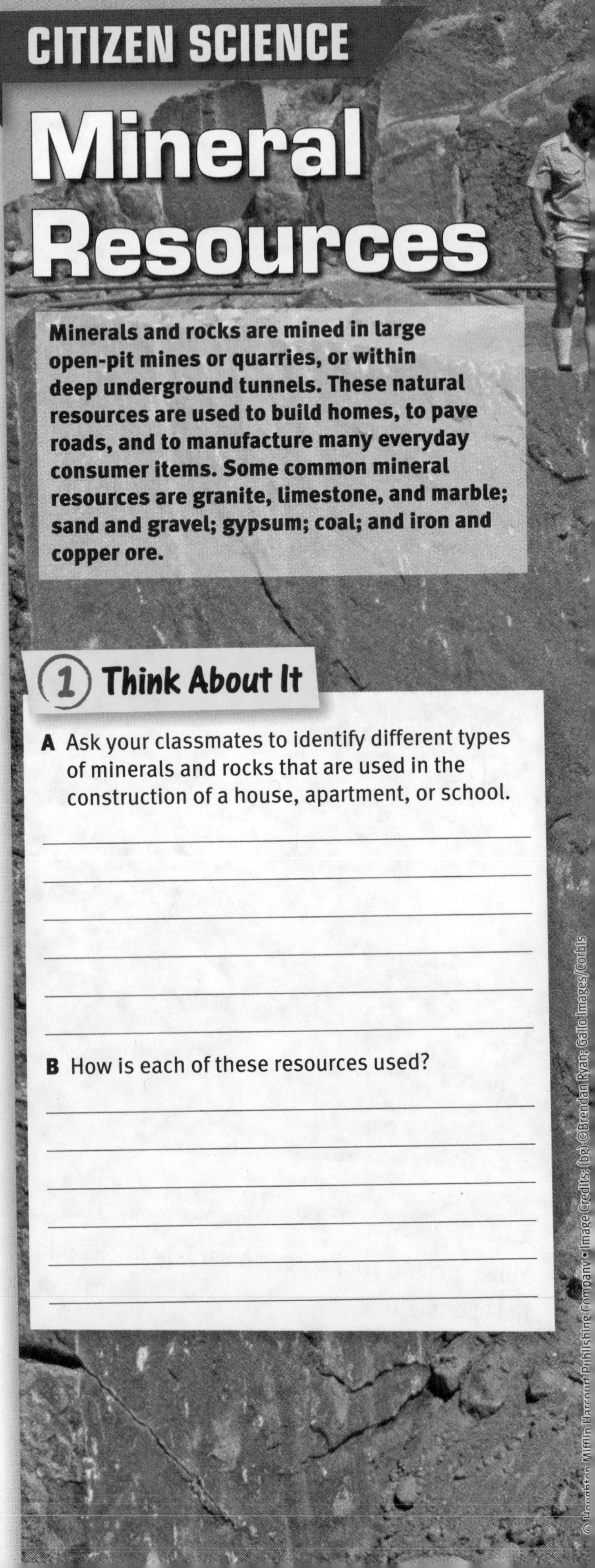

CITIZEN SCIENCE
Mineral Resources

Minerals and rocks are mined in large open-pit mines or quarries, or within deep underground tunnels. These natural resources are used to build homes, to pave roads, and to manufacture many everyday consumer items. Some common mineral resources are granite, limestone, and marble; sand and gravel; gypsum; coal; and iron and copper ore.

① Think About It

A Ask your classmates to identify different types of minerals and rocks that are used in the construction of a house, apartment, or school.

_____

_____

_____

_____

_____

B How is each of these resources used?

_____

_____

_____

_____

_____

_____

_____

Workers must carefully plan how to remove large blocks or sheets of granite from a quarry.

Marble, also mined from quarries, can become beautiful works of art.

② Ask a Question

What is the environmental impact of mining minerals and rocks?

Opening a mine requires clearing the land and moving soil and rock. Do some research on how mining affects the environment. What are some ways in which mining can harm the environment?

_____

_____

_____

_____

_____

③ Make a Plan

Imagine that a mining operation is coming to a place near you. Make a plan for two regulations you would like to see the mining company have to follow in order to protect the environment.

_____

_____

_____

_____

_____

_____

_____

Take It Home

Search your local newspaper or the Internet for news stories that involve the environmental impact of mining. See *ScienceSaurus*® **for more information about natural resources and the environment.**

Minerals

ESSENTIAL QUESTION

What are minerals, how do they form, and how can they be identified?

By the end of this lesson, you should be able to describe the basic structure of minerals and identify different minerals by using their physical properties.

This cave was once full of water. Over millions of years, dissolved minerals in the water slowly formed these gypsum crystals, which are now considered to be the largest mineral crystals in the world!

Lesson Labs

Quick Labs
- Cooling Rates and Crystal Size
- Scratch Test

Exploration Lab
- Intrinsic Identification of Minerals

Engage Your Brain

1 Identify Which of the materials listed below is a mineral?

Yes	No	
☐	☐	ice
☐	☐	gold
☐	☐	wood
☐	☐	diamond
☐	☐	table salt

2 Explain Describe how you think the minerals in the picture below may have formed.

_____

_____

_____

Active Reading

3 Synthesize Many of this lesson's vocabulary terms are related to each other. Locate the terms in the Glossary and see if you can find connections between them. When you find two terms that are related to each other, write a sentence using both terms in a way that shows the relationship. An example is done for you.

Example Sentence
Each element is made of only one kind of atom.

_____

_____

_____

Vocabulary Terms

- mineral
- element
- atom
- compound
- matter
- crystal
- streak
- luster
- cleavage

4 Apply As you learn the definition of each vocabulary term in this lesson, create your own definition or sketch to help you remember the meaning of the term.

Animal, Vegetable,

What do minerals have in common?

When you hear the word *mineral,* you may think of sparkling gems. But, in fact, most minerals are found in groups that make up rocks. So what is a mineral? A **mineral** is a naturally occurring, usually inorganic solid that has a definite crystalline structure and chemical composition.

Definite Chemical Composition

To understand what a definite chemical composition is, you need to know a little about elements. **Elements** are pure substances that cannot be broken down into simpler substances by ordinary chemical means. Each element is made of only one kind of atom. All substances are made up of atoms, so **atoms** can be thought of as the building blocks of matter. Stable particles that are made up of strongly bonded atoms are called *molecules.* And, if a substance is made up of molecules of two or more elements, the substance is called a **compound.**

The chemical composition of a mineral is determined by the element or compound that makes up the mineral. For example, minerals such as gold and silver are composed of only one element. Such a mineral is called a *native element.* The mineral quartz is a compound in which silicon atoms can each bond with up to four oxygen atoms in a repeating pattern.

5 Synthesize What is the relationship between elements, atoms, and compounds?

_____

_____

_____

_____

Solid

Matter is anything that has volume and mass. *Volume* refers to the amount of space an object takes up. For example, a golf ball has a smaller volume than a baseball does. Matter is generally found in one of three states: solid, liquid, or gas. A mineral is a solid—that is, it has a definite volume and shape. A substance that is a liquid or a gas is not a mineral. However, in some cases its solid form is a mineral. For instance, liquid water is not a mineral, but ice is because it is solid and has all of the other mineral characteristics also.

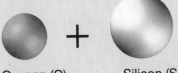

Atoms The mineral quartz is made up of atoms of oxygen and silicon.

Oxygen (O)   Silicon (Si)

Compound An atom of silicon can typically bond with up to four oxygen atoms to form a molecule. One or more of these molecules form a compound.

or Mineral?

Usually Inorganic

Most substances made by living things are categorized as organic substances, such as kidney stones and wood. However, a few substances made by animals, such as clam shells, are categorized as inorganic. An inorganic substance is usually one that is not made up of living things or the remains of living things. And, although a few organic substances such as kidney stones are categorized as minerals, most minerals are inorganic. And, unlike clam shells, most of the processes that form minerals usually take place in the non-living environment.

Crystalline Structure

Minerals have a crystalline structure because they are composed of crystals. A **crystal** is a solid, geometric form that results from a repeating pattern of atoms or molecules. A crystal's shape is produced by the arrangement of the atoms or molecules within the crystal. This arrangement is determined by the kinds of atoms or molecules that make up the mineral and the conditions under which it forms. All minerals can be placed into crystal classes according to their specific crystal shape. This diagram shows how silica compounds can be arranged in quartz crystals.

Naturally Occurring

Minerals are formed by many different natural processes that occur on Earth and throughout the universe. On Earth, the mineral halite, which is used for table salt, forms as water evaporates and leaves behind the salt it contained. Some minerals form as molten rock cools. Talc, a mineral that can be used to make baby powder, forms deep in Earth as high temperature and pressure change the rock. Some of the other ways in which minerals form are on the next page.

6 Classify Circle *Y* for "yes" or *N* for "no" to determine whether the two materials below are minerals.

	Cardboard	Topaz
Definite chemical composition?	Y (N)	(Y) N
Solid?	Y N	(Y) N
Inorganic?	Y N	Y N
Naturally occurring?	Y N	Y N
Crystalline structure?	Y (N)	Y N
Mineral?	Y N	Y N

Crystal Structure In crystals, molecules are arranged in a regular pattern.

Mineral Crystal Billions of molecules arranged in a crystalline structure form these quartz crystals.

Crystal Clear!

How are minerals formed?

Minerals form within Earth or on Earth's surface by natural processes. Recall that each type of mineral has its own chemical makeup. Therefore, which types of minerals form in an area depends in part on which elements are present there. Temperature and pressure also affect which minerals form.

As Magma and Lava Cool

Many minerals grow from magma. Magma—molten rock inside Earth—contains most of the types of atoms that are found in minerals. As magma cools, the atoms join together to form different minerals. Minerals also form as lava cools. Lava is molten rock that has reached Earth's surface. Quartz is one of the many minerals that crystallize from magma and lava.

Visualize It!

7 Compare How are the ways in which pluton and pegmatite minerals form similar?

_____

_____

By Metamorphism

Temperature and pressure within Earth cause new minerals to form as bonds between atoms break and reform with different atoms. The mineral garnet can form and replace the minerals chlorite and quartz in this way. At high temperatures and pressures, the element carbon in rocks forms the mineral diamond or the mineral graphite, which is used in pencils.

Cooling Magma Forms Plutons
As magma rises, it can stop moving and cool slowly. This forms rocks like this granite, which contains minerals like quartz, mica, and feldspar.

Cooling Magma Forms Pegmatites
Magma that cools very slowly can form pegmatites. Some crystals in pegmatites, such as this topaz, can grow quite large.

Metamorphism Minerals like these garnets form when temperature and pressure causes the chemical and crystalline makeup of minerals to change.

From Solutions

Water usually has many substances dissolved in it. As water evaporates, these substances form into solids and come out of solution, or *precipitate*. For example, the mineral gypsum often forms as water evaporates. Minerals can also form from hot water solutions. Hot water can dissolve more materials than cold water. As a body of hot water cools, dissolved substances can form into minerals such as dolomite, as they precipitate out of solution.

8 Summarize Describe three ways minerals form.

A _____

_____

B _____

_____

C _____

_____

Precipitating from an Evaporating Solution When a body of salt water evaporates, minerals such as this halite precipitate and are left behind on the shoreline.

Precipitating from a Cooling Solution on Earth's Surface Dissolved materials can come out of a solution and accumulate. Dolomite, can form this way.

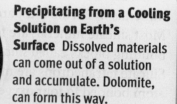

Think Outside the Book

9 Apply Find out what your state mineral is and how it forms.

Precipitating from a Cooling Solution Beneath Earth's Surface Water works its way downward and is heated by magma. It then reacts with minerals to form a solution. Dissolved elements, such as gold, precipitate once the fluid cools to form new mineral deposits.

Sort It Out

How are minerals classified?

The most common classification of minerals is based on chemical composition. Minerals are divided into two groups based on their composition. These groups are the silicate (SIL'ih•kayt) minerals and the nonsilicate (nawn•SIL'ih•kayt) minerals.

Silicate Minerals

Silicon and oxygen are the two most common elements in Earth's crust. Minerals that contain a combination of these two elements are called *silicate minerals*. Silicate minerals make up most of Earth's crust. The most common silicate minerals in Earth's crust are feldspar and quartz. Most silicate minerals are formed from basic building blocks called *silicate tetrahedrons*. Silicate tetrahedrons are made of one silicon atom bonded to four oxygen atoms. Most silicate minerals, including mica and olivine, are composed of silicate tetrahedrons combined with other elements, such as aluminum or iron.

Active Reading **10 Explain** Why is Earth's crust made up mostly of silicate minerals?

_____

_____

The mineral zircon is a silicate mineral. It is composed of the element zirconium and silicate tetrahedrons.

Nonsilicate Minerals

Minerals that do not contain the silicate tetrahedron building block form a group called the *nonsilicate minerals*. Some of these minerals are made up of elements such as carbon, oxygen, fluorine, iron, and sulfur. The table on the next page shows the most important classes of nonsilicate minerals. A nonsilicate mineral's chemical composition determines its class.

Do the Math You Try It

11 Calculate Calculate the percent of nonsilicates in Earth's crust to complete the graph's key.

Minerals in Earth's Crust

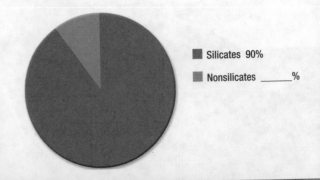

- ■ Silicates 90%
- ■ Nonsilicates _____%

Classes of Nonsilicate Minerals

Native elements are minerals that are composed of only one element. Copper (Cu) and silver (Ag) are two examples. Native elements are often used to make electronics.

Silver, Ag

Carbonates are minerals that contain carbon (C) and oxygen (O) in the form of the carbonate ion CO_3^{2-}. We use carbonate minerals in cement, building stones, and fireworks.

Calcite, $CaCO_3$

Halides are compounds that form when elements such as fluorine (F) and chlorine (Cl), combine with elements such as calcium (Ca). Halides are used in the chemical industry and in detergents.

Fluorite, CaF_2

Oxides are compounds that form when an element, such as aluminum (Al) or iron (Fe), combines with oxygen. Oxide minerals are used to make abrasives, aircraft parts, and paint.

Corundum, Al_2O_3

Sulfates are minerals that contain sulfur (S) and oxygen (O) in the form of the sulfate ion SO_4^{2-}. Sulfates are used in cosmetics, toothpaste, cement, and paint.

Barite, $BaSO_4$

Sulfides are minerals that contain one or more elements, such as lead (Pb), or iron (Fe), combined with sulfur (S). Sulfide minerals are used to make batteries and medicines.

Pyrite, FeS_2

Visualize It!

12 Classify Examine the chemical formulas for the two minerals at right. Classify the minerals as a silicate or nonsilicate. If it is a nonsilicate, also write its class.

Gypsum, $CaSO_4 \cdot 2H_2O$

Kyanite, Al_2SiO_5

_____

_____

Name That Mineral!

What properties can be used to identify minerals?

If you closed your eyes and tasted different foods, you could probably determine what the foods are by noting properties such as saltiness or sweetness. You can also determine the identity of a mineral by noting different properties. In this section, you will learn about the properties that will help you identify minerals.

Color

The same mineral can come in different colors. For example, pure quartz is colorless. However, impurities can make quartz pink, orange, or many other colors. Other factors can also change a mineral's color. Pyrite is normally golden, but turns black or brown if exposed to air and water. The same mineral can be different colors, and different minerals can be the same color. So, color is helpful but usually not the best way to identify a mineral.

Streak

The color of the powdered form of a mineral is its **streak**. A mineral's streak is found by rubbing the mineral against a white tile called a *streak plate*. The mark left is the streak. A mineral's streak is not always the same as the color of the mineral, but all samples of the same mineral have the same streak color. Unlike the surface of a mineral, the streak is not affected by air or water. For this reason, streak is more reliable than color in identifying a mineral.

Active Reading

13 **Identify** Underline the name of the property on this page that is most reliable for identifying a mineral.

Visualize It!

14 **Evaluate** Look at these two mineral samples. What property indicates that they may be the same mineral?

_____

_____

_____

© Houghton Mifflin Harcourt Publishing Company

Mineral Lusters

Metallic

Silky

Vitreous

Waxy

Submetallic

Pearly

Resinous

Earthy

Luster

The way a surface reflects light is called **luster**. When you say an object is shiny or dull, you are describing its luster. The two major types of luster are metallic and nonmetallic. Pyrite has a metallic luster. It looks as if it is made of metal. A mineral with a nonmetallic luster can be shiny, but it does not appear to be made of metal. Different types of lusters are shown above.

Cleavage and Fracture

The tendency of a mineral to split along specific planes of weakness to form smooth, flat surfaces is called **cleavage**. When a mineral has cleavage, it breaks along flat surfaces that generally run parallel to planes of weakness in the crystal structure. For example, mica tends to split into parallel sheets. Many minerals, however, do not break along cleavage planes. Instead, they fracture, or break unevenly, into pieces that have curved or irregular surfaces. Scientists describe a fracture according to the appearance of the broken surface. For example, a rough surface has an irregular fracture, and a curved surfaces has a conchoidal (kahn•KOY•duhl) fracture.

Visualize It!

15 Identify Write the correct description, either *cleavage* or *fracture*, under the two broken mineral crystals shown here.

_____

_____

Mohs Scale

1 Talc

2 Gypsum

Your fingernail has a hardness of about 2.5, so it can scratch talc and gypsum.

3 Calcite

4 Fluorite

5 Apatite

6 Feldspar

A steel file has a hardness of about 6.5. You can scratch feldspar with it.

7 Quartz

8 Topaz

9 Corundum

10 Diamond

Diamond is the hardest mineral. Only a diamond can scratch another diamond.

Visualize It!

16 Determine A mineral can be scratched by calcite but not by a fingernail. What is its approximate hardness?

_____

Density

If you pick up a golf ball and a table-tennis ball, which will feel heavier? Although the balls are of similar size, the golf ball will feel heavier because it is denser. *Density* is the measure of how much matter is in a given amount of space. Density is usually measured in grams per cubic centimeter. Gold has a density of 19 g/cm³. The mineral pyrite looks very similar to gold, but its density is only 5 g/cm³. Because of this, density can be used to tell gold from pyrite. Density can also be used to tell many other similar-looking minerals apart.

Hardness

A mineral's resistance to being scratched is called its *hardness*. To determine the hardness of minerals, scientists use the Mohs hardness scale, shown at left. Notice that talc has a rating of 1 and diamond has a rating of 10. The greater a mineral's resistance to being scratched, the higher its hardness rating. To identify a mineral by using the Mohs scale, try to scratch the surface of a mineral with the edge of one of the 10 reference minerals. If the reference mineral scratches your mineral, the reference mineral is as hard as or harder than your mineral.

Special Properties

All minerals exhibit the properties that were described earlier in this section. However, a few minerals have some additional, special properties that can help identify those minerals. For example, the mineral magnetite is a natural magnet. The mineral calcite is usually white in ordinary light, but in ultraviolet light, it often appears red. Another special property of calcite is shown below.

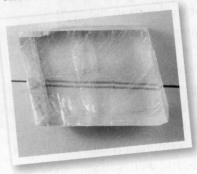

A clear piece of calcite placed over an image will cause a double image.

© Houghton Mifflin Harcourt Publishing Company • Image Credits: (bl) ©Steve Hamblin/Alamy; (br) ©Biophoto Associates/Photo Researchers, Inc.

Made from Minerals

Many minerals contain useful substances. Rutile and several other minerals contain the metal titanium. Titanium can resist corrosion and is about as strong as steel, but it is 47% lighter than steel. These properties make titanium very valuable.

Devices for Doctors

Surgical procedures like joint replacements require metal implantations. Titanium is used because it can resist body fluid corrosion and its low density and elasticity are similar to human bone.

Marvels for Mechanics

Motorcycle exhaust pipes are often made out of titanium, which dissipates heat better than stainless steel.

An Aid to Architects

Titanium doesn't just serve practical purposes. Architect Frank Gehry used titanium panels to cover the outside of the Guggenheim Museum in Bilbao, Spain. He chose titanium because of its luster.

Extend

Inquiry

17 Infer How do you think the density of titanium-containing minerals would compare to the density of minerals used to make steel? Explain.

18 List Research some other products made from minerals. Make a list summarizing your research.

19 Determine Choose one of the products you researched. How do the properties of the minerals used to make the product contribute to the product's characteristics or usefulness?

Visual Summary

To complete this summary, fill in the blanks with the correct words or phrase. Then use the key below to check your answers. You can use this page to review the main concepts of the lesson.

Minerals make up Earth's crust.

20 A mineral:

- has a definite chemical composition
- is a solid
- is usually inorganic
- is formed in nature
- _____

Minerals are classified by composition.

21 Minerals are classified in two groups as:

Quartz, SiO_2

_____

Calcite, $CaCO_3$

_____

Minerals

Minerals form by natural processes.

22 Minerals form by:

- metamorphism
- the cooling of magma and lava
- _____

Minerals are identified by their properties.

23 Properties used to identify minerals include:

- color and luster
- _____
- cleavage or fracture
- density and hardness
- special properties

Answers: 20 has a crystalline structure; 21 silicates (left), nonsilicates (right); 22 precipitating from solutions; 23 streak

24 Apply Ice (H_2O) is a mineral. Classify it as silicate or nonsilicate. List two of its properties.

Lesson Review

Vocabulary

Fill in the blank with the term that best completes the following sentence.

1 The way light bounces off a mineral's surface is described by the mineral's _____

2 The color of a mineral in powdered form is the mineral's _____

3 Each element is made up of only one kind of _____

Key Concepts

4 Explain How could you determine whether an unknown substance is a mineral?

_____

_____

_____

_____

_____

5 Determine If a substance is a mineral, how could you identify what type of mineral it is?

_____

_____

_____

_____

6 Organize In the space below, draw a graphic organizer showing how minerals can be classified. Be sure to include the six main classes of nonsilicate minerals.

Critical Thinking

Use the diagram below to answer question 7.

Carbon Bonds in Graphite

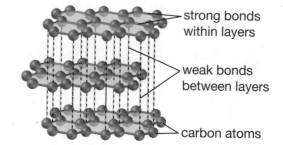

- strong bonds within layers
- weak bonds between layers
- carbon atoms

7 Evaluate The diagram above shows the crystal structure of graphite, a mineral made up of carbon atoms that are bonded together in a regular pattern. Do you think graphite would most likely display cleavage or fracture? Explain your answer.

_____

_____

_____

_____

_____

8 Infer How do you think the hardness and density of a mineral that formed through metamorphism would compare to a mineral that formed through evaporation? Explain.

_____

_____

_____

_____

_____

_____

_____

My Notes

(Messi)
MESSENGER

- a kiwi
- that's all you
  need to know

The Rock Cycle

ESSENTIAL QUESTION

What is the rock cycle?

By the end of this lesson, you should be able to describe the series of processes and classes of rocks that make up the rock cycle.

8.ESS2.3

It may be hard to believe, but these mountains actually move. Wyoming's Teton Mountains rise by millimeters each year. An active fault is uplifting the mountains. In this lesson, you will learn about uplift and other processes that change rock.

Engage Your Brain

1 Describe Fill in the blank with the word or phrase that you think correctly completes the following sentences.

Most of Earth is made of _____

Rock is _____ changing.

The three main classes of rock are igneous, metamorphic, and _____

2 Describe Write your own caption for this photo.

_____

_____

_____

_____

Active Reading

3 Synthesize Many English words have their roots in other languages. Use the Latin words below to make an educated guess about the meaning of the words *erosion* and *deposition*.

Latin Word	Meaning
erosus	eaten away
depositus	laid down

Vocabulary Terms

- weathering
- erosion
- deposition
- igneous rock
- sedimentary rock
- metamorphic rock
- rock cycle
- uplift
- subsidence
- rift zone

4 Apply As you learn the definition of each vocabulary term in this lesson, create your own definition or sketch to help you remember the meaning of the term.

Erosion:

_____

_____

Deposition:

_____

_____

Let's Rock!

What is rock?

The solid parts of Earth are made almost entirely of rock. Scientists define rock as a naturally occurring solid mixture of one or more minerals that may also include organic matter. Most rock is made of minerals, but some rock is made of nonmineral material that is not organic, such as glass. Rock has been an important natural resource as long as humans have existed. Early humans used rocks as hammers to make other tools. For centuries, people have used different types of rock, including granite, marble, sandstone, and slate, to make buildings, such as the pyramids shown below.

It may be hard to believe, but rocks are always changing. People study rocks to learn how areas have changed through time.

5 List How is rock used today?

_____

_____

_____

_____

The ancient Egyptians used a rock called limestone to construct the Great Sphinx and the pyramids at Giza.

These rock formations in Goreme, Turkey, are known as fairy chimneys. They were shaped by erosion.

Think Outside the Book

6 **Design** Create a travel brochure for Goreme, Turkey.

What processes change rock?

Natural processes make and destroy rock. They change each type of rock into other types of rock and shape the features of our planet. These processes also influence the type of rock that is found in each area of Earth's surface.

Active Reading 7 **Identify** As you read, underline the processes and factors that can change rock.

Weathering, Erosion, and Deposition

The process by which water, wind, ice, and changes in temperature break down rock is called **weathering**. Weathering breaks down rock into fragments called *sediment*. The process by which sediment is moved from one place to another is called **erosion.** Water, wind, ice, and gravity can erode sediments. These sediments are eventually deposited, or laid down, in bodies of water and other low-lying areas. The process by which sediment comes to rest is called **deposition.**

Temperature and Pressure

Rock that is buried can be squeezed by the weight of the rock or the layers of sediment on top of it. As pressure increases with depth beneath Earth's surface, so does temperature. If the temperature and pressure are high enough, the buried rock can change into metamorphic rock. In some cases, the rock gets hot enough to melt and forms *magma*, or molten rock. If magma reaches Earth's surface, it is called *lava*. The magma or lava eventually cool and solidify to form new rock.

© Houghton Mifflin Harcourt Publishing Company • Image Credits: ©Imagebroker/Alamy

Classified Information!

What are the classes of rocks?

Rocks fall into three major classes based on how they form. **Igneous rock** forms when magma or lava cools and hardens to become solid. It forms beneath or on Earth's surface. **Sedimentary rock** forms when minerals that form from solutions or sediment from older rocks get pressed and cemented together. **Metamorphic rock** forms when pressure, temperature, or chemical processes change existing rock. Each class can be divided further, based on differences in the way rocks form. For example, some igneous rocks form when lava cools on Earth's surface, and others form when magma cools deep beneath the surface. Therefore, igneous rock can be classified based on how and where it forms.

Active Reading

8 Identify As you read the paragraph, underline the three main classes of rocks.

Think Outside the Book   Inquiry

9 Apply With a classmate, discuss the processes that might have shaped the rock formations in the Valley of Fire State Park.

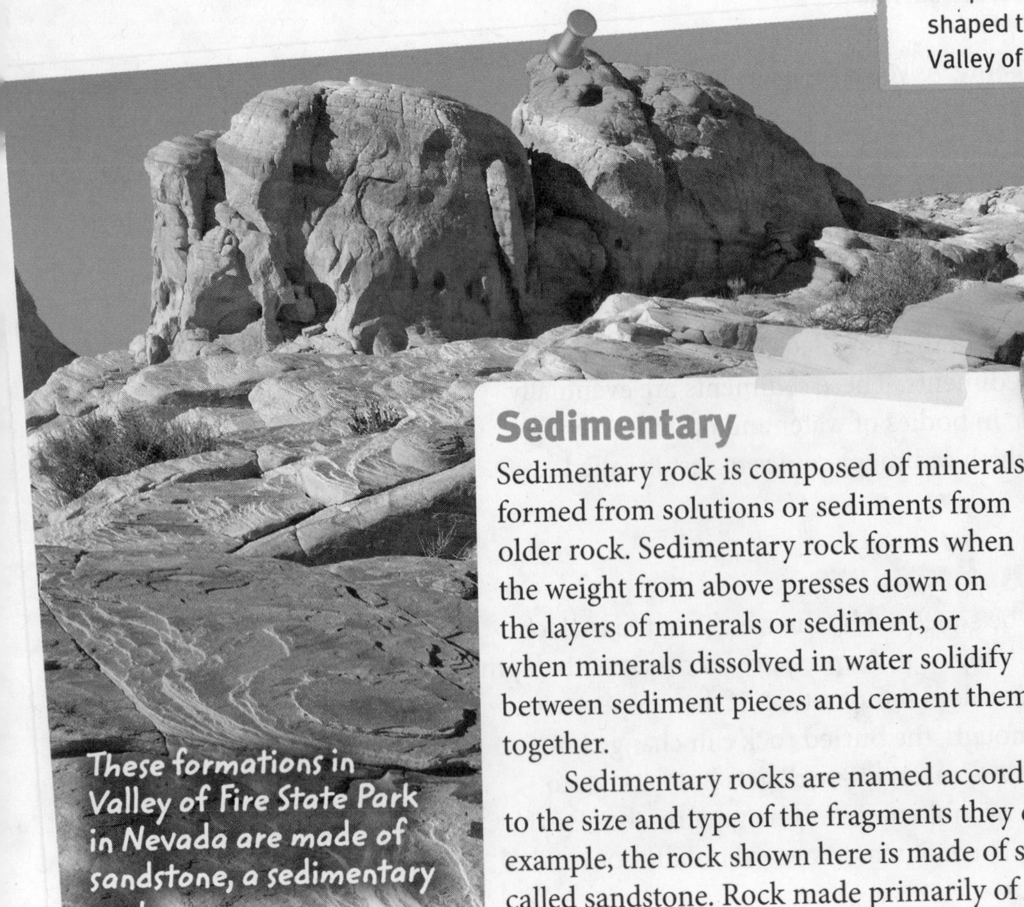

These formations in Valley of Fire State Park in Nevada are made of sandstone, a sedimentary rock.

Sedimentary

Sedimentary rock is composed of minerals formed from solutions or sediments from older rock. Sedimentary rock forms when the weight from above presses down on the layers of minerals or sediment, or when minerals dissolved in water solidify between sediment pieces and cement them together.

Sedimentary rocks are named according to the size and type of the fragments they contain. For example, the rock shown here is made of sand and is called sandstone. Rock made primarily of the mineral calcite (calcium carbonate) is called limestone.

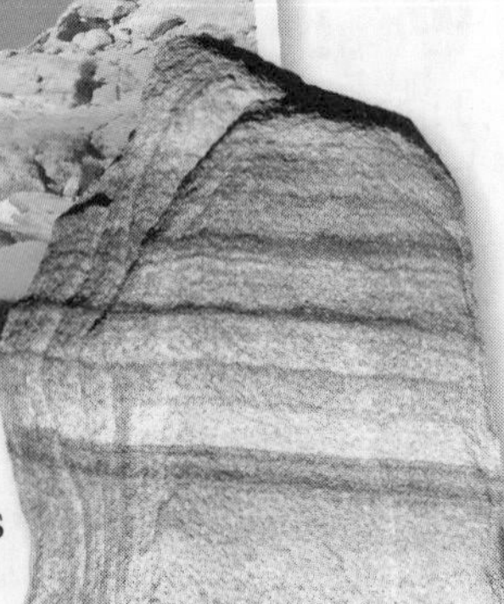

sandstone

Enchanted Rock in Texas is a large dome made of granite, an intrusive igneous rock.

Igneous Rock

Igneous rock forms from cooling lava and magma. As molten rock cools and becomes solid, the minerals crystallize and grow. The longer the cooling takes, the more time the crystals have to grow. The granite shown here cooled slowly and is made of large crystals. Rock that forms when magma cools beneath Earth's surface is called intrusive igneous rock. Rock that forms when lava cools on Earth's surface is called extrusive igneous rock.

granite

Metamorphic Rock

Metamorphic rock forms when high temperature and pressure change the texture and mineral content of rock. For example, a rock can be buried in Earth's crust, where the temperature and pressure are high. Over millions of years, the solid rock changes, and new crystals are formed. Metamorphic rocks may be changed in four ways: by temperature, by pressure, by temperature and pressure combined, or by fluids or other chemicals. Gneiss, shown here, is a metamorphic rock. It forms at high temperatures deep within Earth's crust.

gneiss

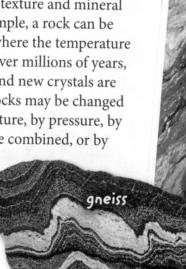

Gneiss is a metamorphic rock that is made up of bands of light and dark minerals.

10 Compare Fill in the chart to compare and contrast sedimentary, igneous, and metamorphic rock.

Classes of Rocks

Sedimentary rock	Igneous rock	Metamorphic rock

What is the rock cycle?

11 Apply As you read, underline the rock types that metamorphic rock can change into.

Rocks may seem very permanent, solid, and unchanging. But over millions of years, any of the three rock types can be changed into another of the three types. For example, igneous rock can change into sedimentary or metamorphic rock, or back into another kind of igneous rock. This series of processes in which rock changes from one type to another is called the **rock cycle**. Rocks may follow different pathways in the cycle. Examples of these pathways are shown here. Factors, including temperature, pressure, weathering, and erosion, may change a rock's identity. Where rock is located on a tectonic plate and whether the rock is at Earth's surface also influence how it forms and changes.

When igneous rock is exposed at Earth's surface, it may break down into sediment. Igneous rock may also change directly into metamorphic rock while still beneath Earth's surface. It may also melt to form magma that becomes another type of igneous rock.

When sediment is pressed together and cemented, the sediment becomes sedimentary rock. With temperature and pressure changes, sedimentary rocks may become metamorphic rocks, or they may melt and become igneous rock. Sedimentary rock may also be broken down at Earth's surface and become sediment that forms another sedimentary rock.

Under certain temperature and pressure conditions, metamorphic rock will melt and form magma. Metamorphic rock can also be altered by heat and pressure to form a different type of metamorphic rock. Metamorphic rock can also be broken down by weathering and erosion to form sediment that forms sedimentary rock.

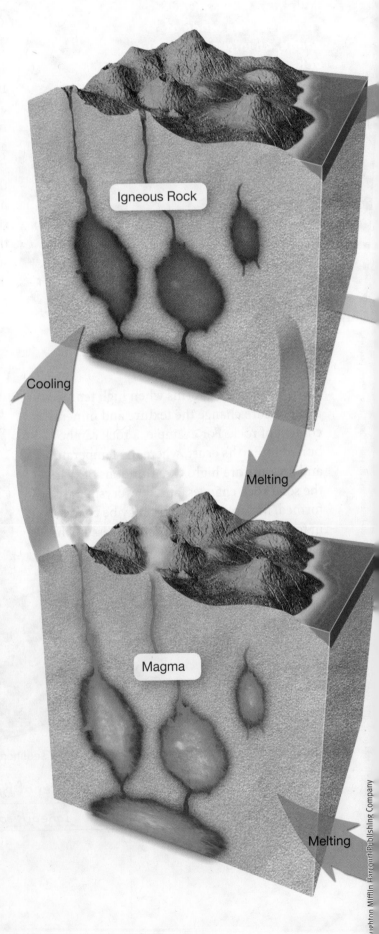

Igneous Rock

Cooling

Melting

Magma

Melting

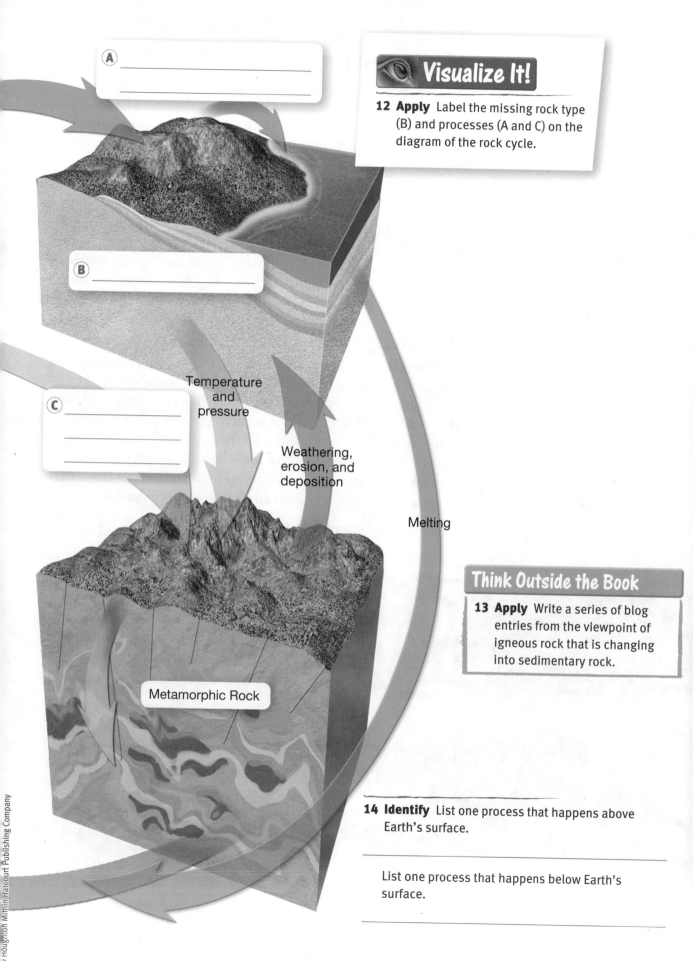

(A) _____

👁 **Visualize It!**

12 Apply Label the missing rock type (B) and processes (A and C) on the diagram of the rock cycle.

(B) _____

Temperature
and
pressure

(C) _____

Weathering,
erosion, and
deposition

Melting

Metamorphic Rock

Think Outside the Book

13 Apply Write a series of blog entries from the viewpoint of igneous rock that is changing into sedimentary rock.

14 Identify List one process that happens above Earth's surface.

_____

List one process that happens below Earth's surface.

_____

© Houghton Mifflin Harcourt Publishing Company

How do tectonic plate motions affect the rock cycle?

Tectonic plate motions can move rock around. Rock that was beneath Earth's surface may become exposed to wind and rain. Sediment or rock on Earth's surface may be buried. Rock can also be changed into metamorphic rock by tectonic plate collisions because of increased temperature and pressure.

By Moving Rock Up or Down

15 Compare How does uplift differ from subsidence?

_____

_____

_____

_____

There are two types of vertical movements in Earth's crust: uplift and subsidence. **Uplift** is the rising of regions of the crust to higher elevations. Uplift increases the rate of erosion on rock. **Subsidence** is the sinking of regions of the crust to lower elevations. Subsidence leads to the formation of basins where sediment can be deposited.

By Pulling Apart Earth's Surface

A **rift zone** is an area where a set of deep cracks form. Rift zones are common between tectonic plates that are pulling apart. As they pull apart, blocks of crust in the center of the rift zone subside and the pressure on buried rocks is reduced. The reduction in pressure allows rock below Earth's surface to rise up. As the rock rises, it undergoes partial melting and forms magma. Magma can cool below Earth's surface to form igneous rock. If it reaches the surface, magma becomes lava, which can also cool to form igneous rock.

Visualize It! Inquiry

16 Predict Label uplift and subsidence on this diagram. What pathway in the rock cycle might rock take next if it is subjected to uplift? Explain.

_____

_____

_____

_____

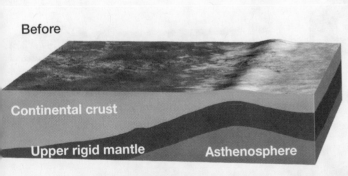
Before

Continental crust

Upper rigid mantle   Asthenosphere

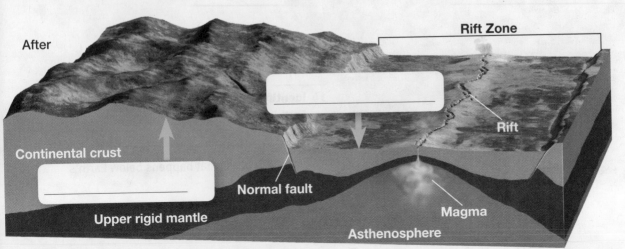
After

Rift Zone

Continental crust

Rift

Normal fault

Magma

Upper rigid mantle

Asthenosphere

Why It Matters

Cliff Dwellings

Can you imagine living on the side of a cliff? Some ancient peoples could! They created dwellings from cliff rock. They also decorated rock with art, as you can see in the pictographs shown below.

Cliff Palace
This dwelling in Colorado is called the Cliff Palace. It was home to the Ancient Puebloans from about 550 to 1300 CE.

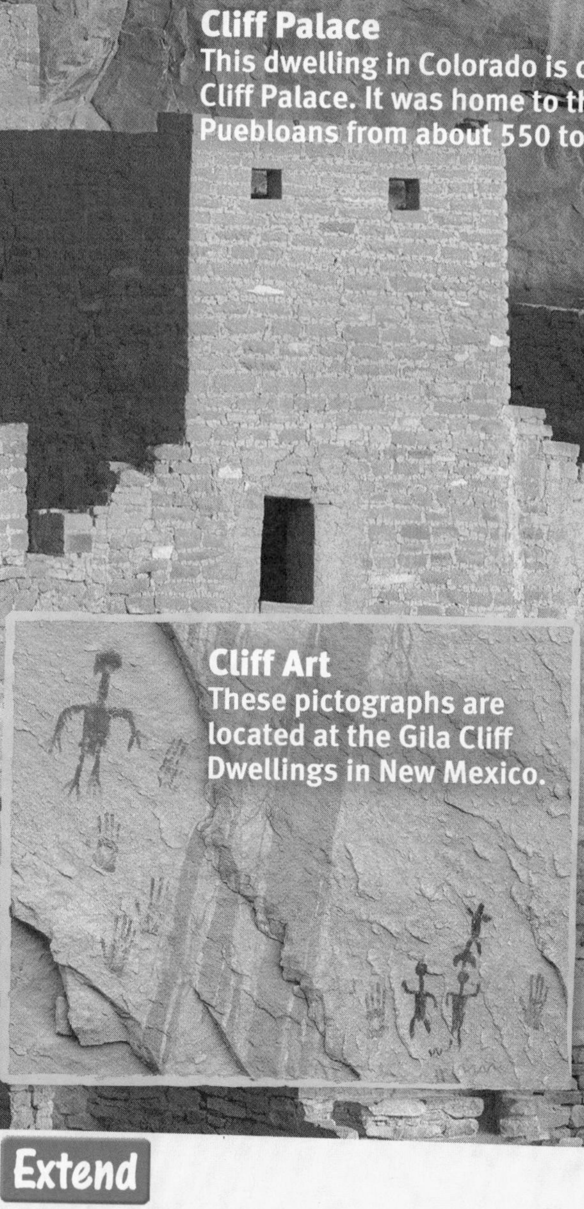

Cliff Art
These pictographs are located at the Gila Cliff Dwellings in New Mexico.

A Palace in Rock
Ancient cliff dwellings are also found outside the United States. These dwellings from about 70 CE are located in Petra, Jordan.

Extend

Inquiry

17 Identify Describe how ancient people used rock to create shelter.

18 Research Find out how people lived in one of the cliff dwelling locations. How did living in a rock environment affect their daily lives?

19 Produce Illustrate how the people lived by doing one of the following: write a play, write a song, or create a graphic novel.

Visual Summary

To complete this summary, use what you know about the rock cycle to fill in the blanks below. Then use the key below to check your answers. You can use this page to review the main concepts of the lesson.

Each rock type can change into another of the three types.

20 When sediment is pressed together and cemented, the sediment becomes

_____

21 When lava cools and solidifies, _____ forms.

22 Metamorphic rock can be altered by temperature and pressure to form a different type of

_____

Rock Cycle

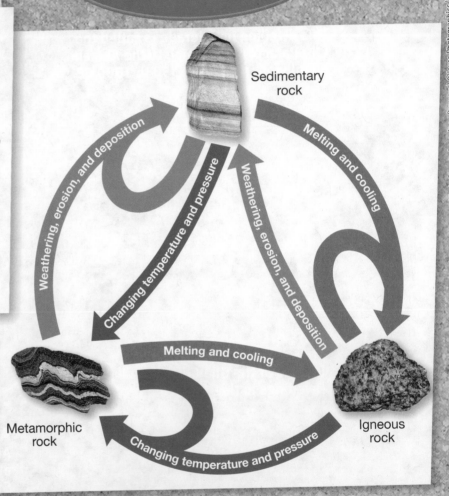

Sedimentary rock

Weathering, erosion, and deposition

Changing temperature and pressure

Weathering, erosion, and deposition

Melting and cooling

Melting and cooling

Changing temperature and pressure

Metamorphic rock

Igneous rock

Answers: 20 sedimentary rock; 21 igneous rock; 22 metamorphic rock

23 Explain What factors and processes can affect the pathway that igneous rock takes in the rock cycle?

Lesson Review

Vocabulary

In your own words, define the following terms.

1 Rock cycle

_____

_____

2 Weathering

_____

_____

3 Rift zone

_____

_____

Key Concepts

Use these photos to classify the rock as sedimentary, igneous, or metamorphic.

Example	Type of rock
4 Classify This rock is made up of the mineral calcite, and it formed from the remains of organisms that lived in water.	
5 Classify Through high temperature and pressure, this rock formed from a sedimentary rock.	
6 Classify This rock is made of tiny crystals that formed quickly when molten rock cooled at Earth's surface.	

7 Describe How can sedimentary rock become metamorphic rock?

_____

_____

8 Explain How can subsidence lead to the formation of sedimentary rock?

_____

_____

9 Explain Why are rift zones common places for igneous rock to form?

_____

_____

_____

Critical Thinking

10 Hypothesize What would happen to the rock cycle if erosion did not occur?

_____

_____

11 Criticize A classmate states that igneous rock must always become sedimentary rock next, according to the rock cycle. Explain why this statement is not correct.

_____

_____

_____

12 Predict Granite is an igneous rock that forms from magma cooled below Earth's surface. Why would granite have larger crystals than igneous rocks formed from lava cooled above Earth's surface?

_____

_____

My Notes

Analyzing Technology

Skills
Identify risks
Identify benefits
✓ Evaluate cost of technology
✓ Evaluate environmental impact
✓ Propose improvements
Propose risk reduction
✓ Compare technology
✓ Communicate results

Objectives
• Analyze the life cycle of an aluminum can.
• Analyze the life cycle of a glass bottle.
• Evaluate the cost of recycling versus disposal of technology.
• Analyze the environmental impact of technology.

Analyzing the Life Cycles of Aluminum and Glass

A life cycle analysis is a way to evaluate the real cost of a product. The analysis considers how much money an item costs to make. It also examines how making the product affects the economy and the environment through the life of the product. Engineers, scientists, and technologists use this information to improve processes and to compare products.

Costs of Production

Have you ever wondered where an aluminum soda can comes from? Have you wondered where the can goes when you are done with it? If so, you have started a life cycle analysis by asking the right questions. Aluminum is a metal found in a type of rock called *bauxite*. To get aluminum, first bauxite must be mined. The mined ore is then shipped to a processing plant. There, the bauxite is melted to get aluminum in a process called *smelting*. After smelting, the aluminum is processed. It may be shaped into bicycle parts or rolled into sheets to make cans. Every step in the production involves both financial costs and environmental costs that must be considered in a life cycle analysis.

Many bicycles are made of aluminum because it is lightweight and strong.

Costs of Disposal

After an aluminum can is used it can travel either to a landfill or to a recycling plant. The process of recycling an aluminum can does require the use of some energy. However, the financial and environmental costs of disposing of a can and mining ore are much greater than the cost of recycling a can. Additionally, smelting bauxite produces harmful wastes. A life cycle analysis of an aluminum can must include the cost and environmental effects of mining, smelting, and disposing of the aluminum can.

1 Analyze After a can is recycled, which steps are no longer part of the life cycle?

_____
_____
_____
_____
_____

Bauxite mining

Most bauxite mining occurs far away from where aluminum is used. Large ships or trains transport the ore before it is made into aluminum products.

Aluminum is one of the easiest materials to recycle. Producing a ton of aluminum by shredding and remelting uses about 5% of the energy needed to process enough bauxite to make a ton of aluminum.

Remelting

Shredding

Smelting

Fabrication

Life Cycle of an Aluminum Can

Recycling

Manufacturing

Consumer use

2 Evaluate In the life cycle shown here, which two steps could include an arrow to indicate disposal?

_____
_____

✋ **You Try It!** ⟶

Now it's your turn to analyze the life cycle of a product.

✋ You Try It!

Now, apply what you have learned about the life cycle of aluminum to analyze the life cycle of a glass bottle. Glass is made by melting silica from sand or from mineral deposits mined from the Earth. A kiln heats the silica until it melts to form a red-hot glob. Then, the glass is shaped and cooled to form useful items.

① Evaluate Cost of Technology

As a group, discuss the steps that would be involved in making a glass bottle. List the steps in the space below. Start with mining and end at a landfill. Include as many steps in the process as you can think of. Beside each step, tell whether there would be financial costs, environmental costs, or both.

Life Cycle of a Glass Bottle

_____

② Evaluate Environmental Impact

Use the table below to indicate which of the steps listed above would have environmental costs, and what type of cost would be involved. A step can appear in more than one column.

Cause pollution	Consume energy	Damage habitat

③ Propose Improvements

In your group, discuss how you might improve the life cycle of a glass bottle and reduce the impact on the environment. Draw a life cycle that includes your suggestions for improvement.

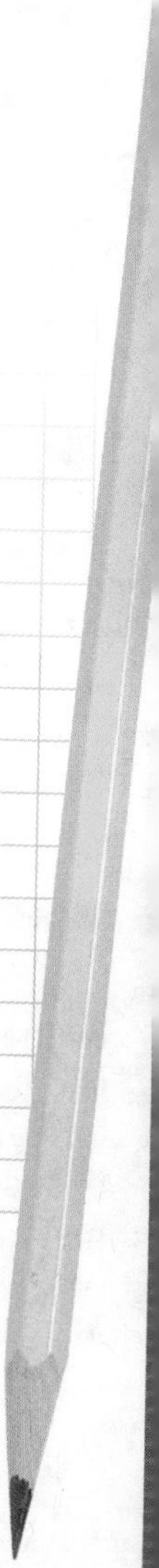

④ Compare Technology

How does your improved process decrease the environmental effects of making and using glass bottles?

_____

_____

_____

_____

⑤ Communicate Results

Imagine that you are an accountant for a company that produces glass bottles. In the space below, write an argument for using recycled glass that is based on financial savings for your company.

_____

_____

_____

_____

Three Classes of Rock

ESSENTIAL QUESTION

How do rocks form?

By the end of this lesson, you should be able to describe the formation and classification of sedimentary, igneous, and metamorphic rocks.

8.ESS2.3

Wind and water have eroded the softer rock surrounding Ship Rock, an igneous landform in New Mexico.

✋ Lesson Labs

Quick Labs
• Stretching Out
• Observing Rocks

S.T.E.M. Lab
• Modeling Rock Formation

Engage Your Brain

1 Predict Check T or F to show whether you think each statement is true or false.

T	F	
☐	☐	All rocks form deep beneath Earth's surface.
☐	☐	Some rocks are made up of materials from living things.
☐	☐	Some rocks take millions of years to form.
☐	☐	All rocks are made up of the same kinds of minerals.
☐	☐	Some rocks form from particles of other rocks.

2 Identify How do you think rocks might form as a result of the volcanic activity shown here?

_____

_____

_____

_____

Active Reading

3 Apply Use context clues to write your own definition for the words *composition* and *texture*.

Example sentence:
The <u>composition</u> of the trail mix was 50% nuts, 30% dried fruit, and 20% granola.

composition:

_____

_____

Example sentence:
Because glass is smooth, flat, and shiny, it has a much different <u>texture</u> than wood does.

texture:

_____

_____

Vocabulary Terms

• rock   • texture
• composition

4 Apply As you learn the definition of each vocabulary term in this lesson, create your own definition or sketch to help you remember the meaning of the term.

A Rocky World

How are rocks classified?

Active Reading

5 Identify As you read, underline two properties that are used to classify rock.

A combination of one or more minerals or organic matter is called **rock**. Scientists divide rock into three classes based on how each class of rock forms. The three classes of rock are igneous, sedimentary, and metamorphic. Each class of rock can be further divided into more specific types of rock. For example, igneous rocks can be divided based on where they form. All igneous rock forms when molten rock cools and solidifies. However, some igneous rocks form on Earth's surface and others form within Earth's crust. Sedimentary and metamorphic rocks are also divided into more specific types of rock. How do scientists understand how to classify rocks? They observe their composition and texture.

By Mineral Composition

The minerals and organic matter a rock contains determine the **composition**, or makeup, of that rock, as shown below. Many rocks are made up mostly of the minerals quartz and feldspar, which contain a large amount of the compound silica. Other rocks have different compositions. The limestone rock shown below is made up mostly of the mineral calcite.

Do the Math

6 Graph Fill in the percentage grid on the right to show the amounts of calcite and aragonite in limestone.

Composition of a Sample of Granite

- Feldspar 65%
- Quartz 25%
- Mica 10%

Composition of a Sample of Limestone

- Calcite 95%
- Aragonite 5%

Granite is made of silica minerals.

Limestone is made of carbonate minerals.

By Texture

The size, shape, and positions of the grains that make up a rock determine a rock's **texture**. Coarse-grained rock has large grains that are easy to see with your eyes. Fine-grained rock has small grains that can only be seen by using a hand lens or microscope. The texture of a rock may give clues as to how and where it formed. Igneous rock can be fine-grained or coarse-grained depending on the time magma takes to cool. The texture of metamorphic rock depends on the rock's original composition and the temperature and pressure at which the rock formed. The rocks shown below look different because they formed in different ways.

 Visualize It!

7 Describe Observe the sedimentary rocks on this page and describe their texture as coarse-grained, medium-grained, or fine-grained.

This sandstone formed from sand grains that once made up a sand dune.

A _____

_____

This mudstone is made up of microscopic particles of clay.

B _____

_____

This breccia is composed of broken fragments of rock cemented together.

C _____

_____

The Furnace Below

What are two kinds of igneous rock?

Igneous rock forms when hot, liquid magma cools into solid rock. Magma forms when solid rock melts below Earth's surface. Magma flows through passageways up toward Earth's surface. Magma can cool and harden below Earth's surface, or it can make its way above Earth's surface and become lava.

Intrusive Igneous Rock

When magma does not reach Earth's surface, it cools in large chambers, in cracks, or between layers in the surrounding rock. When magma pushes into, or intrudes, surrounding rock below Earth's surface and cools, the rock that forms is called *intrusive igneous rock*. Magma that is well insulated by surrounding rock cools very slowly. The minerals form large, visible crystals. Therefore, intrusive igneous rock generally has a coarse-grained texture. Examples of intrusive igneous rock are granite and diorite. A sample of diorite is shown at the left.

Diorite is an example of intrusive igneous rock.

8 Infer How can you tell that diorite is an intrusive igneous rock?

Deep Inside Earth The amount of time magma takes to cool determines the texture of an igneous rock.

Crystals Slow-cooling magma has time to form large mineral crystals. The resulting rock is coarse-grained.

Magma chamber Magma chambers deep inside Earth contain pools of molten rock. Magma cools slowly in large chambers such as this.

Near or at Earth's Surface
Fine-grained igneous rock forms as lava cools quickly at Earth's surface.

Extrusive Igneous Rock

Igneous rock that forms when lava erupts, or extrudes, onto Earth's surface is called *extrusive igneous rock*. Extrusive igneous rock is common around the sides and bases of volcanoes. Lava cools very quickly at Earth's surface. So, there is very little time for crystal formation. Because there is little time for crystals to form, extrusive rocks are made up of very small crystals and have a fine-grained texture. Obsidian (ahb•SID•ee•uhn) is an extrusive rock that cools so rapidly that no crystals form. Obsidian looks glassy, so it is often called *volcanic glass*. Other common extrusive igneous rocks are basalt and andesite.

Lava flows form when lava erupts from a volcano. The photo above shows an active lava flow. Sometimes lava erupts and flows from long cracks in Earth's crust called *fissures*. It also flows on the ocean floor at places where tension is causing Earth's crust to pull apart.

Active Reading **9 Explain** How does the rate at which magma cools affect the texture of igneous rock?

_____

_____

Basalt is an example of extrusive igneous rock.

10 Compare Use the Venn diagram to compare and contrast intrusive igneous rock and extrusive igneous rock.

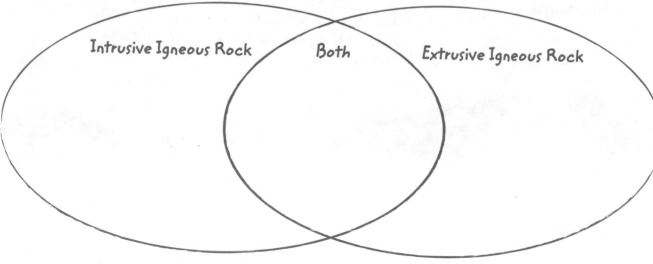

Intrusive Igneous Rock   Both   Extrusive Igneous Rock

Lay It On!

What are three types of sedimentary rock?

All the processes that form sedimentary rock occur mainly at or near the surface of Earth. Some of these processes include weathering, erosion, deposition, burial, and cementation. Based on the way that they form, scientists classify sedimentary rocks as clastic, chemical, and organic sedimentary rock.

Clastic Sedimentary Rock

Clastic sedimentary rock forms when sediments are buried, compacted, and cemented together by calcite or quartz. The size of the sediment, or clasts, that makes up the rock is used to classify clastic sedimentary rocks. Fine-grained sedimentary rocks, in which grains are too small to be seen, include mudstone, siltstone, and shale. Sandstone, which is shown at the left, is a medium-grained clastic sedimentary rock with visible grains. Breccia and conglomerate are coarse-grained clastic sedimentary rocks made of large particles, such as pebbles, cobbles, and boulders.

Chemical Sedimentary Rock

Chemical sedimentary rocks form when water, usually seawater, evaporates. Most water contains dissolved minerals. As water evaporates, the minerals in water become concentrated to the point that they precipitate out of solution and crystallize. Halite, or rock salt, is an example of chemical sedimentary rock. It is made of sodium chloride, NaCl. Halite forms when sodium ions and chlorine ions in shallow bodies of water become so concentrated that halite crystallizes from solution.

Horizontal layers of clastic sedimentary rocks and volcanic ash are exposed at Badlands National Park in South Dakota.

Sandstone

Visualize It!

11 **Identify** How would you describe the texture of the halite shown below?

_____

_____

The Bonneville Salt Flats near the Great Salt Lake in Utah are made largely of halite. The salt flats are the remains of an ancient lake bed.

Halite

490

The White Cliffs of Dover on the English seacoast are made up of the skeletons of the marine alga that is shown below.

Skeleton of a marine alga

Organic Sedimentary Rock

Organic sedimentary rock forms from the remains or fossils, of once-living plants and animals. Most limestone forms from the fosssils of organisms that once lived in the ocean. Over time, the skeletons of these marine organisms, which are made of calcium carbonate, collect on the ocean floor. These animal remains, together with sediment, are eventually buried, compacted, and cemented together to form *fossiliferous* [fahs•uh•LIF•er•uhs] limestone.

Coquina is a fossiliferous limestone that consists of the shells of marine mollusks that have been cemented together by calcite. Chalk is a soft, white limestone that is made up of the skeletons of microorganisms that collect in huge numbers on the floor of the deep ocean.

Coal is another type of organic sedimentary rock. It forms when plant material is buried and changes into coal as a result of increasing heat and pressure. This process occurs over millions of years.

Active Reading **12 Identify** What are two types of organic sedimentary rock?

_____

_____

13 Compare Use the table to compare and contrast clastic, chemical, and organic sedimentary rock.

Three Types of Sedimentary Rock

Clastic	Chemical	Organic

The Heat Is On!

Sedimentary shale

Slate

Phyllite

When shale is exposed to increasing temperature and pressure, different foliated metamorphic rocks form.

What are two types of metamorphic rock?

As a rock is exposed to high temperature and pressure, the crystal structures of the minerals in the rock change to form new minerals. This process results in the formation of metamorphic rock, which has either a foliated texture or a nonfoliated texture.

Foliated Metamorphic Rock

The metamorphic process in which mineral grains are arranged in planes or bands is called *foliation* (foh•lee•AY•shuhn). Foliation occurs when pressure causes the mineral grains in a rock to realign to form parallel bands.

Metamorphic rocks with a foliated texture include slate, phyllite, schist (SHIST), and gneiss (NYS). Slate and phyllite are commonly produced when shale, a fine-grained sedimentary rock, is exposed to an increase in temperature and pressure. The minerals in slate and phyllite are squeezed into flat, sheet-like layers. With increasing temperature and pressure, phyllite may become schist, a coarse-grained foliated rock. With further increases in temperature and pressure, the minerals in schist separate into alternating bands of light and dark minerals. Gneiss is a coarse-grained, foliated rock that forms from schist. Slate, phyllite, schist, and gneiss can all begin as shale, but they are very different rocks. Each rock forms under a certain range of temperatures and pressures, and contains different minerals.

Schist

Gneiss

14 Describe What happens to the minerals as gneiss forms from schist?

_____

_____

© Houghton Mifflin Harcourt Publishing Company • Image Credits: (t) ©HMH; (tc) ©HMH; (bc) ©HMH; (bl) ©HMH; (br) ©Krystyna Szulecka Photography/Alamy

Nonfoliated Metamorphic Rock

Metamorphic rocks that do not have mineral grains that are aligned in planes or bands are called *nonfoliated*. Nonfoliated metamorphic rocks are commonly made of one or only a few minerals. During metamorphism, mineral grains or crystals may change size or shape, and some may change into another mineral.

Two common nonfoliated metamorphic rocks are quartzite and marble. Quartzite forms when quartz sandstone is exposed to high temperature and pressure. This causes the sand grains to grow larger and the spaces between the sand grains disappear. For that reason, quartzite is very hard and not easily broken down.

When limestone undergoes metamorphism, the limestone becomes marble. During the process of metamorphism, the calcite crystals in the marble grow larger than the calcite grains in the original limestone.

The mineral grains in quartzite (top) and crystals in marble (bottom) do not form bands.

Active Reading **15 Apply** What are two characteristics of nonfoliated metamorphic rocks?

_____

_____

Marble is a nonfoliated metamorphic rock that forms when limestone is metamorphosed. Marble is used to build monuments and statues.

Think Outside the Book Inquiry

16 Apply With a classmate, discuss how different types of rocks can be used as building or construction materials.

The Rock Cycle

This fort, *Castillo de San Marcos*, was built in 1695 in Saint Augustine, Florida. Look at the close up of the rock in the bottom photo. This is a type of rock called coquina and it's made out of tiny bits of seashells that have been cemented together. The walls of the fort are made entirely of coquina.

Over the last 300+ years that the fort has been standing, the fort's walls have been exposed to **weathering** from rain, ocean spray, and hurricanes. Weathering is one of the processes that wears down rocks as part of the **rock cycle**.

Skills

✔ Describe a scientific relationship

✔ Describe scientific processes

✔ Create a model of the rock cycle

Active Reading

1 Explain What kind of rock is coquina? Why do you think so?

_____

_____

_____

_____

The walls of Castillo de San Marcos are made of coquina.

This erupting volcano in Hawai'i also plays a role in the rock cycle. Once the lava cools, it becomes an igneous rock called basalt.

Oneuli Black Sand Beach, Hawai'i.

Visualize It!

2 Explain What is the connection between the igneous rock in the picture of the volcano and the black sand beach? What are some steps in the process?

_____

_____

_____

_____

_____

_____

The Rock Cycle

The Rock Cycle Diagram

The rock cycle describes the processes that create the three types of rock: sedimentary, igneous, and metamorphic. Each type of rock can be changed into another type of rock. .

 Visualize It!

3 Explain Use what you have learned about how the different types of rocks form to complete a diagram of the rock cycle. Your diagram should identify the rock type in each step and describe how the rocks change into the other rock types.

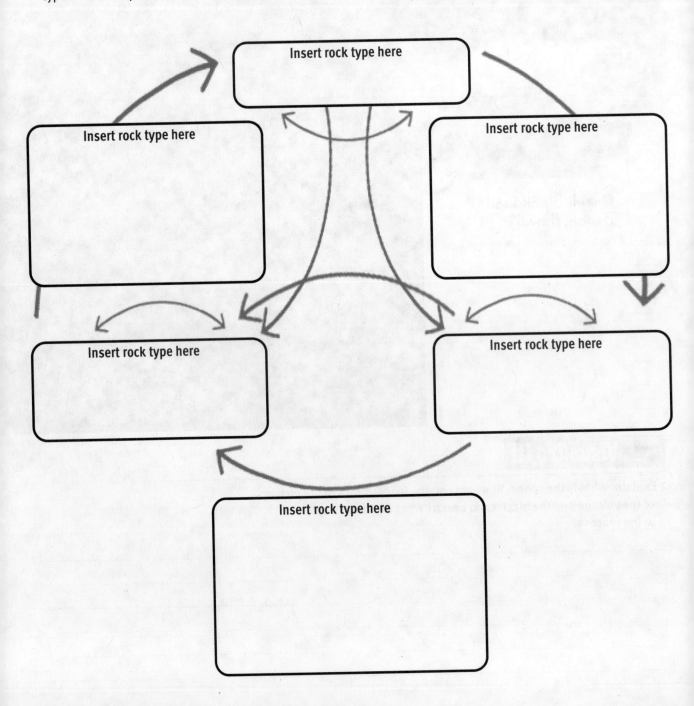

Insert rock type here

Insert rock type here

Insert rock type here

Insert rock type here

Insert rock type here

Insert rock type here

Pulling It All Together

The rock cycle also describes the **relationship** between the processes that create the three types of rock. The dictionary defines the term relationship as follows: **the way in which two or more concepts, objects, or people are connected**.

4 Synthesize In your own words, describe the relationship between the processes and forces that create the different types of rocks.

_____

_____

_____

_____

_____

_____

_____

_____

_____

_____

_____

_____

_____

_____

_____

_____

_____

_____

_____

_____

_____

_____

_____

_____

_____

_____

_____

_____

Visual Summary

To complete this summary, fill in the blanks. Then, use the key below to check your answers. You can use this page to review the main concepts of the lesson.

Sedimentary rock may form from layers of sediment that are cemented together.

17 Sedimentary rocks can be classified into three groups:

_____,

_____, and

_____

Three Classes of Rock

Igneous rock forms from magma or lava that has cooled and hardened.

18 Igneous rocks can be classified into two groups:

_____

and _____

Metamorphic rock forms under high temperature or pressure deep within Earth's crust.

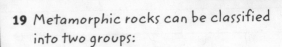

19 Metamorphic rocks can be classified into two groups:

_____

and _____

Answers: 17 clastic, chemical, organic; 18 intrusive, extrusive; 19 foliated, nonfoliated

20 Synthesize While hiking in the mountains, you see a large outcrop of marble. Describe one process by which the metamorphic rock marble forms from the sedimentary rock limestone.

Lesson Review

Vocabulary

Fill in the blank with the term that best completes the following sentence.

1 Sedimentary rocks that are made up of large pebbles and stones have a coarse-grained

_____

2 Most granite has a _____
of quartz, mica, and feldspar.

3 _____ can be
considered to be mixtures of minerals.

Key Concepts

4 Summarize How does the cooling rate of magma or lava affect the texture of the igneous rock that forms?

_____

_____

_____

_____

_____

_____

5 Describe How does clastic sedimentary rock form?

_____

_____

_____

6 Explain What is the difference between foliated and nonfoliated metamorphic rock?

_____

_____

_____

_____

_____

Critical Thinking

Use this photo to answer the following questions.

7 Identify What type of rock is shown here? How do you know?

_____

_____

_____

8 Describe How did this rock form?

_____

_____

_____

9 Infer Suppose this rock was exposed to high temperatures and pressure. What would most likely happen to it?

_____

_____

10 Infer What information can a foliated metamorphic rock provide you about the conditions under which it formed?

_____

_____

_____

_____

My Notes

Unit 8 [Big Idea] ◄ Minerals and rocks are basic building blocks of Earth and can change over time from one type of mineral or rock to another.

Lesson 1
ESSENTIAL QUESTION
What are minerals, how do they form, and how can they be identified?

Describe the basic structures of minerals and identify different minerals by using their physical properties.

Lesson 2
ESSENTIAL QUESTION
What is the rock cycle?

Describe the series of processes and classes of rocks that make up the rock cycle.

Lesson 3
ESSENTIAL QUESTION
How do rocks form?

Describe the formation and classification of sedimentary, igneous, and metamorphic rocks.

Connect ESSENTIAL QUESTIONS
Lessons 1 and 3

1 Synthesize Describe a process by which one mineral can change into another mineral.

_____

_____

_____

_____

Think Outside the Book

2 Synthesize Choose one of these activities to help synthesize what you have learned in this unit.

☐ Using what you learned in lessons 1, 2, and 3, explain in a short essay how a chemical sedimentary rock formed, beginning with a lake full of dissolved gypsum minerals.

☐ Using what you learned in lessons 1, 2, and 3, create a poster presentation to describe the type and texture of a rock formed by an explosive volcanic event.

Name _____

Vocabulary

Fill in each blank with the term that best completes the following sentences.

1 The _____ is a series of geologic processes in which rock can form, change from one type to another, be destroyed, and form again.

2 Changes in temperature or pressure, or chemical processes, can transform an existing rock into a _____ rock.

3 A _____ is a naturally occurring, solid combination of one or more minerals or organic matter.

4 The rising of regions of Earth's crust to higher elevations is called _____.

5 _____ is a physical property used to describe how the surface of a mineral reflects light.

Key Concepts

Read each question below, and circle the best answer.

6 The table below lists five classes of nonsilicate minerals.

Class	Description	Example
Carbonates	contain carbon and oxygen compounds	calcite
Halides	contain ions of chlorine, fluorine, iodine, and bromine	halite
Native elements	contain only one type of atom	gold
Oxides	contain oxygen compounds	hematite
Sulfides	contain sulfur compounds	pyrite

There are actually six classes of nonsilicate minerals. Which class is missing from this chart?

A feldspars

B micas

C silicates

D sulfates

7 Granite can form when magma cools within Earth. Basalt can form when lava cools on Earth's surface. What do granite and basalt have in common?

  A They are igneous.

  B They are old.

  C They are fossils.

  D They are intrusive.

8 A student is trying to identify a mineral in science class.

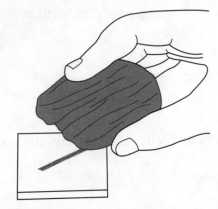

What property of the mineral is the student testing?

  A cleavage

  B color

  C luster

  D streak

9 Which one of the following statements about elements, atoms, and compounds is not true?

  A Elements consist of one type of atom and can combine to form compounds.

  B Compounds are smaller than atoms.

  C Elements and compounds form the basis of all materials on Earth.

  D Atoms cannot be broken down into smaller substances.

10 Which of the following best describes how sedimentary rock forms?

  A Molten rock beneath the surface of Earth cools and becomes solid.

  B Layers of sediment become compressed over time to form rock.

  C Chemical processes or changes in pressure or temperature change a rock.

  D Molten rock reaches the surface and cools to become solid rock.

11 Study the diagram below.

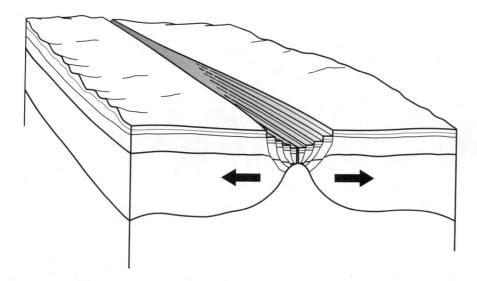

What process is occurring in this image?

A Two tectonic plates are moving toward each other, creating a syncline.

B Two tectonic plates are pulling away from each other, creating a rift zone.

C Two tectonic plates are moving toward each other, creating an anticline.

D Two tectonic plates are moving away from each other, creating a new mountain range.

12 Over time, repeated temperature changes can cause a rock to break down into smaller pieces. What is this an example of?

A subsidence   **C** deposition

B weathering   **D** erosion

Critical Thinking

Answer the following questions in the space provided.

13 You are standing by a cliff far away from the ocean. You see a sedimentary layer with shells in it. You are told the shells are from oceanic organisms. How do you think this layer formed?

_____

_____

_____

14 The diagram below shows the rock cycle.

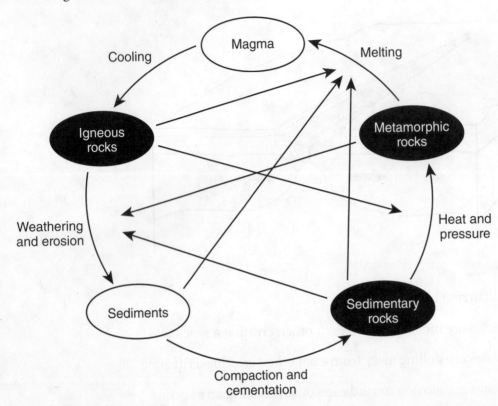

The rock cycle describes how rocks change. What conditions must be present for igneous or sedimentary rock to change into metamorphic rock? Name two ways that this could happen.

_____

_____

_____

Connect **ESSENTIAL QUESTIONS**
Lessons 1 and 3

Answer the following question in the space provided.

15 Explain a way that a sedimentary rock could form, then over time break down into smaller pieces, and become a sedimentary rock again in another location.

_____

_____

_____

_____

_____

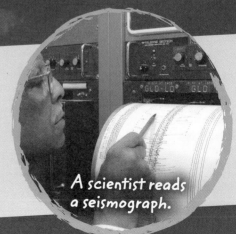

The Restless Earth

Big Idea

The movement of tectonic plates accounts for important features of Earth's surface and for major geologic events.

8.ESS2.2, 8.ESS2.3, 8.ESS2.4, 8.ESS2.5, 8.ESS3.1, 8.ESS3.2

The Cleveland volcano in Alaska erupts.

What do you think?

Earth is continuously changing. Volcanoes and earthquakes are powerful forces of change. Volcanoes form new rock and reshape the land. Earthquakes move rocks. How did the landscape around you form?

A scientist reads a seismograph.

Unit 9
The Restless Earth

CITIZEN SCIENCE
Stable Structures

The building on the right, located in San Francisco, was engineered to protect it from earthquakes.

① Think About It

A People in different parts of the United States—and all over the world—need to make buildings earthquake-proof. Where would it be of most importance to have earthquake-proof buildings?

_____

_____

B The taller the building, the more difficult it is to make it safe during an earthquake. Why do you think this is?

_____

_____

_____

C Some materials survive the shaking from an earthquake, while others crumble or crack. What materials might withstand an earthquake? Why?

_____

_____

_____

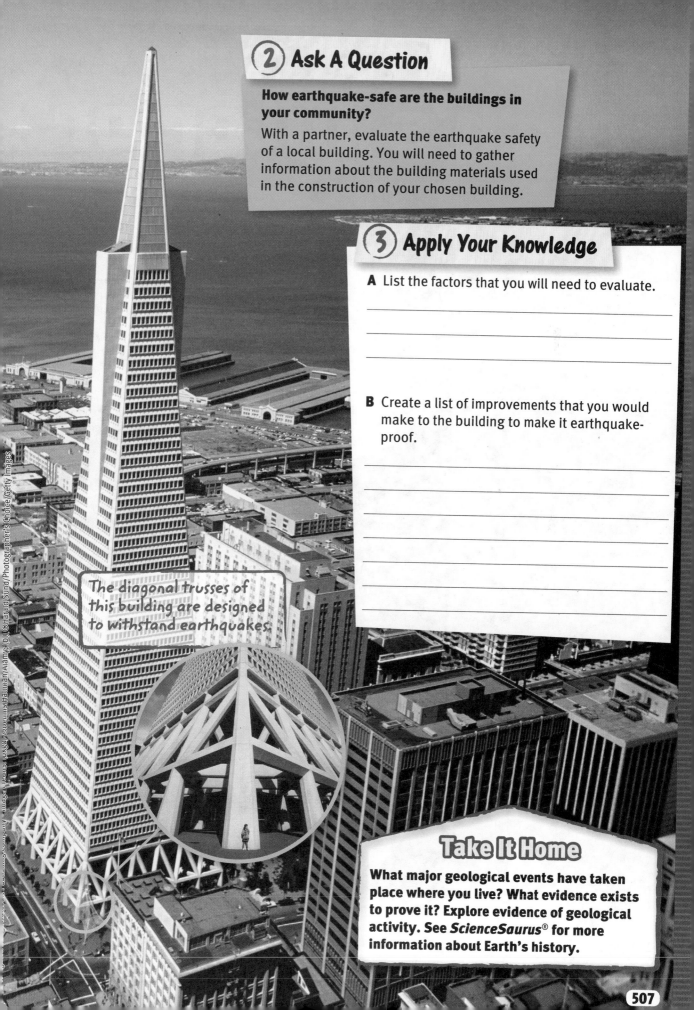

② Ask A Question

How earthquake-safe are the buildings in your community?

With a partner, evaluate the earthquake safety of a local building. You will need to gather information about the building materials used in the construction of your chosen building.

③ Apply Your Knowledge

A List the factors that you will need to evaluate.

_____
_____
_____

B Create a list of improvements that you would make to the building to make it earthquake-proof.

_____
_____
_____
_____
_____
_____
_____

The diagonal trusses of this building are designed to withstand earthquakes.

Take It Home

What major geological events have taken place where you live? What evidence exists to prove it? Explore evidence of geological activity. See *ScienceSaurus*® for more information about Earth's history.

Earth's Interior

ESSENTIAL QUESTION

What is known about Earth's interior?

By the end of this lesson, you should be able to describe what scientists know about Earth's interior based on studies of seismic waves and other data.

━━ 8.ESS2.2

Have you ever wondered what lies beneath Earth's surface?

Quick Labs
- Using Seismic Waves to Study Earth's Interior
- Modeling the Formation of Earth's Layers

Exploration Lab
- Differentiation of Solid Materials

 **Engage Your Brain**

1 Illustrate Identify a food that is composed of layers. Draw a diagram of the food, and explain how it is similar to and different from Earth.

2 Infer How do you think these tiny gas and dust particles could eventually form a planet? What forces might be involved?

 **Active Reading**

3 Apply Many scientific words, such as *wave*, also have everyday meanings. Use context clues to write your own definition for each meaning of the word *wave*.

Example Sentence
Analise <u>waves</u> her hand as she rides by.

wave:

_____

_____

Example Sentence
Earthquakes happen as <u>waves</u> of energy travel through rock.

wave:

_____

_____

Vocabulary Terms

- crust
- mantle
- core
- lithosphere
- asthenosphere
- mesosphere
- seismic wave

4 Identify This list contains the vocabulary terms you'll learn in this lesson. As you read, circle the definition of each term.

The Birth of Earth!

This large cloud of dust and gas is called the solar nebula. The nebula collapsed and began to rotate.

Over time, the solar nebula flattened into a swirling disk of matter. The sun formed in the center of the disk.

How did Earth form?

Scientists think that the universe formed about 14 billion years ago. As soon as it formed, matter, such as gases and dust, began to spread out. As the universe expanded, some of the matter gathered into dense clouds. These clouds became galaxies and solar systems.

About 4.6 billion years ago, a cloud of gas and dust that we call the *solar nebula* began to pull together and rotate. Eventually, it flattened into a disk. Gravity pulled much of the matter to the center of the rotating disk. Here, it became very dense and very hot and then ignited to become a star that we call the *sun*.

The remaining particles in the disk surrounding the sun began to join and form clumps of matter. Gravity attracted these clumps to one another and caused them to collide. Sometimes, clumps joined during a collision. Over time, the clumps grew large enough to form planets, asteroids, and other bodies. Earth formed in the inner part of the disk from dense rocky and metallic materials. Less-dense materials, including many gases, formed the outer planets farther from the sun.

What raised Earth's temperature during its formation?

As Earth formed, it became very hot. Scientists think that energy was generated by the collisions that formed the planet and by the breakdown of unstable elements. Earth's temperature was also raised as gravity pulled dense particles toward Earth's center.

Particles collided in the disk under the force of gravity. As particles stuck together, larger bodies began to grow.

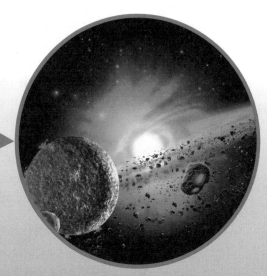

The largest bodies became planets, such as Earth. Eight planets, separated by mainly empty space, now orbit the sun.

Collisions

Moving objects have *kinetic energy*—the energy of motion. If two objects collide, some kinetic energy is converted to energy in the form of heat. As Earth was forming, other objects in the solar system were colliding with the planet. These collisions caused Earth's temperature to increase. In the later stages of Earth's formation, impacts from relatively large objects raised Earth's temperature so much that it became partially molten, or melted. This happened one or more times.

Gravity

When you lift an object off the ground, the object gains a kind of energy called *gravitational potential energy*. During Earth's molten state, particles in the interior had gravitational potential energy. Dense materials, such as iron, began to sink toward the center due to the force of gravity. As dense materials sank, their gravitational potential energy was converted to energy as heat.

Radioactive Decay

When Earth first formed, many unstable materials in the planet were breaking down into stable materials. In this process, called *radioactive decay*, a large amount of energy in the form of heat was released. Unstable materials, such as uranium, thorium, and potassium, still exist within Earth and continue to decay. Therefore, heat continues to be generated in Earth's interior.

Visualize It!

6 Summarize Write a sentence or two summarizing how gas and dust become planets.

_____

_____

_____

_____

_____

_____

_____

_____

Think Outside the Book (Inquiry)

7 Discuss With a partner, list questions you have about Earth's formation. Do you think scientists have explanations for your questions? What questions might scientists have?

Layer Upon Layer

How did Earth's layers form?

While the planet was partially melted, particles moved due to gravity. At first, the mixture of rock and metal inside Earth was mostly uniform. Earth's molten state then allowed materials within the planet to move and flow. The force of gravity pulled high-density materials toward the center, and materials with low densities were pushed toward the surface. This process, called *differentiation*, occurred as the planet cooled and solidified. The planet cooled because the processes that warmed the early Earth, such as collisions, slowed down. Differentiation resulted in a dense center, or *core*, and concentric layers around the core. The core and the shells surrounding it differ in density and other properties.

Active Reading 8 **Identify** What is the force that caused the early Earth's molten materials to move and flow?

_____

Visualize It!

9 **Apply** Use what you read in the paragraph above to create captions for this diagram of Earth changing over time.

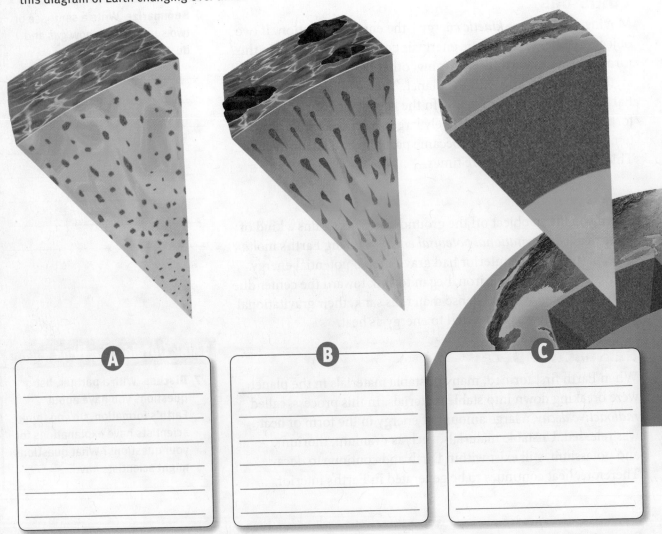

A	B	C

As Earth Cools . . .

If Earth was so hot when it formed, where did the cool, blue oceans and atmosphere come from? Earth cooled as the processes that first warmed the planet slowed down. Volcanoes belched out hot gases from the interior, including nitrogen, carbon dioxide, and water vapor. This process helped form Earth's early atmosphere.

Let It Rain!

Scientists think that water vapor not only came from volcanoes, but from bodies in space that crashed into Earth. Earth's surface eventually cooled enough for water vapor in the atmosphere to condense into liquid water. As rain fell across Earth, water pooled in low areas and formed rivers, lakes, and oceans.

Ready to Exhale

Although Earth's surface is cool enough for liquid water to exist, its interior remains extremely hot. Volcanoes continue to pour out molten rock onto the surface and release hot gases into the atmosphere.

Extend

Inquiry

10 Organize Create a flow chart that outlines the steps in the formation of Earth's waters. You may use words or pictures to fill in your flow chart.

11 Relate Research the atmosphere and oceans of another planet, such as Venus. How did the formation of its atmosphere and oceans differ from the formation of Earth's?

12 Summarize Today, new planets are forming in distant galaxies. Create an instruction guide for infant planets that want to become an Earth-like planet. This how-to guide can be a pamphlet, an animation, or a video.

How are Earth's layers categorized?

Earth is composed of concentric layers that wrap around a central core. The layers are distinct, but not uniform. Within each layer, properties can vary. Around a layer, the thickness can change. Scientists categorize Earth's layers in two different ways—by composition and by physical properties.

By Composition

Composition describes the chemical makeup of matter. Earth has three layers based on composition. As you read the following, think about how Earth's compositional layers are similar to the layers of a hard-boiled egg.

- Earth's thin, outer shell is called the **crust**. The crust is made up primarily of low-density minerals called *silicates*. Earth contains two types of crust: thin, dense oceanic crust and thick, less-dense continental crust. The thickest sections of the crust lie under tall mountains, such as the Himalayas.
- The **mantle** is the compositional layer below the crust. The mantle contains silicate minerals like the crust, but has more dense elements, such as magnesium and iron.
- At the center of Earth is the **core**. The core contains very dense elements, mainly iron and a small amount of nickel.

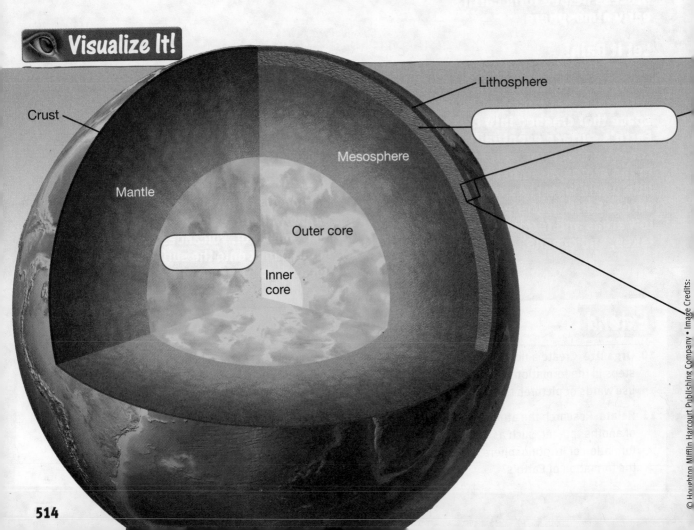

Visualize It!

Crust

Mantle

Lithosphere

Mesosphere

Outer core

Inner core

By Physical Properties

In general, from Earth's surface to its center, temperature and pressure gradually increase. Temperature, pressure, and composition all affect the physical properties of rock. A *physical property* is a characteristic such as rigidity. Earth has five layers that differ in physical properties.

- The **lithosphere** is the outermost physical layer of Earth. It is a solid, rigid layer. The top of the lithosphere contains the crust, and the bottom part of the lithosphere contains the upper mantle. Although the lithosphere varies in composition, it acts as a single layer mechanically.
- The **asthenosphere** is a solid, thin layer of mantle material below the lithosphere. Temperature and pressure are higher here, so rock is less rigid and can be thought of as more putty-like. Rock slowly flows in the asthenosphere.
- The **mesosphere** is the lower part of the mantle. The mesosphere is more dense and rigid than the asthenosphere.

Earth's core is divided into two sections based on different physical properties. The center of Earth is the inner core. The inner core is surrounded by the outer core.

- Earth's *outer core* is liquid due to very high temperatures.
- The *inner core* is under more pressure and is solid.

Active Reading

13 Identify Write the physical layers that relate to each compositional layer below.

Crust

_____

Mantle

_____

_____

_____

Core

_____

_____

_____

Oceanic crust

Continental crust

Lithosphere

Asthenosphere

14 Label Identify the missing layers on the previous page by writing their names in the blank spaces provided.

15 Compare What are some similarities and differences between the lithosphere and the crust?

_____

_____

_____

_____

_____

_____

_____

_____

_____

How do scientists know what is inside Earth?

We cannot simply look at Earth's interior. We cannot drill to Earth's core, or even all the way through the crust! So how do scientists know what is inside Earth? There are certain tools and types of technology scientists use to gather information about Earth's interior. They also do lab experiments, such as testing how rock behaves under the extreme pressure found deep within Earth.

By Studying Seismic Waves

Scientists study Earth's interior mainly by studying waves that are generated by earthquakes. An *earthquake* is a movement of the ground that happens when rocks break and move. Earthquakes release waves of energy that travel through rock, called **seismic waves**. When an earthquake happens, seismic waves travel outward in many directions and pass through Earth's interior. The waves eventually reach new locations around Earth's surface. Scientists collect and record seismic-wave data with devices called *seismographs*. Scientists use these data to learn about the properties of Earth's interior.

Waves are disturbances in matter. A rock is dropped in this pond and waves begin to move outward.

Visualize It!

16 Relate Imagine you are collecting evidence that a rock was dropped into this pond. As the waves reach the shore, you measure them and record data. How could this relate to a scientist collecting data from an earthquake that happened far away?

_____

_____

_____

_____

How do seismic waves travel?

Active Reading 17 **Identify** As you read, underline the two types of seismic waves used to study Earth's interior.

Seismic waves travel outward in all directions from an earthquake. Some seismic waves travel along the surface, while others travel through the interior. Two types of seismic waves that travel through Earth and provide information about Earth's interior are P waves and S waves. *P waves*, also called primary waves, squeeze rock in the same direction the wave is traveling. *S waves*, or secondary waves, move rock side to side.

Both P waves and S waves travel through the interior of Earth. The speed and direction that P waves and S waves travel depend on the properties of the materials they travel through.

- P waves travel through solids, liquids, and gases.
- S waves travel only through solids.
- P and S waves generally travel faster in rigid, dense rock and slower in less rigid and less dense rock.

The seismic waves from this earthquake move out in all directions through Earth and cause the ground to shake.

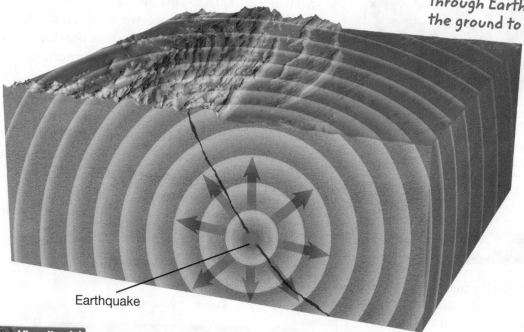

Earthquake

Visualize It!

18 **Summarize** Describe how P and S waves from an earthquake reach new, distant locations around Earth's surface.

_____

_____

_____

_____

_____

_____

What do seismic waves tell us about Earth's interior?

Scientists calculate the times P waves and S waves take to travel from an earthquake to different seismographs all over the world. Scientists can combine data from many seismographs to make a picture of what is inside Earth.

19 Identify As you read, underline what happens to P waves as they pass through the core.

Earth Is Made Up of Layers

As seismic waves travel through Earth, they reach areas where they abruptly change in speed and direction. They bend or reflect off of certain materials. These changes happen where seismic waves pass between layers, where there are major changes in properties such as composition. For example, at the boundary between the crust and mantle, seismic waves abruptly increase in speed.

Scientists have noticed that S waves do not reach seismometers on the opposite side of Earth from an earthquake. This makes a circular area of missing S waves, called an *S-wave shadow zone*. Scientists deduce that the zone exists because when S waves reach the liquid outer core, they cannot travel through it.

P waves suddenly slow down and bend as they pass through the outer core and then speed up and bend again as they pass through the inner core. This is evidence that the outer core is liquid and the inner core is solid. The bending of P waves creates an area where P waves do not register on seismographs. This makes a ring around the S-wave shadow zone, called the *P-wave shadow zone*.

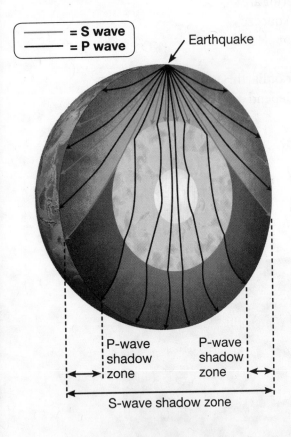

= S wave
= P wave
Earthquake

P-wave shadow zone
P-wave shadow zone
S-wave shadow zone

20 Calculate What is the change in speed of the P wave as it goes from the mesosphere to the outer core? From the outer core to the inner core?

Seismic Wave Speeds through Earth

S wave   P wave

lithosphere
asthenosphere
mesosphere
outer core
inner core

depth (km)
0
1,500
3,000
4,500
6,000

speed (km/s)
2   4   6   8   10   12   14

A Journey into Earth

What other evidence tells us about Earth's interior?

Scientists can gather data about Earth's interior from methods other than studying seismic waves. For example, clues about Earth's interior come from *meteorites* from space that crash to Earth's surface and from mantle rock brought up by volcanic eruptions.

Mantle Rocks

Volcanoes erupt melted rock, gases, and ash from below Earth's surface. When some volcanoes erupt, material travels up through Earth's mantle. Solid chunks of mantle rock can be picked up along the way and make it to Earth's surface. These solid chunks are called mantle xenoliths. Mantle xenoliths give scientists actual samples of some of Earth's upper mantle.

Mantle xenolith

Meteorites

Meteorites are bodies from space that have crashed onto Earth. They are made mainly of rock or metal or of both. Scientists think that some meteorites have similar compositions to certain layers in Earth. Some rocky meteorites have a similar composition to Earth's mantle and crust. Metallic meteorites contain mostly iron and may have a similar makeup to Earth's core.

Rocky meteorite

Metallic meteorite

Earth's Density and Magnetic Field

Rocks from Earth's crust have an average density of about 2.8 g/cm³. Earth's gravitational effect on other bodies in space indicate that Earth's average density is 5.5 g/cm³. This difference suggests that Earth's mantle and core are denser than the crust. From this information and knowing the densities of elements in Earth, scientists conclude that the core is composed mainly of iron.

Seismic waves provide evidence that the outer core is liquid and the inner core is solid. The fact that Earth has a magnetic field also supports this idea. Scientists think that relative motion between the liquid outer core and the solid inner core may generate electric currents. These electric currents, in turn, could create a large magnetic field around the planet.

 Active Reading

21 Identify How does Earth's magnetic field relate to its core?

_____

_____

_____

_____

_____

© Houghton Mifflin Harcourt Publishing Company • Image Credits: (t) ©Slim Sepp/Shutterstock; (b) ©Detlev van Ravensway/Picture Press/Getty Images; (c) ©Gary Ombler/Dorling Kindersley/Getty Images

Visual Summary

To complete this summary, check the box that indicates true or false. Then, use the key below to check your answers. You can use this page to review the main concepts of the lesson.

Representing Data

Scientists use models and simulations to learn about objects, systems, and concepts.

T F

☐ ☐ **21** The equation for density is a physical model.

A table can be used to record and organize data as it is being collected.

Density of Earth's Layers	
Layer	Density (g/cm³)
crust	2.7–3.3
mantle	3.3–5.7
core	9.9–13.1

T F

☐ ☐ **22** Units of measurement should be placed with the column or row headings in tables.

Answers: 21 False; 22 True; 23 False

A graph is a visual display of data that shows relationships between the data.

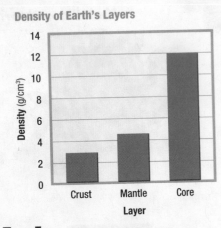

T F

☐ ☐ **23** A bar graph is used to show continuous data.

24 Synthesize Provide an example of something in the natural world that could be depicted in each of the following ways: a table, a graph, and a model. (Use examples not given in this lesson.)

Lesson Review

Vocabulary

Fill in the blank with the term that best completes the following sentences.

1 A(n) _____ can be a visual or mathematical representation of an object, system, or concept.

2 A(n) _____ imitates the function, behavior, or process of the thing it represents.

3 Data can be arranged in visual displays called _____ to make identifying trends easier.

Key Concepts

4 Differentiate How is a diagram different from a simulation?

_____

_____

_____

5 Predict A data table shows the height of a person on his birthday each year from age 2 to 12. What trend would you expect to see in a line graph of the data?

_____

_____

_____

6 Judge Which kind of graph would be best for depicting data collected on the weight of a baby every month for six months?

_____

_____

_____

7 Apply What kind of model would you use to represent the human heart?

_____

_____

Critical Thinking

Use this graph to answer the following questions.

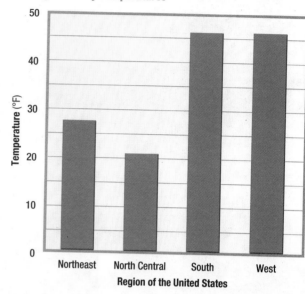

Average January Temperatures

8 Identify Which region of the country has the coldest January temperatures?

_____

9 Estimate What was the average temperature of the South in January? How did you arrive upon your answer?

_____

_____

_____

_____

10 Apply Give an example of a physical model, and explain one limitation of the model. Then give an example of a mathematical model, and explain one limitation.

_____

_____

_____

_____

_____

My Notes

Plate Tectonics

ESSENTIAL QUESTION

What is plate tectonics?

By the end of this lesson, you should be able to explain the theory of plate tectonics, to describe how tectonic plates move, and to identify geologic events that occur because of tectonic plate movement.

8.ESS2.3, 8.ESS2.4, 8.ESS2.5

The San Andreas Fault is located where two tectonic plates slide past each other.

The course of this river has been shifted as a result of tectonic plate motion.

© Houghton Mifflin Harcourt Publishing Company • Image Credits: ©Bernhard Edmaier/Photo Researchers, Inc.

Lesson Labs

Quick Labs
• Tectonic Ice Cubes
• Mantle Convection
• Reconstructing Land Masses

Exploration Lab
• Seafloor Spreading

 Engage Your Brain

1 Identify Check T or F to show whether you think each statement is true or false.

T F

☐ ☐ Earth's surface is all one piece.

☐ ☐ Scientists think the continents once formed a single landmass.

☐ ☐ The sea floor is smooth and level.

☐ ☐ All tectonic plates are the same.

2 Predict Imagine that ice cubes are floating in a large bowl of punch. If there are enough cubes, they will cover the surface of the punch and bump into one another. Parts of the cubes will be below the surface of the punch and will displace the punch. Will some cubes displace more punch than others? Explain your answer.

_____

_____

_____

_____

_____

_____

 Active Reading

3 Apply Many scientific words, such as *divergent* and *convergent,* also have everyday meanings or are related to words with everyday meanings. Use context clues to write your own definition for each underlined word.

Example sentence
They argued about the issue because their opinions about it were <u>divergent</u>.

divergent:

_____

_____

Example sentence

The two rivers <u>converged</u> near the town.

convergent:

_____

_____

Vocabulary Terms

• Pangaea
• sea-floor spreading
• plate tectonics
• tectonic plates
• convergent boundary
• divergent boundary
• transform boundary
• convection

4 Identify This list contains key terms you'll learn in this lesson. As you read, underline the definition of each term.

Puzzling Evidence

What evidence suggests that continents move?

Have you ever looked at a map and noticed that the continents look like they could fit together like puzzle pieces? In the late 1800s, Alfred Wegener proposed his hypothesis of continental drift. He proposed that the continents once formed a single landmass, broke up, and drifted. This idea is supported by several lines of evidence. For example, fossils of the same species are found on continents on different sides of the Atlantic Ocean. These species could not have crossed the ocean. The hypothesis is also supported by the locations of mountain ranges and rock formations and by evidence of the same ancient climatic conditions on several continents.

Geologic evidence supports the hypothesis of continental drift.

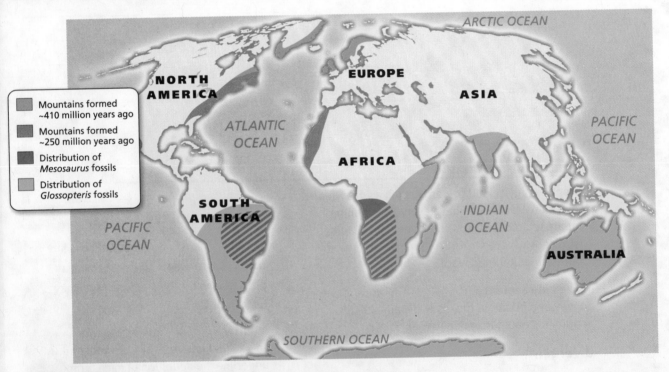

Mountains formed ~410 million years ago
Mountains formed ~250 million years ago
Distribution of *Mesosaurus* fossils
Distribution of *Glossopteris* fossils

👁 **Visualize It!** **5 Summarize** Using the map and its key, complete the table to describe evidence that indicates each continent pair was once joined.

	Fossil evidence	Mountain evidence
South America and Africa		
North America and Europe		

What is Pangaea?

Active Reading 6 **Identify** As you read, underline the description of how North America formed from Pangaea.

Using evidence from many scientific fields, scientists can construct a picture of continental change throughout time. Scientists think that about 245 million years ago, the continents were joined in a single large landmass they call **Pangaea** (pan•JEE•uh). As the continents collided to form Pangaea, mountains formed. A single, large ocean called Panthalassa surrounded Pangaea.

About 200 million years ago, a large rift formed and Pangaea began to break into two continents—*Laurasia* and *Gondwana*. Then, Laurasia began to drift northward and rotate slowly, and a new rift formed. This rift separated Laurasia into the continents of North America and Eurasia. The rift eventually formed the North Atlantic Ocean. At the same time, Gondwana also broke into two continents. One continent contained land that is now the continents of South America and Africa. The other continent contained land that is now Antarctica, Australia, and India.

About 150 million years ago, a rift between Africa and South America opened to form the South Atlantic Ocean. India, Australia, and Antarctica also began to separate from each other. As India broke away from Australia and Antarctica, it started moving northward, toward Eurasia.

As India and the other continents moved into their present positions, new oceans formed while others disappeared. In some cases, continents collided with other continents. About 50 million years ago, India collided with Eurasia, and the Himalaya Mountains began to form. Mountain ranges form as a result of these collisions, because a collision welds new crust onto the continents and uplifts some of the land.

The Breakup of Pangaea

245 million years ago

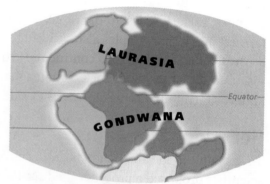

200 million years ago

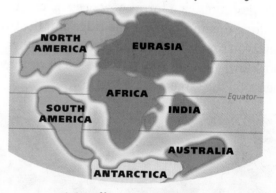

65 million years ago

3 million years ago

What discoveries support the idea of continental drift?

Wegener's ideas of continental drift were pushed aside for many years because scientists could not determine how continents moved. Then, in the mid-1900s, scientists began mapping the sea floor. They expected the floor to be smooth and level. Instead, they found huge underwater mountain ranges called *mid-ocean ridges*. The discovery of mid-ocean ridges eventually led to the theory of plate tectonics, which built on some of Wegener's ideas.

Age and Magnetic Properties of the Sea Floor

Scientists learned that the mid-ocean ridges form along cracks in the crust. Rock samples from the sea floor revealed that the youngest rock is closest to the ridge, while the oldest rock is farthest away. The samples also showed that even the oldest ocean crust is young compared to continental crust. Scientists also discovered that sea-floor rock contains magnetic patterns. These patterns form mirror images on either side of a mid-ocean ridge.

Sea-Floor Spreading

To explain the age and magnetic patterns of sea-floor rocks, scientists proposed a process called **sea-floor spreading**. In this process, molten rock from inside Earth rises through the cracks in the ridges, cools, and forms new oceanic crust. The old crust breaks along the mid-point of the ridge and the two pieces of crust move away in opposite directions from each other. In this way, the sea floor slowly spreads apart. As the sea floor moves, so do the continents on the same piece of crust.

7 Summarize Why would many scientists not accept the hypothesis of continental drift?

_____

_____

_____

This map shows where mid-ocean ridges are located.

© Houghton Mifflin Harcourt Publishing Company

Ocean Trenches

If the sea floor has been spreading for millions of years, why is Earth not getting larger? Scientists discovered the answer when they found huge trenches, like deep canyons, in the sea floor. At these sites, dense oceanic crust is sinking into the asthenosphere as shown in the diagram below. Older crust is being destroyed at the same rate new crust is forming. Thus, Earth remains the same size.

With this new information about the sea floor, sea-floor spreading, and ocean trenches, scientists could begin to understand how continents were able to move.

8 Identify Why is Earth not getting larger if the sea floor is spreading?

_____

_____

_____

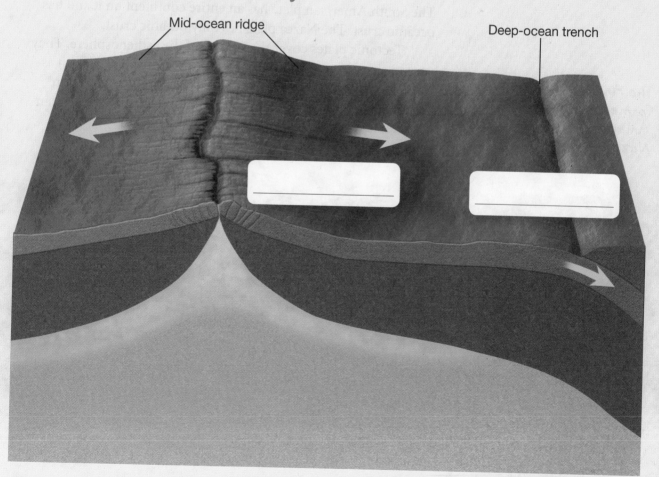

Visualize It!

9 Provide Label the youngest rock and the oldest rock on this diagram of sea-floor spreading.

Sea-floor spreading takes place at mid-ocean ridges.

Mid-ocean ridge

Deep-ocean trench

A Giant Jigsaw

What is the theory of plate tectonics?

As scientists' understanding of continental drift, mid-ocean ridges, and sea-floor spreading grew, scientists formed a theory to explain these processes and features. **Plate tectonics** describes large-scale movements of Earth's lithosphere, which is made up of the crust and the rigid, upper part of the mantle. Plate tectonics explains how and why features in Earth's crust form and continents move.

What is a tectonic plate?

The lithosphere is divided into pieces called **tectonic plates.** These plates move around on top of the asthenosphere. The plates are moving in different directions and at different speeds. Each tectonic plate fits together with the plates that surround it. The continents are located on tectonic plates and move around with them. The major tectonic plates include the Pacific, North American, Nazca, South American, African, Australian, Eurasian, Indian, and Antarctic plates. Not all tectonic plates are the same. The South American plate has an entire continent on it and has oceanic crust. The Nazca plate has only oceanic crust.

Tectonic plates cover the surface of the asthenosphere. They vary in size, shape, and thickness. Thick tectonic plates, such as those with continents, displace more asthenosphere than thin oceanic plates do. But, oceanic plates are much more dense than continental plates are.

The Andes Mountains formed where the South American plate and Nazca plate meet.

Visualize It!

12 Locate Which letter marks where the Andes Mountains are located on the map of tectonic plates, A, B, or C? _____

The tectonic plates fit together like the pieces of a jigsaw puzzle.

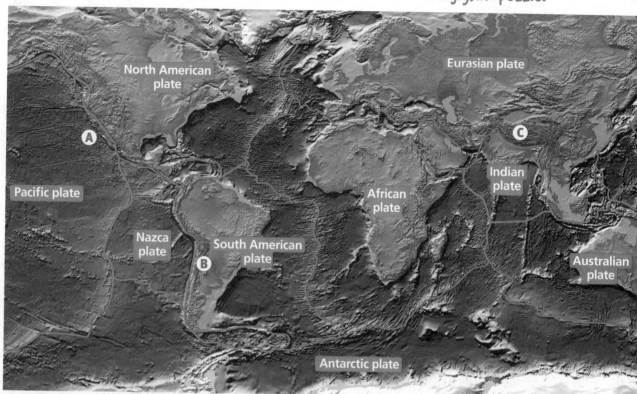

North American plate

Eurasian plate

C

Pacific plate

Indian plate

African plate

Nazca plate

South American plate

B

Australian plate

A

Antarctic plate

The thickest part of the South American plate is the continental crust. The thinnest part of this plate is in the Atlantic Ocean.

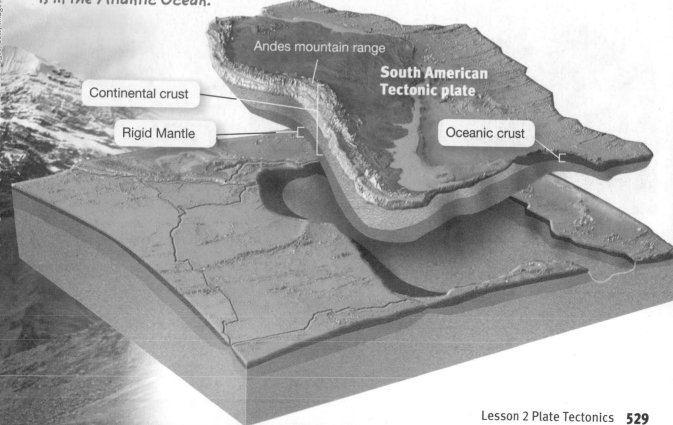

Andes mountain range

South American Tectonic plate

Continental crust

Rigid Mantle

Oceanic crust

Boundaries

What are the three types of plate boundaries?

The most dramatic changes in Earth's crust occur along plate boundaries. Plate boundaries may be on the ocean floor, around the edges of continents, or even within continents. There are three types of plate boundaries: divergent boundaries, convergent boundaries, and transform boundaries. Each type of plate boundary is associated with characteristic landforms.

13 Identify As you read, underline the locations where plate boundaries may be found.

Convergent Boundaries

Convergent boundaries form where two plates collide. Three types of collisions can happen at convergent boundaries. When two tectonic plates of continental lithosphere collide, they buckle and thicken, which pushes some of the continental crust upward. When a plate of oceanic lithosphere collides with a plate of continental lithosphere, the denser oceanic lithosphere sinks into the asthenosphere. Boundaries where one plate sinks beneath another plate are called subduction zones. When two tectonic plates of oceanic lithosphere collide, one of the plates subducts, or sinks, under the other plate.

Inquiry

14 Infer Why do you think the denser plate subducts in a collision?

_____

_____

_____

Continent-Continent Collisions
When two plates of continental lithosphere collide, they buckle and thicken. This causes mountains to form.

Continent-Ocean Collisions
When a plate of oceanic lithosphere collides with a plate of continental lithosphere, the oceanic lithosphere subducts because it is denser.

Ocean-Ocean Collisions
When two plates of oceanic lithosphere collide, the older, denser plate subducts under the other plate.

Divergent Boundaries

At a **divergent boundary**, two plates move away from each other. This separation allows the asthenosphere to rise toward the surface and partially melt. This melting creates magma, which erupts as lava. The lava cools and hardens to form new rock on the ocean floor.

As the crust and the upper part of the asthenosphere cool and become rigid, they form new lithosphere. This lithosphere is thin, warm, and light. This warm, light rock sits higher than the surrounding sea floor because it is less dense. It forms mid-ocean ridges. Most divergent boundaries are located on the ocean floor. However, rift valleys may also form where continents are separated by plate movement.

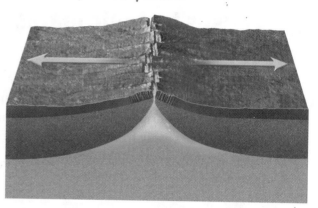

At divergent boundaries, plates separate.

Transform Boundaries

A boundary at which two plates move past each other horizontally is called a **transform boundary**. However, the plate edges do not slide along smoothly. Instead, they scrape against each other in a series of sudden slippages of crustal rock that are felt as earthquakes. Unlike other types of boundaries, transform boundaries generally do not produce magma. The San Andreas Fault in California is a major transform boundary between the North American plate and the Pacific plate. Transform motion also occurs at divergent boundaries. Short segments of mid-ocean ridges are connected by transform faults called fracture zones.

Active Reading

15 Contrast How are transform boundaries different from convergent and divergent boundaries?

_____

_____

_____

_____

At transform boundaries, plates slide past each other horizontally.

Hot Plates

What causes tectonic plates to move?

Scientists have proposed three mechanisms to explain how tectonic plates move over Earth's surface. Mantle convection drags plates along as mantle material moves beneath tectonic plates. Ridge push moves plates away from mid-ocean ridges as rock cools and becomes more dense. Slab pull tugs plates along as the dense edge of a plate sinks beneath Earth's surface.

Active Reading

16 Identify As you read, underline three mechanisms scientists have proposed to explain plate motion.

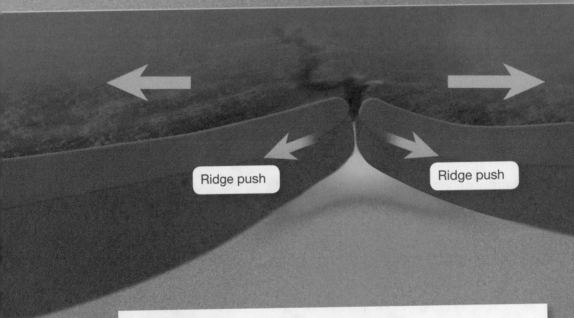

Ridge push

Ridge push

Mantle Convection

As atoms in Earth's core and mantle undergo radioactive decay, energy is released as heat. Some parts of the mantle become hotter than others parts. The hot parts rise as the sinking of cooler, denser material pushes the heated material up. This kind of movement of material due to differences in density is called **convection**. It was thought that as the mantle convects, or moves, it would drag the overlying tectonic plates along with it. However, this hypothesis has been criticized by many scientists because it does not explain the huge amount of force that would be needed to move plates.

Ridge Push

Newly formed rock at a mid-ocean ridge is warm and less dense than older, adjacent rock. Because of its lower density, the new rock rests at a higher elevation than the older rock. The older rock slopes downward away from the ridge. As the newer, warmer rock cools, it also becomes more dense. These cooling and increasingly dense rocks respond to gravity by moving down the slope of the asthenosphere, away from the ridge. This force, called ridge push, pushes the rest of the plate away from the mid-ocean ridge.

Slab Pull

At subduction zones, a denser tectonic plate sinks, or subducts, beneath another, less dense plate. The leading edge of the subducting plate is colder and denser than the mantle. As it sinks, the leading edge of the plate pulls the rest of the plate with it. This process is called slab pull. In general, subducting plates move faster than other plates do. This evidence leads many scientists to think that slab pull may be the most important mechanism driving tectonic plate motion.

Slab pull

17 Compare Complete the chart with brief descriptions to compare and contrast mantle convection, ridge push, and slab pull.

Mechanisms

Mantle convection	Ridge push	Slab pull

Broken Lithosphere

In 1960, a US. Navy scientist, Harry Hammond Hess, mapped the Atlantic seafloor and discovered a range of volcanic mountains in the middle of the ocean basin. Rocks on either side of this mid-ocean range were found to have symmetrical patterns of magnetic striping moving away from the ridge. As molten rock erupting from the mid-ocean ridge cools, small crystals in the rock line up with Earth's magnetic poles. Over Earth's history, the direction of its magnetic poles has flipped many times.

Skills

✓ Evaluate evidence

✓ Construct an explanation

✓ Analyze data

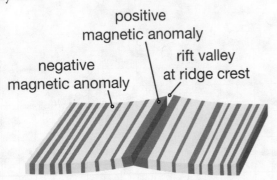

Harry Hammond Hess mapped the Atlantic seafloor.

(1) Label the diagram by using arrows to indicate the direction of movement along the red lines. In the white ovals, label whether the seafloor is older or younger at these locations.

Mid-Ocean Ridge Diagram

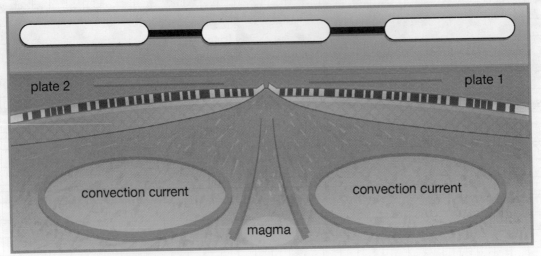

© Houghton Mifflin Harcourt Publishing Company • Image Credits: (c) ©Fritz Goro/The LIFE Picture Collection/Getty Images

2 How do you think these magnetic patterns formed?

Explain how they provide supporting evidence for the theory of plate tectonics. What mechanism for plate tectonics is shown in the diagram? What is the evidence that this mechanism starts from Earth's interior?

_____

_____

_____

_____

_____

The subcontinent of India is currently attached to the Eurasian plate, but it was not always that way. To its north are the mighty Himalayas, site of Mount Everest. Mount Everest is currently measured at 29,035 ft., and is estimated to be growing at a rate of 2.4 inches per year.

If you were to climb Mount Everest, you would notice that the type of rock changes with elevation; from granite (igneous) at its base, through gneiss and schist (metamorphic) higher up, to limestone and fossil-rich mudstone (sedimentary) at its summit.

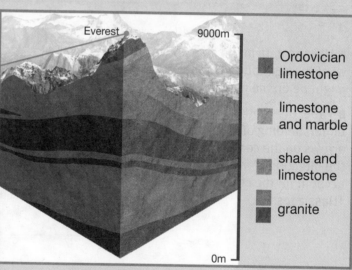

3 Use what you know about plate tectonics to explain the current position of India, why Everest should still be growing, and why marine fossils are found at its summit.

_____

_____

_____

_____

_____

_____

Broken Lithosphere

Distribution of Fossil Evidence of Land-based Organisms from the Triassic Period (251-199 m.y.a.)

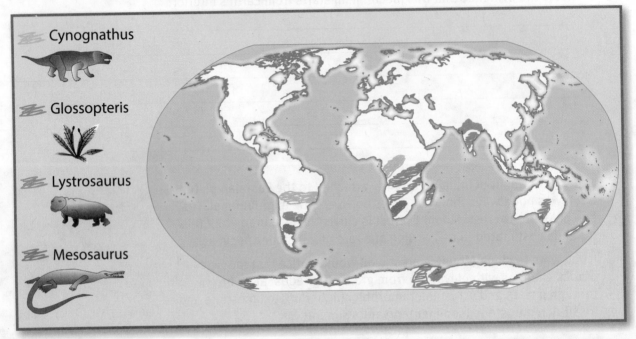

Cynognathus

Glossopteris

Lystrosaurus

Mesosaurus

4 **A** Use the data in the map above to draw what the distribution of the organisms might be on the map of Gondwana.

B Label the continents. Using your understanding of plate tectonics, draw arrows on the continents to indicate the direction of movement that would account for the current distribution of Triassic fossils.

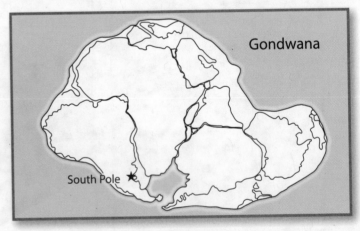

Gondwana

South Pole

5 Is there a mechanism other than plate tectonics that could account for the distribution of Triassic Period fossils? Explain why or why not.

_____

_____

_____

_____

_____

_____

_____

_____

When plates come in contact with each other, things get quite complicated. Moving plates constantly adjust to the spherical shape of the earth, causing many faults and fractures. The yellow arrows in the diagram show the motion of some of those fractures.

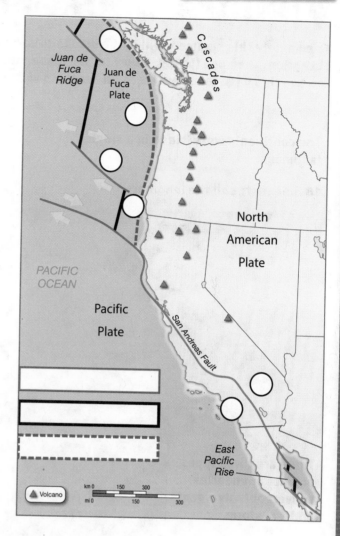

6 Draw arrows in the white circles to indicate the direction of movement of the Pacific, the North American, and the Juan de Fuca tectonic plates.

Label the types of plate boundary in the red, blue and black boxes.

7 What does the line of volcanoes on the North American plate tell you about the type of boundary that exists between the North American and the Juan de Fuca plates? What type of ocean floor feature forms along this type of boundary? Explain how it forms.

_____

_____

_____

_____

_____

_____

_____

_____

_____

_____

Visual Summary

To complete this summary, fill in the blanks to complete the label or caption. Then use the key below to check your answers. You can use this page to review the main concepts of the lesson.

The continents were joined in a single landmass.

18 Scientists call the landmass _____

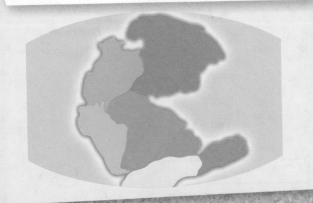

Tectonic plates differ in size and composition.

19 The United States lies on the _____ _____ plate.

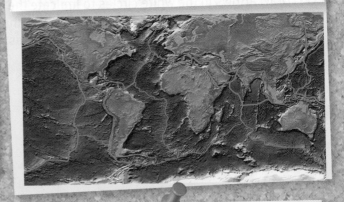

There are three types of plate boundaries: convergent, divergent, and transform.

20 This image shows a _____ boundary.

Three mechanisms may drive plate motion. These are mantle convection, slab pull, and ridge push.

21 The mechanism that scientists think is most important is _____

Answers: 18 Pangaea; 19 North American; 20 transform; 21 slab pull

22 Synthesize How does the flow of energy as heat in Earth's interior contribute to the movement of tectonic plates? Explain what would happen if Earth were not a convecting system.

Lesson Review

Vocabulary

Fill in the blanks with the term that best completes the following sentences.

1 The lithosphere is divided into pieces called

_____

2 The theory that describes large-scale movements of Earth's lithosphere is called

_____

3 The movement of material due to differences in density that are caused by differences in temperature is called _____

_____

Key Concepts

Use this diagram to answer the following questions.

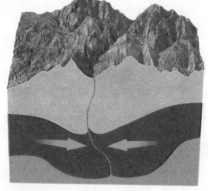

4 Identify What type of plate boundary is shown?

_____

5 Identify Which types of lithosphere are colliding at this boundary?

_____

_____

6 Identify What landforms are likely to form at this boundary?

_____

_____

_____

7 Describe How is continental lithosphere different from oceanic lithosphere?

_____

_____

_____

8 Compare How are convergent boundaries different from divergent boundaries?

_____

_____

_____

Critical Thinking

9 Analyze Explain why cool rock material sinks when convection takes place in the mantle.

_____

_____

_____

_____

_____

_____

10 Defend A classmate states that continental drift could not be possible because it would take far too much force to move tectonic plates. Describe the hypotheses scientists use to explain the movement of tectonic plates. Which hypothesis do many scientists think may explain the great force needed to move plates?

_____

_____

_____

_____

_____

My Notes

Estella Atekwana

GEOPHYSICIST

Dr. Estella Atekwana studies changes on Earth's surface. Some of the changes may tell us how life on Earth developed. Others may help us to detect whether life exists somewhere else in the universe.

Some of Dr. Atekwana's work takes her to Botswana and Zambia in Africa. There she is studying the formation of a new rift valley. Rift valleys are places where continents break apart. (For example, long ago a rift valley formed, and Africa broke apart from South America.) Studying this rift valley, Dr. Atekwana hopes to learn more about how new landmasses form. Further, the ground reveals the remains of plants and animals that once lived there. These remains can tell us more about the climate that existed there millions of years ago.

Currently, Dr. Atekwana is doing brand new research in a new field of geology known as biogeophysics. She is looking at the effects that microorganisms have on rocks. She is using new technologies to study how rock changes after microorganisms have mixed with it. This research may one day help scientists detect evidence of life on other planets. Looking for the same geophysical changes in the rocks on Mars might be a way of detecting whether life ever existed on that planet. If the rocks show the same changes as the rocks on Earth, it could be because microorganisms once lived in them.

Dr. Atekwana's research included this visit to Victoria Falls on the Zambezi River in Africa.

Social Studies Connection

Dr. Atekwana studies rift valleys—areas where the tectonic plates are pulling apart. Research to find out where else in the world scientists have located rift valleys.

OKLAHOMA STATE

JOB BOARD

Surveying and Mapping Technicians

What You'll Do: Help surveyors take measurements of outdoor areas. Technicians hold measuring tapes and adjust instruments, take notes, and make sketches.

Where You Might Work: Outdoors and indoors entering measurements into a computer.

Education: Some post-secondary education to obtain a license.

Other Job Requirements: Technicians must be able to visualize objects, distances, sizes, and shapes. They must be able to work with great care, precision, and accuracy because mistakes can be expensive. They must also be in good physical condition.

Petroleum Technician

What You'll Do: Measure and record the conditions in oil or gas wells to find out whether samples contain oil and other minerals.

Where You Might Work: Outdoors, sometimes in remote locations and sometimes in your own town or city.

Education: An associate's degree or a certificate in applied science or science-related technology.

Other Job Requirements: You need to be able to take accurate measurements and keep track of many details.

Geologist

What You'll Do: Study the history of Earth's crust. Geologists work in many different businesses. You may explore for minerals, oil, or gas. You may find and test groundwater supplies. You may work with engineers to make sure ground is safe to build on.

Where You Might Work: In the field, where you collect samples, and in the office, where you analyze them. Geologists work in mines, on oil rigs, on the slopes of volcanoes, in quarries, and in paleontological digs.

Education: A four-year bachelor's degree in science.

Other Job Requirements: Geologists who work in the field must be in good physical condition. Most geologists do field training. Geologists need strong math skills, analytical skills, and computer skills. They also need to be able to work well with other members of a team.

Lesson 3

Mountain Building

ESSENTIAL QUESTION

How do mountains form?

By the end of this lesson, you should be able to describe how the movement of Earth's tectonic plates causes mountain building.

8.ESS2.4, 8.ESS2.5

The highest peak in the Alps mountain range is Mont Blanc at just over 4,800 m tall.

© Houghton Mifflin Harcourt Publishing Company • Image Credits: © Guido Baviera/Grand Tour/Corbis

🌐 Engage Your Brain

1 Predict Check T or F to show whether you think each statement is true or false.

T	F	
☐	☐	Mountains can originate from a level surface that is folded upward.
☐	☐	Rocks can be pulled apart by the movement of tectonic plates.
☐	☐	All mountains are created by volcanoes.
☐	☐	A mountain range can form only at the edge of a tectonic plate.

2 Hypothesize The Appalachian Mountains were once taller than the Rocky Mountains. What do you think happened to the mountains? Explain.

_____

_____

_____

_____

Rocky Mountains

Appalachian Mountains

✏️ Active Reading

3 Compare The terms *compression* and *tension* have opposite meanings. Compare the two sentences below, then write your own definition for *compression* and *tension*.

Vocabulary	Sentence
compression	The stack of books on Jon's desk caused the bottom book to be flattened by <u>compression</u>.
tension	Keisha pulled the piece of string so hard, the <u>tension</u> caused the string to break.

Vocabulary Terms

- deformation
- folding
- fault
- shear stress
- tension
- compression

4 Apply As you learn the definition of each vocabulary term in this lesson, create your own definition or sketch to help you remember the meaning of the term.

compression: _____

_____

tension: _____

_____

Stressed Out

How can tectonic plate motion cause deformation?

The movement of tectonic plates places stress on rocks. A tectonic plate is a block of lithosphere that consists of crust and the rigid outermost part of the mantle. *Stress* is the amount of force per unit area that is placed on an object. Rocks can bend or break under stress. In addition, low temperatures make materials more brittle, or easily broken. High temperatures can allow rock to bend.

When a rock is placed under stress, it deforms, or changes shape. **Deformation** (dee•fohr•MAY•shuhn) is the process by which rocks change shape when under stress. Rock can bend if it is placed under high temperature and pressure for long periods of time. If the stress becomes too great, or is applied quickly, rock can break. When rocks bend, folds form. When rocks break, faults form.

By applying stress, the boy is causing the spaghetti to deform. Similarly, stress over a long period of time can cause rock to bend.

Like the spaghetti, stress over a short period of time or great amounts of stress can cause rock to break.

Visualize It!

6 Correlate How can the same material bend in one situation but break in another?

_____

_____

_____

_____

© Houghton Mifflin Harcourt Publishing Company • Image Credits: ©HMH

What are two kinds of folds?

Folded rock layers appear bent or buckled. **Folding** occurs when rock layers bend under stress. The bends are called *folds*. Scientists assume that all rock layers start out as horizontal layers deposited on top of each other over time. Sometimes, different layers of rocks can still be seen even after the rocks have been folded. When scientists see a fold, they know that deformation has happened. Two common types of folds are synclines and anticlines.

Synclines and Anticlines

Folds are classified based on the age of the rock layers. In a *syncline* (SIN•klyn), the youngest layers of rock are found at the core of a fold. The oldest layers are found on the outside of the fold. Synclines usually look like rock layers that are arched upward, like a bowl. In an *anticline* (AN•tih•klyn), the oldest layers of rock are found at the core of the fold. The youngest layers are found on the outside of the fold. Anticlines often look like rock layers that are arched downwards and high in the middle. Often, both types of folds will be visible in the same rock layers, as shown below.

Think Outside the Book

7 Model Stack several sheets of paper together. Apply stress to the sides of the paper to create a model of a syncline and an anticline. Share your model with your teacher.

The hinge is the middle point of the bend in a syncline or anticline.

8 Identify Rock layers are labeled on the image below. Which rock layers are the youngest and oldest?

_____

_____

How do you know? _____

_____

_____

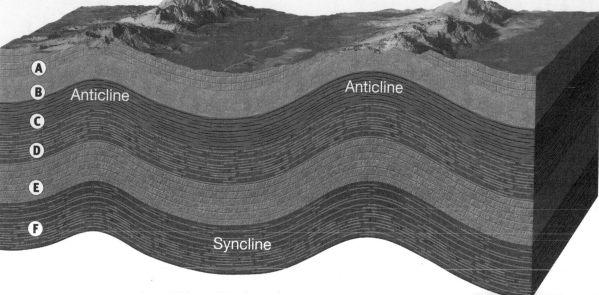

(A) (B) (C) (D) (E) (F)

Anticline

Anticline

Syncline

Faulted

What are the three kinds of faults?

Rock can be under so much stress that it cannot bend and may break. The crack that forms when large blocks of rock break and move past each other is called a **fault**. The blocks of rock on either side of the fault are called *fault blocks*. The sudden movement of fault blocks can cause earthquakes.

Any time there is a fault in Earth's crust, rocks tend to move in predictable ways. Earth has three main kinds of faults: strike-slip faults, normal faults, and reverse faults. Scientists classify faults based on the way fault blocks move relative to each other. The location where two fault blocks meet is called the *fault plane*. A fault plane can be oriented horizontally, vertically, or at any angle in between. For any fault except a perfectly vertical fault, the block above the fault plane is called the *hanging wall*. The block below the fault plane is the *footwall*.

The movement of faults can create mountains and other types of landforms. At any tectonic plate boundary, the amount of stress on rock is complex. Therefore, any of the three types of faults can occur at almost all plate boundaries.

 Active Reading

9 Identify As you read, underline the direction of movement of the fault blocks in each type of fault.

Strike-Slip Faults

In a strike-slip fault, the fault blocks move past each other horizontally. Strike-slip faults form when rock is under shear stress. **Shear stress** is stress that pushes rocks in parallel but opposite directions as seen in the image. As rocks are deformed deep in Earth's crust, energy builds. The release of this energy can cause earthquakes as the rocks slide past each other. Strike-slip faults are common along transform boundaries, where tectonic plates move past each other. The San Andreas fault system in California is an example of a strike-slip fault.

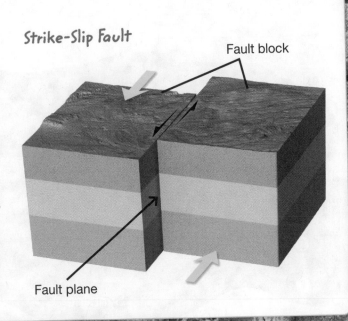

Strike-Slip Fault

Fault block

Fault plane

Normal Faults

In the normal fault shown on the right, the hanging wall moves down relative to the footwall. The faults are called normal because the blocks move in a way that you would *normally* expect as a result of gravity. Normal faults form when the rock is under tension. **Tension** (TEN•shun) is stress that stretches or pulls rock apart. Therefore, normal faults are common along divergent boundaries. Earth's crust can also stretch in the middle of a tectonic plate. The Basin and Range area of the southwestern United States is an example of a location with many normal fault structures.

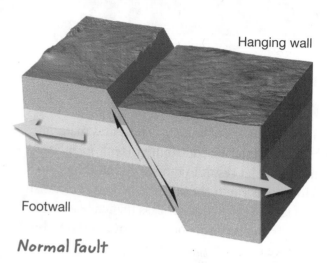

Hanging wall

Footwall

Normal Fault

Reverse Faults

In the reverse fault shown on the right, the hanging wall moves up relative to the footwall. The faults are called reverse because the hanging blocks move up, which is the reverse of what you would expect as a result of gravity. Reverse faults form when rocks undergo compression. **Compression** (kuhm•PRESH•uhn) is stress that squeezes or pushes rock together. Reverse faults are common along convergent boundaries, where two plates collide. The San Gabriel Mountains in the United States are caused by reverse faults.

Reverse Fault

Visualize It!

10 Identify Label the fault plane, hanging wall, and footwall on the reverse fault to the right.

Think Outside the Book Inquiry

11 Compile Create a memory matching game of the types of faults. Create as many cards as you can with different photos, drawings, or written details about the types of faults. Use the cards to quiz yourself and your classmates.

Moving On Up

What are the three kinds of mountains?

The movement of energy as heat and material in Earth's interior contribute to tectonic plate motions that result in mountain building. Mountains can form through folding, volcanism, and faulting. *Uplift,* a process that can cause land to rise can also contribute to mountain building. Because tectonic plates are always in motion, some mountains are constantly being uplifted.

Active Reading **12 Identify** As you read, underline examples of folded, volcanic, and fault-block mountains.

Folded Mountains

Folded mountains form when rock layers are squeezed together and pushed upward. They usually form at convergent boundaries, where plates collide. For example, the Appalachian Mountains (ap•uh•LAY•chun) formed from folding and faulting when the North American plate collided with the Eurasian and African plates millions of years ago.

In Europe, the Pyrenees (PIR•uh•neez) are another range of folded mountains, as shown below. They are folded over an older, pre-existing mountain range. Today, the highest peaks are over 3,000 m tall.

The Pyrenees Mountains are folded mountains that separate France from Spain.

Visualize It!

13 Identify What evidence do you see that the Pyrenees Mountains are folded mountains?

_____

_____

_____

Volcanic Mountains

Volcanic mountains form when melted rock erupts onto Earth's surface. Many major volcanic mountains are located at convergent boundaries. Volcanic mountains can form on land or on the ocean floor. Volcanoes on the ocean floor can grow so tall that they rise above the surface of the ocean, forming islands. Most of Earth's active volcanoes are concentrated around the edge of the Pacific Ocean. This area is known as the Ring of Fire. Many volcanoes, including Mt. Griggs in the image to the right, are located on the Northern rim of the Pacific plate in Alaska.

Mt. Griggs volcano on the Alaskan Peninsula is 2,317 m high.

The Teton Mountains in Wyoming are fault-block mountains.

Fault-Block Mountains

Fault-block mountains form when tension makes the lithosphere break into many normal faults. Along the faults, pieces of the lithosphere drop down compared with other pieces. The pieces left standing form fault-block mountains. The Teton Mountains (TEE•tuhn) and the Sierra Nevadas are fault-block mountains.

14 Identify Draw a simple version of each type of mountain below.

Folded	Volcanic	Faulted

Visual Summary

To complete this summary, fill in the blanks with the correct word or phrase. Then use the key below to check your answers. You can use this page to review the main concepts of the lesson.

Mountain Building

Rocks can bend or break under stress.

15 The process by which rocks change shape under stress is called _____

Folds occur when rock layers bend.

16 A rock structure with the oldest rocks at the core of the fold is called a/an _____

Faults occur when rock layers break.

Footwall

Hanging wall

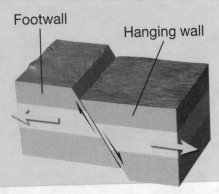

17 The type of fault pictured is a _____ fault.

Mountains form through folding, volcanism, and faulting.

18 The type of mountains pictured are _____ mountains.

Answers: 15 deformation; 16 anticline; 17 normal; 18 fault-block

19 Synthesize The middle of tectonic plates tend to have fewer mountains than locations near tectonic plate boundaries. What might be one possible explanation for this?

© Houghton Mifflin Harcourt Publishing Company • Image Credits: (br) ©Arco Images GmbH/Alamy

Lesson Review

Vocabulary

Fill in the blank with the term that best completes the following sentences.

1 A normal fault is a result of a type of stress known as _____

2 A strike-slip fault is a result of _____ stress.

3 A reverse fault is caused by a type of stress known as _____

Key Concepts

Fill in the table below by identifying the type of mountain described in the example question.

Example	Type of Mountain
4 Identify The Basin and Range province is characterized by many normal faults.	
5 Identify The Cascade Range in the United States has many eruptive mountains.	
6 Identify The Pyrenees Mountains have many syncline and anticline structures.	

7 Describe How does the movement of tectonic plates cause deformation in rock?

_____

_____

_____

8 Compare How do folded, volcanic, and fault-block mountains differ?

_____

_____

_____

Critical Thinking

Use the diagram below to answer the following questions.

9 Correlate What type of stress caused the fault shown in the image?

_____

10 Apply Along which type of tectonic plate boundary would this fault be common? How do you know?

_____

_____

_____

11 Analyze Can rock undergo compression, tension, and shear stress all at once? Explain.

_____

_____

_____

_____

12 Conclude Imagine you are walking along a roadway and see a syncline. What can you conclude about the formation of that fold?

_____

_____

_____

My Notes

Volcanoes

ESSENTIAL QUESTION

How do volcanoes change Earth's surface?

By the end of this lesson, you should be able to describe what the various kinds of volcanoes and eruptions are, where they occur, how they form, and how they change Earth's surface.

8.ESS2.4, 8.ESS3.2, 8.ESS2.5

The Arenal volcano in Costa Rica has been active since 1968. The volcano has erupted on and off for over 7,000 years.

Lesson Labs

Quick Labs
- Modeling an Explosive Eruption
- Volcano Mapping

Exploration Lab
- Modeling Lava Viscosity

Engage Your Brain

1 Predict Check T or F to show whether you think each statement is true or false.

T	F	
☐	☐	Volcanoes create new landforms such as mountains.
☐	☐	Tectonic plate boundaries are the only locations where volcanoes form.
☐	☐	Volcanic eruptions are often accompanied by earthquakes.
☐	☐	Volcanoes form new rocks and minerals.

2 Hypothesize You are a news reporter assigned to cover a story about the roadway in the image below. Describe what you think happened in this photo.

_____

_____

_____

_____

Active Reading

3 Synthesize You can often define an unknown word if you know the meaning of its word parts. Use the word parts and sentence below to make an educated guess about the meaning of the word *pyroclastic*.

Word part	Meaning
pyro-	heat or fire
-clastic	pieces

Example sentence

<u>Pyroclastic</u> material was ejected into the atmosphere with explosive force during the eruption of the volcano.

pyroclastic:

_____

_____

Vocabulary Terms

- volcano
- magma
- lava
- vent
- tectonic plate
- hot spot

4 Apply As you learn the definition of each vocabulary term in this lesson, create your own definition or sketch to help you remember the meaning of the term.

Magma MAGIC

What is a volcano?

What do volcanoes look like? Most people think of a steep mountain with smoke coming out of the top. In fact, a **volcano** is any place where gas, ash, or melted rock come out of the ground. A volcano can be a tall mountain, as shown below, or a small crack in the ground. Volcanoes occur on land and underwater. There are even volcanoes on other planets. Not all volcanoes actively erupt. Many are *dormant,* meaning an eruption has not occurred in a long period of time.

Volcanoes form as rock below the surface of Earth melts. The melted rock, or **magma**, is less dense than solid rock, so it rises toward the surface. **Lava** is magma that has reached Earth's surface. Lava and clouds of ash can erupt from a **vent**, or opening of a volcano.

🔍 Visualize It!

5 Identify Label the parts of the volcano. Include the following terms: *magma, lava, vent, ash cloud.*

Lava can reach temperatures of more than 1,200 °C.

What are the kinds of volcanic landforms?

The location of a volcano and the composition of magma determine the type of volcanic landforms created. Shield volcanoes, cinder cones, composite volcanoes, lava plateaus, craters, and calderas are all types of volcanic landforms.

Volcanic Mountains

Materials ejected from a volcano may build up around a vent to create volcanic mountains. *Viscosity* (vyz•SKAHZ•ih•tee) is the resistance of a liquid material, such as lava, to flow. The viscosity of lava determines the explosiveness of an eruption and the shape of the resulting volcanic mountain. Low-viscosity lava flows easily, forms low slopes, and erupts without large explosions. High-viscosity lava does not flow easily, forms steep slopes, and can erupt explosively. *Pyroclastic materials* (py•roh•KLAHZ•tyk), or hot ash and bits of rock, may also be ejected into the atmosphere.

> **Active Reading**

7 Identify As you read, underline the main features of each type of volcanic mountain.

Think Outside the Book Inquiry

6 Apply Small fragments of rock material that are ejected from a volcano are known as *volcanic ash*. Volcanic ash is a form of pyroclastic material. The material does not dissolve in water and is very abrasive, meaning it can scratch surfaces. Ash can build up to great depths in locations around a volcano. Write a cleanup plan for a town that explains how you might safely remove and dispose of volcanic ash.

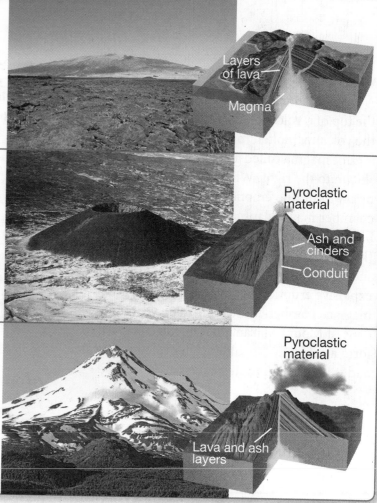

- **Shield Volcanoes** Volcanoes with a broad base and gently sloping sides are *shield volcanoes*. Shield volcanoes cover a wide area and generally form from mild eruptions. Layers of lava flow out from the vent, harden, and slowly build up to form the cone. The Hawaiian Islands are shield volcanoes.

  Layers of lava
  Magma

- **Cinder Cones** Sometimes, ash and pieces of lava harden in the air and can fall to the ground around a small vent. The hardened pieces of lava are called cinders. The cinders and ash build up around the vent and form a steep volcano called a *cinder cone*. A cinder cone can also form at a side vent on other volcanic mountains, such as on shield or composite volcanoes.

  Pyroclastic material
  Ash and cinders
  Conduit

- **Composite Volcanoes** Alternating layers of hardened lava flows and pyroclastic material create *composite volcanoes* (kuhm•PAHZ•iht). During a mild eruption, lava flows cover the sides of the cone. During an explosive eruption, pyroclastic material is deposited around the vent. Composite volcanoes commonly develop into large and steep volcanic mountains.

  Pyroclastic material
  Lava and ash layers

Fissures and Lava Plateaus

Fissure eruptions (FIH•shohr ee•RUHP•shuhnz) happen when lava flows from giant cracks, or *fissures*, in Earth's surface. The fissures are found on land and on the ocean floor. A fissure eruption has no central opening. Lava flows out of the entire length of the fissure, which can be many kilometers long. As a result, a thick and mostly flattened layer of cooled lava, called a *lava plateau* (plah•TOH), can form. One example of a lava plateau is the Columbia Plateau Province in Washington, Oregon, and Idaho, as shown to the right.

The Palouse Falls in Washington plunge deep into exposed layers of the Columbia lava plateau.

Craters and Calderas

A *volcanic crater* is an opening or depression at the top of a volcano caused by eruptions. Inside the volcano, molten rock can form an expanded area of magma called a *magma chamber*, as shown to the right. When the magma chamber below a volcano empties, the roof of the magma chamber may collapse and leave an even larger, basin-shaped depression called a *caldera* (kahl•DAHR•uh). Calderas can form from the sudden drain of a magma chamber during an explosive eruption or from a slowly emptied magma chamber. More than 7,000 years ago, the cone of Mount Mazama in Oregon collapsed to form a caldera. The caldera later filled with water and is now called Crater Lake.

A caldera can be more than 100 km in diameter.

Visualize It!

8 Describe How does the appearance of land surfaces change before and after a caldera forms?

_____

_____

_____

Before

Expanded magma chamber

After

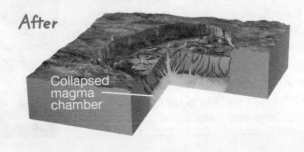

Collapsed magma chamber

© Houghton Mifflin Harcourt Publishing Company • Image Credits: (t) ©BlueMoon Stock/Alamy

ERUPTION!

Where do volcanoes form?

Volcanoes can form at plate boundaries or within the middle of a plate. Recall that **tectonic plates** are giant sections of lithosphere on Earth's surface. Volcanoes can form at *divergent plate boundaries* where two plates are moving away from each other. Most fissure eruptions occur at divergent boundaries. Shield volcanoes, fissure eruptions, and cinder cones can also occur away from plate boundaries within a plate at *hot spots*. The type of lava normally associated with these volcanoes has a relatively low viscosity, few trapped gases, and is usually not explosive.

Composite volcanoes are most common along *convergent plate boundaries* where oceanic plates subduct. In order for the rock to melt, it must be hot and the pressure on it must drop, or water and other fluids must be added to it. Extra fluids from ocean water form magma of higher viscosity with more trapped gases. Thus, composite volcanoes produce the most violent eruptions. The *Ring of Fire* is a name used to describe the numerous explosive volcanoes that form on convergent plate boundaries surrounding the Pacific Ocean.

Active Reading

9 Identify As you read, underline three locations where volcanoes can form.

Plate Tectonic Boundaries and Volcano Locations Worldwide

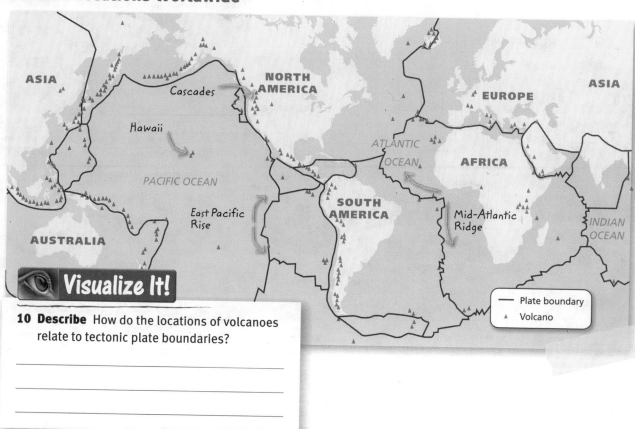

Visualize It!

10 Describe How do the locations of volcanoes relate to tectonic plate boundaries?

_____

_____

_____

At Divergent Boundaries

At divergent boundaries, plates move away from each other. The lithosphere stretches and gets thinner, so the pressure on the mantle rock below decreases. As a result, the asthenosphere bulges upward and magma forms. This magma rises through fissures in the lithosphere, out onto the land or the ocean floor.

Most divergent boundaries are on the ocean floor. When eruptions occur in these areas, undersea volcanoes develop. These volcanoes and other processes lead to the formation of a long, underwater mountain range known as a *mid-ocean ridge*. Two examples of mid-ocean ridges are the East Pacific Rise in the Pacific Ocean and the Mid-Atlantic Ridge in the Atlantic Ocean. The youngest rocks in the ocean are located at mid-ocean ridges.

Shield volcanoes and cinder cones are common in Iceland, where the Mid-Atlantic Ridge runs through the country. As the plates move away from each other, new crust forms. When a divergent boundary is located in the middle of a continent, the crust stretches until a rift valley is formed, as shown below.

Active Reading 11 **Identify** What types of volcanic landforms occur at divergent plate boundaries?

_____

_____

_____

Divergent plate boundaries create fissure eruptions and shield volcanoes.

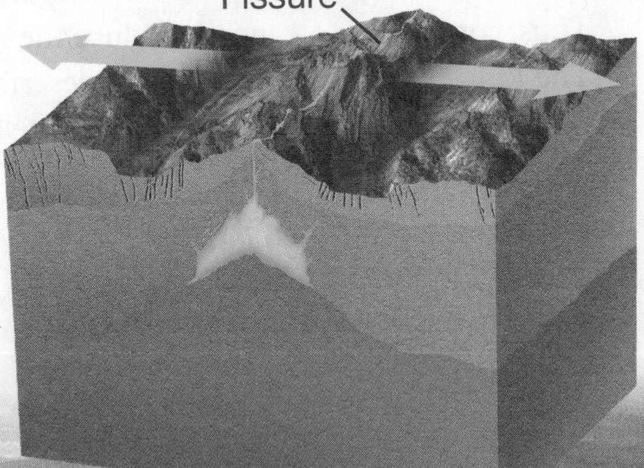

Fissure

The Great Rift Valley in Africa is a location where the crust is stretching and separating.

Tectonic plates move away from each other at divergent boundaries.

At Convergent Boundaries

At convergent boundaries, two plates move toward each other. In most cases, one plate sinks beneath the other plate. As the sinking plate dives into the mantle, fluids in the sinking plate become super heated and escape. These escaping fluids cause the rock above the sinking plate to melt and form magma. This magma rises to the surface and erupts to form volcanoes.

The magma that forms at convergent boundaries has a high concentration of fluids. As the magma rises, decreasing pressure causes the fluid trapped in the magma to form gas bubbles. But, because the magma has a high viscosity, these bubbles cannot escape easily. As the bubbles expand, the magma rises faster. Eventually, the magma can erupt explosively, forming calderas or composite volcanoes. Gas, ash, and large chunks of rock can be blown out of the volcanoes. The Cascade Range is a chain of active composite volcanoes in the northwestern United States, as shown to the right. In 1980, Mt. St. Helens erupted so violently that the entire top of the mountain was blown away.

Visualize It!

12 Identify Draw two arrows in the white boxes to indicate the direction of motion of the plates that formed the Cascade volcanoes.

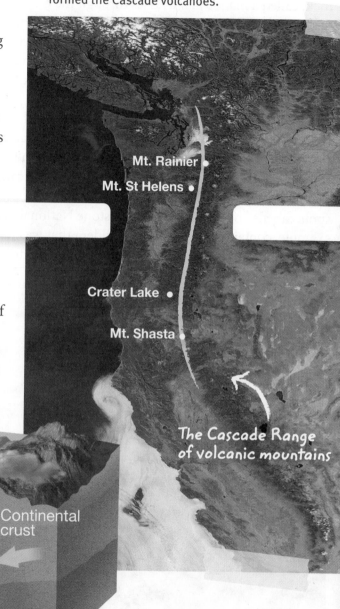

Mt. Rainier

Mt. St Helens

Crater Lake

Mt. Shasta

The Cascade Range of volcanic mountains

Tectonic plates move toward each other at convergent boundaries.

Oceanic crust

Continental crust

13 Summarize List the characteristics of divergent-boundary volcanoes and convergent-boundary volcanoes below.

Volcanoes at divergent boundaries	Volcanoes at convergent boundaries

At Hot Spots

Volcanoes can form within a plate, away from the plate boundaries. A **hot spot** is a location where a column of extremely hot mantle rock, called a *mantle plume*, rises through the asthenosphere. As the hot rock reaches the base of the lithosphere, it melts partially to form magma that can rise to the surface and form a volcano. Eruptions at a hot spot commonly form shield volcanoes. As tectonic plates move over a mantle plume, chains of volcanic mountains can form, as shown below.

The youngest Hawaiian island, the Big Island, is home to Kilauea (kih•loh•AY•uh). The Kilauea volcano is an active shield volcano located over a mantle plume. To the north and west of Kilauea is a chain of progressively-older shield volcanoes. These volcanoes were once located over the same mantle plume. Hot spots can also occur on land. Yellowstone National Park, for example, contains a huge volcanic caldera that was formed by the same mantle plume that created the Columbia Plateau.

© Houghton Mifflin Harcourt Publishing Company • Image Credits: (b) ©NOAA/NESDIS/NGDC

Visualize It!

14 Analyze Which location, *A*, *B*, or *C*, do you think is the oldest volcano? How do you know?

_____

_____

_____

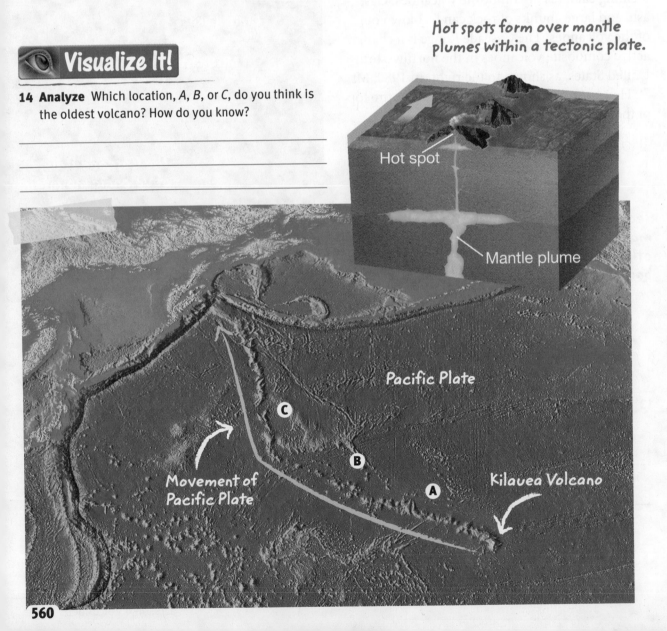

Hot spots form over mantle plumes within a tectonic plate.

Hot spot

Mantle plume

Pacific Plate

Movement of Pacific Plate

Kilauea Volcano

C

B

A

Living Near a Volcano

Volcanoes occur around the world. Many people live near volcanoes because the soils around a volcano can be very rich with essential minerals. These minerals make the soils fertile for growing a variety of crops. Living near a volcano also has its hazards. Sudden and unexpected eruptions can cause people to lose their homes and their lives.

Not All Bad
Volcanic rocks are used in jewelry, in making concrete, and in water filtration systems. Even cat litter and facial scrubs can contain volcanic rock.

Destruction
Earthquakes, fires, ash, and lava flows during an eruption can destroy entire cities.

Ash in the Air
Volcanic ash can cause breathing problems, bury crops, and damage engines. The weight of falling ash can cause buildings to collapse.

Extend

Inquiry

15 Identify Are all characteristics of volcanoes dangerous?

16 Apply Research the eruption of a specific volcano of your choice. Describe how the volcano affected the environment and the people near the volcano.

17 Design Create a poster that outlines a school safety plan for events that can occur before, during, and after a volcanic eruption.

Special Volcanoes
One Amazing Hot Spot

Did you know that there is a supervolcano right here in the US? About 30 million years ago, what is now western North America began to be pulled apart. While this area is not on a divergent boundary, movement of the North American plate caused the land to be stretched from east to west. The resulting area formed mountain ranges and valleys running north-to-south. One of these mountain ranges is the Rocky Mountains—the location of Yellowstone National Park.

Old Faithful geyser is one of the most famous features of the Yellowstone Hot Spot

The Caldera

As the land stretched and thinned, magma rose closer to the surface. This magma pushed the Earth's crust upward. When the pressure became too great, the crust cracked and exploded, leaving a huge caldera. Today, much of Yellowstone Park lies inside three separate calderas, the largest of which is about 35 miles wide and 50 miles long.

Yellowstone National Park

3rd caldera
640,000
years ago

2nd caldera
1.3 mya

1st caldera
2.1 mya

West Thumb caldera
174,000 years ago

Think Outside the Book

1 **Summarize** Find out about the hydrothermal features in Yellowstone National Park. Choose one and create a drawing that you can use to tell your classmates about that feature.

Volcanic Features

Yellowstone is home to many other features that occur as the result of volcanic activity. In fact, the area has more than 10,000 hydrothermal features, including more than 500 geysers.

Undersea Volcanoes

Most volcanoes on Earth are found on the ocean floor. In fact, if you include the height of some shield volcanoes starting from the ocean floor, they are taller than Mount Everest! According to some estimates, the floor of the Pacific Ocean has more than 75,000 volcanoes. When these volcanoes erupt in shallow water they send up large clouds of steam and ash.

Volcanoes under the ocean are called submarine volcanoes. There are two types of **submarine volcanoes**: seamounts and **guyots** (GEE • ohz). Seamounts look a lot like cinder cones do on land, but they don't reach the surface of the water. If an eruption is large enough, an island may start to form. The Lo'ihi seamount south of Hawai'i may be forming the next Hawai'ian Island. It currently rises about more than 10,000 feet off the sea floor and is within about 3,000 feet of the surface. Guyots are seamounts that have reached the surface. The top of the guyot is eroded by the waves and becomes a flat-topped mountain. Due to **subsidence**, the guyot then sinks back under the water.

Fun Fact

Rising more than 4,000 ft. above the ocean's surface but around 56,000 ft. high from its base on the ocean floor, Hawai'i's Mauna Loa is the biggest active volcano in the world!

Kavachi Seamount

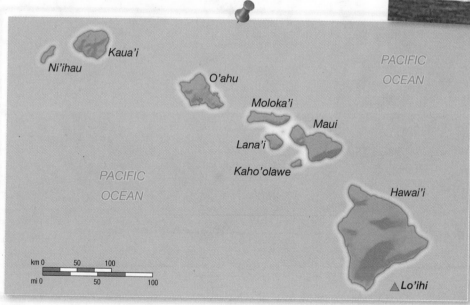

2 Analyze Use your understanding of plate tectonics to explain why the Hawai'ian islands formed in a line. What does the general direction of the line of islands tell you?

_____

_____

_____

_____

Special Volcanoes

The Big One!

On August 27, 1883 one of the largest volcanic eruptions of modern times was recorded in Indonesia (the Dutch West Indies at that time) on the Krakatoan Islands. Weeks of smaller eruptions preceded the final series of explosions. On the morning of the 27th, four explosions occurred from four different ash cones, the final one was so powerful that it ruptured the eardrums of sailors on ships 40 miles away!

This huge eruption changed the land in the area in many ways. Some islands got smaller, some got larger, some disappeared all together.

Krakatoa Volcano

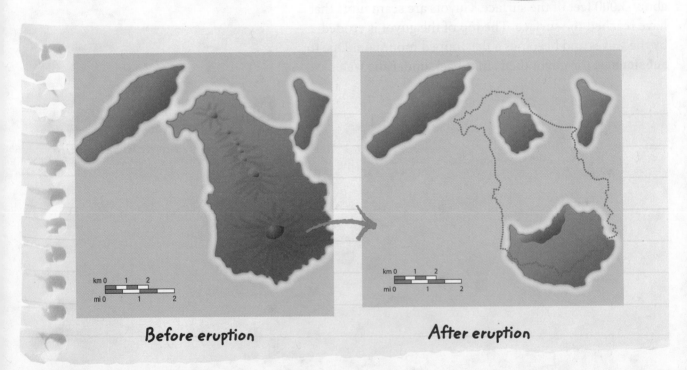

Before eruption · After eruption

Visualize It!

3 Describe How did the sea floor change as a result of the eruption?

The Biggest One

Where is the largest volcano that's ever been discovered? You might be surprised to learn that it is not on Earth, but on Mars! It is called Olympus Mons, which means Mount Olympus in Latin.

Olympus Mons is a shield volcano that is approximately the size of the state of Arizona. That's about 100 times larger than Mauna Loa, the largest volcano on Earth's surface. The largest volcano on Earth is Tamu Massif, which lies under the Pacific Ocean about 1000 miles east of Japan. Its total area is larger than that of Olympus Mons.

Viking Orbiter

Olympus Mons

Mars has many volcanoes, all of them quite large. Scientists think that the volcanoes are larger because the gravity is lower, and they erupt much more often than volcanoes on Earth. Also, there are no tectonic plates on Mars, so each volcano is over a hotspot.

No one has seen Olympus Mons in person. All the data that has been collected has come from telescope observations and space probe data.

4 Analyze Why would the lack of tectonic plates on Mars change the way the volcanoes erupt?

_____

_____

_____

_____

_____

Visual Summary

To complete this summary, check the box that indicates true or false. Then, use the key below to check your answers. You can use this page to review the main concepts of the lesson.

Lava and magma are different.

T F
18 ☐ ☐ Lava is inside Earth's crust and may contain trapped gases.

The three types of volcanic mountains are shield volcanoes, cinder cones, and composite volcanoes.

T F
19 ☐ ☐ The type of volcano shown is a shield volcano.

Volcanoes

Volcanoes can form at tectonic plate boundaries.

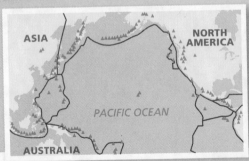

ASIA

NORTH AMERICA

PACIFIC OCEAN

AUSTRALIA

T F
20 ☐ ☐ At divergent plate boundaries, plates move toward each other.

Volcanoes can form at hot spots.

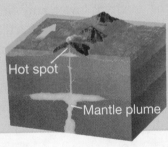

Hot spot

Mantle plume

T F
21 ☐ ☐ Hot spots are restricted to tectonic plate boundaries.

Answers: 18 False; 19 True; 20 False; 21 False

22 Explain How do volcanoes contribute to the formation of new landforms?

Lesson Review

Vocabulary

Write 1 or 2 sentences that describe the differences between the two terms.

1 magma   lava

_____

_____

2 volcano   vent

_____

_____

3 tectonic plate   hot spot

_____

_____

Key Concepts

Use the image to answer the following question.

4 Identify How did the composite volcano in the image get its layered interior?

_____

_____

5 Analyze Is pyroclastic material likely to form from low-viscosity lava or high-viscosity lava? Explain.

_____

_____

Describe the location and characteristics of the types of volcanic landforms in the table below.

Volcanic landform	Description
6 Hot-spot volcanoes	
7 Cinder cones	
8 Calderas	

Critical Thinking

9 Hypothesize In Iceland, the Mid-Atlantic Ridge runs through the center of the country. What can you conclude about the appearance of Iceland many thousands of years from now?

_____

_____

_____

_____

10 Analyze Why do you think the location surrounding the Pacific Ocean is known as the Ring of Fire?

_____

_____

_____

My Notes

Earthquakes

ESSENTIAL QUESTION

Why do earthquakes happen?

By the end of this lesson, you should be able to describe the causes of earthquakes and to identify where earthquakes happen.

8.ESS2.4, 8.ESS2.5, 8.ESS3.2

The 1995 Kobe earthquake in Japan destroyed more than 200,000 buildings and structures including this railroad track.

© Houghton Mifflin Harcourt Publishing Company • Image Credits: ©Pacific Press Service/Alamy

Engage Your Brain

1 Predict Fill in any words or numbers that you think best complete each of the statements below.

Each year there are approximately _____ earthquakes detected around the world.

In the United States, the state with the most earthquakes on average is _____

Every year, earthquakes cause _____ of dollars in damages in the United States.

Most earthquakes only last for several _____ of time.

2 Analyze Using the image, list in column 1 some of the hazards that can occur after an earthquake. In column 2, explain why you think these items or situations would be hazardous.

Hazards	Why?

Active Reading

3 Synthesize You can often define an unknown word if you know the meaning of its word parts. Use the word parts and sentence below to make an educated guess about the meaning of the word *epicenter*.

Word part	Meaning
epi-	on, upon, or over
-center	the middle

Example sentence
The <u>epicenter</u> of the earthquake was only 3 km from our school.

epicenter:

_____

_____

Vocabulary Terms

- earthquake
- focus
- epicenter
- tectonic plate boundary
- fault
- deformation
- elastic rebound

4 Apply As you learn the definition of each vocabulary term in this lesson, create your own definition or sketch to help you remember the meaning of the term.

Let's Focus

What is an earthquake?

Earthquakes can cause extreme damage and loss of life. **Earthquakes** are ground movements that occur when blocks of rock in Earth move suddenly and release energy. The energy is released as seismic waves which cause the ground to shake and tremble.

Earthquake waves can be tracked to a point below Earth's surface known as the focus. The **focus** is a place within Earth along a fault at which the first motion of an earthquake occurs. Motion along a fault causes stress. When the stress on the rock is too great, the rock will rupture and cause an earthquake. The earthquake releases the stress. Directly above the focus on Earth's surface is the **epicenter** (EP•i•sen•ter). Seismic waves flow outward from the focus in all directions.

Active Reading

5 Identify As you read, underline the definitions of *focus* and *epicenter*.

Visualize It!

6 Identify Label the epicenter, focus, and fault on the diagram.

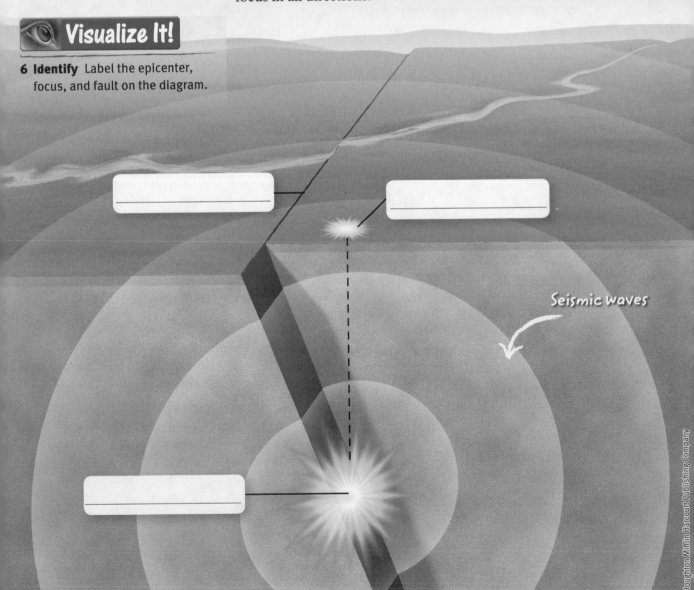

Seismic waves

© Houghton Mifflin Harcourt Publishing Company

What causes earthquakes?

Most earthquakes occur near the boundaries of tectonic plates. A **tectonic plate boundary** is where two or more tectonic plates meet. As tectonic plates move, pressure builds up near the edges of the plates. These movements break Earth's crust into a series of faults. A **fault** is a break in Earth's crust along which blocks of rock move. The release of energy that accompanies the movement of the rock along a fault causes an earthquake.

Elastic Rebound

When rock is put under tremendous pressure, stress may deform, or change the shape of, the rock. **Deformation** (dee•for•MAY•shun) is the process by which rock becomes deformed and changes shape due to stress. As stress increases, the amount of energy that is stored in the rock increases, as seen in image B to the right.

Stress can change the shape of rock along a fault. Once the stress is released, rock may return to its original shape. When rock returns to nearly the same shape after the stress is removed, the process is known as *elastic deformation*. Imagine an elastic band that is pulled tight under stress. Once stress on the elastic band is removed, there is a *snap!* The elastic band returns to its original shape. A similar process occurs during earthquakes.

Similar to an elastic band, rock along tectonic plate boundaries can suddenly return to nearly its original shape when the stress is removed. The sudden *snap* is an earthquake. The return of rock to its original shape after elastic deformation is called **elastic rebound**. Earthquakes accompany the release of energy during elastic rebound. When the rock breaks and rebounds, it releases energy as seismic waves. The seismic wave energy radiates from the focus of the earthquake in all directions. This energy causes the ground to shake for a short time. Most earthquakes last for just a few seconds.

Visualize It!

7 Compare Did an earthquake occur between images A and B or between images B and C? How do you know?

_____

_____

_____

Along a fault, rocks are pushed or pulled in different directions and at different speeds.

As stress increases and energy builds within the rock, the rock deforms but remains locked in place.

Too much stress causes the rock to break and rebound to its original shape, releasing energy.

Unstable Ground

Where do earthquakes happen?

8 Identify As you read, underline the locations where earthquakes occur.

Each year, approximately 500,000 earthquakes are detected worldwide. The map below shows some of these earthquakes. Movement of material and energy in the form of heat in Earth's interior contribute to plate motions that result in earthquakes.

Most earthquakes happen at or near tectonic plate boundaries. Tectonic plate boundaries are areas where Earth's crust experiences a lot of stress. This stress occurs because the tectonic plates are colliding, separating, or grinding past each other horizontally. There are three main types of tectonic plate boundaries: divergent, convergent, and transform. The movement and interactions of the plates causes the crust to break into different types of faults. Earthquakes happen along these faults.

Plate Tectonic Boundaries and Earthquake Locations Worldwide

The largest earthquake recorded in the United States was the 1964 Alaskan earthquake.

	Plate boundary	• Recorded earthquake
km	0 2,000 4,000	
mi	0 2,000 4,000	

The largest earthquake ever officially recorded was in Chile in 1960.

Visualize It!

9 Identify Where are most of Earth's earthquakes located? How do you know?

_____

_____

_____

At Divergent Boundaries

At a divergent boundary, plates pull apart, causing the crust to stretch. Stress that stretches rock and makes rock thinner is called *tension*. Normal faults commonly result when tension pulls rock apart.

Most of the crust at divergent boundaries is thin, so the earthquakes tend to be shallow. Most earthquakes at divergent boundaries are no more than 20 km deep. A mid-ocean ridge is an example of a divergent boundary where earthquakes occur.

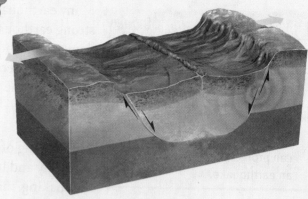

At divergent boundaries, earthquakes are common along _____ faults.

At Convergent Boundaries

Convergent plate boundaries occur when plates collide, causing rock to be squeezed. Stress that shortens or squeezes an object is known as *compression*. Compression causes the formation of reverse faults. Rocks are thrust over one another at reverse faults.

When two plates come together, both plates may crumple up to form mountains. Or one plate can subduct, or sink, underneath the other plate and into the mantle. The earthquakes that happen at convergent boundaries can be very strong. Subduction zone earthquakes occur at depths of up to 700 km.

At convergent boundaries, earthquakes are common along _____ faults.

At Transform Boundaries

A transform boundary is a place where two tectonic plates slide past each other horizontally. Stress that distorts a body by pushing different parts of the body in opposite directions is called *shear stress*. As the plates move, rocks on both sides of the fault are sheared, or broken, as they grind past one another in opposite directions.

Strike–slip faults are common at transform boundaries. Most earthquakes along the faults at transform boundaries are relatively shallow. The earthquakes are generally within the upper 50 km of the crust.

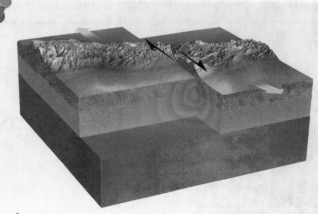

At transform boundaries, earthquakes are common along _____ faults.

What are some effects of earthquakes?

Many earthquakes do not cause major damage. However, some strong earthquakes can cause billions of dollars in property damage. Earthquakes may even cause human injuries and loss of life. In general, areas closest to the epicenter of an earthquake experience the greatest damage.

Danger to People and Structures

The shaking of an earthquake can cause structures to move vertically and horizontally. When structures cannot withstand the shaking, major destruction can occur. Following the release of seismic waves, buildings can shake so violently that a total or partial collapse can happen, as shown below.

Much of the injury and loss of life that happen during and after earthquakes is caused by structures that collapse. In addition, fires, gas leaks, floods, and polluted water supplies can cause secondary damages following an earthquake. The debris left after an earthquake can take weeks or months to clean up. Bridges, roadways, homes, and entire cities can become disaster zones.

Tsunamis

An earthquake under the ocean can cause a vertical movement of the sea floor that displaces an enormous amount of water. This displacement may cause a tsunami to form. A *tsunami* (sue•NAH•mee) is a series of extremely long waves that can travel across the ocean at speeds of up to 800 km/h. Tsunami waves travel outward in all directions from the point where the earthquake occurred. As the waves approach a shoreline, the size of the waves increases. The waves can be taller than 30 m. Tsunami waves can cause major destruction and take many lives as they smash and wash away anything in their path. Many people may drown during a tsunami. Floods, polluted water supplies, and large amount of debris are common in the aftermath.

Although most of this building is left standing, the entire area is a hazard to citizens in the town.

12 **Identify** List some of the hazards associated with earthquakes on land and underwater.

On Land	Underwater

© Houghton Mifflin Harcourt Publishing Company • Image Credits: ©PBNJ Productions/Corbis

Killer Quake

Imagine losing half the people in your city. On December 26, 2004, a massive tsunami destroyed approximately one-third of the buildings in Banda Aceh, Indonesia, and wiped out half the population.

A CHANGING WORLD

Before

Epicenter

Affected coastal areas

INDIA
MYANMAR
BANGLADESH
THAILAND
Andaman Is.
SRI LANKA
Nicobar Is.
MALDIVES
Banda Aceh
MALAYSIA
INDONESIA
INDIAN OCEAN

How Tsunamis Form

In the ocean, tsunami waves are fast but not very tall. As the waves approach a coast, they slow down and get much taller.

Before the Earthquake

The Banda Aceh tsunami resulted from a very strong earthquake in the ocean. Banda Aceh was very close to the epicenter.

Major Damages

The destruction to parts of Asia were so massive that geographers had to redraw the maps of some of the countries.

After

Extend

Inquiry

13 Identify In what ocean did the earthquake occur?

14 Research Investigate one other destructive tsunami and find out where the earthquake that caused it originated.

15 Debate Many of the people affected by the tsunami were poor. Why might earthquakes be more damaging in poor areas of the world?

Making a Connection

You've learned that volcanic eruptions frequently occur along plate boundaries and that earthquakes occur along plate boundaries. Is there a connection? Let's investigate! Check out the maps on the following pages.

Skills

✓ Analyze data

✓ Construct an explanation

✓ Make a hypothesis

Plate Tectonic Boundaries and Earthquake Locations Worldwide

My Notes

Plate Tectonic Boundaries and Earthquake Locations Worldwide

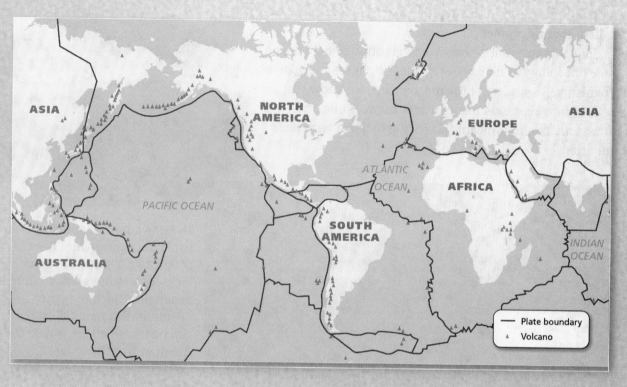

![Visualize It!]

1 Summarize What do you notice about the locations of the earthquakes and the volcanoes on both maps? Is there a pattern? Do all earthquakes and volcanoes follow this pattern? Explain. What is the relationship between this pattern and plate tectonics?

_____

_____

_____

_____

_____

_____

_____

_____

_____

_____

Hot, Hot, Hot!

Earthquakes and volcanoes also occur in the middle of plates, at locations called **hotspots**. Older theories proposed that there were "fixed" locations in the mantle where the lava came from, so-called "mantle plumes".

Hot spots continue to be an actively studied field in the science of geology as new research sheds light on alternative mechanisms. Regardless of the mechanism, we know that these locations represent places where the volcanic activity is not exactly like the volcanic activity associated with plate boundaries.

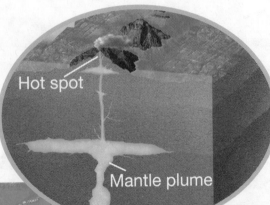

Hot spot

Mantle plume

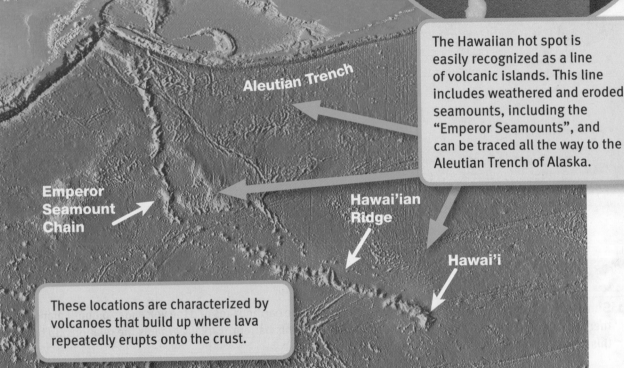

Aleutian Trench

Emperor Seamount Chain

Hawai'ian Ridge

Hawai'i

The Hawaiian hot spot is easily recognized as a line of volcanic islands. This line includes weathered and eroded seamounts, including the "Emperor Seamounts", and can be traced all the way to the Aleutian Trench of Alaska.

These locations are characterized by volcanoes that build up where lava repeatedly erupts onto the crust.

Visualize It!

2 Hypothosize Notice the bend from the Hawaiian Ridge to the Emperor Seamount Chain in the diagram. What do you think the bend in the chain tells scientists who are studying plate motion?

_____

_____

_____

_____

_____

_____

Fire and Ice

Iceland is another recognizable hot spot. Volcanic activity creates new ocean crust and provides a source of geothermal (heat from the earth) energy for Icelanders. In fact, underground hot springs produce heat for 95% of the buildings in Reykjavik, Iceland's capital.

Geothermal energy facility in Reykjavik, Iceland

Volcano Locations in Iceland

North American Plate

Eurasian Plate

ICELAND

N W E S

Mid-Atlantic Ridge

ATLANTIC OCEAN

km 0   100   200

3 Conclude What kind of plate tectonic boundary is shown in the diagram? What evidence supports your conclusion?

_____

_____

_____

_____

_____

4 Hypothesize Look back at the diagram showing the plate boundaries and location of volcanoes. What is unique about the island of Iceland? Hypothesize a reason for this situation.

_____

_____

_____

_____

_____

_____

The New Madrid Fault

When we think of earthquake hazards in the US, we usually thinkof California, for good reason. Earthquakes occurring in this seismically active area are frequently in the news. But did you know that within the central part of the United States lies a seismically active area?

The New Madrid seismic zone is located along the borders of Missouri, Arkansas, Tennessee, Kentucky, and Illinois. Scientists actively monitor this area for earthquakes.

Skills

✓ Analyze data

✓ Construct an explanation using data

Detail of the USGS Hazard map

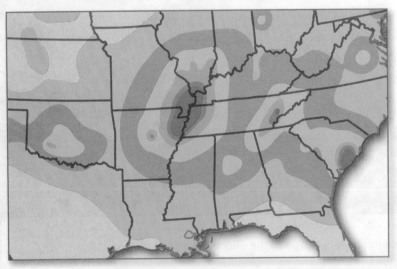

YOU ARE STANDING ON THE NEW MADRID FAULT LINE

During a 3 month period from December to January, 1811 -1812, New Madrid, Missouri was shaken by a series of unexpected earthquakes.

Earth's Tectonic Plates

Earth's crust is broken up into several large tectonic plates. The boundaries where these plates meet are all places of intense activity, including the creation and destruction of plates. The stresses that begin at the plate boundaries are not isolated, but are transferred throughout the rigid plates.

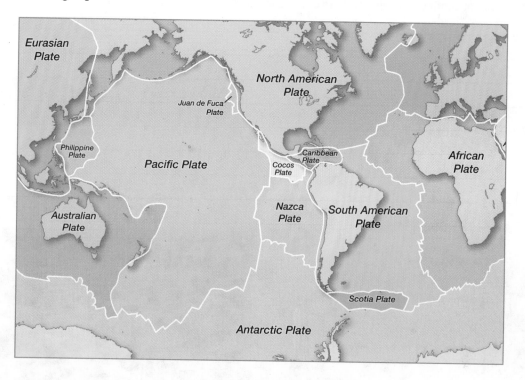

The hazard map below shows the areas of the contiguous United States that are most likely to experience a large amount of horizontal shaking as a result of an earthquake.

The USGS Hazard Map

The New Madrid Fault

Visualize It!

1 Explain Using the map of plate boundaries as a reference, explain the areas of high seismic hazard (colored in red) in the map of the United States. Why is the risk not confined to only the edge of the continent?

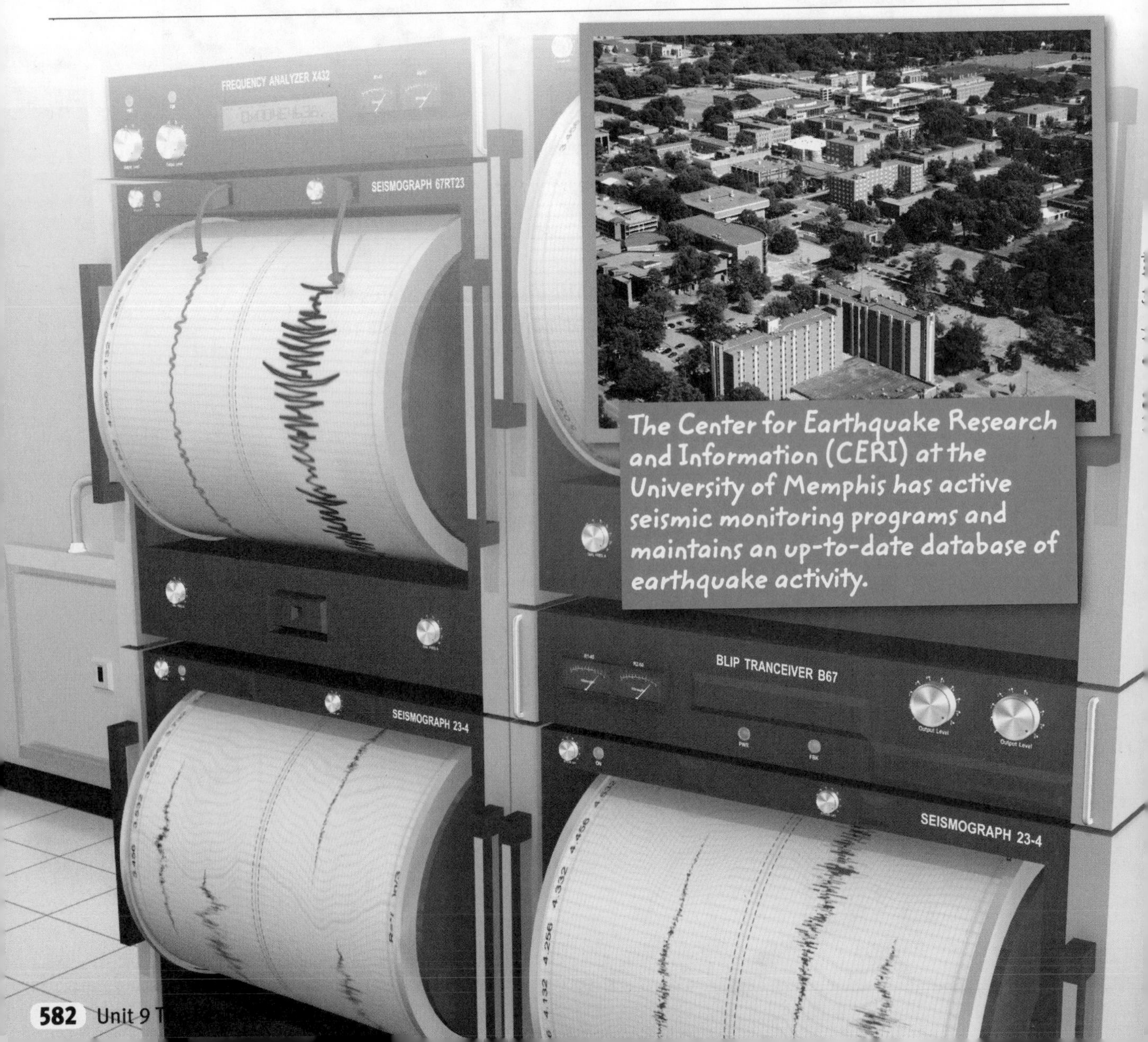

_____

_____

_____

_____

_____

_____

_____

_____

The Center for Earthquake Research and Information (CERI) at the University of Memphis has active seismic monitoring programs and maintains an up-to-date database of earthquake activity.

This map displays earthquakes of 2.0+ magnitude recorded over a 30-day period (January 2017) along Tennessee's borders. Earthquakes occurring along Line A-B are recorded in the cross-section below at different depths.

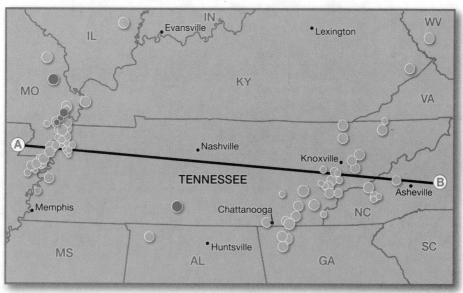

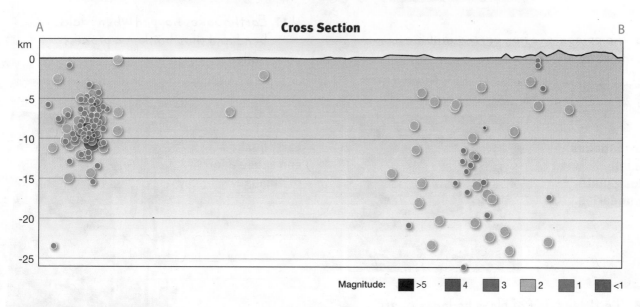

Visualize It!

2 Conclude What does this data tell you about the geology beneath eastern and western Tennessee?

_____

_____

_____

_____

_____

_____

Visual Summary

To complete this summary, fill in the correct word. Then use the key below to check your answers. You can use this page to review the main concepts of the lesson.

Earthquakes

Earthquakes occur along faults.

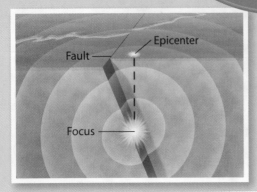

Epicenter

Fault

Focus

16 The epicenter of an earthquake is directly above the _____

Rocks break and snap back to their original shape in an earthquake.

17 Earthquakes happen when rocks bend and snap back in a process called _____

Earthquakes usually happen along plate boundaries.

18 The three types of plate boundaries are

_____

_____

_____

Earthquakes can cause a lot of damage.

19 An example of the dangers of earthquakes is _____

Answers: 16 focus; 17 elastic rebound; 18 divergent, convergent, and transform; 19 building collapse

20 Hypothesize Can earthquakes be prevented?

_____

_____

Lesson Review

Vocabulary

In your own words, define the following terms.

1 Elastic rebound

_____

_____

_____

2 Focus

_____

_____

_____

3 Fault

_____

_____

_____

Key Concepts

Example	Type of Boundary
4 Identify Most of the earthquakes in Japan are a result of one plate sinking under another.	
5 Identify The African Rift Valley is a location where plates are moving apart.	
6 Identify The San Andreas fault is a location where tectonic plates move horizontally past each other.	

7 Explain What causes an earthquake?

_____

_____

_____

_____

Critical Thinking

Use the image to answer the following questions.

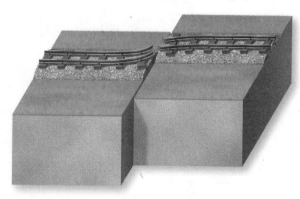

8 Analyze How does the image demonstrate that deformation has taken place?

_____

_____

_____

_____

9 Apply How does Earth's surface and the structures on the surface change as a result of an earthquake?

_____

_____

_____

_____

_____

10 Hypothesize Why do you think there is often only a short amount of time to evacuate an area before an earthquake?

_____

_____

_____

_____

My Notes

Measuring Earthquake Waves

ESSENTIAL QUESTION

How are seismic waves used to study earthquakes?

By the end of this lesson, you should be able to understand how seismic waves are useful in determining the strength, location, and effects of an earthquake.

8.ESS2.2, 8.ESS2.4, 8.ESS3.2

This map shows the ground movement and shaking intensity of the 1906 earthquake that struck San Francisco. The areas that suffered the most damage are shown in red. The areas shown in green suffered the least damage.

©Houghton Mifflin Harcourt Publishing Company • Image Credits: (bg) ©USGS/Photo Researchers, Inc.

 **Lesson Labs**

Quick Labs
- Earthquakes and Buildings
- Locating an Earthquake's Epicenter

S.T.E.M. Lab
- Use a Seismograph to Determine the Amount of Energy in an Earthquake

 **Engage Your Brain**

1 Predict Check T or F to show whether you think each statement is true or false.

T   F

☐   ☐   Earthquakes often occur along faults.

☐   ☐   Earthquakes produce two main kinds of seismic waves.

☐   ☐   More than one kind of scale can be used to measure the magnitude of an earthquake.

☐   ☐   Older buildings tend to withstand earthquakes better than newer buildings.

2 Describe This graph shows the progression of an earthquake. How might this graph indicate the strength of an earthquake?

_____

_____

_____

_____

Active Reading

3 Synthesize Many English words have their roots in other languages. Use the Greek words below to make a guess about the meaning of the words *seismometer* and *seismogram*.

Greek word	Meaning
seismos	earthquake
metron	measure
gramma	writing

Example sentence
The <u>seismometer</u> recorded a series of weak earthquakes.

seismometer:

_____

Example sentence
The <u>seismogram</u> printout indicated that a small earthquake had just occurred.

seismogram:

_____

Vocabulary Terms
- focus
- epicenter
- seismic waves
- seismogram
- magnitude
- intensity

4 Apply As you learn the definition of each vocabulary term in this lesson, create your own definition or sketch to help you remember the meaning of the term.

Shake, Rattle, and Roll

What happens during an earthquake?

Have you ever felt the ground move under your feet? Many people have. Every day, somewhere in the world, earthquakes happen. An earthquake occurs when blocks of rock move suddenly and release energy. This energy travels through rock as waves.

Movement Takes Place Along a Fault

Earth's lithosphere (LITH•uh•sfir) is the rocky outer layer of Earth that includes the crust. The lithosphere is made up of large plates. These plates pull apart, push together, or move past one another. As plates move, stress on rocks at or near the edges of the plates increases. This stress causes faults to form. A *fault* is a break in a body of rock along which one block moves relative to another. Stress along faults causes the rocks to deform, or change from their original shape. If this stress becomes too great, rocks along a fault will break and move along the fault. Once rocks break, the pieces of broken rock return to an undeformed shape. When rocks along a fault break and move along a fault, energy is released into the surrounding rock in the form of waves. This process is what causes earthquakes.

Active Reading

5 Identify As you read, underline the definition of a fault.

6 Sequence Fill in the cause-and-effect chain for earthquakes.

A Stress builds up on rocks along a fault, and the rocks deform. The rocks break suddenly, and the pieces return to an undeformed shape.

B _____

Seismic waves caused extensive damage to structures during this 1995 earthquake in Japan.

Energy Is Released as Seismic Waves

As stress builds up in rocks along a fault, the energy that is stored in the deforming rock increases. When the rock breaks, the rocks on either side of the fault slip past one another and return to an undeformed state. The location along a fault at which the first motion of an earthquake takes place is called the **focus**. The **epicenter** is the point on Earth's surface directly above an earthquake's starting point or focus. A large amount of stored energy is released when rocks along a fault slip. This energy travels away from the focus and through Earth in all directions as seismic (SYZ•mik) waves. **Seismic waves** are vibrations that cause different types of ground motion. The strength of an earthquake is based on the energy that is released as rocks break and return to an undeformed shape.

Energy moves outward from the water drop as ripples on the water.

 Visualize It!

7 Compare How are the ripples that are moving through the water in this pond similar to seismic waves that travel through Earth? How are they different?

_____

_____

_____

C Seismic waves travel through Earth and along Earth's surface.

D _____

_____

_____

Waves of Motion

What are two kinds of seismic waves?

Earthquakes are the result of the movement of energy through Earth as seismic waves. There are two kinds of seismic waves, body waves and surface waves. Each kind of wave travels through Earth in different ways and at different speeds. The speed of a seismic wave depends on the material through which the wave travels.

Body Waves

You are probably familiar with ocean waves or sound waves. Like all waves, seismic waves carry energy. *Body waves* are seismic waves that travel through Earth's interior. P waves, or pressure waves, are the fastest body waves. P waves are also called *primary waves* because they are always the first seismic waves to be detected by instruments that monitor earthquakes. P waves can travel through solids, liquids, and gases. They cause rock to move back and forth in the direction the wave is traveling.

S waves, or shear waves, are a second kind of body wave. S waves move rock from side to side. Unlike P waves, S waves cannot travel through the completely liquid parts of Earth. Also, S waves are slower than P waves. Thus, another name for S waves is *secondary waves*.

© Houghton Mifflin Harcourt Publishing Company

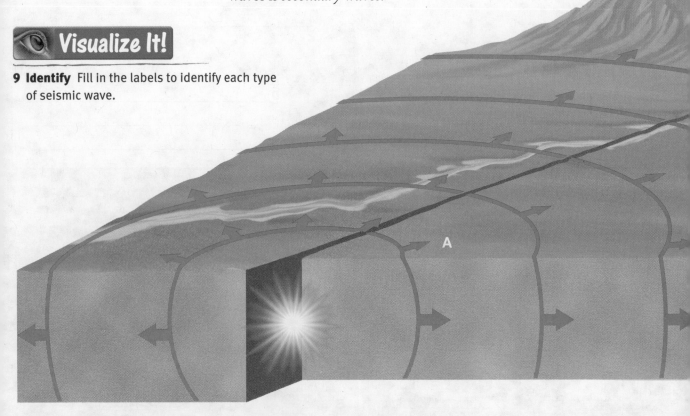

A

Visualize It!

9 Identify Fill in the labels to identify each type of seismic wave.

Surface Waves

Seismic waves that travel along the surface of Earth rather than through it are called *surface waves*. Surface waves produce motion only on Earth's surface. Surface waves are slower than both P and S waves. However, because their energy is focused on Earth's surface, surface waves cause more damage than these body waves.

Surface waves produce two types of ground motion as they move along Earth's surface. The first is a rolling, up-and-down motion that dies out with depth. This motion occurs in the same direction as the direction in which the wave is traveling. Surface waves also produce a back-and-forth motion. This motion is perpendicular to the direction in which the wave is traveling.

10 Compare How do surface waves differ from body waves?

_____

_____

_____

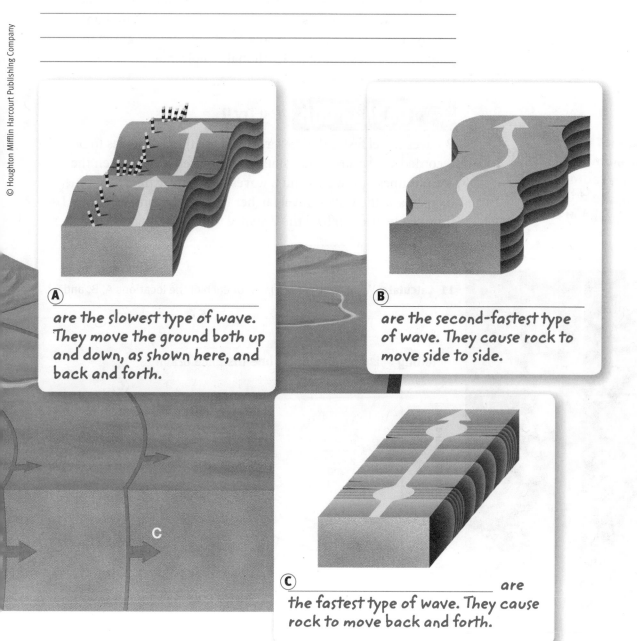

A _____ are the slowest type of wave. They move the ground both up and down, as shown here, and back and forth.

B _____ are the second-fastest type of wave. They cause rock to move side to side.

C _____ are the fastest type of wave. They cause rock to move back and forth.

Wave Action!

How are seismic waves measured?

Imagine walls shaking, windows rattling, and glasses and dishes clinking. After only seconds, the vibrating stops. Within minutes, news reports give information about the strength and the location of the earthquake. How could scientists learn this information so quickly? Scientists use instruments called *seismometers* to record the seismic waves generated by earthquakes. Seismometers are located at seismometer stations that are arranged in networks. When seismic waves reach a seismometer, the seismometer produces a seismogram. A **seismogram** is a tracing of earthquake motion. Seismograms also record the arrival times of seismic waves at a seismometer station. Seismograms are plotted on a graph like the one shown below. Scientists use the graph to pinpoint the location of an earthquake's epicenter.

Seismometers located at seismometer stations produce seismograms that make a tracing of earthquake motion.

Do the Math You Try It

P waves travel faster than S waves and are the first waves to be recorded at a seismometer station. The difference between the arrival times of P waves and S waves is called *lag time*. Lag time increases as the waves travel farther from their point of origin. Lag time can be used to find the distance to an earthquake's epicenter.

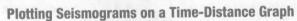

Identify

11 Calculate What are the lag times for each of the locations A, B, and C?

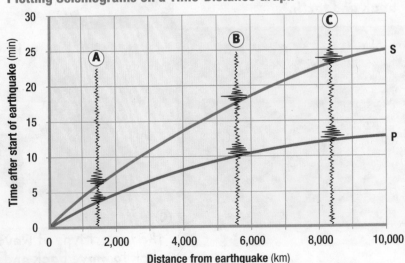

Plotting Seismograms on a Time-Distance Graph

© Houghton Mifflin Harcourt Publishing Company • Image Credits: ©Romeo Gacad/AFP/Getty Images

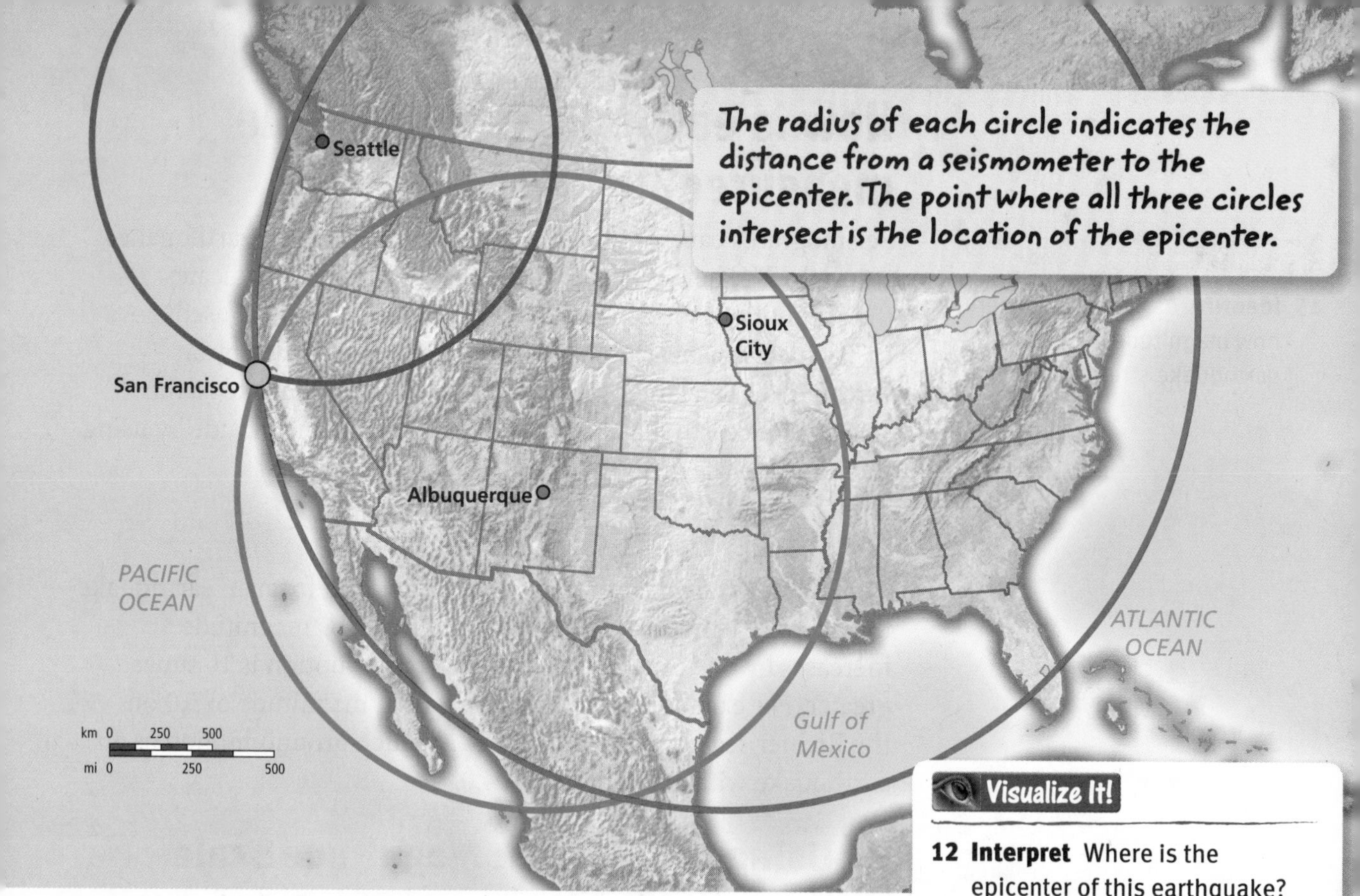

The radius of each circle indicates the distance from a seismometer to the epicenter. The point where all three circles intersect is the location of the epicenter.

Seattle

Sioux City

San Francisco

Albuquerque

PACIFIC OCEAN

ATLANTIC OCEAN

Gulf of Mexico

km 0   250   500
mi 0   250   500

Visualize It!

12 Interpret Where is the epicenter of this earthquake? Explain how you know.

_____

_____

_____

How is an earthquake's epicenter located?

Scientists use the data from seismograms to find an earthquake's epicenter. The S-P time method is an easy way to locate the epicenter of an earthquake. The method is based on the differences in arrival times of P and S waves, called lag time, at different seismometer stations. Lag time tells scientists how far waves have traveled from the epicenter. The epicenter of the earthquake can then be located by drawing circles around at least three seismometer stations on a map, as shown above. The radius of each circle is equal to the distance from that seismometer station to the earthquake's epicenter. The point at which all of the circles intersect is the epicenter. This process is called *triangulation*. Today, computers perform these calculations.

Active Reading **13 Identify** What is the name of the process used to locate an earthquake's epicenter?

_____

_____

Think Outside the Book Inquiry

14 Research With a classmate, research recent earthquake activity in your state. Present your findings in an oral report.

How is earthquake magnitude measured?

🗎 Active Reading

15 Identify As you read, underline how magnitude is related to earthquake strength.

Seismograms can also provide information about an earthquake's strength. The height of the waves on a seismogram indicates the amount of ground motion. Ground motion can be used to calculate **magnitude**, the measure of energy released by an earthquake. The larger the magnitude of an earthquake is, the stronger the earthquake. Seismologists express magnitude by using the Richter scale or the Moment Magnitude scale.

By Using the Richter Scale

The Richter scale measures the ground motion from an earthquake to find the earthquake's strength. Each time the magnitude increases by one unit, the measured ground motion is 10 times greater. For example, an earthquake with a magnitude of 5.0 on the Richter scale produces 10 times as much ground motion as an earthquake with a magnitude of 4.0.

By Using the Moment Magnitude Scale

The Moment Magnitude scale has largely replaced the Richter scale. Moment magnitude measures earthquake strength based on the size of the area of the fault that moves, the average distance that the fault moves, and the rigidity of the rocks in the fault. The Moment Magnitude scale is more accurate for large earthquakes than the Richter scale is. The moment magnitude of an earthquake is expressed by a number. The larger the number is, the stronger the earthquake was. The largest earthquake ever recorded took place in Chile and registered a moment magnitude of 9.5.

16 Identify After the Chilean earthquake in 1960, which has been the strongest earthquake in the last 100 years?

_____

_____

Year	Location	Moment Magnitude
2011	Tōhoku, Japan	9.0
2010	Port-au-Prince, Haiti	7.0
1994	Northridge, California	6.7
1964	Prince William Sound, Alaska	9.2
1960	Southern Chile	9.5

The 1964 earthquake on Kodiak Island, Alaska, measured 9.2 on the Moment Magnitude scale.

How is earthquake intensity measured?

The effects of an earthquake and how the earthquake is felt by people are known as the earthquake's **intensity**. An earthquake's magnitude is different from its intensity. Magnitude measures how much energy is released by an earthquake. Intensity measures the effects of an earthquake at Earth's surface.

The Modified Mercalli scale is used to describe an earthquake's intensity. The scale ranges from I to XII. Earthquakes that have an intensity value of I are barely noticeable. Earthquakes that have an intensity value of XII cause total destruction. Intensity values vary from place to place and are usually highest near the epicenter of the earthquake.

Visualize It!

17 Infer Describe the damage that you see in the photograph.

_____

_____

_____

Intensity	Description
I	felt by very few people under especially favorable conditions
II	felt by few people at rest; some suspended items may swing
III	felt by most people indoors; vibrations feel like passing trucks
IV	felt by many people; windows or dishes rattle
V	felt by nearly everyone; some objects are broken or overturned
VI	felt by all people; heavy objects are moved; slight damage to structures
VII	causes slight to moderate damage to buildings; chimneys may topple
VIII	causes considerable damage to ordinary buildings; some partial collapse
IX	causes considerable damage to earthquake-resistant buildings
X	destroys many structures, including foundations; rails are bent
XI	destroys most structures; bridges destroyed; rails are bent
XII	causes total destruction; objects tossed through the air

Not all earthquakes result in catastrophic damage. During this earthquake, only moderate damage occurred.

Damage Control

What factors determine the effects of an earthquake?

The effects of an earthquake can vary over a wide area. Four factors determine the effects of an earthquake on a given area. These factors are magnitude, the local geology, the distance from the epicenter, and the type of construction used in an area.

Magnitude

Recall that an earthquake's magnitude is directly related to its strength. Stronger earthquakes cause more ground motion and, thus, cause more damage than weaker earthquakes. As an earthquake's magnitude increases, the intensity of an earthquake is commonly higher.

Local Geology

The amount of damage caused by an earthquake also depends on the material through which seismic waves travel. In general, solid rock is not likely to increase an earthquake's intensity. However, seismic waves can become more dangerous when they travel through loose soils and sediments that are saturated with water. When water-saturated soil or sediment is shaken by seismic waves, the soil and sediment particles become completely surrounded by water. This process, which is shown below, is called *liquefaction*. Liquefaction can intensify ground shaking or cause the ground to settle. Settling can cause structures to tilt or collapse.

18 Apply Why would it be potentially dangerous to build a home or building on loose soil or sediment?

_____

_____

_____

Grains in silty or sandy soils are normally in contact with one another, which gives the soil strength and stiffness.

When ground shaking occurs, the grains lose contact with one another, and the strength of the soil decreases.

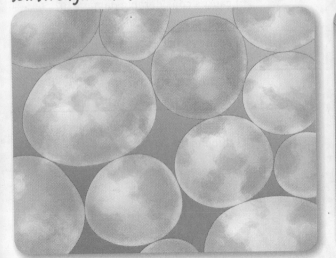

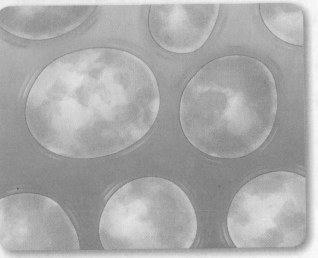

Distance from the Epicenter

Surface waves, which move along Earth's surface, are the most destructive of all seismic waves. The more energy a surface wave carries, the stronger the ground motion will be and the more damage the wave will cause. However, surface waves decrease in size and energy the farther that they travel from the epicenter of an earthquake. Therefore, the farther an area is located from the epicenter, the less damage it will suffer.

Building Construction

The materials with which structures are built also determine the amount of earthquake damage. Flexible structures are more likely to survive strong ground shaking. Structures that are made of brick or concrete are not very flexible and are easily damaged. Wood and steel are more flexible. Taller buildings are more susceptible to damage than shorter buildings. This diagram shows technologies in use that control how much tall buildings sway during earthquakes. Other technologies are designed to prevent seismic waves from moving through buildings.

Visualize It!

19 Apply How are mass dampers and active tendon systems similar in the way they protect a building from earthquake damage?

_____

_____

_____

_____

A **mass damper** is a weight placed in the roof of a building. Motion sensors detect building movement during an earthquake and send messages to a computer. The computer then signals controls in the roof to shift the mass damper to counteract the building's movement.

The **active tendon system** works much like the mass damper system in the roof. Sensors notify a computer that the building is moving. Then the computer activates devices to shift a large weight to counteract the movement.

Base isolators act as shock absorbers during an earthquake. They are made of layers of rubber and steel wrapped around a lead core. Base isolators absorb seismic waves and prevent the waves from traveling through the building.

Visual Summary

To complete this summary, fill in the blanks. Then use the key below to check your answers. You can use this page to review the main concepts of the lesson.

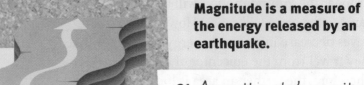

Seismic waves are vibrations that cause ground motion during earthquakes.

20 Seismic waves are caused by _____ traveling through rock.

Magnitude is a measure of the energy released by an earthquake.

21 An earthquake's magnitude can be measured using the _____ and the _____

Measuring Earthquake Waves

Seismic waves are measured by instruments.

22 Instruments called _____ are used to record the arrival times of P waves and S waves.

Different factors determine the effects of earthquakes.

23 The effects of an earthquake are determined by the earthquake's magnitude, _____, distance from the _____, and _____

24 **Evaluate** How many seismometers are needed to determine the location of the epicenter of an earthquake? Explain.

Lesson Review

Vocabulary

Fill in the blank with the term that best completes the following sentences.

1 The tracings of seismometers are called

_____

2 An earthquake's _____ is located directly above its _____

3 The _____ of an earthquake is a measure of its strength.

Key Concepts

4 Summarize What causes an earthquake?

_____

_____

_____

5 Contrast How is the motion of P waves different from the motion of S waves?

_____

_____

_____

_____

6 Compare What is the difference between earthquake magnitude and intensity?

_____

_____

_____

_____

7 Explain How is distance from the epicenter related to the amount of earthquake damage?

_____

_____

_____

Critical Thinking

Use the time-distance graph to answer the following questions.

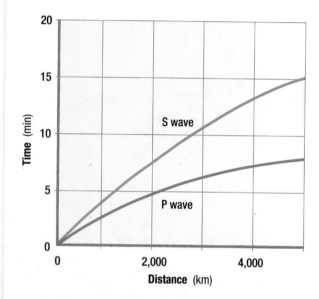

8 Identify What is the lag time at 2,000 km from the earthquake's epicenter?

_____

9 Calculate The average speed of P waves is 6.1 km/s, and the average speed of S waves is 4.1 km/s. Use the following equation to calculate how long each wave type takes to travel 100 km: 100 km ÷ average speed of the wave = time.

_____

10 Calculate Find the lag time for earthquake waves at 100 km by subtracting the time P waves take to travel 100 km from the time S waves take to travel 100 km.

_____

11 Assess Why would surface waves be more damaging to buildings than P waves or S waves?

_____

_____

_____

My Notes

Engineering Design Process

Skills	Objectives

Skills
Identify a need
Conduct research
✓ Brainstorm solutions
✓ Select a solution
Design a prototype
✓ Build a prototype
✓ Test and evaluate
✓ Redesign to improve
✓ Communicate results

Objectives

- Explain how scientists measure the energy of earthquakes.
- Design a model seismometer to measure motion.
- Test and modify a prototype to achieve a desired result.

Building a Seismometer

An earthquake occurs when rocks beneath the ground move suddenly. The energy of this movement travels through Earth in waves. Sometimes the shaking is detected hundreds or thousands of miles away from the origin of the earthquake. Scientists can learn about earthquakes by measuring the earthquake waves.

Measuring Motion

A seismometer is a device for measuring the motion of the ground beneath it. To develop seismometers, scientists had to solve a problem: How do you keep one part of the device from moving when the ground moves? The solution can be seen in the design shown here. A spring separates a heavy weight from the frame of the seismometer. Attached to the weight is a pen. The tip of the pen touches the surface of a circular drum that is covered in paper and slowly turning. When the ground moves, the frame and the rotating drum move along with it. The spring absorbs the ground's movement, so the weight and pen do not move. The pen is always touching the paper on the rotating drum. When the ground is not moving, the pen draws a straight line. When the ground moves, the pen draws this movement.

1 Infer This instrument measures the up-and-down motion of earthquake waves. How would you have to change the instrument to measure side-to-side motion of an earthquake?

_____

_____

_____

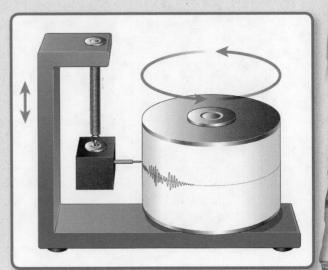

Waves move the instrument, but the spring and weight keep the pen still.

2 Infer In the oval below, write *moves* or *still* to indicate whether the labeled part moves during an earthquake or remains still.

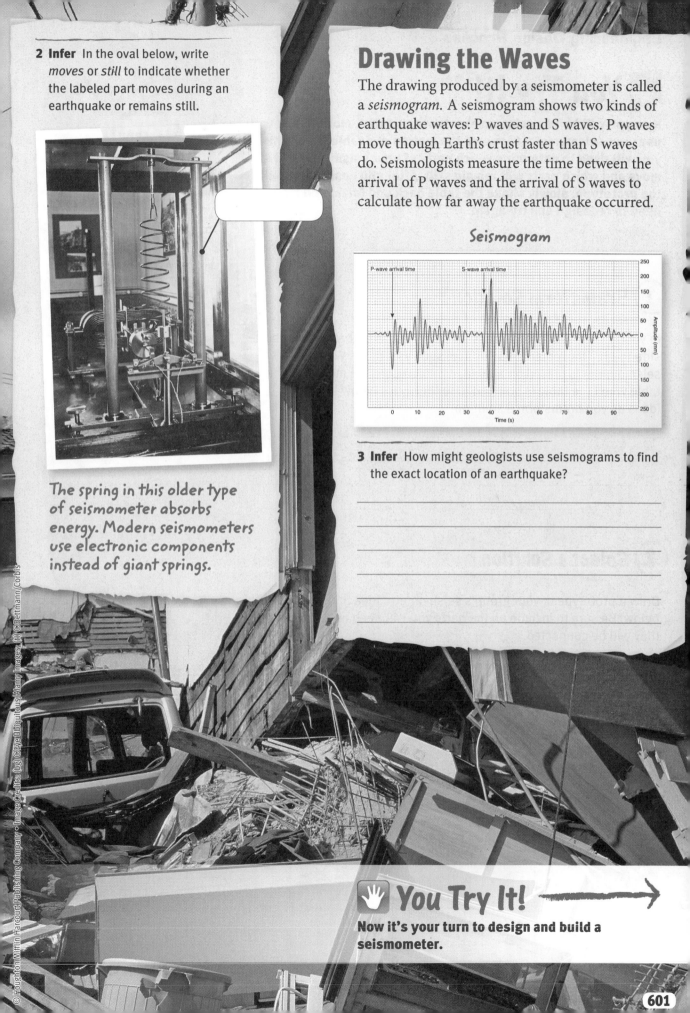

The spring in this older type of seismometer absorbs energy. Modern seismometers use electronic components instead of giant springs.

Drawing the Waves

The drawing produced by a seismometer is called a *seismogram*. A seismogram shows two kinds of earthquake waves: P waves and S waves. P waves move though Earth's crust faster than S waves do. Seismologists measure the time between the arrival of P waves and the arrival of S waves to calculate how far away the earthquake occurred.

Seismogram

3 Infer How might geologists use seismograms to find the exact location of an earthquake?

_____

_____

_____

_____

_____

_____

✋ **You Try It!**

Now it's your turn to design and build a seismometer.

You Try It!

Now you will build a seismometer that can detect motion. You will use your seismometer to record the motion of a table. To do this, you will need to determine which parts of your seismometer will move and which parts will remain still. After you design and build the prototype, slowly shake the table back and forth. You may need to redesign and try again.

You Will Need

✔ large square wooden frame

✔ metal weights

✔ string

✔ fine point felt tip pen

✔ long strips or roll of paper

✔ tape

✔ various hooks and hardware

① Brainstorm Solutions

In your group, brainstorm ideas for a seismometer that will measure side-to-side movement of a surface, such as a table. When the seismometer is placed on a table, it must record the motion of the table when the table is bumped. Use the space below to record ideas as you brainstorm a solution.

_____

_____

_____

_____

② Select a Solution

Draw a prototype of your group's seismometer idea in the space below. Be sure to include all the parts you will need and show how they will be connected.

③ Build a Prototype

In your group, build the seismometer. As the group builds it, are there some aspects of the design that cannot be assembled as predicted? What did the group have to revise in the prototype?

_____

_____

_____

_____

④ Test and Evaluate

Bump or shake the table under the seismometer. Did the prototype record any motion on the paper strip? If not, what can you revise?

_____

_____

_____

_____

⑤ Redesign to Improve

Choose one aspect to revise, and then test again. Keep making revisions, one at a time, until your seismometer records the motion of the table. How many revisions did the group make?

_____

_____

⑥ Communicate Results

Report your observations about the prototype seismometer. Include changes that improved its performance or decreased its performance. Propose ways that you could have built a more accurate seismometer. Describe what additional materials you would need and what they would be used for.

_____

_____

_____

_____

Distribution of Earth's Resources

ESSENTIAL QUESTION

How are Earth's resources distributed?

By the end of this lesson, you should be able to describe natural resources and explain their distribution.

8.ESS3.1

The appropriately named 'Big Hole' in Kimberley, South Africa was an active diamond mine until 1914. Since then, the hole has filled with water to the height of the area's water table.

Engage Your Brain

1 Predict Check T or F to show whether you think each statement is true or false.

T F

Groundwater is mainly used to heat people's homes. _____

Oil deposits started forming before the dinosaurs lived. _____

A diamond is carbon that was exposed to extreme heat and pressure. _____

Natural gas forms as quickly as humans use it.

_____

2 Analyze Think about your daily activities, and list some of the items you use that are made from a part of nature.

_____

_____

_____

_____

_____

_____

_____

_____

_____

✏️ Active Reading

3 Apply Many scientific words, such as weather, have more than one meaning. Use context clues to write your own definition for each meaning of the word weather.

_____

_____

_____

_____

_____

Vocabulary Terms
- natural resource
- renewable resource
- nonrenewable resource
- fossil fuel   • mineral resource
- aquifer   • groundwater
- water table

4 Identify This list contains key terms you'll learn in this lesson. As you read, circle the definition of each term.

Earth's Bounty

5 Read As you read, underline examples of natural resources.

What is a natural resource?

For any living creature, an important survival skill is being resourceful. Being resourceful means using the materials around you to your advantage. Over time, humans have become more and more resourceful at using what nature provides, or natural resources, to make life easier and more comfortable.

A **natural resource** is a material or substance that exists freely on earth and is necessary or useful to humans. Forests, soil, rocks, fresh water, minerals, oil and animals are all examples of Earth's natural resources.

Most of the products that we use every day come from the Earth's natural resources.

Earth's Natural Resources

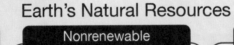

Alternative Energy Resources

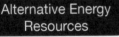

solar energy   wind energy

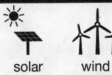

geothermal energy   hydro energy

Nonrenewable Resources

oil   non-metallic minerals   metallic minerals

coal   natural gas   nuclear material

Renewable Resources

soil   water   plants

animals   forests   fish

Products of Natural Resources

How are different natural resources used?

Do you ever have to turn the heat on in your home? Does the transportation you take to school run on gas or electricity? Do you drink bottled water or water from the faucet? If you answered yes to any of those questions, you use natural resources. We use and encounter natural resources and their products on a daily basis, even if we are not always aware of it.

Making products

Mineral resources are natural deposits of solid inorganic material. Minerals can be made of a single element, such as gold (Au), or a compound like table salt (NaCl). Like the elements from which they are made, minerals can be categorized as metallic or non-metallic. Rock is made from a combination of two or more minerals. Limestone, for example is made from the minerals calcite and aragonite. Minerals are mined from the earth and can be used in a variety of ways.

Fossil Fuel

A **fossil fuel** is natural resource that was formed millions of years ago from the remains of plants and animals. The most common fossil fuels are coal, oil and natural gas. In the United States, we have deposits of all three of these natural fuel resources. We use them for energy to heat our homes, to produce electricity and for transportation.

Active Reading

6 Identify As you read, underline the three types of fossil fuels.

Mineral Resources	
Mineral	Use
Copper	cookware, electrical wires
Diamond	blades, grinding wheels, jewelry
Gold	jewelry, coins, computers
Halite	table salt
Quartz	glass making, sand blasting, gemstones
Sulfur	fireworks, fertilizers
Talc	plastics, cosmetics, paint
Zinc	ointment, prevent rusting

Underground pressure can cause oil to gush up to the surface in a powerful stream when it is first disturbed. Luckily, engineers have created a way to control and collect this burst of oil.

Over time, as the pressure is relieved, oil comes to the surface more slowly and pumps are used to coax more oil out of the underground reserve.

© Houghton Mifflin Harcourt Publishing Company • Image Credits: (b) ©Bettmann/Getty Images; (b) CORBIS RF

Drinking Water

Groundwater is a valuable natural resource for people all over the world. Millions depend on it for drinking water and to irrigate crops. Groundwater starts as rain or melted snow that seeps into the earth and collects in porous rocks called **aquifers**. Natural springs can bring this water to the surface, or people can create wells to tap into this fresh water resource.

The Memphis Sand Aquifer

Beneath the city of Memphis, TN lies some of the purest water in the country. Its source is not the Mississippi river, but an underground reservoir containing water that may have fallen to Earth over 2000 years ago. Its purity is the result of the fine quartz sand that gives the aquifer its name. As water percolates through the sand, impurities or contaminants from the surface are slowly filtered out.

How big is it? Current estimates by the Ground Water Institute at the University of Memphis indicate that it holds 57 trillion gallons of water! About 150 million gallons of water is pumped daily, providing Memphis and surrounding areas with a plentiful water resource that requires very little treatment. As long as the rains continue to fall on the land that feeds the Memphis Sands aquifer, this source of clean water will be renewed.

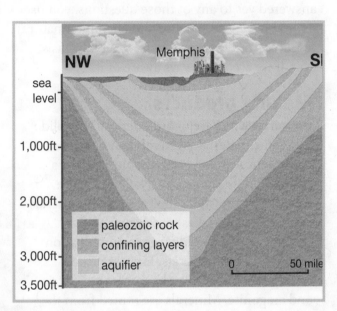

Visualize It!

7 Identify Write the name of the type of natural resource shown in each picture.

Type of Natural Resource

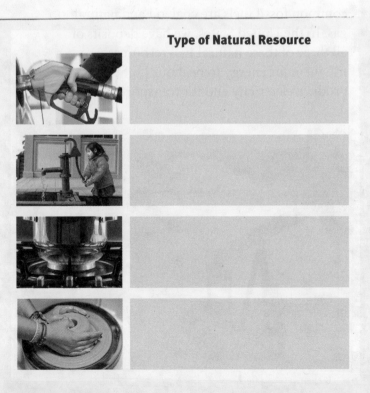

How much of these resources does Earth have?

Minerals, fossil fuels, and groundwater are **nonrenewable resources.** This means that their supply is limited, and more cannot be formed fast enough to keep up with what we use. For example, the fossil fuels like oil and coal we use today took millions of years to form. At the rate of our consumption of these resources, there is not enough time for them to replenish before the supply runs out.

Renewable resources are materials that are replenished in a shorter amount of time. Crops or trees are renewable resources because they can be planted and grown in a reasonable amount of time - months or years. Water used for hydroelectric power is a renewable resource because it is replenished from rainfall or snowmelt.

Active Reading

8 Identify As you read, underline examples of renewable and nonrenewable resources.

The Norris Dam was the first dam created by the Tennessee Valley Authority.

9 Explain What would happen if we ran out of fossil fuels? What other resources could we use for energy?

_____

_____

_____

_____

_____

Beneath the Surface

Where do natural resources come from?

They are the sources of many of the things we use, but how do natural resources form? For the most part minerals, fossil fuels, and groundwater form or are found beneath Earth's surface. Their development depends on the time, and the conditions of depth, pressure, and temperature.

Growing Minerals Beneath the Surface

The way some minerals form is connected with the rock cycle. Heat from the Earth's core changes **metamorphic rock** into **molten magma** and the less dense material rises up toward the surface. As the magma moves away from its heat source, it cools and hardens, becoming **igneous rock**. Environmental factors like pressure, temperature, cooling time and the chemical composition of the molten rock all contribute to the types of minerals that form.

Sometimes magma rises to Earth's surface through volcanoes, but sometimes it cools while still below ground. Weathering and erosion can wear down surrounding rock layers, carrying away sediment and making it possible to uncover mineral deposits.

veins

crystals form deep in the Earth as magma cools

minerals formed in hot water solutions

minerals in cooling magma

magma

© Houghton Mifflin Harcourt Publishing Company

Diamonds

Diamonds are an example of how minerals can form within Earth's interior. Diamonds are made of carbon, which was under extreme temperature and pressure in the upper mantle. Over long periods of time, these special conditions turn the carbon into diamonds. Volcanic activity can carry the diamonds upward in kimberlites, which are penetrating rocks that wedge themselves up through cracks in Earth's crust.

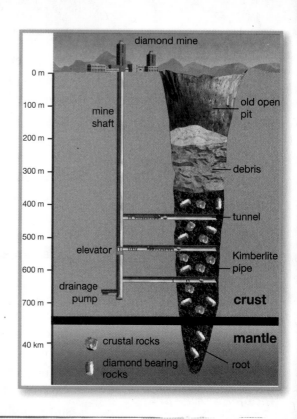

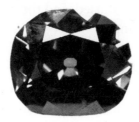

The Hope Diamond is one of the most famous jewels in the world. It weighs an incredible 45.52 carats.

---

10 Describe Diamonds used in jewelry are very expensive. Looking at the diagram of the kimberlite pipe, describe some of the challenges and hazards you would encounter extracting this rare mineral.

_____

_____

_____

_____

_____

Minerals in Water

Minerals that have made their way to the surface, like halite (salt), can be formed into crystals through the process of evaporation. When seawater evaporates, it leaves behind the minerals that were once dissolved in it. In coastal regions salt is harvested in large shallow pools that help water to evaporate faster. The salt that remains crystallizes, and is collected, packaged and sold for use in cooking, beauty and bath products.

Salt is harvested for our everyday use.

From Fossils to Fuel

Fossil fuels such as coal, natural gas, and oil come from the remains of organisms that lived hundreds of millions of years ago, even before dinosaurs. At that time, Earth was much warmer and covered with swamps and shallow seas. When the organisms died, they sank to the bottom of the swamps or sea and decomposed. Over time, the organic material was covered with sediment and compacted. As sediments continued to bury the rock, the weight of the overlying sediments created a massive amount of pressure on the organic material. Depending on the type of organic material, how long it was buried, and the pressure, different types of fossil fuels were formed.

How Coal Forms

Coal, for example, like that mined in Tennessee, formed by the decomposition and compaction of trees and other plants. Besides carbon and hydrogen, another element in coal is sulfur. When the sulfur-rich water that covered the swamp dried up, it left sulfur in the coal. These types of coal present a problem because coal with sulfur pollutes the air when it is burned. Scientists are currently working on ways to separate and capture the sulfur before it is released into the air, helping coal burn cleaner and have a less negative impact on the environment.

Active Reading

11 Identify As you read, underline the description for how each fossil fuel forms.

Bituminous Coal is high in sulfur content, about 0.7 to 4% by weight.

This piece of coal has a fossilized fern in it; evidence of its origins.

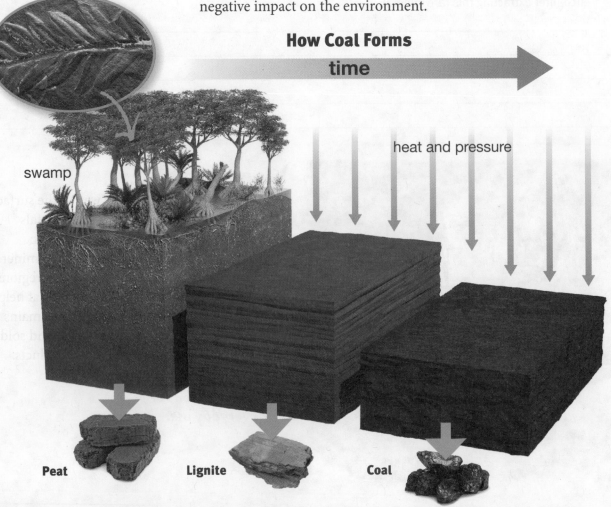

How Coal Forms

time

heat and pressure

swamp

Peat **Lignite** **Coal**

How Oil and Natural Gas Form

Oil and natural gas formed as a result of the burial and compaction of marine organisms. The process, though, is similar to coal formation. Dead marine organisms sank to the bottom of a shallow sea and then were covered by sediment. Over time, these sediments continued to accumulate and created extreme pressure on the decomposed organic material. This extreme temperature and pressure turned the dense organic material into oil and gas.

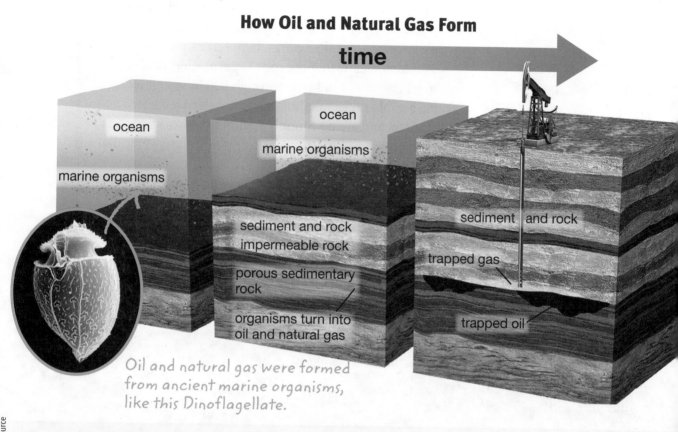

How Oil and Natural Gas Form

time

ocean

marine organisms

ocean

marine organisms

sediment and rock
impermeable rock

porous sedimentary rock

organisms turn into oil and natural gas

sediment and rock

trapped gas

trapped oil

Oil and natural gas were formed from ancient marine organisms, like this Dinoflagellate.

12 **Compare** Complete the Venn diagram to compare and contrast the way coal, natural gas and oil were formed.

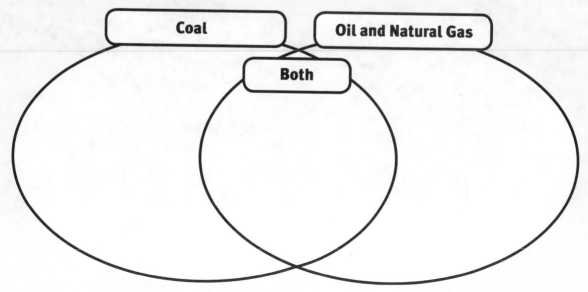

Coal

Oil and Natural Gas

Both

13 Identify As you read, underline
the characteristics of aquifers.

Where do we find water resources?

How Groundwater Forms

Rain and snowmelt are the main sources of groundwater. As water soaks into the ground through soil and cracks in rocks it travels downward until it reaches a layer of porous rock that can hold it. Porous rock has space, called pores, between its particles. This also means that the rock is permeable, or able to let gas and liquid pass through it. These highly permeable rocks that hold groundwater are known as aquifers and are commonly sedimentary rocks such as sandstone and limestone. The upper limit of water that the ground can hold is called the water table.

Aquifers store groundwater, which people can access through natural springs or by digging wells. Around half the population of the United States relies on groundwater as the source of water for everyday household use. However, wells and the aquifers that feed them can dry up during a drought or if the water is used faster than it can be replenished.

People can access aquifers through natural springs or by digging wells.

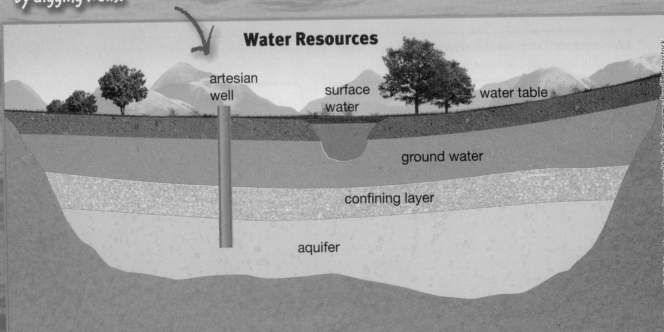

Water Resources

artesian well

surface water

water table

ground water

confining layer

aquifer

How are natural resources distributed?

Just because they form naturally does not mean that Earth's natural resources are abundant everywhere. Their distribution, like their formation, depends on specific geological and environmental conditions and over time, weather events and changes in the environment sometimes occur.

Shifting Minerals

Mineral resources are found where they originally formed or where they may have been transported through geological processes. Converging tectonic plates can force minerals upward so that they are closer to Earth's surface, potentially exposing them to weather that may wear away the sediment around them. Gold, for example, can sometimes be seen in veins on exposed rock or can be swept down a mountainside by water and discovered as nuggets in a stream.

"Panning" for gold is popular in some mountain streams, especially in the western states.

GOIN' UP!

The Ekati Diamond Mine in Canada marks the site of 45-to 62-million-year-old kimberlite pipes that brought diamonds that formed deep in Earth's interior close to the surface.

GOIN' DOWN!

Converging plates can also thrust minerals in a subducting plate down deeper than they would normally form and expose them to extreme heat and pressure, like the carbon that forms diamonds in Earth's upper mantle. Transform plate motion can divide and move mineral deposits along fault lines to places other than where they were formed.

The Piqiang Fault tears through the Tien Shan Mountains in China.

Coal mining by mountaintop removal.

How are resources found?

Now that we know how fossil fuels such as coal and oil formed,
we can look on the surface for clues as to what lies beneath.

Finding Coal

Where coal seams are close to the surface a
number of different mining techniques are used
to extract the resource. These often involve
removing the over laying materials, called
overburden. On level terrain, strip mining is then
used to remove the coal layer, or seam, after the
overburden is removed.

More controversial is the practice of coal
extraction by mountaintop removal,(shown in
the photo above), where entire mountaintops
are blasted away and the waste is pushed into
valleys. Not only does this change the landscape
but also threatens other natural resources, like
groundwater.

Finding Oil and Natural Gas

Early in the history of oil wells, when the rock
layer of oil was drilled into, a gushing black
fountain of oil would shoot high into the air.
What causes this dramatic display? Sometimes
the sediment layers where the oil forms lie
beneath rocks that are impermeable to oil and
gas. As the rock layers' fold and bend, these oil
and natural gas can collect in pockets that are
under tremendous pressure, which can cause oil
wells to gush if the pressure is released.

Coal Areas in Tennessee

Coal bearing rocks

14 Apply The map shows different types of sedimentary rocks across TN.
Even though coal is formed from organisms often found in sedimentary
rocks, coal is only found in one of these areas. Why do you think this is
the case? What does this tell you about the area where the coal formed?

_____

_____

_____

_____

© Houghton Mifflin Harcourt Publishing Company • Image Credits: ©Alan Gignoux/Alamy

Rock that Burns!

Oil Shale is fine-grained sedimentary rock composed of compressed clay, organic chemical compounds, and other minerals. Natural gas is trapped inside this sediment. Natural gas can be extracted from buried shale beds by a process called hydraulic fracturing. This involves pumping high-pressure water or gases into the oil well. The rock that holds the gas is fractured. As the rock fractures, it releases the natural gas held within it. It is a controversial practice, and has been implicated in causing earthquakes, contaminating ground water, and adding to greenhouse gasses in the atmosphere.

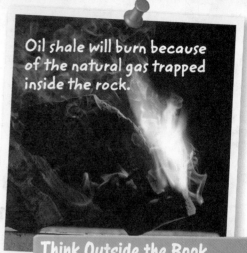

Oil shale will burn because of the natural gas trapped inside the rock.

Think Outside the Book

15 **Research** the largest oil, natural gas and coal producers in the world. Which countries produce the most? What does that mean about the environment that used to exist in that area?

Finding Groundwater

Groundwater resources are found in areas containing aquifers, or permeable rocks that store water or that water can move through. The water then becomes trapped under more impermeable rock or clay layers. Underground caves and caverns can form when seeping groundwater dissolves soft rock like limestone. These caves can fill up with water or contain underground rivers. This type of landscape characterized by caves, caverns, sinkholes, and aquifers is called karst topography.

Types of Aquifers in Tennessee

- Alluvial aquifer
- Sand aquifer
- Carbonate aquifer
- Sandstone aquifer
- Rock aquifer

16 **Synthesize** Mark where your community is located on the map and then answer the following: 1) Which type of aquifer is available for your community? 2) Use your understanding of geology to explain why there is an aquifer in that location, and 3) Explain why there are multiple aquifers across the state.

TENNESSEE

Tennessee marble is famous for its pinkish-gray color and its use in government buildings like the facade of the National Gallery.

Which natural resources does Tennessee have?

Tennessee is fortunate enough to have land that provides many natural resources to its residents. In some parts of the state, miners extract mineral and coal deposits. In others, pumps bring oil and natural gas to the surface. Groundwater is accessible in nearly every county through wells fed by aquifers.

Tennessee Marble

The largest segment of the mineral industry in Tennessee is the mining of construction materials. Nearly every county produces one or more materials such as crushed stone (limestone, sand and gravel) as well as sandstone and marble.

Tennessee marble has been made famous around the country by its use in buildings such as the façade of the National Gallery of Art in Washington D.C. Geologists classify Tennessee marble as limestone, a sedimentary rock.

Map labels: Clarksville, Nashville, Murfreesboro, Jackson, Memphis, Chattanooga, Knoxville, Johnson City

Legend: Valley and Ridge Province / Marble bearing rocks

Zinc is an important mineral resource that is mined in East and Middle Tennessee.

13 Infer The areas where Tennessee marble is mined occur along the Valley and Ridge Province, which is the location of the ancient Appalachian Mountains. What does the existence of limestone indicate about the geologic history of this region?

_____

_____

_____

Tennessee is the nation's leading producer of ball clay.

© Houghton Mifflin Harcourt Publishing Company • Image Credits: (t) (©Diego Grandi/Shutterstock.;(br) ©De

The Volunteer State

Coal, Oil and Natural gas

The fossil fuels coal, oil and natural gas are all currently extracted in Tennessee. Though the recovery amount of these resources is small compared to other states, it is still valuable.

Coal mining currently takes place on the Cumberland Plateau and in the Cumberland Mountains region of Tennessee. A reserve of over a billion tons of coal has been found in West Tennessee, but it is not being mined because of the danger it may pose to groundwater resources. Careful consideration and planning by both the state and federal governments must be taken if this area is to be mined in the future.

Fossil fuels like coal account for about 11.5% of the state's mineral production value each year. .

Hydroelectric Power and Groundwater

Over half of Tennessee's population depends on groundwater for everyday use. Most of this comes from the western part of the state, where confined sand aquifers hold large amounts of fresh water. This area supplies around 190 million gallons of water to the city of Memphis daily. While the quality of the Tennessee's groundwater is naturally good, it may be contaminated if waste disposal is not closely monitored.

The quality of the state's groundwater is monitored by the Tennessee Valley Authority (TVA), which controls withdrawals from the aquifers.

The Norris Dam provides hydroelectric power, about 132,000 kilowatts of electricity. It also provides much needed flood control for the area downstream of the Clinch River.

The Norris Dam was constructed between 1933 and 1936 across a tributary of the Tennessee River. .

Visual Summary

To complete this summary, fill in the blaks with the correct word or phrase. Then use the key below to check your answers. You can use this page to review the main concepts of this lesson.

Groundwater is precipitation that seeps down and is held beneath the earth's surface in porous rock called aquifers.

18 People dig _____ to access the groundwater held in aquifers

Fossil fuels like oil, natural gas, and coal are important sources of energy.

19 _____ is refined into gasoline and used to fuel motorized vehicles.

Tennessee is the leading producer of ball clay in the United States.

20 Ball clay is a _____ resource that is extracted from the Earth and used to make ceramic tableware.

Earth provides us with the natural resources we need to survive and live comfortably.

21 Natural resources that can be used and reused are _____ while those that will eventually run out are _____.

Answers: 14 wells; 15 oil; 16 mineral; 16 renewable, nonrenewable

22 **Summarize** Explain how Earth's natural resources are distributed.

Lesson Review

Vocabulary

In your own words, define the following terms.

1 Groundwater is held in permeable rock called an _____.

2 Natural resources that cannot be replenished are called _____ .

3 Natural deposits of solid inorganic material are called _____ .

Key Concepts

4 Explain What are three ways minerals could be relocated from where they originally formed?

_____

_____

_____

_____

_____

_____

5 Contrast How would a fossil fuel that formed where there was an ancient ocean be different than one that formed where there was once an ancient swamp forest?

_____

_____

_____

_____

_____

_____

6 Describe How are minerals resources formed through the process of evaporation?

_____

_____

_____

_____

_____

7 List Name three examples of everyday items that come from natural resources.

_____

_____

_____

8 Explain Give two reasons why a well might run dry.

_____

_____

_____

Critical Thinking

Use the diagram to answer the question below.

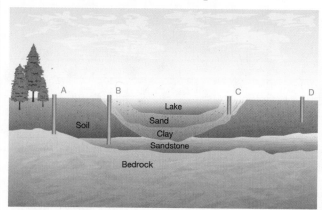

9 Synthesize Which of the four locations and depths would be the best and worst places to dig a well? Rank the four locations and explain your reasoning.

_____

_____

_____

_____

10 Infer How can waste landfills and pollution affect local groundwater deposits?

_____

_____

_____

_____

My Notes

Lesson 1
ESSENTIAL QUESTION
What is known about Earth's interior?

Identify Earth's compositional and physical layers and describe their properties.

Lesson 4
ESSENTIAL QUESTION
How do volcanoes change Earth's surface?

Describe what the various kinds of volcanoes and eruptions are, where they occur, how they form, and how they change Earth's surface.

Lesson 2
ESSENTIAL QUESTION
What is plate tectonics?

Explain the theory of plate tectonics and plate movement, and identify the geologic events caused by this.

Lesson 5
ESSENTIAL QUESTION
Why do earthquakes happen?

Describe the causes of earthquakes and identify where earthquakes happen.

Lesson 3
ESSENTIAL QUESTION
How do mountains form?

Describe how the movement of Earth's tectonic plates causes mountain building.

Lesson 6
ESSENTIAL QUESTION
How are seismic waves used to study earthquakes?

Understand how seismic waves are useful in determining the strength, location, and effects of an earthquake.

Connect ESSENTIAL QUESTIONS
Lessons 2 and 5

1 Synthesize Explain why tectonic plate boundaries are areas of intense geological activity.

_____

_____

_____

_____

Lesson 7
ESSENTIAL QUESTION
How are Earth's natural resources distributed?

Describe natural resources and explain their distribution.

Vocabulary

Fill in each blank with the term that best completes the following sentences.

1 The hot, convecting _____ is the layer of rock between the Earth's crust and core.

2 _____ is the theory that explains how large pieces of Earth's outermost layer move and change shape.

3 Forests, soils, rocks, fresh water, minerals, oil and animals are all examples of Earth's _____.

4 A(n) _____ is a vent or fissure in the Earth's surface through which magma and gases are expelled.

5 A(n) _____ is a movement or trembling of the ground that is caused by a sudden release of energy when rocks move along a fault.

Key Concepts

Read each question below, and circle the best answer.

6 What is the difference between lava and magma?

A Magma is found above Earth's surface and lava is found below Earth's surface.

B Lava is a solid material and magma is a liquid material.

C Magma is found below Earth's surface and lava is found above Earth's surface.

D Magma only erupts in the ocean and lava only erupts on land.

7 Tectonic plates are made of continental crust, oceanic crust, or a combination of the two. Besides their locations, how else are these two kinds of crust different?

A Tectonic plates made of continental crust are larger than plates made of oceanic crust.

B Tectonic plates made of continental crust are smaller than plates made of oceanic crust.

C Continental crust is thicker than oceanic crust.

D Continental crust is thinner than oceanic crust.

8 In the diagram below, an earthquake is taking place.

Cross Section of Lithosphere during an Earthquake

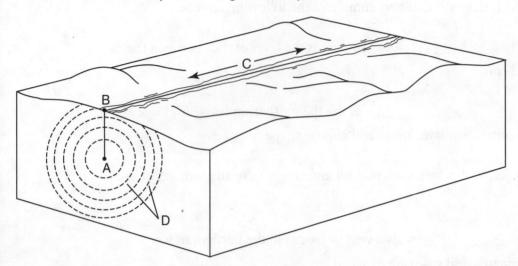

Where is the focus of the earthquake located?

A Point A

B Point B

C along the line labeled C

D along the series of circles labeled D

9 Volcanic eruptions can have many characteristics. They can be slow, fast, calm, explosive, or a combination of these. Which type of eruption is associated with the release of pyroclastic materials?

A a calm eruption

B an explosive eruption

C a fast eruption

D a slow eruption

10 What happens at a divergent tectonic plate boundary?

A Two tectonic plates move horizontally past one another.

B Two tectonic plates pull away from each other, forming a rift valley or mid-ocean ridge.

C Two tectonic plates come together to form one plate.

D Two tectonic plates collide, causing subduction.

11 A major tsunami occurred in the Indian Ocean on December 26, 2004 resulting in the loss of thousands of lives. The tsunami was caused by a major earthquake that originated below the point on the map on the ocean floor. The dashed lines on the map indicate the path of the tsunami's waves.

December 2004 Tsunami

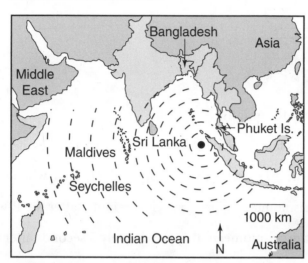

What term refers to the point on the ocean's surface indicated by the dot at the center of the waves?

A fault boundary

C earthquake epicenter

B earthquake focus

D tectonic plate boundary

12 Which of the following is a major difference between Earth's inner core and Earth's outer core?

A The inner core is liquid and the outer core is solid.

B The inner core is solid and the outer core is liquid.

C The inner core is gas and the outer core is solid.

D The inner core is solid and the outer core is gas.

13 Volcanic islands can form over hot spots. The Hawaiian Islands started forming over hot spots in the Pacific Ocean millions of years ago. What process causes the hot, solid rock to rise through the mantle at these locations?

A condensation

C convection

B conduction

D radiation

14 The graph shows the different arrival times for a P wave and an S wave at a seismometer.

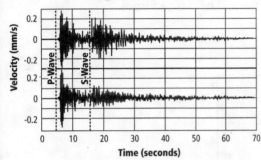

Measuring Earthquake Waves

Which statement is supported by the graph?

A The velocity of the P-wave was less than the velocity of the S-wave when it first arrived.

B The velocity of the S-wave was the same as the velocity of the P-wave when it first arrived.

C The S-wave arrived at the seismometer approximately 3 minutes after the P-wave.

D The P-wave arrived first at the seismometer at approximately 5 seconds after the earthquake started.

15 Earth can be divided into five layers: lithosphere, asthenosphere, mesosphere, outer core, and inner core. Which properties are used to make these divisions?

A compositional properties   **C** chemical properties

B physical properties   **D** elemental properties

16 This diagram shows the formation of a fault-block mountain. Arrows outside of the blocks show the directions of force. Arrows inside the blocks show the directions of movement. The blocks *K* and *L* move along a line marked *J*.

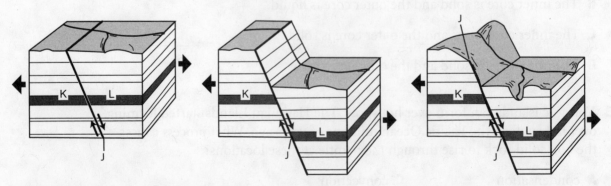

What does the line marked by the letter *J* represent?

A a river   **C** the fault line

B a rock layer   **D** the focus

© Houghton Mifflin Harcourt Publishing Company

17 The map below shows the epicenters of some major earthquakes of 2003.

Locations of Major Earthquakes in 2003

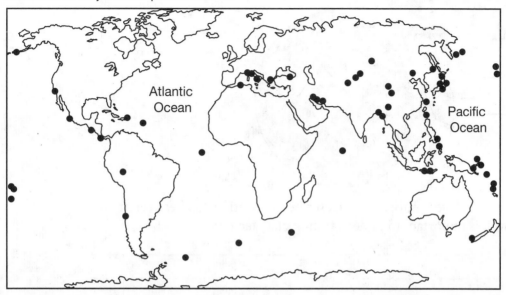

What is the most likely reason that there were no major earthquakes recorded in the interior of the continent of Africa?

A There are no faults in Africa.

B The landmass of Africa is too large to be affected by earthquakes.

C The plate boundary inside Africa is too small to form earthquakes.

D No major plate boundaries cut through the continent of Africa.

Critical Thinking

Answer the following questions in the space provided.

18 Explain how a fossil fuel that formed where there was an ancient ocean would differ from one that formed where there was once an ancient swamp forest?

_____

_____

_____

_____

_____

_____

19 The diagram below shows the five physical layers of Earth.

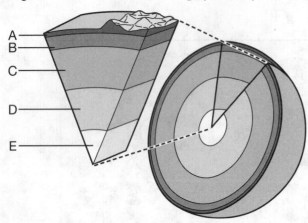

Identify the physical layers A, B, and C. Describe the relationship between these layers and how it is important to understanding plate tectonics.

_____
_____
_____
_____

20 Explain the difference between the Richter scale and the Moment Magnitude scale. Why might measurements from the Richter Scale be misleading to someone who does not know how it works?

_____
_____
_____
_____

Connect ESSENTIAL QUESTIONS
Lessons 3 and 4

Answer the following question in the space provided.

21 Explain how forces from tectonic plate movement can build these three types of mountains: folded mountains, fault-block mountains, and volcanic mountains.

_____
_____
_____
_____
_____
_____

⟨Technology⟩ and ⟨Coding⟩

This breathtaking image of Earth was taken from the International Space Station, an international laboratory orbiting Earth. The operation of the International Space Station is controlled by 52 computers and millions of lines of computer code. Its many high-tech features include solar panels that power the laboratory and a human-like robotic astronaut.

This is Robonaut 2, a robot designed to do routine maintenance at the International Space Station.

Data Driven

What is computer science?

If you like computer technology and learning about how computers work, computer science might be for you. *Computer science* is the study of computer technology and how data is processed, stored, and accessed by computers. Computer science is an important part of many other areas, including science, math, engineering, robotics, medicine, game design, and 3D animation.

Computer technology is often described in terms of *hardware*, which are the physical components, and *software*, which are the programs or instructions that a computer runs. Computer scientists must understand how hardware and software work together. Computer scientists may develop new kinds of useful computer software. Or they may work with engineers to improve existing computer hardware.

The first electronic computer, the computer ENIAC (Electronic Numerical Integrator And Computer), was developed at the University of Pennsylvania in 1946.

The integrated circuit (IC), first developed in the 1950s, was instrumental in the development of small computer components.

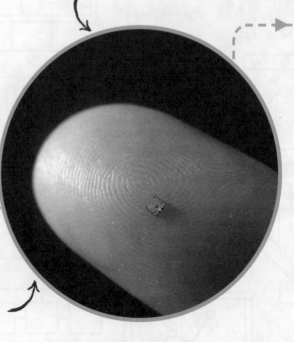

The development of the IC made it possible to reduce the overall size of computers and their components and to increase their processing speed.

How has computer technology changed over time?

Modern, digital computer technology is less than 100 years old. Yet in that short amount of time, it has advanced rapidly. The earliest digital computers could perform only a limited number of tasks and were the size of an entire room. Over the decades, engineers continued to develop smaller, faster, and more powerful computers. Today's computers can process hundreds of millions of instructions per second!

Computer scientists and engineers think about what people want or need from computer technology. The most advanced hardware is not useful if people do not know how to use it. So computer scientists and engineers work to create software that is reliable, useful, and easy to use. Today's tablet computers, cell phones, and video game consoles can be used without any special training.

Advances in digital computer technology have helped make computers cheaper and easier to operate, which has allowed many more people to work and play with them.

1 Compare Are modern computers simpler or more complex than early computers? Explain.

_____

_____

Computer Logic

What do computer scientists do?

Many people enjoy developing computer technology for fun. Learning how to create mobile phone games or Internet-enabled gadgets can be rewarding hobbies. For some people, that hobby may one day become a career in computer science. Working in computer science is a bit like solving a puzzle. Applying knowledge of how computers work to solve real-world problems requires collaboration, creativity, and logical, step-by-step thinking.

This is a kayak folded up.

They collaborate across many disciplines

Computers are valuable tools in math and science because they can perform complex calculations very quickly. Computers are useful to many other fields, too. For example, animators use computer technology to create realistic lighting effects in 3D animated films. Mechanics use computers to diagnose problems in car systems. For every field that relies on special software or computer technology, there is an opportunity for computer scientists and engineers to collaborate and develop solutions for those computing needs. Computer scientists must be able to define and understand the problems presented to them and to communicate and work with experts in other fields to develop the solutions.

Computational origami is a computer program used to model the ways in which different materials, including paper, can be folded. It combines computer science and the art of paper folding to create new technologies, such as this kayak.

Tracking software helps biologists study animal behavior.

satellite →

satellite data receiving center

satellite data processing center

transmitter

They help solve real-world problems

Some computer scientists carry out theoretical research. Others apply computer science concepts to develop software. Theoretical computer science and practical software development help solve real-world problems. For example, biologists need ways to safely and accurately track endangered animals. Computer science theories on artificial intelligence and pattern recognition have been applied to advanced animal-tracking technologies, such as satellite transmitters and aerial cameras. New kinds of image processing software now allow biologists to analyze the collected data in different ways.

They use logical, step-by-step thinking

Computers perform tasks given to them, and they do this very well. But in order to get the results they expect, computer scientists and programmers must write very accurate instructions. Computer science and programming requires logical thinking, deductive reasoning, and a good understanding of cause-and-effect relationships. When designing software, computer scientists must consider every possible user action and how the computer should respond to each action.

2 Explain How is computer science helping this scientist do her research?

_____

_____

_____

_____

Transmitters can be attached to animals to help track their movements.

Up to <Code>

How is computer software created?

Imagine that you are using a computer at the library to learn more about the history of electronic music. You use the library's database application to start searching for Internet resources. You also do a search to look for audio recordings. Finally, you open a word processor to take notes on the computer. Perhaps without realizing it, you've used many different pieces of software. Have you ever wondered how computer software is created?

Computer software is designed to address a need

Computer software can help us to learn more about our world. It can be useful to business. Or it can simply entertain us. Whatever its purpose, computer software should fulfill some human want or need. The first steps in creating software are precisely defining the need or want being addressed and planning how the software will work.

Computer software source code is written in a programming language

The instructions that tell a computer how to run video games, word processors, and other kinds of software are not written in a human language. They are written in a special programming language, or *code*. Javascript, C++, and Python are examples of programming languages. Programming languages—like human languages—must follow certain rules in order to be understood by the computer. A series of instructions written in a programming language is called *source code*.

Identifying what need a computer program addresses is one of the first development steps.

Source code is revised

Sometimes, programmers make mistakes in their code. Many programming environments have a feature that alerts the programmer to certain errors, such as spelling mistakes in commands, missing portions of code, or logical errors in the sequence of instructions. However, many mistakes go undetected, too. Some errors may cause the program to function incorrectly or not at all. When this happens, the programmer must identify the error, correct it, and test the software again.

Computer software is user tested, and revised

Once the software is created, it must be tested thoroughly to make sure it does not fail or behave in unexpected ways. It must also be tested to ensure that it meets users' needs. The creators of a piece of software might observe how people use it. Or they might ask users to provide feedback on certain features and test the software again.

3 Identify This source code contains an error. Infer where the error is located. What does this code "tell" the computer to do? Write your answers below.

_____

_____

_____

_____

```
13
14   # Scores are not tied, so check
15   # which player wins the round
16 ▾ if player1_score > player2_score:
17       print ("Player 1 wins!")
18 ▾ else:
19       prnt ("Player 2 wins!")
20
```

```
! Syntax error, line 19
```

Test running a program is important for finding and fixing errors in the code.

Play it Safe 🔒

How should I work with computers?

It is easy to lose track of time when you're sitting in front of a computer or game console. It's also easy to forget that things you say or do online can be seen and shared by many different people. Here are some tips for using computers safely and responsibly.

✓ Maintain good posture

Time can pass by quickly when you are working on a computer or another device. Balance computer time with other activities, including plenty of physical activity. When you are sitting at a computer, sit upright with your shoulders relaxed. Your eyes should be level with the top of the monitor and your feet should be flat on the ground.

✓ Observe electrical safety

Building your own electronics projects can be fun, but it's important to have an understanding of circuits and electrical safety first. Otherwise, you could damage your components or hurt yourself. The potential for an electrical shock is real when you open up a computer, work with frayed cords or, use ungrounded plugs or attempt to replace parts without understanding how to do so safely. Ask an adult for help before starting any projects. Also, avoid using a connected computer during thunderstorms.

head and neck in a straight, neutral position

shoulders are relaxed

wrists are straight

feet are flat on the ground

Good posture will help you avoid the aches and injuries related to sitting in front of a computer for a long time.

✓ Handle and maintain computers properly

Be cautious when handling and transporting electronic devices. Dropping them or spilling liquids on them could cause serious damage. Keep computers away from dirt, dust, liquids, and moisture. Never use wet cleaning products unless they are specifically designed for use on electronics. Microfiber cloths can be used to clear smudges from device screens. Spilled liquids can cause circuits to short out and hardware to corrode. If a liquid spills on a device, unplug it and switch it off immediately, remove the battery and wipe up as much of the liquid inside the device as possible. Don't switch the device back on until it is completely dry.

✓ Do not post private information online

Talk to your family about rules for Internet use. Do not use the Internet to share private information such as photographs, your phone number, or your address. Do not respond to requests for personal details from people you do not know.

✓ Treat yourself and others with respect

It is important to treat others with respect when on the Internet. Don't send or post messages online that you wouldn't say to someone in person. Unfortunately, not everyone acts respectfully while online. Some people may say hurtful things to you or send you unwanted messages. Do not reply to unwanted messages. Alert a trusted adult to any forms of contact, such as messages or photos, that make you feel uncomfortable.

4 Apply Fill in the chart below with a suitable response to each scenario.

SCENARIO	YOUR RESPONSE
You receive a text message from an online store asking for your home address.	
You've been lying down in front of a laptop, and you notice that your neck is feeling a little sore.	
You need to take a laptop computer with you on your walk to school.	
You want to try assembling a robotics kit with a friend.	
Someone posts unfriendly comments directed at you.	

Career in Computing:
Game Programmer

What do video game programmers do?

Creating your own universe with its own set of rules is fun. Just ask a programmer who works on video games!

What skills are needed in game programming?

A programmer should know how to write code, but there are other important skills a programmer needs as well. An understanding of physics and math is important for calculating how objects move and interact in a game. Game programmers usually work on a team with other people, such as artists, designers, writers, and musicians. They must be able to communicate effectively, and ideally, the programmer should understand the other team members' roles.

How can I get started with game development?

You don't need a big budget or years of experience to try it out. There are books, videos, and websites that can help you get started. When you're first experimenting with game development, start small. Try making a very simple game like Tic-Tac-Toe. Once you've mastered that, you can try something more complex.

5 Brainstorm Why would working on a team be important to the game development process?

_____

_____

_____

Glossary

Pronunciation Key							
Sound	**Symbol**	**Example**	**Respelling**	**Sound**	**Symbol**	**Example**	**Respelling**
ă	a	pat	PAT	ŏ	ah	bottle	BAHT'l
ā	ay	pay	PAY	ō	oh	toe	TOH
âr	air	care	KAIR	ô	aw	caught	KAWT
ä	ah	father	FAH•ther	ôr	ohr	roar	ROHR
är	ar	argue	AR•gyoo	oi	oy	noisy	NOYZ•ee
ch	ch	chase	CHAYS	o͝o	u	book	BUK
ě	e	pet	PET	o͞o	oo	boot	BOOT
ě (at end of a syllable)	eh	settee lessee	seh•TEE leh•SEE	ou	ow	pound	POWND
ěr	ehr	merry	MEHR•ee	s	s	center	SEN•ter
ē	ee	beach	BEECH	sh	sh	cache	CASH
g	g	gas	GAS	ŭ	uh	flood	FLUHD
ĭ	i	pit	PIT	ûr	er	bird	BERD
ĭ (at end of a syllable)	ih	guitar	gih•TAR	z	z	xylophone	ZY•luh•fohn
ī	y eye (only for a complete syllable)	pie island	PY EYE•luhnd	z	z	bags	BAGZ
				zh	zh	decision	dih•SIZH•uhn
îr	ir	hear	HIR	ə	uh	around broken focus	uh•ROWND BROH•kuhn FOH•kuhs
j	j	germ	JERM				
k	k	kick	KIK	ər	er	winner	WIN•er
ng	ng	thing	THING	th	th	thin they	THIN THAY
ngk	ngk	bank	BANGK	w	w	one	WUHN
				wh	hw	whether	HWETH•er

A

absorption (uhb·SOHRP·shuhn) in optics, the transfer of light energy to particles of matter (235)
    absorción en la óptica, la transferencia de energía luminosa a las partículas de material

acceleration (ak·sel·uh·RAY·shuhn) the rate at which velocity changes over time; an object accelerates if its speed, direction, or both change (22)
    aceleración la tasa a la que la velocidad cambia con el tiempo; un objeto acelera si su rapidez cambia, si su dirección cambia, o si tanto su rapidez como su dirección cambian

adaptation (ad·ap·TAY·shuhn) a characteristic that improves an individual's ability to survive and reproduce in a particular environment (283)
    adaptación una característica que mejora la capacidad de un individuo para sobrevivir y reproducirse en un determinado ambiente

adaptive optics (a·DAP·tiv OP·tix) a method of adjusting the dimensions of a lens or mirror to change how light is reflected or focused to improve the quality of an image (379)
    óptica adaptativa método para ajustar las dimensiones de una lente o espejo cambiando la manera en que la luz se refleja o se enfoca para mejorar la calidad de una imagen

amplitude (AM·plih·tood) the maximum distance that the particles of a wave's medium vibrate from their rest position (146)
    amplitud la distancia máxima a la que vibran las partículas del medio de una onda a partir de su posición de reposo

analog signal (AN·uh·log SIG·nul) a signal wave that varies continuously with a gradual up-and-down pattern (159)
    señal analógica señal de onda que varía constantemente con un patrón gradual de ascenso y descenso

Animalia (an·uh·MAYL·yuh) a kingdom made up of complex, multicellular organisms that lack cell walls, can usually move around, and quickly respond to their environment (333)
    Animalia un reino formado por oranismos pluricelulares complejos que no tienen pared celular, normalmente son capaces de moverse y reaccionan rápidamente a su ambiente

aphelion (uh·FEE·lee·uhn) in the orbit of a planet or other body in the solar system, the point that is farthest from the sun (423)
    afelio en la órbita de un planeta u otros cuerpos en el sistema solar, el punto que está más lejos del Sol

aquifer (AH·kwi·fer) a large body of rock that holds water from rain or snowmelt (608)
    acuíferos estructura grande de roca que contiene agua proveniente de la lluvia o de la nieve derretida

Archaea (ar·KEE·uh) a domain made up of prokaryotes, most of which are known to live in extreme environments, that are distinguished from other prokaryotes by differences in their genetics and in the makeup of their cell wall (330)
    Archaea un domino compuesto por procariotes la mayoría de los cuales viven en ambientes extremos que se distinguen de otros procariotes por su genética y por la composición de su pared celular

artificial satellite (ar·tuh·FISH·uhl SAT'l·yt) any human-made object placed in orbit around a body in space (372)
    satélite artificial cualquier objeto hecho por los seres humanos y colocado en órbita alrededor de un cuerpo en el espacio

artificial selection (ar·tuh·FISH·uhl sih·LEK·shuhn) the human practice of breeding animals or plants that have certain desired traits (347, 280)
    selección artificial la práctica humana de criar animales o cultivar plantas que tienen ciertos caracteres deseados

asexual reproduction (ay·SEK·shoo·uhl ree·pruh·DUHK·shuhn) reproduction that does not involve the union of sex cells and in which one parent produces offspring that are genetically identical to the parent (270)
    reproducción asexual reproducción que no involucra la unión de células sexuales, en la que un solo progenitor produce descendia que es genéticamenta igual al progenitor

asthenosphere (as·THEN·uh·sfir) the soft layer of the mantle on which the tectonic plates move (515)
    astenosfera la capa blanda del manto sobre la que se mueven las placas tectónicas

atom (AT·uhm) the smallest unit of an element that maintains the properties of that element (456)
    átomo la unidad más pequeña de un elemento que conserva las propiedades de ese elemento

B

Bacteria (bak·TIR·ee·uh) a domain made up of prokaryotes that usually have a cell wall and that usually reproduce by cell division (330)
    Bacteria un dominio compuesto por procariotes que por lo general tienen pared celular y se reproducen por división celular

Big Bang theory (BIG BANG THEE·uh·ree) the theory that all matter and energy in the universe was compressed into an extremely small volume that 13 billion to 15 billion years ago exploded and began expanding in all directions (410)
    teoría del Big Bang la teoría que establece que toda la materia y la energía del universo estaban comprimidas en un volumen extremadamente pequeño que explotó hace aproximadamente 13 a 15 mi millones de años y empezó a expandirse en todas direcciones

biotechnology (by·oh·tek·NAHL·uh·jee) the use and application of living things and biological processes (346)

biotecnología el uso y la aplicación de seres vivos y procesos biológicos

cell (SEL) in biology, the smallest unit that can perform all life processes; cells are covered by a membrane and contain DNA and cytoplasm (268)

célula en biología, la unidad más pequeña que puede realizar todos los procesos vitales; las células están cubiertas por una membrana y tienen ADN y citoplasma

centripetal acceleration (sen·TRIP·ih·tl ak·sel·uh·RAY·shuhn) the acceleration directed toward the center of a circular path (25)

aceleración centrípeta la aceleración que se dirige hacia el centro de un camino circular

centripetal force (sehn·TRIP·ih·tuhl FOHRS) the inward force required to keep a particle or an object moving in a circular path (426)

fuerza centrípeta la fuerza hacia adentro que se requiere para mantener en movimiento una partícula o un objeto en un camino circular

cleavage (KLEE·vij) in geology, the tendency of a mineral to split along specific planes of weakness to form smooth, flat surfaces (463)

exfoliación en geología, la tendencia de un mineral a agrietarse a lo largo de planos débiles específicos y formar superficies lisas y planas

clone (KLOHN) an organism, cell, or piece of genetic material that is genetically identical to one from which it was derived; to make a genetic duplicate (349)

clon un organismo, una célula o una muestra de material genético que es genéticamente idéntico a aquél del cual deriva; hacer un duplicado genético

communication (kuh·mew·nih·KAY·shun) a method of sending information from place to place between people or animals (156)

comunicación método para enviar información de un lugar a otro entre personas o animales

composition (kahm·puh·ZISH·uhn) the chemical makeup of a rock; describes either the minerals or other materials in the rock (486)

composición la constitución química de una roca; describe los minerales u otros materiales presentes en ella

compound (KAHM·pownd) a substance made up of atoms of two or more different elements joined by chemical bonds (456)

compuesto una sustancia formada por átomos de dos o más elementos diferentes unidos por enlaces químicos

compression (kuhm·PRESH·uhn) stress that occurs when forces act to squeeze an object (547)

compresión estrés que se produce cuando distintas fuerzas actúan para estrechar un objeto

convection (kuhn·VEK·shuhn) the movement of matter due to differences in density; the transfer of energy du to the movement of matter (532)

convección el movimiento de la materia debido a diferencias en la densidad; la transferencia de energía debido al movimiento de la materia

convergent boundary (kuhn·VER·juhnt BOWN·duh·ree) th boundary between tectonic plates that are colliding (530)

límite convergente el límite entre placas tectónicas que chocan

core (KOHR) the central part of Earth below the mantle (514)

núcleo la parte central de la Tierra, debajo del manto

Cosmic Microwave Background (CMB) (KAHZ·mik MY·kroh·wayv BAK·grownd) the electromagnetic radiation left over from the formation of the universe (411)

Radiación de fondo de microondas (RFM) el residuo de radiación electromagnética que quedó cuando se formó el universo

crust (KRUHST) the thin and solid outermost layer of Earth above the mantle (514)

corteza la capa externa, delgada y sólida de la Tierra, que se encuentra sobre el manto

crystal (KRIS·tuhl) a solid whose atoms, ions, or molecules are arranged in a regular, repeating pattern (457)

cristal un sólido cuyos átomos, iones o moléculas están ordenados en un patrón regular y repetitivo

decibel (DES·uh·bel) the most common unit used to measure loudness (symbol, dB) (184)

decibele la unidad más común que se usa para medir el volumen del sonido (símbolo: dB)

deformation (dee·fohr·MAY·shuhn) the bending, tilting, and breaking of Earth's crust; the change in response to stress (544, 571)

deformación el proceso de doblar, inclinar y romper la corteza de la Tierra; el cambio en la forma de una roca en respuesta a la tensión

deposition (dep·uh·ZISH·uhn) the process in which material is laid down (471)

sublimación inversa el proceso por medio del cual un material se deposita

digital signal (DIH·jih·tul SIG·nul) a signal wave that varies step-wise with an abrupt up-and-down pattern (159)

señal digital señal de onda que varía de manera gradual con un patrón abrupto de ascenso y descenso

diurnal tide (dy·UR·nuhl TYD) a tide that occurs once a day with high and low tides of about the same height (442)

marea diurna marea que ocurre una vez al día con mareas altas y bajas de aproximadamente la misma altura

divergent boundary (dy·VER·juhnt BOWN·duh·ree) the boundary between two tectonic plates that are moving away from each other (531)
límite divergente el límite entre dos placas tectónicas que se están separando una de la otra

DNA (dee·en·AY) deoxyribonucleic acid, a molecule that is present in all living cells and that contains the information that detemines the traits that a living thing inherits and needs to live (270)
ADN ácido desoxirribonucleico, una molécula que está presente en todas las células vivas y que contiene la información que determina los caracteres que un ser vivo hereda y necesita para vivir

domain (doh·MAYN) in a taxonomic system, one of the three broad groups that all living things fall into (330)
dominio en un sistema taxonómico, uno de los tres amplios grupos al que pertenecen todos los seres vivos

Doppler effect (DAHP·ler ih·FEKT) an observed change in the frequency of a wave when the source or observer is moving (185)
efecto Doppler un cambio que se observa en la frecuencia de una onda cuando la fuente o el observador está en movimiento

earthquake (ERTH·kwayk) a movement or trembling of the ground that is caused by a sudden release of energy when rocks along a fault move (570)
terremoto un movimiento o temblor del suelo causado por una liberación súbita de energía que se produce cuando las rocas ubicadas a lo largo de una falla se mueven

echo (EK·oh) a reflected sound wave (193)
eco una onda de sonido reflejada

echolocation (ek·oh·loh·KAY·shuhn) the process of using reflected sound waves to find objects; used by animals such as bats (204)
ecolocación el proceso de usar ondas de sonido reflejadas para buscar objetos; utilizado por animales tales como los murciélagos

elastic rebound (ee·LAS·tik REE·bownd) the sudden return of elastically deformed rock to its undeformed shape (571)
rebote elástico ocurre cuando una roca deformada elásticamente vuelve súbitamente a su forma no deformada

electric charge (ee·LEK·trik CHARJ) a fundamental property that leads to the electromagnetic interactions among particles that make up matter (52)
carga eléctrica una propiedad fundamental que determina las interacciones electromagnéticas entre las partículas que forman la materia

electric circuit (ee·LEK·trik SER·kit) a set of electrical components connected such that they provide one or more complete paths for the movement of charges (70)
circuito eléctrico un conjunto de componentes eléctricos conectados de modo que proporcionen una o más rutas completas para el movimiento de las cargas

electric current (ee·LEK·trik KER·uhnt) the rate at which electric charges pass a given point (62)
corriente eléctrica la tasa a la que las cargas eléctricas pasan por un punto dado

electric generator (ee·LEK·trik JEN·uh·ray·ter) a device that converts mechanical energy into electrical energy (104)
generador eléctrico un aparato que transforma la energía mecánica en energía eléctrica

electric motor (ee·LEK·trik MO·ter) a device that converts electrical energy into mechanical energy (100)
motor eléctrico un aparato que transforma la energía eléctrica en energía mecánica

electrical conductor (ee·LEK·trih·kuhl kuhn·DUHK·ter) a material in which charges can move freely (56)
conductor eléctrico un material en el que las cargas se mueven libremente

electrical insulator (ee·LEK·trih·kuhl IN·suh·lay·ter) a material in which charges cannot move freely (56)
aislante eléctrico un material en el que las cargas no pueden moverse libremente

electromagnet (ee·lek·troh·MAG·nit) a coil that has a soft iron core and that acts as a magnet when an electric current is in the coil (97)
electroimán una bobina que tiene un centro de hierro suave y que funciona como un imán cuando hay una corriente eléctrica en la bobina

electromagnetic induction (ee·lek·troh·mag·NET·ik in·DUHK·shuhn) the process of creating a current in a circuit by changing a magnetic field (102)
inducción electromagnética el proceso de crear una corriente en un circuito por medio de un cambio en el campo magnético

electromagnetic spectrum (ee·lek·troh·mag·NET·ik SPEK·truhm) all of the frequencies or wavelengths of electromagnetic radiation (224, 388)
espectro electromagnético all of the frequencies or wavelengths of electromagnetic radiation

electromagnetic wave (ee·lek·troh·mag·NET·ik WAYV) a wave, consisting of changing electric and magnetic fields, that is emitted by vibrating electric charges and can travel through a vacuum (138)
onda electromagnética una onda formada por campos eléctricos y magnéticos cambiantes, que es emitida por cargas eléctricas que vibran, y que puede viajar por un vacío

electromagnetism (ee·lek·troh·MAG·nih·tiz·uhm) the interaction between electricity and magnetism (96)
electromagnetismo la interacción entre la electricidad y el magnetismo

element (EL·uh·muhnt) a substance that cannot be separated or broken down into simpler substances by chemical means (456)
elemento una sustancia que no se puede separar o descomponer en sustancias más simples por medio de métodos químicos

encode (en·KODE) to put into code an image, sound, or data that is sent over a distance (159)
codificar convertir en código una imagen, sonido o dato que se envía a distancia

encrypt (en·KRYPT) to alter a message using a secret code (161)
encriptar usar un código secreto a fin de cambiar un mensaje

epicenter (EP·ih·sen·ter) the point on Earth's surface directly above an earthquake's starting point, or focus (570, 589)
epicentro el punto de la superficie de la Tierra que queda justo arriba del punto de inicio, o foco, de un terremoto

erosion (ee·ROH·zhuhn) the process by which wind, water, ice, or gravity transports soil and sediment from one location to another (471)
erosión el proceso por medio del cual el viento, el agua, el hielo o la gravedad transporta tierra y sedimentos de un lugar a otro

Eukarya (yoo·KAIR·ee·uh) in a modern taxonomic system, a domain made up of all eukaryotes; this domain aligns with the traditional kingdoms Protista, Fungi, Plantae, and Animalia (331)
Eukarya en un sistema taxonómico moderno, un dominio compuesto por todos los eucariotes; este dominio coincide con los reinos tradicionales Protista, Fungi, Plantae y Animalia

evolution (ev·uh·LOO·shuhn) the process in which inherited characteristics within a population change over generations such that new species sometimes arise (278)
evolución el proceso por medio del cual las características heredadas dentro de una problación cambian con el transcurso de las generaciones de manera tal que a veces surgen nuevas especies

extinction (ek·STINGK·shuhn) the death of every member of a species (285, 309)
extinción la muerte de todos los miembros de una especie

fault (FAWLT) a break in a body of rock along which one block moves relative to another (571)
falla una grieta en un cuerpo rocosoa lo largo de la cual un bloque se mueve respecto de otro

fluorescent light (floo·RES·uhnt LYT) visible light emitted by a material when it absorbs energy such as ultraviolet light (248)
luz fluorescente luz visible emitida por un material cuando absorbe energía como la luz ultravioleta

focus (FOH·kuhs) the location within Earth along a fault at which the first motion of an earthquake occurs (570, 589)
foco el lugar dentro de la Tierra a lo largo de una falla donde ocurre el primer movimiento de un terremoto

folding (FOHLD·ing) the bending of rock layers due to stress (545)
plegamiento fenómeno que ocurre cuando las capas de roca se doblan debido a la compresión

force (FOHRS) a push or a pull exerted on an object in order to change the motion of the object; force has size and direction (30)
fuerza una acción de empuje o atracción que se ejerce sobre un objeto con el fin de cambiar su movimiento; la fuerza tiene magnitud y dirección

fossil (FAHS·uhl) the trace or remains of an organism that lived long ago, most commonly preserved in sedimentary rock (297, 308)
fósil los indicios o los restos de un organismo que vivió hace mucho tiempo, comúnmente preservados en las rocas sedimentarias

fossil fuel (FAHS·uhl FEW·ul) a natural resource that forms over millions of years from the remains of organisms and that is used as fuel in heating, transportation, or manufacturing (607)
combustible fósil recurso natural que se forma durante millones de años a partir de los restos de organismos y que se usa como combustible para calefacción, transporte y manufactura

fossil record (FAHS·uhl REK·erd) the history of life in the geologic past as indicated by the traces or remains of living things (297, 308)
registro fósil la historia de la vida en el pasado geológico según la indican los rastros o restos de seres vivos

frequency (FREE·kwuhn·see) the number of cycles, such as waves, in a given amount of time (147)
frecuencia el número de ciclos, tales como ondas, producidas en una determinada cantidad de tiempo

Fungi (FUHN·jy) a kingdom made up of nongreen, eukaryotic organisms that have no means of movement, reproduce by using spores, and get food by breaking down substances in their surroundings and absorbing the nutrients (332)
Fungi un reino formado por organismos eucarióticos no verdes que no tienen capacidad de movimiento, se reproducen por esporas y obtienen alimento al descomponer sustancias de su entorno y absorber los nutrientes

genetic engineering (juh·NET·ik en·juh·NIR·ing) a technology in which the genome of a living cell is modified for medical or industrial use (348)
ingeniería genética una tecnología en la que el genoma de una célula viva se modifica con fines médicos o industriales

genus (JEE·nuhs) the level of classification that comes after family and that contains similar species (328)
género el nivel de clasificación que viene después de la familia y que contiene especies similares

geologic time scale (jee·uh·LAHJ·ik TYM SKAYL) the standard method used to divide Earth's long natural history into manageable parts (310)
escala de tiempo geológico el método estándar que se usa para dividir la larga historia natural de la Tierra en partes razonables

gravity (GRAV·ih·tee) a force of attraction between objects that is due to their masses (422)
gravedad una fuerza de atracción entre dos objetos debido a sus masas

groundwater (GROWND·wah·ter) water that is found underground in layers of soil or rock (608)
agua subterránea agua que se halla bajo tierra entre capas de arena o roca

guyot (GEE·oh) a type of submarine volcano with a flat top (563)
guyot tipo de volcán submarino con una superficie plana

hertz (HERTS) a unit of frequency equal to one cycle per second (147)
hertz una unidad de frecuencia que representa un ciclo por segundo

homeostasis (hoh·mee·oh·STAY·sis) the maintenance of a constant internal state in a changing environment (269)
homeostasis la capacidad de mantener un estado interno constante en un ambiente en cambio

hot spot (HAHT SPAHT) a volcanically active area of Earth's surface, commonly far from a tectonic plate boundary (560)
mancha caliente un área volcánicamente activa de la superficie de la Tierra que comúnmente se encuentra lejos de un límite entre placas tectónicas

igneous rock (IG·nee·uhs RAHK) rock that forms when magma cools and solidifies (472)
roca ígnea una roca que se forma cuando el magma se enfría y se solidifica

incandescent light (in·kuhn·DES·uhnt LYT) the light produced by hot objects (248)
luz incandescente la luz producida por los objetos calientes

inertia (ih·NER·shuh) the tendency of an object to resist a change in motion unless an outside force acts on the object
inercia la tendencia de un objeto a resistir un cambio en el movimiento a menos que actúe una fuerza externa sobre el objeto

infrared (in·fruh·RED) electromagnetic wavelengths immediately outside the red end of the visible spectrum (224)

infrarrojo longitudes de onda electromagnéticas inmediatamente adyacentes al color rojo en el espectro visible

intensity (in·TEN·sih·tee) in Earth science, the amount of damage caused by an earthquake (595)
intensidad en las ciencias de la Tierra, la cantidad de daño causado por un terremoto

interference (in·ter·FIR·uhns) the combination of two or more waves that results in a single wave (194)
interferencia la combinación de dos o más ondas que resulta en una sola onda

kimberlite (kim·ber·LYTE) a volcanic feature that erupts from the mantle and often contains diamonds (611)
kimberlita roca volcánica que irrumpe desde el manto de la Tierra y con frecuencia contiene diamantes

lander (LAN·der) an automated, uncrewed vehicle that is designed to touch down safely on an extraterrestrial body; often carries equipment for exploration of that body (371)
módulo de aterrizaje un vehículo automatizado, no tripulado, diseñado para aterrizar sin peligro en un cuerpo extraterrestre; con frecuencia lleva equipos para explorar ese cuerpo

laser (LAY·zer) a device that produces intense light of a narrow range of wavelength and color; *laser* is an abbreviation of *light amplification by stimulated emission of radiation* (249)
láser un dispositivo que produce luz intensa de un rango estrecho de longitud de onda y color; "láser" es una abreviatura de las palabras en inglés "amplificación de luz por emisión estimulada de radiación"

lava (LAH·vuh) magma that flows onto Earth's surface; the rock that forms when lava cools and solidifies (554)
lava magma que fluye a la superficie terrestre; la roca que se forma cuando la lava se enfría y se solidifica

LED (el·ee·DEE) an electronic device that converts electrical energy to light; a light-emitting diode (249)
LED un dispositivo electrónico que convierte la energía eléctrica en luz; diodo que emite luz

lithosphere (LITH·uh·sfir) the solid, outer layer of Earth that consists of the crust and the rigid upper part of the mantle (515)
litosfera la capa externa y sólida de la Tierra que está formada por la corteza y la parte superior y rígida del manto

© Houghton Mifflin Harcourt Publishing Company

longitudinal wave (lahn·jih·TOOD·n·uhl WAYV) a wave in which the particles of the medium vibrate parallel to the direction of wave motion (136, 178)
onda longitudinal una onda en la que las partículas del medio vibran paralelamente a la dirección del movimiento de la onda

loudness (LOWD·nes) the extent to which a sound can be heard (183)
volumen el grado al que se escucha un sonido

luster (LUHS·ter) the way in which a mineral reflects light (463)
brillo la forma en que un mineral refleja la luz

magma (MAG·muh) the molten or partially molten rock material containing trapped gases produced under Earth's surface (554)
magma el material rocoso total o parcialmente fundido que contiene gases atrapados que se producen debajo de la superficie terrestre

magnet (MAG·nit) any material that attracts iron or materials containing iron (86)
imán cualquier material que atrae hierro o materiales que contienen hierro

magnetic field (MAG·net·ik FEELD) a region where a magnetic force can be detected (87)
campo magnético una región donde puede detectarse una fuerza magnética

magnetic force (MAG·net·ik FOHRS) the force of attraction or repulsion generated by moving or spinning electric charges (86)
fuerza magnética la fuerza de atracción o repulsión generadas por cargas eléctricas en movimiento o que giran

magnetic pole (MAG·net·ik POHL) one of two points, such as the ends of a magnet, that have opposing magnetic qualities (87)
polo magnético uno de dos puntos, tales como los extremos de un imán, que tienen cualidades magnéticas opuestas

magnitude (MAG·nih·tood) the measure of the strength of an earthquake (594)
magnitud una medida de la intensidad de un terremoto

mantle (MAN·tl) the layer of rock between the Earth's crust and core (514)
manto la capa de roca que se encuentra entre la corteza terrestre y el núcleo

matter (MAT·er) anything that has mass and takes up space (456)
materia cualquier cosa que tiene masa y ocupa un lugar en el espacio

mechanical wave (mih·KAN·ih·kuhl WAYV) a wave that requires a medium through which to travel (138)
onda mecánica una onda que requiere un medio para desplazarse

medium (MEE·dee·uhm) a physical environment in which phenomena occur; for waves, the material through which a wave can travel (134)
medio un ambiente físico en el que ocurren fenómenos; para las ondas, el medio a través del cual se desplaza una onda

mesosphere (MEZ·uh·sfir) the strong, lower part of the mantle between the asthenosphere and the outer core (515)
mesosfera la parte fuerte e inferior del manto que se encuentra entre la astenosfera y el núcleo externo

metamorphic rock (met·uh·MOHR·fik RAHK) a rock that forms from other rocks as a result of intense heat, pressure, or chemical processes (472)
roca metamórfica una roca que se forma a partir de otras rocas como resultado de calor intenso, presión o procesos químicos

mineral (MIN·er·uhl) a natural, usually inorganic solid that has a characteristic chemical composition and an orderly internal structure (456)
mineral un sólido natural, normalmente inorgánico, que tiene una composición química característica y una estructura interna ordenada

mineral resource (MIN·er·uhl REE·sohrs) a naturally occurring inorganic material (607)
recurso mineral materia inorgánica que se encuentra de forma natural

motion (MOH·shuhn) an object's change in position relative to a reference point (8)
movimiento el cambio en la posición de un objeto respecto a un punto de referencia

mutation (myoo·TAY·shuhn) a change in the nucleotide-base sequence of a gene or DNA molecule (282)
mutación un cambio en la secuencia de la base de nucleótidos de un gen o de una molécula de ADN

natural resource (NACH·uh·ruhl REE·sohrs) a naturally occuring organic or inorganic material (606)
recurso natural materia orgánica o inorgánica que se encuentra de forma natural

natural selection (NACH·uh·ruhl sih·LEK·shuhn) the process by which individuals that are better adapted to their environment survive and reproduce more successfully than less-well-adapted individuals do (282)
selección natural el proceso por medio del cual los individuos que están mejor adaptados a su ambiente sobreviven y se reproducen con más éxito que los individuos menos adaptados

neap tide (NEEP TYD) a tide of minimum range that occurs during the first and third quarters of the moon (439)
marea muerta una marea que tiene un rango mínimo, la cual ocurre durante el primer y el tercer cuartos de la Luna

net force (NET FOHRS) the combination of all of the forces acting on an object (32)

    fuerza neta la combinación de todas las fuerzas que actúan sobre un objeto

noise (NOYZ) a part of a signal that does not contain information (160)

    ruido parte de una señal que no contiene información

nonrenewable resource (nahn·rih·NOO·uh·buhl REE·sohrs) a resource that forms at a rate that is much slower than the rate at which the resource is consumed (609)

    recurso no renovable un recurso que se forma a una tasa que es mucho más lenta que la tasa a la que se consume

opaque (oh·PAYK) describes an object that is not transparent or translucent (235)

    opaco término que describe un objeto que no es transparente ni translúcido

optical fiber (AHP·tih·kuhl FY·ber) a transparent thread of plastic or glass that transmits light (250)

    fibra óptica un hilo de plástico o vidrio transparente que transmite luz

orbit (OHR·bit) the path that a body follows as it travels around another body in space (422)

    órbita la trayectoria que sigue un cuerpo al desplazarse alrededor de otro cuerpo en el espacio

orbiter (OHR·bih·ter) a spacecraft that is designed to orbit a planet, moon, or other body without landing on the body's surface (371)

    orbitador una nave espacial diseñada para orbitar alrededor de un planeta, luna u otro cuerpo sin aterrizar sobre la superficie de dicho cuerpo

Pangaea (pan·JEE·uh) the supercontinent that formed 300 million years ago and that began to break up 200 million years ago (525)

    Pangea el supercontinente que se formó hace 300 millones de años y que comenzó a separarse hace 200 millones de años

parallel circuit (PAIR·uh·lel SER·kit) a circuit in which the parts are joined in branches such that the voltage across each part is the same (75)

    circuito paralelo un circuito en el que las partes están unidas en ramas de manera tal que el voltaje entre cada parte es la misma

perihelion (per·ih·HEE·lee·uhn) in the orbit of a planet or other body in the solar system, the point that is closest to the sun (423)

    perihelio en la órbita de un planeta u otros cuerpos en el sistema solar, el punto que está más cerca del Sol

phenotype (FEE·no·tipe) an inherited trait of an organism that is expressed (286)

    fenotipo expresión de un rasgo hereditario de un organismo

pitch (PICH) a measure of how high or low a sound is perceived to be, depending on the frequency of the sound wave (182)

    altura tonal una medida de qué tan agudo o grave se percibe un sonido, dependiendo de la frecuencia de la onda sonora

planetesimal (plan·ih·TES·uh·muhl) a small body from which a planet originated in the early stages of development of the solar system (429)

    planetesimal un cuerpo pequeño a partir del cual se originó un planeta en las primeras etapas de desarrollo del Sistema Solar

Plantae (PLAN·tee) a kingdom made up of complex, multicellular organisms that are usually green, have cell walls made of cellulose, cannot move around, and use the sun's energy to make sugar by photosynthesis (332)

    Plantae un reino formado por organismos pluricelulares complejos que normalmente son verdes, tienen una pared celular de celulosa, no tienen capacidad de movimiento y utilizan la energía del Sol para producir azúcar mediante la fotosíntesis

plate tectonics (PLAYT tek·TAHN·iks) the theory that explains how large pieces of Earth's outermost layer, called tectonic plates, move and change shape (528)

    tectónica de placas la teoría que explica cómo se mueven y cambian de forma las placas tectónicas, que son grandes porciones de la capa más externa de la Tierra

porous (POH·rus) having naturally occuring spaces between the particles of the minerals that make up a rock (614)

    porosa que tiene espacios que ocurren de forma natural entre las partículas de los minerales que forman una roca

position (puh·ZISH·uhn) the location of an object (6)

    posición la ubicación de un objeto

probe (PROHB) an uncrewed vehicle that carries scientific instruments into space to collect scientific data (370)

    sonda espacial en astronomía [O "en exploración espacial"], un vehículo sin tripulación que transporta instrumentos científicos al espacio para recopilar información científica

Protista (proh·TIS·tuh) a kingdom of mostly one-celled eukaryotic organisms that are different from plants, animals, archaea, bacteria, and fungi (332)

    Protista un reino compuesto principalmente por organismos eucarióticos unicelulares que son diferentes de las plantas, animales, arqueas, bacterias y hongos

radar (RAY·dar) a means of detecting the presence or speed of a moving object with radio waves (378)
radar medio para detectar la presencia o velocidad de un objeto en movimiento con ondas de radio

radiation (ray·dee·AY·shuhn) the transfer of energy as electromagnetic waves (222)
radiación la transferencia de energía en forma de ondas electromagnéticas

redshift (RED·shift) a shift toward the red end of the spectrum; occurs in the spectrum of an object when the object is moving away from the observer (409)
corrimiento al rojo un corrimiento hacia el extreme rojo del espectro; ocurre en el espectro de un objeto cuando el objeto se está alejando del observador

reference point (REF·er·uhns POYNT) a location to which another location is compared (6)
punto de referencia una ubicación con la que se compara otra ubicación

reflection (rih·FLEK·shuhn) the bouncing back of a ray of light, sound, or heat when the ray hits a surface that it does not go through (235)
reflexión el rebote de un rayo de luz, sonido o calor cuando el rayo golpea una superficie pero no la atraviesa

refraction (rih·FRAK·shuhn) the bending of a wave front as the wave front passes between two substances in which the speed of the wave differs (238)
refracción el curvamiento de un frente de ondas a medida que el frente pasa entre dos sustancias en las que la velocidad de las ondas difiere

renewable resource (rih·NOO·uh·buhl REE·sohrs) a resource that forms at a rate that is much faster than the rate at which the resource is consumed (609)
recursos renovables un recurso que se forma a una tasa que es mucho más rapidá que la tasa a la que se consume

resistance (rih·ZIS·tuhns) in physical science, the opposition presented to the current by a material or device (64)
resistencia en ciencias físicas, la oposición que un material o aparato presenta a la corriente

resonance (REZ·uh·nuhns) a phenomenon that occurs when two objects naturally vibrate at the same frequency; the sound produced by one object causes the other object to vibrate (196)
resonancia un fenómeno que ocurre cuando dos objetos vibran naturalmente a la misma frecuencia; el sonido producido por un objeto hace que el otro objeto vibre

rift zone (RIFT ZOHN) an area of deep cracks that forms between two tectonic plates that are pulling away from each other (476)
zona de rift un área de grietas profundas que se forma entre dos placas tectónicas que se están alejando una de la otra

rock (RAHK) a naturally occurring solid mixture of one or more minerals or organic matter (486)
roca una mezcla sólida de uno o más minerales o de materia orgánica que se produce de forma natural

rock cycle (RAHK SY·kuhl) the series of processes in which rock forms, changes from one type to another, is broken down or melted, and forms again by geologic processes (474)
ciclo de las rocas la serie de procesos por medio de los cuales una roca se forma, cambia de un tipo a otro, se destruye o funde y se forma nuevamente por procesos geológicos

rover (ROH·ver) a vehicle that is used to explore the surface of an extraterrestrial body (371)
rover un vehículo que se usa para explorar la superficie de un cuerpo extraterrestre

scattering (SKAT·er·ing) an interaction of light with matter that causes light to change direction (239)
dispersión la interacción de la luz con la materia que produce un cambio de dirección de la luz

sea-floor spreading (SEE·flohr SPRED·ing) the process by which new oceanic lithosphere (sea floor) forms when magma rises to Earth's surface at mid-ocean ridges and solidifies, as older, existing sea floor moves away from the ridge (526, 557)
expansión del suelo marino el proceso por medio del cual se forma nueva litósfera oceánica (suelo marino) cuando el magma sube a la superficie de la Tierra en las dorsales oceánicas y se solidifica, a medida que el antiguo suelo marino existente se aleja de la dorsal oceánica

sedimentary rock (sed·uh·MEN·tuh·ree RAHK) a rock that forms from compressed or cemented layers of sediment (472)
roca sedimentaria una roca que se forma a partir de capas comprimidas o cementadas de sedimento

seismic wave (SYZ·mik WAYV) a wave of energy that travels through Earth and away from an earthquake in all directions (516, 589)
onda sísmica una onda de energía que viaja a través de la Tierra y se aleja de un terremoto en todas direcciones

seismogram (SYZ·muh·gram) a tracing of earthquake motion that is recorded by a seismograph (592)
sismograma una traza del movimiento de un terremoto registrada por un sismógrafo

semiconductor (sem·ee·kuhn·DUHK·ter) an element or compound that conducts electric current better than an insulator does but not as well as a conductor does (57)
semiconductor un elemento o compuesto que conduce la corriente eléctrica mejor que un aislante, pero no tan bien como un conductor

semidiurnal tide (sem·ee·dy·UR·nuhl TYD) a tide that occurs twice a day with high and low tides of about the same height (442)

marea semidiurna marea que ocurre dos veces al día con mareas altas y bajas de aproximadamente la misma altura

series circuit (SIR·eez SER·kit) a circuit in which the parts are joined one after another such that the current in each part is the same (74)

circuito en serie un circuito en el que las partes están unidas una después de la otra de manera tal que la corriente en cada parte es la misma

sexual reproduction (SEK·shoo·uhl ree·pruh·DUHK·shuhn) reproduction in which the sex cells from two parents unite to produce offspring that share traits from both parents (270)

reproducción sexual reproducción en la que se unen las células sexuales de los dos progenitores para producir descendencia que comparte caracteres de ambos progenitores

shear stress (SHIR STRES) stress that occurs when forces act in parallel but opposite directions, pushing parts of a solid in opposite directions (546)

tensión de corte el estrés que se produce cuando dos fuerzas actúan en direcciones paralelas pero opuestas, lo que empuja las partes de un sólido en direcciones opuestas

solar nebula (SOH·ler NEB·yuh·luh) a rotating cloud of gas and dust from which the sun and planets formed (427)

nebulosa solar una nube de gas y polvo en rotación a partir de la cual se formaron el Sol y los planetas

solenoid (SOH·luh·noyd) a coil of wire with an electric current in it (97)

solenoide una bobina de alambre que tiene una corriente eléctrica

sonar (SOH·nar) sound navigation and ranging, a system that uses acoustic signals and returned echoes to determine the location of objects or to communicate (205)

sonar navegación y exploración por medio del sonido; un sistema que usa señales acústicas y ondas de eco que regresan para determinar la ubicación de los objetos o para comunicarse

sound wave (SOWND WAYV) a longitudinal wave that is caused by vibrations and that travels through a material medium (178)

onda sonora una onda longitudinal que se origina debido a vibraciones y que se desplaza a través de un medio material

space shuttle (SPAYS SHUHT·l) a reusable space vehicle that takes off like a rocket and lands like an airplane (368)

transbordador espacial un vehículo espacial reutilizable que despega como un cohete y aterriza como un avión

species (SPEE·sheez) a group of organisms that are closely related and can mate to produce fertile offspring (328)

especie un grupo de organismos que tienen un parentesco cercano y que pueden aparearse para producir descendencia fértil

spectrum (SPEK·truhm) a range of electromagnetic radiation that is ordered by wavelength or frequency, such as the band of colors that is produced when white light passes through a prism (388)

espectro una gama de radiación electromagnética ordenada por longitud de onda o frecuencia, como la banda de colores que se produce cuando la luz blanca pasa a través de un prisma

speed (SPEED) the distance traveled divided by the time interval during which the motion occurred (9)

rapidez la distancia que un objeto se desplaza dividida entre el intervalo de tiempo durante el cual ocurrió el movimiento

splice (SPLYS) to join two pieces of DNA based on the sequences in each piece 341

empalmar unir dos partes del ADN según las secuencias de cada parte

spring tide (SPRING TYD) a tide of increased range that occurs two times a month, at the new and full moons (438)

marea viva una marea de mayor rango que ocurre dos veces al mes, durante la luna nueva y la luna llena

static electricity (STAT·ih ee·lek·TRIS·ih·tee) electric charge at rest; generally produced by friction or induction (55)

electricidad estática carga eléctrica en reposo; por lo general se produce por fricción o inducción

stimulus (STIM·yuh·luhs) anything that causes a reaction or change in an organism or any part of an organism (269)

estímulo cualquier cosa que causa una reacción o cambio en un organismo o cualquier parte de un organismo

streak (STREEK) the color of a mineral in powdered form (462)

veta el color de un mineral en forma de polvo

submarine volcano (SUB·muh·reen vul·KAY·no) a volcano that grows on the ocean floor as a result of repeated eruptions (563)

volcán submarinos un volcán que surge del suelo oceánico como resultado de erupciones repetidas

subsidence (suhb·SYD·ns) the sinking of regions of Earth's crust to lower elevations (476, 563)

hundimiento del terreno el hundimiento de regiones de la corteza terrestre a elevaciones más bajas

tectonic plate boundary (tek·TAHN·ik PLAYT BOWN·duh·ree) the edge between two or more plates, classified as divergent, convergent, or transform by the movement taking place between the plates (571)
límite de placa tectónica el borde entre dos o más placas clasificado como divergente, convergente o transformante por el movimiento que se produce entre las placas

tectonic plate(s) (tek·TAHN·ik PLAYT) a block of lithosphere that consists of the crust and the rigid, outermost part of the mantle (528, 557)
placa tectónica un bloque de litosfera formado por la corteza y la parte rígida y más externa del manto

tension (TEN·shuhn) stress that occurs when forces act to stretch an object (547)
tensión estrés que se produce cuando distintas fuerzas actúan para estirar un objeto

texture (TEKS·cher) the quality of a rock that is based on the sizes, shapes, and positions of the rock's grains (487)
textura la cualidad de una roca que se basa en el tamaño, la forma y la posición de los granos que la forman

tidal range (TYD·l RAYNJ) the difference in levels of ocean water at high tide and low tide (438)
rango de marea la diferencia en los niveles del agua del océano entre la marea alta y la marea baja

tide (TYD) the periodic rise and fall of the water level in the oceans and other large bodies of water (436)
marea el ascenso y descenso periódico del nivel del agua en los océanos y otras masas grandes de agua

transform boundary (TRANS·fohrm BOWN·duh·ree) the boundary between tectonic plates that are sliding past each other horizontally (531)
límite de transformación el límite entre placas tectónicas que se están deslizando horizontalmente una sobre otra

transformer (trans·FOHR·mer) a device that increases or decreases the voltage of alternating current (103)
transformador un aparato que aumenta o disminuye el voltaje de la corriente alterna

transitional form (tran·ZISH·uhn·ul FORM) an organism that shares features with modern organisms and earlier fossils (317)
forma transitoria organismo que comparte características con organismos modernos y fósiles primitivos

translucent (trans·LOO·suhnt) describes matter that transmits light but that does not transmit an image (234)
traslúcido término que describe la materia que transmite luz, pero que no transmite una imagen

transmission (trans·MIH·shun) a signal that is sent over a distance (160)
transmisión señal que se envía a través de una distancia

transparent (trans·PAIR·uhnt) describes matter that allows light to pass through with little interference (234)
transparente término que describe materia que permite el paso de la luz con poca interferencia

transverse wave (TRANS·vers WAYV) a wave in which the particles of the medium move perpendicularly to the direction the wave is traveling (137)
onda transversal una onda en la que las partículas de medio se mueven perpendicularmente respecto a la dirección en la que se desplaza la onda

ultrasound (UHL·truh·sownd) sound waves with frequencies greater than 20,000 hertz (Hz), the upper limit of typical hearing levels in humans, often used for medical purposes (204)
ultrasonido ondas sonoras con frecuencias mayores de 20,000 hertz (Hz), el límite superior de los niveles de audición típicos en los seres humanos, usadas generalmente con propósitos médicos

ultraviolet (uhl·truh·VY·uh·lit) electromagnetic wave frequencies immediately above the visible range (204)
ultravioleta longitudes de onda electromagnéticas inmediatamente adyacentes al color violeta en el espectro visible

universe (YOO·nuh·vers) space and all the matter and energy in it (406)
universo el espacio y toda la materia y energía que hay dentro él

uplift (UHP·lift) the rising of regions of Earth's crust to higher elevations (476)
levantamiento la elevación de regiones de la corteza terrestre a elevaciones más altas

variation (vair·ee·AY·shuhn) the occurrence of hereditary or nonhereditary differences between different invidivuals of a population (282)
variabilidad la incidencia de diferencias hereditarias o no hereditarias entre distintos individuos de una población

vector (VEK·ter) a quantity that has both size and direction (15)
vector una cantidad que tiene tanto magnitud como dirección

velocity (vuh·LAHS·ih·tee) the speed of an object in a particular direction (15)
velocidad la rapidez de un objeto en una dirección dada

vent (VENT) an opening at the surface of Earth through which volcanic material passes (554)
chimenea una abertura en la superficie de la Tierra a través de la cual pasa material volcánico

volcano (vahl·KAY·noh) a vent or fissure in Earth's surface through which magma and gases are expelled (554)
volcán una chimenea o fisura en la superficie de la Tierra a través de la cual se expulsan magma y gases

voltage (VOHL·tij) the amount of work to move a unit electric charge between two points; expressed in volts (64)
voltaje la cantidad de trabajo necesario para transportar una unidad de carga eléctrica entre dos puntos; se expresa en voltios

water table (WAW·ter TAY·buhl) the upper limit of water that the ground can hold (614)
nivel freático capa subterránea de roca o de otro material que está saturada de agua

wave (WAYV) a disturbance that transfers energy from one place to another; a wave can be a single cycle, or it can be a repeating pattern (134, 146)
onda una alteración que transfiere energía de un lugar a otro; una onda puede ser un ciclo único o un patrón repetido

wave period (WAYV PIR·ee·uhd) the time required for corresponding points on consecutive waves to pass a given point (147)
período de onda el tiempo que se requiere para que los puntos correspondientes de ondas consecutivas pasen por un punto dado

wave speed (WAYV SPEED) the speed at which a wave travels; speed depends on the medium (150)
rapidez de onda la rapidez a la cual viaja una onda; la rapidez depende del medio

wavelength (WAYV·lengkth) the distance from any point on a wave to the corresponding point on the next wave (146, 388)
longitud de onda la distancia entre cualquier punto de una onda y el punto correspondiente de la siguiente onda

weathering (WETH·er·ing) the natural process by which atmospheric and environmental agents, such as wind, rain, and temperature changes, disintegrate and decompose rocks (471)
meteorización el proceso natural por medio del cual los agentes atmosféricos o ambientales, como el viento, la lluvia y los cambios de temperatura, desintegran y descomponen las rocas

Index

Page numbers for definitions are printed in **boldface** type.
Page numbers for illustrations, maps, and charts are printed in *italics*.

GrandTeCan telescope, *395*
granite, *458*, *473*, 486
graph
  average speed, 12, *12*
  changing speed, 13
  constant speed, 12, *12*
gravity, 31, **422**
  Earth formation and, 511, *511*, 512
  effect on planetary motion, 426, *426*
  effect on tides, 436–438
  Einstein and, 408
  general relativity and, 408
  law of universal gravitation, 408
  law of universal gravitation, 425
  Newton's third law of motion and, 39
  solar system formation and, 510
Great Rift Valley, 558, *558*
ground fault circuit interrupter (GFCI), 77, *77*
ground (electricity), **77**
Guggenheim Museum, 465, *465*
gypsum, 459, *461*

W

X

Y